MACHINE LEARNING
WITH PYTHON
Theory and Applications

MACHINE LEARNING WITH PYTHON

Theory and Applications

G. R. Liu

University of Cincinnati, USA

NEW JERSEY · LONDON · SINGAPORE · BEIJING · SHANGHAI · HONG KONG · TAIPEI · CHENNAI · TOKYO

Published by

World Scientific Publishing Co. Pte. Ltd.

5 Toh Tuck Link, Singapore 596224

USA office: 27 Warren Street, Suite 401-402, Hackensack, NJ 07601

UK office: 57 Shelton Street, Covent Garden, London WC2H 9HE

Library of Congress Cataloging-in-Publication Data
Names: Liu, G. R. (Gui-Rong), author.
Title: Machine learning with Python : theory and applications / G.R. Liu, University of Cincinnati, USA.
Description: Singapore ; Hackensack, NJ : World Scientific Publishing Co. Pte. Ltd., [2023] |
    Includes bibliographical references and index.
Identifiers: LCCN 2022001048 | ISBN 9789811254178 (hardcover) |
    ISBN 9789811254185 (ebook for institutions) | ISBN 9789811254192 (ebook for individuals)
Subjects: LCSH: Machine learning. | Python (Computer program language)
Classification: LCC Q325.5 .L58 2023 | DDC 006.3/1--dc23/eng20220328
LC record available at https://lccn.loc.gov/2022001048

British Library Cataloguing-in-Publication Data
A catalogue record for this book is available from the British Library.

First published 2023 (hardcover)
Reprinted 2025 (in paperback edition)
ISBN 9789819814091 (pbk)

For any available supplementary material, please visit
https://www.worldscientific.com/worldscibooks/10.1142/12774#t=suppl

Desk Editors: Jayanthi Muthuswamy/Steven Patt

Typeset by Stallion Press
Email: enquiries@stallionpress.com

About the Author

 **G. R. Liu** received his Ph.D from Tohoku University, Japan, in 1991. He was a post-doctoral fellow at Northwestern University, USA, from 1991–1993. He was a Professor at the National University of Singapore until 2010. He is currently a Professor at the University of Cincinnati, USA. He is the founder of the Association for Computational Mechanics (Singapore) (SACM) and served as the President of SACM until 2010. He served as the President of the Asia-Pacific Association for Computational Mechanics (APACM) (2010–2013) and an Executive Council Member of the International Association for Computational Mechanics (IACM) (2005–2010; 2020–2026). He has authored a large number of journal papers and books including two bestsellers — *Mesh Free Method: Moving Beyond the Finite Element Method* and *Smoothed Particle Hydrodynamics: A Meshfree Particle Methods*. He is the Editor-in-Chief of the *International Journal of Computational Methods* and served as an Associate Editor for IPSE and MANO. He is the recipient of numerous awards, including the Singapore Defence Technology Prize, NUS Outstanding University Researcher Award and Best Teacher Award, APACM Computational Mechanics Awards, JSME Computational Mechanics Awards, ASME Ted Belytschko Applied Mechanics Award, Zienkiewicz Medal from APACM, the AJCM Computational Mechanics Award, and the Humboldt Research Award. He has been listed as a world top 1% most influential scientist (Highly Cited Researchers) by Thomson Reuters in 2014–2016, 2018, and 2019. ISI citations by others: $\sim$22000; His journal and book credentials include the following. ISI H-index: $\sim$85; Google Scholar H-Index: 110.

Contents

4 Statistics and Probability-based Learning Model   **157**

14 Overfitting and Regularization 501

Chapter 1

Introduction

1.1 Naturally Learned Ability for Problem Solving

We are constantly dealing with all kinds of problems every day, and would like to solve these problems for timely decisions and actions. We may notice that for many of the daily-life problems, our decisions are often made spontaneously, swiftly without much consciousness. This is because we have been constantly learning to solve such problems in the past since we were born, and therefore the solutions have already been encoded in the neuron cells in our brain. When facing similar problems, our decision is spontaneous.

For many complicated problems, especially in science and engineering, one would need to think harder and even conduct extensive research and study on the related issues before we can provide a solution. What if we want to give spontaneous reliable solutions to these types of problems as well? Some scientists and engineers may be able to do this for some problems, but not many. Those scientists are intensively trained or educated in specially designed courses for dealing with complicated problems.

What if a normal layman would also like to be able solve these challenging types of problems? One way is to go through a special learning process. The alternative may be through machine learning, to develop a special computer model with a mechanism that can be trained to extract features from experience or data to provide a reliable and instantaneous solution for a type of problem.

1.2 Physics-Law-based Models

Problems in science and engineering are usually much more difficult to solve. This is because we humans can only experience or observe the phenomena associated with the problem. However, many phenomena are not easily observable and have very complicated underlying logic. Scientists have been trying to unveil the underlying logic by developing some theories (or laws or principles) that can help to best describe these phenomena. These theories are then formulated in the form of algebraic, differential, or integral system equations that govern the key variables involved in the phenomena. The next step is then to find a method that can solve these equations for these variables varying in space and with time. The final step is to find a way to validate the theory by observation and/or experiments to measure the values of these variables. The validated theory is used to build models to solve problems that exhibit the same phenomena. This type of model is called physics-law-based model.

The above-mentioned process is essentially what humans on earth have been doing in trying to understand nature, and we have made tremendous progress so far. In this process, we have established a huge number of areas of studies, physics, mathematics, biology, etc., which are now referred to as sciences.

Understanding nature is only a part of the story. Humans want to invent and build new things. A good understanding of various phenomena enables us to do so, and we have practically built everything around us, buildings, bridges, airplanes, space stations, cars, ships, computers, cell phones, internet, communication systems, and energy systems. Such a list is endless. In this process, we humans established a huge number of areas of development, which we are now referred to as engineering.

Understanding biology helped us to discover medicines, treatments for illnesses of humans and animals, treatments for plants and the environment, as well as proper measures and policies dealing with the relationships between humans, animals, plants, and environments. In this process, we humans established a huge number of areas of studies, including medicine, agriculture, and ecology.

In the relentless quest by humans in history, countless theories, laws, techniques, methods, etc., have been developed in various areas of science, engineering, and biology. For example, in the study of a small area of computational mechanics for designing structural systems, we have developed the finite element method (FEM) [1], smoothed finite element method (S-FEM) [2], meshfree methods [3, 4], inverse techniques [5], etc., just to name a few that the author has been working on. It is not possible and necessary to list all of these kinds of methods and techniques. Our discussion here is just to provide an overall view of how a problem can be solved based on physics laws.

Note that there are many problems in nature, engineering, and society for which it is difficult to describe and find proper physics laws to accurately and effectively solve them. Alternative means are thus needed.

1.3 Machine Learning Models, Data-based

There is a large class of complicated problems (in science, engineering, biology, and daily-life) that do not yet have known governing physics laws, or the solutions to the governing laws' equations are too expensive to obtain. For this type of problem, on the other hand, we often have some data obtained and accumulated through observations or measurements or historic records. When the data are sufficiently large and of good quality, it is possible to develop computer models to learn from these data. Such a model can then be used to find a solution for this type of problem. This kind of computer model is defined as a data-based model or machine learning model in this book.

Different types of effective artificial Neural Networks (NNs) with various configurations have been developed and widely used for practical problems in sciences and engineering, including multilayer perceptron (MLP) [6–9], Convolutional Neural Networks (CNNs) [10–14], and Recurrent Neural Networks (RNNs) [15–17]. TrumpetNets [8] and TubeNets [9, 18–20] were also recently proposed by the author for creating two-way deepnets using physics-law-based models as trainers, such as the FEM [1] and S-FEM [2]. The unique feature of TrumpetNets and TubeNets is their effectiveness for both forward and inverse problems [5]. It has a unique net architecture. Most importantly, solutions to inverse problems can be analytically derived in explicit formulae for the first time. This implies that when a data-based model is built properly, one can find solutions very efficiently.

Machine learning is essentially to mimic the natural learning process occurring in biological brains that can have a huge number of neurons. In terms of usage of data, we may have three major categories:

1. Supervised Learning, using data with true labels (teachers).
2. Unsupervised Learning, using data without labels.
3. Reinforcement Learning, using a predefined environment.

In terms of problems to solve, there are the following:

1. Binary classification problems, answer in probability to yes or no.
2. k-classification problems, answer in probabilities to k classes.
3. k-clustering problems, answer in k clusters of data-points.

4. Regression (linear or nonlinear), answer in predictions of continuous functions.
5. Feature extraction, answer in key features in the dataset.
6. Abnormality detection, answer in abnormal data.
7. Inverse analysis, answer in prediction on features from known responses.

In terms of learning methodology or algorithms, we have the following:

1. Linear and logistic regression, supervised.
2. Decision Tree, supervised.
3. Support Vector Machine (SVM), supervised.
4. Naive Bayes, supervised.
5. Multi-Layer Perceptron (MLP) or artificial Neural Networks (NNs), supervised.
6. k-Nearest Neighbors (kNN), supervised.
7. Random Forest, supervised.
8. Gradient Boosting types of algorithms, supervised.
9. Principal Components Analysis (PCA), unsupervised.
10. K-means, Mean-Shift, unsupervised.
11. Autoencoders, unsupervised.
12. Markov Decision Process, reinforcement Learning.

This book will cover most of these algorithms, but our focus will be more on neural network-based models because rigorous theory and predictive models can be established.

Machine learning is a very active area of research and development. New models, including the so-called cognitive machine learning models, are being studied. There are also techniques for manipulating various ML models. This book, however, will not cover those topics.

1.4 General Steps for Training Machine Learning Models

General steps for training machine learning models are summarized as follows:

1. Obtaining the dataset for the problem, by your own means of data generation, or imported from other existing sources, or computer syntheses.
2. Clean up the dataset if there are objectively known defaults in it.
3. Determine the type of hypothesis for the model.

4. Develop or import proper module for the needed algorithm for the problem. The learning ability (number of the learning parameters) of the model and the size of the dataset shall be properly balanced, if possible. Otherwise, consider the use of regularization techniques.

5. Randomly initialize the learning parameters, or import some known pre-trained learning parameter.

6. Perform the training with proper optimization techniques and monitoring measures.

7. Test the trained model using an independent test dataset. This can also be done during the training.

8. Deploy the trained and tested model to the same type of problems, where the training and testing datasets are collected/generated.

1.5 Some Mathematical Concepts, Variables, and Spaces

We shall define variables and spaces often used in this book for ease of discussion. We first state that this book deals with only real numbers, unless specified when geometrically closed operations are required. Let us introduce two toy examples.

1.5.1 *Toy examples*

Toy Example-1, Regression: Assume we are to build a machine learning model to predict the quality of fruits. Based on its three **features**, size, weight, and roundness (that can easily observe and measure), we aim to establish a machine learning regression model to predict the values of two characteristics, sweetness and vitamin-C content (that are difficult to quantify nondestructively), for any given fruit. To build such a model, we make 8,000 measurements to randomly selected fruits from the market and create a **dataset** with 8,000 paired data-points. Each data-point records the values of these three features and pairs with the values of these two characteristics. The values of these two characteristics are called **labels** (ground truth) to the data-point. The dataset is called labeled dataset that can be used systematically to train a machine learning model.

Toy Example-2, Classification: Assume we are to build a machine learning model to classify the type of fruits based on its three **features** (size, weight, and roundness). In this case, we want a machine to predict whether any given frait is an apple or orange, so that it can be packaged separately in an automatic manner. To achieve this, we make 8,000 measurements to randomly selected fruits of these two types from the market, and create a **dataset** with 8,000 paired data-points. Each data-point records the values of these three features and pairs with two **labels** (ground truth) of yes-or-no for apple or yes-or-no for orange. The dataset is also called labeled dataset for model training.

With an understanding of these two typical types of examples, it should be easy to extend this to many other types of problems for which a machine learning model can be effective.

1.5.2 *Feature space*

Feature space $\mathbb{X}^p$: Machine learning uses datasets that contain observed or measured p variables of real numbers in $\mathbb{R}$, often called *features*. In our two toy examples, $p = 3$. We may define a p-dimensional feature space $\mathbb{X}^p$ which is a vector space (https://en.wikipedia.org/wiki/Vector_space) over real numbers in $\mathbb{R}$ with inner product defined. A vector in $\mathbb{X}^p$ for an arbitrary point $(x_1, x_2, \ldots, x_p)$ is written as

$$\mathbf{x} = [x_1, x_2, \ldots, x_p], \quad \mathbf{x} \in \mathbb{X}^p \tag{1.1}$$

The origin of $\mathbb{X}^p$ is at $\mathbf{x} = [0, 0, \ldots, 0]$ following the standard for all vector spaces. Note that we use italic for scalar variables, bold face for all vectors and matrices, and blackboard bold for spaces (or sets or of that nature), and this convention is followed throughout this book. Also, we define, in general, all vectors in row vectors by default, as we usually do in Python programming. A column vector is treated as special case of 2D array (matrix) with only one column.

It is clear that the feature space $\mathbb{X}^p$ is a special (with vector operations defined) case of the real space $\mathbb{R}^p$. Thus, $\mathbb{X}^p \in \mathbb{R}^p$.

Also, $x_i(i = 1, 2, \ldots, p)$ is called linear basis functions (not to be confused with the basis vectors), because a linear combination of x_i gives a new x that is still in $\mathbb{X}^p$. A two-dimensional (2D) feature space $\mathbb{X}^2$ is the black plane $x_1 - x_2$ shown in Fig. 1.1.

An observed data-point $\mathbf{x}_i$ with p features is a discrete point in the space, and the corresponding vector $\mathbf{x}_i$ is expressed as

$$\mathbf{x}_i = [x_{i1}, x_{i2}, \ldots, x_{ip}], \quad \mathbf{x}_i \in \mathbb{X}^p, \forall \ i = 1, 2, \ldots, m \tag{1.2}$$

where m is the number of measurements or observations or data-points in the dataset. It is also often referred as number of samples in a dataset. For these two toy examples, $m = 8,000$. For the example shown in Fig. 1.1, these 4 blue vectors are for four data-points in space $\mathbb{X}^2$, and $m = 4$.

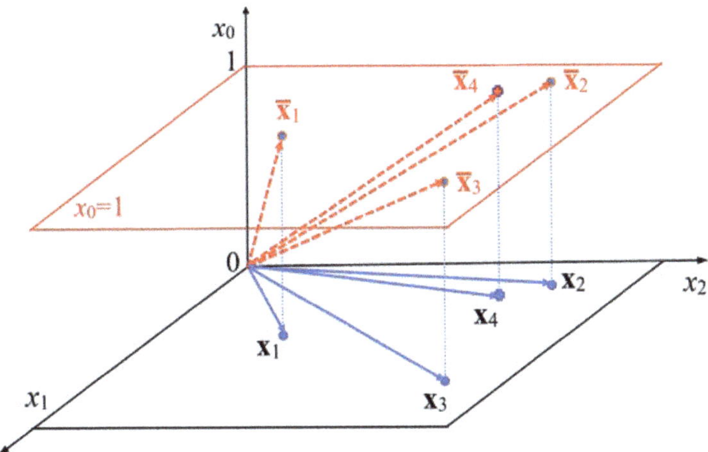

Figure 1.1: Data-points in a 2D feature space $\mathbb{X}^2$ with blue vectors: $\mathbf{x}_i = [x_{i1}, x_{i2}]$; and the same data-points in the augmented feature space $\overline{\mathbb{X}}^2$, called affine space, with red vectors: $\overline{\mathbf{x}}_i = [1, x_{i1}, x_{i2}]$; $i = 1, 2, 3, 4$.

These data-points $\mathbf{x}_i (i = 1, 2, \ldots, m)$ can be stacked to form a **dataset** noted as $\mathbf{X} \in \mathbb{X}^p$. This is for convenience in formulation. We do not form such a matrix in computation because it is usually very large for big datasets with large m.

1.5.3 *Affine space*

Affine space $\overline{\mathbb{X}}^p$: It is an **augmented feature space**. It is the red plane shown in Fig. 1.1. It has a "complete" linear bases (or basis functions):

$$\overline{\mathbf{x}} = [1, x_1, x_2, \ldots, x_p] \tag{1.3}$$

By complete linear bases, we mean all bases up to the 1st order of all the variables including the 0th order. The 0th order basis is the constant basis 1 that provides the **augmentation**. Affine space is not a vector space, because $\mathbf{0} \notin \overline{\mathbb{X}}^p$ and $(\overline{\mathbf{x}}_i + \overline{\mathbf{x}}_j) \notin \overline{\mathbb{X}}^p$ where $i, j = 1$ or 2 or 3 or 4 in Fig. 1.1. This special and fundamentally useful space always has a constant 1 as a component, and thus it does not have an origin by definition. Operation that occurs on an affine space and still stays in an affine space is called affine transformation. It is the most essential operation in major machine learning models, and the fundamental reason for such models being predictive.

An observed data-point with p features can also be presented as an augmented discrete point in the $\overline{\mathbb{X}}^p$ space and can be expressed by

$$\overline{\mathbf{x}}_i = [1, x_{i1}, x_{i2}, \ldots, x_{ip}], \quad \overline{\mathbf{x}}_i \in \overline{\mathbb{X}}^p, \ \forall \, i = 1, 2, \ldots, m \tag{1.4}$$

A $\overline{\mathbb{X}}^p$ space can be created by first spanning $\mathbb{X}^p$ by one dimension to $\mathbb{X}^{p+1}$ via introduction of a new variable x_0 as

$$[x_0, x_1, x_2, \ldots, x_p] \tag{1.5}$$

and then set $x_0 = 1$. These 4 red vectors shown in Fig. 1.1 live in an affine space $\overline{\mathbb{X}}^2$.

Note that the affine space $\overline{\mathbb{X}}^p$ is neither $\mathbb{X}^{p+1}$ nor $\mathbb{X}^p$, and is quite special. A vector in a $\overline{\mathbb{X}}^p$ is in $\mathbb{X}^{p+1}$, but the tip of the vector is confined in "hyperplane" of $x_0 = 1$. For convenience of discussion in this book, we say that an affine space has a **pseudo-dimension** that is $p + 1$. Its true dimension is p, but it is a hyperplane in a $\mathbb{X}^{p+1}$ space.

In terms of function approximation, the linear bases given in Eq. (1.3) can be used to construct any arbitrary linear function in the feature space. A *proper* linear combination of these complete linear bases is still in the affine space. Such a combination can be used to perform an **affine transformation**, which will be discussed in detail in Chapter 5.

These data-points $\overline{\mathbf{x}}_i (i = 1, 2, \ldots, m)$ are stacked to form an **augmented dataset** $\overline{\mathbf{X}} \in \overline{\mathbb{X}}^p$, which is the well-known **moment matrix** in function approximation theory [1–4]. Again, this is for convenience in formulation. We may not form such a matrix in computation.

1.5.4 *Label space*

Label space $\mathbb{Y}^k$: Consider a labeled dataset for a supervised machine learning model creation. We shall introduce variables $(y_1, y_2, \ldots, y_k)$ of real numbers in $\mathbb{R}$. For toy example-1, $k = 2$. We may define a label space $\mathbb{Y}^k$ over real numbers. It is a vector space. A vector in space $\mathbb{Y}^k$ for can be written as

$$\mathbf{y} = [y_1, y_2, \ldots, y_k], \quad \mathbf{y} \in \mathbb{Y}^k \in \mathbb{R}^k \tag{1.6}$$

A label in a dataset is paired with a data-point. The label for data-point $\mathbf{x}_i$ which is denoted as $\mathbf{y}_i$ can be expressed as

$$\mathbf{y}_i = [y_{i1}, y_{i2}, \ldots, y_{ik}], \quad \mathbf{y}_i \in \mathbb{Y}^k, \ \forall i = 1, 2, \ldots, m \tag{1.7}$$

For the toy example-1, $y_{ij} (i = 1, 2, \ldots, 8000; \ j = 1, 2)$ are 8,000 real numbers in 2D space $\mathbb{Y}^2$. For the toy example-2, each label, y_{i1} or y_{i2}, has a value of 0 or 1 (or -1 or 1), but the labels can still be viewed living in $\mathbb{Y}^2$.

These labels $\mathbf{y}_i (i = 1, 2, \ldots, m)$ can be stacked to form a label set $\mathbf{Y} \in \mathbb{Y}^k$, although we may not really do so in computation.

Typically, affine transformations end at the output layer in a neural network and produces a vector in a label space, so that a loss function can be constructed there for "terminal control".

1.5.5 *Hypothesis space*

The learning parameters $\hat{\mathbf{w}}$ in a machine learning model are continuous variables that live in a **hypothesis space** noted as $\mathbb{W}^P$ over the real numbers. Learning parameters are also called training or trainable parameters. We use these terms interchangeably. The learning parameters include weights and biases in each and all the layer. The hat above $\mathbf{w}$ implying that it is a collection of all weights and biases, so that we have single notation in a vector for all learning parameters. Its dimension P depends on type of hypothesis used including the configuration of neural networks or ML models. These parameters always work with feature vectors, resulting in intermediate feature vectors in a new feature space or in a label space, thorough a properly designed architecture.

These parameters need to be updated which involves vector operations. To ensure convergence, we would need the vector of all learning parameters obey important vector properties, such as inner products, norms and the Cauchy-Schwartz inequality, etc. We will do such proofs multiple times in this book. Therefore, we require $\mathbb{W}^P$ be a vector space, so that each update to the current learning parameters results new parameters that are still in the same vector space, until they converge.

Note that the learning parameters, in general, are in matrix form or column vectors (that can be viewed as a special case of matrix). In a typical machine learning model, there could be multiple matrices of different sizes. These matrices form **affine transformation matrices** that operates on features on affine spaces. A component in a "vector" of the hypothesis space can be in fact a matrix in general, and thus it is not easy to comprehend intuitively. The easiest (and valid) way is to "flatten" all the matrix and then "concatenate" them together to form a tall vector, and then treat it as a usual vector. We do this kind of flattening and concatenation all the time in Python. Such a flattened tall vector $\hat{\mathbf{w}}$ in the hypothesis space $\mathbb{W}^P$ can be written generally as,

$$\hat{\mathbf{w}} = [w_0, w_1, \ldots, w_P]^\top \in \mathbb{W}^P \tag{1.8}$$

We will discuss in later chapters the details about $\mathbb{W}^P$ for various models including estimation of the dimension P.

1.5.6 *Definition of a typical machine learning model, a mathematical view*

Finally, we can define mathematically ML models for prediction as a mapping operator:

$$\mathbb{M}(\hat{\mathbf{w}} \in \mathbb{W}^P; \overline{\mathbf{X}} \in \overline{\mathbb{X}}^p, \mathbf{Y} \in \mathbb{Y}^k) : \mathbb{X}^p \to \mathbb{Y}^k \tag{1.9}$$

It reads that the ML model $\mathbb{M}$ uses a given dataset $\mathbf{X}$ with $\mathbf{Y}$ to train its learning parameters $\hat{\mathbf{w}}$, and produces a map (or giant functions) that makes a prediction in the label space for any point in the feature space.

The ML model shown in Eq. (1.9) is in fact a **data-parameter converter**: it converts a given dataset to learning parameters during training and then converts the parameters back in making a prediction for a given set of feature variables. It can also be mathematically viewed as a giant function with k components in the feature space $\mathbb{X}^p$ and controlled (parameterized) by the training parameters in $\mathbb{W}^P$. When the parameters are tuned, one gets a set of k giant functions over the feature space.

On the other hand, this set of k giant functions can also be viewed as continuous (differentiable) functions of these parameters for any given data-point in the dataset, which can be used to form a loss function that is also differentiable. Such a loss function can be the error between these k giant functions and the corresponding k labels given in the dataset. It can be viewed as a **functional** of prediction functions that in turn are functions of $\hat{\mathbf{w}}$ in the vector space $\mathbb{W}^P$. The training is to minimize such a loss function for all the data-points in the dataset, by updating the training parameters to become minimizers. This overview picture will be made explicitly into a formula in later chapters. The success factors for building a quality ML model include: (1) type of hypothesis, (2) number of learning parameters in $\mathbb{W}^P$, (3) quality (representativeness to the underlaying problem to be modeled, including correctness, size, data-point distribution over the features space, and noise level) of the dataset in $\mathbb{X}^p$, and (4) techniques to find the **minimizer** of learning parameters to best produce the label in the dataset. We will discuss this in detail in later chapters for different machine learning models.

Concepts on spaces are helpful in our later analysis of the predictive properties of machine learning models. Readers may find difficulty in comprehending these concepts at this stage, and thus are advised to just have some rough idea for now and to revisit this section when reading relevant chapters. Readers may jump to Section 13.1.5 and take a look at Eq. (13.13) there just for a quick glance on how the spaces evolve in a deepnet.

Note also that there are ML models for discontinuous feature variables, and the learning parameters may not need to be continuous. Such methods are often developed based on proper intuitive rules and techniques, and we will discuss some of those. The concepts on spaces may not be directly applicable but can often help.

1.6 Requirements for Creating Machine Learning Models

To train a machine learning model, one would need the following:

1. A dataset, which may be obtained via observations, experiments, and physics-law-based models. The dataset is usually divided (in a random manner) into two mutually independent subsets, training dataset and testing dataset, typically at a rate of 75:25. The independence of the testing dataset is critical, because ML models are determined largely by the training dataset, and hence their reliability depends on objective testing.
2. Labels with the dataset, if possible.
3. Prior information on the dataset if possible, such as the quality of the data and key features of the data. This can be useful in choosing a proper algorithm for the problem, and in application of regularization techniques in the training.
4. Proper computer software modules and/or effective algorithms.
5. A computer, preferably connected to the internet.

1.7 Types of Data

Data are the key to any data-based models. There are many types of data available for different types of problems that one may make use of as follows:

- **Images**: photos from cameras (more often now cellphones), images obtained from the open websites, computer tomography (CT), X-ray, ultrasound, Magnetic resonance imaging (MRI), etc.
- **Computer-generated data**: data from proven physics-law-based models, other surrogate models, other reliable trained machine learning models, etc.
- **Text**: unclassified text documents, books, emails, webpages, social media records, etc.
- **Audio and video**: audio and video recordings.

Note that the quality and the sampling domain of the dataset play important roles in training reliable machine learning models. Use of a trained model beyond the data sampling domain requires a special caution, because it can go wrong unexpectedly, and hence be very dangerous.

1.8 Relation Between Physics-Law-based and Data-based Models

Machine learning models are in general **slow learners, fast predictors**, while physics-law-based models do not need to learn (using existing laws), but are slow in prediction. This is because the strategies for physics-law-based models and those for data-based models are quite different. ML models use datasets to train the parameters, but physics-law-based models use laws to determine the parameters.

However, at the detailed computational methodology level, many techniques used in both models are in fact the same or quite similar. For example, when we express a variable as a function of other variables, both models use basis functions (polynomial, or radial basis function (RBF), or both). In constructing objective functions, the least squares error formulation is used in both. In addition, the regularization methods used are also quite similar. Therefore, one should not study these models in total isolation. The ideas and techniques may be deeply connected and mutually adaptable. This realization can be useful in better understanding and further development of more effective methods for both models, by exchanging the ideas and techniques from one to another. In general, for physics-law-based computational methods, such as the general form of meshfree methods, we understand reasonably well why and how a method works in theory [3]. Therefore, we are quite confident about what we are going to obtain when a method is used for a problem. For data-based methods, however, this is not always true. Therefore, it is of importance to develop fundamental theories for data-based methods. The author made some attempts [21] to reveal the relationship between physics-law-based and data-based models, and to establish some theoretical foundation for data-based models. In this book, we will try to discuss the similarities and differences, when a computational method is used in both models.

1.9 This Book

This book offers an introduction to general topics on machine learning. Our focus will be on the basic concepts, fundamental theories, and essential computational techniques related to creation of various machine learning models. We decided not to provide a comprehensive document for all the machine learning techniques, models, and algorithms. This is because the topic of machine learning is very extensive and it is not possible to be comprehensive in content. Also, it is really not possible for many readers to learn all the content. In addition, there are in fact plenty of documents and codes available publicly online. There is no lack of material, and there is no need to simply reproduce these materials. In the opinion of the author, the best learning approach is to learn the most essential basics and build a strong foundation, which is sufficient to learn other related topics, methods, and algorithms. Most importantly, readers with strong fundamentals can even develop innovative and more effective machine models for their problems.

Based on this philosophy, the highlights of the book that cannot be found easily or in good completion in the open literature are listed as follows, many of which are the outcomes of author's study in the past years:

1. Detailed discussion on and demonstration of predictability for arbitrary linear functions of the basic hypothesis used in major ML models.
2. Affine transformation properties and their demonstrations, affine space, affine transformation unit, array, chained arrays, roles of the weights and biases, and roles of activation functions for deepnet construction.
3. Examination of predictability of high-order functions and a Universal Prediction Theory for deepnets.
4. A concept of data-parameter converter, parameter encoding, and uniqueness of the encoding.
5. Role of affine transformation in SVM, complete description of SVM formulation, and the kernel trick.
6. Detailed discussion on and demonstration of activation functions, Neural-Pulse-Unit (NPU), leading to the Universal Approximation Theorem for wide-nets.
7. Differentiation of a function with respect to a vector and matrix, leading to automatic differentiation and Autograd.
8. Solution Existence Theory, effects of parallel data-points, and predictability of the solution against the label.
9. Neurons-Samples Theory gives, for the first time, a general rule of thumb on relationship between the number of data-points and the number neurons in a neural network (or the total pseudo-dimensions of affine spaces involved).
10. Detailed discussion on and demonstration of Tikhonov regularization effects.

The author has made substantial effort to write Python codes to demonstrate the essential and difficult concepts and formulations, which allows readers to comprehend each chapter earlier. Based on the learning experience of the author, this can make the learning more effective.

The chapters of this book are written, in principle, readable independently, by allowing some duplicates. Necessary cross-references between chapters provided are kept minimum.

1.10 Who May Read This Book

The book is written for beginners interested to learn the basics of machine learning, including university students who have completed their first year, graduate students, researchers, and professionals in engineering and sciences. Engineers and practitioners who want to learn to build machine learning models may also find the book useful. Basic knowledge of college mathematics is helpful in reading this book smoothly.

This book may be used as a textbook for undergraduates (3rd year or senior) and graduate students. If this book is adopted as a textbook, the instructor may contact the author (liugr100@gmail.com) directly for some homework and course projects and solutions.

Machine learning is still a fast developing area of research. There still exist many challenging problems, which offer ample opportunities for research to develop new methods and algorithms. Currently, it is a hot topic of research and applications. Different techniques are being developed every day, and new businesses are formed constantly. It is the hope of the author that this book can be helpful in studying existing and developing machine learning models.

1.11 Codes Used in This Book

The book has been written using Jupiter Notebook with codes. Readers who purchased the book may contact the author directly (mailto:liugr100@gmail.com) to request a softcopy of the book with codes (which may be updated), free for academic use after registration. The conditions for use of the book and codes developed by the author, in both hardcopy and softcopy, are as follows:

1. Users are entirely at their own risk using any of part of the codes and techniques.

2. The book and codes are only for your own use. You are not allowed to further distribute without permission from the author of the code.
3. There will be no user support.
4. Proper reference and acknowledgment must be given for the use of the book, codes, ideas, and techniques.

Note that the handcrafted codes provided in the book are mainly for studying and better understanding the theory and formulation of ML methods. For production runs, well-established and well-tested packages should be used, and there are plenty out there, including but not limited to Scikit learn, PyTouch, TensorFlow, and Keras. Also, our codes provided are often run with various packages/modules. Therefore, care is needed when using these codes, because the behavior of the codes often depends on the versions of Python and all these packages/modules. When the codes do not run as expected, version mismatch could be one of the problems. When this book was written, the versions of Python and some of the packages/modules were as follows:

- Python 3.6.13 :: Anaconda, Inc.
- Jupyter Notebook (web-based) 6.3.0
- TensorFlow 2.4.1
- keras 2.4.3
- gym 0.18.0

When issues are encountered in running a code, readers may need to check the versions of the packages/modules used. If Anaconda Navigator is used, the versions of all these packages/modules installed with the Python environment are listed when the Python environment are highlighted. You can also check the versions of a package in a code cell of the Jupyter Notebook. For example, to check the version of the current environment of Python, one may use

```
!python -V            #! is used to execute an external command
```

```
Python 3.6.13 :: Anaconda, Inc.
```

To check the version of a package/module, one may use

- import package_name
- print('package_name version',package_name)

For example,

```python
import keras
print('keras version',keras.__version__)
import tensorflow as tf
print('tensorflow version',tf.version.VERSION)
```

```
keras version 2.4.3
tensorflow version 2.4.1
```

If the version is indeed an issue, one would need to either modify the code to fit the version or install the correct version in your system, by may be creating an alternative environment. It is very useful to query on the web using the error message, and solutions or leads can often be found. This is the approach the author often takes when encountering an issue in running a code. Finally, this book has used materials and information available on the web with links. These links may change over time, because of the nature of the web. The most effective way (and often used by the author) to dealing with this matter is to use keywords to search online, if the link is lost.

References

[1] G.R. Liu and S.S. Quek, *The Finite Element Method: A Practical Course*, Butterworth-Heinemann, London, 2013.

[2] G.R. Liu and T.T. Nguyen, *Smoothed Finite Element Methods*, Taylor and Francis Group, New York, 2010.

[3] G.R. Liu, *Mesh Free Methods: Moving Beyond the Finite Element Method*, Taylor and Francis Group, New York, 2010.

[4] G.R. Liu and Gui-Yong Zhang, *Smoothed Point Interpolation Methods: G Space Theory and Weakened Weak Forms*, World Scientific, New Jersey, 2013.

[5] G.R. Liu and X. Han, *Computational Inverse Techniques in Nondestructive Evaluation*, Taylor and Francis Group, New York, 2003.

[6] F. Rosenblatt, *Principles of Neurodynamics: Perceptrons and the Theory of Brain Mechanisms*, New York, 1962. https://books.google.com/books?id=7FhRAA AAMAAJ.

[7] D.E. Rumelhart, G.E. Hinton and R.J. Williams, *Learning Internal Representations by Error Propagation*, 1986.

[8] G.R. Liu, FEA-AI and AI-AI: Two-way deepnets for real-time computations for both forward and inverse mechanics problems, *International Journal of Computational Methods*, **16**(08), 1950045, 2019.

[9] G.R. Liu, S.Y. Duan, Z.M. Zhang *et al.*, TubeNet: A special trumpetnet for explicit solutions to inverse problems, *International Journal of Computational Methods*, **18**(01), 2050030, 2021. https://doi.org/10.1142/S0219876220500309.

[10] Fukushima Kunihiko, Neocognitron: A self-organizing neural network model for a mechanism of pattern recognition unaffected by shift in position, *Biological Cybernetics*, **36**(4), 193–202, Apr 1980. https://doi.org/10.1007%2Fbf00344251.

[11] D. Ciregan, U. Meier and J. Schmidhuber, Multi-column deep neural networks for image classification, *2012 IEEE Conference on Computer Vision and Pattern Recognition*, 2012.

[12] M.V. Valueva, N.N. Nagornov, P.A. Lyakhov *et al.*, Application of the residue number system to reduce hardware costs of the convolutional neural network implementation, *Mathematics and Computers in Simulation*, **177**, 232–243, 2020.

[13] Duan Shuyong, Ma Honglei, G.R. Liu *et al.*, Development of an automatic lawnmower with real-time computer vision for obstacle avoidance, *International Journal of Computational Methods*, Accepted, 2021.

[14] Duan Shuyong, Lu Ningning, Lyu Zhongwei *et al.*, An anchor box setting technique based on differences between categories for object detection, *International Journal of Intelligent Robotics and Applications*, **6**, 38–51, 2021.

[15] M. Warren and P. Walter, A logical calculus of ideas immanent in nervous activity, *Bulletin of Mathematical Biophysics*, **5**, 127–147, 1943.

[16] J. Schmidhuber, *Habilitation Thesis: An Ancient Experiment with Credit Assignment Across 1200 Time Steps or Virtual Layers and Unsupervised Pre-training for a Stack of Recurrent NNs*, 1993, TUM. https://people.idsia.ch//~juergen/habilitation/node114.html.

[17] Yu Yong, Si Xiaosheng, Hu Changhua *et al.*, A review of recurrent neural networks: LSTM cells and network architectures, *Neural Computation*, **31**(7), 1235–1270, 2019. https://direct.mit.edu/neco/article/31/7/1235/8500/A-Review-of-Recurrent-Neural-Networks-LSTM-Cells.

[18] L. Shi, F. Wang, S. Duan *et al.*, Two-way TubeNets uncertain inverse methods for improving positioning accuracy of robots based on interval, *The 11th International Conference on Computational Methods (ICCM2020)*, 2020.

[19] Duan Shuyong, Shi Lutong, G.R. Liu *et al.*, An uncertainty inversion technique using two-way neural network for parameter identification of robot arms, *Inverse Problems in Science & Engineering*, **29**, 3279–3304, 2021.

[20] Duan Shuyong, Wang Li, G.R. Liu *et al.*, A technique for inversely identifying joint-stiffnesses of robot arms via two-way TubeNets, *Inverse Problems in Science & Engineering*, **13**, 3041–3061, 2021.

[21] G.R. Liu, A neural element method, *International Journal of Computational Methods*, **17**(07), 2050021, 2020.

Chapter 2

Basics of Python

This chapter discusses basics of Python language for coding machine learning models. Python is a very powerful high-level programming language with the need for compiling, but with some level of efficiency of machine-level language. It has become the top popular tool for the development of tools and applications in the general area of machine learning. It has rich libraries for open access, and new libraries are constantly being developed. The language itself is powerful in terms of functionality. It is an excellent tool for effective and productive coding and programming. It is also fast, and the structure of the language is well built for making use of bulky data, which is often the case in machine learning.

This chapter is not a formal training on Python, but just to help readers have a smoother start in learning and practicing the materials in the later chapters. Our focus will be on some useful simple tricks that are familiar to the author, and some behavior subtleties that often affect our coding in ML. Readers familiar with Python may simply skip this chapter. We will use the Jupyter Notebook as the platform for the discussions, so that the documentation and demonstration can be all in a single file.

You may go online and have the Jupyter Notebook installed at, for example, https://www.anaconda.com/distribution/, where you can have the Jupyter Notebook and Python installed at the same time, and maybe along with another useful Python IDE (Integrated Development Environment) called Spyder. In my laptop, I have all three pieces ready to use.

A Jupyter Notebook consists of "cells" of different types: cells for codes and cells for text called "makedown". Each cell is framed with color borders, and the color shows up when the cell is clicked on. A green color border indicates that this cell is in the input mode, and one can type and edit the contents. Pressing "ctrl + Enter" within the cell, the green border changes to blue color, indicating that this cell is formatted or executed, and may produce an outcome. Double clicking on the blue framed cell sets it back to the input mode. The right vertical border is made thicker for better viewing. This should be sufficient for us to get going. One will get more skills (such as adding cells, deleting cells, and converting cell types) by playing and navigating among the menu bars on the top of the Notebook window.

Googling the open online sources is excellent for getting help when one has a question. The author does this all the time. Sources of the reference materials include the following:

- https://docs.python.org/3.7/
- https://docs.scipy.org/doc/numpy/reference/?v=20191112052936
- https://medium.com/ibm-data-science-experience/markdown-for-jupyter-notebooks-cheatsheet-386c05aeebed
- https://www.dataquest.io/blog/jupyter-notebook-tips-tricks-shortcuts/
- https://www.python.org/about/
- https://www.learnpython.org/
- https://en.wikipedia.org/wiki/Python_(programming_language)
- https://www.learnpython.org/en/Basic_Operators+
- https://www.python.org/+
- https://jupyter.org/
- https://www.youtube.com/watch?v=HW29067qVWkb
- https://pynative.com/

The following lists the details of versions of modules related to jupyter-notebook in the current installation in the author's laptop (Use "!" to execute an external command):

```
!jupyter --version
```

```
jupyter core     : 4.7.1
jupyter-notebook : 6.3.0
qtconsole        : not installed
ipython          : 7.16.1
ipykernel        : 5.3.4
jupyter client   : 6.1.12
jupyter lab      : not installed
nbconvert        : 6.0.7
ipywidgets       : 7.6.3
nbformat         : 5.1.3
traitlets        : 4.3.3
```

2.1 An Exercise

Let us have a less conventional introduction here. Different from other books on computer languages, we start the discussion on how to make use of our own codes that we may develop during the course of study.

First, we "import" the Python system library or module from external or internal sources, so that functions (also called methods) there can be used in our code for interaction with your computer system. The most important environment setting is the path.

```python
import sys # import an external module "sys" which
            # provides tools for accessing the computer system.
sys.path.append('grbin')
            # I made a code in folder grbin in the current
            # working directory, and want to use it later.
#print(sys.path)
            # check the current paths To execute this or any
            # cell use Ctrl-Enter (hold on Ctrl and press Enter)
```

Note that "#" in a code cell starts a comment line. It can be put anywhere in a line in a code. Everything in the line behind # becomes comments, and is not treated as a part of the code.

One may remove "#" in front of print(sys.path), execute it, and a number of paths will be printed. Many of them were set during the installations of the system and various codes, including the Anaconda and Python. "grbin" in the current working directory has just been added in using the sys.path.append().

When multiple lines of comments are needed, we use "doc-strings" as follows:

```python
'''Inside here are all comments with multiple lines. It is \
a good way to convey information to users, co-programmers. \
Use a backslash to break a line.'''
```

```
'Inside here are all comments with multiple lines. It is a
good way to convey information to users, co-programmers.
Use a backslash to break a line.'
```

Just for demonstration purposes, we now import our own "module" (a Python file named as grcodes.py) "grcodes", and then give it an alias "gr" for easy reference later, when accessing the attributes, functions, classes, etc., inside the module.

```python
import grcodes as gr   # a Python code grcodes.py in 'grbin'.
```

The following cell contains the Python code "grcodes.py". Readers may create the "grcodes.py" file and put it in the folder "grbin" (or any other folder), so that the cell above can be executed and "gr.printx()" can be used.

```python
from __future__ import print_function   # import external module
import sys
# Define function
def printx(name):
    """ This prints out both the name and its value together.
    usage: name = 88.0;  printx('name') """
    frame=sys._getframe(1)
    print(name,'=',repr(eval(name,frame.f_globals,frame.f_locals)))
```

Let us try to use a function in the imported module grcodes, using its alias gr.

```python
x = 1.0                 # Assign x a value.
print(x)                # The Python built-in print() function prints
                        # the value of the given argument x.

gr.printx('x')          # a function from the gr module. It prints the
                        # argument name, and its value at the same time.
```

```
1.0
x = 1.0
```

```python
help(gr.printx)     # Find out the usage of the gr.printx function
```

```
Help on function printx in module grcodes:

printx(name)
    This prints out both the name and its value together.
    usage: name = 88.0;  printx('name')
```

Nice. I have actually completed a simple task of printing out "x" using Python, and in two ways. The gr.printx function is equivalent to doing the following:

```python
print('x=',x)       # you must type the same x twice
```

```
x= 1.0
```

Notice in this case that you must type the same x twice, which gives room for error. A good code should have as little as possible repetition, allowing easy maintenance. When a change is needed, the programmer (or others using or maintaining the code) shall just need to do it once.

Alternatively, one can import functions from a module in the following alternative manner:

```python
from grcodes import printx   # you may import more functions
        # by adding the function names separated with ",".
#from grcodes import *       # Import everything from grcodes
        # This is not a very good practice, because it can
        # lead to problems when some function names in
        # grcodes happened to be the same as those in the code.
```

In this case, we can now use the imported functions as if it is written in the current file (notebook).

```python
gr.printx('x')
printx('x')              # Notice that "gr." is no longer needed.
```

```
x = 1.0
x = 1.0
```

2.2 Briefing on Python

Now, what is Python? Python was created by Guido van Rossum and first released in 1991. Python's design philosophy emphasizes code "readability". It uses an object-oriented approach aiming to help programmers to write clear, less repetitive, logical codes for small- and large-scale projects that may have teams of people working together.

Python is open source, and its interpreters are available for many operating systems. A global community of programmers develops and maintains CPython, an open-source reference implementation. A non-profit organization, the Python Software Foundation, manages and directs resources for Python and CPython development.

The language's core philosophy is summarized in the document The Zen of Python (PEP 20), which includes aphorisms such as the following:

- Beautiful is better than ugly.
- Explicit is better than implicit.
- Simple is better than complex.
- Complex is better than complicated.
- Readability counts.

Guido van Rossum manages Python development projects together with a steering council. There are two major Python versions, Python 2 and Python 3, and they are quite different. Python 3.0, released 2008, was a major revision. It is not completely backward-compatible with Python 2. Due to the number of codes written for Python 2, support for Python 2.7 (the last release in the 2.x series) was extended to 2020. At the time of writing this book, Python 3.9 had already been released. This tutorial uses Python 3.6 because it supports more existing libraries and modules.

There are a huge number (probably in the order of hundreds) of computer programming languages developed so far. The author's first experience with computer programming languages was in the 1970s, when learning BASICS for programming. He used ALGOL60 later and then FORTRAN for a long time from the 1970s till today, along with limited use of Matlab, C, C++, and now Python. Any programming language has a complicated syntax and deeply organized logic. For a user like the author, the best approach to learn a computer programming language is via examples and practice, while paying attention to the syntax, property, and the behavior. For a beginner, following examples is probably the best approach to get started. This will be the guidance in writing this section of the book. For rigorous syntax, readers may read the relevant documentations that are readily available online. We will give a lot of examples, with explanations in the form of comments (as a programmer often does). All these examples may be directly executed within this book while reading, so that readers can have a real-time feeling for easy observation of the behavior and hence comprehension. Readers may also make use of it via a simple copy and paste to form his/her notebook. Because of this example-based approach, the discussions on different topics may jump a little here and there.

To write and execute a Python code, one often uses an IDE. Jupyter Notebook, PyCharm, and Spyder are among the popular IDEs. In this book, we use Jupyter Notebook (https://jupyter.org/) via the distributor Anaconda (https://www.anaconda.com/). Jupyter Notebook can be used not only as an IDE but also as a nice document generator allowing description text (markdown cells) and code cells to be edited together in one document. The lecture notes used in the author's machine learning course have also been mostly developed using Jupyter Notebook. The documents created using Jupyter Notebook can be exported in various types of documents, including ascii doc, html, latex, markdown, pdf, Python(.py), and slides(.slides.html). Readers and students may use this notebook as a template for your documents (project reports, homeworks, etc.), if so desired. If one needs to use a spelling check when typing in the markdown cells in a Jupyter Notebook, the following commands should be executed in the Anaconda Prompt:

- %pip install jupyter_contrib_nbextensions.
- %jupyter contrib nbextension install --user.
- %jupyter nbextension enable spellchecker/main.

This would mark the misspelled words for you (but will not provide suggestions). Other necessary modules with add-on functions may also be installed in a similar manner.

This book covers in a brief manner a tiny portion of Python.

2.3 Variable Types

Python is said to be object oriented. Every variable in Python is an object. It is "dynamically typed": the variable type is determined at the point when it is typed. You do not need to declare variables before using them, or declare their types. It has some basic types of variables: Numbers and Strings. These variables can stand alone, or form a Tuple, List, Dictionary, Set, Numpy Arrays, etc. They all can be subjected to various operations (arithmetic, boolean, logical, formatting, etc.) in a code. Note that the variable is loosely defined, meaning it could be a Tuple, List, Dictionary, etc. For example, a List can be in a List, a Tuple in a List, or a List in a Tuple.

2.3.1 *Numbers*

Python supports three types of numbers — **integers**, **floating point numbers**, and **complex numbers**.

To define an integer variable, one can simply assign it with an integer.

```python
my_int = 48   # by this assignment, my_int becomes an integer
print(my_int); printx('my_int')
```

```
48
my_int = 48
```

```python
type(my_int)  # Check the type of the variable. print() is not
              # needed, if it is the last line in the cell
```

```
int
```

```python
my_int = 5.0            # by this my_int becomes now a float
```

```python
type(my_int)
```

```
float
```

```python
my_complex=8.0+5.0j # by this my_complex is a complex number
print(my_complex)
printx('my_complex')
```

```
(8+5j)
my_complex = (8+5j)
```

```python
my_int, my_float, my_string = 20, 10.0, "Hello!"

if my_string == "Hello!":    # comparison operators: ==, !=, <, <=, >, >=
    print("A string: %s" % my_string) # Indented 4 spaces

if isinstance(my_float, float) and my_float == 10.0:
#isinstance():returns if an object is an instance of a class
    print("This is a float, and it is %f" % my_float)

if isinstance(my_int, int) and my_int == 20:
    print("This is an integer, and it is: %d" % my_int)
```

```
A string: Hello!
This is a float, and it is 10.000000
This is an integer, and it is: 20
```

To list all variables, functions, modules currently in the memory, try this:

```python
#%whos                   # you may remove "#" and try this
```

The type of a variable can be converted:

```python
my_float = 5.0 # by this assignment, my_float becomes a float
print(my_float)
my_float = float(6)
    # create a float, by converting an integer, using float()
print(my_float)
print(int(7.0))        # float is converted to integer.
printx('int(7.0)')
```

```
5.0
6.0
7
int(7.0) = 7
```

To check the memory address of a variable, use

```python
a = 1.0
print('a=',a, 'at memory address:',id(a))
```

```
a= 1.0 at memory address: 1847993237600
```

```python
b = a
print('b=',b, 'at memory address: ',id(b))
```

```
b= 1.0 at memory address:  1847993237600
```

Notice that 'b' has the same address of 'a'.

```python
a, b = 2.0, 3.0
print('a=',a, 'at memory address: ',id(a))
print('b=',b, 'at memory address: ',id(b))
```

```
a= 2.0 at memory address:  1847974064064
b= 3.0 at memory address:  1847974063944
```

Notice the change in address when the value of a variable changes.

2.3.2 *Underscore placeholder*

```python
n1=100000000000
n_1=100_000_000_000                  # for easy reading
print('Yes, n1 is same as n_1') if n1==n_1 else print('No')
                                 # Ternary if Statement
n2=1_000_000_000
print('Total=',n1+n2)
print('Total=',f'{n1+n2:,}') # f-string (Python3.6 or later)
total=n1+n2
print('Total=',f'{total:_}')
```

```
Yes, n1 is same as n_1
Total= 101000000000
Total= 101,000,000,000
Total= 101_000_000_000
```

2.3.3 *Strings*

Strings are bits of text, which are very useful in coding in generating labels and file names for outputs. Strings can be defined with anything between quotes. The quote can be either a pair of single quotes or a pair of double quotes.

```python
my_string = "How are you?"
  # spring is defined, the characters in it can be indexed
print(my_string, my_string[0:3],my_string[5],my_string[10:])
my_string = 'Hello,' + " hello!" + " I am here."
  # note "+" operator for strings is concatenation
print(my_string)
```

```
How are you? How r u?
Hello, hello! I am here.
```

Although both single and double quotes can all be used, when there are apostrophes in a string, one should use double quotes, or these apostrophes would terminate the string if single quotes are used and vice versa. For example,

```
my_string = "Do not worry, just use double quotes to 'escape'."
print(my_string)
```

```
Do not worry, just use double quotes to 'escape'.
```

One may exchange the role of these two types of quotes:

```
my_string = 'Do not worry about "double quotes".
print(my_string)
```

```
Do not worry about "double quotes"
```

One shall refer to the Python documentation, when needing to include things such as carriage returns, backslashes, and Unicode characters. Below are some more handy and clean operators applied to numbers and strings. You may try it out and get some experience.

```
one, two, three = 1, 2, 3          # Assign values to variables.
summation = one + two + three
print('summation=',summation)      # printx('summation')
```

```
summation= 6
```

```
one, two, three = 1, 2, 3.0        # variable type can be mixed!
summation = one + two + three
print('Summation=',summation)
```

```
Summation= 6.0
```

```
one3 = two3 = three3 = 3   # Assign a same value to variables
print(one3, two3, three3)
```

```
3 3 3
```

More handy operations:

```python
hello, world = "Hello,", "world!"
helloworld = hello + " " + world + "!!" # concatenate strings
print(helloworld, '   ', hello + " " + world)
lhw=len(helloworld)  # length of the string, counting the space
                     # and the punctuations.
print('The length of the "helloword" is',lhw)
```

```
Hello, world!!!     Hello, world!
The length of the "helloword" is 15
```

You can split the string to a list of strings, each of which is a word.

```python
the_words = helloworld.split(" ") # creates a list of strings
                  # Similar operations on Lists later
print("Split the words of the string: %s" % the_words)
print('Joined together again with a space as separator:',' '
      '.join(the_words))
```

```
Split the words of the string: ['Hello,', 'world!!!']
Joined together again with a space as separator: Hello, world!!!
```

To find a letter (character) in a string, try this:

```python
my_string = "Hello world!"
print('"o" is right after the',my_string.index("o"),\
      'th letter.')   # "\" is used to break a line
print('The first letter "l" is right after the', \
      my_string.index("l"), 'nd letter.')
```

```
"o" is right after the 4 th letter.
The first letter "l" is right after the  2 nd letter.
```

Do not like the white-spaces between "4" and "th" "2" and "nd"? use string concatenation:

```python
print('The position of the letter "o" is right after the ' +
      str(my_string.index("o")) + 'th letter.')
                # "+" concatenate
print('The 1st letter "l" is right after the ' +
      str(my_string.index("l")) + 'nd letter.')
```

```
The position of the letter "o" is right after the 4th letter.
The 1st letter "l" is right after the 2nd letter.
```

You may need to find the frequency of each element in a list.

```python
from collections import Counter    # import Counter module.
my_list = ['a','a','b','b','b','c','d','d','d','d','d']
count = Counter(my_list) # Counter object is a dictionary
print(count)    # of frequencies of each element in the list
                # See also Dictionary later
```

```
Counter({'d': 5, 'b': 3, 'a': 2, 'c': 1})
```

```python
print('The frequency of "b" is', count['b'])
                # frequency of an element indexed by its key
```

```
The frequency of "b" is 3
```

Note Python (and many other programming languages) starts counting at 0 instead of 1.

We list below more operations that can be useful.

Conversion between uppercase and lowercase of a string

```python
my_string = "Hello world!"
print(my_string.upper(),my_string.lower(),my_string.title())
# convert to uppercase and lowercase, respectively.
```

```
HELLO WORLD! hello world! Hello World!
```

- Reversion of a string using slicing (also see section on Lists).

```python
my_string = "ABCDEFG"
reversed_string = my_string[::-1]
print(reversed_string)
```

```
GFEDCBA
```

The title() function of string class

```python
my_string = "my name is professor g r liu"
new_string = my_string.title()
print(new_string)
```

```
My Name Is Professor G R Liu
```

Use of repetitions

```python
n  = 8
my_list = [0]*n
print(my_list)
```

```
[0, 0, 0, 0, 0, 0, 0, 0]
```

```python
my_string = "abcdefg "
print(my_string*2)    #concatenated n times and then print out
```

```
abcdefg abcdefg
```

```python
lotsofhellos = "Hello " * 5   #concatenate 5 times
print(lotsofhellos)
```

```
Hello Hello Hello Hello Hello
```

```python
my_list = [1,2,3,4,5]
print(my_list*2)      #concatenate 2 times and then print out
```

```
[1, 2, 3, 4, 5, 1, 2, 3, 4, 5]
```

Length of a given argument using len()

```python
print('The length of "ABCD" is', len('ABCD'))
```

The length of "ABCD" is 4

```python
print('The length of',my_string,'is', len(my_string))
```

The length of abcdefg is 8

```python
even_numbers, odd_numbers= [2,4,6,8], [1,3,5,7]
```

```python
length = len(even_numbers)      #get the length using len()
all_numbers = odd_numbers + even_numbers    #concatenation
print(all_numbers,' The original length is',
length, '. The new length is',len(all_numbers))
```

[1, 3, 5, 7, 2, 4, 6, 8] The original length is 4 . The new
   length is 8

Sort the elements using sorted()

```python
print(sorted('BACD'),sorted('ABCD',reverse=True))
print(sorted(all_numbers), sorted(all_numbers,reverse=True))
```

['A', 'B', 'C', 'D'] ['D', 'C', 'B', 'A']
[1, 2, 3, 4, 5, 6, 7, 8] [8, 7, 6, 5, 4, 3, 2, 1]

Multiplying each element in a list by a same number

```python
original_list, n = [1,2,3,4], 2
new_list = [n*x for x in original_list]
            # list comprehension for element-wise operations
print(new_list)
```

[2, 4, 6, 8]

Generating index for a list using enumerate()

```python
my_list = ['a', 'b', 'c']
for index, value in enumerate(my_list):
    print('{0}: {1}'.format(index+1, value))
```

```
1: a
2: b
3: c
```

```python
for index, value in enumerate(my_list):   # generate indices
    print(f'{index+1}: {value}')           # f-string
```

```
1: a
2: b
3: c
```

Error exception tracks code while avoiding stop execution

```python
a, b = 1,2
try:
    print(a/b)                      # exception raised when b=0
except ZeroDivisionError:
    print("division by zero")
else:
    print("no exceptions raised")
finally:
    print("Regardless of what happened, run this always")
```

```
0.5
no exceptions raised
Regardless of what happened, run this always
```

Get the memory size in bytes

```python
import sys                          #import sys module
num = "AAA"
print('The memory size is %d'%sys.getsizeof(num),'bytes')
                                    # memory size of string
```

```
The memory size is 52 bytes
```

```
num = 21099
print('The memory size is %d'%sys.getsizeof(num),'bytes')
                              # memory size of integer
```

```
The memory size is 28 bytes
```

```
num = 21099.0
print('The memory size is %d'%sys.getsizeof(num),'bytes')
                              # memory size of float
```

```
The memory size is 24 bytes
```

Check whether the string starts with or ends with something

```
astring = "Hello world!"
print(astring.startswith("Hello"),astring.endswith("asdf"),\
      astring.endswith("!"))
```

```
True False True
```

The first one printed True, as the string starts with "Hello". The second one printed False, as the string certainly does not end with "asdf". The third printed True, as the string ends with "!". Their boolean values are useful when creating conditions. More such functions:

```
my_string="Hello World!"
my_string1="HelloWorld"
my_string2="HELLO WORLD!"
print (my_string.isalnum())     #check if all char are numbers
print (my_string1.isalpha())    #check if all char are alphabetic
print (my_string2.isupper())    #test if string is upper case
```

```
False
True
True
```

```python
my_string3, my_string4, my_string5="hello world!","   ", "8888a"
print (my_string3.istitle()) #test if contains title words
print (my_string3.islower()) #test if string is lower case
print (my_string4.isspace()) #test if string is spaces
print (my_string5.isdigit()) #test if string is digits
```

```
False
True
True
False
```

Checking the type and other attributes of variables

```python
n, x, s = 8888,8.0, 'string'
print (type(n), type(x), type(s))    # check the type of an object
print (len(s),len(str(n)),len(str(x)))
```

```
<class 'int'> <class 'float'> <class 'str'>
6 4 3
```

2.3.4 *Conversion between types of variables*

When one of the variables is a floating point number in an operation with other integers, the variable becomes a floating point number.

```python
a = 2
print('a=',a, ' type of a:',type(a))
b = 3.0; a = a + b
print('a=',a, ' type of a:',type(a))
print('b=',b, ' type of a:',type(b))
```

```
a= 2  type of a: <class 'int'>
a= 5.0  type of a: <class 'float'>
b= 3.0  type of a: <class 'float'>
```

The type of a variable can be converted to other types.

```python
n, x, s = 8888,8.5, 'string'
sfn = str(n)           #integer to string
print(sfn,type(sfn))
sfx = str(x)           #float to string
print(sfx,type(sfx))
```

```
8888 <class 'str'>
8.5 <class 'str'>
```

```python
xfn = float(n)         #integer to float
print(xfn,type(xfn))
nfx = int(x)           #float to integer
print(nfx,type(nfx))
```

```
8888.0 <class 'float'>
8 <class 'int'>
```

```python
#a = int('Hello')      # string to integer: produces ValueError
#a = int('8.5')        # string to integer: produces ValueError
a = int('85')          # works, '85' is converted to an integer
print(a,type(a))
```

```
85 <class 'int'>
```

```python
a = float('85')        # how about this one?
print(a,type(a))
```

```
85.0 <class 'float'>
```

```python
8.0 + float("8.0")     #try this
```

```
16.0
```

```python
a = int(False)         # check this out
print(a,type(a))
```

```
0 <class 'int'>
```

However, operators with mixed numbers and strings are not permitted, and it triggers a TypeError:

```python
my_mix = my_float + my_string
```

```
---------------------------------------------------------------
TypeError               Traceback  (most recent call last)
<ipython-input-67-8c4f7138852e> in <module>
----> 1 my_mix = my_float + my_string

TypeError: unsupported operand type(s) for +: 'float' and 'str'
```

2.3.5 *Variable formatting*

Formatting is very useful in printing out variables. Python uses C-style string formatting to create new, formatted strings. The "%" operator is used to format a set of variables enclosed in a "tuple", which is a fixed size list (to be discussed later). It produces a normal text at a location given by one of the "argument specifiers" like "%s", "%d", "%f", etc. The best way to understand this is through examples.

```python
name = "John"
print("Hello, %s! how are you?" % name)    # %s is for string
# for two or more argument specifiers, use a tuple:
name, age = "Kevin", 23
print("%s is %d years old." % (name,age)) # %d is for digit
```

```
Hello, John! how are you?
Kevin is 23 years old.
```

```python
print(f"{name} is {age} years old.")
                          # f-string Python 3.6 or later.
```

```
Kevin is 23 years old.
```

Any object that is not a string (a list for example) can also be formatted using the %s operator. The %s operator formats the object as a string using the "repr" method and returns it. For example:

```python
list1,list2,x=[1,2,3],['John','Ian'],21.5 # multi- assignment
print("List1:%s; List2:%s\n x=%s,x=%f,x=%.3f,x=%e" \
    % (list1,  list2,  x,   x,   x,    x))
```

```
List1:[1, 2, 3]; List2:['John', 'Ian']
 x=21.5,x=21.500000,x=21.500,x=2.150000e+01
```

```
print(f"List1:{list1};List2:{list2};x={x},x={x:.2f}, x={x:.3e}")
                                        # powerful f-string
```

```
List1:[1, 2, 3]; List2:['John', 'Kevin']; x=21.5,x=21.50,x=2.150e+01
```

Often used formatting argument specifiers (if not using f-string):

- %s - String (or any object with a string representation, like numbers).
- %d - Integers.
- %f - Floating point numbers.
- %.f - Floating point numbers with a fixed number-of-digits to the right of the dot.
- %e - scientific notation: a float multiplied by the specified power of 10.
- %x/%X - Integers in hex representation (lowercase/uppercase).

2.4 Arithmetic Operators

Addition, subtraction, multiplication, and division operators can be used with numbers.

2.4.1 *Addition, subtraction, multiplication, division, and power*

$+ - * /$ $//$(floor division) % (remainder of integer division or modulo) $**$

```
number = 1 + 2 * 3 / 4.0
print(number)
```

2.5

The modulo (%) operator returns the integer remainder of the division: dividend % divisor = remainder.

```
numerator, denominator = 11, 2
floor = numerator // denominator   #floor division
print(str(numerator)+'//'+str(denominator)+ '=', floor)
remainder = numerator % denominator
print(str(numerator) +'%'+ str(denominator) +'=', remainder)
print(floor*denominator + remainder)
```

```
11//2= 5
11%2= 1
11
```

Using two multiplication symbols makes a power relationship.

```python
squared, cubed = 7 ** 2, 2 ** 3
print('7 ** 2 =', squared, ', and 2 ** 3 =',cubed)
```

```
7 ** 2 = 49 , and 2 ** 3 = 8
```

```python
bwlg_XOR = 7^2
print(bwlg_XOR)      # ^ is XOR (bitwise logic gate) operator!
```

5

Python allows simple swap operation between two variables.

```python
a, b = 100, 200
print('a=',a,'b=',b)
a, b = b, a          # swapping without using a "mid-man"
print('a=',a,'b=',b)
```

```
a= 100 b= 200
a= 200 b= 100
```

2.4.2 *Built-in functions*

Python provides a number of build-in functions and types that are always available. For a quick glance, see the following table, or find more details at https://docs.python.org/3/library/functions.html.

Built-in Functions

abs()	delattr()	hash()	memoryview()	set()
all()	dict()	help()	min()	setattr()
any()	dir()	hex()	next()	slice()
ascii()	divmod()	id()	object()	sorted()
bin()	enumerate()	input()	oct()	staticmethod()
bool()	eval()	int()	open()	str()
breakpoint()	exec()	isinstance()	ord()	sum()
bytearray()	filter()	issubclass()	pow()	super()
bytes()	float()	iter()	print()	tuple()
callable()	format()	len()	property()	type()
chr()	frozenset()	list()	range()	vars()
classmethod()	getattr()	locals()	repr()	zip()
compile()	globals()	map()	reversed()	__import__()
complex()	hasattr()	max()	round()	

```python
#help(all)           # to find out what a builtin function does
```

2.5 Boolean Values and Operators

Boolean values are two constant objects: True and False. When used as an argument to an arithmetic operator, they behave like the integers 0 and 1, respectively. The built-in function bool() can be used to cast any value to a Boolean. The definitions are as follows:

```python
print(bool(5),bool(-5),bool(0.2),bool(-0.1),bool(str('a')),
      bool(str('0')))
#      True   True   True   True   True   True
print(bool(0),bool(-0.0)) # These are all zero
#      False     False
print(bool(''),bool([]),bool({}),bool(()))    # all empty (0)
#      False   False    False    False
```

```
True True True True True True
False False
False False False False
```

bool() returns False, only if the value is zero or the container is empty. Otherwise, True. Note that str('0') is neither zero nor empty.

Boolean operators include "and" and "or".

```python
print(True and True, False or True, True or True,)
#          True              True              True
print(False and False, False and True)
#          False                 False
```

```
True True True
False False
```

2.6 Lists: A diversified variable type container

We already saw **Lists** a few times. This Section gives more details. A list is a collection of variables, and it is very similar to **arrays** (see Numpy Array section for more details). A list may contain any type of variables, and as many variables as one likes. These variables are held in a pair of square brackets [ ]. Lists can be iterated over for operations when needed. It is one of the "iterables". Let us look at the following examples.

2.6.1 *List creation, appending, concatenation, and updating*

```python
x_list = []       # Use [] to define a placeholder for x_list.
                  # It is empty but with an address assigned.
print('x_list=',x_list)
print(hex(id(x_list)))   # memory address in hexadecimal
```

```
x_list= []
0x1ae44e9f548
```

```python
x_list.append(1)   # 1 is appended as the 0th member in this list
x_list.append(2)   # 2 is appended as the 1st member
x_list.append(3.)  # Variable type changed!
print(x_list[0])   # prints 1, the 0th element ...
print(x_list[1])   # prints 2
print(x_list[2])   # prints 3
print(x_list)      # print all in the list
```

```
3.0
[1, 2, 3.0]
```

```python
for x in x_list:    # prints out 1,2,3.0 in an iteration
    print(x, end=',')

print('\n')
x_list2 = x_list*2
    # concatenation of 2 x_list (not element-wise
    # multiplication!) this creates an independent new x_list2
print(x_list2)
```

```
1,2,3.0,

[1, 2, 3.0, 1, 2, 3.0]
```

```python
print(id(x_list),id(x_list2))   # addresses are different
```

```
1847992120648 1847993139592
```

```python
id(x_list[1])          # Again, print() function is not needed
                       # because this is the last line in the cell
```

```
1594536160
```

```python
x_list3 = x_list    # assignment is a "pointer" to x_list3
print(x_list,'   ',x_list3,)
```

```
[1, 2, 3.0]     [1, 2, 3.0]
```

```python
print(id(x_list),id(x_list3))   # They share the same address
```

```
1847992120648 1847992120648
```

```python
x_list4 = x_list.copy()      # copy() function creates x_list4
                             # it is a new independent list
print(x_list,'   ',x_list4)
```

```
[1, 2, 3.0]     [1, 2, 3.0]
```

```
print(id(x_list),id(x_list4))  # x_list4 has its own address
```

1847992120648 1847993186760

```
x_list[0] = 4.0          # Assign the 0th element a new value
print(x_list)
```

[4.0, 2, 3.0]

```
print(x_list3,' ',x_list4) # x_list3 is changed with x_list,
   # because assignment creates a "pointer". x_list4 is not
   # changed, because it was created using copy() function.
```

[4.0, 2, 3.0]   [1, 2, 3.0]

```
print(x_list2)    # Changes to x_list has no affect
```

[1, 2, 3.0, 1, 2, 3.0]

Creating a list by unpacking a string of digits:

```
num = 19345678
list_of_digits=list(map(int, str(num)))    #list iterable
print(list_of_digits)
list_of_digits=[int(x) for x in str(num)] #list comprehension
print(list_of_digits)
```

[1, 9, 3, 4, 5, 6, 7, 8]
[1, 9, 3, 4, 5, 6, 7, 8]

2.6.2 *Element-wise addition of lists*

Element-wise addition of lists needs a little trick. The best ways, including the use of numpy arrays, will be discussed in the list comprehension section. Here, we use a primitive method to achieve this.

```python
list1, list2= [20, 30, 40], [5, 6, 8]
print (list1, '  ', list2, '  ', list1+list2)
print ("Original list 1: " + str(list1))
print ("Original list 2: " + str(list2))

print ('"+" is not addition, but concatenation:',list1+list2)
```

```
[20, 30, 40]    [5, 6, 8]    [20, 30, 40, 5, 6, 8]
Original list 1: [20, 30, 40]
Original list 2: [5, 6, 8]
"+" is not addition, it is concatenation:  [20, 30, 40, 5, 6, 8]
```

```python
# We shall use a for-loop to achieve element-wise addition:
add_list = []
for i in range(0, len(list1)):  # for-loop to add up one-by-one!
    add_list.append(list1[i] + list2[i])

print ("Element-wise addition of 2 lists is: " + str(add_list))
```

```
Element-wise addition of 2 lists: [25, 36, 48]
```

```python
id(add_list[0])                        # check the address of the list
```

```
1594536896
```

```python
id(list1[0])
```

```
1594536736
```

```python
add_list = []
for i1,i2 in zip(list1,list2): # for-loop and zip() to add it up
    add_list.append(i1+i2)

print ("The element-wise addition of 2 lists: ",add_list)
```

```
The element-wise addition of 2 lists:  [25, 36, 48]
```

2.6.3 *Slicing strings and lists*

Slicing is a useful and efficient operation to manipulate parts of a string, list, or array (to be discussed later). Our discussion starts from slicing strings, and then lists.

```python
my_string = "Hello world!"
            #123456789TET              # conventional order
print('0123456789TE')                  # ordering in Python
print (my_string)
print('5th=',my_string[4])             # take the 5th character
print('7-11th=',my_string[6:11])   # 7th to 11th
```

```
0123456789TE
Hello world!
5th= o
7-11th= world
```

```python
print('[6:-1]=',my_string[6:-1])
        # "-1" for the last slice from the 6th to (last-1)th
print('[:]=',my_string[:])     # all characters in the string
print('[6:]=',my_string[6:])   # slice from 7th to the end
print('[:-1]=',my_string[:-1]) # to (last-1)th
```

```
[6:-1]= world
[:]= Hello world!
[6:]= world!
[:-1]= Hello world
```

```python
my_string = "Hello world!"
            #123456789TET                  # conventional order
print('[3:9:2]=',my_string[3:9:2]) # 4th to 9th step 2
                                   # Syntax:[start:stop:step]
my_string = "Hello world!"
```

```
[3:9:2]= l o
```

Using a negative step, we can easily reverse a string, as we have seen earlier:

```python
my_string = "Hello world!"
print('string:',my_string)
print('[::-1]=',my_string[::-1])   # all but from the last
```

```
string: Hello world!
[::-1]= !dlrow olleH
```

In summary, if we just have one number in the brackets, the slicing takes the character at the (number +1)th position. This is because Python counts from zero. A colon stands for all available. If it is used alone, the slice is the entire string. If there is a number on its left, the slice is from the number to the right-end, and vice versa. A negative number means it counts the number but is from the right-end: −3 means "the 3rd character from the right-end". One can also use the step option for skipping.

Note that when accessing a string with an index which does not exist, it generates an exception of IndexError.

```python
print('[14]=',my_string[14])      # index out of range error
```

```
-------------------------------------------------------------
IndexError        Traceback (most recent call last)
<ipython-input-102-024f17c69a4f> in <module>
----> 1 print('[14]=',my_string[14]) # gives an index out of range error

IndexError: string index out of range
```

```python
print('[14:]=',my_string[14:])      # This will not give an
            # error, but gives nothing: nothing can be sliced
```

```
[14:]=
```

The very similar rules detailed above for strings apply also to a list, by treating a variable in the list as a character.

```python
# Create my_list that contains mixed type variables:
list2=[]
my_list=[0, 1, 2, 3,'4E', 5, 6, 7,[8,8], 9]
 # 1, 2, 3, 4, 5,   6, 7, 8,  9,  10 -> indices
 # 0, 1, 2, 3, 4,   5, 6, 7,  8,   9 -> Python indices
 #-10 -9,-8,-7,-6, -5,-4,-3, -2,  -1 -> Python reverse indices

print(my_list[0:10:1])    # [start:end:step]  end is inclusive!
print(my_list[:])         # A colon stands for all variable
```

```
[0, 1, 2, 3, '4E', 5, 6, 7, [8, 8], 9]
[0, 1, 2, 3, '4E', 5, 6, 7, [8, 8], 9]
```

```python
print(my_list[0:])        # from (0+1)st to the end
print(my_list[1:])        # from (1+1)th to the end
print(my_list[8:])        # from the (8+1)th to the end
print(my_list[8:9])       # Gives a list in list
```

```
[0, 1, 2, 3, '4E', 5, 6, 7, [8, 8], 9]
[1, 2, 3, '4E', 5, 6, 7, [8, 8], 9]
[[8, 8], 9]
[[8, 8]]
```

```python
print(my_list[:])         # A colon stands for all variable
print(my_list[:3])        # 0,1,2,
print(my_list[:1])        # from 1st to 1st: 0
print(my_list[:0])        # from 1st to 0th: empty []
print(my_list[-1])        # reads out the last: 9
print(my_list[-1:])       # Slices out the last:
print(my_list[::-1])      # reverse the list
```

```
[0, 1, 2, 3, '4E', 5, 6, 7, [8, 8], 9]
[0, 1, 2]
[0]
[]
9
[9]
[9, [8, 8], 7, 6, 5, '4E', 3, 2, 1, 0]
```

When accessing a list with an index that does not exist, it generates an exception of IndexError.

```python
#print(my_list[11]) # will give an index out of range error
```

```python
print(my_list[10:]) # from the (10+1)th to the end: no more
                    # there, not out of range, but an empty list
```

```
[]
```

2.6.4 *Underscore placeholders for lists*

```python
nlist = [10, 20, 30, 40, 50, 6.0, '7H']   # Mixed variables
_, _, n3,_,*nn = nlist                     # when only the 3rd is needed,
                                           # skip one, and then the rest
print ('n3=',n3, 'the rest numbers',*nn)

nlist = [10, 20, 30, 40, 50, 60, 70]
_, _, n3, *nn, nlast = nlist               # The 3rd, last and the rest
                                           # in between are needed
print('n3=',n3,', the last=', nlast,', and all the rest numbers',*nn)
```

```
n3= 30 the rest numbers 50 6.0 7H
n3= 30 , the last= 70 , and all the rest numbers 40 50 60
```

2.6.5 *Nested list (lists in lists in lists)*

```python
nested_list = [[11, 12], ['2B',22], [31, [32,3.2]]]
                # A nested list of mixed types of variables
printx('nested_list')
print(len(nested_list)) #number of sub-lists in nested_list
```

```
nested_list = [[11, 12], ['2B', 22], [31, [32, 3.2]]]
3
```

```python
print(nested_list[0])      #1st sub-list in the nested_list
print(nested_list[1])      #2nd sub-list in the nested_list
print(nested_list[2])      #3rd sub-list in the nested_list
print(nested_list)         #print all for easy viewing
```

```
[11, 12]
['2B', 22]
[31, [32, 3.2]]
[[11, 12], ['2B', 22], [31, [32, 3.2]]]
```

```python
print(nested_list[0][0])    #1st element in 1st sub-list
print(nested_list[0][1])    #2nd element in 1st sub-list
```

```
11
12
```

```python
print(nested_list)
print(nested_list[1][0])    # Try this: what would this be?
print(nested_list[2][1])    #?
print(nested_list[2][1][0]) #?
```

```
[[11, 12], ['2B', 22], [31, [32, 3.2]]]
2B
[32, 3.2]
32
```

2.7 Tuples: Value preserved

After the discussion about the List, discussing Tuples becomes straightforward. This is because they are essentially the same, and the major difference is as follows:

- A Tuple is usually enclosed with (), but a List is with [].
- A Tuple is immutable, but a List is mutable. This means that tuples cannot be changed after they are created. Values in Tuples are preserved.

Because a Tuple is immutable, we use it to store data that needs to be preserved. Thus, its use is very much limited. It is used to store constants preventing them from being changed. Also, operating on Tuples is faster.

Except these differences, a Tuple behaves like a List. It can be accessed via index, iterated over, and assigned to other variables. Below are some examples.

```python
ttuple = (10, 20, 30, 40, 50, 6.0, '7H')     # create a Tuple
gr.printx('ttuple')                           # print(ttuple)
aa = ttuple[0]
print('aa=',aa)
print(ttuple[1], '    ',ttuple[6],'    ',ttuple[-1])
```

```
ttuple = (10, 20, 30, 40, 50, 6.0, '7H')
aa= 10
20      7H      7H
```

```python
for i, data in enumerate(ttuple):
    # use enumerate function to get both index and content
    if i < 3:
        print(i, ':', data)
```

```
0 : 10
1 : 20
2 : 30
```

```python
# ttuple[2] = 300                          # this gives an error
```

The above may be all we need to know about Tuples. We now discuss another useful data structure in Python.

2.8 Dictionaries: Indexable via keys

A dictionary is a data type similar to a list. It contains paired keys and values. The key is a string and can be used for indexing. The value can be any type of object: a string, a number, a list, etc. Because the key and value are paired, each value stored in a dictionary can be accessed using the corresponding key. A dictionary does not contain any duplicated keys. The values may be with duplication.

2.8.1 *Assigning data to a dictionary*

For example, phone numbers can be assigned to a dictionary in the following format:

```python
phonebook1 = {}                         # placeholder for a dictionary
phonebook1["Kevin"] = 513476565
phonebook1["Richard"] = 513387234
phonebook1["Jim"] = 513682762
phonebook1["Mark"] = 513387234    # A duplicated value
gr.printx('phonebook1')
print(phonebook1)
```

```
phonebook1 = {'Kevin': 513476565, 'Richard': 513387234,
      'Jim': 513682762, 'Mark': 513387234}
{'Kevin': 513476565, 'Richard': 513387234, 'Jim': 513682762,
      'Mark': 513387234}
```

A dictionary can also be initialized in the following means:

```python
phonebook2 = {'Joanne': 656477456, 'Yao': 656377243,
   'Das': 656662798}
print(phonebook2)
```

```
{'Joanne': 656477456, 'Yao': 656377243, 'Das': 656662798}
```

```python
phonebook0 = {
   "John" : [788567837,788347278],
                     # this is a list, John has 2 phonenumbers
   'Mark': 513683222,
   'Joanne': 656477456
}
print(phonebook0)
```

```
{'John': [788567837, 788347278], 'Mark': 513683222, 'Joanne':
   656477456}
```

2.8.2 *Iterating over a dictionary*

Like lists, dictionaries can be iterated over. Because keys and values are recorded in pairs, we may use for-loop to access them.

```python
for name, number in phonebook1.items():
    print("Phone number of %s is %d" % (name, number))
```

```
Phone number of Kevin is 513476565
Phone number of Richard is 513387234
Phone number of Jim is 513682762
Phone number of Mark is 513387234
```

```python
for key, value in phonebook1.items():
    print(key, value)
```

```
Kevin 513476565
Richard 513387234
Jim 513682762
Mark 513387234
```

```python
for key in phonebook1.keys():
    print(key)
```

```
Kevin
Richard
Jim
Mark
```

```python
for value in phonebook1.values():
    print(value)
```

```
513476565
513387234
513682762
513387234
```

2.8.3 *Removing a value*

To delete a pair of records, we use the build-in function del or pop, by using the keys.

```python
phonebook2 = {'Joanne': 656477456, 'Yao': 656377243,
              'Das': 656662798}
del phonebook2["Yao"]
print(phonebook2)
value = phonebook2.pop("Das")
print(phonebook2)
print('value for poped out key',value)
```

```
{'Joanne': 656477456, 'Das': 656662798}
{'Joanne': 656477456}
value for poped out key 656662798
```

2.8.4 *Merging two dictionaries*

First, use update() method.

```python
phonebook1.update(phonebook2)          # phonebook1 is updated
print(phonebook1)
```

```
{'Kevin': 513476565, 'Richard': 513387234, 'Jim': 513682762,
    'Mark': 513387234, 'Joanne': 656477456}
```

Now, use a simpler means called double-star. This allows one to create a 3rd new dictionary that is a combination of two dictionaries, without affecting the original two.

```python
phonebook3 = {**phonebook1, **phonebook0}
print(phonebook3)
```

```
{'Kevin': 513476565, 'Richard': 513387234, 'Jim': 513682762,
    'Mark': 513683222,
'Joanne': 656477456, 'John': [788567837, 788347278]}
```

Duplicated keys (if any) are removed in the new dictionary:

```python
dict_1 = {'Apple': 7, 'Banana': 5}
dict_2 = {'Banana': 3, 'Orange': 4}    #'Banana' is in dict_1
```

```python
combined_dict = {**dict_1, **dict_2}
    #'Banana' in dict_1 will be replaced in the new dictionary
print(combined_dict)
```

```
{'Apple': 7, 'Banana': 3, 'Orange': 4}
```

2.9 Numpy Arrays: Handy for scientific computation

Numpy arrays are similar to Lists, and much easier to work with for scientific computations. Operations on Numpy arrays are usually much faster for bulky data.

2.9.1 *Lists vs. Numpy arrays*

(1) Similarities:

- Both are **mutable** (the elements there can be added and removed after the creation. A mutating operation is also called "destructive", because it modifies the list/array in place instead of returning a new one).
- Both can be indexed.
- Both can be sliced.

(2) Differences:

- For using arrays, one needs to import Numpy module, but lists are build-in.
- Array works for element-wise operations, but lists cannot (need some coding to do that).
- Data types in an array must be the same, but a list can have different types of data (part of the reason why element-wise operation is not generally accepted).
- Numpy array can be multi-dimensional.
- Operations with arrays are, in general, much faster than those on lists.
- Storing arrays uses less memory than storing lists.
- Numpy arrays are more convenient to use for mathematical operations and machine learning algorithms.

2.9.2 *Structure of a numpy array*

We first brief on the structure of a numpy array in comparison with a list we discussed earlier. To start the discussion, we import the numpy package.

```python
import numpy as np        # Import numpy & give it an alias np
```

```python
#dir(np)                  #try this (remove #)
```

```python
x1 = np.array([28, 3, 28, 0]) # a one-dimensional (1D) numpy array
print('x1=',x1)                  # A numpy array looks like a list.
gr.printx('x1')                  # This specifies that it is an array.
```

```
x1 = [28  3 28  0]
x1 = array([28,  3, 28,  0])
```

As shown above, a numpy array is "framed" in a pair of square brackets (same as a list).

```python
x2 = np.array([[51,22.0],[0,0],(18+9j,3.)]) # mixed types
print('x2=',x2)                         # All become complex-valued
```

```
x2= [[51.+0.j 22.+0.j]
 [ 0.+0.j  0.+0.j]
 [18.+9.j  3.+0.j]]
```

This is a 2D numpy array. It is framed in a double pair of square brackets. A list does not have multi-dimensionality, except in the form of nesting: lists in lists.

We can also create numpy arrays using lists. In the following, we create first two lists, and then create Numpy arrays using these two lists:

```python
list_w = [57.5, 64.3, 71.6, 68.2]   # list, peoples' weights (Kg)
list_h = [1.5,  1.6,  1.7,  1.65]   # list heights (m)
print('list_w=',list_w, ';  list_h= ',list_h)
```

```
list_w= [57.5, 64.3, 71.6, 68.2] ;  list_h=  [1.5, 1.6, 1.7, 1.65]
```

```python
narray_w = np.array(list_w)        # convert list to numpy array
narray_h = np.array(list_h)
print('narray_w=',narray_w, ';  narray_h= ',narray_h)
```

```
narray_w= [57.5 64.3 71.6 68.2] ;  narray_h=  [1.5  1.6  1.7  1.65]
```

Let us create a function that prints out the information of a given numpy array.

```python
def getArrayInfo(a):
    '''Get the information about a given array:
    getArrayInfo(array)'''
    print('elements of the first axis of the array:',a[0])
    print('type:',type(a))
    print('number of dimensions, a.ndim:', a.ndim)
    print('a.shape:', a.shape)
    print('number of elements, a.size:', a.size)
    print('a.dtype:', a.dtype)
    print('memory address',a.data)
```

```python
help(getArrayInfo)        # may try this
```

```
Help on function getArrayInfo in module __main__:

getArrayInfo(a)
    Get the information about a given array: getArrayInfo(array)
```

We see here that """" useful to provide a simple instruction for the use of a created function. Let us now use it to get the information for nist_w.

```python
getArrayInfo(narray_w)
```

```
elements of the first axis of the array: 57.5
type: <class 'numpy.ndarray'>
number of dimensions, a.ndim: 1
a.shape: (4,)
number of elements, a.size: 4
a.dtype: float64
memory address <memory at 0x000001AE7D549408>
```

We note that narray_w is 1D in dimension, and has a shape of (4,) meaning it has four entries. The shape of a numpy array is given in a tuple.

Slicing also works for a numpy array, in the similar way as for lists. Let us take a slice for an array.

```python
print(list_w[1:3])        # a slice between the 2nd and 3rd elements
```

```
[64.3, 71.6]
```

```python
print(narray_w[1:3])        # a slice between the 2nd and 3rd elements
```

```
[64.3 71.6]
```

Let us now append an element to both the list and the numpy array.

```python
# For lists, we use:
list_w.append(59.8)
print(list_w)
# For numpy array we shall use:
print(np.append(narray_w,59.8))
```

```
[57.5, 64.3, 71.6, 68.2, 59.8]
[57.5 64.3 71.6 68.2 59.8]
```

```python
print(list_w,'   ',narray_w)
print(type(list_w),'   ',type(narray_w))
print(len(list_w),'   ', narray_w.ndim) # Use len() to get the length
```

```
[57.5, 64.3, 71.6, 68.2, 59.8]    [57.5 64.3 71.6 68.2]
<class 'list'>    <class 'numpy.ndarray'>
5    1
```

```python
nwh = (narray_w,narray_h)   # This forms a tuple of np arrays
print(nwh)
```

```
(array([57.5, 64.3, 71.6, 68.2]), array([1.5 , 1.6 , 1.7 , 1.65]))
```

To form a multi-dimensional array, we may use the following (more on this later):

```python
arr = np.array([narray_w,narray_h])
arr
```

```
array([[57.5 , 64.3 , 71.6 , 68.2 ],
       [ 1.5 ,  1.6 ,  1.7 ,  1.65]])
```

```python
getArrayInfo(arr)
```

```
elements of the first axis of the array: [57.5 64.3 71.6 68.2]
type: <class 'numpy.ndarray'>
number of dimensions, a.ndim: 2
a.shape: (2, 4)
number of elements, a.size: 8
a.dtype: float64
memory address <memory at 0x000001AE44FB12D0>
```

We note that arr is of dimension 2, and has a shape of (2, 4), meaning it has two entries along axis 0 and 4 entries along axis 1. We see again that the shape of a numpy array is given in a tuple. A multi-dimensional numpy array can be transported:

```python
arrT = arr.T
print(arrT)
getArrayInfo(arrT)    # see the change in shape from (2,4) to (4,2)
```

```
[[57.5   1.5 ]
 [64.3   1.6 ]
 [71.6   1.7 ]
 [68.2   1.65]]
elements of the first axis of the array: [57.5  1.5]
type: <class 'numpy.ndarray'>
number of dimensions, a.ndim: 2
a.shape: (4, 2)
number of elements, a.size: 8
a.dtype: float64
memory address <memory at 0x000001AE44FB12D0>
```

It is seen that the dimension remains 2, but the shape is changed from (2,4) to (4,2). The value of an entry in a numpy array can be changed.

```python
arr = np.array([[57.5 , 64.3 , 71.6 , 68.2 ],
                [ 1.5 ,  1.6 ,  1.7 ,  1.65]])
arrb = arr
printx('arrb')
arr[0,0]= 888.0     # change is done to arr only
printx('arrb')
```

```
arrb = array([[57.5 , 64.3 , 71.6 , 68.2 ],
       [ 1.5 ,  1.6 ,  1.7 ,  1.65]])
arrb = array([[888.  , 64.3 , 71.6 , 68.2 ],
       [ 1.5 ,  1.6 ,  1.7 ,  1.65]])
```

Notice the behavior of the array created via an assignment: changes in an array will affect the other. This behavior was observed for lists. To create an independent array, use copy() function.

```python
arr = np.array([[57.5 , 64.3 , 71.6 , 68.2 ],
                [ 1.5 ,  1.6 ,  1.7 ,  1.65]])
arrc = arr.copy()    #This is expensive. Do it only it is necessary
printx('arrc')
arr[0,0]= 77.0
printx('arr')
printx('arrc')
```

```
arrc = array([[57.5 , 64.3 , 71.6 , 68.2 ],
       [ 1.5 ,  1.6 ,  1.7 ,  1.65]])
arr = array([[77.  , 64.3 , 71.6 , 68.2 ],
       [ 1.5 ,  1.6 ,  1.7 ,  1.65]])
arrc = array([[57.5 , 64.3 , 71.6 , 68.2 ],
       [ 1.5 ,  1.6 ,  1.7 ,  1.65]])
```

2.9.3 *Axis of a numpy array*

Axis is an important concept for numpy array operations. A 1D array has axis 0, a 2D array has two axes, 0 and 1, and so on. The definition is given in Fig. 2.1.

Multidimensional numpy array structure and axes:
We can now use an axis to stack up arrays to form new arrays, as follows:

```
arr=np.stack([narray_w,narray_h],axis=0)
                                #stack up 1D arrays along axis 0
print(arr)
```

```
[[57.5  64.3  71.6  68.2 ]
 [ 1.5   1.6   1.7   1.65]]
```

We can use np.ravel to flatten an array.

```
print(arr)
rarr=np.ravel(arr)
print(rarr)
getArrayInfo(rarr)
```

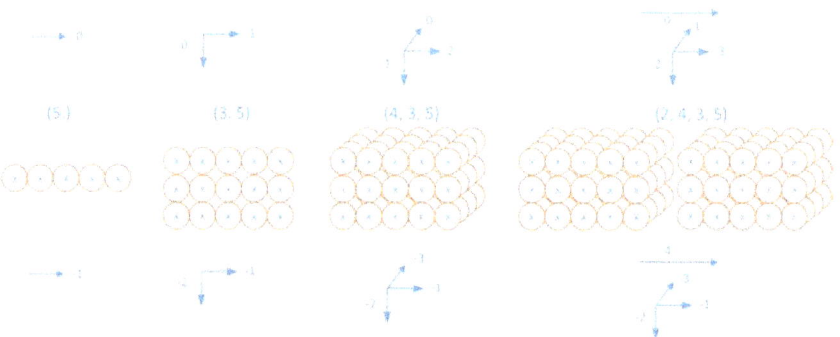

Figure 2.1:   Picture modified from that in "Introduction to Numerical Computing with NumPy", SciPy 2019 Tutorial, by Alex Chabot-Leclerc.

```
[[57.5  64.3  71.6  68.2 ]
 [ 1.5   1.6   1.7   1.65]]
[57.5  64.3  71.6  68.2   1.5   1.6   1.7   1.65]
elements of the first axis of the array: 57.5
type: <class 'numpy.ndarray'>
number of dimensions, a.ndim: 1
a.shape: (8)
number of elements, a.size: 8
a.dtype: float64
memory address <memory at 0x000001AE7D5494C8>
```

It is seen that the dimension is changed from 2 to 1, and the shape is changed from (2,4) to (8,).

In machine learning computations, we often perform summation of entries of an array along an axis of the array. This can be done easily using the np.sum function.

```
print(arr)
print('Column-sum:',np.sum(arr,axis=0),np.sum(arr,axis=0).shape)
print('row-sum:',np.sum(arr,axis=1),np.sum(arr,axis=1).shape)
```

```
[[57.5  64.3  71.6  68.2 ]
 [ 1.5   1.6   1.7   1.65]]
Column-sum: [59.   65.9  73.3  69.85] (4,)
row-sum: [261.6    6.45] (2,)
```

Notice that the dimension of the summed array is reduced.

2.9.4 *Element-wise computations*

Element-wise computation using Numpy arrays is very handy, which is very much different from that for lists.

```
print('listwh=',list_w+list_h)     # + is a concatenation for lists.
```

```
listwh= [57.5, 64.3, 71.6, 68.2, 59.8, 1.5, 1.6, 1.7, 1.65]
```

```
print('narraywh=',narray_w+narray_h)
                    # + is element-wise addition for numpy arrays.
```

```
narraywh= [59.   65.9  73.3  69.85]
```

Let us compute the weights in pounds, using 1kg = 2.20462 lbs.

```
print(narray_w * 2.20462)          # element-wise multiplication
```

```
[126.76565  141.757066 157.850792 150.355084]
```

Let us compute the Body Mass Index or BMI using these narrays.

```python
bmi = narray_w / narray_h ** 2     # formula to compute the BMI
print(bmi)
```

```
[25.55555556 25.1171875  24.77508651 25.05050505]
```

This includes element-wise power operation and division as well.

```python
# lbmi = list_w / list_h ** 2          # would this work? Try it!
```

We discussed element-wise operations for lists earlier, and used special operations (list comprehension) and special functions such as zip(). The alternative is the "numpy-way". This is done by first converting the lists to numpy arrays, then performing the operations in numpy using these arrays, and finally converting the results back to a list. When the lists are large in size, this numpy-way can be much faster, because all these operations can be performed in bulk in numpy, without element-by-element accessing of the memories.

```python
import numpy as np
list1 = [20, 30, 40, 50, 60]
list2 = [4,  5,  6,  2,  8]
(np.array(list1) + np.array(list2)).tolist()
```

```
[24, 35, 46, 52, 68]
```

The results are the same as those we obtained before using special list element-wise operations.

2.9.5 *Handy ways to generate multi-dimensional arrays*

In machine learning and mathematical computations in general, multi-dimensional arrays are frequently used, because one has to deal with big data frequently. Numpy supports the necessary functions (tools) to generate, manipulate, and operate multi-dimensional arrays.

```python
np.arange(2, 8, 0.5, dtype=np.float)   # equally spaced values
```

```
array([2. , 2.5, 3. , 3.5, 4. , 4.5, 5. , 5.5, 6. , 6.5, 7. , 7.5])
```

```python
np.linspace(1., 4., 6)
     # arrays with a specified number of elements with equal value spacing
```

```
array([1. , 1.6, 2.2, 2.8, 3.4, 4. ])
```

```python
a = np.array([1.,2.,3.])
a.fill(9.9)               # all entries with the same value
print(a)
```

```
[9.9 9.9 9.9]
```

```python
x = np.empty((3, 4))   # shape (dimension) of (3,4) specified,
                       # without initializing entries
print(x)
```

```
[[2.   2.5 3.   3.5]
 [4.   4.5 5.   5.5]
 [6.   6.5 7.   7.5]]
```

```python
x = np.zeros((6,6))    # initialized with zero
x
```

```
array([[0., 0., 0., 0., 0., 0.],
       [0., 0., 0., 0., 0., 0.],
       [0., 0., 0., 0., 0., 0.],
       [0., 0., 0., 0., 0., 0.],
       [0., 0., 0., 0., 0., 0.],
       [0., 0., 0., 0., 0., 0.]])
```

```python
y = np.ones((2,2))*2   # a 2 by 2 array with 1.0 in all the entries
print(y)
```

```
[[2. 2.]
 [2. 2.]]
```

```python
x[3:5,3:5] += y          # Assign y to a sliced portion in x
print(x)
```

```
[[0. 0. 0. 0. 0. 0.]
 [0. 0. 0. 0. 0. 0.]
 [0. 0. 0. 0. 0. 0.]
 [0. 0. 0. 2. 2. 0.]
 [0. 0. 0. 2. 2. 0.]
 [0. 0. 0. 0. 0. 0.]]
```

2.9.6 *Use of external package: MXNet*

For computations in machine learning, a number of useful packages/modules/
libraries have been developed for creating large-scale machine learning models.
MXNet is one of those. We will also make use of it in this book. Because it is
an external package, MXNet needs to be installed in your computer system using
pip.

    pip install mxnet

Note that if an error message like "No module named 'xyz'" is encountered, which is likely during this course using our codes, one shall perform the installation of "xyz" module in a similar way, so that all the functions and variables defined there can be made use of. Note also that there are a huge number of modules/libraries/packages openly available, and it is not possible to install all of them. The practical way is installing it only when it is needed. One may encounter issues in installations, many of which are related to compatibility of versions of the involved packages. Searching online for help can often resolve these issues, because the chance is high that someone has already encountered similar issues earlier, and the huge online community has already provided some solution.

After mxnet module is installed, we import it to our code.

```python
import mxnet as mx
mx.__version__
```

```
'1.7.0'
```

```python
np.set_printoptions(formatter={'float': '{: 0.3f}'.format})
from mxnet import nd       # import Mxnet library/package
                           # see https://gluon.mxnet.io for details
x = nd.empty((3, 4))       # Try also x = nd.ones((3, 4))
print(x)
print(x.size)              # print the size (number of elements) of a
                           # multi-dimensional mxnet or nd.array
```

```
[[ 0.000  0.000  0.000  0.000]
 [ 0.000  0.000  0.000  0.000]
 [ 0.000  0.000  0.000  0.000]]
<NDArray 3x4 @cpu(0)>
12
```

We often create arrays with randomly sampled values when working with neural networks. In such cases, we initialize an array using a standard normal distribution with zero mean and unit variance. For example,

```python
y = nd.random_normal(0, 1, shape=(3, 4))     # 0 mean, variance 1
printx('y')
y
```

```
y =
[[-0.681 -0.135  0.377  0.410]
 [ 0.571 -2.758  1.076 -0.614]
 [ 1.831 -1.147  0.054 -2.507]]
<NDArray 3x4 @cpu(0)>

[[-0.681 -0.135  0.377  0.410]
 [ 0.571 -2.758  1.076 -0.614]
```

```
 [ 1.831 -1.147  0.054 -2.507]]
<NDArray 3x4 @cpu(0)>
```

Element-wise operations of addition, multiplication, and exponentiation all work for multi-dimensional arrays.

```
x=nd.exp(y)
x
```

```
[[ 0.506  0.873  1.458  1.507]
 [ 1.771  0.063  2.934  0.541]
 [ 6.239  0.318  1.055  0.081]]
<NDArray 3x4 @cpu(0)>
```

Often used matrix (2D array) transpose can be obtained as follows:

```
y.T
```

```
[[-0.681  0.571  1.831]
 [-0.135 -2.758 -1.147]
 [ 0.377  1.076  0.054]
 [ 0.410 -0.614 -2.507]]
<NDArray 4x3 @cpu(0)>
```

Now, we can multiply matrices with comparable dimensions. Now we can multiply matrices with comparable dimensions using dot-product in both numpy and MXNet:

```
nd.dot(x, y.T)                           # x: 3×4; y.T: 4×3
```

```
[[ 0.705 -1.476 -3.776]
 [ 0.114  3.662  1.970]
 [-3.860  3.774 10.910]]
<NDArray 3×3 @cpu(0)>
```

Note that nd arrays behave differently from np arrays. They do not usually work together without proper conversion. Therefore, special care is need. When strange behavior is observed, one may print out the variable to check the array type. The same is generally true when numpy arrays work with arrays in other external modules, because the array objects are, in general, different from one module to another. One may use asnumpy() to convert an nd-array to an np-array, when so desired. Given below is an example (more on this later):

```
np.dot(x.asnumpy(), y.T.asnumpy())
        # convert nd array to np array and then use numpy np.dot()
```

```
array([[ 0.705, -1.476, -3.776],
       [ 0.114,  3.662,  1.970],
       [-3.860,  3.774, 10.910]], dtype=float32)
```

2.9.7 *In-place operations*

In machine learning, we frequently deal with bigdata. To avoid expensive and very complicated moving data operations, we prefer in-place operations. Let us first take a look at the following computations and the locations of the data:

```python
print('id(y) before operation:', id(y))
y = y + x                              # x and y must be shape compatible
print('id(y) after operation:', id(y))# location of y changes
```

```
id(y) before operation: 1847926752760
id(y) after  operation: 1847462282128
```

For in-place operations, we do this:

```python
print('id(y) before operation:', id(y))
y[:] = x + y
        # addition first, put it in a temporary buffer, then copy to y[:]
print('id(y) after  operation:', id(y))    # memory of y remains the same
```

```
id(y) before operation: 1847462282128
id(y) after  operation: 1847462282128
```

To perform an in-place addition without using even a temporary buffer, we do this in MXNet:

```python
print('id(y) before operation:', id(y))
print(nd.elemwise_add(x, y, out=y))    # for mxnet nd.arrays
print('id(y) after  operation:', id(y))
                                       # memory location un-changed
```

```
id(y) before operation: 1847462282128

[[ 0.837   2.485   4.752   4.931]
 [ 5.883  -2.568   9.878   1.009]
 [ 20.547 -0.194   3.220  -2.263]]
<NDArray 3x4 @cpu(0)>
id(y) after  operation: 1847462282128
```

If we do not plan to reuse x, then the result can be assigned to x itself. We may do this in MXNet:

```python
print('id(x) before operation:', id(x))
x += y
print(x)
print('id(x) after  operation:', id(x))
```

```
id(x) before operation: 1847462202168
```

```
[[ 1.343   3.358   6.210   6.438]
 [ 7.653 -2.504   12.811   1.550]
 [ 26.785   0.124   4.275 -2.182]]
<NDArray 3x4 @cpu(0)>
id(x) after  operation: 1847462202168
```

2.9.8 *Slicing from a multi-dimensional array*

To read the second and third rows from x, we do this:

```
print(x)
x[1:3]                    # read the second and third rows from x
```

```
[[ 1.343   3.358   6.210   6.438]
 [ 7.653 -2.504   12.811   1.550]
 [ 26.785   0.124   4.275 -2.182]]
<NDArray 3x4 @cpu(0)>

[[ 7.653 -2.504   12.811   1.550]
 [ 26.785   0.124   4.275 -2.182]]
<NDArray 2x4 @cpu(0)>
```

```
x[1:2,1:3]                # read the 2nd raw, 2nd to 3rd column from x
```

```
[[-2.504   12.811]]
<NDArray 1x2 @cpu(0)>
```

```
x[1,2] = 88.0             # change the value at the 2nd raw 3rd column
print(x)
x[1:2,1:3] = 88.0
        # change the values from the 2nd raw and 2nd to 3rd column
print(x)
```

```
[[ 1.343   3.358   6.210   6.438]
 [ 7.653 -2.504   88.000   1.550]
 [ 26.785   0.124   4.275 -2.182]]
<NDArray 3x4 @cpu(0)>

[[ 1.343   3.358   6.210   6.438]
 [ 7.653   88.000   88.000   1.550]
 [ 26.785   0.124   4.275 -2.182]]
<NDArray 3x4 @cpu(0)>
```

2.9.9 *Broadcasting*

What would happen if one adds a vector (1D array) y to a matrix (2D array) X? In Python, this can be done, and is often done in machine learning. Such an operation is performed using a procedure called "broadcasting": the low-dimensional array is duplicated along any axis with dimension 1 to match the shape of the high-dimensional array, and then the desired operation is performed.

```python
import numpy as np
y = np.arange(6)              # y has an initial of shape (6), or (1,6)
print('y = ', y,'Shape of y:', y.shape)
x = np.arange(24)
print('x = ', x,'Shape of x:', x.shape)
```

```
y =  [0 1 2 3 4 5] Shape of y: (6,)
x =  [ 0  1  2  3  4  5  6  7  8  9 10 11 12 13 14 15 16 17 18 19
     20 21 22 23]
Shape of x: (24,)
```

```python
X = np.reshape(x,(4,6))      # reshape to (4,6), to match (6,) of y
print(X.shape)
print('X = \n', X,'Shape of X:', X.shape)
print('X + y = \n', X + y)   # y's shape expands to (4,6) by copying
                             # the data along axis 0,then the addition
```

```
(4, 6)
X =
 [[ 0  1  2  3  4  5]
 [ 6  7  8  9 10 11]
 [12 13 14 15 16 17]
 [18 19 20 21 22 23]] Shape of X: (4, 6)
X + y =
 [[ 0  2  4  6  8 10]
 [ 6  8 10 12 14 16]
 [12 14 16 18 20 22]
 [18 20 22 24 26 28]]
```

```python
print('shape of X is:',X.shape, '   shape of y is:',y.shape)
print(np.dot(X,y))
```

```
shape of X is: (4, 6)    shape of y is: (6,)
[ 55 145 235 325]
```

```python
z = np.reshape(X,(2,3,4))
print (z)
```

```
[[[ 0  1  2  3]
  [ 4  5  6  7]
  [ 8  9 10 11]]
```

```
[[12 13 14 15]
 [16 17 18 19]
 [20 21 22 23]]]
```

```
a = np.arange(12).reshape(3,4)
a.fill(100)
a
```

```
array([[100, 100, 100, 100],
       [100, 100, 100, 100],
       [100, 100, 100, 100]])
```

```
z + a
```

```
array([[[100, 101, 102, 103],
        [104, 105, 106, 107],
        [108, 109, 110, 111]],

       [[112, 113, 114, 115],
        [116, 117, 118, 119],
        [120, 121, 122, 123]]])
```

```
a = np.arange(4)
a.fill(100)
a
```

```
array([100, 100, 100, 100])
```

```
z + a
```

```
array([[[100, 101, 102, 103],
        [104, 105, 106, 107],
        [108, 109, 110, 111]],

       [[112, 113, 114, 115],
        [116, 117, 118, 119],
        [120, 121, 122, 123]]])
```

Broadcasting Rules: https://docs.scipy.org/doc/numpy/user/basics.broadcasting.html.

When operating on two arrays, NumPy compares their shapes element-wise. It starts with the trailing dimensions and works its way forward. Two dimensions are *compatible* when

1. they are equal, or
2. one of them is 1.

If these conditions are met, the dimensions are *compatible*, otherwise *not compatible* hence a ValueError. Figure 2.2 shows some examples.

Broadcasting operations:

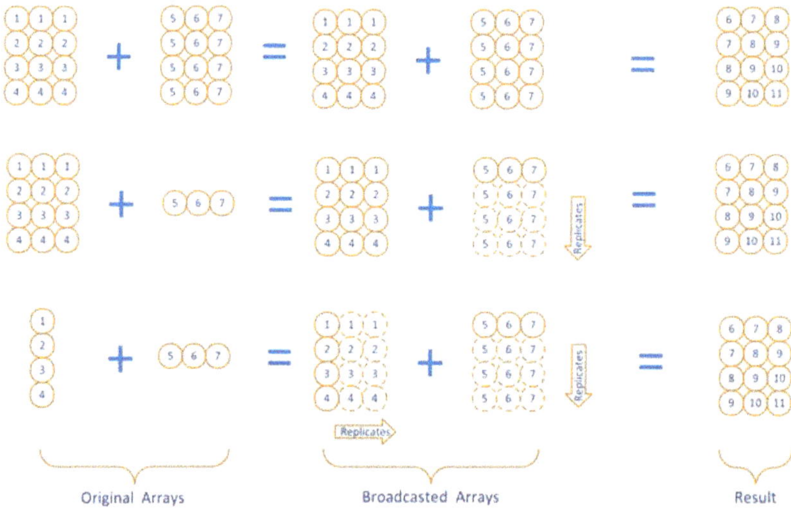

Figure 2.2: Picture modified from that in "Introduction to Numerical Computing with NumPy", SciPy 2019 Tutorial, by Alex Chabot-Leclerc.

2.9.10 *Converting between MXNet NDArray and NumPy*

Converting between MXNet NDArrays and NumPy arrays is easy. The converted arrays do not share memory.

```python
import numpy as np
x = np.arange(24).reshape(4,6)
y = np.arange(6)
```

```python
x
```

```
array([[ 0,  1,  2,  3,  4,  5],
       [ 6,  7,  8,  9, 10, 11],
       [12, 13, 14, 15, 16, 17],
       [18, 19, 20, 21, 22, 23]])
```

```python
from mxnet import nd
ndx = nd.array(x)
npa = ndx.asnumpy()
type(npa)
```

```
numpy.ndarray
```

```
npa
```

```
array([[ 0.000,   1.000,   2.000,   3.000,   4.000,   5.000],
       [ 6.000,   7.000,   8.000,   9.000,  10.000,  11.000],
       [ 12.000,  13.000,  14.000,  15.000,  16.000,  17.000],
       [ 18.000,  19.000,  20.000,  21.000,  22.000,  23.000]],
      dtype=float32)
```

```
ndy = nd.array(npa)
ndy
```

```
[[ 0.000   1.000   2.000   3.000   4.000   5.000]
 [ 6.000   7.000   8.000   9.000  10.000  11.000]
 [ 12.000  13.000  14.000  15.000  16.000  17.000]
 [ 18.000  19.000  20.000  21.000  22.000  23.000]]
<NDArray 4x6 @cpu(0)>
```

To figure out the detailed differences between the MXNet NDArrays and the NumPy arrays, one may refer to https://gluon.mxnet.io/chapter01_crashcourse/nd array.html.

2.9.11 *Subsetting in Numpy*

Another feature of numpy arrays is that they are easy to subset.

```
print(bmi[bmi > 25])          # Print only those with BMI above 25
```

```
[ 25.556   25.117   25.051]
```

2.9.12 *Numpy and universal functions (ufunc)*

NumPy is a useful library for the Python for large-scale numerical computations including but not limited to machine learning. It supports efficient operations for bulky data in multi-dimensional arrays (ndarrays) of large size. It also offers a large collection of high-level mathematical functions to operate on these arrays [1]. In 2005, Travis Oliphant created NumPy by incorporating features of Numarray into Numeric, which was originally created by Jim Hugunin with several other developers with extensive modifications. More details can be found at https://en.wikipedia. org/wiki/NumPy.

The Numpy documentation states that "a universal function (or ufunc for short) is a function that operates on ndarrays in an element-by-element fashion, supporting array broadcasting, type casting, and several other standard features. A ufunc is a "vectorized" wrapper for a function that takes a fixed number of specific inputs and produces a fixed number of specific outputs. In NumPy, universal functions are instances of the numpy.ufunc class (to be discussed later). Many of the built-in functions are implemented in compiled C code. The basic ufuncs operate on scalars, but there is also a generalized kind for which the basic elements are sub-arrays (vectors, matrices, etc.), and broadcasting is done over other dimensions. One can also produce custom ufunc instances using the frompyfunc factory function".

More details of unfuncs can be found at scipy documentation (https://docs.sc ipy.org/doc/numpy/reference/ufuncs.html). Given below are two of many ufuncs. exp(x, /[, out, where, casting, order, ...]) Calculate the exponential of all elements in the input array. log(x, /[, out, where, casting, order, ...]) Natural logarithm, element-wise. One may use the following for more details.

```
# help(np.log)          # use this to find out what a ufunc does
```

2.9.13 *Numpy array and vector/matrix*

Numpy uses primarily the structure of arrays. The behavior of a numpy array is similar, and yet quite different from the conventional concepts of vector and matrix that we learned from linear algebra. It can be quite confusing and even frustrating during coding and debugging. The author has bothered by such differences quite frequently in the past. The items below are some of the issues one may need to pay attention to.

(1) Numpy array is in principle multidimensional

First, we note that numpy array is far more than 1D vector and 2D matrix. By default, we can have as many as 32D, and that can also be changed. Thus, numpy array is extremely powerful, and is a data structure works well for complex machine learning models that use multidimensional dataset and data flows. All the element-wise operations, broadcasting, handling of flows of large volume data, etc. work very efficiently. It, however, does not follow precisely the concept of vectors, matrices that we established in the conventional linear algebra and most frequently used. This is essentially the root of confusion in many cases, in the author's opinion. Understanding the following key points is a good start to mitigate the confusion.

(2) Numpy 1D array vs. vector

Numpy 1D array is similar to the usual vector concept in linear algebra. The difference is that 1D array does not distinguish row or column vector. It is just a 1D array with a shape of $(n,)$, where n is the length of the array. It behaves largely like the row vector, but not quite. For example, transpose() has no effect on it. This is because what the transpose() function does is to swap two axises of an array with two or more axises.

The column vector in linear algebra should be treated in numpy as a special case of 2D array with only one column. One can create an array like the column vector in linear algebra, by adding an additional axis to the 1D array. See the following examples.

```
a = np.array([1, 2, 3])                # create an 1D array with length 3
print(a, a.T, a.shape, a.T.shape)      # its shape will be (3,)
```

```
[1 2 3] [1 2 3] (3,) (3,)
```

As shown, ".T" for transpose() has no effect to the 1D array.

```
an = a[:,np.newaxis]      # add in a newaxis, shape becomes (3, 1)
print(an, an.shape)       # it's a column vector, a special 2D array
```

```
[[1]
 [2]
 [3]] (3, 1)
```

```
print(an.T, an.T.shape)               # .T works, it comes row vector
```

```
[[1 2 3]] (1, 3)
```

The axis added array becomes a 2D array, and the transpose() function works. It creates a "real" row vector that is a special case of a 2D array in numpy.

The same can also be achieved using the following tricks.

```
a1 = a.reshape(a.shape+(1,))     # reshape, adds one more dimension
print(a1, a1.shape)
aN = a[:,None]             # adds in a new dimension without elements
print(aN, aN.shape)
```

```
[[1]
 [2]
 [3]] (3, 1)
[[1]
 [2]
 [3]] (3, 1)
```

Adding an axis can be done at any axis:

```
a0 = a[np.newaxis,:]      # the new axis is added to the 0-axis
print(a0, a0.shape)       # shape becomes (1,3), an row vector
```

```
[[1 2 3]] (1, 3)
```

```
print(an+a0)   # interesting trick to create a Hankel matrix
```

```
[[2 3 4]
 [3 4 5]
 [4 5 6]]
```

Once knowing how to create arrays equivalent to the usual row and column vectors in the conventional linear algebra, we shall be much more comfortable in debugging codes when encountering strange behavior.

Another often encountered example is when solving linear system equations. From the conventional linear algebra, we know that the right-hand-side (rhs) should be a column vector, and the solution also should be a column vector. In using numpy.linalg.solve() for a linear algebraic equation, we can feed in with a 1D array as the rhs vector, and it will return a solution that is also a 1D array. Of course, we can also feed in with a column vector (a 2D array with only one column). In that case we will get the solution in a 2D array with only one column. We shall see examples in Section 3.1.11, and many cases in later chapters. These behaviors are all expected and correct in numpy

(3) Numpy 2D array vs. matrix

Numpy 2D array is similar to the usual matrix in linear algebra largely, but not quite. For example, the matrix multiplication in linear algebra is often done in numpy using the dot-product, such as np.dot() or the "@" operator in numpy (version 3.5 or later). The "*" operator is an element-wise multiplication, as shown in Section 2.9.4. We will see more examples in Chapter 3 and later chapters. Also, some operations to a numpy array can results in dimension change. For example, when mean() is applied to an array, the dimension is reduced. Thus, care is required on which axis is collapsed.

Note that there is a numpy matrix class (see definition of class in Section 2.14) that can be used to create matrix objects. These objects behavior quite similar as the matrix in linear algebra. We try not to use it, because it will be deprecated one day, as announced in the online document numpy-ref.pdf.

Based on the author's limited experience, once we are aware of these differences and behavior subtleties (more discussion later when we encountered one), we can then pay attention to the behavior subtleties. It is often helpful to frequently checking the shape of the arrays. This allows us to work more effectively with powerful numpy arrays, including performing proper linear algebra analysis. At this moment, it is quite difficult to discuss the theorems in linear algebra using 1D, 2D or higher dimensional array concepts. In the later chapters, we will still follow the general rules, principles, and use the terms of vector and matrix in the conventional linear algebra, because many theoretical findings and arguments are based on it. A vector refers generally to a 1D numpy array, and a matrix to a 2D numpy array. When examine the outcomes in numpy codes, we shall notice the behavior subtleties of the numpy arrays.

2.10 Sets: No Duplication

A set is a list, but with no duplicate entries.

```python
sentence1 = "His first name is Mark and Mark is his first name"
words1 = sentence1.split()    # use split() to form a set of words
print(words1)                 # whole list of these words is printed
word_set1 = set(words1)       # convert to a set
print(word_set1)              # print. No duplication
```

```
['His', 'first', 'name', 'is', 'Mark', 'and', 'Mark', 'is', 'his',
    'first', 'name']
{'and', 'His', 'is', 'first', 'Mark', 'his', 'name'}
```

Using a set to get rid of duplication is useful for many situations. Many other useful operations can be applied to sets. For example, we may want to find the intersection of two sets. To show this, let us create a new list and then a new set.

```python
sentence2 = "Her first name is Jane and Jane is her first name"
words2 = sentence2.split()
print(words2)                 # whole list of these words is printed.
word_set2 = set(words2)       # convert to a set
print(word_set2)              # print. No duplication
```

```
['Her', 'first', 'name', 'is', 'Jane', 'and', 'Jane', 'is', 'her',
    'first', 'name']
{'her', 'Jane', 'Her', 'is', 'first', 'and', 'name'}
```

2.10.1 *Intersection of two sets*

```python
print(word_set1.intersection(word_set2)) #intersection of two sets
```

```
{'first', 'and', 'name', 'is'}
```

2.10.2 *Difference of two sets*

```python
print(word_set1.difference(word_set2))
```

```
{'his', 'His', 'Mark'}
```

This finds words in word_set1 that are not in word_set2.

We may also want to find the words in word_set2 that are not in word_set1 as follows:

```python
print(word_set1.symmetric_difference(word_set2))
```

```
{'her', 'His', 'Jane', 'Her', 'Mark', 'his'}
```

Can we do similar operations to lists? Try this.

```python
#print(words1.intersection(words2))    # intersection of two list?
                                       # No. It throws an AttributeError.
```

2.11 List Comprehensions

We used list comprehension for particular situations a few times. List comprehension is a very powerful tool for operations on all iterables including lists and numpy arrays. When used on a list, it creates a new list based on another list, in a single, readable line.

In the following example, we would like to create a list of integers which specify the length of each word in a sentence, but only if the word is not "the". The natural way to do this is as follows:

```python
sentence="Raises the Sun and comes the light" # Create a string.
words = sentence.split() # Create a list of words using split().
word_lengths = []          # Empty list for the lengths of the words
words_nothe = []       # Empty list for the words that are not "the"
for word in words:
    if word != "the":
        word_lengths.append(len(word))
        words_nothe.append(word)

print(words_nothe, '   ',word_lengths)
```
```
['Raises', 'Sun', 'and', 'comes', 'light']    [6, 3, 3, 5, 5]
```

With a list comprehension, we simply do this:

```python
words = sentence.split()
word_lengths = [len(word) for word in words if word != "the"]
words_nothe = [word for word in words if word != "the"]
print(words_nothe, '   ',word_lengths)
```
```
['Raises', 'Sun', 'and', 'comes', 'light']    [6, 3, 3, 5, 5]
```

The following is even better:

```python
words_nothe2=[]     # Empty list to hold the lists of word & length
                    # for words that are not "the", lists in list
words_nothe2=[[word,len(word)] for word in words if word != "the"]
                    # one may use () instead of the inner []
print(words_nothe2)
```
```
[['Raises', 6], ['Sun', 3], ['and', 3], ['comes', 5], ['light', 5]]
```

The following example uses list comprehension to numpy arrays:

```python
import numpy as np
np.set_printoptions(formatter={'float': '{: 0.3f}'.format})
fx = []
x = np.arange(-2, 2, 0.5) # Numpy array with equally spaced values
fx = np.array([-(-xi)**0.5 if xi < 0.0 else xi**0.5 for xi in x])
    # Creates a piecewise function (such as activation function).
    # The created list is then converted to a numpy array.
print('x =',x); print('fx=',fx)
```

```
x = [-2.000 -1.500 -1.000 -0.500  0.000  0.500  1.000  1.500]
fx= [-1.414 -1.225 -1.000 -0.707  0.000  0.707  1.000  1.225]
```

2.12 Conditions, "if" Statements, "for" and "while" Loops

In machine learning programming, one frequently uses conditions, "if" statements, "for" and "while" loops. Boolean variables are used to evaluate conditions. The boolean values True or False are returned when an expression is compared or evaluated.

2.12.1 *Comparison operators*

Comparison operators include ==, <, <=, >, >=, !=. The == operator compares the values of both the operands and checks for value equality, while "!=" checks for "inequality", and others check for inequality and/or equality.

```python
x = 2
print(x == 2) # The comparison result in a boolean value: True
print(x == 3) # The comparison result in a boolean value: False
print(x < 3)  # The comparison result in a boolean value: True
```

```
True
False
True
```

```python
x = 2
if x == 2:
    print("x equals 2!")
else:
    print("x does not equal to 2.")
```

```
x equals 2!
```

```python
name, age = "Richard", 18
if name == "Richard" and age == 18:              # if-block!
    print("He is famous. His name is", name, \
          "and he is only",age,"years old.")
```

```
He is famous. His name is Richard and he is only 18 years old.
```

```python
temp_critical = 48.0                    #unit: degree Celsius (C).
current_temp = 50.0
if current_temp >= temp_critical:
    print("The current temperature is", current_temp, \
          "degree C. It is above the critical temperature of",\
          temp_critical,"degree C. Actions are needed. ")
else:
    print("The current temperature is", current_temp, \
          "degree C. It is below the critical temperature of",\
          temp_critical, "degree C. No action is needed for now.")

# Notice the use of block, and "\" to break a long line.
```

```
The current temperature is 50.0 degree C. It is above the
critical temperature of 48.0 degree C. Actions are needed.
```

2.12.2 The "in" operator

The "in" operator is used to check if a specified object exists within an iterable object container, such as a list.

```python
name1, name2 = "Kevin", 'John'
groupA= ["Kevin", "Richard"]             # a list with two strings.
if name1 in groupA:
    print("The person's name is either",groupA[0], "or", groupA[1])

if name2 in groupA:
    print("The person's name is either",groupA[0], "or", groupA[1])
else:
    print(name2, "is not found in group A")
```

```
The person's name is either Kevin or Richard
John is not found in group A
```

2.12.3 The "is" operator

Unlike the double equals operator "==", the "is" operator does not check the values of the operands. It checks whether both the operands refer to the same object or not. For example,

```python
x, y = ['a','b'], ['a','b']
z = y # makes z pointing to y

print(x == y,' x=',x,'y=',y,hex(id(x)),hex(id(y))) # Prints True,
                        # because the values in x and y are equal

print(x is y,'x=',x,'y=',y,hex(id(x)),hex(id(y)))  # Prints False,
                        # because x and y with different ID

print(y is z,' y=',y,'z=',z,hex(id(y)),hex(id(z)))  # True, y is z
```

```
True  x= ['a', 'b'] y= ['a', 'b'] 0x1ae25570188 0x1ae25570208
False x= ['a', 'b'] y= ['a', 'b'] 0x1ae25570188 0x1ae25570208
True  y= ['a', 'b'] z= ['a', 'b'] 0x1ae25570208 0x1ae25570208
```

```python
y[1]='x'                                # change the 2nd element
print('After change one value in y')
print(x == y,'x=',x,'y=',y,hex(id(x)),hex(id(y)))   # Prints False,
                        # their values are no longer equal

print(x is y,'x=',x,'y=',y,hex(id(x)),hex(id(y)))
                                # False, x is # NOT y

print(y is z,' y=',y,'z=',z,hex(id(y)),hex(id(z))) # True, y is z:
                                # they change together!
```

```
After change one value in y
False x= ['a', 'b'] y= ['a', 'x'] 0x1ae25570188 0x1ae25570208
False x= ['a', 'b'] y= ['a', 'x'] 0x1ae25570188 0x1ae25570208
True  y= ['a', 'x'] z= ['a', 'x'] 0x1ae25570208 0x1ae25570208
```

```python
y.append(x)
print('After change one value in y')
print(x == y,'x=',x,'y=',y,hex(id(x)),hex(id(y))) # Prints False,
                                # their values are no longer equal
print(x is y,'x=',x,'y=',y,hex(id(x)),hex(id(y)))
                                # False, x is # NOT y
print(y is z,' y=',y,'z=',z,hex(id(y)),hex(id(z))) # True, y is z:
                                # they change together!
```

```
After change one value in y
False x= ['a', 'b'] y= ['a', 'x', ['a', 'b'], ['a', 'b']]
  0x1ae25570188 0x1ae25570208
```

```
False x= ['a', 'b'] y= ['a', 'x', ['a', 'b'], ['a', 'b']]
   0x1ae25570188 0x1ae25570208
True  y= ['a', 'x', ['a', 'b'], ['a', 'b']] z= ['a', 'x', ['a',
   'b'], ['a', 'b']]  0x1ae25570208 0x1ae25570208
```

2.12.4 *The 'not' operator*

Using "not" before a boolean expression inverts the value of the expression.

```
print(not False)                          # Prints out True
print(not False == False)                 # Prints out False
```

```
True
False
```

The "**not**" operator can also be used with "is" and "in": "is not","not in":

```
x, y = [1,2,3], [1,2,3]
z = y                       # makes z pointing to same object as y
print(x == y,' x=',x,'y=',y,hex(id(x)),hex(id(y)))        # True,
                       # because the values in x and y are equal

print(x is not y,'x=',x,'y=',y,hex(id(x)),hex(id(y))) # False, the
                       # values in x in NOT y
print(y is z,' y=',y,'z=',z,hex(id(y)),hex(id(z)))  # True, y is z
```

```
True  x= [1, 2, 3] y= [1, 2, 3] 0x1ae25570348 0x1ae255702c8
True x= [1, 2, 3] y= [1, 2, 3] 0x1ae25570348 0x1ae255702c8
True  y= [1, 2, 3] z= [1, 2, 3] 0x1ae255702c8 0x1ae255702c8
```

2.12.5 *The "if" statements*

As any other language, the "if" statement is often used for programming, we have already seen some earlier. The following are more examples for using Python's conditions in the "if" statement with code blocks:

```
temp_good = 22.0            # unit: degree Celsius (C).
temp_now1 = 48.0            # Readers may change this value and try
statement1=(temp_now1<=(temp_good+10.0))&(temp_now1>=(temp_good-10.0))
                                        # comfortable
statement2 = temp_now1 < (temp_good-10.0)      # cold
statement3 = temp_now1 > (temp_good+10.0)      # hot
if statement1 is True:    # do not forget ":"
   print("Okay, it is",temp_now1,"degree C. Comfortable. Let's go.")
   pass                                 # do something
elif statement2 is True: # do not forget ":"
   print("No, it is",temp_now1,"degree C. Too cold. We cannot go.")
   pass                                 # do something else
```

```python
elif statement3 is True:
    print("No, it",temp_now1,"degree C. Too hot. We cannot go.")
    pass                                        # do something else
else:
    print("Let's check the temperature.")       # do another thing
    pass
```

```
No, it 48.0 degree C. Too hot. We cannot go.
```

Note that there is no limit in Python on how many blocks one can use in an if statement.

2.12.6 *The "for" loops*

There are two types of loops in Python, for and while. We have used "for" loops already. We discuss it here in more detail together with the while loops. A for loop iterates over a given iterable sequence. The starting and stopping points and the step-size are controlled by the sequence, as shown in the following example. It is sequence controlled.

```python
primes = [2, 3, 5]              # define a list (that is iterable)
for prime in primes:           # do not forget ":"
    print(prime, end='  ')
```

```
2   3   5
```

For loops can iterate over a sequence of numbers using the "range" function. The range() is a built-in function which returns a range object: a sequence of integers. It generates integer numbers between the given start-integer and the stop-integer. It is generally used to iterate over with for loops.

```python
print('Member in range(10) are')
for n in range(10):            # Syntax: range(start, stop[, step])
    print(n, end=',')

print('\nMembers in range(3, 8) are')
for n in range(3, 8):          # Default step is 1
    print(n, end=',')
```

```
Member in range(10) are
0,1,2,3,4,5,6,7,8,9,
Members in range(3, 8) are
3,4,5,6,7,
```

```python
print('Members in range(3, 10, 2) are')
for n in range(-3, 10, 2):     # starting from a negative value
    print(n, end=',')
```

```
print('\nMembers in range(10, -3, -2) are')
for n in range(10, -3, -2):        # reverse range
    print(n, end=',')
```

```
Members in range(3, 10, 2) are
-3,-1,1,3,5,7,9,
Members in range(10, -3, -2) are
10,8,6,4,2,0,-2,
```

For a given list of five numbers, let us display each element that doubled, using a for loop and range() function.

```
print("Double the numbers in a list, using for-loop and range()")
given_list = [10, 30, 40, 50]
for i in range(len(given_list)):
    print("Index["+str(i)+"]","Value in the given list is",
            given_list[i],", and its double is", given_list[i]*2)
```

```
Double the numbers in a list, using for-loop and range()
Index[0] Value in the given list is 10 , and its double is 20
Index[1] Value in the given list is 30 , and its double is 60
Index[2] Value in the given list is 40 , and its double is 80
Index[3] Value in the given list is 50 , and its double is 100
```

The range() function returns an immutable sequence object of integers, so it is possible to convert a range() output to a list, using the list class. For example,

```
print("Converting python range() output to a list")
list_rng = list(range(-10,12,2))
print(list_rng)
```

```
Converting python range() output to a list
[-10, -8, -6, -4, -2, 0, 2, 4, 6, 8, 10]
```

2.12.7 *The "while" loops*

The "while" loops repeat as long as a certain boolean condition is met. The condition controls the operations. For example,

```
#To print out 0,1,2,3,4,5,6,7,8,9,
count = 0
while count < 10:              # do not forget ":"
    print(count, end=',')
    count += 1                 # This is the same as count = count + 1
```

```
0,1,2,3,4,5,6,7,8,9,
```

"**break**" and "**continue**" statements: break is used to exit a "for" loop or a "while" loop, whereas continue is used to skip the current block, and return to the "for" or "while" statement.

```python
# print all digits limited by a given number.
count = 0
while True:
    print(count,end=',')
    count += 1
    if count >= 10:
        break
print('\n')
# Prints out only even numbers: 0,2,4,6,8,
for n in range(10):           # for-loop to control the range
    if n % 2 != 0:            # Check condition, control what to print
        continue              # continue to count on (in the for-loop)
    print(n,end=',')
```

```
0,1,2,3,4,5,6,7,8,9,


0,2,4,6,8,
```

When the loop condition fails, then the code part in "else" is executed. If break statement is executed inside the for loop, then the "else" part is skipped. Note that the "else" part is executed even if there is a continue statement before it.

```python
# Prints out 0,1,2,3,4 and then it prints "count value reached 5"
count=0
nlimit = 5
while(count<nlimit):
    print(count, end=',')
    count +=1
else:
    print("count value reached %d" %(nlimit))

# Prints out 1,2,3,4
for i in range(1, 10):
    if(i%5 == 0):  #  modulo division (%)
        break
    print(i, end=',')
else:
    print("This is not printed because for-loop is terminated due\
        to the break but not due to fail in condition")
```

```
0,1,2,3,4,count value reached 5
1,2,3,4,
```

2.12.8 *Ternary conditionals*

The following 4-line code

```
condition=True
if condition:
    x=1
else:
    x=0
print(x)
```

1

can be written in one line, with ternary conditionals:

```
condition=True
x=1 if condition else 0
print(x)
```

1

It is simple, readable and dry. Thus conditionals are frequently used in Python.

2.13 Functions (Methods)

Functions offer a convenient way to divide a code into useful blocks that can be called unlimited times when needed. This can drastically reduce the repeat of codes, and make codes clean, more readable, and easy to maintain. In addition, functions are good ways to define interfaces for easy sharing of the codes among programmers.

2.13.1 *Block structure for function definition*

A function has a "block" structure. Block keywords include those we have already seen, such as "if", "for", and "while". Functions in Python are defined using the block keyword "def", followed by a function name that is also the block's name. The function is called using the function name followed by (), which brackets the arguments, if any. Try this simplest function:

```
def print_hello():                    # do not forget ":"
    print("Hello, welcome to this simple function!")
print_hello()
```

```
Hello, welcome to this simple function!
```

2.13.2 *Function with arguments*

In the simple case given above, no argument is required. Functions are often created with required arguments that are variables passed from the caller to the function.

```python
def greeting_student(username, greeting):
    print(f"Hello, {username}, greetings! Wish you {greeting}")
greeting_student("Kevin", "a fun journey in using functions!")
```

```
Hello, Kevin, greetings! Wish you a fun journey in using functions!
```

Functions may be created with return values to the caller, using the keyword "return".

```python
def sum_two_numbers(a, b):
    return a + b

x, y = 2.0, 8.0
apb = sum_two_numbers(x, y)
print(f'{x} + {y} = {apb}') # print('%f + %f = %f'%(x,y,apb))
x, y = 20, 80
apb = sum_two_numbers(x, y)
print(f'{x} + {y} = {apb}, perfect!')
                        #print('%d + %d = %d: perfect!'%(x,y,apb))
print(f'{x + y}, perfect!') #f-string allow the use of operations
```

```
2.0 + 8.0 = 10.0
20 + 80 = 100, perfect!
100, perfect!
```

Variable scope: LEGB rule (local, enclosing, global, buildings) defines the sequence for Python to search for a variable. The searching terminates when the variable is found.

```python
def sum_two_numbers(a, b):
    a += 1
    print('Inside the function, a=',a)
    print('Inside the function x=',x)
    return a + b

x, y = 2.0, 8.0
print('Before the function is called,x=',x,'y=',y)
apb = sum_two_numbers(x, y)
print('After the function is called, %f + %f = %f'%(x,y,apb))
```

```
Before the function is called,x= 2.0 y= 8.0
Inside the function, a= 3.0
Inside the function x= 2.0
After the function is called, 2.000000 + 8.000000 = 11.000000
```

2.13.3 *Lambda functions (Anonymous functions)*

Lambda function is a single-line function. It may be the simplest form of functions and the most useful. The linear functions can be defined simply as

```python
f = lambda x, k, b: k * x + b          # do not forget ":"
print(f(1,1,1),f(2,2,2),f(1,2,3))
```

2 6 5

The quadratic functions can be defined as

```python
f = lambda x, a, b, c: a*x**2 + b*x +c
print(f(2,2,-4,6))
```

6

Often Lambda functions are used together with the normal functions, especially for returning a value where a single-line function comes in handy.

```python
def func2nd_order(a,b,c):
    return lambda x: a*x**2 + b*x +c

f2 = func2nd_order(2,-4,6)
print('f2(2)=',f2(2), 'or', func2nd_order(2,-4,6)(2))
```

f2(2)= 6 or 6

2.14 Classes and Objects

A class is a single entity that encapsulates variables and functions (or methods). A class is essentially a template to create class objects. One can create unlimited number of class objects with it, and each class object gets the structure, variables/attributes and-functions (or methods) from the class. References used in this section includes the following:

- https://www.python-course.eu/python3_class_and_instance_attributes.php.
- https://realpython.com/instance-class-and-static-methods-demystified/.

2.14.1 *A simplest class*

```python
class C:  # Define a lass named C
    ''' A simplest possible class named "C" '''
    ca = "class attribute" # an attribute defined in the class
```

```python
help(C)                       # check out what has been created
```

```
Help on class C in module __main__:

class C(builtins.object)
 |  A simplest possible class named "C"
 |
 |  Data descriptors defined here:
 |
 |  __dict__
 |      dictionary for instance variables (if defined)
 |
 |  __weakref__
 |      list of weak references to the object (if defined)
 |
 |  ----------------------------------------------------------------
 |  Data and other attributes defined here:
 |
 |  ca = 'class attribute'
```

This example shows how a Class is structured, comments given in """" in the class definition are used to convey a message to the user, and how an attribute can be created in the class. We can now use it to observe some behavior of a class attribute and instance attributes.

```python
i1 = C()        # an instance i1 (a class object) is created.
i2 = C()        # an instance i2 (another class object) is created.
print('i1.ca=',i1.ca)    # prints: 'class attribute!'
print('i2.ca=',i2.ca)    # prints: 'class attribute!'
print('C.ca =',C.ca)     # prints: 'class attribute!'
#print('ca=',ca)         # NameError:'ca' is not defined
```

```
i1.ca= class attribute
i2.ca= class attribute
C.ca = class attribute
```

```python
C.ca = "This is a changed class attribute 'ca'"
                        # Changing the class attribute, via class
print('C.ca =',C.ca)
print('i1.ca=',i1.ca)
print('i2.ca=',i2.ca)
```

```
C.ca = This is a changed class attribute 'ca'
i1.ca= This is a changed class attribute 'ca'
i2.ca= This is a changed class attribute 'ca'
```

Note the values in the instances are also changed.

```python
i1.ca = "This is a changed instance attribute 'ca'"
                              # Changing an instance attribute
print('i1.ca=',i1.ca)         # Changed
print('C.ca =',C.ca)          # Unchanged
print('i2.ca=',i2.ca)         # Unchanged
```

```
i1.ca= This is a changed instance attribute 'ca'
C.ca = This is a changed class attribute 'ca'
i2.ca= This is a changed class attribute 'ca'
```

The change is only effective for the instance attribute that is changed.

```python
C.ca = "The 2nd changed class attribute 'ca'"
                        # Changing the class attribute, via class
print('C.ca =',C.ca)    # should change accordingly
print('i1.ca=',i1.ca)   # Will not change! No longer follow C
                        # because it made a change after creation
print('i2.ca=',i2.ca)   # should change according to class C
                        # because it has not been changed creation
```

```
C.ca = The 2nd changed the class attribute 'ca'
i1.ca= This is a changed instance attribute 'ca'
i2.ca= The 2nd changed class attribute 'ca'
```

Class attributes and object instance attributes are stored in separate dictionaries:

```python
C.__dict__
```

```
mappingproxy({'__module__': '__main__',
              '__doc__': ' A simplest possible class named "C" ',
              'ca': "The 2nd changed the class attribute 'ca'",
              '__dict__': <attribute '__dict__' of 'C' objects>,
              '__weakref__': <attribute '__weakref__' of 'C' objects>})
```

```python
i1.__dict__
```

```
{'ca': "This is a changed instance attribute 'ca'"}
```

It is clear that a dictionary has been created when a change is made at the instance level, departing from the class level.

```python
i2.__dict__
```

```
{}
```

No dictionary has been created, because no change is made at the instance level. It stays with the class.

```python
i2.ca = "Make now a change at the instance y to the attribute 'ca'"
```

```python
i2.__dict__
```

```python
{'ca': "Make now a change at the instance y to the attribute 'ca'"}
```

A dictionary has now been created, because the change is made at the instance level. It departed from the class level. Any future change at the class level to this attribute will no longer affect the attribute at this instance level.

2.14.2 *A class for scientific computation*

Let us look at an example for simple scientific computations. We first create a class called Circle to compute the area of a circle for given radius. The following is the code:

```python
class Circle:
    ''' Class "Circle": Compute the area of a circle '''
    pi = 3.14159     #class attribute of constants used class-wide
                     # and class specific

    def __init__(self, radius): # a special constructor
        # __init__ is executed when the class is called.
        # it is used to initiate a class. For this simple
        # task we need only one variable: radius.
        # "self" is used to reserve an argument place for an
        # instance (to-be-created) itself to pass along.
        # It is used for all the functions in a class.
        self.radius = radius     # This allows the instance accessing
                                 # the variable: radius.
        def circle_area(self):   # function computes circle area
        return self.pi * self.radius **2  # pi gets in there via
                                 # the object instance itself
```

```python
#help(Circle)       # check out what has been created
```

We can now use this class to perform computations.

```python
r = 10
c10 = Circle(r)       # create an instance c10. c10 is now passed to
                      # self inside the class definition
                      # 10 is passed to the self.radius
print('Circle.pi before re-assignment',Circle.pi)
                      # access pi via class
```

```python
print('Radius=',c10.radius)
    # access via object c10.radius is the self.radius in __init__
print('c10.pi before re-assignment', c10.pi)
    # The class attribute is accessed via instance attribute
```

```
Circle.pi before re-assignment 3.14159
Radius= 10
c10.pi before re-assignment 3.14159
```

```python
c10.pi=3.14    # this will change the constant for instance c10
               # It will not change the class-wide pi value
print('c10.pi after re-assignment via c10.pi:',c10.pi)
print('Circle.pi after re-assignment via c10.pi:',Circle.pi)
print('circle_area of c10 =',c10.circle_area())
print('circle_area of Circle100=',Circle(100).circle_area())
```

```
c10.pi after re-assignment via c10.pi: 3.14
Circle.pi after re-assignment via c10.pi: 3.14159
circle_area of c10 = 314.0
circle_area of Circle100= 31415.899999999998
```

It is seen that the Class Circle works well. Let us now create a subclass.

2.14.3 *Subclass (class inheritance)*

Subclasses can often be used, to take the advantages of the inheritance feature in Python. This allows us to create new classes by fully making use of an existing class for its entire structure (attributes and functions), without affecting the ongoing use of the existing class. It is thus also useful in upgrading the existing programs because of the reduced duplications.

Assume that the Circle code created above has already been distributed and used by many. We now decide to create another class to compute the area of a partial Circle, given the value of the portion of the circle. We can now create a subclass for this purpose, called P_circle, without affecting the use of the already distributed Circle. The following is the code:

```python
class P_circle(Circle):
            # Subclass P_circle referring the base (or parent)
            # Circle in (). This establishes the inheritance
    ''' Subclass "P_circle" based on Class "Cirle": Compute the\
        area of a circle portion '''
    def __init__(self,radius,portion):
            # with 3 attributes: self, radius, and portion.
    super().__init__(radius)   # This brings in base attributes
                               # from the base class Circle.
        self.portion = portion # Subclass attribute.
```

```
    def pcircle_area(self):
        # define a function to compute the area of a partial circle
        return self.portion*self.circle_area() # New function in
        # subclass. The base class Circle is used here.
```

```
#help(P_circle)     # check out what has been created
```

Readers may remove "#" in above cell, execute it, and take a moment to read through this information, and see how the subclass is structured, its connection with the base class, how self is been used to prepare for connections with the future objects to be assigned, and what are the attributes and functions that are newly created and inherited from the base class.

```
pc10 = P_circle(10.,0.5) # create an object instance using the
            # subclass, with argument radius=10 and portion =50%
pc10.pi     # we have the same attribute from the base class
```

```
3.14159
```

```
pc10.radius     # we have the same attribute from the base class
```

```
10.0
```

```
pc10.pcircle_area()         # area of a 50% partial circle is computed
```
```
157.0795
```

Let us now make a change to constant pi via subclass instance.

```
pc10.pi = 3.14
pc10.pi
```
```
3.14
```

It changed. Let us check pi via the base class c10.

```
c10.pi
```
```
3.14
```

It remains unchanged. Actions to the subclass are not affecting the base class.

2.15 Modules

We now touch upon modules. A module is a piece of Python file that has a specific functionality. For example, when writing a finite element program, we may write one module for creating the stiffness matrix and another for solving the system equations. Each module is a separated Python file, which can be written and edited independently. This helps a lot in organizing and maintaining large programs.

A module in Python is a Python file with .py extension. The file name will be the module name. Such a module can have a set of functions, classes, and variables defined. In a module, one can import other modules in the procedure mentioned in the beginning of this chapter.

2.16 Generation of Plots

Python is also very powerful in generating plots. This is done by import modules that are openly available. Here, we shall present a simple demo plot of scattered circles.

First, we import the modules needed.

```python
import numpy as np
import matplotlib.pyplot as plt
    # matplotlib.pyplot is a plot function in the matplotlib module
%matplotlib inline
    # to have the plot generated inside the notebook
    # Otherwise, it will be generated in a new window
```

We now generate sample data, and then plot 80 randomly generated circles.

```python
n=80
x=np.random.rand(n)      # Coordinates randomly generated
y=np.random.rand(n)
colors=np.random.rand(n)
areas=np.pi*(18*np.random.rand(n))**2
                        # circle radiuses from 0~20 randomly generated
plt.scatter(x,y,s=areas,c=colors,alpha=0.8)
plt.show()
```

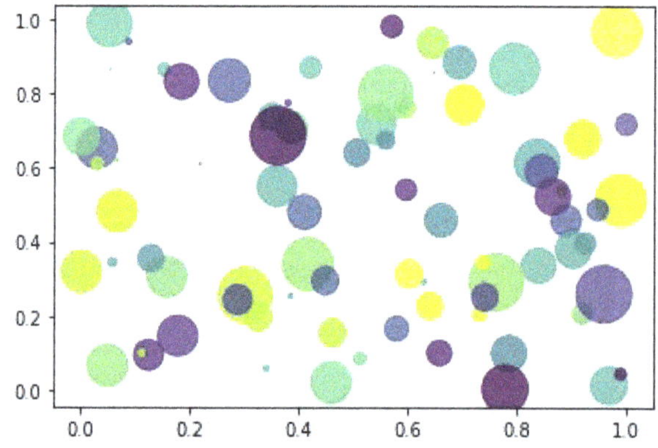

Figure 2.3:   Randomly generated circular areas filled with different colors.

```python
# Plost a curve
x = range(1000)
y = [i ** 2 for i in x]
plt.plot(x,y)
plt.show();
```

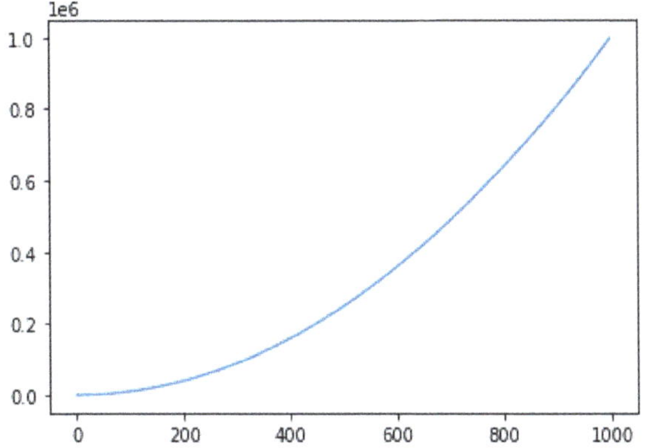

Figure 2.4:   Curve for a quadratic function.

```python
x = np.linspace(0, 1, 1000)**1.5
plt.hist(x);
```

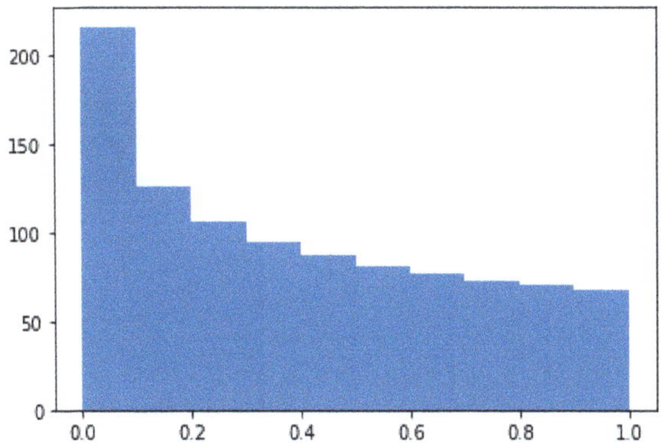

Figure 2.5:   An example of a histogram.

2.17 Code Performance Assessment

Performance assessment on a code can be done in two ways. Typical example codes are given below. Readers may make use of these codes for accessing computational performance to his/her codes.

```python
import time                                # import time module
import numpy as np

g=list(range(10_000_000))
#print(g)
q=np.array(g,'float64')
#print(q)
start = time.process_time()
sg=sum(g)
t_elapsed = (time.process_time() - start)
print(sg,'Elapsed time=',t_elapsed)

start = time.process_time()
sq=np.sum(q)
t_elapsed = (time.process_time() - start)
print(sq,t_elapsed)
```

```
49999995000000 Elapsed time= 0.28125
49999995000000.0 0.03125
```

```python
%%timeit                                #use timeit
sg=sum(g)
```

```
329 ms ± 70.7 ms per loop (mean ± std. dev. of 7 runs, 1 loop each)
```

2.18 Summary

With the basic knowledge of Python and its related modules, and the essential techniques for coding, we are now ready to learn to code for computations and machine learning techniques. In this process one can also gradually improve his/her Python coding skills.

Reference

[1] C.R. Harris, K.J. Millman and J.v.d.W. Stéfan *et al.* Array programming with NumPy, *Nature*, **585**(7825), 357–362, Sep 2020. http://dx.doi.org/10.1038/s41586-020-2649-2.

Chapter 3

Basic Mathematical Computations

This chapter discusses typical scientific computations using codes in Python. We will focus on how numerical data are represented mathematically, how they are structured or organized, stored, manipulated, operated upon, or computed in effective manners. Subtleties in those operations in Python will be examined. At the end of this chapter, techniques for initial treatment of datasets will also be discussed. The reference materials used in the chapter include Numpy documentation, Scipy documentation, https://gluon. mxnet.io/, and https://jupyter.org/. Our discussion shall start with some basic linear algebra operations on data with a structure of vector, matrix and tensor.

3.1 Linear Algebra

Linear algebra is most essential for any computations that involve big data, such as in machine learning. We plan to briefly review basic linear algebraic operations, through the use of Python programming, using modules that have already been developed in the Python community at large. We shall go through the basic concepts, the mathematical notation, data structure, and the computation procedure. Readers feel free to skim or skip this chapter if you are already confident in the basic linear algebra computations. Our discussion will start from the data structure. First, we import necessary modules and functions.

```
import sys                  # import "sys" module
sys.path.append('grbin')    # current/relative directory,
                            # like ..\\..\\code
            # Or absolute folder like 'F:\\xxx\\...\\code'
```

```
import grcodes as gr       # grcodes module is placed in the
                           # folder above
from grcodes import printx    # import a particular function
import numpy as np            # Import Numpy package
```

We will also use the MXNet package. If not done yet, we shall have MXNet installed using: pip install mxnet.

After the installation, we import the MXNet.

```
from mxnet import nd # Import NDArray and give it a alias nd
```

3.1.1 *Scalar numbers*

As discussed in Chapter 2, scalar numerical numbers for mathematical computations have three major types: integer, real number, and complex number. In Python, such a numerical number is assigned with a unique name and a given address. It is accessed by calling its name, can be updated, and used as an argument of a properly defined function (built-in, defined in a code or in an imported module). In Python programming, all these operations on a number are straightforward. The most often encountered problem in computation is that the number may get out of the bound of the digits of the computer (over- or under-flow), and may become illegal as an argument for a function. Also, we assume that the numbers generated in Python can cover the entire real space with the machine accuracy of limit.

3.1.2 *Vectors*

A vector refers to an object that has more than one component stacked along one dimension. It can give a physical meaning depending on the type of the physics problem. For example, a force vector in three-dimensional (3D) space has three components, each representing the projection of the force vector onto one of the three axes of the space. It is also known as the degrees of freedom (DoF). Higher dimensions are encountered in discretized numerical models, such as the finite element method or FEM (e.g., [1]). In the FEM, the solid structure is discretized in space with elements and nodes. The DoFs of such a discretized model depend on the number of nodes, which can be very large, often in the order of millions. Therefore, we form vectors with millions of components or entries. In machine learning models, the features and labels can be written in vector form.

In this chapter, we will not discuss much about the physical problems. Instead, we discuss general aspects of a vector in abstract, and issues on computational operations that we may perform to the vector for a given coordinate system. The DoF for a vector is also referred as the **length**. A vector of length p has a **shape** denoted in Python as (p').

```python
p = 15                      # Length of the vector
x = nd.arange(p)            # Create a vector that is an nd-array
                            # using nd.arange() function

gr.printx('x')              # x is now a vector with n components
printx('x')                 # Use the printx function directly
print(x.shape)
```

```
x =
[ 0.  1.  2.  3.  4.  5.  6.  7.  8.  9. 10. 11. 12. 13. 14.]
<NDArray 15 @cpu(0)>
x =
[ 0.  1.  2.  3.  4.  5.  6.  7.  8.  9. 10. 11. 12. 13. 14.]
<NDArray 15 @cpu(0)>
(15,)
```

Note that in mathematics, the notation of vector is often presented as a column vector. In Python, is shows as a raw vector.

```python
print(x.T)                              # Transpose of x
print(x.T.shape)
```

```
[ 0.  1.  2.  3.  4.  5.  6.  7.  8.  9. 10. 11. 12. 13. 14.]
<NDArray 15 @cpu(0)>
(15,)
```

In mathematics, the transpose of a (column) vector shall become a raw vector, and vice versa. In MXNet NDArray, The transformed vector is stored in the same place but marked as transpose, so that operations, such as multiplication, can be performed properly. This saves operations for physically copying and moving the data, improving efficiency. To confirm this, we just print out the addresses, as follows.

```python
print(id(x))
print(id(x.T))                          # Transpose of x
```

```
2212173184080
2212173184080
```

It is clear that in NDArray, a vector is a vector. One does not distinguish whether it is a column or row vector. Its transport is just a marker on it and only one set of data is stored. This is an example that MXNet pays special attention to not moving the data in memory unnecessarily. We do not seem to observe this behavior in numpy arrays, as shown below.

```python
xnp = np.arange(15)              # an Numpy array is generated
print(id(xnp), xnp.shape)
print(id(xnp.T),xnp.T.shape)    # address is changed
```

```
2212173195344 (15,)
2212173195424 (15,)
```

The shape of the numpy array is unchanged (still structured as row-vector or vector), but its transpose is given a separated address.

3.1.3 *Matrices*

A matrix refers to an object that has more than one dimensions of data structure, in which each dimension has more than one component. It can be viewed as stacks of vectors of some length. It again can have a physical meaning depending on the type of physics problem. For example, the stiffness (and mass) matrix created based on a discretized numerical model for a solid structure, such as the FEM, has a two-dimensional (2D) structure. In each of the dimensions, the number of components is the same as that of the DoFs. The whole matrix is a kind of spatially distributed "stiffness" of the structure [1]. In machine learning models, the input data points in the feature space, and learning parameters in the hypothesis space may be written in a matrix form.

Again, we will not discuss much about the physical problem here. Instead, we discuss general aspects of a matrix in abstract, and issues on computational operations that we may perform to the matrix. Such an abstract matrix can be presented in arrays of multi-dimensions known as **shape** in Python defined in Chapter 2.

```python
A = x.reshape((3, 5))        # Create a 2D matrix by reshaping
                             # a 1D array
print("A=", A, "\n  A.T=", A.T)
```

```
A=
[[ 0.  1.  2.  3.  4.]
 [ 5.  6.  7.  8.  9.]
```

```
 [10. 11. 12. 13. 14.]]
<NDArray 3x5 @cpu(0)>

  A.T=
[[ 0.   5.  10.]
 [ 1.   6.  11.]
 [ 2.   7.  12.]
 [ 3.   8.  13.]
 [ 4.   9.  14.]]
<NDArray 5x3 @cpu(0)>
```

```python
print(A.shape, A.T.shape)
```

```
(3, 5) (5, 3)
```

The shape or the dimension of the matrix A is 3 by 5, and that of its transpose becomes (5, 3).

As discussed in Chapter 2 in detail, each of the components (or entries) in the vector or matrix can be accessed by indexing or slicing.

```python
print('A[1, 2] = ', A[1, 2])               # via index
print('row 2', A[2, :])    # slice the 3rd row (count from 0)
print('column 1', A[:, 1])                 # slice the 2nd column
```

```
A[1, 2] =
[7.]
<NDArray 1 @cpu(0)>
row 2
[10. 11. 12. 13. 14.]
<NDArray 5 @cpu(0)>
column 1
[ 1.  6. 11.]
<NDArray 3 @cpu(0)>
```

The matrix can also be transposed.

```python
A.T                        # A transpose, shape becomes 5 by 3
print(id(A), id(A.T))
```

```
2212173182960 2213649918832
```

It is found that the transposed matrix has its own address also in MXNet.

3.1.4 *Tensors*

The term of "Tensor" requires some clarification. In mathematics or physics, tensor has a specific well-defined meaning. It refers to a structured data (a single number, a vector, or a multi-dimensional matrix) that obeys a certain tensor transformation rule under coordinate transformations. Therefore, tensor is a very special group of structured data or object, and not all matrices can be called a tensor. In fact, most of them are not. So long as the tensor transformation rules are obeyed, it can be classed in different orders. Scalars are 0th order tensors, vectors are 1st-order tensors, and 2D matrices are 2nd-order tensors, and so on.

Having said that, in the machine learning (ML) community, however, any matrix with dimension higher than 2 is called a tensor. It can be viewed as stacks of matrices of same shape. This ML tensor seems to carry a meaning of big data that needs to be structured in high dimensions. The ML tensor is now used as a general way of representing an array with an arbitrary dimension or arbitrary number of axes. The use of ML tensors becomes more convenient when dealing with, for example, images that can have 3D data structures, with axes corresponding to the height, width, and the three color (RGB) channels. In numpy, a tensor is a multidimensional array.

Because there is usually no such a coordinate transformation performed in machine learning, there will be no possible confusion caused in our discussion in this book. From now onwards, we will call the ML tensor a tensor, with the understanding that it may not obey the real-tensor transformation rules and we do not perform such a transformation in machine learning programming.

We now use nd.range() and then the reshape() to create a 3D nd-array.

```python
X = nd.arange(24).reshape((2, 3, 4))
print('X.shape =', X.shape)
print('X =', X)
```

```
X.shape = (2, 3, 4)
X =
[[[ 0.  1.  2.  3.]
  [ 4.  5.  6.  7.]
  [ 8.  9. 10. 11.]]
```

```
 [[12. 13. 14. 15.]
  [16. 17. 18. 19.]
  [20. 21. 22. 23.]]]
<NDArray 2x3x4 @cpu(0)>
```

Element-wise operations are applicable to all tensors.

```python
A = nd.arange(8).reshape((2, 4))
B = nd.ones_like(A)*8 # get shape of A, assign uniform entries
print('A =', A, '\n B =', B)
print('A + B =', A + B, '\n A * B =', A * B)
```

```
A =
[[0. 1. 2. 3.]
 [4. 5. 6. 7.]]
<NDArray 2x4 @cpu(0)>
 B =
[[8. 8. 8. 8.]
 [8. 8. 8. 8.]]
<NDArray 2x4 @cpu(0)>
A + B =
[[ 8.  9. 10. 11.]
 [12. 13. 14. 15.]]
<NDArray 2x4 @cpu(0)>
 A * B =
[[ 0.  8. 16. 24.]
 [32. 40. 48. 56.]]
<NDArray 2x4 @cpu(0)>
```

3.1.5 *Sum and mean of a tensor*

```python
x = nd.arange(5)
print(x)
```

```
[0. 1. 2. 3. 4.]
<NDArray 5 @cpu(0)>
```

```python
nd.sum(x) # summation of all entries/elements: 0+1+2+3+4=10
```

```
[10.]
<NDArray 1 @cpu(0)>
```

```
X = nd.ones(15).reshape(3,5)
X
```

```
[[1. 1. 1. 1. 1.]
 [1. 1. 1. 1. 1.]
 [1. 1. 1. 1. 1.]]
<NDArray 3x5 @cpu(0)>
```

```
nd.sum(X)                       # summation of all entries/elements
```

```
[15.]
<NDArray 1 @cpu(0)>
```

```
print(nd.mean(X),  nd.sum(X)/X.size) # same as nd.mean()
```

```
[1.]
<NDArray 1 @cpu(0)>
[1.]
<NDArray 1 @cpu(0)>
```

3.1.6 *Dot-product of two vectors*

Dot-product may be one of the most, if not the most, widely used operations in scientific computation including machine learning. We discussed about it briefly in Section 2.9. Here, we shall discuss more on its use for vectors that may have different data structure resulting in some subtleties, as mentioned in Section 2.9.13

Given two vectors $\mathbf{a}$ and $\mathbf{b}$, their dot-product is often written in linear algebra as $\mathbf{a}^\top\mathbf{b}$ or $\mathbf{a}\cdot\mathbf{b}$. Essentially, it is just a sum of their element-wise products, which results in a scalar. This implies that the shape of $\mathbf{a}$ and $\mathbf{b}$ must be compatible: both have the same length. Let us see some examples.

```
a = nd.arange(5)
b = nd.ones_like(a) * 2          #This ensures the compatibility
print(f"a={a},a.shape={a.shape} \nb={b},b.shape={b.shape}")
printx('nd.dot(a, b)')
printx('nd.dot(a, b).shape')
print(f"np.dot(a,  b)={np.dot(a.asnumpy(), b.asnumpy())}")
```

```
print(f"np.dot(a.T,b)={np.dot(a.asnumpy().T, b.asnumpy())}")
printx('np.dot(a.asnumpy(), b.asnumpy()).shape')
```

```
a=
[0. 1. 2. 3. 4.]
<NDArray 5 @cpu(0)>,a.shape=(5,)
b=
[2. 2. 2. 2. 2.]
<NDArray 5 @cpu(0)>,b.shape=(5,)
nd.dot(a, b) =
[20.]
<NDArray 1 @cpu(0)>
nd.dot(a, b).shape = (1,)
np.dot(a, b)=20.0
np.dot(a.T,b)=20.0
np.dot(a.asnumpy(), b.asnumpy()).shape = ()
```

Note that the transpose() to the vector will have not effect, because transpose() in numpy swaps the axes of a 2D array. An numpy 1D array has a shape of (n,) and hence no action can be taken. A numpy 1D array is not treated as a matrix, as discussed in Section 2.9.13. When $\mathbf{b}$ is a column vector, a special case of 2D array, it then has two axes like a matrix. The dot-product $\mathbf{a} \cdot \mathbf{b}$ is same as the matrix-product $\mathbf{ab}$ (where $\mathbf{a}$ is defined as a row vector and $\mathbf{b}$ a column vector), in terms of the scalar value resulted. Thus, in our formulation, we do not distinguish them mathematically, and we often use the following equality.

$$\mathbf{a} \cdot \mathbf{b} = \mathbf{ab} \tag{3.1}$$

In computations in numpy, however, there are some subtleties. The dot-product of two (1D array) vectors gives a scalar, and the dot-product of a (1D array) vector with a column vector gives an 1D array with the same scalar as the sole element. In NDArray, such subtleties are not observed. Readers may examine the following code carefully to make sense of this.

```
b_c = b.reshape(-1, 1)                # convert a 1D array to a column vector
print(b_c, 'b_c.shape=', b_c.shape)
printx('np.dot(a.asnumpy(),b.asnumpy())')        # np dot-product (scalar)
printx('np.dot(a.asnumpy(),b_c.asnumpy())')      # np dot-product (array)
print(a.asnumpy()@b_c.asnumpy())                 # np matrix-product (array)
printx('nd.dot(a, b)')                            # nd dot-product (array)
printx('nd.dot(a, b_c)')                          # nd dot-product (array)
printx('nd.dot(a, b_c).shape')
```

```
[[2.]
 [2.]
 [2.]
 [2.]
 [2.]]
<NDArray 5x1 @cpu(0)> b_c.shape= (5, 1)
np.dot(a.asnumpy(),b.asnumpy()) = 20.0
np.dot(a.asnumpy(),b_c.asnumpy()) = array([20.], dtype=float32)
[20.]
nd.dot(a, b) =
[20.]
<NDArray 1 @cpu(0)>
nd.dot(a, b_c) =
[20.]
<NDArray 1 @cpu(0)>
nd.dot(a, b_c).shape = (1,)
```

As seen, all these give the same scalar value but in a different data structure.

The dot-product of two column vectors (special matrices) $\mathbf{a}$ and $\mathbf{b}$ of equal length is written linear algebra as $\mathbf{a}^\top\mathbf{b}$ or $\mathbf{b}^\top\mathbf{a}$, which gives the same scalar (but in a 2D array or a matrix with only one element).

```python
a_c = a.reshape(-1, 1)        # convert a 1D array to a column vector
print(a_c),
printx('np.dot(a_c.asnumpy().T,b_c.asnumpy())') # scalar in 2D array
printx('np.dot(b_c.asnumpy().T,a_c.asnumpy())')
printx('np.dot(b_c.asnumpy().T,a_c.asnumpy()).shape')
```

```
[[0.]
 [1.]
 [2.]
 [3.]
 [4.]]
<NDArray 5x1 @cpu(0)>
np.dot(a_c.asnumpy().T,b_c.asnumpy()) = array([[20.]], dtype=float32)
np.dot(b_c.asnumpy().T,a_c.asnumpy()) = array([[20.]], dtype=float32)
np.dot(b_c.asnumpy().T,a_c.asnumpy()).shape = (1, 1)
```

To access the scalar value in a 2D array of shape (1, 1), simply use.

```python
print(np.dot(a_c.asnumpy().T,b_c.asnumpy())[0][0])
```

```
20.0
```

One may use flatten() to make a column vector back to a row vector.

```python
printx('np.dot(a_c.asnumpy().flatten(),b_c.asnumpy())')
printx('np.dot(a_c.asnumpy().flatten(),b_c.asnumpy()).shape')
```

```
np.dot(a_c.asnumpy().flatten(),b_c.asnumpy()) = array([20.], dtype=float32)
np.dot(a_c.asnumpy().flatten(),b_c.asnumpy()).shape = (1,)
```

To access the scalar value in a 1D array of shape (1,), simply use,

```python
printx('np.dot(a_c.asnumpy().flatten(),b_c.asnumpy())[0]')
```

```
np.dot(a_c.asnumpy().flatten(),b_c.asnumpy())[0] = 20.0
```

One may use ravel() to convert a multidimensional array to a 1D array (in this case no copy of the array is made).

```python
printx('np.dot(a_c.asnumpy().T,b_c.asnumpy()).ravel()')
printx('np.dot(a_c.asnumpy().T,b_c.asnumpy()).ravel()[0]')
```

```
np.dot(a_c.asnumpy().T,b_c.asnumpy()).ravel() = array([20.], dtype=float32)
np.dot(a_c.asnumpy().T,b_c.asnumpy()).ravel()[0] = 20.0
```

3.1.7 *Outer product of two vectors*

Given two vectors $\mathbf{a}$ and $\mathbf{b}$, the outer product $\mathbf{a} \otimes \mathbf{b}$ becomes a matrix; in its ij position, the element is $a_i b_j$. Thus, the shapes of $\mathbf{a}$ and $\mathbf{b}$ are always compatible.

```python
a = np.arange(3)
b = np.ones(5) * 2
print(a, b)
print('np.outer=\n',np.outer(a, b))
```

```
[0 1 2] [2. 2. 2. 2. 2.]
np.outer=
 [[0. 0. 0. 0. 0.]
 [2. 2. 2. 2. 2.]
 [4. 4. 4. 4. 4.]]
```

A matrix (2D array) is created using two 1D arrays of arbitrary lengths, with the help of the np.outer() function. One can achieve the same results using the @ operator, but $\mathbf{a}$ needs to be a column vector with shape (n, 1) and **b** needs to be a row vector with shape (1, m). Readers may try this as an exercise. Note that although we may get the same results, using the built-in np.outer() is recommended, because it is usually much faster, and does not need additional operations. This recommendation applies to all the other similar situations.

3.1.8 *Matrix-vector product*

When the dimensionality (shape) is compatible (or made compatible via "broadcasting"), one can obtain a matrix-vector product, using the np.dot() function.

```python
A35 = nd.arange(15).reshape(3,5)
d5 = nd.ones(A35.shape[1]) # get the 2nd element of shape A35
print(A35,A35.shape, d5, d5.shape)
f = nd.dot(A35, d5)            # shape compatible:[3,5]X[5]->vector
                              # of length 3

print(f,f.shape)
```

```
[[ 0.  1.  2.  3.  4.]
 [ 5.  6.  7.  8.  9.]
 [10. 11. 12. 13. 14.]]
<NDArray 3x5 @cpu(0)> (3, 5)
[1. 1. 1. 1. 1.]
<NDArray 5 @cpu(0)> (5,)


[10. 35. 60.]
<NDArray 3 @cpu(0)> (3,)
```

```python
#nd.dot(d5,A35)          # shape error: [5]X[3,5] not compatible
```

```python
d3 = nd.ones(A35.shape[0])
nd.dot(d3,A35)      # this works:[3]X[3,5]-> vector of length 5
```

```
[15. 18. 21. 24. 27.]
<NDArray 5 @cpu(0)>
```

3.1.9 *Matrix-matrix multiplication*

Further, dot-product can also be used for matrix-matrix multiplications, as long as the shape is compatible.

```python
A23 = nd.ones(shape=(2, 3))
B35 = nd.ones(shape=(3, 5))
print(A23,B35)
nd.dot(A23, B35)        # [2,3]X[3,5]: shape compatible ->[2,5]
```

```
[[1. 1. 1.]
 [1. 1. 1.]]
<NDArray 2x3 @cpu(0)>
[[1. 1. 1. 1. 1.]
 [1. 1. 1. 1. 1.]
 [1. 1. 1. 1. 1.]]
<NDArray 3x5 @cpu(0)>

[[3. 3. 3. 3. 3.]
 [3. 3. 3. 3. 3.]]
<NDArray 2x5 @cpu(0)>
```

```python
#nd.dot(B35,A23) # this would give a dot shape error: [4,5]X[3,4]
```

In numpy, we have similar ways to perform matrix-matrix dot-product operation.

```python
import numpy as np
print('np.dot():\n',np.dot(A23.asnumpy(),B35.asnumpy()))
print('numpy @ operator:\n',A23.asnumpy() @ B35.asnumpy())
```

```
np.dot():
 [[3. 3. 3. 3. 3.]
 [3. 3. 3. 3. 3.]]
numpy @ operator:
 [[3. 3. 3. 3. 3.]
 [3. 3. 3. 3. 3.]]
```

Care is needed in dealing with matrix-vector, matrix-matrix operations, because of the requirement of dimension compatibility. It is important to always check the consistency of the dimensions of all the terms in the same equation. Readers may need to struggle a while to get used to it. Operations between one-dimensional arrays (row vectors) in Python are rather simpler, because there is only on dimension to check and we usually use only the dot-product (inner product).

3.1.10　*Norms*

A norm is used in Python to measure how "big" a vector or matrix is. There are types of norm measures, but they all produce a non-negative value for the measure. The most often used or default one is the L2-norm. It is the square root of the sum of the squared elements in the vector or matrix or tensor. For matrices, it is often called the Frobenius norm. The computation is by calling a norm() function:

```python
d = nd.ones(9)                        # create an array (vector)
print(d,nd.sum(d))
printx('nd.norm(d)')                  # use nd.norm()
print(np.linalg.norm(d.asnumpy()))    # use numpy linalg.norm()
```

```
[1. 1. 1. 1. 1. 1. 1. 1. 1.]
<NDArray 9 @cpu(0)>
[9.]
<NDArray 1 @cpu(0)>
nd.norm(d) =
[3.]
<NDArray 1 @cpu(0)>
3.0
```

Note the difference that the nd.norm returns an NDArray, but np.linalg.norm gives a float.

```python
#help(nd.norm)                        # when wondering, use this
```

```python
print(nd.norm(A23),np.sqrt(6*1**2))   # nd.norm() for matrix,
                                       # default L2
print(np.linalg.norm(A23.asnumpy()))  # numpy linalg.norm()
                                       # for matrix
```

```
[2.4494898]
<NDArray 1 @cpu(0)> 2.449489742783178
2.4494898
```

```python
print(nd.norm(A23,ord=2, axis=1))     # nd.norm() for matrix,
                                       # along axis 1
print(np.linalg.norm(A23.asnumpy(),ord=2, axis=1))
                                       # numpy linalg.norm() for matrix
```

```
[1.7320508 1.7320508]
<NDArray 2 @cpu(0)>
[1.7320508 1.7320508]
```

The L1-norm of a vector is the sum of the absolute value of the elements in a vector. The L1-norm of a matrix can be defined as the maximum of L1-norm of column vectors of the matrix. For computing the L1-norms of a vector, we use the following:

```
printx('nd.sum(nd.abs(d))')        # use nd.norm() for vector
printx('nd.norm(d,1)')
```

```
nd.sum(nd.abs(d)) =
[9.]
<NDArray 1 @cpu(0)>
nd.norm(d,1) =
[9.]
<NDArray 1 @cpu(0)>
```

```
print(np.sum(np.abs(d.asnumpy())))      # numpy for vector
print(np.linalg.norm(d.asnumpy(),1))    # np.linalg.norm() for vector
```

```
9.0
9.0
```

```
print(np.linalg.norm(A23.asnumpy(),1))      # np.linalg.norm()
                                            # for matrix
```

```
2.0
```

3.1.11 *Solving algebraic system equations*

We can use numpy.linalg.solve to solve a set of linear algebraic system equations given as follows:

$$\mathbf{K}\,\mathbf{D} = \mathbf{F} \tag{3.2}$$

where $\mathbf{K}$ is a given positive-definite (PD) square matrix (stiffness matrix in FEM, for example), $\mathbf{F}$ is a given vector (nodal forces in FEM), and $\mathbf{D}$ is the unknown vector (the nodal displacements). The $\mathbf{K}$ matrix is a symmetric-positive-definite (SPD) for well-posed FEM models [1].

```python
import numpy as np
np.set_printoptions(formatter={'float': '{: 0.3f}'.format})


K = np.array([[1.5, 1.], [1.5, 2.]])        # A square matrix
print('K:',K)
F = np.array([1, 1])    # one may try F = np.array([[2], [1]])
print('F:',F)
D = np.linalg.solve(K,F)
print('D:',D)
```

```
K: [[ 1.500   1.000]
 [ 1.500   2.000]]
F: [1 1]
D: [ 0.667   0.000]
```

If careful, one should see that the input F is a 1D numpy array, and the result is also a 1D array, which is not the convention of linear algebra, as discussed in Section 2.9.13. One can also purposely define a column vector (a 2D array with only on column) following the convention of linear algebra, and get the solution. In this case, however, the returned solution will be the same, but is in a column vector. Readers may try this as an exercise.

Note that solving linear algebraic system equations numerically can be very time consuming and expensive, especially for large systems. With the development of computer hardware and software in the past decades, numerical algorithms for solving linear algebraic systems are well developed. The most effective solver for very large systems uses iterative methods. It converts the problem of solving algebraic equations to a minimization problem with a properly defined error residual function as a cost or loss function. A gradient-based algorithm, such as the conjugate gradient methods and Krylov methods, can be used to minimize the residual error. These methods are essentially the same as those used in machine learning. The numpy.linalg.solve uses routines from the widely used efficient Linear Algebra PACKage or LAPACK.

For a matrix that is not square, we shall use the least-square solvers for a best solution with minimized least-square error. The function in numpy is numpy.linalg.lstsq(). We will see examples later when discussing interpolations.

3.1.12 *Matrix inversion*

Readers may notice that the solution to Eq. (3.2) can be written as

$$\mathbf{D} = \mathbf{K}^{-1}\mathbf{F} \tag{3.3}$$

where $\mathbf{K}^{-1}$ is the inverse of $\mathbf{K}$. Therefore, if one can compute $\mathbf{K}^{-1}$, the solution is simply a matrix-vector product. Indeed, for small systems, this approach does work, and is used by many. We now use numpy.linalg.inv() to compute the inverse of a matrix.

```python
from numpy.linalg import inv   # import the inv() function
Kinv = inv(K)
print(Kinv)
```

```
[[ 1.333 -0.667]
 [-1.000  1.000]]
```

```python
print(np.allclose(np.dot(K, Kinv), np.eye(2)))
print(np.allclose(np.dot(Kinv, K), np.eye(2)))
```

```
True
True
```

The solution to Eq. (3.2) is obtained as follows:

```python
D = np.dot(Kinv,F)
print('D:',D)
```

```
D: [ 0.667  0.000]
```

which is the same as the one obtained earlier.

Multiple matrices can be inverted at once.

```python
a = np.array([[[1., 2.], [3., 4.]], [[1, 3], [3, 5]]])
print(a)
inv(a)
```

```
[[[ 1.000  2.000]
  [ 3.000  4.000]]

 [[ 1.000  3.000]
  [ 3.000  5.000]]]
```

```
array([[[-2.000,  1.000],
        [ 1.500, -0.500]],

       [[-1.250,  0.750],
        [ 0.750, -0.250]]])
```

```
a = np.array([[1.5, 1.], [1.5, 1.]])
                           # A singular matrix, because its
print(a)                   # two columns are parallel
#ainv = inv(a)             # This would give a Singular matrix error
```

```
[[ 1.500  1.000]
 [ 1.500  1.000]]
```

Note that computing numerically the inverse of a matrix of large size is much more expensive, compared to solving the algebraic system equations. Therefore, one would like to avoid the computation of inverse matrix. In many cases, we can change the matrix inversion problem to a set of problems of solving algebraic equations.

In machine learning computations, one may encounter matrices that are singular, which do not have an inverse, leading to breakdown in computations. More often, the matrices are nearly singular, which may allow the computation to continue but can lead to serious error, showing as some unexpected, strange behavior. When such behavior is observed, the chance is high that the system matrix may be "bad-conditioned", and one should check for possible errors in the data or the formulation procedure that may lead to the nearly singular system matrix. If the problem is rooted in the data itself, one may need to clean up the data or check for data error. After this is exhausted, one may resort to mathematical means, one of which is the use of singular value decomposition (SVD) to get the best possible information from the data. See later in this chapter on SVD.

The key point we would like to make here is that the most important factor that controls whether we can solve an algebraic system equation for quality solution is the property (or characteristics or condition) of the system matrix. Therefore, studying the property of a matrix is of fundamental importance.

Eigenvalues (if they exist) and their corresponding eigenvectors are the characteristics of a matrix.

3.1.13 *Eigenvalue decomposition of a matrix*

A diagonalizable matrix can have an eigenvalue decomposition, which gives a set of eigenvalues and the corresponding eigenvectors. The original matrix can be decomposed into a diagonal matrix with eigenvalues at the diagonal and a matrix consisting of eigenvectors. In particular, for real symmetric matrices, eigenvalue decomposition is useful, and the computation can be fast, because the eigenvalues are all real and the eigenvectors can be made real and orthonormal. Consider a real symmetric square matrix $\mathbf{A}$ that is positive-definite (PD). It has the following eigenvalue decomposition:

$$\mathbf{A} = \mathbf{V}\mathbf{\Lambda}\mathbf{V}^\top \tag{3.4}$$

where $\top$ stands for transpose, $\mathbf{\Lambda}$ is a diagonal matrix with eigenvalues at the diagonal, and matrix $\mathbf{V}$ is formed with eigenvectors corresponding to the eigenvalues. It is an orthonormal matrix, because

$$\mathbf{V}\mathbf{V}^\top = \mathbf{I} \tag{3.5}$$

which implies also that the inverse of $\mathbf{V}$ equals its transpose.

$$\mathbf{V}^{-1} = \mathbf{V}^\top \tag{3.6}$$

In addition, once a matrix is decomposed, computing the inverse of it becomes trivial simply by matrix multiplications. To see this, we start from the definition of inverse of a matrix, $\mathbf{A}\mathbf{A}^{-1} = \mathbf{I}$, and use Eqs. (3.4) and (3.6), which leads to

$$\mathbf{A}^{-1} = \mathbf{V}\mathbf{\Lambda}^{-1}\mathbf{V}^\top \tag{3.7}$$

Because the matrix is PD, its inverse exists and all the eigenvalues are nonzero (positive-definite). The inverse of the diagonal matrix $\mathbf{\Lambda}$ is simply the same diagonal matrix with diagonal terms replaced by the reciprocals of the eigenvalues.

Eigenvalue decomposition can be viewed as a special case of SVD. For general matrices that we often encounter in machine learning, the SVD is more widely used for matrix decomposition and will be discussed later in this chapter, because it exists for all matrices.

In this section, let us see an example of how the eigenvalues and the corresponding eigenvectors can be computed in Numpy.

```
import numpy as np
from numpy import linalg as lg    # import linalg module
A = np.array([[1, 0, 0], [0, 1, 0], [0, 0, 1]]) # Identity matrix
print('A=',A)
e, v = lg.eig(A)
print('Eigenvalues:',e)
print('Eigenvectors:\n',v)
```

```
A= [[1 0 0]
 [0 1 0]
 [0 0 1]]
Eigenvalues: [ 1.000  1.000  1.000]
Eigenvectors:

[[ 1.000  0.000  0.000]
 [ 0.000  1.000  0.000]
 [ 0.000  0.000  1.000]]
```

It is clearly seen that the identity matrix has three eigenvalues all of 1, and their corresponding eigenvectors are three linearly independent unit vectors. Let us look at a more general symmetric matrix.

```
A = np.array([[1, 0.2, 0], [0.2, 1, 0.5], [0, 0.5, 1]])
                                          # Symmetric A
print('A:\n',A)
e, v = lg.eig(A)
print('Eigenvalues:',e,  '\n Eigenvectors:\n',v)
```

```
A:
 [[ 1.000  0.200  0.000]
 [ 0.200  1.000  0.500]
 [ 0.000  0.500  1.000]]
Eigenvalues: [ 1.539  1.000  0.461]
 Eigenvectors:
 [[-0.263  0.928  0.263]
 [-0.707 -0.000 -0.707]
 [-0.657 -0.371  0.657]]
```

We obtain three eigenvalues and their corresponding eigenvectors, and they are all real numbers. These eigenvectors are orthonormal. To see this, lets compute:

```python
print(np.dot(v,v.T))
```

```
[[ 1.000  0.000  0.000]
 [ 0.000  1.000 -0.000]
 [ 0.000 -0.000  1.000]]
```

This means that all these three eigenvectors are orthogonal with each other, and the dot-product between them becomes a unit. We are now ready to recover the original matrix A, using these eigenvalues and eigenvectors.

```python
print(A)
lamd = np.eye(3)*e
A_recovered = v@lamd@v.T
print(A_recovered)
```

```
[[ 1.000  0.200  0.000]
 [ 0.200  1.000  0.500]
 [ 0.000  0.500  1.000]]
[[ 1.000  0.200  0.000]
 [ 0.200  1.000  0.500]
 [ 0.000  0.500  1.000]]
```

It is clear that matrix A is recovered with the machine error. This means that the information in matrix **A** is fully kept in its eigenvalues and eigenvectors.

Next, we use the eigenvalues and eigenvectors to compute its inverse, using Eq. (3.7).

```python
lamd_inv = np.eye(3)/e
A_inv = v@lamd_inv@v.T
print(A_inv)
```

```
[[ 1.056 -0.282  0.141]
 [-0.282  1.408 -0.704]
 [ 0.141 -0.704  1.352]]
```

which is the same as that obtained directly using the numpy.linalg.inv() function:

```python
from numpy.linalg import inv
print(inv(A))
```

```
[[ 1.056 -0.282  0.141]
 [-0.282  1.408 -0.704]
 [ 0.141 -0.704  1.352]]
```

Let us now compute the eigenvalues and eigenvectors of an asymmetric matrix.

```python
A = np.array([[1,-0.2, 0], [0.1, 1,-0.5], [0, 0.3, 1]])
                                        # Symmetric A
print('A:\n',A)
e, v = lg.eig(A)
print('Eigenvalues:',e, '\n Eigenvectors:\n',v)
```

```
A:
 [[ 1.000 -0.200  0.000]
 [ 0.100  1.000 -0.500]
 [ 0.000  0.300  1.000]]
Eigenvalues: [1.+0.j      1.+0.4123j 1.-0.4123j]
Eigenvectors:
[[-0.9806+0.j        0.     +0.3651j   0.     -0.3651j]
 [ 0.    +0.j        0.7528+0.j        0.7528-0.j      ]
 [-0.1961+0.j       -0.     -0.5477j  -0.     +0.5477j]]
```

We now see one real eigenvalue, but the other two eigenvalues are complex valued. These two complex eigenvalues are conjugates of each other. Similar observations are made for the eigenvectors. We conclude that a real asymmetric matrix can have complex eigenvalues and eigenvectors. Complex valued matrices shall in general have complex eigenvalues and eigenvectors. A special class of complex valued matrices called the Hermitian matrix (self-adjoint matrix) has real eigenvalues. This example shows that the complex space is geometrically closed, but the real space is not. An n by n real matrix should have n eigenvalues (and eigenvectors), but they may not be all in the real space. Some of them get into the complex space (that with the real space as its special case).

3.1.14 *Condition number of a matrix*

The condition number of a matrix is a measure of the "level" of singularity. There are a number of options of norms for computing the condition number. It is always larger than or equal to 1 for any measure. This implies that the best condition of a matrix is 1, which is the condition number of any unit matrix that has no (the lowest) singularity. Any other matrix shall have some level of singularity. The condition number for a matrix with the highest level of singularity is infinite. Let us see some examples.

```python
from numpy import linalg as lg
A = np.array([[1, 0, 0], [0, 1, 0], [0, 0, 1]])
                                    # A unit matrix
            # Clearly, it has 3 eigenvalues of all 1.0
print(A, '\n Condition number of A=',lg.cond(A))
                                    # or lg.cond(A,2)
                        # Option 2-> L2 more measure
```

```
[[1 0 0]
 [0 1 0]
 [0 0 1]]
Condition number of A= 1.0
```

Because matrix A is a unit matrix, we got a condition number of 1, as expected. Another example is as follows:

```python
A = np.array([[1, 0, 0], [0, 1, 0], [0, 0, 0]])
                                    # A singular matrix
    # It has 2 eigenvalues of all 1.0, and 1 eigenvalue of 0
print(A, '\n Condition number of A=',lg.cond(A))
```

```
[[1 0 0]
 [0 1 0]
 [0 0 0]]
Condition number of A= inf
```

Because matrix A is singular, its condition number is inf which is a numpy number for infinity, as expected. More examples are as follows:

```python
A = np.array([[1, 0, 0], [0, 1, 0], [0, 0, 10.]])
                                    # Last entry is 10.
print(A, '\n Condition number of A=',lg.cond(A))
```

```
[[ 1.000  0.000   0.000]
 [ 0.000  1.000   0.000]
 [ 0.000  0.000  10.000]]
Condition number of A= 10.0
```

The condition number of this A is 10.0, which is 10.0/1.0. Again, the condition number is the ratio of the largest eigenvalue and the smallest eigenvalue. We can now conclude that if the largest eigenvalue of a matrix is very large or the smallest eigenvalue of the matrix is very small, the matrix is likely singular, depending on their ratio.

This finding implies that a normalization to a matrix (which is often done in machine learning) will not in theory change its condition number. It may help in reducing the loss of significant digits (because of the limited presentation of floats in computer hardware).

3.1.15 *Rank of a matrix*

We mentioned rank before. If a square matrix has a full rank, it implies that all the columns (or rows) are mutually linearly independent. Such a matrix is not singular. For a singular matrix, its rank should be less than full, which is called rank deficiency. One can further ask what the level of rack deficiency is. The answer is the deficit number of its rank. Essentially, if the matrix has a rank of 2, we know that two linearly independent vectors can be formed using these columns (or rows) in the matrix.

For a non-square matrix, the full rank is the number of its columns or rows, whichever is smaller. Similarly, it can also have rank deficiency if the rank is smaller than the full rank.

Let us now examine it in more detail using Numpy.

```python
from numpy.linalg import matrix_rank, eig
print('Rank=',matrix_rank(np.eye(4)))    # Identity matrix
```

```
Rank= 4
```

It is seen that the identity matrix has a shape of 4×4. It has a full rank.

```python
A = np.array([[1,-0.2, 0], [0.1, 1,-0.5], [0.1, 1,-0.5]])
                                          # singular A
print(A, '\n Rank=', matrix_rank(A))
```

```
[[ 1.000 -0.200  0.000]
 [ 0.100  1.000 -0.500]
 [ 0.100  1.000 -0.500]]
Rank= 2
```

This singular matrix has two linearly independent columns, and hence a rank of 2. It has a rank deficiency of 1. Thus, it should also have a zero eigenvalue, as shown below. If the matrix has a rank deficiency of n, it shall have n zero eigenvalues. This is easy checked out using Numpy.

```python
np.set_printoptions(formatter={'float': '{: 0.3f}'.format})
eig(A)
```

```
(array([ 0.956,  0.544, -0.000]),
 array([[ 0.955, -0.296,  0.088],
        [ 0.209, -0.675,  0.438],
        [ 0.209, -0.675,  0.894]]))
```

```python
A = np.array([[1, -0.2, 0], [0.1, 1, -0.5]])
print('A:',A, '\n Rank=',matrix_rank(A))
```

```
A: [[ 1.000 -0.200  0.000]
 [ 0.100  1.000 -0.500]]
Rank= 2
```

The matrix has only two rows, and a rank of 2. It has a full rank.

3.2 Rotation Matrix

For two-dimensional cases, the coordinate transformation (rotation) matrix can be given as follows:

$$\mathbf{T} = \begin{bmatrix} \cos\theta & -\sin\theta \\ \sin\theta & \cos\theta \end{bmatrix} \tag{3.8}$$

where $\mathbf{T}$ is the transformation (or rotation) matrix, and θ is the rotation angle. A given vector (displacement, force, for example) can be written with two components in the coordinate system as follows:

$$\mathbf{d} = [u \; v] \tag{3.9}$$

The new coordinates of the vector $\mathbf{d}_\theta$ that is rotated by θ can be computed using the rotation matrix.

```python
import numpy as np
theta = 45                              # Degree
thetarad = np.deg2rad(theta)
c, s= np.cos(thetarad), np.sin(thetarad)
T = np.array([[c, -s],
              [s,  c]])
print('Transformation matrix T:\n',T)
```

```
Transformation matrix T:
 [[ 0.707 -0.707]
 [ 0.707  0.707]]
```

```python
d = np.array([1, 0])                  # Original vector
```

```python
T @ d                                 # rotated by theta
array([ 0.707,  0.707])
```

```python
T @ (T@d)                             # rotated by 2 thetas
array([-0.000,  1.000])
```

```python
T @ T                                 # 2 theta rotations
array([[ 0.000, -1.000],
       [ 1.000, -0.000]])
```

```python
T @ (T@(T @ T))                       # 4 theta rotations
array([[-1.000,  0.000],
       [ 0.000, -1.000]])
```

```python
T@(T @ (T@(T @ (T @ (T@(T @ T))))))   # 8 theta rotations =
                                      # no rotation
array([[ 1.000,  0.000],
       [-0.000,  1.000]])
```

3.3 Interpolation

Interpolation is a frequently used numerical technique for getting an approximate date based on known data. Machine learning is in some way quite similar to the interpolation. This section studies general issues related to interpolation, using numpy. Interpolation is also known as curve fitting. We show here some examples of function interpolation and approximation, using values given at discrete points in a space.

Let us try numpy.interp first. More descriptions can also be found in Scipy documentation (https://docs.scipy.org/doc/numpy-1.13.0/reference/generated/numpy.interp.html).

3.3.1 *1-D piecewise linear interpolation using numpy.interp*

```python
# Data available
xn = [1, 2, 3]              # data: given coordinates x
fn = [3, 2, 0]              # data: given function values at x
# Query/Prediction f at a new location of x
x = 1.5
f = np.interp(x, xn, fn)  # get approximated value at x
print(f'f({x:.3f})≈{f:.3f}')
```

```
f(1.500)≈2.500
```

```python
np.interp(2, xn, fn)    # Is it a data-passing interpolation?
```

```
2.0
```

```python
np.interp([0, 1, 1.5, 2.72, 3.14], xn, fn)   # querying at
                                             # more points
```

```
array([ 3.000,  3.000,  2.500,  0.560,  0.000])
```

```python
np.interp(4, xn, fn)
```

```
0.0
```

In practice, we know that interpolation can be a quite dangerous operation, and hence extra care is required, especially when extrapolating. To avoid or to be made aware of an extrapolation, one can set a warning when the interpolation occurs outside the domain that the data covers.

```python
out_of_domain = -109109109.0      # A warning number is used
print(np.interp(2.9, xn, fn,right=out_of_domain))
            # print out the number when extrapolation occurs
print(np.interp(3.5, xn, fn,right=out_of_domain))
```

```
0.20000000000000018
-109109109.0
```

Interpolation using higher-order polynomials can be more accurate but can also be a bigger problem. Piecewise linear approximation has often been found to be much safer and can be very effective, when dense data are available. Given below is an example using piecewise linear interpolation for the approximation of a sine function.

```python
import matplotlib.pyplot as plt # module for plot the results
x = np.linspace(0, 2*np.pi, 20)  # data: x values
y = np.sin(x)                    # data: function values at x
xvals = np.linspace(0, 2*np.pi, 50) # generate dense x data
                                 # at which the values are
                                 # obtained via interpolation
yinterp = np.interp(xvals, x, y)
plt.plot(x, y, 'o')              # plot the original data points
plt.plot(xvals, yinterp, '-x')   # plot interpolated data points
plt.show()                       # show the plots
```

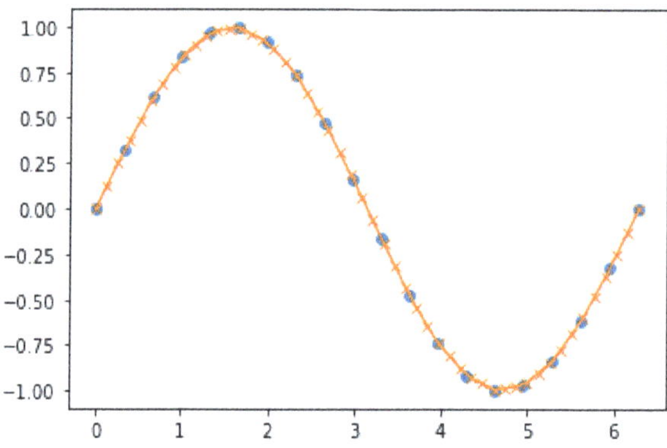

Figure 3.1:   Fitted sine curve.

3.3.2 *1-D least-square solution approximation*

This is to fit a given set of data with a straight line in $x - y$ plane

$$y = wx + b \tag{3.10}$$

We shall determine the gradient w and bias b, using the data pair $[x_i, y_i]$. In this example, Eq. (3.10) can be rewritten as

$$y = \mathbf{X} \cdot \mathbf{w} \tag{3.11}$$

where $\mathbf{X} = [x,\ 1]$ and $\mathbf{w} = [w, b]$. Now, we can use the np.linalg.lstsq to solve for $\mathbf{w}$:

```python
w_true,b_true = 1.0, -1.0              # used for generating data
x = np.array([0, 1, 2, 3])             # x value at which data
                                       # will be generated
X = np.vstack([x, np.ones(len(x))]).T # Form the matrix of data
X
```

```
array([[ 0.000,   1.000],
       [ 1.000,   1.000],
       [ 2.000,   1.000],
       [ 3.000,   1.000]])
```

```python
y = w_true*x+b_true+np.random.rand(len(x))/1.0
                        # generate y data random noise added
print(y)
w, b = np.linalg.lstsq(X, y, rcond=None)[0]
w, b
```

```
[-0.686  0.754  1.643  2.702]
```

```
(1.1055249814646126, -0.5550392342429096)
```

```python
#help(np.linalg.lstsq) # to find out the details of this function.
```

```python
import matplotlib.pyplot as plt
plt.plot(x, y, 'o', label='Original data', markersize=10)
plt.plot(x, w*x + b, 'r', label='Fitted line')
plt.legend()
plt.show()
```

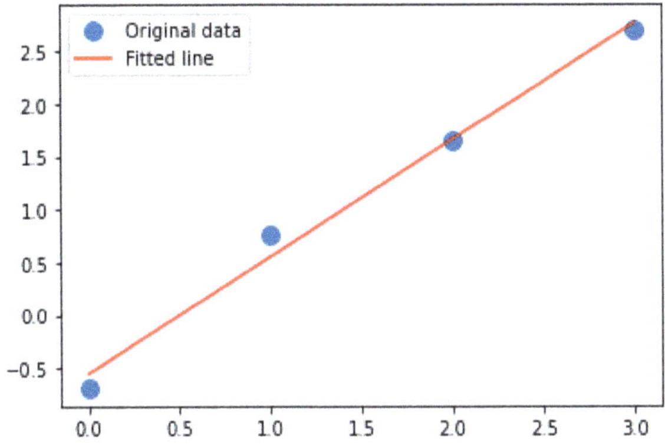

Figure 3.2:   Least square approximation of data via a straight line.

We have, in fact, created the simplest machine learning model, known as linear regression.

Scipy package offers efficient functions for machine learning computations, including interpolation. Let us examine some examples that are available at the Scipy documentation (https://docs.scipy.org/doc/scipy/reference/tutorial/interpolate.html).

3.3.3 *1-D interpolation using interp1d*

```python
import numpy as np
from scipy import interpolate
from scipy.interpolate import interp1d
import matplotlib.pyplot as plt
x0, xL = 0, 18
x = np.linspace(x0, xL, num=11, endpoint=True)
                                # x data points
y = np.sin(-x**3/8.0)           # y data points
print('x.shape:',x.shape,'y.shape:',y.shape)
f = interp1d(x, y)              # linear interpolation
f2 = interp1d(x, y, kind='cubic') # Cubit interpolation
                                # try also quadratic
xnew = np.linspace(x0,xL,num=41,endpoint=True)
                                # x prediction points
plt.plot(x, y, 'o', xnew, f(xnew), '-', xnew, f2(xnew), '--')
plt.legend(['data', 'linear', 'cubic'], loc='best')
plt.show()
```

x.shape: (11,) y.shape: (11,)

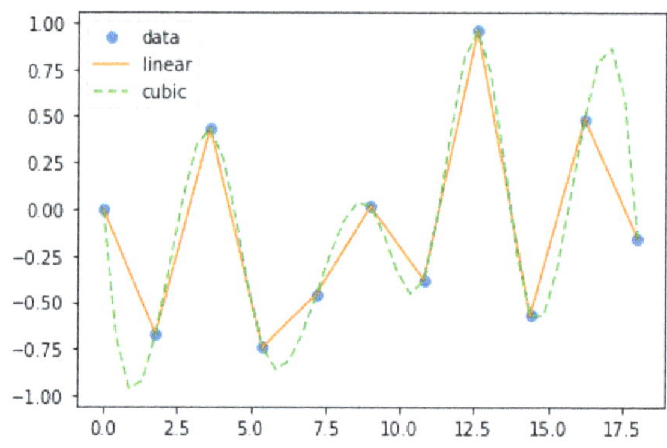

Figure 3.3:   Interpolation using Scipy.

3.3.4 *2-D spline representation using bisplrep*

```python
x, y = np.mgrid[-1:1:28j, -1:1:28j]         # x, y data grid
z = (x**2+y**2)*np.exp(-2.0*(x*x+y*y+x*y)) # z data
plt.figure()
```

```python
plt.pcolor(x, y, z, shading='auto')  # plot the initial data
plt.colorbar()
plt.title("Function sampled at discrete points")
plt.show()
```

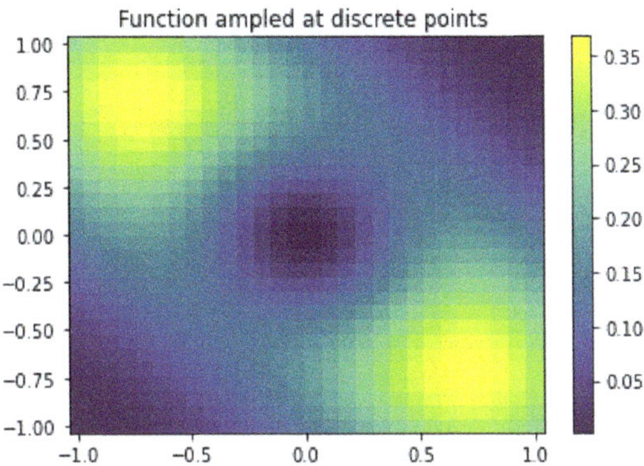

Figure 3.4:   Spline representation using bisplrep, coarse grids.

```python
xnew, ynew = np.mgrid[-1:1:88j, -1:1:88j]        # for view at grid
tck = interpolate.bisplrep(x, y, z, s=0)         # B-spline
znew = interpolate.bisplev(xnew[:,0], ynew[0,:], tck) # z value
plt.figure()
plt.pcolor(xnew, ynew, znew, shading='auto')
plt.colorbar()
plt.title("Interpolated function.")
plt.show()
```

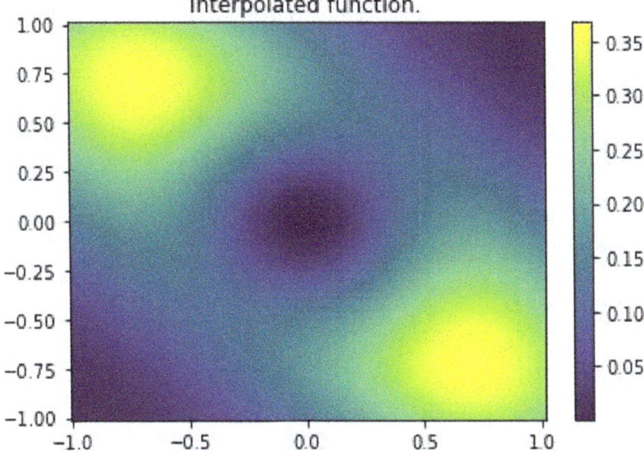

Figure 3.5:   Spline representation using bisplrep, fine grids.

3.3.5 *Radial basis functions for smoothing and interpolation*

Radial basis functions (RBFs) are useful basis functions for approximation of functions. RBFs are distance functions, and hence work well for irregular grids (even randomly distributed points), in high dimensions, and are often found less prone to overfitting. They are also used for constructing meshfree methods [2]. In using Scipy, the choices of RBFs are as follows:

- "multiquadric": sqrt((r/self.epsilon)**2 + 1)
- "inverse": 1.0/sqrt((r/self.epsilon)**2 + 1)
- "gaussian": exp(-(r/self.epsilon)**2)
- "linear": r
- "cubic": r**3
- "quintic": r**5
- "thin_plate": r**2 * log(r).

The default is "multiquadric".
First, let us look at one-dimensional examples.

```python
import numpy as np
from scipy.interpolate import Rbf, InterpolatedUnivariateSpline
import matplotlib.pyplot as plt
```

```python
# Generate data
np.set_printoptions(formatter={'float': '{: 0.3f}'.format})
x = np.linspace(0, 10, 9)
print('x=',x)
y = np.sin(x)
print('y=',y)
                # fine grids for plotting the interpolated data
xi = np.linspace(0, 10, 101)
                # use fitpack2 method
ius=InterpolatedUnivariateSpline(x,y)   # interpolation
                                        # function
yi = ius(xi)            # interpolated values at fine grids
plt.subplot(2, 1, 1)    # have 2 sub-plots plotted together
plt.plot(x, y, 'bo')    # original data points in blue dots
plt.plot(xi, np.sin(xi), 'r') # original function, red line
```

```
plt.plot(xi, yi, 'g')     # Spline interpolated, green line
plt.title('Interpolation using univariate spline')
plt.show()
                          # use RBF method
rbf = Rbf(x, y)
fi = rbf(xi)
plt.subplot(2, 1, 2)      # have 2 plots plotted together
plt.plot(x, y, 'bo')      # original data points in blue dots
plt.plot(xi, np.sin(xi), 'r')   # original function, red line
plt.plot(xi, fi, 'g')     # RBF interpolated, green line
plt.title('Interpolation using RBF - multiquadrics')
plt.show()
```

```
x= [ 0.000   1.250   2.500   3.750   5.000   6.250   7.500   8.750
     10.000]
y= [ 0.000   0.949   0.598  -0.572  -0.959  -0.033   0.938   0.625
     -0.544]
```

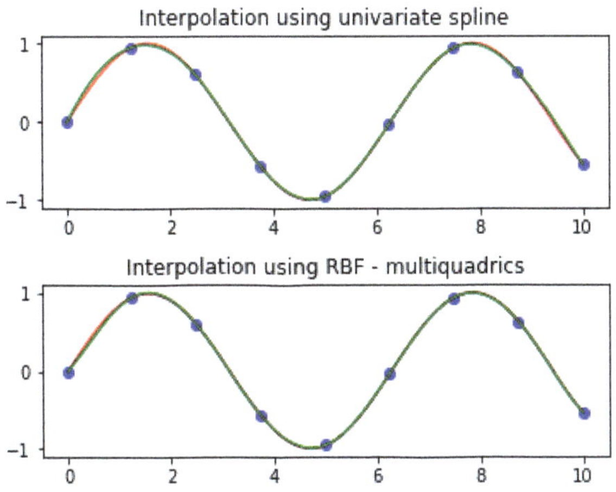

Figure 3.6:   Comparison of interpolation using spline and radial basis function (RBF).

We now examine some two-dimensional examples.

```
import numpy as np
from scipy.interpolate import Rbf
import matplotlib.pyplot as plt
from matplotlib import cm
```

```python
# 2-d tests - setup scattered data
x = np.random.rand(108)*4.0-2.0
y = np.random.rand(108)*4.0-2.0
z = (x+y)*np.exp(-x**2-y**2+x*y)
di = np.linspace(-2.0, 2.0, 108)
XI, YI = np.meshgrid(di, di)
```

```python
# use RBF https://docs.scipy.org/doc/scipy/reference/
# generated/scipy.
# interpolate.Rbf.html#scipy.interpolate.Rbf
rbf = Rbf(x, y, z, epsilon=2)
ZI = rbf(XI, YI)
```

```python
# plot the result
plt.pcolor(XI, YI, ZI, cmap=cm.jet, shading='auto')
plt.scatter(x, y, 88, z, cmap=cm.jet)
plt.title('RBF interpolation - multiquadrics')
plt.xlim(-2, 2)
plt.ylim(-2, 2)
plt.colorbar();
```

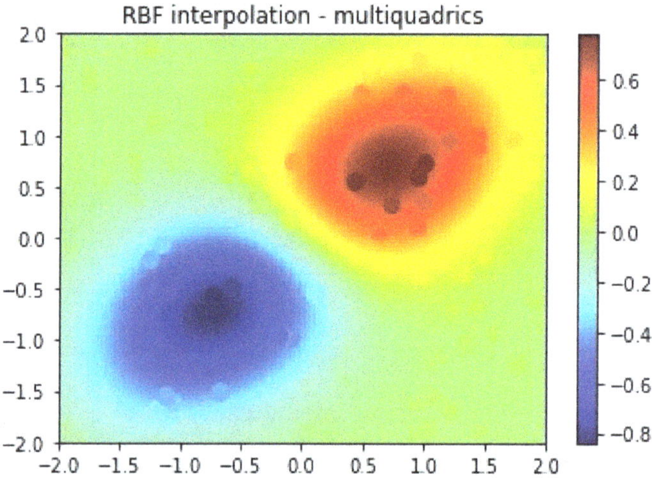

Figure 3.7:   Two-dimensional interpolation using RBF.

RBFs can be used for interpolation over N-dimensions. Below is an example for 3D.

```python
from scipy.interpolate import Rbf
x, y, z, d = np.random.rand(4, 20)
                              # randomly generated data 0~1
                              # 4D, 50 points in each dimension
#print(d)                     # original data
rbfi = Rbf(x, y, z, d)        # RBF interpolator
xi = yi = zi = np.linspace(0, 1, 10)
di = rbfi(xi, yi, zi)         # interpolated values
print(di)
```

```
[-0.378 -0.058  0.450  0.832  0.825  0.665  0.559  0.512
    0.430  0.497]
```

3.4 Singular Value Decomposition

3.4.1 *SVD formulation*

Singular value decomposition (SVD) is an essential tool for many numerical operations on matrices, including signal processing, statistics, and machine learning. It is a general factorization of a matrix (real or complex) that may be singular and of any shape. It is very powerful, because any such a matrix exists an SVD and can be found numerically. It is a generalization of the eigenvalue decomposition that works for diagonalizable square matrices, which was discussed earlier in this chapter.

A general (real or complex, square, or not square) $m \times p$ matrix $\mathbf{A}$ has the following singular value decomposition:

$$\mathbf{A} = \mathbf{U\Sigma V}^* \tag{3.12}$$

where * stands for Hessian (transpose of the matrix and conjugate to the complex values).

- $\mathbf{U}$ is an $m \times m$ unitary matrix.
- $\mathbf{\Sigma}$ is an $m \times p$ rectangular diagonal matrix with non-negative real numbers on the diagonal entries.
- $\mathbf{V}$ is a $p \times p$ unitary matrix.
- The diagonal entries σ_i in $\mathbf{\Sigma}$ are known as the singular values of $\mathbf{A}$.
- The columns of $\mathbf{U}$ are called the left-singular vectors of $\mathbf{A}$.
- The columns of $\mathbf{V}$ are called the right-singular vectors of $\mathbf{A}$.

More detailed discussions on SVD can be found at Wikipedia (https://en.wikipedia.org/wiki/Singular_value_decomposition).

3.4.2　*Algorithms for SVD*

Computation of SVD for large matrices can be very expensive. The often used SVD algorithm is based on the QR decomposition (https://en.wikipedia.org/wiki/QR_decomposition) and its variations. The basic idea is to decompose the given matrix into an orthogonal matrix Q and an upper triangular matrix R. Readers can refer to the Wikipedia page for more details and the leads there on the related topic. Here, we discuss a simple approach to compute SVD based on the well-established eigenvalue decomposition. This approach is not used for numerical computation of SVD. This is because it uses a normal matrix that with condition number squared, leading to numerical instability issues for large systems. For our theoretical analysis and formula derivation, this is not an issue, and thus will be used here. For this simple approach to work, we would need to impose some condition on matrix $\mathbf{A}$.

Consider a general $m \times p$ matrix $\mathbf{A}$ of real numbers with $m > p$, and assume it has a rank of p. Such a matrix is often encountered in machine learning. We first form a normal matrix $\mathbf{B}$:

$$\mathbf{B} = \mathbf{A}^\top \mathbf{A} \tag{3.13}$$

which will be a $p \times p$ symmetric square matrix (smaller in size). Therefore, $\mathbf{B}$ will be orthogonally diagonalizable. Because matrix $\mathbf{A}$ has a rank of p, $\mathbf{B}$ will also be symmetric-positive-definite (SPD). Thus, $\mathbf{B}$ has an eigenvalue decomposition, we perform such a decomposition. The results can be written in the form of

$$\mathbf{B} = \mathbf{V}_e \mathbf{\Lambda} \mathbf{V}_e^\top \tag{3.14}$$

where $\mathbf{V}_e$ is a $p \times p$ orthonormal matrix of p eigenvectors of the $\mathbf{B}$ matrix. $\mathbf{\Lambda}$ is a $p \times p$ square diagonal matrix. The diagonal entries are the eigenvalues that are positive real numbers.

On the other hand, we know that matrix $\mathbf{A}$ has an SVD decomposition; we thus also have

$$\mathbf{A} = \mathbf{U} \mathbf{\Sigma} \mathbf{V}^\top \tag{3.15}$$

Because matrix $\mathbf{A}$ has a rank of p, the singular value in $\mathbf{\Sigma}$ shall all be positive real numbers. Using Eq. (3.15), we have

$$\mathbf{A}^\top \mathbf{A} = \left(\mathbf{U} \mathbf{\Sigma} \mathbf{V}^\top \right)^\top \left(\mathbf{U} \mathbf{\Sigma} \mathbf{V}^\top \right) = \mathbf{V} \mathbf{\Sigma} \mathbf{U}^\top \mathbf{U} \mathbf{\Sigma} \mathbf{V}^\top = \mathbf{V} \mathbf{\Sigma}^2 \mathbf{V}^\top = \mathbf{B} \tag{3.16}$$

In the above derivation, we used the fact that $\mathbf{U}$ is unitary: $\mathbf{U}^\top\mathbf{U} = \mathbf{I}$, and $\mathbf{\Sigma}$ is diagonal (not affected by the transpose). Comparing Eq. (3.16) with Eq. (3.14), we have

$$\mathbf{V} = \mathbf{V}_e \tag{3.17}$$

$$\mathbf{\Sigma} = \sqrt{\mathbf{\Lambda}} \tag{3.18}$$

Using now Eq. (3.15), and the orthonormal property of $\mathbf{V}$: $\mathbf{V}^\top\mathbf{V} = \mathbf{I}$, we have

$$\mathbf{AV} = \mathbf{U}\mathbf{\Sigma} \tag{3.19}$$

Because $\mathbf{\Sigma}$ has all positive eigenvalues, we finally obtain

$$\mathbf{U} = \mathbf{AV}\mathbf{\Sigma}^{-1} \tag{3.20}$$

It is easy to confirm $\mathbf{U}$ is unitary. Finally, if $\mathbf{A}$ is rank deficient (rank($\mathbf{A}$)$< p$), matrix $\mathbf{B}$ will have zero eigenvalues. In such cases, we simply discard all the zero-eigenvalues and their corresponding eigenvectors. This will still give us an SVD in a reduced form, and all the process given above still holds

Readers may derive the similar set of equations for an $m \times p$ matrix $\mathbf{A}$ of real numbers with $p > m$, and assume it has a rank of m.

The above analysis proves in theory that any matrix has a SVD. In practical computations, we usually do not use the above procedure to compute the SVD. This is because the condition number of matrix $\mathbf{B}$ is squared, as seen in Eq. (3.13), leading to numerical instability. The practical SVD algorithms often use the QR decomposition of $\mathbf{A}$, which avoids forming $\mathbf{B}$. With the theoretical foundation, we now use some simple examples to demonstrate the SVD process using Python.

3.4.3 *Numerical examples*

```python
import numpy as np
a = np.random.randn(3, 6)      # matrix with random numbers
print(a)
```

```
[[-1.582  0.398  0.572 -1.060  1.000 -1.532]
 [ 0.257  0.435 -1.851  0.894  1.263 -0.364]
 [-1.251  1.276  1.548  1.039  0.165 -0.946]]
```

```python
u, s, vh = np.linalg.svd(a, full_matrices=True)
print(u.shape, s.shape, vh.shape)
```

```
(3, 3) (3,) (6, 6)
```

```python
print('u=',u,'\n','s=',s,'\n','vh=',vh)
```

```
u= [[-0.677  0.283  0.679]
 [ 0.202  0.959 -0.198]
 [-0.707  0.003 -0.707]]
 s= [ 3.412  2.466  1.881]
 vh= [[ 0.589 -0.318 -0.544  0.048 -0.158  0.479]
 [-0.083  0.216 -0.652  0.227  0.606 -0.318]
 [-0.128 -0.382 -0.180 -0.867  0.166 -0.159]
 [-0.510 -0.736 -0.110  0.412 -0.115 -0.066]
 [ 0.300 -0.343  0.476  0.115  0.723  0.171]
 [-0.529  0.218 -0.083 -0.104  0.210  0.781]]
```

```python
smat = np.zeros((3, 6))
smat[:3, :3] = np.diag(s)
print(smat)
```

```
[[ 3.412  0.000  0.000  0.000  0.000  0.000]
 [ 0.000  2.466  0.000  0.000  0.000  0.000]
 [ 0.000  0.000  1.881  0.000  0.000  0.000]]
```

```python
np.allclose(a, np.dot(u, np.dot(smat, vh)))
                                    # Is original a recovered?
```

```
True
```

```python
print(a)
print(np.dot(u, np.dot(smat, vh)))
```

```
[[-1.582  0.398  0.572 -1.060  1.000 -1.532]
 [ 0.257  0.435 -1.851  0.894  1.263 -0.364]
 [-1.251  1.276  1.548  1.039  0.165 -0.946]]
[[-1.582  0.398  0.572 -1.060  1.000 -1.532]
 [ 0.257  0.435 -1.851  0.894  1.263 -0.364]
 [-1.251  1.276  1.548  1.039  0.165 -0.946]]
```

We note here that the SVD of a matrix keeps the full information of the matrix: using all these singular values and vectors, one can recover the original matrix. What if one uses only some of these singular values (and the corresponding singular vectors)?

3.4.4 *SVD for data compression*

We can use SVD to compress data, by discarding some (often many) of these singular values and vectors of the data matrix. The following is an example of compressing an $m \times n$ array of an image data.

```python
from pylab import imshow,gray,figure
from PIL import Image, ImageOps
import matplotlib.pyplot as plt
import numpy as np
%matplotlib inline
np.set_printoptions(formatter={'float': '{: 0.3f}'.format})


A = Image.open('../images/hummingbird.jpg')   # open an image
print(np.shape(A))    # check the shape of A, it is a 3D tensor
A = np.mean(A,2)      # get 2-D array by averaging RBG values
m, n = len(A[:,0]), len(A[1])
r = m/n               # Aspect ratio of the original image
print(r,len(A[1]),A.shape,A.size)
fsize, dpi = 3, 80  # inch, dpi (dots per inch, resolution)
plt.figure(figsize=(fsize,fsize*r), dpi=dpi)
gray()
imshow(A)
U, S, Vh = np.linalg.svd(A, full_matrices=True)
print(U.shape, S.shape, Vh.shape)
                      # Recover the image
k = 20                # use first k singular values
S = np.resize(S,[m,1])*np.eye(m,n)
Compressed_A=np.dot(U[:,0:k],np.dot(S[0:k,0:k],Vh[0:k,:]))
#print(Compressed_A.shape, 'Compressed_A=',Compressed_A)
plt.figure(figsize=(fsize,fsize*r), dpi=dpi)
gray()
imshow(Compressed_A)
```

```
(405, 349, 3)
1.160458452722063 349 (405, 349) 141345
(405, 405) (349,) (349, 349)
```

```
<matplotlib.image.AxesImage at 0x203185a7080>
```

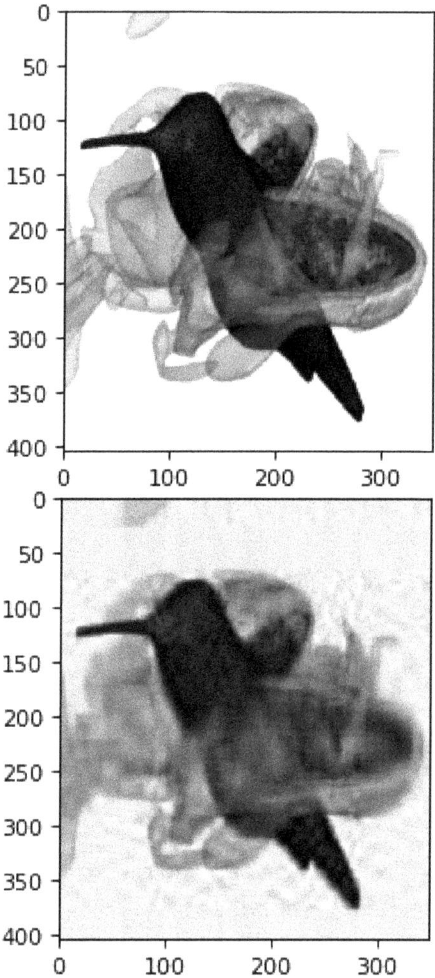

Figure 3.8:   Reproduced image using compressed data in comparison with the original image.

It is clear that when $k = 20$ (out of 349) singular values are used, the reconstructed image is quite close to the original one. Readers may estimate how much the storage can be saved if one keeps 10% of the singular values (and the corresponding singular vectors), assuming the reduced quality is acceptable.

3.5 Principal Component Analysis

Principal component analysis (PCA) is an effective technique to extract features from datasets. It was invented in 1901 by Karl Pearson [3]. It is a procedure that converts a dataset of p observations (raw features) of a possibly correlated to a reduced set of variables (extracted features), using an orthogonal transformation. The principal components produced via a PCA are not linearly correlated and are sorted by their variance values. Principal components at the top of the sorted list account for higher variability in the dataset. It is an effective way to reduce the dimension of feature spaces of datasets, so that machine learning models such as the neural network can work more effectively [4, 5]. Note that PCA is known to be sensitive to the relative scaling of the original observations, see Wikipedia (https://en.wikipedia.org/wiki/Principal_component_analysis#cite_note-1) for more details.

PCA can be performed at least in two ways. One is to use a regression approach which finds the set of orthogonal axes in an iterative manner. The other is to use eigenvalue decomposition algorithms. The following examples use the 2nd approach.

3.5.1 *PCA formulation*

Consider a general $m \times p$ matrix $\mathbf{A}$ of real numbers with $m > p$. We first form a matrix $\mathbf{B}$:

$$\mathbf{B} = \mathbf{A}^\top \mathbf{A} \tag{3.21}$$

which is a $p \times p$ symmetric square matrix with reduced size. Thus, it will be at least semi-positive-definite, and often SPD. We can perform an eigenvalue decomposition to it, which gives

$$\mathbf{B} = \mathbf{V} \boldsymbol{\Sigma} \mathbf{V}^\top \tag{3.22}$$

These decomposed matrices are as follows:

- $\mathbf{V}$ is a $p \times p$ orthonormal matrix of p eigenvectors of the $\mathbf{B}$ matrix.
- $\boldsymbol{\Sigma}$ is a $p \times p$ square diagonal matrix. The diagonal entries are the eigenvalues that are non-negative real numbers.

The PCA is then given as

$$\mathbf{A}_{PCA} = \mathbf{A} \mathbf{V} \tag{3.23}$$

which is the projection of $\mathbf{A}$ on these p orthonormal eigenvectors. It has the same shape as the original $\mathbf{A}$ that is $m \times p$.

One may reconstruct $\mathbf{A}$ using the following formula, if using all the eigenvectors:

$$\mathbf{A}_r = \mathbf{A}_{PCA}\mathbf{V}^\top = \mathbf{A}\mathbf{V}\mathbf{V}^\top = \mathbf{A} \tag{3.24}$$

This is because eigenvectors are orthonormal. It is often that the first few (ranked by the value of the eigenvalues in descending order) eigenvectors contain most of the overall information of the original matrix $\mathbf{A}$. In this case, we can use only a small number of eigenvectors to reconstruct the $\mathbf{A}$ matrix. For example, if we use $k \ll p$ number of eigenvectors, we have

$$\begin{aligned}
\mathbf{A}_r &= \mathbf{A}_{PCA}[0:m, 0:k]\mathbf{V}^\top[0:k, 0:p] \\
&= \mathbf{A}[0:m, 0:p]\mathbf{V}[0:p, 0:k]\mathbf{V}^\top[0:k, 0:p] \neq \mathbf{A}
\end{aligned} \tag{3.25}$$

This will, in general, not equal the original $\mathbf{A}$, but can be often very close to it. In this case, the storage becomes $m \times k + k \times p$ which can be much smaller than the original size of $m \times p$. In Eq. (3.25), we used the Python syntax, and hence it is very close to that in the Python code.

Note that if matrix $\mathbf{A}$ has dimensions of $m < p$, we simply treat its transpose in the same way mentioned above.

One can also perform a similar analysis by forming a normal matrix $\mathbf{B}$ using the following equation instead:

$$\mathbf{B} = \mathbf{A}\mathbf{A}^\top \tag{3.26}$$

which will be an $m \times m$ symmetric square matrix of reduced size. Assuming it is at least semi-positive-definite, we can perform an eigenvalue decomposition to it, which gives

$$\mathbf{B} = \mathbf{V}\Sigma\mathbf{V}^\top \tag{3.27}$$

In this case, these decomposed matrices are as follows:

- $\mathbf{V}$ is an $m \times m$ orthonormal matrix of m eigenvectors of the $\mathbf{B}$ matrix.
- Σ is an $m \times m$ square diagonal matrix. The diagonal entries are the eigenvalues that are non-negative real numbers.

The PCA is then given as

$$\mathbf{A}_{PCA} = \mathbf{V}^\top\mathbf{A} \tag{3.28}$$

It has the same shape as the original $\mathbf{A}$ that is $m \times p$. One may reconstruct $\mathbf{A}$ using the following formula and all the eigenvectors (that are orthonormal):

$$\mathbf{A}_r = \mathbf{V}\mathbf{A}_{PCA} = \mathbf{V}\mathbf{V}^\top\mathbf{A} = \mathbf{A} \tag{3.29}$$

We can use only a small number of eigenvectors to reconstruct the $\mathbf{A}$ matrix. For example, if we use $k \ll m$ number of eigenvectors, we have

$$\mathbf{A}_r = \mathbf{V}[0:k, 0:m]\mathbf{V}^\top[0:m, 0:k]\mathbf{A}_{PCA}[0:k, 0:p]$$
$$\neq \mathbf{A} \tag{3.30}$$

Note that for large systems, we do not really form the normal matrix $\mathbf{B}$, perform eigenvalue decomposition, and then compute $\mathbf{V}$ numerically. Instead, the QR transformation type of algorithms are used. This is because of the instability reasons mentioned in the beginning of Section 3.4.2.

3.5.2 *Numerical examples*

3.5.2.1 *Example 1: PCA using a three-line code*

We show an example of PCA code with only three lines. It is from glowing-python (https://glowingpython.blogspot.com/2011/07/principal-component-analysis-with-numpy.html), with permission. It is inspired by the function princomp of matlab's statistics toolbox and quite easy to follow. We modified the code to exactly follow the PCA formulation presented above.

```python
import numpy as np
from pylab import plot,subplot,axis,show,figure
def princomp(A):
    """ PCA on matrix A. Rows: m observations; columns:
        p variables. A will be zero-centered and normalized
    Returns:
    coeff: eig-vector of A^T A. Row-reduced observations,
           each column is for one principal component.
    score: the principal component - representation of A in
           the principal component space.Row-observations,
           column-components.
    latent: a vector with the eigenvalues of A^T A.
    """

    # eigenvalues and eigenvectors of covariance matrix
    # modified. It was:
    # M = (A-np.mean(A.T,axis=1))
```

```python
    # [latent,coeff] = np.linalg.eig(np.cov(M))
    # score = np.dot(coeff.T,M)
    A=(A-np.array([np.mean(A,axis=0)])) # subtract the mean
    [latent,coeff] = np.linalg.eig(np.dot(A.T,A))
    score = np.dot(A,coeff)    # projection on the new space
    return coeff,score,latent
```

Let us test the code using a 2D dataset.

```python
# A simple 2D dataset
np.set_printoptions(formatter={'float': '{: 0.2f}'.format})

Data = np.array([[2.4,0.7,2.9,2.5,2.2,3.0,2.7,1.6,1.8,1.1,
                  1.6,0.9],
                 [2.5,0.5,2.2,1.9,1.9,3.1,2.3,2.0,1.4,1.0,
                  1.5,1.1]])
A = Data.T                  # Note: transpose to have A with m>p
print('A.T:\n',Data)
coeff, score, latent = princomp(A) # change made. It was A.T
print('p-by-p matrix, eig-vectors of A:\n',coeff)
print('A.T in the principal component space:\n',score.T)
print('Eigenvalues of A, latent=\n',latent)
figure(figsize=(50,80))
figure()
subplot(121)
# every eigenvector describe the direction of a principal
# component.
m = np.mean(A,axis=0)
plot([0,-coeff[0,0]*2]+m[0], [0,-coeff[0,1]*2]+m[1],'--k')
plot([0, coeff[1,0]*2]+m[0], [0, coeff[1,1]*2]+m[1],'--k')
plot(Data[0,:],Data[1,:],'ob')          # the data points
axis('equal')
subplot(122)
# New data produced using the s
plot(score.T[0,:],score.T[1,:],'*g')  # Note: transpose back
axis('equal')
show()
```

```
A.T:
 [[ 2.40  0.70  2.90  2.50  2.20  3.00  2.70  1.60  1.80
    1.10  1.60  0.90]
  [ 2.50  0.50  2.20  1.90  1.90  3.10  2.30  2.00  1.40  1.00
    1.50  1.10]]
p-by-p matrix, eig-vectors of A:
 [[ 0.74 -0.67]
  [ 0.67  0.74]]
A.T in the principal component space:
 [[ 0.82 -1.79  0.98  0.49  0.26  1.66  0.90 -0.11 -0.37
    -1.16 -0.45 -1.24]
  [ 0.23 -0.11 -0.33 -0.28 -0.08  0.27 -0.12  0.40 -0.18 -0.01
    0.03  0.20]]
Eigenvalues of A, latent=
 [ 11.93  0.58]

<Figure size 3600x5760 with 0 Axes>
```

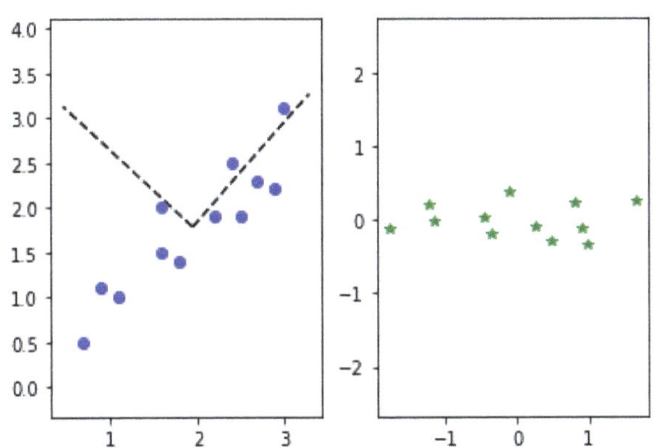

Figure 3.9:   Data process with PCA.

3.5.2.2 *Example 2: Truncated PCA*

This example is a modified PCA based on the previous code. The test is done for an image compression application. The code is from glowingpython (https://glowingpython.blogspot.com/2011/07/pca-and-image-compression-with-numpy.html), with permission.

```python
import numpy as np
def princomp(A,numpc=0):
    # computing eigenvalues and eigenvectors of covariance
    # matrix A
    A = (A-np.array([np.mean(A,axis=0)]))
                        # subtract the mean (along columns)
    [latent,coeff] = np.linalg.eig(np.dot(A.T,A))
    #was: A = (A-np.mean(A.T,axis=1)).T # subtract the mean
    #was: [latent,coeff] = np.linalg.eig(np.cov(M))


    p = np.size(coeff,axis=1)
    idx = np.argsort(latent)     # sorting the eigenvalues
    idx = idx[::-1]              # in ascending order
    # sorting eigenvectors according to eigenvalues
    coeff = coeff[:,idx]
    latent = latent[idx]                    # sorting eigenvalues
    if numpc < p and numpc >= 0:
        coeff = coeff[:,range(numpc)]    # cutting some PCs


    #score = np.dot(coeff.T,M) # projection on the new space
    score = np.dot(A,coeff)
                        # projection of the data on the new space
    return coeff,score,latent
```

The following code computes the PCA of matrix A, which is an image in
color scale. It first converts Image A into gray scale. After the PCA is done,
a different reduced number of principal components are used to reconstruct
the image.

```python
from pylab import imread,subplot,imshow,title,gray,figure,
    show,NullLocator
from ipykernel import kernelapp as app
from PIL import Image, ImageOps
%matplotlib inline
#A = Image.open('./images/hummingbirdcapsized.jpg')
A = Image.open('../images/hummingbird.jpg')  # open an image
#A = ImageOps.flip(B)            # flip it if so required
# or use A = imread('./images/hummingbirdcapsized.jpg')
A = np.mean(A,2)                # to get a 2-D array
```

```python
full_pc = np.size(A,axis=1)
    # numbers of all the principal components
r = len(A[:,0])/len(A[1])
print(r,len(A[1]),A.shape,A.size)
i = 1
dist = []
figure(figsize=(11,11*r))
for numpc in range(0,full_pc+10,50): # 0 50 100 ... full_pc
    coeff, score, latent = princomp(A,numpc)
    print(numpc,'coeff, score, latent \n',
    coeff.shape,  score.shape, latent.shape)
    Ar = np.dot(score,coeff.T)+np.mean(A,axis=0)
    #was:Ar = np.dot(coeff,score).T+np.mean(A,axis=0)
    # difference in Frobenius.norm
    dist.append(np.linalg.norm(A-Ar,'fro'))
    # showing the pics reconstructed with less than 50 PCs
    if numpc <= 250:
        ax = subplot(2,3,i,frame_on=False)
        ax.xaxis.set_major_locator(NullLocator())
        ax.yaxis.set_major_locator(NullLocator())
        i += 1
        imshow(Ar)                      #imshow(np.flipud(Ar))
        title('PCs # '+str(numpc))
        gray()
figure()
imshow(A)                               #imshow(np.flipud(A))
title('numpc FULL: '+str(len(A[1])))
gray()
show()
```

```
1.160458452722063 349 (405, 349) 141345
0 coeff, score, latent
 (349, 0) (405, 0) (349,)
50 coeff, score, latent
 (349, 50) (405, 50) (349,)
100 coeff, score, latent
 (349, 100) (405, 100) (349,)
150 coeff, score, latent
 (349, 150) (405, 150) (349,)
200 coeff, score, latent
```

```
 (349, 200) (405, 200) (349,)
250 coeff, score, latent
 (349, 250) (405, 250) (349,)
300 coeff, score, latent
 (349, 300) (405, 300) (349,)
350 coeff, score, latent
 (349, 349) (405, 349) (349,)
```

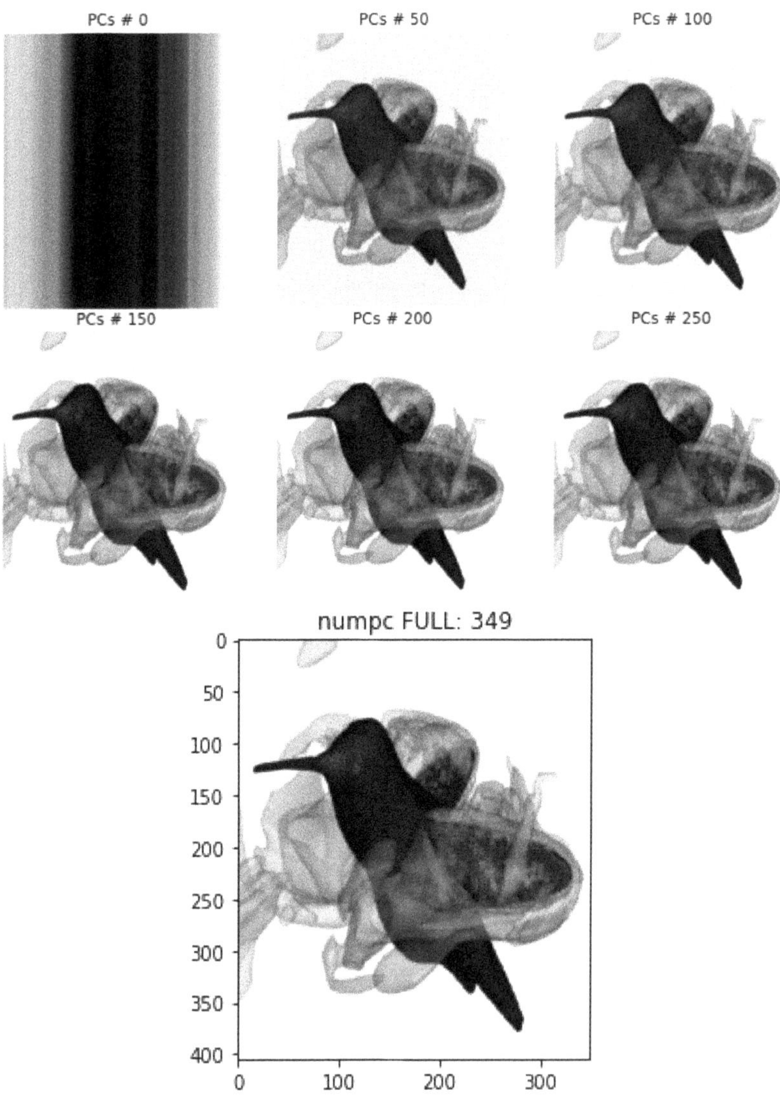

Figure 3.10:   Images reconstructed using reduced PCA components, in comparison with the original image.

We can see that 50 principal components give a pretty good quality image, compared to the original one.

To assess the quality of the reconstruction quantitatively, we compute the distance of the reconstructed images from the original one in the Frobenius norm, for a different number of eigenvalues/eigenvectors used in the reconstruction. The results are plotted in Fig. 3.11, with the x-axis for the number of eigenvalues/eigenvectors used. The sum of the eigenvalues is plotted in the blue curve, and the Frobenius norm is plotted in the red curve. The sum of the eigenvalues relates to the level of variance contribution.

```python
from pylab import plot, axis, cumsum
figure()
perc = cumsum(latent)/sum(latent)
dist = dist/max(dist)
plot(range(len(perc)),perc,'b',range(0,full_pc+10,50), dist,'r')
axis([0,full_pc,0,1.1])
show()
```

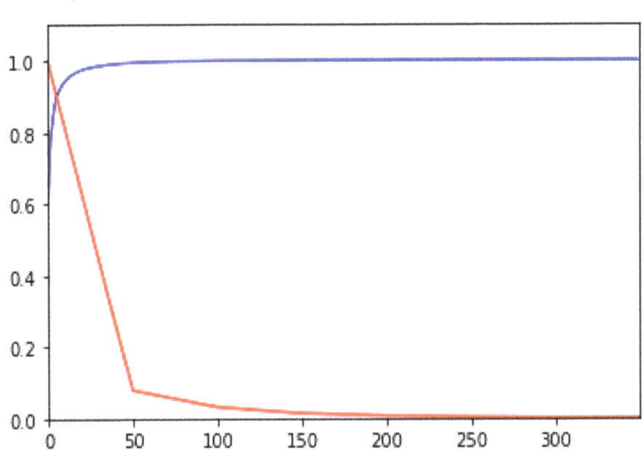

Figure 3.11: Quality of the reconstructed images.

In practical computations, the QR decomposition can be used to compute the eigenvectors $\mathbf{V}$, to avoid numerical stability, as discussed earlier for SVD.

3.6 Numerical Root Finding

Module scipy.optimize offers a function fsolve() to find roots of a set of given nonlinear equations defined by $\mathbf{f}(\mathbf{x}) = \mathbf{0}$, with estimated locations of the roots. The fsolve() is a wrapper around the algorithms in MINPACK that uses essentially a variant of the Newton iteration method (https://en.wikipedia.org/wiki/Newton%27s_method), which finds the root using the

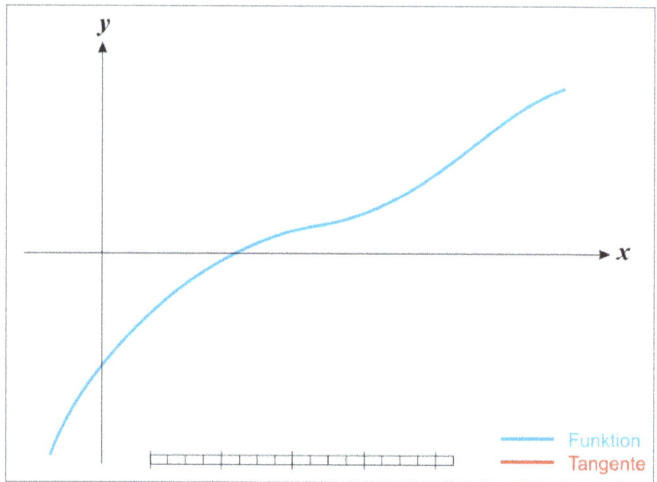

Figure 3.12: The Newton Iteration: The function is shown in blue and the tangent line at local x_i is in red. We see that x_i gets closer and closer to the root of the function when the number of iterations i increases (https://en.wikipedia.org/wiki/Newton%27s_method#/media/File:NewtonIteration_Ani.gif) under the CC BY-SA 3.0. (https://creativecommons.org/licenses/by-sa/3.0/) license.

function derivative to approximate the function locally. This process can be easily viewed from the animation nicely made by Ralf Pfeifer shown in Fig. 3.12.

Let us define two functions, one with a single variable and another with two variables, as examples to demonstrate how to find the roots. For functions with a single variable x, we define the following function that is often encountered in structural mechanics problems:

```python
import numpy as np
def BeamOnFoundation(bz):      # Deflection of a beam on foundation
    return np.exp(-bz)*(np.sin(bz)+np.cos(bz))
def f(x):                      # function whose root to be found
    return 2*BeamOnFoundation(x/2)-1-BeamOnFoundation(x)
```

```python
from scipy.optimize import fsolve
starting_guess = 5   # specify estimated location of the root
x_root=fsolve(f, starting_guess)
print('x_root=',x_root)
np.isclose(f(x_root), 0)    # check if f(x_root)=0.0.
```

```
x_root= [ 1.86]
```

```
array([ True])
```

Let us now consider a set of two functions with two variables.

```python
def f2d(x):
    return [x[0]*np.sin(x[1])-5,x[1]*x[0]-x[1]-8]
                         # x is an array   function-1   function-2
x_roots = fsolve(f2d, [3, 2])        # specify 2 estimated roots
print('x_roots=',x_roots)
np.isclose(f2d(x_roots), [0.0, 0.0]) # check if f(x_root)=0.0.
```

```
x_roots= [ 5.25  1.88]
```

```
array([ True,  True])
```

Note in general, a polynomial (or other algebraic equation) can have complex roots, even though their coefficients are all real. This is another case where the complex space is geometrically closed, but the real space is not. A polynomial of nth order should have n roots, but they may not be all in the real space. Some of them get into the complex space.

3.7 Numerical Integration

Numerical integration is one of the routine operations in computations for practical problems in sciences and engineering. This is because only simple functions can be analytically integrated, and one has to resort to numerical means for real-life problems. Different types of numerical integration techniques have been developed in the past, and numpy made the computation easy to implement and use. Our discussion on this topic starts from the classical trapezoid rule that may be familiar to many readers. More reference materials can be found from the Scipy.integrate documentation (https://docs.scipy.org/doc/scipy/reference/tutorial/integrate.html) and notebook. community (https://notebook.community/sodafree/backend/build/ipyth on/docs/examples/notebooks/trapezoid_rule).

3.7.1 *Trapezoid rule*

The trapezoid rule for definite integration uses the following formula:

$$\int_a^b f(x)\,dx \approx \frac{1}{2}\sum_{k=1}^{n_s}(x_k - x_{k-1})\left(f(x_k) + f(x_{k-1})\right). \qquad (3.31)$$

We define a simple polynomial function and sample it in a finite range $[a, b]$ at n_s number of sampling points equally spaced.

```python
%matplotlib inline
import numpy as np
import matplotlib.pyplot as plt
np.set_printoptions(formatter={'float': '{: 0.3f}'.format})
```

```python
def f(x):
    return 9*x**3-8*x**2-7*x+6    # define a polynomial function
a, b, n = -1., 2, 400    # large n for plotting the curve
x = np.linspace(a, b, n) # x at n points in [a,b]
y = f(x)                 # compute the function values
```

The function is integrated over $[a, b]$, by sampling a small number of points.

```python
ns = 6                         # sample ns points for integration
xint = np.linspace(a, b, ns)
yint = f(xint)
```

Plot the function curve and the trapezoidal (shaded) areas below it.

```python
plt.plot(x, y, lw=2) # plot the function as a line of width 2
#plt.axis([a, b, 0, 150])           # plot x and y axes
plt.fill_between(xint, 0, yint, facecolor='gray', alpha=0.4)
   # plot the shaded area over which the integration is done
plt.text((a+b)/2,12,r"$\int_a^b f(x)dx$", horizontalalignment=\
   'center',fontsize=15); # use \ to change line in code
```

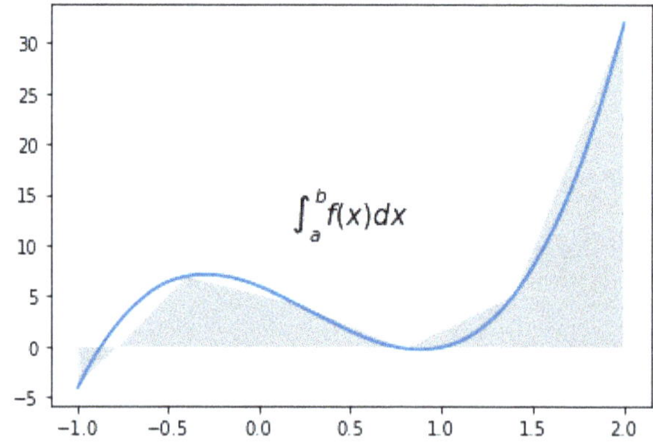

Figure 3.13:　Integration using the trapezoidal rule.

The trapezoid integration computes the shaded area. Thus, it is likely an approximation as shown.

```python
from scipy.integrate import quad  # quadrature (integration)
integral, error = quad(f, a, b)
                            # shall give the results and the error
integral_trapezoid=sum((xint[1:]-xint[:-1])*(yint[1:]+yint[:-1]))/2
                            # use the trapezoid formula
print("The results should be:", integral, "+/-", error)
print("The results by the trapezoid approximation with",len(xint),
      "points is:", integral_trapezoid)
```

```
The results should be: 17.25 +/- 1. 97757701330077287e-13
The results by the trapezoid approximation with 6 points are:
      18.240000000000002
```

3.7.2 *Gauss integration*

Gauss integration (or quadrature) is regarded as one of the most effective numerical integration techniques. It samples the integrand function at specific points called the Gauss points and sums up these sampled function values weighted by the Gauss weights for these points. It can produce exact values (to machine accuracy) for the integration of a polynomial integrand, because the Gauss point locations are the roots of the Legendre polynomials defined in the natural coordinates in $[-1, 1]$.

The Gauss integration is widely applied in numerical integration if the fixed locations of sampling points are not a concern. It is a standard integration scheme used in the FEM [1]. Here, we show an example using the p_roots() function available in Scipy module to find the roots of polynomials, and then carry out the integration.

```python
from pylab import *
from scipy.special.orthogonal import p_roots
```

```python
def gauss(f,n,a,b):
    [x,w] = p_roots(n+1)    # roots of the Legendre polynomial
                            # and weights
    G=0.5*(b-a)*sum(w*f(0.5*(b-a)*x+0.5*(b+a)))
                            # in natural coordinates
    # sample the function values at these roots and sum up.
    return G
```

```python
def my_f(x):
    return 9*x**3-8*x**2-7*x+6 # define a polynomial function
ng = 2
integral_Gauss = gauss(my_f,ng,a,b)
print("The results should be:", integral, "+/-", error)
print("The results by the trapezoid approximation with",
      len(xint),"points is:", integral_trapezoid)
print("The results by the Gauss integration with", ng,
      'Gauss points:', "points is:", integral_Gauss)
```

```
The integral results should be: 17.25 +/-
    1.9775770133077287e-13
The results by the trapezoid approximation with 6 points is:
    18.240000000000002
The results by the Gauss integration with 2 Gauss points:
    points is: 17.250000000000007
```

It is observed that the Gauss integration gives a much more accurate solution with a much smaller number of sampling points. In fact, the solution is exact (within the machine error) for this example because the integrand is a polynomial of the order of 3. We need only 2 Gauss points to obtain the exact solution. The general formula for polynomial integrands is $n_g = \frac{n+1}{2}$, where n is the order of the polynomial integrand and n_g is the number of Gauss points needed to obtain the exact solution for the integral. Note that when the trapezoid integration rule is used with 6 sampling points, the solution is still quite far off.

For general complicated integrand functions, Gauss integration may not give the exact solution. The accuracy, however, will still be much better compared to the trapezoid rule or the rectangular rule (which we did not discuss, but very similar to the trapezoid rule). In other words, for solutions of similar accuracy, Gauss integration uses less sampling points.

3.8 Initial data treatment

Finally, let us introduce techniques often used for initial treatment for datasets. Consider a given training dataset $\mathbf{X} \in \mathbb{X}^{m \times p}$. In machine learning models, m is the number of data-points in the dataset, and p is the number of feature variables. The values of the data are often in a wide range for real-life problems. For numerical stability reasons, we usually perform normalization to the given dataset before feeding it to a model. There are mainly two techniques are used: min-max feature scaling and standard scaling. Such a scaling or normalization is also called transformation in many ML modules.

3.8.1 *Min-max scaling*

For formulation for min-max scaling is given as follows.

$$\mathbf{X}_{scaled} = \frac{\mathbf{X} - \mathbf{X}.\min(axis = 0)}{\mathbf{X}.\max(axis = 0) - \mathbf{X}.\min(axis = 0)} \tag{3.32}$$

where $\mathbf{X}.\min$ and $\mathbf{X}.\min$ will be (row) vectors, and we used the Python syntax of broadcasting rules and element-wise divisions. This would bring all values for each feature into $[0, 1]$ range. A more generalized formula that can bring these values to an arbitrary range of $[a, b]$ is given as follows.

$$\mathbf{X}_{scaled} = a + \frac{\mathbf{X} - \mathbf{X}.\min(axis = 0)}{\mathbf{X}.\max(axis = 0) - \mathbf{X}.\min(axis = 0)}(b - a) \tag{3.33}$$

Here we used again the Python syntax so that scalars, vectors and matrix are all in the same formula.

Once such a scaling transformation to the training dataset is done, $\mathbf{X}.\min$ and $\mathbf{X}.\min$ can be used to perform exactly the same transformation to the testing dataset to ensure consistency for proper predictions.

The following is a simple code to perform min-max scaling using Eq.(3.32).

```python
np.set_printoptions(precision=4)
X = [[-1,  2,   8],              # an assumed toy training dataset
     [2.5, 6, 1.5],              # with 4 samples, and 3 features
     [3,   11, -6],
     [21,  7,   2]]
print(f"Original training dataset X:\n{X}")
X = np.array(X)
X_scaled = (X - X.min(axis=0)) / (X.max(axis=0) - X.min(axis=0))
print(f"Scaled training dataset X:\n{X_scaled}")
print(f"Maximum values for each feature:\n{X.max(axis=0)}")
print(f"Minimum values for each feature:\n{X.min(axis=0)}")
```

```
Original training dataset X:
[[-1, 2, 8], [2.5, 6, 1.5], [3, 11, -6], [21, 7, 2]]
Scaled training dataset X:
[[0.     0.     1.    ]
 [0.1591 0.4444 0.5357]
```

```
[0.1818 1.      0.    ]
 [1.      0.5556 0.5714]]
```

```
Maximum values for each feature:
[21. 11.  8.]
Minimum values for each feature:
[-1.  2. -6.]
```

We can now perform the same transformation to the testing dataset using
X. min and **X**. min of the training dataset.

```python
Xtest = [[-2,  3,   7],              # assumed testing dataset
         [5,   4, 5.5]]
Xt_scaled = (Xtest - X.min(axis=0)) / (X.max(axis=0) - X.min(axis=0))
print(f"Scaled corresponding testing dataset Xtest:\n{Xt_scaled}")
```

```
Scaled corresponding testing dataset Xtest:
[[-0.0455  0.1111  0.9286]
 [ 0.2727  0.2222  0.8214]]
```

The inverse transformation can be done with ease.

```python
X_back = X_scaled*(X.max(axis=0) - X.min(axis=0))+ X.min(axis=0)
print(f"Back transformed training dataset:\n{X_back}")

Xt_back = Xt_scaled*(X.max(axis=0) - X.min(axis=0))+ X.min(axis=0)
print(f"Back transformed testing dataset Xtest:\n{Xt_back}")
```

```
Back transformed training dataset:
[[-1.   2.   8. ]
 [ 2.5  6.   1.5]
 [ 3.  11.  -6. ]
 [21.   7.   2. ]]
Back transformed testing dataset Xtest:
[[-2.   3.   7. ]
 [ 5.   4.   5.5]]
```

It is clearly seen that the min-max scaling does no harm to the dataset.
One can get it back as needed.

The same min-max scaling can be done using Sklearn.

```python
from sklearn.preprocessing import MinMaxScaler
scaler = MinMaxScaler()                 # create an instance
scaler.fit(X)                           # fit with the training dataset
X_scaled = scaler.transform(X)    # perform the scaling transformation
print(f"Scaled training dataset X:\n{X_scaled}")
print(f"Maximum values for each feature:\n{scaler.data_max_}")
print(f"Minimum values for each feature:\n{scaler.data_min_}")
```

```
Scaled training dataset X:
[[0.      0.      1.     ]
 [0.1591 0.4444 0.5357]
 [0.1818 1.      0.     ]
 [1.      0.5556 0.5714]]
Maximum values for each feature:
[21. 11.  8.]
Minimum values for each feature:
[-1.  2. -6.]
```

```python
Xtest = [[-2,  3,   7],                 # assumed testing dataset
         [5,   4, 5.5]]
Xt_scaled = scaler.transform(Xtest)
print(f"Scaled corresponding testing dataset:\n{Xt_scaled}")
```

```
Scaled corresponding testing dataset:
[[-0.0455  0.1111  0.9286]
 [ 0.2727  0.2222  0.8214]]
```

```python
X_back = scaler.inverse_transform(X_scaled)
print(f"Back transformed training dataset:\n{X_back}")

Xt_back = scaler.inverse_transform(Xt_scaled)
print(f"\nBack transformed testing dataset Xtest:\n{Xt_back}")
```

```
Back transformed training dataset:
[[-1.   2.   8. ]
 [ 2.5  6.   1.5]
 [ 3.  11.  -6. ]
 [21.   7.   2. ]]


Back transformed testing dataset Xtest:
[[-2.   3.   7. ]
 [ 5.   4.   5.5]]
```

3.8.2 *"One-hot" encoding*

Many ML datasets use categorical features. For example, a color variable may have values of "red", "green", and "blue". These values must be converted to numerical numbers for building a ML model. Consider a single column feature vector is given originally as [[green], [red], [0], [blue]], one can simply encode this feature vector as [[1], [2], [0], [3]], where the integers are arbitrary but distinct. The treatment to dataset coded in this manner will be the same as any ordinary dataset we discussed before. However, this implies that the colors are having significance in values, which may not be what we want.

To avoid such a problem, we often use the so-called "one-hot" encoding. The single column dataset is then encoded to a matrix $\mathbf{X}$ with three columns, as shown in the code below. Thus, one-hot encoding results in a significant increase in the number of feature vectors, so that the features can all be made unique, and the categories are not given any value significance. Let us scale such kind of dataset.

```python
#     red   green  blue
X = [[0,    1,    0 ],        # a 'one-hot' training dataset
     [1,    0,    0 ],
     [0,    0,    0 ],
     [0,    0,    1 ]]
scaler.fit(X)
print(f"Original 'one-hot' training dataset X:\n{X}")
X_scaled = scaler.transform(X)   # perform the scaling transformation
print(f"Scaled 'one-hot' training dataset X:\n{X_scaled}")
print(f"Maximum values for each feature:\n{scaler.data_max_}")
print(f"Minimum values for each feature:\n{scaler.data_min_}")
```

```
Original 'one-hot' training dataset X:
[[0, 1, 0], [1, 0, 0], [0, 0, 0], [0, 0, 1]]
Scaled 'one-hot' training dataset X:
[[0. 1. 0.]
 [1. 0. 0.]
 [0. 0. 0.]
 [0. 0. 1.]]
Maximum values for each feature:
[1. 1. 1.]
Minimum values for each feature:
[0. 0. 0.]
```

It is seen that the min-max scaling used has not changed anything to the one-hot dataset, as expected. They do not have value significance.

3.8.3 *Standard scaling*

When the dataset has a distribution that is close to the normal distribution, one can use the standard scaling. The formulation for the standard scaling is given as follows.

$$\mathbf{X}_{scaled} = \frac{\mathbf{X} - \mathbf{X}.mean(axis = 0)}{\mathbf{X}.std(axis = 0)} \tag{3.34}$$

The following is a simple code to perform min-max scaling using Eq.(3.34).

```python
X = [[-1,   2,    8],        # an assumed toy training dataset
     [2.5, 6, 1.5],
     [3,    11, -6],
     [21,   7,    2]]
print(f"Original training dataset X:\n{X}")
X = np.array(X)
X_scaled = (X - X.mean(axis=0)) / X.std(axis=0)
print(f"Standard scaled training dataset X:\n{X_scaled}")
print(f"Mean value for each feature:\n{X.mean(axis=0)}")
print(f"Standard deviation for each feature:\n{X.std(axis=0)}")
```

```
Original training dataset X:
[[-1, 2, 8], [2.5, 6, 1.5], [3, 11, -6], [21, 7, 2]]
Standard scaled training dataset X:
[[-0.8592 -1.4056  1.3338]
 [-0.4515 -0.1562  0.0252]
 [-0.3932  1.4056 -1.4848]
 [ 1.7039  0.1562  0.1258]]
Mean value for each feature:
[6.375 6.5    1.375]
Standard deviation for each feature:
[8.5832 3.2016 4.9671]
```

Note that the values are not confirmed in $[-1, 1]$. It follows a normal distribution. We can now perform the same transformation to the corresponding testing dataset using the fitted instance of the training dataset.

```python
Xtest = [[-2,   3,    7],      # an assumed testing dataset
         [5,    4, 5.5]]
Xt_scaled = (Xtest - X.mean(axis=0)) / X.std(axis=0)
print(f"Standard scaled corresponding testing dataset Xtest:
        \n{Xt_scaled}")
```

```
Standard scaled corresponding testing dataset Xtest:
[[-0.9757 -1.0932  1.1325]
 [-0.1602 -0.7809  0.8305]]
```

The inverse transformation can be done with ease.

```python
X_back = X_scaled*X.std(axis=0) + X.mean(axis=0)
print(f"Back transformed training dataset:\n{X_back}")


Xt_back = Xt_scaled*X.std(axis=0) + X.mean(axis=0)
print(f"Back transformed corresponding testing dataset Xtest:
         \n{Xt_back}")
```

```
Back transformed training dataset:
[[-1.    2.    8. ]
 [ 2.5  6.    1.5]
 [ 3.   11.   -6. ]
 [21.    7.    2. ]]
Back transformed corresponding testing dataset Xtest:
[[-2.    3.    7. ]
 [ 5.    4.    5.5]]
```

It is clearly seen that the standard scaling does no harm to the dataset.
One can get it back as needed.

The same standard scaling can be done using Sklearn.

```python
from sklearn.preprocessing import StandardScaler
scaler = StandardScaler()    # create an instance
scaler.fit(X)
X_scaled = scaler.transform(X)
print(f"Scaled dataset X:\n{X_scaled}")
print(f"Mean values for each feature:\n{scaler.mean_}")
print(f"Standard deviations for each feature:\n{np.sqrt(scaler.var_)}")
```

```
Scaled dataset X:
[[-0.8592 -1.4056  1.3338]
 [-0.4515 -0.1562  0.0252]
 [-0.3932  1.4056 -1.4848]
 [ 1.7039  0.1562  0.1258]]
Mean values for each feature:
[6.375 6.5    1.375]
Standard deviations for each feature:
[8.5832 3.2016 4.9671]
```

```
Xtest = [[-2,  3,   7],          # assumed testing dataset
         [5,   4, 5.5]]
Xt_scaled = scaler.transform(Xtest)
print(f"Scaled corresponding testing dataset Xtest:\n{Xt_scaled}")
```

```
Scaled corresponding testing dataset Xtest:
[[-0.9757 -1.0932  1.1325]
 [-0.1602 -0.7809  0.8305]]
```

```
X_back = scaler.inverse_transform(X_scaled)
print(f"Back transformed training dataset:\n{X_back}")

Xt_back = scaler.inverse_transform(Xt_scaled)
print(f"\nBack transformed testing dataset Xtest:\n{Xt_back}")
```

```
Back transformed training dataset:
[[-1.    2.    8. ]
 [ 2.5  6.    1.5]
 [ 3.  11.   -6. ]
 [21.   7.    2. ]]
```

```
Back transformed testing dataset Xtest:
[[-2.    3.    7. ]
 [ 5.    4.    5.5]]
```

Note that the same scaling can be done for the labels in the training dataset, if they are not probability distribution types of data. When perform the testing on the trained model or prediction using the trained model, the labels should be scaled back to the original really data unit.

Also, it is a good practice to take look at the distribution of the data-points. This is usually done after scaling so that the region of the data-points is normalized. One may simply plot the so-called kernel density estimation (KDE) using, for example, seaborn.kdeplot().

References

[1] G.R. Liu and S.S. Quek, *The Finite Element Method: A Practical Course*, Butterworth-Heinemann, 2013. London.
[2] G.R. Liu, *Mesh Free Methods: Moving Beyond the Finite Element Method*, Taylor and Francis Group, New York, 2010.

[3] K. Pearson, On lines and planes of closest fit to systems of points in space, *Philosophical Magazine*, **2**(1), 559–572, 1901.

[4] G.R. Liu, S.Y. Duan, Z.M. Zhang *et al.*, Tubenet: A special trumpetnet for explicit solutions to inverse problems, *International Journal of Computational Methods*, **18**(01), 2050030, 2021. https://doi.org/10.1142/S0219876220500309.

[5] Shuyong Duan, Zhiping Hou, G.R. Liu *et al.*, A novel inverse procedure via creating tubenet with constraint autoencoder for feature-space dimension-reduction, *International Journal of Applied Mechanics*, **13**(08), 2150091, 2021.

Chapter 4

Statistics and Probability-based Learning Model

This chapter discusses some topics of probability and statistics related to machine learning models and the computation techniques using Python. Referenced materials include codes from Numpy documentation (https:// numpy.org/doc/), Jupyter documentation (https://jupyter.org/), and Wikipedia (https://en.wikipedia.org/wiki/Main_Page). Codes from mxnet-the-straight-dope (https://github.com/zackchase/mxnet-the-straight-dope) are also used under the Apache-2.0 License.

Building a machine learning model is mostly for prediction, classification, or identification, based on the data available and the knowledge about the data. Predictions can be deterministic and probabilistic. We often want to predict the probability of the occurrence of an event, which can be very useful and more practical for some problems.

For example, for aircraft maintenance, the engineers might want to assess how likely it is for the engine of the aircraft to get into an unhealthy state, based on records and/or diagnostic data. For a doctor, he/she may want to predict the possibility of a patient having a critical illness in the next period of time, based on the patient's health records, diagnostic data, and the current health environment. Health care organizations want to predict the likelihood of the occurrence of a pandemic. For all these types of tasks, we need to resort to means of quantifying the probability of the occurrence of the event. It can be a complicated topic of study and research, and machine learning models may help.

This chapter focuses on some of the basic concepts, theories, formulations, and computational techniques that we may need to build machine learning models using probability and statistics. At the end of this chapter, we will introduce a Naive Bayes classification model.

4.1　Analysis of Probability of an Event

4.1.1　*Random sampling, controlled random sampling*

In machine learning, one often needs to sample numbers in a random manner. This can be done numerically. In Python, we import random module to do so. The random() can then be used to generate "simulated" random numbers.

First, let us use a code to produce random integers. We shall use random.randint() for this, which samples numbers uniformly in a given range.

```python
# help(random.randint)                        # check it out
```

```python
import random                                 # random module
na, nb, n = 1, 100, 5                         # n integers in na~nb
for i in range(n):                            # First, generate n
    print(random.randint(na,nb),' ',end ='')  # random integers
                                              # in na~nb
print('\n')
for i in range(n):                            # Generate again
    print(random.randint(na,nb),' ',end ='')  # n random integers
```

```
86  61  35  81  40

4  92  95  31  70
```

We generated 5 random integer numbers twice. These generated numbers are "random", because two of the same generations gave two sets of different numbers. One can try to execute the above cell multiple times, and it should be found that each time different sets of numbers are generated.

Now, let us redo the same, but this time we use random.seed() to specify the same seed for each of the generations.

```python
random.seed(1)     # seed value 1 for random number generation
for i in range(n):   # Generate n random integers
    print(random.randint(na, nb),'  ',end ='')
print('\n')
random.seed(1)        # The same seed value (try also seed(2))
for i in range(n):
    print(random.randint(na, nb),'  ',end ='')
```

18   73   98   9   33

18   73   98   9   33

We see now that the same set of numbers is generated, which is some kind of **controlled random sampling** by a seed value. The use of random.seed() may confuse many beginners, but the above example shall eliminate the confusion. Function random.seed() is used just to ensure the repeatability when one reruns the code again, which is important for code development ensuring reproducibility. We will use it quite frequently.

Also, we see the fact that random numbers generated by a computer are not entirely random and are controllable to a certain degree. Naturally, it should be, because any (classic) computer is deterministic in nature. This pseudo-random feature is useful: when we study a probability event, we make use of the randomness of random.randint() or random.random(). When we want our study and code to be repeatable, we make use of random.seed().

Note that the seed value of 1 can be changed to any other number, and with a different seed value used, a different set of random numbers is generated.

Let us now generate real numbers.

```python
#random.seed(1)          #  seed for random number generation
n = 5
for i in range(n):       #generates n random real numbers
    print(random.random())
```

0.11791870367106105
0.7609624449125756
0.47224524357611664
0.37961522332372777
0.20995480637147712

It is seen that real numbers are generated in between 0 and 1. It is produced by generating a random integer first using random.randint() and then dividing it by its maximum range. The reader may switch on and off random.seed(1) or change the seed value to see the difference.

4.1.2 *Probability*

Probability is a numerical measure on the likelihood of the occurrence of an event or a prediction. Assume, for example, the probability of the failure of a structure is 0.1. We can then denote it mathematically as

$$Pr(\text{failure}=\text{``yes''}) = 0.1 \tag{4.1}$$

In this case, there is only one random variable that takes two possible discrete values: "yes" with probability of 0.1, and "no" with probability of 0.9. Such a distribution of a random variable is known as the Bernoulli distribution. For general events, there may be more possible discrete random variables and random variables with continuous distributions. Statistics studies the techniques for sampling, interpreting, and analyzing the data about an event. Machine learning is based on a dataset available for an event, and thus statistical analysis helps us to make sense of a dataset and hopefully produces a prediction in terms of probability.

We use Python to perform statistical analysis to datasets. We first import necessary packages, including the MXNet packages (https://gluon.mxnet.io/).

```python
import numpy as np          # numpy package, give an alias np
import mxnet as mx          # mxnet package, give an alias mx
from mxnet import nd        # ndarray class from mxnet package
mx.random.seed(1)           # seed for random number generation
                            # for repeatability of the code
```

Let us consider a simple event: tossing a die that has six identical surfaces, each of which is marked with a unique digit number, from 1 to 6. In this case, the random variable can take 6 possible discrete values. Assume that such markings do not introduce any bias (fair die), and do not affect in any way the outcome of a tossing. We want to know the probability of getting a particular number on the top surface, after a number of tossings. One can then perform "numerical" experiments: tossing the die the large number of times virtually in a computer and counting the times that the number shows on the top surface. We use the following code to do this:

```python
pr = nd.ones(6)/6           # probability distribution for a
                            # number on top. A total of 6
                            # values. Assume they have the
                            # same Pr (uniform distribution)
```

```
print(pr)
n_top_array = nd.sample_multinomial(pr,shape=(1))
                              # toss once using the
                              # sample_multinomial() function
print('The number on top surface =', n_top_array)
```

```
[0.16666667 0.16666667 0.16666667 0.16666667 0.16666667
 0.16666667]
<NDArray 6 @cpu(0)>
The number on top surface =
[3]
<NDArray 1 @cpu(0)>
```

For this problem, we know (assumed) that the theoretical or the "true" probability for a number showing on the top surface is $1/6 \approx 0.1667$.

The one-time toss above gives an nd-array with just one entry that is the number on the top surface of the die. To obtain a probability, we shall toss for many times for statistics to work. This is done by simply specifying the length of the nd-array in the handy nd.sample_multinomial() function.

```
n_surfaces = 6                 # number of possible values
n_tosses = 18                  # number of tosses
mx.random.seed(1)
toss_results = nd.sample_multinomial(pr, shape=(n_tosses))
                               # toss n_tosses times
print("Tossed", n_tosses,'times.')
print("Toss results", toss_results)
```

```
Tossed 18 times.
Toss results
[3 0 0 3 1 4 4 5 3 0 0 2 2 2 4 2 4 4]
<NDArray 18 @cpu(0)>
```

This time, we tossed 18 times, resulting to an nd-array with 18 entries. Note that if mx.random.seed(1) is not used in the above cell, we would get a different array each tossing, because of the random nature. For this controlled tossing (that readers can repeat) with random.seed(1), we got 1 "5" in 18 times of tossing. We thus have Pr(die="5") = 1/18. We got 3 "3"s, which gives Pr(die="3") = 3/18=1/6, and so on. The values of Pr(die="5") and Pr(die="3") are quite apart. Let us toss some more times.

```
n_t = 20
print(nd.sample_multinomial(pr, shape=(n_t)))   #toss n_t times
```

```
[2 3 5 4 0 0 1 1 0 2 3 0 0 0 2 4 5 2 0 4]
<NDArray 20 @cpu(0)>
```

It is difficult to count and calculate the probabilities manually. Let us use the following code available at the mxnet site to do so:

```
# The code is modified from these at https://github.com/
# zackchase/mxnet-the-straight-dope/blob/master/chapter01_
# crashcourse/probability.ipynb; # Under Apache-2.0 License.
#
n_tosses = 2000                         # number of tosses
toss_results = nd.sample_multinomial(pr, shape=(n_tosses))
                                # toss, record the results
record=nd.zeros((n_surfaces,n_tosses)) # count the event (tossing)
     # results: times of each of 6 surfaces appearing on top

n_digit_number = nd.zeros(n_surfaces)  # Initial with zeros for an
                    # array to hold the probability of on-top
                    # appearances for each of the 6 numbers
for i, digit_number in enumerate(toss_results):
    n_digit_number[int(digit_number.asscalar())] += 1
                                # counts and put in the
                                # corresponding place.
    record[:,i] = n_digit_number    # records the results

n_digit_number[:]=n_digit_number/n_tosses    # compute the Pr
print('Total number of tosses:',n_tosses)
print('Probability of each of the 6 digits:',n_digit_number)
print('Theoretical (true) probabilities:',pr)
```

```
Total number of tosses: 2000
Probability of each of the 6 digits:
[0.1675 0.1865 0.1705 0.1635 0.15   0.162 ]
<NDArray 6 @cpu(0)>
Theoretical (true) probabilities:
[0.16667 0.16667 0.16667 0.16667 0.16667 0. 16667]
<NDArray 6 @cpu(0)>
```

We see the probability values for all the 6 digits getting closer to the theoretical or true probability.

```python
import numpy as np
np.set_printoptions(suppress=True)
print(record)                    # print out the records
```

```
[[  0.    0.    0.  ... 333. 334. 335.]
 [  0.    0.    1.  ... 373. 373. 373.]
 [  0.    1.    1.  ... 341. 341. 341.]
 [  1.    1.    1.  ... 327. 327. 327.]
 [  0.    0.    0.  ... 300. 300. 300.]
 [  0.    0.    0.  ... 324. 324. 324.]]
<NDArray 6x2000 @cpu(0)>
```

We now normalized the data, which we often do in machine learning, by the total number of tosses using the following codes:

```python
x = nd.arange(n_tosses).reshape((1,n_tosses)) + 1
#print(x)
observations = record / x   # Pr of 6 digits for all tosses
print(observations[:,0])    # observations for 1st toss
print(observations[:,10])   # for first 10 toss
print(observations[:,999])  # for first 1000 toss
```

```
[0. 0. 0. 1. 0. 0.]
<NDArray 6 @cpu(0)>


[0.181819 0.272728 0.090909 0.181819 0.090909 0. 181819]
<NDArray 6 @cpu(0)>


[0.175 0.185 0.16  0.164 0.144 0.172]
<NDArray 6 @cpu(0)>
```

This simple experiment gives us 1,000 observations for six possible values of uniform distribution (any of the 6 digits has equal chance to land on top). When the probability of the appearance of each of the six surfaces of the die is computed after 1,000 times of tossing, we got roughly 0.14 to 0.19. These probabilities will change a little each time we do the experiment because of the random nature. If we would do 10,000 times of tossing for each experiment, we shall get all probabilities quite close to the theoretical value of $1/6 \approx 0.1667$. Readers can try this very easily using the code given above.

Let us now plot the "numerical" experimental results. For this, we use matplotlib library.

```python
# The code is modified from these at https://github.com/
# zackchase/mxnet-the-straight-dope/blob/master/chapter01_
# crashcourse/probability.ipynb; Under Apache-2.0 License.
%matplotlib inline
from matplotlib import pyplot as plt
plt.plot(observations[0,:].asnumpy(),label="Observed P(die=1)")
plt.plot(observations[1,:].asnumpy(),label="Observed P(die=2)")
plt.plot(observations[2,:].asnumpy(),label="Observed P(die=3)")
plt.plot(observations[3,:].asnumpy(),label="Observed P(die=4)")
plt.plot(observations[4,:].asnumpy(),label="Observed P(die=5)")
plt.plot(observations[5,:].asnumpy(),label="Observed P(die=6)")
plt.axhline(y=0.166667, color='black', linestyle='dashed')
plt.legend()
plt.show()
```

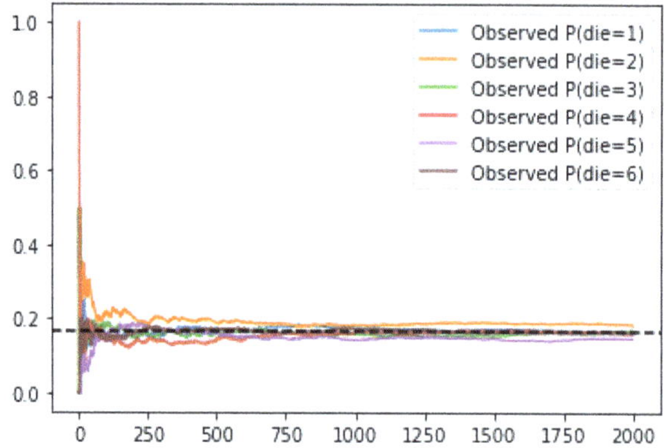

Figure 4.1:　Probabilities obtained via finite sampling from a uniform distribution of a fair die.

It is clear that the more experiments we do, the probability gets closer to the theoretical value of $1/6$.

The above discussion is for very simple events of a die toss. It gives a clear view on some of the basic issues and procedures related to the statistics analysis and probability computation for complicated events.

4.2　Random Distributions

In machine learning, one often needs to sample numbers in a random manner. Depending on types of problems, the distribution of the data of a variable can have different types. Sampling of data numerically shall be based on a given/assumed distribution type. We did so in the beginning for this chapter using uniform distribution. We shall now examine this further.

4.2.1 *Uniform distribution*

These numbers generated based on uniform distribution shall have an equal chance to land anywhere in between the specified range. To check the uniformity of the numbers generated using random.randint(), we can run it for a large number of times, say 1 million, and see how these numbers are distributed. We use the following code to do so:

```python
# This code are modified from these at https://github.com/
# zackchase/mxnet-the-straight-dope/blob/master/chapter01_
# crashcourse/probability.ipynb; Under Apache-2.0 License.
import numpy as np
import matplotlib.pyplot as plt
import random
na, nb, n = 0, 99, 100
counts = np.zeros(n)      # Array to hold counted numbers
fig, axes = plt.subplots(2,3,figsize=(15,8),sharex=True)
axes = axes.reshape(6)
n_samples = 1000001
for i in range(1, n_samples):
    counts[random.randint(na, nb)]+=1   # Random integers
    if i in [10, 100, 1000, 10000, 100000, 1000000]:
        axes[int(np.log10(i))-1].bar(np.arange(na+1,nb+2),counts)
plt.show()
```

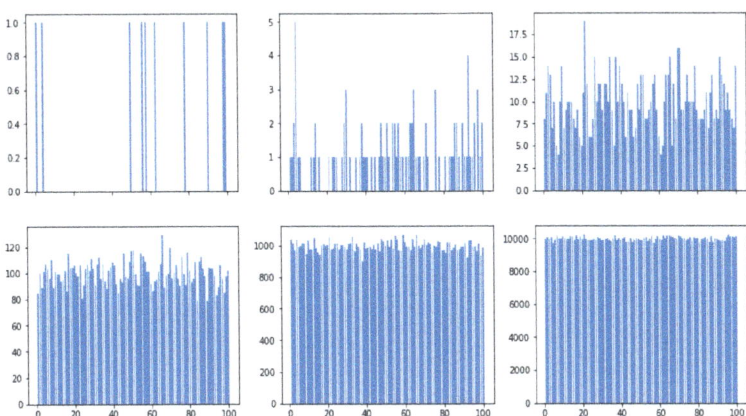

Figure 4.2:   Finite samplings from a uniform distribution.

It is observed that with the increase of sampling, the uniformity increases.

4.2.2 *Normal distribution (Gaussian distribution)*

The normal distribution is also called Gaussian distribution. It is widely used in statistics because many events in nature, science, and engineering obey this distribution. It is defined using the following Gaussian density function of variable x:

$$p(x) = \frac{1}{\sigma\sqrt{2\pi}}e^{-\left(\frac{x-\mu}{\sqrt{2}\sigma}\right)^2} \tag{4.2}$$

where μ and σ are, respectively, the mean and the standard deviation of the distribution. The normal distribution is often denoted as $\mathcal{N}(\mu, \sigma^2)$. In particular, when $\mu = 0$ and $\sigma = 1$, we have the **standard normal distribution** denoted as $\mathcal{N}(0,1)$ and its density function becomes simply $p(x) = \frac{1}{\sqrt{2\pi}}e^{-\left(\frac{x}{\sqrt{2}}\right)^2}$.

The gauss() in the numpy random module can be used to conveniently generate normal distribution numbers.

```python
from random import gauss
mu, sigma, n = 0., 0.1, 10
for i in range(n):                     # generates n random numbers
    print(f'{gauss(mu, sigma):.4f} ', end ='')
                                       # mu: mean; sigma: standard deviation
```

```
-0.1939 0.1794 0.0614 -0.1348 0.1020 0.0432 -0.2144 -0.0636
    0.0502 -0.1377
```

Let us plot out the density function defined in Eq. (4.2). The bell shape of the function may already be familiar to you.

```python
x = np.arange(-0.5, 0.5, 0.001)    # define variable x
def gf(mu,sigma,x):                # define the Gauss function
    return 1/(sigma*np.sqrt(2*np.pi))*np.exp(-.5*((x-mu)/sigma)**2)
mu, sigma = 0, 0.1                 # mean 0, standard deviation 0.1
plt.figure(figsize=(6, 4))
plt.plot(x, gf(mu,sigma,x))
plt.show()
```

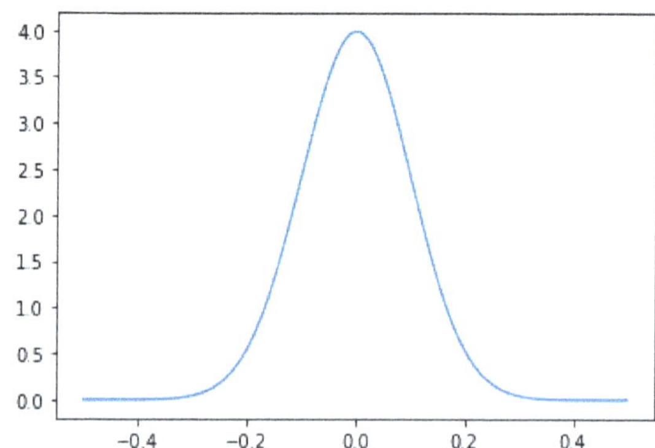

Figure 4.3:   A typical normal distribution (Gaussian distribution).

Let us now generate some random samples of Gauss distribution using np.random.normal(). We then compare the sampled data with the "true" Gaussian distribution.

```python
n = 500
samples = np.random.normal(mu, sigma, n) #generate samples
count, bins, ignored = plt.hist(samples, 80, density=True)
                    # plot histogram of the samples
plt.plot(bins, gf(mu,sigma,bins),linewidth=2, color='r')
                    # plot true Gauss distribution
plt.show()
```

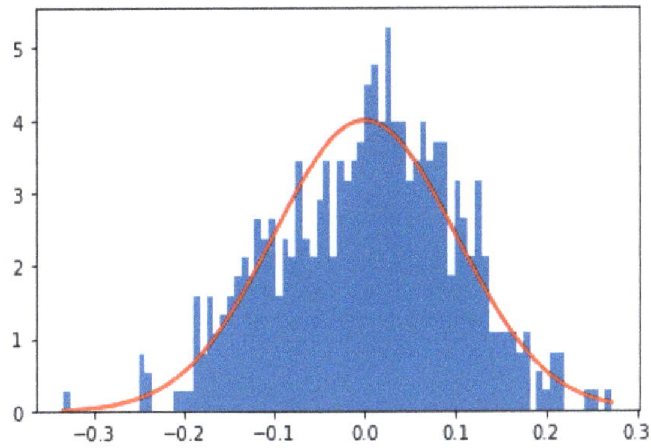

Figure 4.4: Sampling from a normal (Gaussian) distribution.

Numpy can generate samples of about 40 different types of distributions. Readers are referred to the numpy documentation (https://numpy.org/doc/1.16/reference/routines.random.html) for details when needed.

4.3 Entropy of Probability

For given probabilities of random variables of a statistics event, one can evaluate the corresponding *entropy*. It is a measure for *uncertainty* of the probability distribution for the event. It is the dot-product of the probability vector (that holds the probability values of a random variable) with its negative logarithm. The entropy $H_{\mathbf{p}}$ for an event with probability $\mathbf{p}$ is expressed by

$$H_{\mathbf{p}} = -\left(\sum_i p_i \log p_i \right) = -\mathbf{p} \cdot \log(\mathbf{p}) \tag{4.3}$$

where p_i is the probability of the ith possible value of the variable and $\sum_i p_i = 1$. Vector $\mathbf{p}$ is the vector that holds these the probabilities. The negative sign is needed, because entropy is positive and $\log(p_i)$ is always negative for $0 \leq p_i \leq 1$. In the computation, we often have it normalized by dividing it with the total number of possible values. Entropy is used very often in machine learning, especially for constructing objective functions, because it is a measure of the *uncertainty* that needs to be minimized.

Since the logarithm is used frequently, we shall first examine it in more detail using numpy log() function.

```python
import numpy as np
import matplotlib.pyplot as plt
%matplotlib inline
p = np.arange(0.01, 1.0, .01)          # generate variables
logp = -np.log(p)
    # negative sign for positive value: log(p)<0 for 0<p<1
plt.plot(p,logp,color='blue')
plt.xlabel('Probability p')
plt.ylabel('Negative log(p)')
plt.title('Negative log Value of Probability')
plt.show()
```

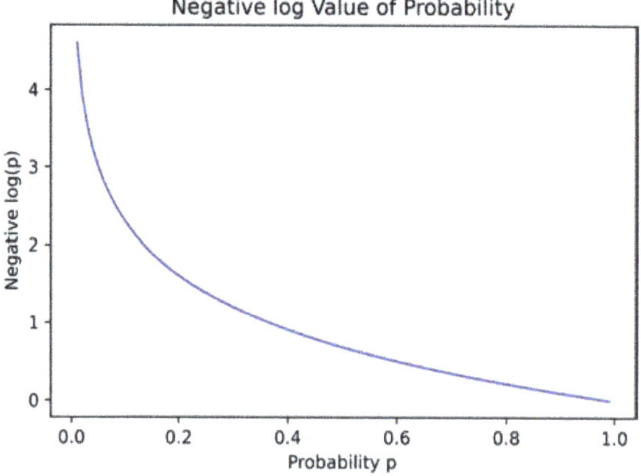

Figure 4.5:   A log function of probability.

Let us mention a few important features, which are the root reasons for why the logarithm is used so often in machine learning.

- $-\log(p)$ is monotonically varying with argument p. The monotonous is important because it does not affect the locations of the stationary points of the original function when it is in logarithm. This is an excellent property for optimization algorithms that are frequently used in machine learning.

- $-\log(p)$ is monotonically decaying with increasing probability. This reverses the trend of the probability, and thus it is the proper behavior for measuring the *entropy* for a high probability range. This is because when the probability is high, the uncertainty level is low (because we are quite certain that it is likely to happen) and so the value of entropy. When the probability is low, the uncertainty should also be low (because we are quite certain that it is unlikely to happen). In this case, we simply make use of the probability itself in the entropy equation.

- Entropy $H_{\mathbf{p}}$ is a combination of both the probability and its negative logarithm in the form of a product, as shown in Eq. (4.3). This combination gives the needed behavior, and it is nicely defined to suit our purpose by making use of the features of the logarithm function.

The following examples demonstrate how the entropy function works:

4.3.1 *Example 1: Probability and its entropy*

Consider an event with a variable that takes two values. We made an observation first, which produces probability vector $\mathbf{q}_1$ with entries of these two probabilities of the corresponding two variables. We then made another observation, which produces probabilities $\mathbf{q}_2$. We would like to evaluate the entropy of the probability of these two observations.

```python
q1 =np.array([0.999, 0.001]) # Pr. distribution with low
    # uncertainty: quite sure whether the event is to
    # happen, because the variable is with either a
    # very high or low chance to be observed.
q2 =np.array([ 0.5,0.5 ]) # Distribution with high uncertainty:
                # Not sure whether the event is to happen,
                # because the variable is with neither a
                # high or low chance to be observed.
                # - sign for getting a positive value:
print('q1=',q1,' -log(q1)=',-np.log(q1))  # log(p): negative
                                           # for 0<p<1
print('q2=',q2,' -log(q2)=',-np.log(q2))
H_q1 = -np.dot(q1,np.log(q1))/len(q1)     #Entropy: Uncertainty
H_q2 = -np.dot(q2,np.log(q2))/len(q2)
print('H_q1=',H_q1,'H_q2=',H_q2)
```

q1= [0.999 0.001] -log(q1)= [0.0010005 6.90775528]
q2= [0.5 0.5] -log(q2)= [0.69314718 0.69314718]
H_q1= 0.003953627556116044 H_q2= 0.34657359027997264

In this example, we see the contradicting behavior of $\mathbf{p}$ and $-\log(\mathbf{p})$. Vector $\mathbf{q}_1$ has either low or high probability values for its two variables, meaning that the uncertainty is low, and hence the computed entropy is low. On the other hand, $\mathbf{q}_2$ have two probabilities in the middle for both variables, meaning that it is very uncertain. The computed entropy is high as expected.

4.3.2 *Example 2: Variation of entropy*

To show this more clearly, we create artificial events $\mathbf{q}_1$ with a variable that takes two possible values, and let the probabilities be v_1 and v_2 for these two values, which change in the reverse manner while the sum of the probabilities equals 1. We write the following code to compute the entropy changing with the changes in the probability of v_1 and v_2:

```python
# An event with a variable that takes two values
v1 = np.arange(0.01, 1.0, .05)
gap = (v1[1]-v1[0])*len(v1)/3.
v1 /= (v1[0]+v1[-1])     # create an array that holds linearly
                         # changing probability values.
v2 = v1[::-1]            # create the revise of v1.
print(v1,np.sum(v1))     # to check it out
print(v2,np.sum(v2))
print(v1+v2,np.sum(v1+v2)/2)
xtick = range(len(v1))   #[0,1,2,3,4]
plt.bar(range(len(v1)),v1,width=gap*1.2,alpha=.9,color='blue')
plt.bar(range(len(v2)),v2,width=gap,alpha=.9,color='red')
plt.xlabel('Event ID, blue: v1, red: v2')
plt.ylabel('Probability')
plt.xticks(xtick)
plt.show()


H_qf = np.array([]) # initialize the array for entropy
for q1 in list(zip(v1,v2)):
    # create a pair of probability compute the entropy and append
    H_qf = np.append(H_qf,-(np.dot(q1,np.log(q1)))/2)


plt.plot(v1,H_qf)
plt.xlabel('Probability, v1 (v2=1-v1)')
plt.ylabel('Entropy of events')
plt.title('Entropy of Events')
plt.show()
```

```
[0.01030928 0.06185567 0.11340206 0.16494845 0.21649485 0.26804124
 0.31958763 0.37113402 0.42268041 0.4742268  0.5257732  0.57731959
 0.62886598 0.68041237 0.73195876 0.78350515 0.83505155 0.88659794
 0.93814433 0.98969072] 10.0
[0.98969072 0.93814433 0.88659794 0.83505155 0.78350515 0.73195876
 0.68041237 0.62886598 0.57731959 0.5257732  0.4742268  0.42268041
 0.37113402 0.31958763 0.26804124 0.21649485 0.16494845 0.11340206
 0.06185567 0.01030928] 9.999999999999998
[1. 1. 1. 1. 1. 1. 1. 1. 1. 1. 1. 1. 1. 1. 1. 1. 1. 1. 1. 1.] 10.0
```

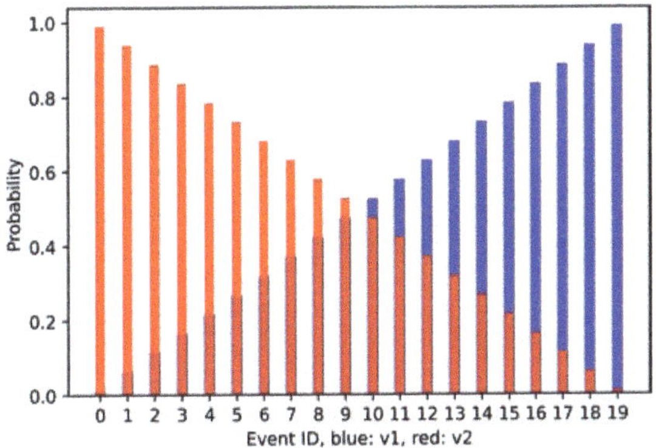

Figure 4.6:   Probabilities of 20 events each of which has two values.

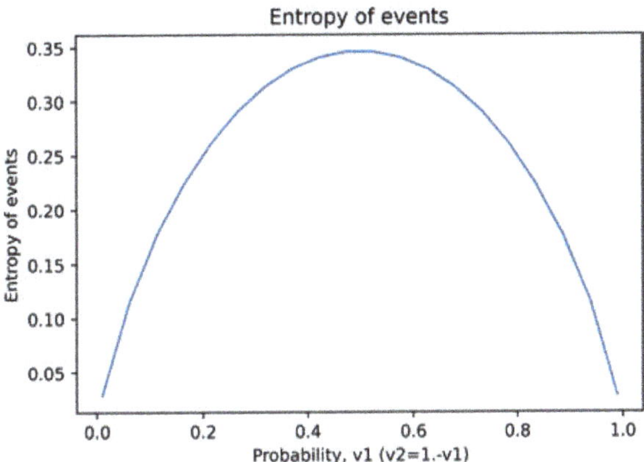

Figure 4.7:   Variation of entropy of the probabilities of the 20 events.

It is clear that when the probability of v_1 and v_2 is at 0.5, the entropy is the largest. The entropy is smallest at two ends, as expected.

4.3.3 *Example 3: Entropy for events with a variable that takes different numbers of values of uniform distribution*

Let us take a look at events with a variable that can take different numbers of possible values. We assume that the probability distribution for the variable is uniform for all these events. We want to find out how the entropy for the probability distribution changes with the number of variables of the events.

```python
# An event with a variable that can take many values of
 ↪uniform probability
N = 0
max_v = 100                      # Events with N variables
                                 # capped at max_values.
Ni = np.array([])                # For the number of v
H_qf = np.array([])              # To hold the entropy
while N < max_v:
    N += 1
    Ni = np.append(Ni,N)
    qf = np.ones(N)
    qf = qf/np.sum(qf)           # uniform sample generated
    H_qf = np.append(H_qf,-np.dot(qf,np.log(qf))/len(qf))

print('Probability distribution:',qf[0:max_v:10])
print('H_qf=', H_qf[0:max_v:10])
import matplotlib.pyplot as plt
import numpy as np
%matplotlib inline
plt.plot(Ni,H_qf)
plt.xlabel('Number of variables, all with same probability')
plt.ylabel('Entropy')
plt.title('Events with variables of uniform distribution')
plt.show()
```

```
Probability distribution: [0.01 0.01 0.01 0.01 0.01 0.01 0.01
    0.01 0.01 0.01]
H_qf= [-0.    0.21799048  0.14497726  0.11077378  0.09057493
    0.07709462  0.06739137  0.06003774  0.05425246  0.04956988]
```

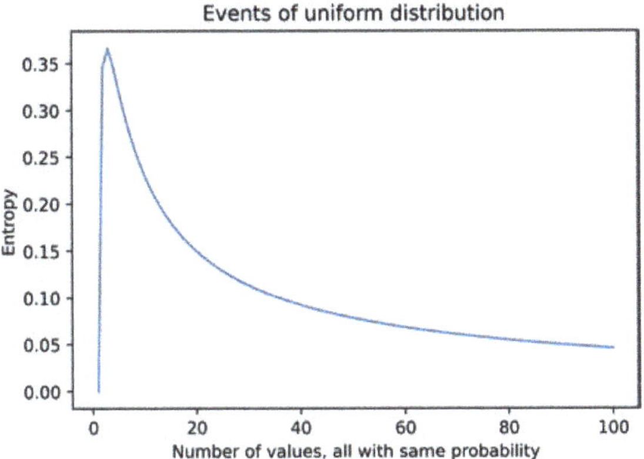

Figure 4.8: Entropy of probability of events with uniform distributions.

We find that (1) the entropy is zero when $N = 1$; (2) it peaks at $N = 3$; and (3) when N get very big, the entropy becomes small, implying that when an event has a very large number of variables, the entropy becomes small. This is because the probability of each of the variables becomes very small due to the uniform probability assumption for all these variables.

4.4 Cross-Entropy: Predicated and True Probability

Let us now look at the cross-entropy, which is an often used concept in statistics. The cross-entropy of a distribution $\mathbf{q}$ relative to the distribution $\mathbf{p}$ is defined as follows:

$$H_{\mathbf{pq}} = -\left(\sum_i p_i \log q_i\right) = -\mathbf{p} \cdot \log(\mathbf{q}) \tag{4.4}$$

In general, the cross-entropy is a measure of the similarity of two distributions (from the same space). In machine learning, we are interested in the cross-entropy of the predicated probability $\mathbf{q}$ with respect to the true one, $\mathbf{p}$. In this case, $H_{\mathbf{pq}}$ can be a measure of the performance of a prediction model, and hence often used as an objective or loss function in machine learning models.

We note the following properties:

- Cross-entropy is not symmetric: $H_{\mathbf{pq}} \neq H_{\mathbf{qp}}$, if $\mathbf{p} \neq \mathbf{q}$, which is obvious from Eq. (4.4).
- We shall have $H_{\mathbf{pq}} \geq H_{\mathbf{p}}$, and $H_{\mathbf{qp}} \geq H_{\mathbf{q}}$. The difference will be the KL-divergence, which is always positive (see the following section).

- When these two distributions are the same, the cross-entropy becomes the entropy studied in the previous section. All these three inequalities above become equal.
- Therefore, in machine learning models, even if the prediction is perfect, the cross-entropy will still not be zero, because the true distribution itself may have an entropy. If $\mathbf{p}$ is the entropy of the true distribution, the cross-entropy $H_{\mathbf{pq}}$ is bounded from below by $H_{\mathbf{p}}$. It can only be zero if the true distribution is without any uncertainty (probabilities of the variables are all zero, except for one of them, which is 1).

We look at some simple examples.

4.4.1 *Example 1: Cross-entropy of a quality prediction*

We examine a simple event with a variable that can take two possible values. Assuming we have a quality prediction, how is it measured in cross-entropy?

```python
# A good prediction case
q_good = np.array([0.9,0.1]) # predicted Pr. of 2 values
y = np.array([0.99,0.01])    # true Pr. of 2 values
p = y                        # Truth
q = q_good                   # prediction
print('p=',p,'  log(p)=',-np.log(p))
print('q=',q,'  log(q)=',-np.log(q))
print(' Entropy: Hp=',-np.dot(p,np.log(p))/len(p),\
             ' Hq=',-np.dot(q,np.log(q))/len(q))
print('\nCross-entropy: Hpq=',-np.dot(p,np.log(q))/len(p),\
                 'Hqp=',-np.dot(q,np.log(p))/len(q))
#Cross-entropy: Hpq>Hp; Hqp>Hq should hold.
```

```
p= [0.99 0.01]    log(p)= [0.01005034 4.60517019]
q= [0.9 0.1]      log(q)= [0.10536052 2.30258509]
 Entropy: Hp= 0.028000767177423672  Hq= 0.1625414866957241


Cross-entropy: Hpq= 0.06366638 Hqp= 0. 234781160
```

It is seen that the cross-entropy $H_{\mathbf{pq}}$ is low, indicating that the prediction $\mathbf{q}$ is good. Notice that $H_{\mathbf{pq}} \neq H_{\mathbf{qp}}$, $H_{\mathbf{pq}} \geq H_{\mathbf{p}}$, and $H_{\mathbf{qp}} \geq H_{\mathbf{q}}$.

4.4.2 *Example 2: Cross-entropy of a poor prediction*

Consider again a simple event with a variable that can take two possible values. This time, we assume a poor-quality prediction, and we examine how it is measured in cross-entropy.

```python
# A totally-off prediction case
q_bad = np.array([0.1,0.9])  # predicted Pr. of 2 values
y = np.array([0.99,0.01])    # true Pr. of 2 values
p = y                        # Truth
q = q_bad                    # prediction
print('p=',p,'  log(p)=',-np.log(p))
print('q=',q,'  log(q)=',-np.log(q))

print(' Entropy: Hp=',-np.dot(p,np.log(p))/len(p),\
                ' Hq=',-np.dot(q,np.log(q))/len(p))
print('\nCross-entropy: Hpq=',-np.dot(p,np.log(q))/len(p),\
                'Hqp=',-np.dot(q,np.log(p))/len(q))
#Cross-entropy: Hpq>Hp; Hqp>Hq should hold.
```

```
p= [0.99 0.01]    log(p)= [0.01005034 4.60517019]
q= [0.1 0.9]      log(q)= [2.30258509 0.10536052]
 Entropy: Hp= 0.028000767177423672  Hq= 0.1625414866957241

Cross-entropy: Hpq= 1.1403064236103417 Hqp= 2.072829100487316
```

It is seen that the cross-entropy $H_{\mathbf{pq}}$ is high, indicating that the prediction $\mathbf{q}$ is bad. Notice again that $H_{\mathbf{pq}} \neq H_{\mathbf{qp}}$, $H_{\mathbf{pq}} \geq H_{\mathbf{p}}$, and $H_{\mathbf{qp}} \geq H_{\mathbf{q}}$.

We are now ready to discuss the KL-divergence.

4.5 KL-Divergence

Kullback-Leibler Divergence or KL-divergence is a measure of the relative entropy from one distribution to another. For the given two distributions $\mathbf{p}$ and $\mathbf{q}$, the KL-divergence from $\mathbf{q}$ to $\mathbf{p}$ is defined as

$$D_{KL}(\mathbf{p}||\mathbf{q}) = \sum_i p_i \cdot [\log p_i - \log q_i] = \mathbf{p} \cdot [\log(\mathbf{p}) - \log(\mathbf{q})] \qquad (4.5)$$

It is also referred to as the relative entropy of $\mathbf{q}$ with respect to $\mathbf{p}$ that can be regarded as the true or reference distribution. Using the definitions for the entropy and the cross-entropy, we shall have

$$D_{KL}(\mathbf{p}\|\mathbf{q}) = H_{\mathbf{pq}} - H_{\mathbf{p}} \tag{4.6}$$

Note that the KL-divergence of $\mathbf{q}$ with respect to $\mathbf{p}$ is different from that of $\mathbf{p}$ with respect to $\mathbf{q}$. We have also

$$D_{KL}(\mathbf{p}\|\mathbf{q}) \geq 0, \text{ equality holds only if } \mathbf{p} = \mathbf{q} \tag{4.7}$$

This is known as the Gibbs' inequality (https://en.wikipedia.org/wiki/Gibbs%27_inequality).

Two simple examples of KL-divergence are given below.

4.5.1 *Example 1: KL-divergence of a distribution of quality prediction*

We examine a simple event with a variable that can take two possible values. Assuming we have a quality prediction of a distribution in relation to the true distribution, how is it measured in KL-divergence?

```python
# Good prediction case
p = y                    # true or reference distribution
q = q_good               # prediction
print('p=',p,'  log(p)=',-np.log(p))
print('q=',q,'  log(q)=',-np.log(q))
Dpq=np.sum(np.dot(p,(np.log(p)-np.log(q))))/len(p)
Dqp=np.sum(np.dot(q,(np.log(q)-np.log(p))))/len(p)
print('Dpq=',Dpq,'  Dqp=',Dqp)
```

```
p= [0.99 0.01]   log(p)= [0.01005034 4.60517019]
q= [0.9 0.1]     log(q)= [0.10536052 2.30258509]
Dpq= 0.035665613538170556   Dqp= 0.07223967373775611
```

It is seen that the KL-divergences $D_{\mathbf{pq}}$ and $D_{\mathbf{qp}}$ are all positive. They all have low values, indicating that the prediction $\mathbf{q}$ is good. Notice that $D_{\mathbf{pq}} \neq D_{\mathbf{qp}}$.

4.5.2 *Example 2: KL-divergence of a poorly predicted distribution*

Consider again a simple event with a variable that can take two possible values. Assume that we have a poor prediction of a distribution in relation to the true or reference distribution. We examine how it is measured in KL-divergence using the following code:

```python
# A bad prediction case
p = y
q = q_bad
print('p=',p,'  log(p)=',-np.log(p))
print('q=',q,'  log(q)=',-np.log(q))
Dpq=np.dot(p,(np.log(p)-np.log(q)))/len(p)
Dqp=np.dot(q,(np.log(q)-np.log(p)))/len(p)
print('Dpq=',Dpq, '  Dqp=',Dqp)
```

```
p= [0.99 0.01]    log(p)= [0.01005034 4.60517019]
q= [0.1 0.9]      log(q)= [2.30258509 0.10536052]
Dpq= 1.112305656432918   Dqp= 1.910287613791592
```

It is seen again that the KL-divergences $D_{\mathbf{pq}}$ and $D_{\mathbf{qp}}$ are all positive. They all have high values, indicating the prediction $\mathbf{q}$ is poor. Notice also that $D_{\mathbf{pq}} \neq D_{\mathbf{qp}}$.

4.6 Binary Cross-Entropy

Let us finally look at the so-called binary cross-entropy used in machine learning. For the given two distributions $\mathbf{p}$ and $\mathbf{q}$, the binary cross-entropy of $\mathbf{q}$ with respect to $\mathbf{p}$ is defined as

$$H_{\mathbf{pq}}^{B} = - \left(\sum_{i} p_i \cdot \log q_i + (1 - p_i) \cdot \log (1 - q_i) \right)$$
$$= -\mathbf{p} \cdot \log(\mathbf{q}) - (1 - \mathbf{p}) \cdot \log(1 - \mathbf{q})$$

(4.8)

In machine learning models, we usually assume that $\mathbf{p}$ is the truth distribution, which can have probability 0 or 1, and hence cannot be subject to logarithm. The binary cross-entropy can be viewed as a measure of the entropy of the predicated probability with respect to the true one. It takes into account both the probability $\mathbf{p}$ and $\mathbf{q}$ and the converse probability $(1 - \mathbf{p})$ and $(1 - \mathbf{q})$, and computes the entropy of both of them. It roughly doubles the cross-entropy, a somewhat enhanced measure of the discrepancy of the predicated distribution from the true distribution. It is often used to measure the performance of a model and used as one type of loss function.

We look at some examples.

4.6.1 *Example 1: Binary cross-entropy for a distribution of quality prediction*

Consider a simple event with a variable that can take four possible values. Assume that we have a good prediction of a distribution in relation to the true or reference distribution. We examine how it is measured in the binary cross-entropy using the following code:

```python
# A good prediction case
import numpy as np
q = np.array([0.9,0.04,0.03,0.03])    # prediction
p = np.array([1.0,0.0,0.,0.])          # truth
p_conv = 1.0 - p                        # converse side of prediction
q_conv = 1.0 - q                        # converse side of truth
print(p, q, ' converse:',p_conv,q_conv)
cHpq = -np.sum(np.dot(p,np.log(q)))/len(p)
bcHpq = -np.sum(np.dot(p,np.log(q))+np.dot(p_conv,
                np.log(q_conv)))/len(p)
print('Cross-entropy cHpq:',cHpq)
print('Binary cross-entropy bcHpq:',bcHpq)
```

```
[1. 0. 0. 0.] [0.9  0.04 0.03 0.03]  converse: [0. 1. 1. 1.]
     [0.1  0.96 0.97 0.97]
Cross-entropy cHpq: 0.02634012891445657
Binary cross-entropy bcHpq: 0.05177523128687465
```

It is found that the binary cross-entropy roughly doubles the cross-entropy value, as expected.

4.6.2 *Example 2: Binary cross-entropy for a poorly predicted distribution*

Consider an event with a variable that can take four possible values. Assume that we have a poor prediction of a distribution in relation to the true distribution. We examine again how it is measured in the binary cross-entropy using the following code:

```python
# A bad prediction case
q = np.array([0.4,0.2,0.3,0.1])    # prediction
p = np.array([1.0,0.0,0.,0.])       # truth
```

```python
p_conv = 1.0 - p          # converse side of prediction
q_conv = 1.0 - q          # converse side of truth
print(p, q, ' converse:',p_conv,q_conv)
cHpq = -np.sum(np.dot(p,np.log(q)))/len(p)
bcHpq = -np.sum(np.dot(p,np.log(q))+np.dot(p_conv,
        np.log(q_conv)))/len(p)
print('Cross-entropy cHpq:',cHpq)
print('Binary cross-entropy bcHpq:',bcHpq)
```

```
[1. 0. 0. 0.] [0.4 0.2 0.3 0.1]   converse: [0. 1. 1. 1.]
    [0.6 0.8 0.7 0.9]
Cross-entropy cHpq: 0.22907268296853875
Binary cross-entropy bcHpq: 0.40036743569623098
```

It is also found that the binary cross-entropy roughly doubles the cross-entropy, leading to an enhanced discrepancy measure.

4.6.3 *Example 3: Binary cross-entropy for more uniform true distribution: A quality prediction*

In the previous two examples, we studied two cases with the true distribution at extreme: its probabilities are 1.0 and zeros. For both examples, we observed an enhanced entropy measure using the binary cross-entropy. In this example, we consider a more even true distribution and examine the behavior of the binary cross-entropy.

```python
# A good prediction case
q = np.array([0.4,0.2,0.3,0.1]) # prediction
p = np.array([0.3,0.3,0.2,0.2]) # truth, rather even distribution
p_conv = 1.0 - p                # converse side of prediction
q_conv = 1.0 - q                # converse side of truth
print(p, q, ' converse:',p_conv,q_conv)
cHpq =-np.sum(np.dot(p,np.log(q)))/len(p)
bcHpq=-np.sum(np.dot(p,np.log(q))+np.dot(p_conv,
        np.log(q_conv)))/len(p)
print('Cross-entropy cHpq:',cHpq)
print('Binary cross-entropy bcHpq:',bcHpq)
```

```
[0.3 0.3 0.2 0.2] [0.4 0.2 0.3 0.1]   converse: [0.7 0.7 0.8
 0. 8] [0.6 0.8 0.7 0.9]
```

```
Cross-entropy cHpq: 0.36475754318911824
Binary cross-entropy bcHpq: 0.5856092407474651
```

In this case, it is also found that the binary cross-entropy does not give enhancement.

4.6.4 *Example 4: Binary cross-entropy for more uniform true distribution: A poor prediction*

Same as the previous example, but consider a case with poor prediction.

```python
# A bad prediction case
q = np.array([0.4,0.05,0.05,0.5]) # prediction
p = np.array([0.1,0.3,0.2,0.2])    # truth, rather even distribution
p_conv = 1.0 - p                   # converse side of prediction
q_conv = 1.0 - q                   # converse side of truth
print(p, q, ' converse:',p_conv,q_conv)
cHpq =-np.sum(np.dot(p,np.log(q)))/len(p)
bcHpq=-np.sum(np.dot(p,np.log(q))+np.dot(p_conv,
           np.log(q_conv)))/len(p)
print('Cross-entropy cHpq:',cHpq)
print('Binary cross-entropy bcHpq:',bcHpq)
```

```
[0.1 0.3 0.2 0.2] [0.4  0.05 0.05 0.5]   converse: [0.9 0.7 0.
    8 0.8] [0.6 0.95 0.95 0.5]
Cross-entropy cHpq: 0.43203116151910004
Binary cross-entropy bcHpq: 0.7048313483737685
```

In this case, we found a similarity: the binary cross-entropy gives an enhancement.

In conclusion, our study on simple vents above shows that the binary cross-entropy enhances the discrepancy measure, by taking into consideration both positive samples (with probability close to 1) and "negative" samples (with probability close to zero).

4.7 Bayesian Statistics

Consider a statistics event with more than one random variable that occurs jointly. When we deal with such multiple random variables, we may want to know the joint probability $\Pr(A,B)$: the probability of both $A = a$ and $B = b$ occurring simultaneously, for given elements a and b.

It is clear that for any values a and b, $\Pr(A,B) \leq \Pr(A=a)$, because $\Pr(A=a)$ is measured regardless of what happens for B. For A and B to happen jointly, A has to happen and B also has to happen (and vice versa). Thus, A,B cannot be more likely than A or B occurring individually.

$\Pr(A,B)\Pr(A)$ is called conditional probability and is denoted by $\Pr(B|A)$, which is the probability that B happens, under the condition that A has happened. This leads to the important Bayes' theorem.

- By construction, we have: $\Pr(A,B) = \Pr(B|A)\Pr(A)$.
- By symmetry, this also holds: $\Pr(A,B) = \Pr(A|B)\Pr(B)$.
- We thus have

$$Pr(A|B) = Pr(B|A)Pr(A)/Pr(B). \tag{4.9}$$

4.8 Naive Bayes Classification: Statistics-based Learning

4.8.1 *Formulation*

Based on the Bayesian statistics, a popular algorithm has been developed known as the Naive Bayes Classifier. Consider an event with p variable $\mathbf{x} = \{x_1, x_2, \ldots, x_p\} \in \mathbb{X}^p$. We assume that any variable x_i is independent of another. For a given label y, the conditional probability for being $\mathbf{x}$ is expressed as

$$p(\mathbf{x}|y) = \prod_i p(x_i|y) \tag{4.10}$$

Based on Bayes' Theorem, we have the following formula:

$$p(y|\mathbf{x}) = \frac{p(\mathbf{x}|y)p(y)}{p(\mathbf{x})} = \frac{\prod_i p(x_i|y)p(y)}{p(\mathbf{x})} \tag{4.11}$$

Although we may not know $p(\mathbf{x})$ (that is the probability that $\mathbf{x}$ occurs in the event), it may not be needed because it is only a matter of normalization in computing $p(y|\mathbf{x})$. Thus, we may just use the following formula instead:

$$p(y|\mathbf{x}) \propto p(\mathbf{x}|y)p(y) = \prod_i p(x_i|y)p(y) \tag{4.12}$$

4.8.2 *Case study: Handwritten digits recognition*

We can now use the code provided at mxnet-the-straight-dope (https://github.com/zackchase/mxnet-the-straight-dope/blob/master/chapter01_crashcourse/probability.ipynb) to show how a Naive Bayes classifier is coded to identify handwritten digits. We will use the well-known MNIST dataset to train this classifier. The MNIST (https://en.wikipedia.org/wiki/MNIST_database) contains a total of 70,000 images (60,000 for training and 10,000 for testing) of handwritten 10 digits from 0 to 9, and all these images are labeled. These images have been taken from American Census Bureau employees and American high school students.

The digit classification problem is then casted to compute the probability of a given image $\mathbf{x}$ being digit y: $p(y|\mathbf{x})$. Any image $\mathbf{x}$ contains p pixels $x_i(i = 1, 2, \ldots, p)$, and each pixel x_i can take a value of 1 (being lighted on) or 0 (being lighted off), and hence is a binary variable.

Equation (4.12) can then be used, in which we need to estimate $p(y)$ and $p(x_i|y)$. Both can be computed using the MNIST training dataset for each digit y. For example, in the total of 60,000 images of digits of the MNIST training dataset, digit 4 is found 5,800 times, and we then have $p(y = 4) = \frac{5800}{60000}$. To estimate $p(x_i|y)$, we can estimate $p(x_i = 1|y)$, because x_i is binary and $p(x_i = 0|y) = 1 - p(x_i = 1|y)$. Estimating $p(x_i = 1|y)$ can be done by counting the times that pixel i is on for label digit y, and then dividing it by the number of occurrences of label y in the dataset. In this simple algorithm, all we need is to count over the MNIST training dataset. It is quite a straightforward strategy, the training is just counting, and we can use the following code to get this done:

4.8.3 *Algorithm for the Naive Bayes classification*

```python
# The codes are modified from these at https://github.com/
# zackchase/mxnet-the-straight-dope/blob/master/chapter01_
# crashcourse/probability.ipynb; Under Apache-2.0 License.
# import all the necessary packages
import numpy as np
import mxnet as mx
from mxnet import nd
```

```python
def transform(data, label):  # define a function to transfer data
    return (nd.floor(data/128)).astype(np.float32),
        label. astype(np.float32)
            # floor of 255/128 = 1   pixel value = 1 when it is on.
# Divide dataset to 2 sets: one for training and one for testing
mnist_train = mx.gluon.data.vision.MNIST(train=True,
    transform=transform)
mnist_test = mx.gluon.data.vision.MNIST(train=False,
    transform=transform)
```

```
print('type:',type(mnist_train))
```

```
type: <class 'mxnet.gluon.data.vision.datasets.MNIST'>
```

```
import matplotlib.pyplot as plt
%matplotlib inline
image_index=8888   # Check one. Any integer <60,000
                   # 8888 is digit with label 3, as printed below
print(mnist_train[image_index][1])    #image in 0; label in 1
plt.imshow(mnist_train[image_index][0].reshape((28, 28)).\
           asnumpy(), cmap='Greys')   #image pixel: 28 by 28
```

```
3.0
```

```
<matplotlib.image.AxesImage at 0x1c5743ba630>
```

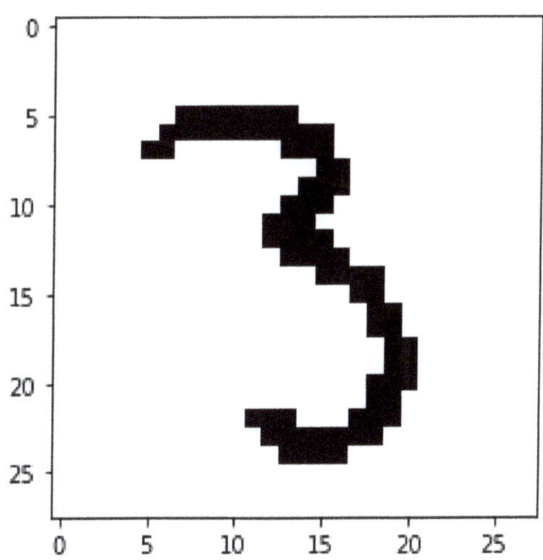

Figure 4.9:   One sample image of handwritten digit from the MNIST dataset.

```
# Initialize arrays for counts for computing p(y), p(xi/y)
# We initialize all numbers with a count of 1 to avoid
# division by zero, known as Laplace smoothing.

ycount = nd.ones(shape=(10))         #10 possible digits
xcount = nd.ones(shape=(784, 10))    #784 (= 28*28) variables
```

```python
# Aggregate the count of the labels in training dataset
# and number of its corresponding pixels being on (value=1)
for data, label in mnist_train:     # loop over the dataset
    x = data.reshape((784,))
    y = int(label)                  # get the digit-number
    ycount[y] += 1                  # add 1 to (digit)th entry
    xcount[:, y] += x               # add the image data to
                                    # the (digit)th column
# compute the probabilities p(xi|y) (divide per pixel counts
# by total count of the label in the training dataset)
for i in range(10):
    xcount[:, i] = xcount[:, i]/ycount[i]
# Compute the probability p(y)
py = ycount / nd.sum(ycount)
```

The model has been trained using the training dataset. We now plot the "trained" model.

```python
import matplotlib.pyplot as plt
%matplotlib inline
fig, figarr = plt.subplots(1, 10, figsize=(15, 15))

for i in range(10):
    figarr[i].imshow(xcount[:,i].reshape((28,28)).asnumpy(),
                     cmap='hot')
    figarr[i].axes.get_xaxis().set_visible(False)
    figarr[i].axes.get_yaxis().set_visible(False)

plt.show()
np.set_printoptions(formatter={'float': '{: 0.3f}'.format})
print(py.asnumpy(),nd.sum(py).asnumpy())
```

Figure 4.10:   A kind of mean appearance of handwritten digits.

```
[0.099  0.112  0.099  0.102  0.097  0.090  0.099  0.104
   0. 098  0.099] [1.000]
```

These pictures show the estimated probability distributions of observing a switched-on pixel for all these 10 digits. These are the mean appearance of these digits, or what a digit shall look like on average based on the training dataset.

4.8.4 *Testing the Naive Bayes model*

We now examine the performance of this statistics-based model using the MNIST test dataset. The training (which is just simple counting over the training dataset) completed above gives us $p(x_i = 1|y)$ and $p(y)$. For a given image $\mathbf{x}$ from the test dataset, we compute the likelihood of the image corresponding to a label y, which is to compute $p(y|\mathbf{x})$ using Eq. (4.12) where $p(\mathbf{x}|y)$ is in turn computed using the trained model. To avoid chain multiplication of small probability numbers, we compute the following logarithms instead (known as "log-likelihood"):

$$\log p(y|\mathbf{x}) \propto \log p(\mathbf{x}|y) + \log p(y) = \sum_i \log p(x_i|y) + \log p(y) \qquad (4.13)$$

For the given image $\mathbf{x}$, a feature x_i is binary and takes values of either 1 or 0. Because we are using the train model to compute the probabilities, we shall have

$$
\begin{aligned}
p(x_i = 1|y) &= p(x_i = 1|y) &&\text{for predicting } x_i \text{ is on} \\
p(x_i = 0|y) &= 1 - p(x_i = 1|y) &&\text{for predicting } x_i \text{ is off}
\end{aligned}
\qquad (4.14)
$$

Equation (4.14) can be written in a single one using a mathematical trick:

$$p(x_i|y) = p(x_i = 1|y)^{x_i}(1 - p(x_i = 1|y))^{1-x_i} \qquad (4.15)$$

This is a general equation of computing the probability of an event with binary variables using a trained model for predicting the probability of the positive variable. We finally have

$$\sum_i \log p(x_i|y) = \sum_i [x_i \log p(x_i = 1|y) + (1 - x_i) \log(1 - p(x_i = 1|y))] \qquad (4.16)$$

It is clear now that the testing is essentially measuring the binary cross-entropy of the distribution of a given image (true distribution) with that of the average image of a labeled letter computed from the dataset (the model distribution). Therefore, we can write out Eq. (4.16) directly using the binary cross-entropy formula.

To avoid re-computing the logarithms repetitively, we pre-compute $\log p(y)$ for all y, and also $\log p(x_i|y)$ and $\log(1 - p(x_i|y))$ for all pixels.

```python
logxcount = nd.log(xcount)                    # pre-computations
logxcountneg = nd.log(1-xcount)
logpy = nd.log(py)
fig, figarr = plt.subplots(2, 10, figsize=(15, 3))
# test and show 10 images
ctr = 0   # initialize the control iterator
y = []
pxm = np.array([])
xi = ()
for data, label in mnist_test:                # for any image
    x = data.reshape((784,))
    y.append(int(label))
    # Incorporate the prior probability p(y) since p(y|x) is
    # proportional to p(x|y) p(y)
    logpx = logpy.copy() #nd.zeros_like(logpy)
    for i in range(10):
        # compute the log probability for a digit
        logpx[i]+=nd.dot(logxcount[:,i],x)+nd.
        dot(logxcountneg[:,i],1-x)

    # normalize to prevent overflow or underflow by
    # subtracting
    # the largest value
    logpx -= nd.max(logpx)
    # and compute the softmax using logpx
    px = nd.exp(logpx).asnumpy()
    px = px*py.asnumpy()   # this proportional to P(y|x)
    px /= np.sum(px)
    pxm = np.append(pxm,max(px))    # use the one with max Pr.
    xi = np.append(xi,np.where(px == np.amax(px)))
    # bar chart and image of digit
    figarr[1, ctr].bar(range(10), px)
    figarr[1, ctr].axes.get_yaxis().set_visible(False)
    figarr[0, ctr].imshow(x.reshape((28,28)).asnumpy(),
                          cmap='hot')
```

```python
    figarr[0, ctr].axes.get_xaxis().set_visible(False)
    figarr[0, ctr].axes.get_yaxis().set_visible(False)
    ctr += 1
    if ctr == 10:
        break
np.set_printoptions(formatter={'float': '{: 0.0f}'.format})
plt.show()
print('True label:          ',y)
xi = np.array(xi)
print('Predicted digits:',xi)
print('Correct?',np.equal(y,xi))
np.set_printoptions(formatter={'float': '{: 0.1f}'.format})
print('Maximum probability:',pxm)
```

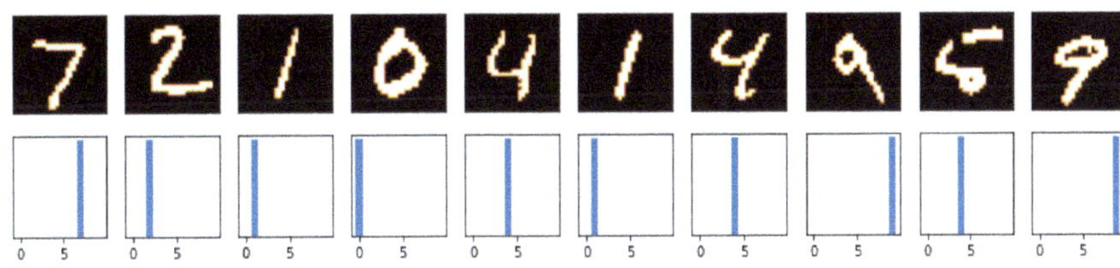

Figure 4.11:   Predicted digits (in probability) using images from the testing dataset of MINST.

```
True label:          [7, 2, 1, 0, 4, 1, 4, 9, 5, 9]
Predicted digits:  [7 2 1 0 4 1 4 9 4 9]
Correct? [True True True True True True True True False True]
Maximum probability: [1.0 1.0 1.0 1.0 1.0 1.0 1.0 1.0 1.0 1.0]
```

4.8.5 *Discussion*

The test shows that this classifier made one wrong classification for the first 10 digits in the testing dataset. The 9th digit should be 5, but classified as 4. For this wrongly classified digit, the confidence level is very close to 1. The wrong prediction may be due to the incorrect assumptions: each pixel is independently generated, depending only on the label. Clearly, a digit is a very complicated function of images, and statistic information alone has a limit. This type of Naive Bayes classifier was popular in the 1980s and 1990s for applications such as spam filtering. For image processing types of problems, we now have effective classifies (such as CNN; for example, see Chapter 15).

Alternatively, we can use the cross-entropy or the binary cross-entropy concept to perform the prediction. Once we obtained $p(x_i|y_j)$, $j = 1, 2, \ldots, 9$ using the training dataset, one can then compute the (binary) cross-entropy between $p(x_i|y_j)$ and $p(x_i|y_{test})$, where y_{test} is any given image from the test dataset (or any other handwritten digit). The y_j that gives the least (binary) cross-entropy should be regarded as the predicted digit.

This simple example does show how statistical analyses are useful in classifications and machine learning in general. We also showed how statistics can be computed for given datasets. Powerful Naive classifiers can be conveniently trained using the existing module at Sklearn (https://scikit-learn.org/stable/modules/naive_bayes.html) for practical problems that are heavily governed by statistics and where the physics laws are unknown, such as medical applications, recommendation systems, text classification, and real-time prediction and recommendation.

Chapter 5

Prediction Function and Universal Prediction Theory

To build an ML model for predictions, one needs to use some hypothesis, which predefines the prediction function to connect the feature variables to the learning parameters. Thus, a proper hypothesis may follow the function approximation theory, which has been studied intensively in physics-law-based models [1–4]. The most essential rule is that the prediction function must be capable of predicting an arbitrary linear function in the feature space by a chosen set of learning parameters. Therefore, the prediction function is assumed as a complete **linear function** of the feature variables, and it is one of the most basic hypotheses.

It turns out such a complete linear prediction function performs affine transformations of patterns in the affine space. Such a transformation preserves **affinity**, meaning that the **ratios of distances** (Euclidean) between points lying on a straight line and the **parallelism** of parallel line segments remain unchanged after the transformation. It may not preserve the angles between line segments and the (Euclidean) distances between points in the original pattern. Further discussion on more general issues with affine transformations can be found in Wikipedia (https://en.wikipedia.org/wiki/Affine_transformation) and the links therein.

The affinity ensures a special unique point-to-point seamless and gapless transformation, meaning that it does not merge two distinct points to one, or split one point to two, when the learning parameters are varying smoothly. The connection between the feature variables and the learning parameters is also smooth. Because an affine transformation is a combination of a linear transformation and a translation controlled by the learning parameters, any function up to the first order in the feature space can be reproduced, which is critically important for machine learning models to be predictive.

This chapter discusses first the formulation and predictability of predication functions, followed by discussion on detailed process, properties, and behavior of affine transformations. We shall focus on two aspects: (1) capability in predicting functions in the feature space, and (2) affine transformation of patterns in the affine space.

Then, the concept of affine transformation unit (ATU) (or linear prediction function unit) is introduced as a building block, and simple neural network codes will be built to perform affine transformations and demonstrate their behavior and property. Feature encodings by learning parameters and the uniqueness of the encodings are then studied, demonstrating the concept of data-parameter converter. Next, an extension of ATU to form an affine transformation array (ATA) and further extensions of the activation function wrapped ATA to form MLPs or deepnets will be studied, which shows how the predictability of a high-order nonlinear function can be established with a deepnet. Finally, a Universal Prediction Theory is presented offering the fundamental basis of why a deepnet can be made predictive.

5.1 Linear Prediction Function and Affine Transformation

Figure 5.1 shows the mechanism of the transmission of neurotransmitters in a synaptic cleft of sensory neurons. Molecules of a neurotransmitter are shown in a pseudo-colored image from a scanning electron microscope. A terminal button (green) has been opened to reveal the synaptic vesicles (orange and blue) inside the neurotransmitter.

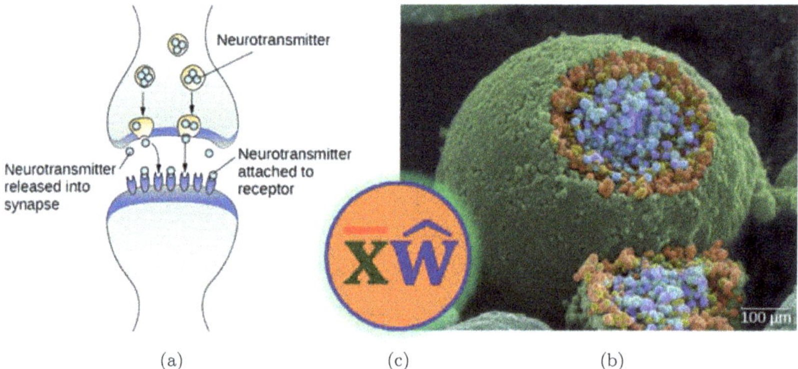

Figure 5.1: (a) Transmission of neurotransmitters; (b) a pseudo-colored image of a neurotransmitter from a scanning electron microscope: a terminal button (green) has been opened to reveal the synaptic vesicles (orange and blue) inside; (c) a typical affine transformation in **xw** formulation in an artificial NN. (Modified based on the image given in the Psychology book (2d) by Rose M. Spielman *et al.* under the CC BY 4.0 License). (Credit b: modification of work by Tina Carvalho, NIH-NIGMS; scale-bar data from Matt Russell).

In an artificial NN, we use a so-called affine transformation between the data-points and the learning parameters in an artificial neuron to somehow mimic the information transformation process in a neurotransmitter. This transformation is of most fundamental importance in many ML models, and thus the related theory is discussed in great detail in this chapter.

5.1.1 *Linear prediction function: A basic hypothesis*

In machine learning models, the basic hypothesis is that the prediction function z is given by the following equation:

$$z(\hat{\mathbf{w}}; \mathbf{x}) = \overline{\mathbf{x}}\,\hat{\mathbf{w}} = \underbrace{[1\ \ \mathbf{x}]}_{\overline{\mathbf{x}}}\underbrace{\begin{bmatrix} b \\ \mathbf{w} \end{bmatrix}}_{\hat{\mathbf{w}}} = \mathbf{x}\mathbf{w} + b$$

$$(5.1)$$

$$= w_1 x_1 + \cdots + w_p x_p + b = \sum_{i=1}^{p} w_i x_i + b$$

where $z(\hat{\mathbf{w}}; \mathbf{x})$ reads as "z is a function of $\hat{\mathbf{w}}$ for given $\mathbf{x}$", and all vectors are defined as

$$\mathbf{x} = [x_1, x_2, \ldots, x_p] \in \mathbb{X}^p \in \mathbb{R}^p$$

$$\overline{\mathbf{x}} = [1\ \ \mathbf{x}] = \left[\underbrace{x_0}_{1}, x_1, x_2, \ldots, x_p\right] \in \overline{\mathbb{X}}^p \in \mathbb{R}^{p+1}$$

$$\mathbf{w} = [w_1, w_2, \ldots, w_p]^\top \in \mathbb{W}^p \in \mathbb{R}^p$$

$$(5.2)$$

$$\hat{\mathbf{w}} = [b\ \ \mathbf{w}]^\top = \left[\underbrace{w_0}_{b}, w_1, w_2, \ldots, w_p\right]^\top \in \mathbb{W}^{p+1} \in \mathbb{R}^{p+1}$$

in which $x_i(i = 1, 2, \ldots, p)$ are feature variables, and here we use only the *linear basis functions*; $w_i(i = 1, 2, \ldots, p) \in \mathbb{R}$ are called weights. Constant $b \in \mathbb{R}$ is called bias, and is also often denoted as $w_0 \in \mathbb{R}$. These real numbers form vectors in corresponding spaces (defined in Chapter 1) and used in the operations above. The hat over $\mathbf{w}$ stands for the basis on top of it. It absorbs the bias and become new vector in the hypothesis space $\mathbb{W}^{p+1}$. Both weights and bias are parameters that can be tuned to predict exactly a desired arbitrary linear function in the feature space. The relations of these spaces are discussed in Chapter 1. Notice the transpose we used for the learning parameters, which implies that they are formed in a matrix (with only one column in this case). The features are formed in row vectors. This is why the learning parameter matrix is acting from the right on the feature vector.

We intentionally put together most used formulas for the prediction function in Eq. (5.1) a single united form, so that the relationship between all these variables can be made clear once for all. Readers may take a movement to digest this formulation, so that the later formulations can be understood more easily.

When we write $z = \mathbf{x}\mathbf{w} + b$, we call it a xw+b formulation. When we write $z = \overline{\mathbf{x}}\,\hat{\mathbf{w}}$, in which the bias b is absorbed by w, we call it an xw formulation. Both formulations will be used in the book interchangeably, because they are essentially the same. The xw+b formulation allows explicit viewing the roles of weights and biases separately during analysis. The xw formulation is more concise in derivation processes, and also allows explicit expressions of affine transformations, which are most essential for major machine learning models.

5.1.2 *Predictability for constants, the role of the bias*

Note that the bias b is a must have. If we set $b = 0$ and used only $\mathbf{w}$, the hypothesis will not be able to even predict a function that is a constant. This can be easily proven as follows.

Consider a given (label) function $y(\mathbf{x}) = c$, where c is a given constant in $\mathbb{R}$ independent of $\mathbf{x}$. This means that at $\mathbf{x} = \mathbf{0}$, $y(\mathbf{x} = \mathbf{0}) = c$. In order to predict c using Eq. (5.1) we must have $z(\mathbf{w}, b; \mathbf{x} = \mathbf{0}) = c$. Now, if we drop b in Eq. (5.1), regardless of what we choose for $\mathbf{w}$, the hypothesis always predicts

$$z = \mathbf{0} \cdot \mathbf{w} = 0 \tag{5.3}$$

This means that the constant $c \in \mathbb{R}$ will never be predicted by the hypothesis without b. This means also that a pure linear transformation through $\mathbf{w}$ is insufficient for proper prediction, because it cannot even predict constants.

On the other hand, when b is there, we simply choose $b = c$, and the constant c is then produced by the hypothesis. This implies also that z must live in an affine space $\overline{\mathbb{X}^p}$, an augmented feature space that lives within $\mathbb{X}^{p+1}$.

5.1.3 *Predictability for linear functions: The role of the weights*

Further, by proper choices of $\mathbf{w}$ and b, any linear function can be produced using Eq. (5.1). This can also be easily proven as follows.

Consider any given (label) linear function $y \in \mathbb{Y}$ of variables $\mathbf{x} \in \mathbb{X}^p$:

$$y(\mathbf{x}) = \mathbf{x}\mathbf{k} + c \tag{5.4}$$

where $c \in \mathbb{R}$ is a given constant and $\mathbf{k}$ is a (column) vector in $\mathbb{W}^p$. Note $\mathbf{k}$ in general may be in $\mathbb{R}^p$, however, we need to perform vector operations on it, it must be confined in the vector space $\mathbb{W}^p$.

By simply choosing $\mathbf{w}^* = \mathbf{k}$, and $b^* = c$, we obtain

$$z(\mathbf{w}^*, b^*; \mathbf{x}) = \mathbf{x}\mathbf{k} + c = y(\mathbf{x}) \tag{5.5}$$

The given linear function is predicted exactly, using such a particular choice of $\mathbf{w}^*$ and b^*. This means that any given arbitrary linear function of $\mathbf{x} \in \mathbb{X}^p$ can be predicted using hypothesis Eq. (5.1).

5.1.4 *Prediction of linear functions: A machine learning procedure*

The above process showed that to predict a label linear function using Eq. (5.1) is straightforward because we can choose these learning parameters by inspection. For more complicated problems, this is not possible, and we would use a minimization process to find these learning parameters. Here, we demonstrate such a process to find $\mathbf{w}^*$ and b^*. This time, let us use the xw formulation. We rewrite Eq. (5.4) to

$$y(\mathbf{x}) = \overline{\mathbf{x}}\,\hat{\mathbf{k}} \tag{5.6}$$

where $\hat{\mathbf{k}} = [c \ \ \mathbf{k}]^\top \in \mathbb{W}^{p+1} \in \mathbb{R}^{p+1}$.

Step 1: define a loss function in terms of the learning parameters. The loss function shall evaluate the error between the hypothesis Eq. (5.1) and the label function Eq. (5.6). It can have various forms. The widely used one is the L2 error function that is the error squared:

$$\begin{aligned}
\mathcal{L}(z(\hat{\mathbf{w}})) &= \|z(\hat{\mathbf{w}}; \overline{\mathbf{x}}) - y(\overline{\mathbf{x}})\|^2 = [z(\hat{\mathbf{w}}; \overline{\mathbf{x}}) - y(\overline{\mathbf{x}})]^2 \\
&= (\overline{\mathbf{x}}\,\hat{\mathbf{w}} - \overline{\mathbf{x}}\,\hat{\mathbf{k}})^\top (\overline{\mathbf{x}}\,\hat{\mathbf{w}} - \overline{\mathbf{x}}\,\hat{\mathbf{k}}) \\
&= (\hat{\mathbf{w}}^\top - \hat{\mathbf{k}}^\top)[\overline{\mathbf{x}}^\top\overline{\mathbf{x}}](\hat{\mathbf{w}} - \hat{\mathbf{k}})
\end{aligned} \tag{5.7}$$

It is clear that the loss function is $\mathcal{L}(z)$ is a scalar function of the prediction function $z(\hat{\mathbf{w}})$ that is in turn a function of the vector of learning parameter $\hat{\mathbf{w}}$. Therefore, $\mathcal{L}(z)$ is in fact a **functional**. It takes a vector $\hat{\mathbf{w}} \in \mathbb{W}^{(p+1)}$ and produces a positive number in $\mathbb{R}$. It is also quadratic in $\hat{\mathbf{w}}$.

In the 2nd line of Eq. (5.7), we first moved the transpose into the first pair of parentheses, and then factor out $\overline{\mathbf{x}}^\top$ and $\overline{\mathbf{x}}$ from these two pairs of parenthesis to form matrix that is the out-product of $[\overline{\mathbf{x}}^\top\overline{\mathbf{x}}]$, which is a $p \times p$ symmetric matrix of rank 1. All these follow the matrix operation rules. Note that $(\hat{\mathbf{w}} - \hat{\mathbf{k}})$ is a vector. Therefore, Eq. (5.7) is a standard quadratic form. If $[\overline{\mathbf{x}}^\top\overline{\mathbf{x}}]$ is SPD, $\mathcal{L}$ has a unique minimum at $(\hat{\mathbf{w}} - \hat{\mathbf{k}}) = 0$ or $\hat{\mathbf{w}}^* = \hat{\mathbf{k}}$. This would prove that the prediction function is *capable* of reproducing any linear function *uniquely* in the feature space, and we are done. However, because $[\overline{\mathbf{x}}^\top\overline{\mathbf{x}}]$ has only rank 1, we need to manipulate a little further for deeper inside.

Step 2: minimize the loss function with respect to $\hat{\mathbf{w}} \in \mathbb{W}^{p+1}$.

This allow us to find $\hat{\mathbf{w}}$ that is the stationary point of $\mathcal{L}$, by setting the gradient to zero.

$$\frac{\partial \mathcal{L}(\hat{\mathbf{w}})}{\partial \hat{\mathbf{w}}} = 2\overline{\mathbf{x}}^\top\overline{\mathbf{x}}(\hat{\mathbf{w}} - \hat{\mathbf{k}}) = 0 \tag{5.8}$$

In above, we used again that $\overline{\mathbf{x}}^\top\overline{\mathbf{x}}$ is symmetric. Regardless its contents, Eq. (5.8) is satisfied when we set $\hat{\mathbf{w}} = \hat{\mathbf{w}}^* = \hat{\mathbf{k}}$, which gives $\mathbf{w}^* = \mathbf{k}$, and $b^* = c$. This is exactly the same as the results obtained previously. This proves that the prediction function is *capable* of reproducing any linear function in the feature space. Because $\overline{\mathbf{x}}^\top\overline{\mathbf{x}}$ is rank deficient (rank =1), the solution of $\hat{\mathbf{w}}^* = \hat{\mathbf{k}}$ is not unique, and there are other (may infinite number of) solutions of $(\hat{\mathbf{w}} - \hat{\mathbf{k}}) \neq 0$ that satisfy Eq. (5.8). These solutions live in the null-space of $\overline{\mathbf{x}}^\top\overline{\mathbf{x}}$. This implies that we need to have more data points to make the null-space zero, for unique solution. All these issues relate to the **solution existence theory** that demands sufficient quality data-points, which will be discussed in Chapter 9.

We have now solved analytically an ML problem using a typical minimization procedure to predict a continuous function. This problem we just examined is simple, but our analysis reveals essential issues in an ML model using predictive functions. For more complicated problems with datasets of discrete data-points, we would usually need computational means to solve it, but the essential concept is the same.

5.1.5 *Affine transformation*

On the other hand, Eq. (5.1) can be used to perform an affine transformation, where weights $w_i(i = 1, 2, \ldots, p)$ are responsible for (pure) linear transformation and bias b is responsible for translation. Both w_i and b are learning parameters in a machine learning model. To show how Eq. (5.1) is explicitly used to perform an affine transformation, we perform the following maneuver in matrix formulations:

First, using each $\hat{\mathbf{w}}_i(i = 1, 2, \ldots, k)$ and Eq. (5.1) we obtain,

$$z_i = \overline{\mathbf{x}}\,\hat{\mathbf{w}}_i \tag{5.9}$$

Now, form the following vector,

$$\mathbf{z} = [z_1, z_2, \ldots, z_k] = \left[\overline{\mathbf{x}} \begin{bmatrix} b_1 \\ \mathbf{w}_1 \end{bmatrix}, \ \overline{\mathbf{x}} \begin{bmatrix} b_2 \\ \mathbf{w}_2 \end{bmatrix}, \ldots, \ \overline{\mathbf{x}} \begin{bmatrix} b_k \\ \mathbf{w}_k \end{bmatrix} \right]$$

$$= \overline{\mathbf{x}} \begin{bmatrix} \mathbf{b} \\ \mathbf{W} \end{bmatrix} = \overline{\mathbf{x}} \underbrace{\begin{bmatrix} \mathbf{W}_0 \\ \mathbf{W} \end{bmatrix}}_{\hat{\mathbf{W}}} \ \text{ or simply } \mathbf{z} = \overline{\mathbf{x}} \, \hat{\mathbf{W}} \tag{5.10}$$

where $\mathbf{b} = [b_1, b_2, \ldots, b_k]$, $\mathbf{W}_0 = [\underbrace{w_{01}}_{b_1}, \underbrace{w_{02}}_{b_2}, \ldots, \underbrace{w_{0k}}_{b_k}] = \mathbf{b}$, and $\mathbf{W} = [\mathbf{w}_1, \mathbf{w}_2, \ldots, \mathbf{w}_k]$.

Notice that $\hat{\mathbf{W}}$ absorbs $\mathbf{b}$ as the hat of $\mathbf{W}$, and hence collects all the learning parameters for predicting $\mathbf{z}$. Our notation $\hat{\mathbf{W}}$ allows easy tracking the variables. It is often used for prediction at the output layer of a neural network, because $\mathbf{z} = \overline{\mathbf{x}} \, \hat{\mathbf{W}}$, and affine transformation is no longer needed at the output layer.

With Eq. (5.10), we can further construct the following matrix operation [6].

$$\underbrace{\begin{bmatrix} 1 \\ \mathbf{z}^\top \end{bmatrix}}_{\overline{\mathbf{z}}^\top} = \underbrace{\begin{bmatrix} 1 & \mathbf{0}^\top \\ \mathbf{b}^\top & \mathbf{W}^\top \end{bmatrix}}_{\overline{\mathbf{W}}^\top} \underbrace{\begin{bmatrix} 1 \\ \mathbf{x}^\top \end{bmatrix}}_{\overline{\mathbf{x}}^\top} = \underbrace{\begin{bmatrix} 1 & \mathbf{0}^\top \\ \mathbf{W}_0^\top & \mathbf{W}^\top \end{bmatrix}}_{\overline{\mathbf{W}}^\top} \underbrace{\begin{bmatrix} 1 \\ \mathbf{x}^\top \end{bmatrix}}_{\overline{\mathbf{x}}^\top} \ \text{ or}$$

$$\underbrace{[1 \ \mathbf{z}]}_{\overline{\mathbf{z}}} = \underbrace{[1 \ \mathbf{x}]}_{\overline{\mathbf{x}}} \underbrace{\begin{bmatrix} 1 & \mathbf{b} \\ \mathbf{0} & \mathbf{W} \end{bmatrix}}_{\overline{\mathbf{W}}} = \underbrace{[1 \ \mathbf{x}]}_{\overline{\mathbf{x}}} \underbrace{\begin{bmatrix} 1 & \mathbf{W}_0 \\ \mathbf{0} & \mathbf{W} \end{bmatrix}}_{\overline{\mathbf{W}}} \ \text{ or simply} \tag{5.11}$$

$$\overline{\mathbf{z}} = \overline{\mathbf{x}} \, \overline{\mathbf{W}}$$

where $\mathbf{0} = [0, 0, \ldots, 0]^\top$ with p zeros. Matrix $\overline{\mathbf{W}}$ we derived is the **affine transformation matrix**. It has a dimension of $(p + 1) \times (k + 1)$ and performs affine transformations an affine transformation from space $\mathbb{X}^p$ to space $\mathbb{X}^k$ for given $\overline{\mathbf{x}}$. It is used in the hidden layers in neural networks, because transformations must occur in the affine space in these layers to ensure proper connections.

Matrix $\overline{\mathbf{W}}$ will be used in Chapter 13 when studying MLPs or deepnets. Note that $\overline{\mathbf{W}}$ can be written as $[\mathbf{e}_1 \ \hat{\mathbf{W}}]$, in which $\mathbf{e}_1 = [1 \ \mathbf{0}]^\top$ is the first base vector of space $\mathbb{W}^{p+1}$. $\overline{\mathbf{W}}$ contains a unit vector (constant) as its column, and thus the trainable parameters are in $\hat{\mathbf{W}}$. In the output layer of an NN, we use only $\hat{\mathbf{W}}$, because affine transformation is no longer needed there. For machine learning models, $\overline{\mathbf{W}}$ can be called **affine transformation weight matrix**.

Formulation given above reveals clearly how the affine transformation weight matrix is derived, and how the traditional weights and biases are involved in the affine transformation weight matrix. Finally, we note the following points:

1. We know that $[1, \mathbf{x}]$ is in $\overline{\mathbb{X}}^p$. Now, after action of $\overline{\mathbf{W}}$ (from the right) on it, the resulting $[1, \mathbf{z}]$ that is clearly also in $\overline{\mathbb{X}}^k$. This is known as the **automorphism** property of an affine transformation. A pattern in an affine space stays in an affine space after affine transformation. We will demonstrate this in the example section.

2. The affine transformation uses only b and $\mathbf{w}$ given in Eq. (5.1), except that it needs to be arranged in a form of $\overline{\mathbf{W}}$ to properly act on $\overline{\mathbf{x}}$. This may be the reason for Eq. (5.1) being often called affine transformation (although not exactly at least in concept). Equation (5.1) is currently used in the actual computations of affine transformation, including many parts in this book. Our Eq. (5.11), however, allows more concise formulation, and shows explicitly the automorphism. The last equation in Eq. (5.11) and Eq. (5.10) can and should, of course, also be used for computation. If we do, the codes and data structure may be even neater, because we have only xw operations, and not b is involved.

3. For given w_0 (or b) and $\mathbf{w}$, $\overline{\mathbf{W}}$ is a linear operator. Weights $\mathbf{w}$ is responsible for stretching-compression (scaling) and rotation, and w_0 is responsible for translation. This property is shown as the **affinity** mentioned earlier. We will discuss this further in the following sections and demonstrate this in the example section.

4. For conveniences, we will use both xw formulation and xw+b formulation.

Let us look at some special cases, when Eq. (5.11) is used to perform affine transformations.

Case 1: if we set all learning parameters to zero, $\hat{\mathbf{W}} = \mathbf{0}$, we will obtain $[1 \quad \mathbf{z}] = [1 \quad \mathbf{0}]$, meaning that any data-point $[1 \quad \mathbf{x}]$ in an affine space collapsed to the same point $[1 \quad \mathbf{0}]$ in another affine space.

Case 2: if we set $\mathbf{b} = \mathbf{0}$ and $\mathbf{W} = \mathbf{I}$ where $\mathbf{I}$ is the identity matrix, we shall have $[1 \quad \mathbf{z}] = [1 \quad \mathbf{x}]$. This means that any original point in affine space is unchanged (no transformation).

Case 3: if we set $\mathbf{b} = \mathbf{c}$ where $\mathbf{c}$ is a constant vector, and $\mathbf{W} = \mathbf{I}$, we shall have $[1 \quad \mathbf{z}] = [1 \quad \mathbf{c} + \mathbf{x}]$. This means that any original point in affine space is translated by $\mathbf{c}$.

Case 4: if we set where $\mathbf{b} = [c, 0, \ldots, 0]$, $\mathbf{W} = [\mathbf{k}, \mathbf{e}_2, \ldots, \mathbf{e}_p]$ where $\mathbf{e}_i$ is a base vector of $\mathbb{W}^p$ (with all zero entries except 1 at the ith entry), we obtain $z_i = x_i (i = 2, \ldots, p)$ and

$$z_1 = \mathbf{x}\,\mathbf{k} + c \tag{5.12}$$

which is Eq. (5.5). This means that the prediction of a linear function in the feature space can be viewed as an affine transformation in the affine space. Since $\mathbf{k}$ in $\mathbf{W}$ is the gradient of the function, it is responsible for rotation.

5.2 Affine Transformation Unit (ATU), A Simplest Network

A $p \to 1$ neural network can be built for predicting arbitrary linear functions in the feature space, or to perform an affine transformations on the affine space. The typical architectures are shown in Fig. 5.2.

This net can be set to predict arbitrary linear functions, or to perform affine transformation defined in Eq. (5.1) for a given data-point $x_i (i = 1, 2, \ldots, p)$ using sets of learning parameters $w_i (i = 1, 2, \ldots, p)$ and b. Clearly, any change in learning parameters shall result in a different value in function z, for a given same data-point $x_i (i = 1, 2, \ldots, p)$.

Note that Fig. 5.2 is a basic unit or a building block that can be used to form a complicated neural network. Therefore, let us write a code to

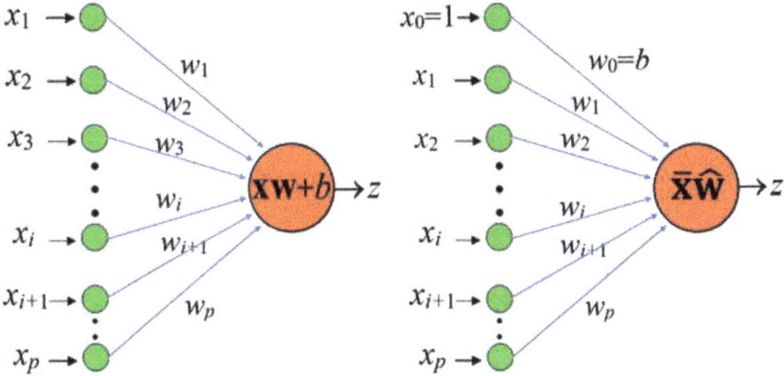

Figure 5.2:   A $p \to 1$ neural network with one layer neurons taking an input of p features, and one output layer of just one single neuron that produces a single prediction function z. This forms an affine transformation unit or ATU (or linear function prediction unit). The net on the left is for xw+b formulation, and on the right is for xw formulation with $p + 1$ neurons in the input layer in which the one at the top is fixed as 1. Both ATUs are essentially identical.

study it in great detail using the following examples. Let us first discuss the data structures. Different ML algorithms may use a different one, and the following one is quite typical.

5.3 Typical Data Structures

$p \to 1$ **nets:**

Equation (5.1) can be written in the matrix form with dimensionality clearly specified as follows:

$$z(\hat{\mathbf{w}}; \mathbf{x}) = \underset{1 \times p}{\mathbf{x}} \underset{p \times 1}{\mathbf{w}} + \underset{1 \times 1}{b} = \underset{1 \times (p+1)}{\overline{\mathbf{x}}} \underset{(p+1) \times 1}{\hat{\mathbf{w}}} \tag{5.13}$$

The prediction function $z \in \overline{\mathbb{X}}^p$ is now clearly specified as a function of $\mathbf{w}$ and b corresponding to any $\mathbf{x} \in \mathbb{X}^p$. For the ith data-point $\mathbf{x}_i$, we have

$$z(\hat{\mathbf{w}}; \mathbf{x}_i) = \underset{1 \times p}{\mathbf{x}_i} \underset{p \times 1}{\mathbf{w}} + \underset{1 \times 1}{b} = \underset{1 \times (p+1)}{\overline{\mathbf{x}}_i} \underset{(p+1) \times 1}{\hat{\mathbf{w}}} \tag{5.14}$$

Note that $z(\hat{\mathbf{w}}; \mathbf{x})$ is still a scalar for one data-point. Also, because no further transformation, $\overline{\mathbf{z}}$ is not needed for one layer nets.

$p \to k$ **nets:**

In hyperspace cases, we would have many, say k, neurons in the output of the current layer, each neuron performing (independently) an affine transformation based on the same dataset (see, Fig. 5.13). Therefore, the output should be an array with k entries. The data may be structured in matrix form:

$$\underset{\mathbf{z}(\mathbf{W},\mathbf{b};\, \mathbf{x}_i)\, 1 \times k}{[z_1\ z_2 \cdots z_k]} = \underset{\mathbf{x}_i\, 1 \times p}{[x_{i1}\ x_{i2} \cdots x_{ip}]} \underset{\mathbf{W}\, p \times k}{\begin{bmatrix} w_{11} & w_{12} & \cdots & w_{1k} \\ w_{21} & w_{22} & \cdots & w_{2k} \\ \vdots & \vdots & \ddots & \vdots \\ w_{p1} & w_{p2} & \cdots & w_{pk} \end{bmatrix}}$$

$$+ \underset{\mathbf{b}\, 1 \times k}{[b_1\ b_2 \cdots b_k]} \tag{5.15}$$

The above matrix can be written in a concise matrix form as follows, with all the dimensionality specified clearly:

$$\mathbf{z}(\hat{\mathbf{W}};\, \mathbf{x}_i) = \underset{1 \times k}{\mathbf{x}_i} \underset{1 \times p}{\underset{p \times k}{\mathbf{W}}} + \underset{1 \times k}{\mathbf{b}} = \underset{1 \times (p+1)}{\overline{\mathbf{x}}_i} \underset{(p+1) \times k}{\hat{\mathbf{W}}} \tag{5.16}$$

Note that one can stack up as many neurons in a layer as needed because these weights for each neuron are independent of the those for any other neuron in the stack. This stacking is powerful because it makes the well-known universal approximation theory (see Chapter 7) workable.

$p \to k$ nets with m data-points:

For a dataset with m points, the data may be structured as matrix $\mathbf{X}_{m \times p}$, by vertically stacking $\mathbf{x}_i$. In this case, m predictions can be correspondingly made, and the formulation in matrix form becomes

$$
\underbrace{\begin{bmatrix} \mathbf{z}_1(\mathbf{W}, \mathbf{b}; \mathbf{x}_1) \\ \mathbf{z}_2(\mathbf{W}, \mathbf{b}; \mathbf{x}_2) \\ \vdots \\ \mathbf{z}_m(\mathbf{W}, \mathbf{b}; \mathbf{x}_m) \end{bmatrix}}_{\mathbf{Z}_{m \times 1}(\mathbf{W}, \mathbf{B}; \mathbf{X})} = \underbrace{\begin{bmatrix} x_{11} & x_{12} & \cdots & x_{1p} \\ x_{21} & x_{22} & \cdots & x_{2p} \\ \vdots & \vdots & \ddots & \vdots \\ x_{m1} & x_{m2} & \cdots & x_{mp} \end{bmatrix}}_{\mathbf{X}_{m \times p}} \underbrace{\begin{bmatrix} w_{11} & w_{12} & \cdots & w_{1k} \\ w_{21} & w_{22} & \cdots & w_{2k} \\ \vdots & \vdots & \ddots & \vdots \\ w_{p1} & w_{p2} & \cdots & w_{pk} \end{bmatrix}}_{\mathbf{W}_{p \times k}} + \underbrace{\begin{bmatrix} \mathbf{b} \\ \mathbf{b} \\ \vdots \\ \mathbf{b} \end{bmatrix}}_{\mathbf{B}_{m \times 1}} \quad (5.17)
$$

where vector $\mathbf{B}$ has the same $\mathbf{b}$ for all entries. The above matrix can be written in a concise matrix form as follows, with all the dimensionality specified clearly:

$$
\underset{m \times 1}{\mathbf{Z}(\mathbf{W}, \mathbf{B})} = \underset{m \times p}{\mathbf{X}} \underset{p \times 1}{\mathbf{W}} + \underset{m \times k}{\mathbf{B}} = \underset{m \times (p+1)}{\overline{\mathbf{X}}} \underset{(p+1) \times k}{\hat{\mathbf{W}}} \quad (5.18)
$$

Note that we do not actually form matrix $\mathbf{Z}$ in practical computations, because when a loss function is constructed, it is a form of a summation over m or a mini-batch size. We will see this frequently in later chapters on actual machine learning models.

5.4 Demonstration Examples of Affine Transformation

We now present a number of examples of affine transformations. This is performed as follows.

For a given geometric pattern defined with a set of multiple data-points $\overline{\mathbf{X}} \in \overline{\mathbb{X}}^2$ (an affine space), its ith row is $\overline{\mathbf{x}}_i = [1, x_{i1}, x_{i2}]$, computed using Eq. (5.1):

$$
z_I = \overline{\mathbf{X}} \hat{\mathbf{w}}_I \quad (5.19)
$$

where $\hat{\mathbf{w}}_I = [b_I, \mathbf{w}_I]^\top$ in which b_I and $\mathbf{w}_I$ are a given set of learning parameters in the hypothesis space $\mathbb{W}^3$, and

$$
z_{II} = \overline{\mathbf{X}} \hat{\mathbf{w}}_{II} \quad (5.20)
$$

where $\hat{\mathbf{w}}_{II} = [b_{II}, \mathbf{w}_{II}]^\top$ in which b_{II} and $\mathbf{w}_{II}$ are a changed set of learning parameters in $\mathbb{W}^3$.

This results in a transformed data-point $\overline{\mathbf{Z}} = [1, z_I, z_{II}] \in \overline{\mathbb{X}}^2$.

The above procedure using affine transformation on the original dataset $\overline{\mathbf{X}} \in \overline{\mathbb{X}}^2$ by varying $\hat{\mathbf{w}}$ for 2 times results in transformed dataset $\overline{\mathbf{Z}}$ that is in the same affine space $\overline{\mathbb{X}}^2$, the automorphism.

We now write a code to demonstrate the affinity of the above transformation. Because $\overline{\mathbb{X}}^2$ is also a 2D plane, we can conveniently plot both original and transformed patterns together in space $\mathbb{R}^2$ using only z_I and z_{II} for visualization and analysis. We first define some functions.

```python
import numpy as np

def logistic0(z):            # The sigmoid/logistic function
    return 1. / (1. + np.exp(-z))

def net(x,w,b):              # An affine transformation net
    y = np.dot(x,w) + b
    return y

def edge(k,dd):              # Define a line pattern in 2D
                             # feature space (x1, x2)
    x = np.arange(-1.0,1.0+dd,dd)     # dd: interval
    x1 = x                   # x1 value.
    x2 = k * x               # x2 value, k slope of the line
    x1 = np.append(x1,0)     # add the center
    x2 = np.append(x2,0)
    X = np.stack((x1, x2), axis=-1)   # X has two components.
    return x1,x2,X

def circle(r,dpi):           # Define a circular pattern in 2D
                             # feature space (x1, x2)
    x = np.arange(0.0,2*np.pi,dpi)
    x1 = r*np.cos(x)         # circle function, for x1 value.
                             # Radius r and scaling factor c.
    x2 = r*np.sin(x)         # for x2 value.
    x1 = np.append(x1,0)     # add the center
    x2 = np.append(x2,0)
    X = np.stack((x1, x2), axis=-1)   # X has two components.
    return x1,x2,X

def rectangle(MinX, MaxX, MinY, MaxY,dd,theta):
    # data for rectangle pattern in 2D space (x1, x2(y))
    x = np.arange(MinX,MaxX+dd,dd)
    ymin= np.full(x.shape,MinY)          #y=x2
    ymax= np.full(x.shape,MaxY)
```

```python
    y = np.arange(MinY,MaxY+dd,dd)
    xmin= np.full(y.shape,MinX)
    xmax= np.full(y.shape,MaxX)

    x1 = np.append(np.append(np.append(x,xmax),np.flip(x)),xmin)
    x2 = np.append(np.append(np.append(ymin,y),ymax),np.flip(y))
    x1 = np.append(x1,(MaxX+MinX)/2) # add the center
    x2 = np.append(x2,(MaxY+MinY)/2)
    X1 = x1*np.cos(theta)+x2*np.sin(theta)
    X2 = x2*np.cos(theta)-x1*np.sin(theta)

    X = np.stack((X1, X2), axis=-1)  # X has two components.
    return X1,X2,X

def spiral(alpha,c):
    # Define a spiral pattern in 2D space (x1, x2)
    xleft,xright,xdelta = 0.0, 40.01, 0.1
    x = np.arange(xleft,xright,xdelta)
    x1 = np.exp(alpha*x)*np.cos(x)/c # logarithmic spiral
    # function, x1 with decay rate alpha & scaling factor c.
    x2 = np.exp(alpha*x)*np.sin(x)/c # x2 value.
    x1 = np.append(x1,0)            # add the center
    x2 = np.append(x2,0)
    X = np.stack((x1, x2), axis=-1)  # X has two components.
    return x1,x2,X
```

Let us now set up learning parameters **w** and b.

```python
# Set w0 & b0,so that original [x1,x2] pattern is reproduced.
w0_I=np.array([1.,0.])    # Initial 2 weights (vector),2D space
b0_I=0                    # Initial bias, so that z_I = x1
w0_II=np.array([0.,1.])   # Initial 2 weights (vector),2D space
b0_II=0                   # Initial bias, so that z_II = x2

# Set wI=w0_I, b_I=b0_I; but w_II, b_II be arbitrary.
#w_I, b_I = w0_I, b0_I   # readers may try this
w_I=np.array([.8,.2])     # Arbitrary values for the two weights
                          # to perform scaling and rotation
b_I = -0.6                # Arbitrary values for the bias to
                          # perform translation
w_II=np.array([.2,.5])    # Arbitrary values for the two weights
                          # to perform scaling and rotation
b_II = 0.6                # Arbitrary values for the bias to
                          # perform translation
```

Next, we define a function for plotting these patterns, initial and affine transformed with $\mathbf{w}_{II}$ and b_{II}, and linear transformed with $\mathbf{w}_{II}$ and $b_{II} = 0$.

```python
%matplotlib inline
import matplotlib.pyplot as plt
def affineplot(x1,x2,X,w0_I,b0_I,w_I,b_I,w_II,b_II):
    plt.figure(figsize=(4.,4.),dpi=90)
    plt.scatter(net(X,w0_I,b0_I),net(X,w0_II,b0_II),label=\
        "Original: w0I=["+str(w0_I[0])+","+str(w0_I[1])+
        "], b0I="+str(b0_I)+"\n w0II=["+str(w0_II[0])+","+
        str(w0_II[1])+"], b0II="+str(b0_II),s=10,c='orange')
        #plot the initial pattern
    plt.scatter(net(X,w_I,b_I),net(X,w_II,b_II),label=\
        "Affine: wI=["+str(w_I[0])+","+str(w_I[1])+
        "], bI="+str(b_I)+"\n wII=["+str(w_II[0])+","+
        str(w_II[1])+"], bII="+str(b_II),s=10,c='blue')
        # plot the affine transformed pattern
    plt.scatter(net(X,w_I,b_I),net(X,w_II,b0_II),label=\
        "Linear: wI=["+str(w_I[0])+","+str(w_I[1])+
        "], bI="+str(b_I)+"\n wII=["+str(w_II[0])+","+
        str(w_II[1])+"], b0II="+str(b0_II),s=10,c='red')
        #plot the linear transformed pattern
    plt.xlabel('$z_{I}$')
    plt.ylabel('$z_{II}$')
    plt.title('linear and affine transformation')
    plt.grid(color='r', linestyle=':', linewidth=0.3)
    plt.legend(loc='center left', bbox_to_anchor=(1, 0.5))
    plt.axis('scaled')
    #plt.ylim(-5,9)
    plt.show()
```

5.4.1 *An edge, a rectangle under affine transformation*

We first create an edge (straight line segment) and a rectangle pattern represented by a set of orange points, perform the affine transformations defined by Eq. (5.1), and plot out these patterns before and after the affine (blue) and linear (red) transformations. Because a rectangle consists of straight lines, it is easy for us to observe the affinity of the transformation.

```python
x1,x2,X = edge(1.5,0.2)
affineplot(x1,x2,X,w0_I,b0_I,w_I,b_I,w_II,b_II)
```

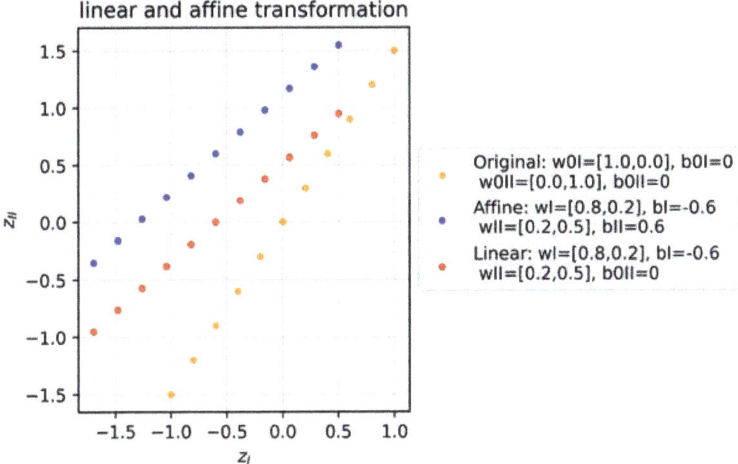

Figure 5.3: Affine transformations of a straight line/edge.

```
x1,x2,X = rectangle(-2.,2.,-1.,1.,0.2,np.pi/4)
affineplot(x1,x2,X,w0_I,b0_I,w_I,b_I,w_II,b_II)
```

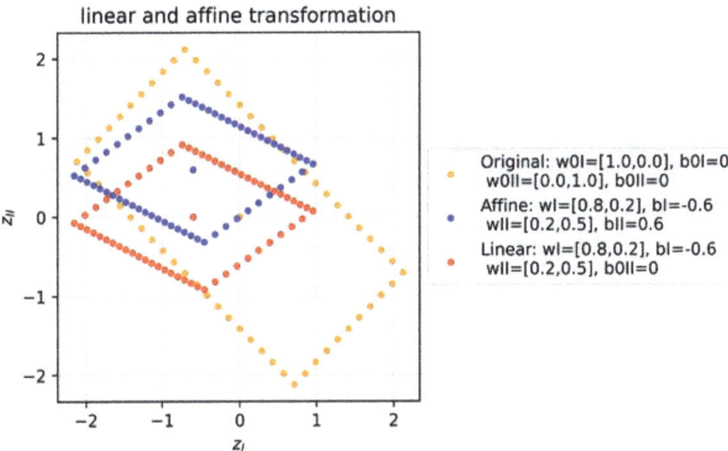

Figure 5.4: Affine transformations of a rectangle.

From the above two figures, the following observations can be made:

1. After the affine transformation, the original (orange) rectangular pattern is only rotated, scaled, sheared, and translated to a new one (blue). Weights **w** is responsible for the linear transformation results in scaling and rotations, and b is responsible for translation.

2. The transformation moves point to point, edge to edge, and quadrilateral to quadrilateral.
3. The transformation preserves the ratio of the lengths of parallel line segments. For example, the ratio of the two longer sides of the orange rectangle is the same as the ratio of the two longer sides of the blue quadrilateral.
4. Parallel line segments remain parallel after the affine transformation.
5. It does not preserve distances between points. It preserves only the ratios of the distances between points lying on a straight line.
6. The affine transformation does not preserve angles between lines.

This simple demonstration helps one to imagine how an affine transformed pattern covers the (same) space by changing $\mathbf{w}$ and b. The pure linear transformation alone does not change the origin, and hence has a much limited coverage.

5.4.2 *A circle under affine transformation*

Let us now take a look at the affine (and linear) transformation to a circle using the same code.

```python
x1,x2,X = circle(1.0,0.1)
affineplot(x1,x2,X,w0_I,b0_I,w_I,b_I,w_II,b_II)
```

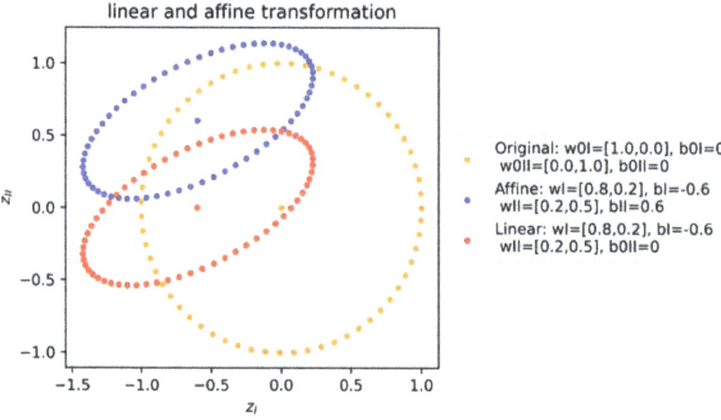

Figure 5.5:　Affine transformations of a circle.

This time, it is clearly seen from Fig. 5.5 that after the transformation, the original (orange) circular pattern is rotated, scaled, sheared, and translated to an ellipse (blue). The points that we have observed for the rectangles are still valid.

5.4.3 *A spiral under affine transformation*

Let us examine the affine (and linear) transformation to a more complicated pattern, spiral.

```
x1,x2,X = spiral(0.1,10.)
affineplot(x1,x2,X,w0_I,b0_I,w_I,b_I,w_II,b_II)
```

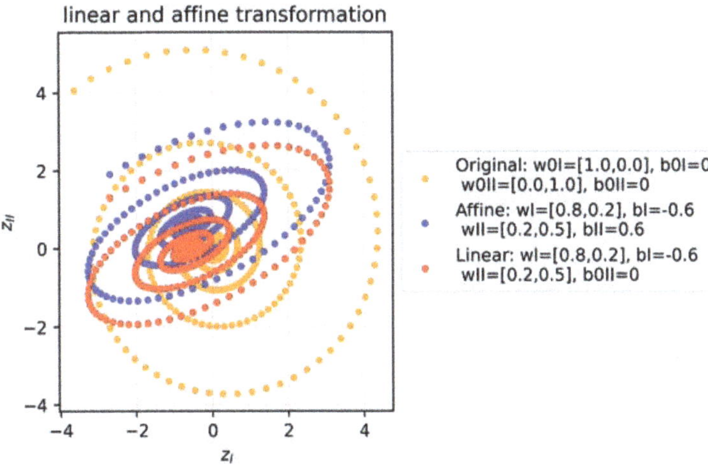

Figure 5.6:   Affine transformations of a spiral.

In this case, the original (orange) spiral is rotated, scaled, sheared, and translated to a new one. The observations made for the above two examples still hold.

5.4.4 *Fern leaf under affine transformation*

Figure 5.7 shows an excellent example of affine transformation available in the public domain provided by António Miguel de Campos (https:// en.wikipedia.org/wiki/Affine_transformation). It is an image of a fractal of Barnsley's fern (https://en.wikipedia.org/wiki/Barnsley_fern). A leaf of the fern is an affine transformation of another by a combination of rotation, scaling, reflection, and translation. The red leaf, for example, is an affine

Figure 5.7:   An image of a leaf of the fern-like fractal is an affine transformation of another.

transformation of the dark blue leaf, or any of the light blue leaves. The fern seems to have this typical pattern coded as an ATU in its DNA. This implies that ATU is as fundamental as DNA.

5.4.5 *On linear prediction function with affine transformation*

One should not confuse the linear prediction function with the affine transformation. They are essentially the same hypothesis, but viewed from different aspects. The former is on the predictability of an arbitrary linear function in the feature space using hypothesis Eq. (5.1), and the latter is on affinity when Eq. (5.1) is used for pattern transformation on the affine space. The predictability of the arbitrary linear function enables affine transformation. The predictability for constants allows translational transformation, and the predictability for the linear function enables variable-wise scaling and rotation, while maintaining the affinity. The prediction of a linear function in the feature space can be viewed as an affine transformation in the affine space. Because of this, we use these two terms interchangeably, knowing this subtle difference.

5.4.6 *Affine transformation wrapped with activation function*

When an affine transformation $z(\mathbf{w}, b; \mathbf{x})$ is wrapped with a nonlinear activation function (see Chapter 7), the output $\phi(z)$ is confined by the activation function, and the affinity is destroyed. However, $\phi(z)$ shall now have some capability to predict nonlinear functions, because the activation functions used in ML are continuous, smooth (at least piecewise differentiable), and vary monotonically with z.

As an example, we wrap the affine transformed pattern with the sigmoid function. In this case, $\phi(z)$ is confined in $(0, 1)$. We write the following code to demonstrate some examples of affine mapping:

```python
# Code for Affine transformation wrapped with sigmoid function
def sigmoidaffine(x1,x2,X,w0_I,b0_I,w0_II,b0_II,w_I,b_I,w_II,b_II):
    # We do the same affine transformation and put the
    # results to a sigmoid.
    plt.figure(figsize=(4.5, 3.0),dpi=100)
    plt.scatter(logistic0(net(X,w0_I,b0_I)),
                logistic0(net(X,w0_II,b0_II)),label=\
        "Original: w0I=["+str(w0_I[0])+","+str(w0_I[1])+
        "], b0I="+str(b0_I)+"\n w0II=["+str(w0_II[0])+","+
        str(w0_II[1])+"], b0II="+str(b0_II),s=10,c='orange')
        #plot the initial pattern
    plt.scatter(logistic0(net(X,w_I,b_I)),
                logistic0(net(X,w_II,b_II)),label=\
        "Affine: wI=["+str(w_I[0])+","+str(w_I[1])+
        "], bI="+str(b_I)+"\n wII=["+str(w_II[0])+","+
        str(w_II[1])+"], bII="+str(b_II),s=10,c='blue')
        # plot the affine transformed pattern
    plt.scatter(logistic0(net(X,w_I,b_I)),
                logistic0(net(X,w_II,b0_II)),label=\
        "Linear: wI=["+str(w_I[0])+","+str(w_I[1])+
        "], bI="+str(b_I)+"\n wII=["+str(w_II[0])+","+
        str(w_II[1])+"], b0II="+str(b0_II),s=10,c='red')
        #plot the linear transformed pattern
    plt.xlabel('$\sigma (z_{I})$')
    plt.ylabel('$\sigma (z_{II})$')
    plt.title('Affine transformation wrapped with sigmoid')
    plt.grid(color='r', linestyle=':', linewidth=0.3)

    plt.legend(loc='center left', bbox_to_anchor=(1, 0.5))
    #plt.axis('scaled')
    plt.ylim(-.05,1.1)
    plt.show()
```

```python
x1,x2,X = edge(5.0,0.1)
sigmoidaffine(x1,x2,X,w0_I,b0_I,w0_II,b0_II,w_I,b_I,w_II,b_II)
```

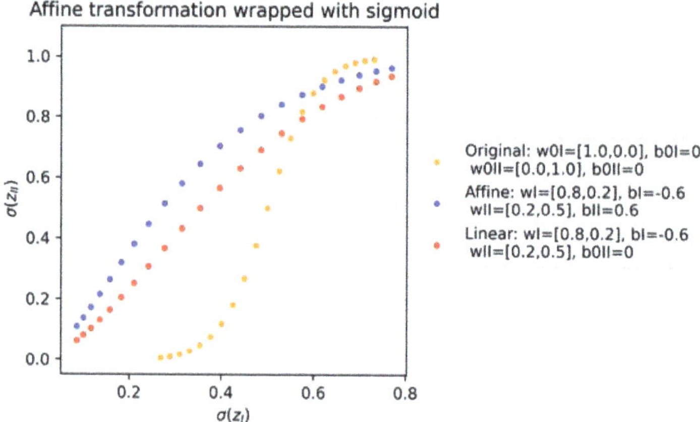

Figure 5.8: Nonlinear activation function wrapped affine transformations of a straight line/edge.

```
x1,x2,X = rectangle(-2.,2.,-1.,1.,0.2,np.pi/4)
sigmoidaffine(x1,x2,X,w0_I,b0_I,w0_II,b0_II,w_I,b_I,w_II,b_II)
```

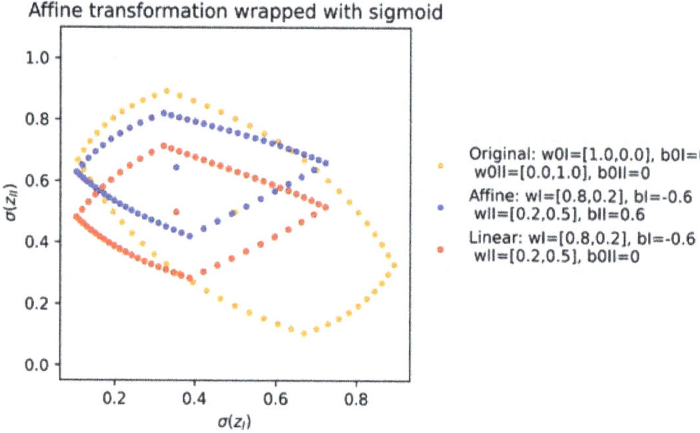

Figure 5.9: Nonlinear activation function wrapped affine transformations of a rectangle.

For this sigmoid wrapped affine transformation, the following observations can be made:

1. The transformation still sends a point to a point, an edge to an edge uniquely. The use of the nonlinear activation function does not change the uniqueness of the point-to-point transformation. This is because the activation functions are continuous, smooth (at least piecewise differentiable), and vary monotonically.

2. The affinity is, however, destroyed: the ratios of distances between points lying on a straight line are changed. Not all the parallel line segments remain parallel after the sigmoid transformation. The use of the sigmoid function clearly brings nonlinearity. This gives the net the following capabilities:

- The output $\phi(z(\hat{\mathbf{w}}; \mathbf{x}))$ is now nonlinearly dependent on the features $\mathbf{x}$. One can now use it for logistic regression for labels given 0, or 1, by training $\hat{\mathbf{w}}$.
- $\phi(z(\hat{\mathbf{w}}; \mathbf{x}))$ is linearly independent of the features $\mathbf{x}$ in the input. This allows further affine transformations to be carried out in a chain to the next layer if needed.
- $\phi(z(\hat{\mathbf{w}}; \mathbf{x}))$ is also linearly independent of the features $\hat{\mathbf{w}}$ used in this layer. When we need more layers in the net, fresh $\hat{\mathbf{w}}$s can now be used for the next layers independently. This enables the creation of deepnets.

Let us now take a look at the wrapped affine transformation to a circle function, using the same code.

```
x1,x2,X = circle(2.5,0.1)
sigmoidaffine(x1,x2,X,w0_I,b0_I,w0_II,b0_II,w_I,b_I,w_II,b_II)
```

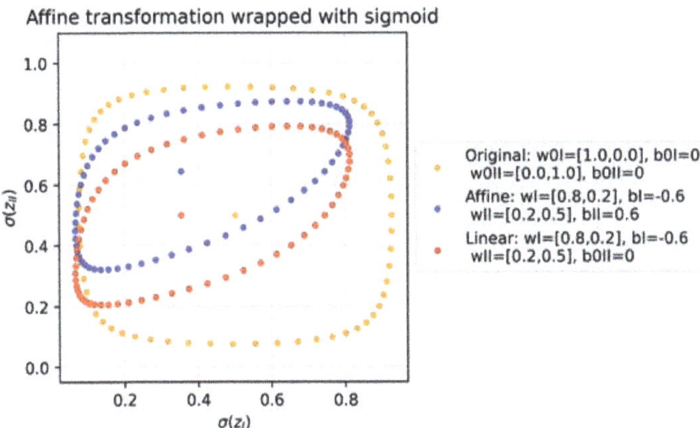

Figure 5.10:   Nonlinear activation function wrapped affine transformations of a circle.

This case shows more server shape destroyed. The uniqueness of the point-to-point transformation is still preserved. The following is for the wrapped affine transformation for the spiral pattern.

```
x1,x2,X = spiral(0.1,10.)
sigmoidaffine(x1,x2,X,w0_I,b0_I,w0_II,b0_II,w_I,b_I,w_II,b_II)
```

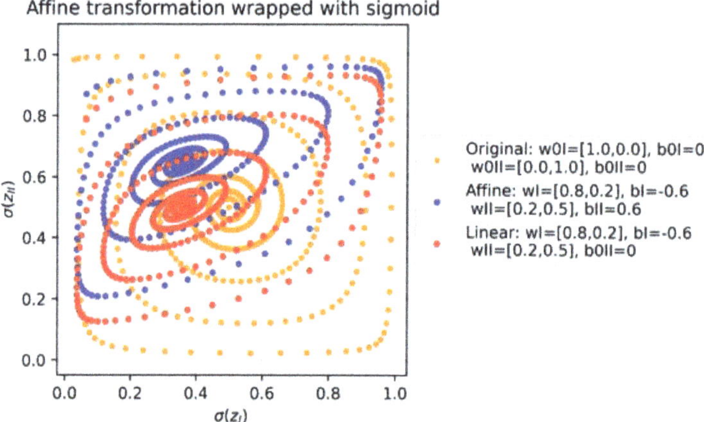

Figure 5.11:   Nonlinear activation function wrapped affine transformations of a spiral.

We see server distortions, due again to the nonlinearity of the nonlinear activation function, sigmoid. The point-to-point transformation is still observed, but when z is near 0.0 and 1.0, the original points and the transformed points are "squashed" closer due to the sigmoid actions. Hence, information near there is getting transmitted much less through updating of these learning parameters $\mathbf{w}$ and b. In other words, the gradient gets close to zero, due again to the properties of the sigmoid function.

5.5 Parameter Encoding and the Essential Mechanism of Learning

5.5.1 *The $\overline{\mathbf{x}}$ to $\hat{\mathbf{w}}$ encoding, a data-parameter converter unit*

Based on Eq. (5.1), we now see a situation where a dataset $(\overline{\mathbf{x}}, z)$ can be encoded in a set of learning parameters $\hat{\mathbf{w}}$ in the hypothesis space. Figure 5.12 shows schematically such an encoded state.

The straight lines in Fig. 5.12 are encoded with a point in the hypothesis space $\mathbb{W}^2$. For example, the red line is encoded by a red dot at $w_0 = 1$ and $w_1 = 1$. In other words, using $w_0 = 1$ and $w_1 = 1$, we can reproduce the red line. The blue line is encoded by a blue dot at $w_0 = 2$ and $w_1 = -0.5$, with which the blue line can be reproduced. The same applies to the black line. A machine learning process is to produce an optimal set of dots using a dataset. After that, one can then produce lines. In essence, a machine learning model converts or encodes the data to w_i. This implies that the size and quality of

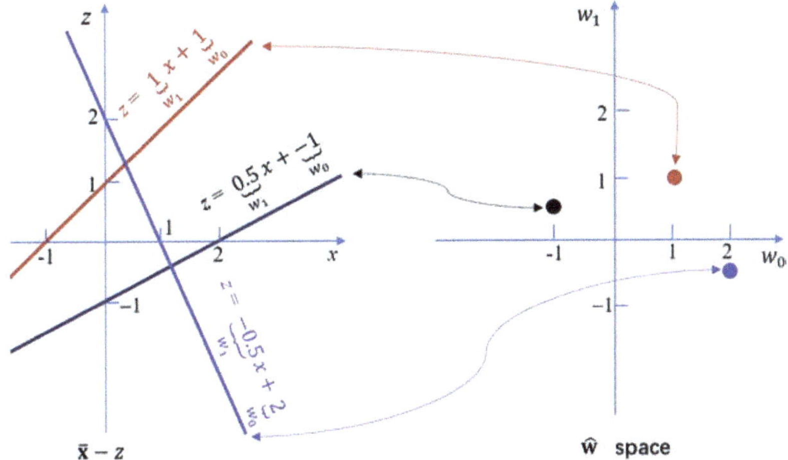

Figure 5.12: Data (on relations of $\overline{\mathbf{x}}$-z or $\overline{\mathbf{x}}$-y for given labels) encoded in model parameters $\hat{\mathbf{w}}$ in the hypothesis space. In essence, a ML model converts data to $\hat{\mathbf{w}}$ during training.

the dataset are directly related to the dimension of the affine spaces used in the model.

On the other hand, if one tunes w_i, different prediction functions can be produced in the label space. Therefore, it is possible to find such a set of w_i that makes the prediction match the given label in the dataset for given data-points. Finding such a set of w_i is the process of learning. Real machine models are a lot more complicated, but this gives the essential mechanism.

5.5.2 Uniqueness of the encoding

We state that the encoding of a line in the $\overline{\mathbf{X}}$-z space to a point in the hypothesis space is unique. It is very easy to prove as follows.

Assume any arbitrary line in the $\overline{\mathbf{X}}$-z space that has two distinct points in the hypothesis space $\hat{\mathbf{w}}^{(1)}$ and $\hat{\mathbf{w}}^{(2)}$; using Eq. (5.9), this line can be expressed as

$$z = \overline{\mathbf{x}}\hat{\mathbf{w}}^{(1)} \tag{5.21}$$

which holds for arbitrary $\overline{\mathbf{x}}$. This same line can also be expressed as

$$z = \overline{\mathbf{x}}\hat{\mathbf{w}}^{(2)} \tag{5.22}$$

which holds also for arbitrary $\overline{\mathbf{x}}$. Using now Eqs. (5.21) and (5.22), we obtain

$$0 = \overline{\mathbf{x}}[\hat{\mathbf{w}}^{(2)} - \hat{\mathbf{w}}^{(1)}] \tag{5.23}$$

Equation (5.23) must also hold for arbitrary $\overline{\mathbf{x}}$. Therefore, we shall have

$$\hat{\mathbf{w}}^{(1)} = \hat{\mathbf{w}}^{(2)} \tag{5.24}$$

which completes the proof.

On the other hand, we also state that a point in the hypothesis space gives a unique line. It can be easily proven as follows.

Given any arbitrary point in the hypothesis space $\hat{\mathbf{w}}$, assume we can construct two lines in the $\overline{\mathbf{X}}$-z space. Using Eq. (5.9), the first line can be expressed as

$$z^{(1)} = \overline{\mathbf{x}}\hat{\mathbf{w}} \tag{5.25}$$

The second line can be expressed as

$$z^{(2)} = \overline{\mathbf{x}}\hat{\mathbf{w}} \tag{5.26}$$

Using Eqs. (5.25) and (5.26), we obtain

$$z^{(2)} - z^{(1)} = 0 \tag{5.27}$$

This means that these two lines are the same, which completes the proof.

In fact, the uniqueness can be clearly observed from Fig. 5.12, because a line is uniquely determined by its slope and bias, and both are given by $\hat{\mathbf{w}}$.

The uniqueness is one of the most fundamental reasons for a quality dataset to be properly encoded with the learning parameters based on the hypothesis of affine transformations, or for a machine learning model to be capable of reliably learning from data.

5.5.3 *Uniqueness of the encoding: Not affected by activation function*

It is observed that the uniqueness of the encoding of an affine transformation wrapped with an activation function is not affected by the activation function. This is because activation functions are all strictly monotonic functions (as will be shown in Chapter 7), which does not change the uniqueness of its argument. The proof is thus essentially the same as that given above.

On the other hand, this property implies that the activation function must be monotonic. This is true for all the activation functions discussed in Chapter 7.

5.6 The Gradient of the Prediction Function

The gradient of the prediction function with respect to the learning parameters has the following simple forms:

$$\nabla_{\mathbf{w}} z = \mathbf{x}$$
$$\nabla_b z = 1$$

(5.28)

which shows that the gradient with respect to weights relates the feature variable (the data). The gradient with respect to bias is, however, a unit. This is because the data corresponding to bias are $x_0 = 1$. This may suggest that when a regularization technique (see Chapter 14) is used, one may choose different regularization parameters for weight and bias.

When the xw formulation is used, we have

$$\nabla_{\hat{\mathbf{w}}} z = \overline{\mathbf{x}}$$

(5.29)

which can be used in an autograd in machine learning processes.

5.7 Affine Transformation Array (ATA)

We can now duplicate vertically the single neuron on the right in Fig. 5.2 for k times and let all neurons become **densely connected**, meaning that each neuron in the output is connected with each of the neurons in the input (also known as fully connected). This forms a mapping of $p \to k$ network.

The prediction functions $\mathbf{z}$ from an ATA can be expressed as

$$\mathbf{z}(\hat{\mathbf{W}}; \mathbf{x}) = \mathbf{x}\mathbf{W} + \mathbf{b} = \overline{\mathbf{x}}\,\hat{\mathbf{W}}$$

(5.30)

where $\mathbf{z}$ is a vector of prediction functions given by

$\mathbf{z}(\hat{\mathbf{W}}; \mathbf{x}) = [z_1(\hat{\mathbf{w}}_1; \mathbf{x}), z_2(\hat{\mathbf{w}}_2; \mathbf{x}), \dots, {}_k(\hat{\mathbf{w}}_k; \mathbf{x})]$, with
$\hat{\mathbf{w}}_j = [w_{0j}, w_{1j}, w_{2j}, \dots, w_{pj}]$ with $w_{0j} = b_j$ are the $(p+1)$ learning parameters for the jth neuron in the output layer,
$\hat{\mathbf{W}} = [\mathbf{b}\ \mathbf{W}]^{\top}$ is a matrix of $(p+1) \times k$ containing all learning parameters for all neurons in the output layer,
$\mathbf{W} = [w_{ij}], (i = 1, 2, \dots, p; j = 1, 2, \dots, k)$ is a matrix of weights (part of the learning parameters), and
$\mathbf{b} = [b_1, b_2, \dots, b_k]$ is a vector of biases (part of the learning parameters).

The vector $\hat{\mathbf{w}}$ of total learning parameters of a $p \to k$ ATA becomes,

$$\hat{\mathbf{w}} = [\hat{\mathbf{w}}_1^{\top}, \hat{\mathbf{w}}_2^{\top}, \dots, \hat{\mathbf{w}}_k^{\top}]^{\top}$$

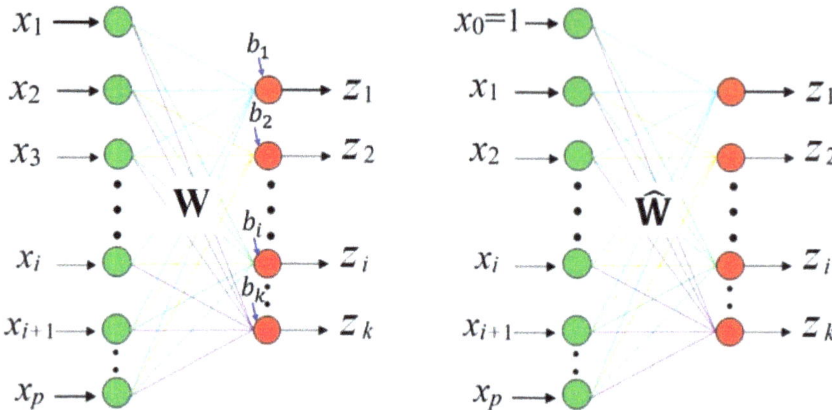

Figure 5.13:   A $p \to k$ neural network with one input layer of p neurons and one output layer of k neurons that produces k prediction functions $z_i(i = 1, 2, \ldots, k)$. Each neuron at the output connects to all the neurons in the input with its own weights. This stack of ATU forms an affine transformation array or ATA. In other words, the $p \to k$ net has the predictability of k functions in the feature space with p dimensions. Left: xw+b formulation; Right: xw formulation.

which can also be regarded as the flattened $\hat{\mathbf{W}}$. The total number of the learning parameters is

$$P = (p + 1) \times k$$

It is clear that the hypothesis space grows fast in multiples for an ATA. Equation (5.30) is the matrix form of a set of affine transformations.

It is important to note that each $z_j(\mathbf{w}_j, b_j)$ is computed using Eq. (5.1), using its own weights $\mathbf{w}_j$ and bias b_j. This enables all $z_j(\mathbf{w}_j, b_j), j = 1, 2, \ldots, k$ being independent of each other. Therefore, the ATA given in Fig. 5.13 creates the simplest mapping that can be used for k-dimensional regression problems using a dataset with p features. Note also that when $k = p$, it can perform the $p \to p$ affine transformation.

5.8 Predictability of High-Order Functions of a Deepnet

5.8.1 *A role of activation functions*

Now, we wrap the stack of prediction functions with nonlinear activation functions. This leads to a vector of

$$\left[\underbrace{\phi(z_1(\mathbf{w}_1, b_1))}_{x_1^{(new)}}, \underbrace{\phi(z_2(\mathbf{w}_2, b_2))}_{x_2^{(new)}}, \ldots, \underbrace{\phi(z_k(\mathbf{w}_k, b_k))}_{x_k^{(new)}} \right] \qquad (5.31)$$

It becomes a set of new features $x_i^{(new)}$, $i = 1, 2, \ldots, k$ that are linearly independent of the original features x_i, $i = 1, 2, \ldots, p$. These new features can then be used as inputs to the next layer. This allows the use of a new set of learning parameters for the next layer.

It is clear that a role of the activation function is to force the outputs from an ATA linearly independent of that of the previous ATA, enabling further affine transformations leading to a chain of ATAs, a deepnet. To fulfill this important role, the activation function must be nonlinear.

Such a chain of stacks of prediction functions (affine transformations) wrapped with nonlinear activation functions gives a very complex deepnet, resulting in a complex prediction function. Further, when affine transformation Eq. (5.1) is replaced with spatial filters, one can build a CNN (see Chapter 15) for object detection, and when replaced with temporal filters, we may have an RNN (see Chapter 16) for time sequential models, and so on.

5.8.2 *Formation of a deepnet by chaining ATA*

These new features given in Eq. (5.31) can now be used as the inputs for the next layer to form a deepnet. To illustrate this more clearly, we consider a simplified deepnet with $4 - 2 - 3$ neurons shown in Fig. 5.14.

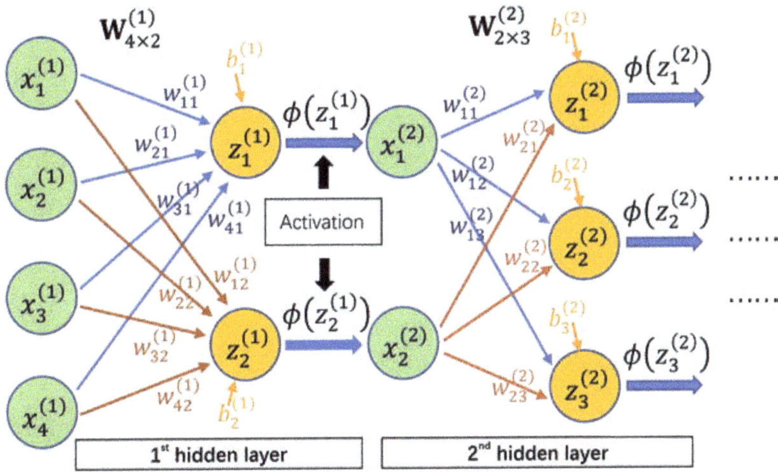

Figure 5.14: Schematic drawing of a chain of stacked affine transformations wrapped with activation functions in a deepnet for approximation of high-order nonlinear functions of high dimensions. This case is an xw+b formulation. A deepnet using xw formulation will be given in Section 13.1.4.

Here, let us use the number in parentheses to indicate the layer number:

1. Based on 4 (independent input) features $x_i^{(1)}$ $(i = 1 \sim 4)$ to the first layer, a stack of 2 affine transformations $z_i^{(1)}$ $(i = 1 \sim 2)$ takes place, using a 4×2 weight matrix $\mathbf{W}^{(1)}$ and biases $b_i^{(1)}$ $(i = 1 \sim 2)$. Affine transformation $z_1^{(1)}$ uses $w_{i1}^{(1)}$ $(i = 1 \sim 4)$ and $b_1^{(1)}$, and $z_2^{(1)}$ uses $w_{i2}^{(1)}$ $(i = 1 \sim 4)$ and $b_2^{(1)}$. Clearly, these are carried out independently using different sets of weights and biases.

2. Next, $z_1^{(1)}$ and $z_2^{(1)}$ are, respectively, subjected to a nonlinear activation function ϕ, producing 2 new features $x_i^{(2)}$ $(i = 1 \sim 2)$. Because of the nonlinearity of ϕ, $x_i^{(2)}$ will no longer linearly depend on the original features $x_i^{(1)}$ $(i = 1 \sim 4)$.

3. Therefore, $x_i^{(2)}$ $(i = 1 \sim 2)$ can now be used as independent inputs for the 2nd layer of affine transformations, using a 2×3 weight matrix $\mathbf{W}^{(2)}$ and biases $b_i^{(2)}$ $(i = 1 \sim 3)$, in the same manner. This results in a stack of 3 affine transformations $z_i^{(3)}$ $(i = 1 \sim 3)$, which can then be wrapped again with nonlinear activation functions. This completes the 2nd layer of 3 stacked affine transformations in a chain.

The above process can continue as desired to increase the depth of the neural network. Note also that the number of neurons in each layer can be arbitrary in theory. Because of the stacking and chaining, the hypothesis space is greatly increased. The stacking causes the increase in multiples, and the chaining in additions. The prediction functions may live in an extremely high dimensional space $\mathbb{W}^P$ for deepnets. For this simple deepnet of $4 - 2 - 3$, the dimension of the hypothesis space becomes $P = (4 \times 2 + 2) + (2 \times 3 + 3) = 19$. In general, for a net of $p - q - r - k$, for example, the formulation should be

$$P = \underbrace{(p \times q + q)}_{\text{layer 1}} + \underbrace{(q \times r + r)}_{\text{layer 2}} + \underbrace{(r \times k + k)}_{\text{layer 3}} \tag{5.32}$$

The vector of all trainable parameters in an MLP becomes,

$$\hat{\mathbf{w}} = \left[\hat{\mathbf{W}}^{(1)}.flatten(), \hat{\mathbf{W}}^{(2)}.flatten(), \ldots, \hat{\mathbf{W}}^{(N_L)}.flatten() \right]^{\top}$$

where N_L is the total number of hidden layers in the MLP. Note that we may not really perform the foregoing flattening in actual ML models. It is just for demonstrating the growth of the dimension of the hypothesis space. In actual computations, we may simply group them in a Python list, and use an important autograd algorithm to automatically perform the needed

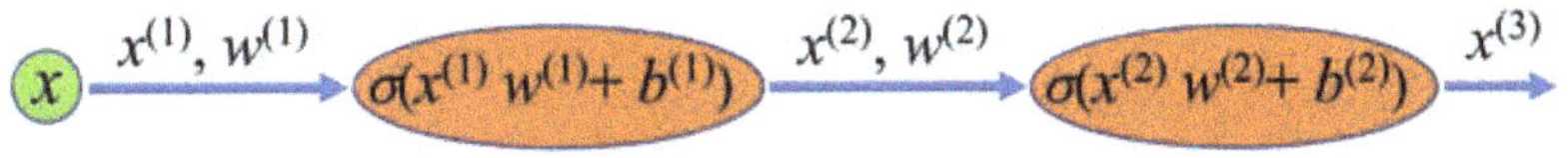

Figure 5.15: $1 \to 1 \to 1$ net with sigmoid activation at the hidden and last layers.

forward and backward computations in training an MLP. The computations over such a high dimension is achieved numerically. This will be discussed in detail in Chapter 8.

The prediction functions are now functions of $\hat{\mathbf{w}}$ in a high dimensional hypothesis space $\mathbb{W}^P$ for MLPs. The formulation on calculating P for more general MLPs will be given in Chapter 13. The Neurons-Samples Theory that gives the relationship between the number of neurons and the number of data-points will be discussed in Section 13.2.1.

5.8.3 *Example: A $1 \to 1 \to 1$ network*

Consider the simplest $1 \to 1 \to 1$ neural network shown in Fig. 5.15. Let us use the same linear prediction function Eq. (5.1) and a sigmoid activation function for the hidden and last layers. In this case, the output at the last layer $x^{(3)}$ can be obtained as follows:

$$x^{(3)} = \sigma\left(z^{(2)}\right) = \sigma\left(w^{(2)} x^{(2)} + b^{(2)}\right) = \frac{1}{1 + e^{-(w^{(2)} x^{(2)} + b^{(2)})}} \tag{5.33}$$

where $x^{(2)}$ is the output from the hidden layer:

$$x^{(2)} = \sigma\left(z^{(1)}\right) = \sigma\left(w^{(1)} x^{(1)} + b^{(1)}\right) = \frac{1}{1 + e^{-(w^{(1)} x + b^{(1)})}} \tag{5.34}$$

in which $x^{(1)} = x$, which is the inputs that can be normalized to be in $(-1, 1)$. The number in the parenthesis in the superscripts stands for the layer number. Because $x^{(2)}$ is in $(0, 1)$, we next use the Taylor expansion consecutively twice to approximate the sigmoid function; we obtain

$$x^{(3)} = c_0 + c_1 x + c_2 x^2 + c_3 x^3 + \cdots \tag{5.35}$$

where these constants are given, through a lengthy but simple derivation, by

$$c_0 = -\frac{1}{16} b^{(1)} b^{(2)} w^{(1)} \left[b^{(1)} - b^{(2)} w^{(1)} \right] - \frac{1}{48} b^{(2)} w^{(1)} \left[\left(b^{(2)}\right)^2 \left(w^{(1)}\right)^2 - 12 \right]$$
$$- \frac{1}{48} b^{(1)} \left[\left(b^{(1)}\right)^2 - 12 \right]$$

$$c_1 = -\frac{1}{16} w^{(1)} w^{(2)} \left[\left(b^{(1)} \right)^2 + 2 b^{(1)} b^{(2)} w^{(1)} + \left(b^{(2)} \right)^2 \left(w^{(1)} \right)^2 - 4 \right] \qquad (5.36)$$

$$c_2 = -\frac{1}{16} \left(w^{(1)} \right)^2 \left(w^{(2)} \right)^2 \left(b^{(1)} + b^{(2)} w^{(1)} \right)$$

$$c_3 = -\frac{1}{48} \left(w^{(1)} \right)^3 \left(w^{(2)} \right)^3$$

It is clear from Eq. (5.36) that by properly setting (training using a dataset) the weights and biases for the neurons in the hidden and output layers, all these constants $c_i, i = 1, 2, 3, 4$ can be determined. The prediction function at the output $x^{(3)}$ becomes a 3rd-order polynomial of the feature x as given in Eq. (5.35). This means that our $1 \to 1 \to 1$ net has the predictability for 3rd-order functions approximately, in contrast to a $1 \to 1$ net that is only capable for 1st-order functions.

Note that the same analysis can be performed for other types of activation functions. Also, if we cut off higher-order terms in the Taylor series, we can approximate even higher-order functions. The point of our discussion here is not about how well to approximate the sigmoid function, but to show the capability of the simple $1 \to 1 \to 1$ net. This simple analysis supports a very important fact that adding layers gives the net the capacity to predict higher-order nonlinear latent behavior. This is the reason why a deepnet is powerful if it can be effectively trained.

We note, without further elaboration, that increasing the depth of a net is equivalent to increasing the order of the shape functions in the physics-law-based models such as the FEM [1] or the meshfree methods [3]. In contrast, increasing the number of neurons in a layer is equivalent to increasing the number of the elements or nodes [5].

5.9 Universal Prediction Theory

A deepnet can be established with the following important properties:

1. The capability of the linear prediction function (affine transformation) in predicting exactly any function up to the first order, and one-to-one unique transformation (with or without activation function) in each ATU.
2. The independence of the function approximation (affine transformation) of a neuron to another in an ATA (due to its independent connections).
3. New independent features are produced in each layer using nonlinear activation functions for each ATA.

4. Chaining of ATA wrapped with nonlinear activation functions provides the capability for predicting complex nonlinear functions to an arbitrarily higher order.

In the opinion of the author, these are the fundamental reasons for various types of deepnets being capable of creating $p \to k$ mappings for extremely complicated problems from p inputs of features to k labels (targeted features) existing in the dataset. We now summarize our discussion to a Universal Prediction Theory [6].

Universal Prediction Theory: *A deepnet with sufficient layers of sufficient neurons wrapped with nonlinear activation functions can be established for predictions of latent features existing in a dataset when properly trained.*

This theory claims only the capability of a deepnet in terms of creating giant prediction functions based on the dataset. How to realize its capability requires a number of techniques, including how to set up a proper structure of the deepnet for given types of problems and how to find these optimal learning parameters reliably and effectively. In addition, the applicability of the trained MLP model depends on the quality of the dataset, as mentioned in Section 1.5.6. The **dataset quality** is defined as its representativeness to the underlaying problem to be modeled, including correctness, size, data-point distribution over the features space, and noise level.

5.10 Nonlinear Affine Transformations

Note that in the above formulations, the features $x_i, i = 1, 2, \ldots, p$ are used in an affine transformation as linear basis functions. However, the basis functions do not have to be linear. Take a one-dimensional problem, for example; when linear approximation is used, the vector of the features should be

$$\overline{\mathbf{x}} = [1, x] \tag{5.37}$$

If one would like to use 2nd-order approximation (often times called nonlinear regression), the vector of the features simply becomes

$$\overline{\mathbf{x}} = \left[1, x, x^2\right] \tag{5.38}$$

If one knows the dataset well and believes that a particular function can be used as a basis function, one may simply add it as an additional feature. For example, one can include $sin(x)$ as a feature in the following form:

$$\overline{\mathbf{x}} = [1, x, sin(x)] \tag{5.39}$$

The use of nonlinear functions as bases for features is also related to the so-called support vector machine (SVM) models that we will discuss in Chapter 6, where we use kernel functions for linearly un-separable classes. This kind of nonlinear feature basis or kernel is sometimes called feature functions.

In our neural network models, higher-order and enrichment basis functions can also be used in higher dimensions. For example, for two-dimensional spaces, we may have features like

$$\overline{\mathbf{x}} = \left[1, x_1, x_2, x_1 x_2, x_1^2, x_2^2, sin(x)\right] \tag{5.40}$$

This has completed 2nd-order polynomial bases functions, and is enriched with a $sin(x)$ function (with proper scaling on x). The dataset $\overline{\mathbf{X}}$ shall also be arranged in the order of all these features. The affine transformation using the nonlinear basis functions can be exactly the same as using linear basis discussed in this chapter. In fact, we have already done the affine transformations for the circle and spiral. Note that for high-dimensional problems, the feature space with nonlinear bases can be in extremely higher dimensions. For such cases, the so-called kernel trick may apply to avoid dimension increase.

5.11　Feature Functions in Physics-Law-based Models

This concept of using higher-order or special feature functions is essentially the same as in the physics-law-based computational methods. In these physics-law-based methods, the feature functions are called **basis functions**. These basis functions are used to approximate the field variables (displacements, stress, velocity, pressure, etc.) that are governed by a physic-law in either strong or weak forms.

For example, in the finite element approximation [1], and the smoothed finite element methods [2], we frequently use higher-order polynomial bases called higher-order elements. Special basis functions are also used but called enrichment functions. For example, when we would like to capture the singular stress field in the domain, we add in $\sqrt{r}$ in the bases [2]. In the meshfree methods [3], one can also use distance basis functions, such as the radial basis functions (RBFs).

In methods used to solve linear mechanics problems governed by physics laws, we often use high-order and special basis functions. The resulting system equations will still be linear in the field variables. The essential concept is the same: to capture necessary features in the system (governed by law or hidden in data), one shall use feature or basis functions of necessary complexity. The resulting models may still be linear in field variables.

References

[1] G.R. Liu and S.S. Quek, *The Finite Element Method: A Practical Course*, Butterworth-Heinemann, London, 2013.

[2] G.R. Liu and T.T. Nguyen, *Smoothed Finite Element Methods*, Taylor and Francis Group, New York, 2010.

[3] G.R. Liu, *Mesh Free Methods: Moving Beyond the Finite Element Method*, Taylor and Francis Group, New York, 2010.

[4] G.R. Liu and Gui-Yong Zhang, *Smoothed Point Interpolation Methods: G Space Theory and Weakened Weak Forms*, World Scientific, London, 2013.

[5] G.R. Liu, *A Neural Element Method, International Journal of Computational Methods*, **17**(07), 2050021, 2020.

[6] G.R. Liu, A thorough study on affine transformations and a novel Universal Prediction Theory, *International Journal of Computational Methods*, **19**(10), in-printing, 2022.

Chapter 6

The Perceptron and SVM

This chapter discusses two fundamentally important supervised machine learning algorithms, the Perceptron and the Support Vector Machine (SVM), for classification. Both are conceptually related, but very much different in formulation and algorithm. In the opinion of the author, there are a number of key ideas used in both classifiers in terms of computational methods. These ideas and the resulting formulations are very inspiring and can be used for many other machine learning algorithms. We hope the presentation in this chapter can help readers to appreciate these ideas. The referenced materials and much of the codes are from the Numpy documentations (https:// numpy.org/doc/), Scikit-learn documentations (https://scikit-learn.org/ stable/), mxnet-the-straight-dope (https://github.com/zackchase/mxnet-the-straight-dope), Jupyter Notebook (https://jupyter.org/), and Wikipedia (https://en.wikipedia.org/wiki/Main_Page).

Our discussion starts naturally from the Perceptron. It is one of the earliest machine learning algorithms by Frank Roseblatt in 1957 [1, 2]. It is used for problems of binary classification and was one of the well-studied problems of classification in 1960s. Here, we first introduce the mathematical model of a typical classification problem with the related formulation and its connection to affine transformation. We then examine in detail Coli's Perceptron algorithm that is made available at mxnet-the-straight-dope (https://github.com/zackchase/mxnet-the-straight-dope) (under the Apache License 2).

The discussion on the Perceptron is naturally followed by that on SVM [3, 4, 9]. A complete description of the SVM formulation is provided, including detailed process leading to a quadratic programming problem, the kernel trick for linearly inseparable datasets, as well as the concept of affine transformation used in SVM.

223

6.1 Linearly Separable Classification Problems

Let us consider the following problem. Given a set of m data-points with p features, the ith data-point is noted as $\mathbf{x}_i = \{x_{i1}, x_{i2}, \ldots, x_{ip},\} \in \mathbb{X}^p$ with its corresponding label $y_i \in \{\pm 1\}$ (meaning the label can be either $+1$ or -1 for a data-point). Such labels distinguish these data-points in two classes: positive points and negative ones. We assume that this set of data-points is *linearly separable*, meaning that these data-points can be separated into these two distinct classes using a hyperplane (a line in higher-dimensional space, $\mathbb{X}^p$).

Consider a simple problem with only 2 features, x_1 and x_2, in a two-dimensional (2D) space $\mathbf{x} = \{x_1, x_2\} \in \mathbb{X}^2$, so that we can have a good visualization. A set of m data-points is scattered in 2D space shown in Fig. 6.1.

All these data-points are labeled into two classes: positive points marked with "+" symbols, and each of the points is labeled with y $= +1$; negative points marked with "−" symbols, and each of them is labeled with y $= -1$. These two classes of points can be separated by straight lines, such as the red-dashed line and the red-dotted line in Fig. 6.1. For datasets in the real world, there are infinite numbers of such lines forming a *street*. Our goal is to develop a computer algorithm to find such a line with a given labeled dataset (the data-points with corresponding labels). This is simple but quite a typical classification problem.

Assume for the moment that we know the orientation of one such red line, say the middle red-dashed line for easy discussion. Hence, we know its normal direction vector $\mathbf{w} = [w_1, w_2]^\top \in \mathbb{W}^2$, although we do not yet know

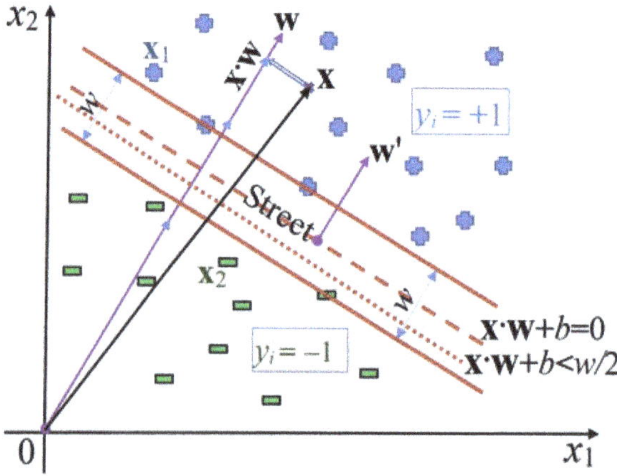

Figure 6.1:   Linearly separable data-points in 2D space.

the *translational* location of the red-dashed line along its normal. We then have the unit normal vector as $\frac{\mathbf{w}}{\|\mathbf{w}\|}$ with a length of 1. For any point (not necessarily the data-point) in the 2D space (marked with a small cross in Fig. 6.1), we can form a vector $\mathbf{x}$ starting at the origin. Now, the dot-product

$$\mathbf{x} \cdot \frac{\mathbf{w}}{\|\mathbf{w}\|} \tag{6.1}$$

becomes the length of the projection of $\mathbf{x}$ on the unit normal $\frac{\mathbf{w}}{\|\mathbf{w}\|}$. Therefore, it is the measure that we need to determine how far point $\mathbf{x}$ is away from the origin in the direction of $\frac{\mathbf{w}}{\|\mathbf{w}\|}$, which is a useful piece of information. Because we do not yet know the translational location of the red line in relation to $\mathbf{x}$, we thus introduce a parameter $\frac{b}{\|\mathbf{w}\|}$, where $b \in \mathbb{W}^1$ is an adjustable parameter to allow the red line move up and down along $\mathbf{w}$.

Notice in Eq. (6.1) that we used dot-product (the inner product). This is the same as the matrix-product we used in the Python implementation, because their shapes match: $\mathbf{x}$ is a (row) vector, and $\mathbf{w}$ is column vector (a matrix with single column) with the same length. Therefore, we use both interchangeably in this book.

The equation for an arbitrary line in relation to given point $\mathbf{x}$ shall have this form:

$$\mathbf{x} \cdot \mathbf{w} + b \tag{6.2}$$

Our task now is to find the red-dashed line by choosing a particular set of $\mathbf{w}$ and b in $\mathbb{W}^3$ that separates the data-points, which is the affine transformation discussed in Chapter 5. The *conditions* should be

$$(\mathbf{x} \cdot \mathbf{w} + b) > 0, \quad \text{for points in upper-right side of the red-dash line: } y = +1 \tag{6.3}$$

$$(\mathbf{x} \cdot \mathbf{w} + b) < 0, \quad \text{for points in lower-left side of the red-dash line: } y = -1 \tag{6.4}$$

Note that Eqs. (6.3) and (6.4) are for ideal situations where these two sets of points might be infinitely close. In practical applications, we often find that these points are in two distinct classes, and they are separated by a *street* with a finite width w (that may be very small). The formulation can now be modified as follows:

$$(\mathbf{x} \cdot \mathbf{w} + b) > w/2, \text{ for points in upper-right side of the red-dash line: } y = +1 \tag{6.5}$$

$$(\mathbf{x} \cdot \mathbf{w} + b) < w/2, \text{ for points in lower-left side of the red-dash line: } y = -1 \tag{6.6}$$

This type of equation is also known as the *decision rule*: when the condition is satisfied by an arbitrary point $\mathbf{x}$, it then belongs to a labeled class ($y = 1$ or $y = -1$), when the parameters $\mathbf{w}$ and b are known. We made excellent progress.

It is obvious that Eqs. (6.5) and (6.6) can be *magically* written in a single equation by putting these two conditions together with their corresponding labels y.

$$y(\mathbf{x} \cdot \mathbf{w} + b) > w/2 \quad \text{or} \quad y(\overline{\mathbf{x}} \cdot \hat{\mathbf{w}}) > w/2 \quad \text{or} \quad m_g > w/2 \qquad (6.7)$$

This is a simplified single-equation decision rule: when the condition is satisfied by an arbitrary point, it belongs to the labeled domain, and is not within the street. This single equation is a lot more convenient for developing the algorithm called a **classifier** to do the task. Note that m_g is called margin, which will be formally discussed in detail in Chapter 11.

We need to now bring in a labeled dataset to find $\mathbf{w}$ and b using the above decision rule. For any data-point (the ith, for example, and regardless of which class it belongs to), it must satisfy the following equation:

$$y_i(\mathbf{x}_i \cdot \mathbf{w} + b) > w/2 \quad \text{or} \quad y_i(\overline{\mathbf{x}}_i \cdot \hat{\mathbf{w}}) > w/2 \quad \text{or} \quad m_{g(i)} > w/2 \qquad (6.8)$$

where $m_{g(i)}$ is the margin for the ith data-point. Because there are an infinite number of lines (such as the red-dashed and red-dotted lines shown in Fig. 6.1) for such a separation, there exist multiple solutions to our problem. We just want to find one of them that satisfies Eq. (6.8) for all data-points in the dataset. This process is called **training**. Because labels are used, it is a supervised training. The trained model can be used to predict the class of a given data-point (which may not be from the training dataset), known as **classification** or **prediction** in general. The following is an algorithm to perform all those: training as well as prediction.

6.2 A Python Code for the Perceptron

The following is an easy-to-follow code available at mxnet-the-straight-dope (https://github.com/zackchase/mxnet-the-straight-dope), under the Apache-2.0 License. We have modified it a little and added in some detailed descriptions as comment lines with the code.

Let us examine the details in this algorithm. As usual, we import the needed libraries.

```python
import mxnet as mx
from mxnet import nd, autograd
import matplotlib.pyplot as plt
import numpy as np
# We now generate a synthetic dataset for this examination.
mx.random.seed(1)       # for repeatable output of this code
        # define a function to generate the dataset that is
        # separable with a margin strt_w
def getfake(samples, dimensions, domain_size, strt_w):
    wfake = nd.random_normal(shape=(dimensions)) # weights
    bfake = nd.random_normal(shape=(1))                 # bias
    wfake = wfake / nd.norm(wfake)                      # normalization
    # generate linearly separable data, with labels
    X = nd.zeros(shape=(samples, dimensions))    # initialization
    Y = nd.zeros(shape=(samples))
    i = 0
    while (i < samples):
        tmp = nd.random_normal(shape=(1,dimensions))
        margin = nd.dot(tmp, wfake) + bfake
        if (nd.norm(tmp).asscalar()<domain_size) & \
                    (abs(margin.asscalar())>strt_w):
            X[i,:] = tmp[0]
            Y[i] = 1 if margin.asscalar() > 0 else -1
            i += 1
    return X, Y, wfake, bfake
# Plot the data with colors according to the labels
def plotdata(X,Y):
    for (x,y) in zip(X,Y):
        if (y.asscalar() == 1):
            plt.scatter(x[0].asscalar(),x[1]. asscalar(),color='r')
        else:
            plt.scatter(x[0].asscalar(),x[1]. asscalar(),color='b')
```

```python
# define a function to plot contour plots over [-3,3] by [-3,3]
def plotscore(w,d):
    xgrid = np.arange(-3, 3, 0.02)                 # generating grids
    ygrid = np.arange(-3, 3, 0.02)
    xx, yy = np.meshgrid(xgrid, ygrid)
    zz = nd.zeros(shape=(xgrid.size, ygrid.size, 2))
    zz[:,:,0] = nd.array(xx)
    zz[:,:,1] = nd.array(yy)
    vv = nd.dot(zz,w) + d
    CS = plt.contour(xgrid,ygrid,vv.asnumpy())
    plt.clabel(CS, inline=1, fontsize=10)
```

```
street_w = 0.1
ndim = 2
X,Y,wfake,bfake = getfake(50,ndim,3,street_w)
 #generates 50 points, in 2D space with a margin of street_w
plotdata(X,Y)
plt.show()
```

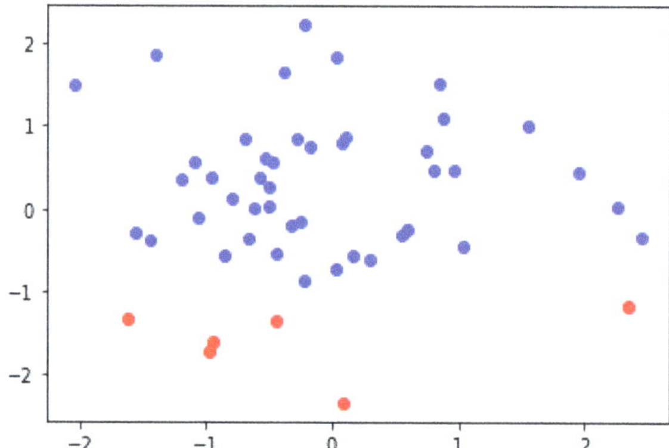

Figure 6.2:   Computer-generated data-points that are separable with a straight line.

We now see a dataset with 50 scattered points in 2D space separated by a street with width street_w. These data-points can be clearly separable by at least one line in between the blue and red data-points.

Let us first take a look at the points after their vectors are all projected on separable with an arbitrary vector **w** and with an arbitrary bias b (an arbitrary affine transformation). We do the same projection using also the true **w** and bias b used to generate all these points for comparison. We write the following code to do so:

```
wa = nd.array([0.5,0.5])              # a given vector
cs = (wa [0]/nd.norm(wa)).asnumpy() # cosine value
si = (wa [1]/nd.norm(wa)).asnumpy() # sine value
ba = 0.5 * nd.norm(wa)              # bias (one may change it)
Xa = nd.dot(X,wa)/nd.norm(wa) + ba  # projection (affine mapping)

plt.plot(Xa.asnumpy()*cs,Xa.asnumpy()*si,zorder=1) # results
for (x,y) in zip(Xa,Y):
        if (y.asscalar() == 1):
            plt.scatter(x.asscalar()*cs,x. asscalar()*si,color='r')
        else:
            plt.scatter(x.asscalar()*cs,x.asscalar()*si, color='b')
cs = (wfake [0]/nd.norm(wfake)).asnumpy() # projection on true norm
```

```
si = (wfake [1]/nd.norm(wfake)).asnumpy()
Xa = nd.dot(X,wfake) + bfake                    # with true bias
```

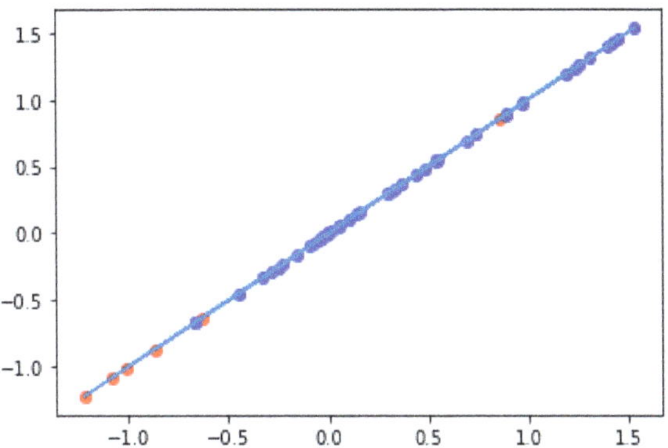

Figure 6.3:   Data-points projected on an arbitrary straight line.

```
plt.plot(Xa.asnumpy()*cs,Xa.asnumpy()*si,zorder=1)
for (x,y) in zip(Xa,Y):
        if (y.asscalar() == 1):
            plt.scatter(x.asscalar()*cs,x. asscalar()*si,color='r')
        else:
            plt.scatter(x.asscalar()*cs,x.asscalar()*si, color='b')
plt.show()
```

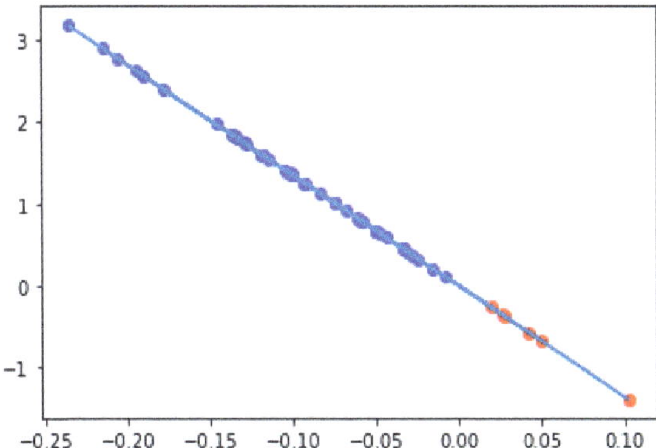

Figure 6.4:   Data-points projected on a straight line that is perpendicular to a line that separates these data-points.

It is seen that

- When these points are projected on a vector that is not the true normal (along the blue line) direction, the blue and red points are mixed along the blue line.

- When the true normal direction is used, all these points are distinctly separated into two classes, blue and red, along the orange line. This dataset is linearly separable.

Let us see how the **Perceptron algorithm** finds a direction and the bias, and hence the red line that separates these two classes. We use again the algorithm available at mxnet-the-straight-dope (https://github.com/zackchase/mxnet-the-straight-dope). The algorithm is based on the following encouragement rule: positive events should be encouraged and negative ones should be discouraged. This rule is used with the decision rule discussed earlier for each data-point in a given dataset.

```python
# The Perceptron algorithm
def Perceptron(w,b,x,y,strt_w):
    if (y*(nd.dot(w,x)+b)).asscalar()<=strt_w/2:
    # Decision rule to check whether the line with
    # the current parameters in the street
        w += y * x              # In the street, update w
        b += y                  # update b
        update = 1
    else:                       # Otherwise (outside the street)
        update = 0              # No action
    return update
```

The above Perception algorithm is used in an iteration to update the learning parameters: the weights in vector **w** and bias b, by looping over the dataset.

```python
w = nd.zeros(shape=(ndim))      #stars with zero (worst case)
b = nd.zeros(shape=(1))
t = 0
print('w:',w.shape,' b:',b.shape,' X:',X.shape,' Y:',Y.shape)
for (x,y) in zip(X,Y):
    update = Perceptron(w,b,x,y,street_w)
    if (update == 1):
        t += 1
        print('In the street: update the parameters')
        print('data{}, label{}'.format(x.asnumpy(),y. asscalar()))
        print('weight{}, bias{}'.format(w.asnumpy(),b. asscalar()))
```

```
plotscore(w,b)        # The plane with updated w and b
plotdata(X,Y)         # data-points
plt.scatter(x[0].asscalar(),x[1]. asscalar(),color='g')
                      # currently updated data-point
plt.show()
```

```
w: (2,)  b: (1,)  X: (50, 2)  Y: (50,)
In the street: update the parameters
data    [ 0.03751943 -0.7298465 ], label -1.0
weight [-0.03751943  0.7298465 ], bias  -1.0
```

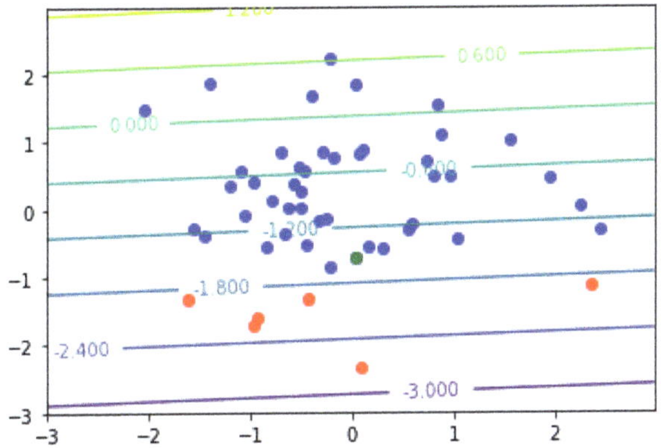

Figure 6.5: Results at the first iteration.

```
In the street: update the parameters
data    [-2.0401056  1.4821309], label -1.0
weight [ 2.0025861 -0.7522844], bias  -2.0
```

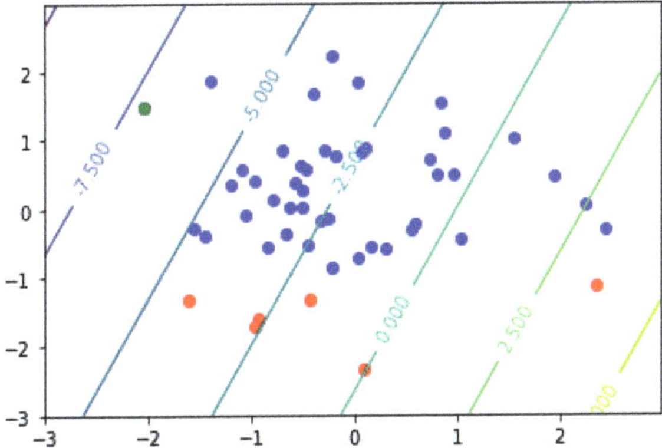

Figure 6.6: Results at the second iteration.

```
In the street: update the parameters
data   [ 1.040828   -0.45256865], label -1.0
weight [ 0.96175814 -0.29971576], bias  -3.0
```

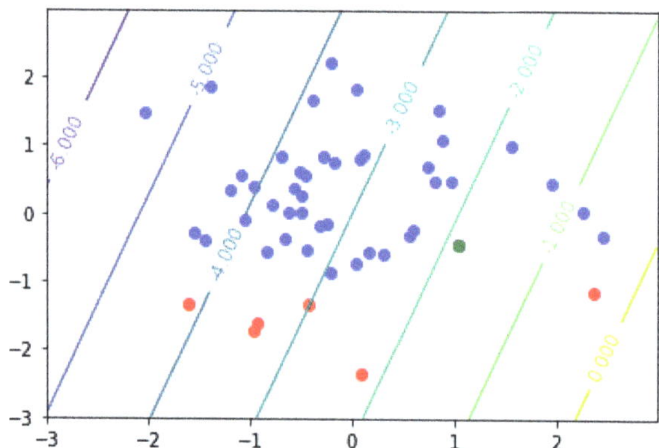

Figure 6.7:   Results at the third iteration.

```
In the street: update the parameters
data   [-0.934901   -1.5937568], label 1.0
weight [ 0.02685714 -1.8934726 ], bias  -2.0
```

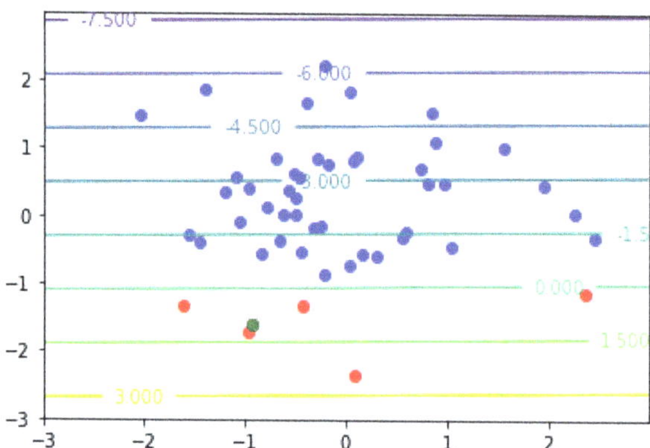

Figure 6.8:   Results at the final iteration.

```
print('Total number of points:',len(Y),'; times of updates:',t)
print('weight {}, bias   {}'.format(w.asnumpy(),b.asscalar()))
print('wfake {}, bfake   {}'.format(wfake.asnumpy(),bfake. asscalar()))
```

```
Total number of points: 50 ; times of updates: 4
weight [ 0.02685714 -1.8934726 ], bias  -2.0
wfake [ 0.0738321  -0.99727064], bfake  -0.9501792788505554
```

It is seen that all the red dots are on the positive side of the straight line of $\mathbf{x} \cdot \mathbf{w} + b = 0$ with the learned parameters of the weight vector $\mathbf{w}^*$ and bias b^*. All the data marked with blue dots are on the negative side of the line. In the entire process, all these points stay still, and the updates are done only on the weight vector $\mathbf{w}$ and bias b. We shall now examine the fundamental reasons for this simple algorithm to work.

6.3 The Perceptron Convergence Theorem

Theorem: Consider a dataset with a finite number of data-points. The ith data-point is paired with its label as $[\mathbf{x}_i, y_i]$. Any data-point $\mathbf{x}_i$ is bounded by $\|\mathbf{x}_i\| \leq R < \infty$, and its label $y_i \in \{\pm 1\}$.

- If the data-points are linearly separable, meaning that there exists at least one pair of parameters $(\mathbf{w}^*, b^*)$ with $\|\mathbf{w}^*\| \leq 1$ and $b^2 \leq 1$, such that $y_i(\mathbf{x}_i \cdot \mathbf{w}^* + b^*) \geq w/2 > 0$ for all data pairs, where w is a given scalar of the street width,
- then the Perceptron algorithm converges after at most $t = 2(R^2+1)/w^2 \propto \left(\frac{R}{w}\right)^2$ iterations, with a pair of parameters $(\mathbf{w}_t, b_t)$ forming a line $\mathbf{x}_i \cdot \mathbf{w}_t + b_t$ that separates the data-points in two classes.

We now prove this Theorem largely following the procedure with codes at mxnet-the-straight-dope (https://github.com/zackchase/mxnet-the-straight-dope/blob/master/chapter01_crashcourse/probability.ipynb), under the Apache-2.0 License. We first check the convergence behavior numerically (this may take minutes to run).

```python
ws = np.arange(0.025,0.45,0.025) #generate a set of street widths
number_iterations = np.zeros(shape=(ws.size))
number_tests = 10
for j in range(number_tests):     #set number of tests to do
    for (i,wi) in enumerate(ws):
        X,Y,_,_=getfake(1000,2,3,wi)  #generate dataset
        for (x,y) in zip(X,Y):
            number_iterations[i] += Perceptron(w,b,x,y,wi)
            #for each test, record the number of updates
number_iterations = number_iterations / 10.0
plt.plot(ws,number_iterations,label='Average number of iterations')
plt.legend()
plt.show()
```

The test results are plotted in Fig. 6.9. It shows that the number of iterations needs to increase with the decrease of the street width w, and

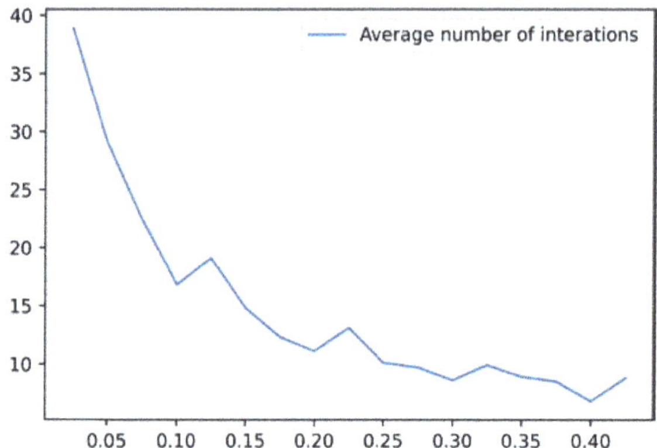

Figure 6.9:   Convergence behavior examined numerically.

the rate is roughly quadratic (inversely). This test supports the convergence theorem. Let us now prove this in a more rigorous mathematical manner.

The proof assumes that the data are linearly separable. Therefore, there exists a pair of parameters $(\mathbf{w}^*, b^*)$ with $\|\mathbf{w}^*\| \leq 1$ and $b^2 \leq 1$. Let us examine the inner product of the current set of parameters $\hat{\mathbf{w}}$ with the assumed existing $\hat{\mathbf{w}}^*$ at each iteration. What we would like the iteration to do is to update the current $\hat{\mathbf{w}}$ to approach $\hat{\mathbf{w}}^*$ iteration by iteration, so that their inner product can get bigger and bigger. Eventually, they can be parallel with each other. Let us see whether this is really what is happening in the Perceptron algorithm given above. Our examination is also iteration by iteration but considers only the iterations when an update is made by the algorithm, because the algorithm does nothing otherwise. This means that we perform update only when $y_t(\overline{\mathbf{x}}_t \cdot \hat{\mathbf{w}}_t) \leq w/2$ at at the tth step.

At the initial setting in the algorithm, $t = 0$, we have no idea on what $\hat{\mathbf{w}}$ should be, and thus set $\hat{\mathbf{w}}_0 = \mathbf{0}$. Here for neat formulation using dot-product. We assume that column vector $\hat{\mathbf{w}}_0$ and $\hat{\mathbf{w}}^*$ are flatten to (row) vectors, so that $\hat{\mathbf{w}}$ can have a dot-product directly with any other (flattened) $\hat{\mathbf{w}}$ resulted in the iteration process. This can be done easily in numpy using the flatten() function. Thus we have at the initial setting,

$$\hat{\mathbf{w}}_0 \cdot \hat{\mathbf{w}}^* = 0$$

At $t = 1$, following the algorithm, we bring in arbitrarily a data-point, say $\overline{\mathbf{x}}_1$ with y_1. We shall find $y_1 (\overline{\mathbf{x}}_1 \cdot \hat{\mathbf{w}}_1) = 0 \leq (w/2)$, because at this point, the current $\hat{\mathbf{w}}_1$ are still all zero. Therefore, data-point $\overline{\mathbf{x}}_1$ with y_1 is in the street defined by the line with current $\hat{\mathbf{w}}_1$. Next, we perform the following updates:

$$\hat{\mathbf{w}}_1 = \hat{\mathbf{w}}_0 + y_1 \overline{\mathbf{x}}_1$$

We thus have,

$$\hat{\mathbf{w}}_1 \cdot \hat{\mathbf{w}}^* = \hat{\mathbf{w}}_0 \cdot \hat{\mathbf{w}}^* + y_1(\overline{\mathbf{x}}_1 \cdot \hat{\mathbf{w}}^*) \geq w/2$$

This is because $y_i(\overline{\mathbf{x}}_i \cdot \hat{\mathbf{w}}^*) \geq w/2$ given by the Theorem as a condition. We see the direction of vector $\hat{\mathbf{w}}_1$ approaches to that of $\hat{\mathbf{w}}^*$ by $w/2$. They are $w/2$ more aligned.

Similarly, at $t = 2$, following the algorithm, we have the following update.

$$\hat{\mathbf{w}}_2 = \hat{\mathbf{w}}_1 + y_2 \overline{\mathbf{x}}_2$$

We now have,

$$\hat{\mathbf{w}}_2 \cdot \hat{\mathbf{w}}^* = \hat{\mathbf{w}}_1 \cdot \hat{\mathbf{w}}^* + y_2(\overline{\mathbf{x}}_2 \cdot \hat{\mathbf{w}}^*) \geq 2(w/2)$$

This is because of the result obtained at $t = 1$ and the new addition of $y_i(\hat{\mathbf{w}}^* \cdot \overline{\mathbf{x}}_i) \geq w/2$ condition given by the Theorem. We see the direction of vector $\hat{\mathbf{w}}_1$ approaches to that of $\hat{\mathbf{w}}^*$ by $2(w/2)$. They are now $2(w/2)$ more aligned.

It is clear that inner product adds one $(w/2)$ in each iteration. Now at tth update, we shall have

$$\hat{\mathbf{w}}_t \cdot \hat{\mathbf{w}}^* \geq t(w/2) \tag{6.9}$$

We see the direction of vector $\hat{\mathbf{w}}_t$ approaches to that of $\hat{\mathbf{w}}^*$ by $t(w/2)$. It is clear that the algorithm drives $\hat{\mathbf{w}}$ more and more in alignment with $\hat{\mathbf{w}}^*$, at a linear rate of $(w/2)$. The wider the street, the faster the convergence.

We next examine the evolution of the length (amplitude) of vector $\hat{\mathbf{w}}_{t+1}$.

$$\begin{aligned}
\|\hat{\mathbf{w}}_{t+1}\|^2 = \hat{\mathbf{w}}_{t+1} \cdot \hat{\mathbf{w}}_{t+1} &= (\hat{\mathbf{w}}_t + y_t \overline{\mathbf{x}}_t) \cdot (\hat{\mathbf{w}}_t + y_t \overline{\mathbf{x}}_t) \\
&= \hat{\mathbf{w}}_t \cdot \hat{\mathbf{w}}_t + 2 y_t \overline{\mathbf{x}}_t \cdot \hat{\mathbf{w}}_t + y_t \overline{\mathbf{x}}_t \cdot y_t \overline{\mathbf{x}}_t \\
&= \|\hat{\mathbf{w}}_t\|^2 + 2 y_t \overline{\mathbf{x}}_t \cdot \hat{\mathbf{w}}_t + y_t^2 \|\overline{\mathbf{x}}_t\|^2
\end{aligned} \tag{6.10}$$

Using the conditions given by the Theorem: $\|\overline{\mathbf{x}}_i\| = \|\mathbf{x}_i\| + 1 \leq R + 1$, and $y_i \in \{\pm 1\}$, and $y_t(\overline{\mathbf{x}}_t \cdot \hat{\mathbf{w}}_t) \leq w/2$ (this is the condition for starting the tth update), we shall have

$$\|\hat{\mathbf{w}}_{t+1}\|^2 \leq \|\hat{\mathbf{w}}_t\|^2 + R^2 + 1 + w$$

When $t = 0$, we have $\|\hat{\mathbf{w}}_0\| = 0$, and hence,

$$\|\hat{\mathbf{w}}_1\|^2 \leq \|\hat{\mathbf{w}}_0\|^2 + R^2 + 1 + w = R^2 + 1 + w$$

When $t = 1$, we shall have,

$$\|\hat{\mathbf{w}}_2\|^2 \leq \|\hat{\mathbf{w}}_1\|^2 + R^2 + 1 + w \leq 2(R^2 + 1 + w)$$

This means that each iteration gives $(R^2 + 1 + w)$.

At the $t = T$ iteration, we shall have

$$\|\hat{\mathbf{w}}_T\| \leq \sqrt{T(R^2 + 1 + w)} \tag{6.11}$$

Using the Cauchy-Schwartz inequality, i.e., $\|a\| \cdot \|b\| \geq a \cdot b$, and then Eq. (6.9), we obtain,

$$\|\hat{\mathbf{w}}_T\| \|\hat{\mathbf{w}}^*\| \geq \hat{\mathbf{w}}_T \cdot \hat{\mathbf{w}}^* \geq T(w/2)$$

Using the conditions given by the Theorem: $\|\hat{\mathbf{w}}^*\| = \|\mathbf{w}^*\| + \|b\| \leq 1 + 1 = 2$, we have

$$\|\hat{\mathbf{w}}_T\| \sqrt{2} \geq T(w/2)$$

Combining this with the inequality Eq. (6.11) yields,

$$\sqrt{2T(R^2 + 1 + w)} \geq T(w/2) \tag{6.12}$$

Let us examine this equation. The number of iterations T is linear on the left and in a square root on the right side of Eq. (6.12), and all others are constants. Thus, this inequality cannot hold for large T. Therefore, T must be limited to satisfy Eq. (6.12), which means that the Perceptron algorithm will converge in a finite number of iterations, and $T \leq \frac{8(R^2+1+w)}{w^2} \propto \left(\frac{R}{w}\right)^2$. This can also be written as

$$\frac{R}{w} \propto \sqrt{T} \tag{6.13}$$

This means that it takes a square root of times for the Perceptron algorithm to converge for a given relative street width.

We now give the following remarks:

1. The Perceptron convergence proof requires that the data-points be separable with a line.

2. The convergence is independent of the dimensionality of the data. This is not a condition used in the proof. It is also independent of the number of observations.
3. The number of iterations increases with the decrease of the street width w, and the rate is (inversely) quadratic. This echoes the numerical test conducted earlier.
4. The number of iterations decreases with the increase of the upper bound of the data R, and the rate is also (inversely) quadratic. This means that if the data-points are generally farther apart, it is easier to separate, which is intuitively understandable.
5. The algorithm updates only for the data-points that are not in alignment. It simply skips the data-points that are already in alignment.

6.4 Support Vector Machine

6.4.1 *Problem statement*

In our discussions above on the Perceptron, it is seen that there are in fact an infinite number of solutions of parameters $\mathbf{w}$ and b in the hypothesis space to form straight lines for a linearly separable dataset, as long as the street width w has a finite value. Readers may observe the different straight lines obtained by simply starting the classifier with different initial weights and biases. One may naturally ask what the best solution is among all these possible solutions. One answer is that the line that separates these two classes of data with largest "street" width and sits in the middle line of the street may be the best. To obtain the widest street **optimal** solution, one can formulate the problem as an optimization one. In fact, one can simply bring in an optimization algorithm to control the Perceptron to try for multiple times to find an optimal solution if the efficiency is not a concern.

Here, we introduce the well-known algorithm known as the support vector machine or SVM. The initial idea was invented in the early 1960s in Vapnik's PhD thesis, and became popular in the 1990s when it (with kernel trick) was applied for handwritten digit recognition [3, 4].

The SVM is an effective algorithm that is constructed using a systematic formulation and the Lagrangian multiply approach. Given below is the detailed description and formulation on SVM. A good reference is the excellent lecture by Prof. Partick Winston at MIT(https://www.youtube.com/watch?v=_PwhiWxHK8o), and also some workings available online (https://towardsdatascience.com/support-vector-machine-python-example-d67d9b63f1c8).

          Machine Learning with Python: Theory and Applications

6.4.2 *Formulation of objective function and constraints*

Our formulation continues from the formulation we derived for the Perceptron. The difference here is that the street width is no longer given in this SVM setting. We just assume it is there. We must find a way to formulate the street width, and then maximize it for a given dataset. We first derive the formula for the street width.

Because we assume that the dataset is linearly separable, there must be a street width of some finite value w. From the decision rule we derived, we know the equation for the middle line of the street can be written in an affine transformation form as

$$\mathbf{x} \cdot \mathbf{w} + b = 0 \tag{6.14}$$

where $b \in \mathbb{W}$ is a learning parameter called bias, $\mathbf{x} \in \mathbb{X}^p$ is a position vector of an arbitrary point in the feature space with linear polynomial bases (features), $x_1, x_2, \ldots, x_p$,

$$\mathbf{x} = [x_1, x_2, \ldots, x_p] \tag{6.15}$$

and $\mathbf{w} \in \mathbb{W}^p$ is a vector of weights that are also learning parameters $w_1, w_2, \ldots, w_p$:

$$\mathbf{w} = [w_1, w_2, \ldots, w_p]^\top \tag{6.16}$$

This middle line in a 2D feature space $\mathbb{X}^2$ is shown in Fig. 6.10 with red dash-dot line, which is approximated using the weights $\mathbf{w}$ and bias b in hypothesis space $\mathbb{W}^3$.

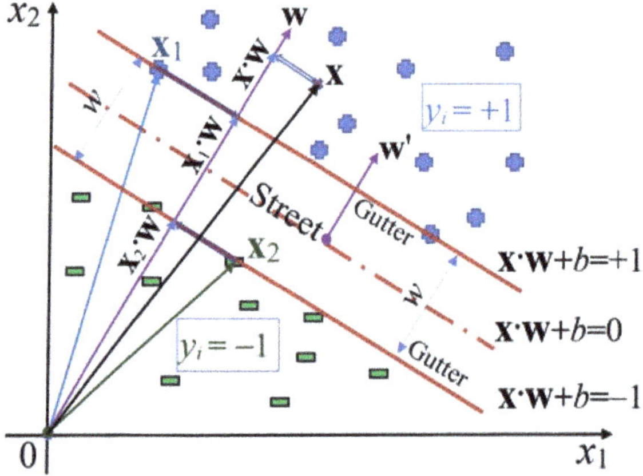

Figure 6.10:   Linearly separable data-points in 2D space, the width of the street is to be maximized using SVM.

On the upper-right gutter, there should be at least one positive data-point, say $\mathbf{x}_1$, right on it. Its vector $\mathbf{x}_1$ is the blue arrow, a *support vector* to the gutter. Because $\mathbf{x}_1$ belongs to the positive class, its label is $+1$. The equation for this gutter line of the street can be given as

$$\mathbf{x}_1 \cdot \mathbf{w} + b = +1 \tag{6.17}$$

This is the decision border for data-point $\mathbf{x}_1$. Similarly, on the lower-left gutter, there is at least one negative data-point, say $\mathbf{x}_2$, right on it. Its vector $\mathbf{x}_2$ supports the gutter. Because $\mathbf{x}_2$ belongs to the negative class, its label is -1. The equation for this gutter line can be given as

$$\mathbf{x}_2 \cdot \mathbf{w} + b = -1 \tag{6.18}$$

Consider now the projections of these two support vectors, $\mathbf{x}_1$ and $\mathbf{x}_2$ on the unit normal of the middle line for the street, $\frac{\mathbf{w}}{\|\mathbf{w}\|}$. The projection of $\mathbf{x}_1$ gives the (Euclidean) distance of the upper-right gutter to the origin along the normalized $\mathbf{w}$. Similarly, the projection of $\mathbf{x}_2$ gives the distance of the lower-left gutter to the origin along the normalized $\mathbf{w}$. Therefore, their difference gives the width of the street:

$$w = \mathbf{x}_1 \cdot \frac{\mathbf{w}}{\|\mathbf{w}\|} + b - \mathbf{x}_2 \cdot \frac{\mathbf{w}}{\|\mathbf{w}\|} - b = \frac{\mathbf{x}_1 \cdot \mathbf{w} - \mathbf{x}_2 \cdot \mathbf{w}}{\|\mathbf{w}\|} \tag{6.19}$$

Substituting Eqs. (6.17) and (6.18) to (6.19), we obtain

$$w = \frac{2}{\|\mathbf{w}\|} \tag{6.20}$$

A very simple formula. Now, we got the equation for the street width, and that depends only on training parameter weights $\mathbf{w}$! This is not so difficult to understand because these weights determine the orientation of the gutter of the street and hence the direction of the street. When the weights change, the street turns accordingly while remaining in touch with both data-points $\mathbf{x}_1$ and $\mathbf{x}_2$, which results in a change in the street width. The bias b affects only the translational location of a line. Because the street width is the difference of the two gutter lines, the bias is thus canceled. Therefore, the bias b should not affect the width. Here, we observe a fact that the affine space is not a vector space (As mentioned in Chapter 1), and the difference of two vectors in the affine space comes back to the feature space (because of the cancellation of the augment 1).

However, why is the street weight inversely related to the norm of the $\mathbf{w}$? This may be seemly counterintuitive, but it is really the mathematics at

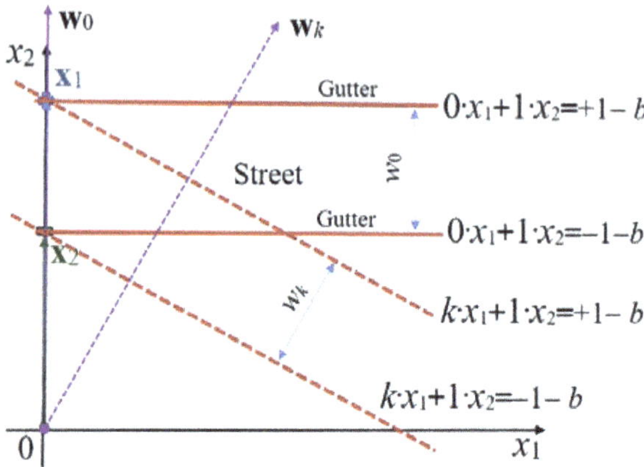

Figure 6.11: Change of width of the street when the street is turned with respect to **w**.

work. To examine and view what is really happening here, let us look at a simpler setting where both $\mathbf{x}_1$ and $\mathbf{x}_2$ (that are on the gutters) are sitting on the x_2-axis, as shown in the Fig. 6.11.

When the gutters are at the horizontal direction, the equation for the upper gutter is

$$0 \cdot x_1 + 1 \cdot x_2 = +1 + b \tag{6.21}$$

The street width is w_0. The normal vector **w** and its norm are given as follows:

$$\mathbf{w} = \begin{bmatrix} 0 & 1 \end{bmatrix}, \quad \|\mathbf{w}\| = \sqrt{0^2 + 1^2} = 1 \tag{6.22}$$

When these gutters rotate to have a slope k while remaining supported by both $\mathbf{x}_1$ and $\mathbf{x}_2$, the equation for the upper gutter becomes

$$k \cdot x_1 + 1 \cdot x_2 = +1 + b \tag{6.23}$$

The new normal vector $\mathbf{w}_k$ and its norm are given as follows:

$$\mathbf{w}_k = \begin{bmatrix} k & 1 \end{bmatrix}, \quad \|\mathbf{w}_k\| = \sqrt{k^2 + 1^2} \tag{6.24}$$

It is obvious that the street width after the rotation, w_k, is clearly smaller than the original street width before the rotation, w_0, while the norm of **w** has increased. This is also true for any value of k. The street width is at the maximum when it is along the horizontal direction which is perpendicular to the vector $\mathbf{x}_1 - \mathbf{x}_2$. We write the following code to plot this relationship:

```python
import matplotlib.pyplot as plt
import numpy as np
%matplotlib inline
fig, figarr = plt.subplots(1, 2, figsize=(11, 4))
def w_norm(k):  # norm of vector w for a line of slope k
    return np.sqrt(1. + k**2)
k = np.arange(-10, 10, .1)
y = 2/w_norm(k) # compute the width of the street
figarr[0].plot(k,y,c='r')
figarr[0].set_xlabel('Slope of the street gutter, $k$')
figarr[0].set_ylabel('Width of the street')
figarr[1].plot(w_norm(k),y)
figarr[1].set_xlabel('Norm of the weight vector')
figarr[1].set_ylabel('Width of the street')
#figarr[1].ax1.set_title('ax1 title')
plt.show()
```

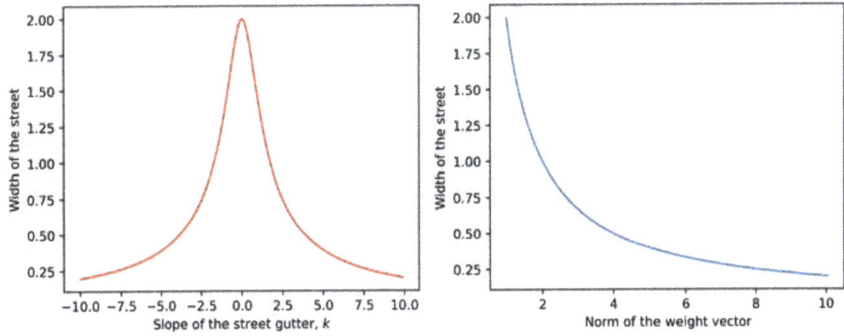

Figure 6.12:   Variation of the street width with the slope of the street gutter (left) and with the norm of the weight vector (right).

It is clear from Fig. 6.12 that the street width is inversely related to the norm of the $\mathbf{w}$.

Most importantly, this analysis shows that if the street width is maximized, $\mathbf{w}$ must be perpendicular to the gutters (decision boundaries). This conclusion is true for the arbitrary pair of data-points $\mathbf{x}_1$ and $\mathbf{x}_2$ on these two gutters.

Now, Eq. (6.19) can be rewritten as

$$w = \underbrace{\left[\mathbf{x}_1 - \mathbf{x}_2\right]}_{\text{Data pair in linear polynomial bases}} \cdot \underbrace{\frac{\mathbf{w}}{\|\mathbf{w}\|}}_{\text{weights or optimization parameters}} \tag{6.25}$$

This means that when w is maximized, the inner production of $[\mathbf{x}_1 - \mathbf{x}_2]$ and $\frac{\mathbf{w}}{\|\mathbf{w}\|}$ is maximized (these two vectors are parallel), where $[\mathbf{x}_1 - \mathbf{x}_2]$ is a vector of pairs of data-points in the linear polynomial bases $x_1, x_2, \ldots$, to approximate a line in the feature space, and $\frac{\mathbf{w}}{\|\mathbf{w}\|}$ is the vector of the normalized weights or tuning/optimization parameters. The use of linear polynomial bases here is because we assume the data-points are linearly separable by a hyperplane.

Remember our original goal is to find maximum street width. Based on Eq. (6.20), this is equivalent to minimizing the norm of $\|\mathbf{w}\|$, which in turn is the same as minimizing $\frac{1}{2}\|\mathbf{w}\|^2$. The benefit of such simple conversions will soon be evidenced. We now have our objective function:

$$\mathcal{L} = \frac{1}{2}\|\mathbf{w}\|^2 = \frac{1}{2}\mathbf{w}^\top \mathbf{w} \tag{6.26}$$

The above function needs to be minimized. We see a nice property of the above formulation: the objective function is *quadratic*, and its Hessian matrix is a unity matrix that is clearly SPD. Therefore, it has one and only one minimal. The local minimal is the global one. This is the fundamental reason why local minimal/optimal is not a concern when an SVM model is used.

Notice that our minimization has to be done under the following condition or constraint:

$$[y_i(\mathbf{x}_i \cdot \mathbf{w} + b) - 1] \geq 0 \tag{6.27}$$

for all the data-points. Assume that there are a total of m data-points for our p dimensional problem. In matrix form, this set of constraint equations has the following form:

$$[\mathbf{y}(\mathbf{X} \cdot \mathbf{w} + \mathbf{1}b) - \mathbf{1}] \geq 0 \tag{6.28}$$

where $\mathbf{y}$ is an $m \times m$ diagonal matrix with all the labels on the diagonal terms, $\mathbf{X}$ is an $m \times p$ rectangular matrix with $\mathbf{x}_i$ sitting on the ith row, $\mathbf{w}$ is a vector of p unknown weight parameters, b is the unknown parameter of bias, and $\mathbf{1}$ is a vector of $m \times 1$ with value 1 for all the entries in it.

6.4.3 *Modified objective function with constraints: Multipliers method*

Because these constraint equations need to be satisfied, our minimization becomes a constrained optimization problem. The objective function is nice (quadratic), but with many constraints. These constraints are linear but in an inequality form.

A very well-known technique for this type of optimization problem is the so-called Lagrangian multipliers method (invented in 1902!), which is widely used in many fields including the finite element methods for imposing the so-called multi-point constraints [5]. The essential idea is that when the parameter in the objective function has to satisfy some equality constraints/conditions, the objective function should be modified. The amount of modification depends on how well these conditions will be satisfied by these parameters. However, before we obtain the solution for these parameters that minimize the objective function, we do not really know. The natural way to take this into consideration in the objective function is to add a cost to it. Such a cost should be tunable by a set of additional parameters, and the number of the additional parameters should correspond to the number of constraints we have. For our case, we have m constraints, and hence we shall have m additional parameters (although some of them will be zero eventually after minimization). These parameters are called Lagrangian multipliers. The modified objective function can be written as

$$\mathcal{L} = \frac{1}{2}\mathbf{w}^\top\mathbf{w} - \boldsymbol{\lambda}^\top[\mathbf{y}(\mathbf{X}\cdot\mathbf{w} + \mathbf{1}b) - 1] \tag{6.29}$$

where $\boldsymbol{\lambda}$ is a vector of $m \times 1$ with m Lagrangian multipliers λ_i that are the additional unknown parameters.

From Eq. (6.29), we can see that when any of these m equations (equality part) in the brackets is fully satisfied, the added cost is zero. If not, the dissatisfaction amount multiplied with $\boldsymbol{\lambda}$ is added into the objective function as an additional cost. This means that any dissatisfaction to the constraints is accounted for a cost. In addition, we purposely put these Lagrangian multipliers in a linear form, so that if we perform the differentiation to the modified objective function with respect to the Lagrangian multipliers to derive the minimization conditions, these constrained equations will be fully recovered. This means that when our modified objective function is minimized, these constraints will be fully satisfied.

Moreover, because of our original constraints, the terms in the square brackets in Eq. (6.29) must be larger than or equal to zero. Therefore, any dissatisfaction will be negative. For the added cost to be positive, we must impose the following constrains to these multipliers (Note the minus sign on the front of $\boldsymbol{\lambda}^\top$):

$$\lambda_i \geq 0 \tag{6.30}$$

Therefore, Eq. (6.30) will be the new constraints on λ_i for our minimization problem using the modified objective function, to ensure the inequality of the original constraints on $\mathbf{w}$. In the algorithm to be discussed later, this set of new constraints will be implemented.

Note that the Lagrangian multiplier method shall be applicable only to equality constraints. However, Eq. (6.29) includes data-points subject to inequality constraints. The justification is given as follows.

When $[y_i(\mathbf{x}_i \cdot \mathbf{w}+b)-1] < 0$, meaning the condition/constraint is violated, λ_i will be driven by the minimization to zero, when the loss is minimized, because λ_i is set nonnegative.

When $[y_i(\mathbf{x}_i \cdot \mathbf{w} + b) - 1] > 0$, the inequality parts of the constraints are satisfied. These constraints can be changed to equality ones by introducing independent slack variables s_i^2:

$$[y_i(\mathbf{x}_i \cdot \mathbf{w} + b) - 1] - s_i^2 = 0$$

The modified loss function with only equality constraints can now be written as,

$$\mathcal{L} = \frac{1}{2}\mathbf{w}^\top\mathbf{w} - \sum_i^m \lambda_i \left([y_i(\mathbf{x}_i \cdot \mathbf{w} + b) - 1] + s_i^2\right)$$

When $\mathcal{L}$ is minimized, it is stationary at the minimizer. Setting the partial differentiation of $\mathcal{L}$ with respect to each s_i to zero gives,

$$\frac{\partial \mathcal{L}}{\partial s_i} = -2\lambda_i s_i = 0$$

This means that the modified loss function with the slack variables is the same as Eq. (6.29) without the slacks. In addition, the foregoing equation can be satisfied, if either λ_i or s_i is zero. Also, when $s_i = 0$, $[y_i(\mathbf{x}_i \cdot \mathbf{w}+b)-1] = 0$, hence we have

$$\lambda_i[y_i(\mathbf{x}_i \cdot \mathbf{w} + b) - 1] = 0$$

Therefore, for all the data-points that satisfies $[y_i(\mathbf{x}_i \cdot \mathbf{w} + b) - 1] > 0$ (data-points away from the street), the corresponding λ_i must be zero, meaning that it is not active. This proves that Eq. (6.29) can be used, because it added only zeros. We will use Eq. (6.29) to derive the equations for our dual problem.

When $[y_i(\mathbf{x}_i \cdot \mathbf{w} + b) - 1] = 0$, the data-points are on the gutters, and the added cost is zero. Thus, λ_i can be positive nonzero. Thus, for it to be bounded, some additional condition on λ_i is needed, which will be naturally obtained through minimization conditions.

When a data-point satisfies the *inequality* in Eq. (6.27), the corresponding λ should be automatically become zero, when the minimization process is completed. The positive nonzero λs correspond to these data-points satisfying the *equality* part of Eq. (6.27), or zero margin data-points that are right on the gutters. These vectors of these data-points is called **supporting vectors**. This will be demonstrated in the example given in Section 6.4.6.

Finally, we note that the constrained optimization problem now has a total of $p + 1 + m$ parameters.

Note that there is another possible method to modify the objective function, known as the penalty method, which does not bring in new parameters. Interested readers may refer to the literature [5].

6.4.4 *Converting to a standard quadratic programming problem*

Equation (6.29) is still quadratic in $\mathbf{w}$ (for fixed λ_is), but now lives in higher-dimensional space. We need to search for the stationary point for the modified objective function by performing its differentiations with respect, first, to $\mathbf{w}$ and then force it to zero, which gives

$$\frac{\partial \mathcal{L}(\mathbf{w}, b, \boldsymbol{\lambda})}{\partial \mathbf{w}} = \mathbf{w} - \mathbf{X}^\top \mathbf{y} \boldsymbol{\lambda} = \mathbf{0} \tag{6.31}$$

Noticing that $\mathcal{L}$ is a scalar, we seek for its partial derivative with respect to a vector $\mathbf{w}$. Therefore, the outcome is a vector, as expected. Equation (6.31) leads to

$$\mathbf{w} = \mathbf{X}^\top \mathbf{y} \boldsymbol{\lambda} = \sum_{i=1}^{n} \lambda_i y_i \mathbf{x}_i \tag{6.32}$$

Equation (6.32) implies that the weight parameter $\mathbf{w}$ is some kind of **linear combination** of the data vectors attached with their corresponding labels. The coefficients for the combination are the Lagrangian multipliers. Observing from Fig. 6.10, this finding does make a lot of sense: vector $\mathbf{w}$ is indeed surrounded by all the data vectors $\mathbf{x}_i$. Their combination should be able to produce $\mathbf{w}$. Because the Lagrangian multipliers are "watching" how these decision rules are obeyed by each of the data vectors, they should have the "right" to decide on the coefficients of the contributions of $\mathbf{x}_i$ to $\mathbf{w}$.

We next take differentiations with respect to b and then force it to zero, which gives

$$\frac{\partial \mathcal{L}(\mathbf{w}, b, \boldsymbol{\lambda})}{\partial b} = \boldsymbol{\lambda}^\top \mathbf{y} \mathbf{1} = 0 \tag{6.33}$$

which leads to

$$\boldsymbol{\lambda}^\top \mathbf{y} \mathbf{1} = \mathbf{1}^\top \mathbf{y} \boldsymbol{\lambda} = \sum_{i=1}^{n} \lambda_i y_i = 0 \tag{6.34}$$

This equation implies that the sum of the label-attached Lagrangian multipliers vanishes. This is somehow interesting: the label of the data-points and the multipliers has come into some kind of "neutral" agreement!

With the above relations obtained, the objective function can be rewritten as follows:

$$\mathcal{L} = \frac{1}{2}\boldsymbol{\lambda}^\top \mathbf{y} \mathbf{X} \mathbf{X}^\top \mathbf{y} \boldsymbol{\lambda} - \boldsymbol{\lambda}^\top \mathbf{y} \mathbf{X} \mathbf{X}^\top \mathbf{y} \boldsymbol{\lambda} - \boldsymbol{\lambda}^\top \mathbf{y} \mathbf{1} b + \mathbf{1}^\top \boldsymbol{\lambda} \tag{6.35}$$

which is reduced to the objective function for the so-called dual problem.

$$\mathcal{L} = \mathbf{1}^\top \boldsymbol{\lambda} - \frac{1}{2}\boldsymbol{\lambda}^\top \mathbf{y} \mathbf{X} \mathbf{X}^\top \mathbf{y} \boldsymbol{\lambda} = \sum_{i=1}^{n} \lambda_i - \sum_{i=1}^{n}\sum_{j=1}^{n} \lambda_i y_i \lambda_j y_j (\mathbf{x}_i \cdot \mathbf{x}_j) \tag{6.36}$$

Note that b is now out of the picture, which echoes Eq. (6.20): the width of the street should not depend on b. This is expected because b affects only the translational location of the street. In addition, the data-points (in the feature space) used in the SVM formulation are in the form of **inner product**: $(\mathbf{x}_i \cdot \mathbf{x}_j)$. This means that what matters is the interrelationship of these data-points. This special formulation of SVM allows the effective use of the so-called nonlinear kernel functions that evaluate the interrelationship of these data-point for problems with nonlinear decision boundaries. We will discuss this further in Section 6.4.10.

In practical computation, we may compute first $\mathbf{X}_y = \mathbf{y}\mathbf{X}$, whose ith row is simply $y_i \mathbf{x}_i$, and can be computed efficiently. Equation (6.36) can now be further simplified as

$$\mathcal{L} = \mathbf{1}^\top \boldsymbol{\lambda} - \frac{1}{2}\boldsymbol{\lambda}^\top \mathbf{P} \boldsymbol{\lambda} \tag{6.37}$$

where

$$\mathbf{P} = [P_{ij}] = \mathbf{X}_y \mathbf{X}_y^\top, \quad \text{where } P_{ij} = y_i y_j (\mathbf{x}_i \cdot \mathbf{x}_j) \tag{6.38}$$

It is clear that matrix $\mathbf{P}$ is symmetric (and of course real). It is non-negative definite. In this case, our objective function is also quadratic in parameter $\boldsymbol{\lambda}$, which is the preferable property for our optimization algorithm. However, we see that the sign on the quadratic term of $\boldsymbol{\lambda}$ is negative. Hence, its curvature is negative with respect to $\boldsymbol{\lambda}$, which is the reverse of the sign in Eq. (6.26). Therefore, our original minimization problem is converted to an optimization problem. In addition, our objective function given in Eq. (6.29) must have a saddle shape: it has a positive curvature along $\mathbf{w}$, and a negative curvature along $\boldsymbol{\lambda}$.

In the theory of Lagrangian multipliers, when the objective function is altered with $\boldsymbol{\lambda}$, the partial differentiations of the modified function can in general only give stationary points where the extrema reside. These points are saddle points, which means that along some parameter axes these points may be minimums, and along other parameter axes they may be maximums. Therefore, whether the extremum is an optimum or minimum needs to be examined carefully. To see the issue more clearly, let us take a look at a simplified problem with a loss function of only two parameters of w and λ. The simplified function still has the same essential behavior, so that we can write a Python code and plot a 3D figure to view what is really going on.

```python
import numpy as np
import matplotlib as mpl
mpl.rcParams['figure.dpi']= 220
import matplotlib.pyplot as plt
from mpl_toolkits import mplot3d
from mpl_toolkits.mplot3d import axes3d
%matplotlib inline
#%matplotlib tk
```

```python
w = np.linspace(-2.0,2.0,100)      # just one weight
l = np.linspace(-4.,4.0,100)       # just one lambda
W, L = np.meshgrid(w, l)           # create grids for 3D plot
c1, c2 = 10.0, 2.0                 # assign some constants
Loss = c1*(W*W) - c2*(L*L)         # simplified loss function
fig_s = plt.figure(figsize=(8,5)) # define sizes for 3D plot
ax = fig_s.add_subplot(1,1,1,projection='3d')
ax.set_xlabel('$w$', fontsize=12, rotation=0)
ax.set_ylabel('$\lambda$', fontsize=12)
ax.set_zlabel('$\mathcal{L}$', fontsize=12, rotation=0)
ax.yaxis._axinfo['label']['space_factor'] = 3.0
#ax.plot_wireframe(X1, X2, Z, color='b',rstride=5, cstride=5)
ax.plot_surface(W,L,Loss,color='b',rstride=2,cstride=2,
                shade=False, cmap="jet", linewidth=1)
plt.title('A simplified loss function with a saddle point,
          +str(c1)+', $c_2$=' +str(c2))
```

```
#plt.legend()
fig_s.tight_layout()    # otherwise y-label will be clipped
plt.show()
```

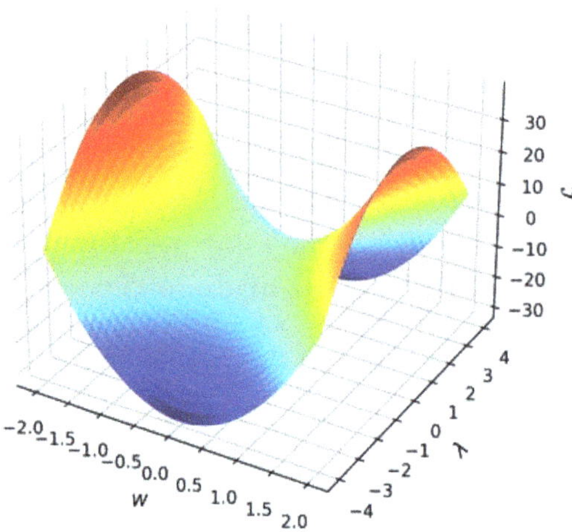

Figure 6.13:   An idealized loss function with a saddle point.

We see a saddle surface and a saddle point at the middle point on the surface. It is clear now that the function has minima along w (for any fixed λ) and maxima along λ (for any fixed w).

Back to our general objective functions $\mathcal{L}$ given in Eq. (6.37), let us look at the 2nd differentiation with respect to λ:

$$\frac{\partial^2 \mathcal{L}(\lambda)}{\partial \lambda^2} = -\mathbf{P} \tag{6.39}$$

which is the Hessian matrix ($-\mathbf{P}$, a measure of curvature), which is a negative definite matrix; because $\mathbf{P}$ is non-negative definite, we can clearly again see that our problem has now become an optimization problem with respect to our newly introduced Lagrangian multiplier λ.

Finally, noticing that our objective function is with constraints given in Eqs. (6.31) and (6.34), our SVM problem can be written as

$$\max_{\lambda} -\frac{1}{2}\lambda^\top \mathbf{P}\lambda + \mathbf{1}^\top \lambda$$
$$\text{subject to } \lambda \geq 0 \tag{6.40}$$
$$\mathbf{1}^\top \mathbf{y}\lambda = 0$$

Note that $\mathbf{1}^\top \mathbf{y}$ is simply a row vector that collects all the labels of the data-points, which can be made use of in the algorithm to avoid unnecessary computation.

Of course, we can easily convert our optimization problem into a minimization problem as follows, by simply revising the sign of the objective function:

$$\min_{\boldsymbol{\lambda}} \ \frac{1}{2}\boldsymbol{\lambda}^\top \mathbf{P}\boldsymbol{\lambda} - \mathbf{1}^\top \boldsymbol{\lambda}$$
$$\text{subject to } \boldsymbol{\lambda} \geq 0 \tag{6.41}$$
$$\mathbf{1}^\top \mathbf{y}\boldsymbol{\lambda} = 0$$

This simple change allows us to plug our problem to a CVXOPT standard solver to obtain the solution.

Let us now take a look at the standard solver at the CVXOPT library (use help(cvxopt.solvers.qp) to check it out). It solves a quadratic program defined as follows:

$$\text{minimize } \frac{1}{2}\mathbf{x}^\top \mathbf{P}\mathbf{x} + \mathbf{q}^\top \mathbf{x}$$
$$\text{subject to } \mathbf{G}\mathbf{x} \leq \mathbf{h} \tag{6.42}$$
$$\mathbf{A}\mathbf{x} = \mathbf{b}$$

Compared with Eq. (6.41), it is seen clearly that our problem is finally formulated as a typical and standard problem with a quadratic (and hence convex) objective function and a set of linear inequality constraints, known as the quadratic programming (QP) problem. Well-established QP techniques can readily be used as standard routines to solve this problem, including the CVXOPT (https://cvxopt.org/), which is a free software package for convex optimization based on Python. Because of the excellent property of convexity, one does not need to worry about the local optimums. It has one and only one optimum (or minimum) and it is the global optimum.

6.4.5 *Prediction in SVM*

After an SVM model is trained, we shall know $\mathbf{w}$ and b. For any given test data-point $\mathbf{x}_j$, we can then make a prediction using

$$\hat{y}_j = \mathbf{x}_j \cdot \mathbf{w} + b = \sum_{i=1}^{n} \lambda_i y_i (\mathbf{x}_i \cdot \mathbf{x}_j) \tag{6.43}$$

When $\hat{y} \geq 1$, $\mathbf{x}_j$ belongs to the positive class, $\hat{y} \leq -1$, it belongs to the negative class, and in the street otherwise.

Note that the prediction also needs only the inner product of the feature variables of the dataset: $(\mathbf{x}_i \cdot \mathbf{x}_j)$.

6.4.6 *Example: A Python code for SVM*

We now use (with permission) the Python code given by Cory Maklin at htt ps://github.com/corymaklin/svm to examine the SVM approach. The code uses the QP tools and solvers.

```python
#Importing the necessary libraries
import numpy as np
import cvxopt    # installation needed, for QP tools & solvers
from sklearn.datasets import make_blobs
from sklearn.model_selection import train_test_split
from matplotlib import pyplot as plt
from sklearn.svm import LinearSVC
from sklearn.metrics import confusion_matrix
print('cvxopt version',cvxopt.__version__)
```

cvxopt version 1.2.6

Define a class called SVM.

```python
class SVM:
    def fit(self, X, y):
        n_samples, n_features = X.shape
        # P = X X^T
        K = np.zeros((n_samples, n_samples))
        for i in range(n_samples):
            for j in range(n_samples):
                K[i,j] = np.dot(X[j], X[i])
        P =  cvxopt.matrix(np.outer(y, y) * K)       #use cvxopt
        print('K.shape',K.shape,'  y.shape',y.shape)
        # q = -1 (1xN)
        q =  cvxopt.matrix(-1*np.ones(n_samples))
        # A = y^T
        A = cvxopt.matrix(y, (1, n_samples))
        # b = 0
        b = cvxopt.matrix(1.0)
        # -1 (NxN)
```

```python
        G = cvxopt.matrix(-1*np.diag(np.ones(n_samples)))
        # 0 (1xN)
        h = cvxopt.matrix(np.zeros(n_samples))
        solution = cvxopt.solvers.qp(P, q, G, h, A, b) # QP
        # Lagrange multipliers
        a = np.ravel(solution['x'])  #flatten to a 1D array
        # Lagrange have nonzero Lagrange multipliers
        sv = a > 1e-5
        ind = np.arange(len(a))[sv]
        self.a = a[sv]
        self.sv = X[sv]
        self.sv_y = y[sv]
        # Intercept
        self.b = 0
        for n in range(len(self.a)):
            self.b += self.sv_y[n]
            self.b -= np.sum(self.aself.sv_yK[ind[n], sv])
        self.b /= len(self.a)
        # Weights
        self.w = np.zeros(n_features)
        for n in range(len(self.a)):
            self.w += self.a[n] * self.sv_y[n] * self.sv[n]

    def project(self, X):
        return np.dot(X, self.w) + self.b
    def predict(self, X):
        return np.sign(self.project(X))
```

We next use the scikit-learn library to generate a set of linearly separable data. We need to label the negative samples as -1 instead of 0 in order to use cvxopt.

```python
X, y = make_blobs(n_samples=255, centers=2,
                  random_state=0, cluster_std=0.65)
y[y == 0] = -1
tmp = np.ones(len(X))
y = tmp * y
# Let us take a look at the data.
print('X.shape',X.shape)
plt.scatter(X[:, 0], X[:, 1], c=y, cmap='winter');
```

```
X.shape (255, 2)
```

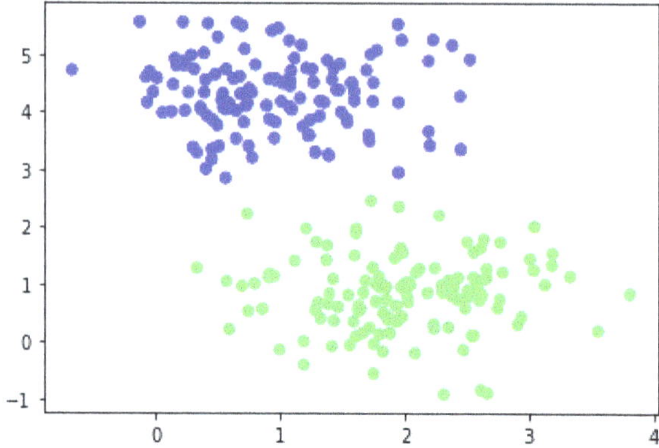

Figure 6.14: Computer-generated data-points that can be separated via a straight line.

Caution: If for some reason a "math domain error" is encountered in running the following cell, try to restart Kernel and re-run the code from the beginning of this subsection.

```python
# We split the data into training and testing sets.
X_train,X_test,y_train,y_test=train_test_split(X,y, random_state=0)
print(X_train.shape,X_test.shape,y_train.shape, y_test.shape)
# Create an instance, and then train the instance of our SVM class.
svm = SVM()
svm.fit(X_train, y_train)
#Plot the decision boundaries and support vectors.
def f(x, w, b, c=0):
    return (-w[0] * x - b + c) / w[1]   #x1.w1 + x2.w2 + b = c

plt.scatter(X_train[:,0],X_train[: ,1],c=y_train, cmap='winter')
# w.x + b = 0
a0 = -1; a1 = f(a0, svm.w, svm.b)
b0 =  4; b1 = f(b0, svm.w, svm.b)
plt.plot([a0,b0], [a1,b1], 'k')
# w.x + b = 1
a0 = -1; a1 = f(a0, svm.w, svm.b, 1)
b0 =  4; b1 = f(b0, svm.w, svm.b, 1)
plt.plot([a0,b0], [a1,b1], 'k--')
# w.x + b = -1
a0 = -1; a1 = f(a0, svm.w, svm.b, -1)
b0 =  4; b1 = f(b0, svm.w, svm.b, -1)
plt.plot([a0,b0], [a1,b1], 'k--')
w_street = 2/np.linalg.norm(svm.w) # compute the street width
print('The width of the street:',w_street)
```

```
(191, 2) (64, 2) (191,) (64,)
K.shape (191, 191)   y.shape (191,)
      pcost          dcost       gap    pres    dres
 0: -2.1259e+01 -4.3138e+01  7e+02  2e+01  2e+00
 1: -3.3107e+01 -3.1685e+01  3e+02  1e+01  8e-01
 2: -5.5227e+01 -3.9785e+01  3e+02  8e+00  6e-01
 3: -1.0725e+02 -3.9083e+01  1e+02  3e+00  3e-01
 4: -1.9273e+01 -1.4357e+01  2e+01  4e-01  3e-02
 5: -1.3042e+01 -1.3209e+01  3e+00  5e-02  4e-03
 6: -1.2960e+01 -1.2963e+01  4e-02  6e-04  5e-05
 7: -1.2961e+01 -1.2961e+01  4e-04  6e-06  5e-07
 8: -1.2961e+01 -1.2961e+01  4e-06  6e-08  5e-09
Optimal solution found.
The width of the street: 0.6301007705116851
```

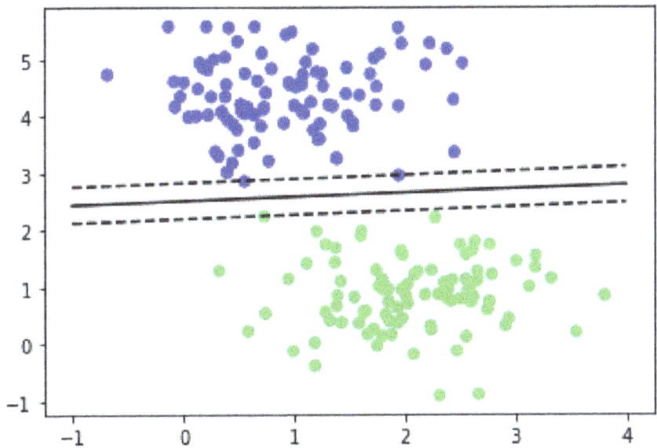

Figure 6.15:   SVM results of a widest street that separates these data-points.

```python
# Finally, the trained model is used for prediction
# using the test dataset.
print('X_test.shape',X_test.shape)
print('y_test.shape',y_test.shape)
y_proj = svm.project(X_test)
y_pred = svm.predict(X_test)
print('Projected:', y_proj[:5])
print('Predicted:', y_pred[:5])
#use a confusion matrix showing its accuracy
confusion_matrix(y_test, y_pred)
```

```
X_test.shape (64, 2)
y_test.shape (64,)
Projected: [ 8.4316 -2.7710 -5.9351  7.9451  5.31072511]
Predicted: [ 1. -1. -1.  1.  1.]
```

```
array([[31,  0],
       [ 0, 33]], dtype=int64)
```

6.4.7 *Confusion matrix*

A confusion matrix $\mathbf{C}$ is generally defined as follows: C_{ij}: the number of observations that are in group i and predicted to be in group j.

For binary classification problems, the count of true negative classes is C_{00} and false negative is C_{10}. The count of true positive classes is C_{11} and false positives is C_{01}.

For our above problem, we had all 31 negative counts and 33 positive counts. There was no false prediction for both classes.

6.4.8 *Example: A Sickit-learn class for SVM*

The above code allows one to modify when it is needed for his/her problems. As an alternative, we also use the existing powerful SVM library to solve the same problem, just for comparison of various approaches. The following codes are from the Scikit-learn [6].

```python
# Import the necessary libraries
import numpy as np
from sklearn.datasets import make_blobs
from sklearn.model_selection import train_test_split
from matplotlib import pyplot as plt
from sklearn.svm import LinearSVC
from sklearn.metrics import confusion_matrix
# Create the dataset
X, y = make_blobs(n_samples=255, centers=2, random_state=0,
                  cluster_std=0.65)
y[y==0] = -1
y = np.ones(len(X)) * y
print('X.shape',X.shape)       # a look at the dataset
plt.scatter(X[:, 0], X[:, 1], c=y, cmap='winter');
# Split the dataset into training and testing sets.
X_train,X_test,y_train,y_test=train_test_split(X,y, random_state=0)
print(X_train.shape,X_test.shape,y_train.shape, y_test.shape)
```

```
X.shape (255, 2)
(191, 2) (64, 2) (191,) (64,)
```

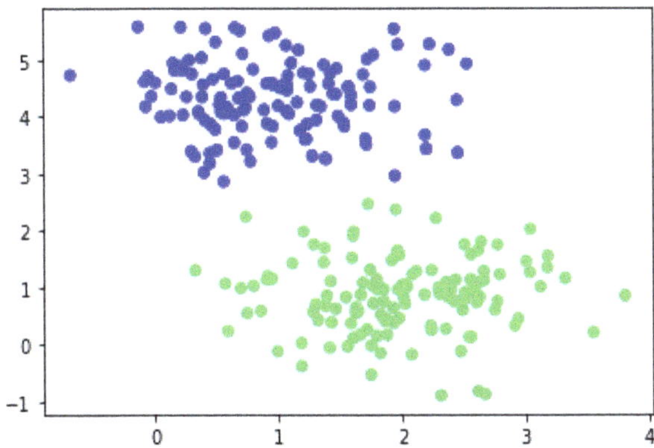

Figure 6.16:   Computer-generated data-points that can be separated via a straight line for sciket-learn SVM classifier.

```python
# scikit-learn SVM class as SVC (support vector classifier)
svc = LinearSVC(tol=0.0001, C=400.0,max_iter=3000) # instance
svc.fit(X_train, y_train)                          # train the model
#Plot the decision boundaries and the support vectors.
plt.scatter(X_train[:,0],X_train[:,1],c=y_train,
            cmap='winter');
ax = plt.gca()
xlim = ax.get_xlim()
w = svc.coef_[0]
a = -w[0] / w[1]
w_street = 2/np.linalg.norm(w)     # compute the street width
print('The width of the street:',w_street)
xx = np.linspace(xlim[0], xlim[1])
yy = a * xx - svc.intercept_[0] / w[1]
plt.plot(xx, yy)
yy = a * xx - (svc.intercept_[0] - 1) / w[1]
plt.plot(xx, yy, 'k--')
yy = a * xx - (svc.intercept_[0] + 1) / w[1]
plt.plot(xx, yy, 'k--');
```

```
The width of the street: 0.6549977642924647
```

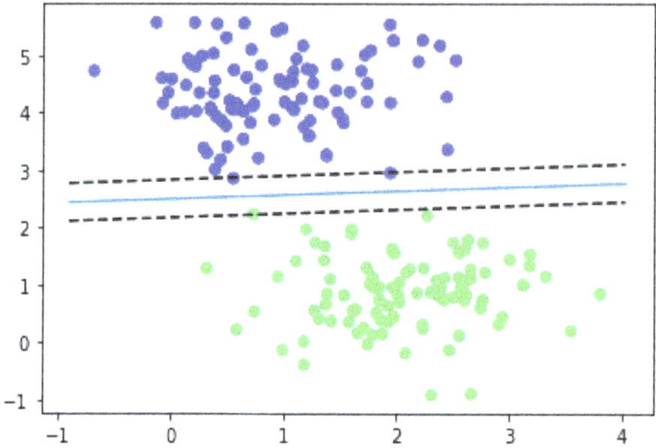

Figure 6.17:   Sciket-learn SVM results of a widest street that separates these data-points.

Notice that the width of the street computed here is a little narrower than that obtained using the previous code. This is because **LinearSVC** allows one to compute the so-called soft decision boundary, by setting the C arguments when creating the svc instance. One may try to change the C value and run the code again to see what happens.

We now make the prediction again using these test samples, and then evaluate the prediction quality in the form of a confusion matrix.

```
y_pred = svc.predict(X_test)
confusion_matrix(y_test, y_pred)
```

```
array([[31,  0],
       [ 0, 33]], dtype=int64)
```

For this example, we also had all 31 negative counts and 33 positive counts. There was no false prediction for both classes.

6.4.9 *SVM for datasets not separable with hyperplanes*

The above examples classify data-points that are all separable by straight lines (or hyperplanes). There are datasets that can only be separated properly by nonlinear curves. The SVM is also an effective approach for such datasets. It is done through expansion of the feature space to higher dimensions, by adding nonlinear basis functions in Eq. (6.14), similar to what we do in the FEM [5]. For example, for a problem with $p = 3$, the preliminary feature variables are

$$\mathbf{x} = \{x_1, x_2, x_3\} \in \mathbb{X}^3 \tag{6.44}$$

We can use the Pascal pyramid to include more nonlinear (NL) basis to form features of

$$\mathbf{x}^{NL} = \Big\{ 1, \sqrt{2}x_1, \sqrt{2}x_2, \sqrt{2}x_3, x_1x_1, x_1x_2, x_1x_3,$$
$$x_2x_1, x_2x_2, x_2x_3, x_3x_1, x_3x_2, x_3x_3 \Big\} \in \mathbb{X}^{13} \tag{6.45}$$

The dimension of the expanded feature space is calculated using $p \times p + p + 1 = 13$. If we use $\mathbf{x}^{NL}$ instead of $\mathbf{x}$, all the formulation for SVM presented above shall hold, but the inner product $(\mathbf{x}_i \cdot \mathbf{x}_j), i, j = 1, 2, 3$ is replaced by the inner product $(\mathbf{x}_I^{NL} \cdot \mathbf{x}_J^{NL}), I, J = 1, 2, \ldots, 13$. Data-points that are separable by a hyperplane may become separable when mapped to a higher-dimensional space. An excellent video demonstrating this can be found at "SVM with polynomial kernel visualization" (https://www.youtube.com/watch?v=OdlNM96sHio&t=0s).

However, when p is a big number, the dimension of the expanded feature space grows drastically, and it can be too costly in computation. Therefore, we do not actually form the expanded features. Instead, we use a **kernel trick** to achieve effects of using expanded features.

6.4.10 *Kernel trick*

The kernel trick places the inner product $(\mathbf{x}_I^{NL} \cdot \mathbf{x}_J^{NL})$ with a proper kernel function that is much cheaper to compute. For the bases in Eq. (6.45), the kernel function is found as

$$k(\mathbf{x}, \mathbf{x}_j) = (\mathbf{x} \cdot \mathbf{x}_j + 1)^2 \tag{6.46}$$

It is not too difficult for readers to verify:

$$(\mathbf{x}_i \cdot \mathbf{x}_j + 1)^2 = \left(\mathbf{x}_I^{NL} \cdot \mathbf{x}_J^{NL} \right) \tag{6.47}$$

Notice that the order of computation for the left is p, but that for the right would be p^2. The saving by using a kernel is significant. The generalized nonlinear polynomial kernels can be given as follows:

$$k(\mathbf{x}, \mathbf{x}_j) = (\mathbf{x} \cdot \mathbf{x}_j + c)^d \tag{6.48}$$

where c and d are predefined constants. Often used constants are $c = 0$ or 1, and $d = 2 \sim 5$. In general cases, we may not know precisely what are the expanded features $\mathbf{x}^{NL}$. Fortunately, we do not need to know. Because of this, many types of kernel functions can be used in SVM without the need to find $\mathbf{x}^{NL}$, including the radial basis functions (RBFs). For example, when the Gaussian basis function (a typical RBF) is used, we have the Gaussian kernel:

$$k(\mathbf{x}, \mathbf{x}_j) = \exp\left(-\frac{\|\mathbf{x} - \mathbf{x}_j\|^2}{2\sigma^2}\right) \tag{6.49}$$

where σ is a predefined parameter which controls the width of the kernel function. Such a kernel is a function of (Euclidean) distance measured from $\mathbf{x}_j$ to $\mathbf{x}$, and hence it is also called a **distance function**. It is sometimes called **similarity function**, because when $\mathbf{x}$ approaches $\mathbf{x}_j$, $k(\mathbf{x}, \mathbf{x}_j)$ approaches 1 and is thus similar. When $\mathbf{x}$ departs from $\mathbf{x}_j$, $k(\mathbf{x}, \mathbf{x}_j)$ approaches zero exponentially, indicating dissimilarity.

With such a simple replacement of the inner product by a kernel, the rest of the operations to find out the optimized parameters for curved decision boundaries remain basically the same. Because of this convenience in using kernels, machine learning packages, such as SK-learn (https://scikit-learn.org/stable/modules/svm.html), allow users to define their own custom kernels that may fit better to their applications.

All the similarity functions can be used as kernel for SVM, by simply replacing P_{ij} in Eq. (6.47) with $P_{ij} = y_i y_j k(\mathbf{x}_i \mathbf{x}_j)$, as long as the kernel is SPD based on the [Mercer's theorem]. RBFs are symmetric, because they are distance functions and hence swapping $\mathbf{x}$ and $\mathbf{x}_j$ gives the same results. It is also positive-definite, hence SPD, as proven by Powell [7]. Care may be needed on the conditioning and computation complexity, when large number of data-points are used.

The concept of kernel is quite generally applicable. It is not just used in SVM, but also possibly in other machine learning techniques, such as the nonlinear PCA, as long as the formulation uses the data-points in an inner product manner. It is also frequently used in physics-law-based methods, such as the meshfree methods [8].

6.4.11 *Example: SVM classification with curves*

The following code from Scikit learn [6] performs nonlinear SVM, which classifies data-points that are separated by curves.

```python
import numpy as np
import matplotlib.pyplot as plt
from sklearn import svm
```

```python
xx, yy = np.meshgrid(np.linspace(-3, 3, 500),
                     np.linspace(-3, 3, 500))
np.random.seed(0)
X = np.random.randn(300, 2)
Y = np.logical_xor(X[:, 0] > 0, X[:, 1] > 0)
# fit the model
clf = svm.NuSVC()
clf.fit(X, Y)
```

```python
# plot the decision function for each datapoint on the grid
Z = clf.decision_function(np.c_[xx.ravel(), yy.ravel()])
Z = Z.reshape(xx.shape)
plt.imshow(Z, interpolation='nearest', extent=(xx.min(),
           xx.max(), yy.min(), yy.max()), aspect='auto',
           origin='lower', cmap=plt.cm.PuOr_r)
contours = plt.contour(xx, yy, Z, levels=[0], linewidths=2)
plt.scatter(X[:, 0], X[:, 1], s=30, c=Y, cmap=plt.cm.Paired)
plt.xticks(())
plt.yticks(())
plt.axis([-3, 3, -3, 3])
plt.show()
```

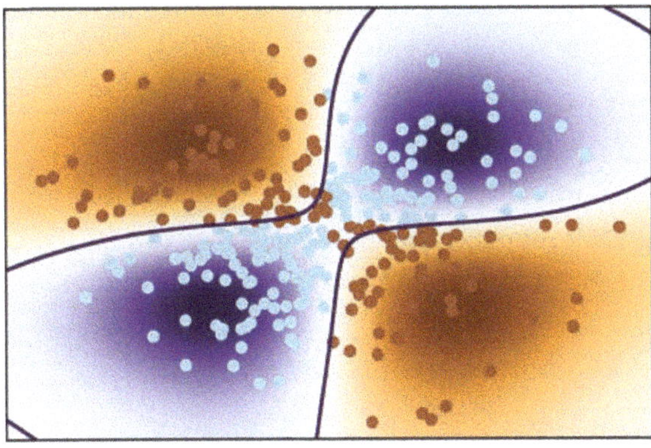

Figure 6.18: SVM classification of data-points with curves via an Sklearn classifier.

It is seen that the Sklearn classifier SVC has also quite correctly classified all these samples in this test dataset.

6.4.12　*Multiclass classification via SVM*

In many machine learning applications, there are datasets of multiple classes. SVM can also be used for such classification tasks. Multiclass reduction techniques are used in multi-classifications, including One-vs-All (also known as One-vs-Rest) and One-vs-One. Let us take a look at the following comparison case study.

6.4.13　*Example: Use of SVM classifiers for iris dataset*

This section introduces a comparison study performed by the Sklearn team. It compares different linear SVM classifiers on a 2D projection of the iris dataset, considering the first two features in the dataset:

- Sepal length.
- Sepal width.

Decision surfaces are produced using SVM classifiers with four different kernels. The linear models `LinearSVC()` and `SVC(kernel='linear')` give slightly different decision boundaries. This is because

- `LinearSVC` minimizes the squared hinge loss, while `SVC` minimizes the regular hinge loss.
- `LinearSVC` uses the One-vs-All (also known as One-vs-Rest) multiclass reduction, while `SVC` uses the One-vs-One multiclass reduction.

```python
%matplotlib inline
print(__doc__)
import numpy as np
import matplotlib.pyplot as plt
from sklearn import svm, datasets
def make_meshgrid(x, y, h=.02):
    """Create a mesh of points to plot in
    Parameters
    ----------

    x: data to base x-axis meshgrid on
    y: data to base y-axis meshgrid on
    h: stepsize for meshgrid, optional
    Returns
    -------
```

```python
    xx, yy : ndarray
    """
    x_min, x_max = x.min() - 1, x.max() + 1
    y_min, y_max = y.min() - 1, y.max() + 1
    xx, yy = np.meshgrid(np.arange(x_min, x_max, h),
                         np.arange(y_min, y_max, h))
    return xx, yy
```

```python
def plot_contours(ax, clf, xx, yy, **params):
    """Plot the decision boundaries for a classifier.
    Parameters
    ----------
    ax: matplotlib axes object
    clf: a classifier
    xx: meshgrid ndarray
    yy: meshgrid ndarray
    params: dictionary of params to pass to contourf, optional
    """
    Z = clf.predict(np.c_[xx.ravel(), yy.ravel()])
    Z = Z.reshape(xx.shape)
    out = ax.contourf(xx, yy, Z, **params)
    return out
```

```python
# import some data to play with
iris = datasets.load_iris()
# Take the first two features. We could avoid this by using a
# two-dim dataset
X = iris.data[:, :2]
y = iris.target
# Create an instance of SVM and fit out data. We do not scale
# data since we want to plot the support vectors
C = 1.0  # SVM regularization parameter
models = (svm.SVC(kernel='linear', C=C),
          svm.LinearSVC(C=C, max_iter=10000),
          svm.SVC(kernel='rbf', gamma=0.7, C=C),
          svm.SVC(kernel='poly', degree=3, gamma='auto', C=C))
models = (clf.fit(X, y) for clf in models)
# title for the plots
titles = ('SVC with linear kernel',
          'LinearSVC (linear kernel)',
          'SVC with RBF kernel',
          'SVC with polynomial (degree 3) kernel')
```

```python
# Set-up 2×2 grid for plotting.
fig, sub = plt.subplots(2, 2, figsize=(10, 8))
plt.subplots_adjust(wspace=0.2, hspace=0.2)
X0, X1 = X[:, 0], X[:, 1]
xx, yy = make_meshgrid(X0, X1)
for clf, title, ax in zip(models, titles, sub.flatten()):
    plot_contours(ax, clf, xx, yy,
                    cmap=plt.cm.coolwarm, alpha=0.8)
    ax.scatter(X0,X1,c=y,cmap=plt.cm.coolwarm,s=40,edgecolors='k')
    ax.set_xlim(xx.min(), xx.max())
    ax.set_ylim(yy.min(), yy.max())
    ax.set_xlabel('Sepal length')
    ax.set_ylabel('Sepal width')
    ax.set_xticks(())
    ax.set_yticks(())
    ax.set_title(title)
plt.show()
```

```
Automatically created module for IPython interactive environment
```

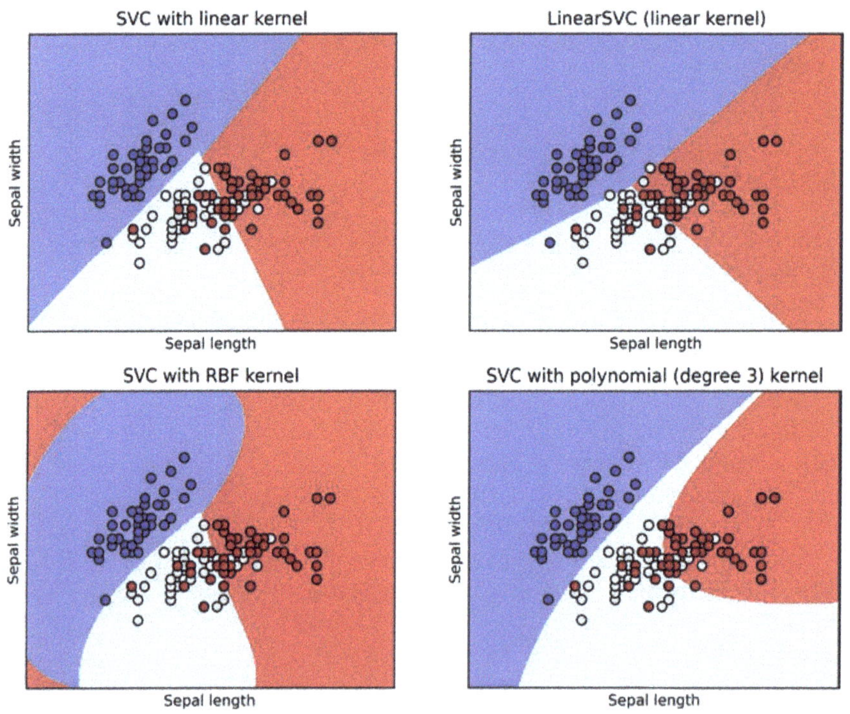

Figure 6.19: Results of Sklearn classifiers of SVM on the iris dataset.

The results show that both linear models have linear decision boundaries of intersecting hyperplanes. The nonlinear kernel models (polynomial or Gaussian RBF) produce more flexible curved decision boundaries. The shapes of the boundaries depend on the kernel type and parameters used. Readers are referred to Sklearn's case studies for more details (https://scikit-learn.org/stable/auto_examples/svm/plot_rbf_parameters.html).

References

[1] F. Rosenblatt, The perceptron: A perceiving and recognizing automation, Report 85-60-1, *Cornell Aeronautical Laboratory*, 1957.

[2] F. Rosenblatt, *Principles of Neurodynamics: Perceptrons and the Theory of Brain Mechanisms*, 1962. https://books.google.com/books?id=7FhRAAAAMAAJ.

[3] C. Corinna and V.N. Vapnik, Support-vector networks, *Machine Learning*, **20**(3), 273–297, 1995.

[4] B.-H. Asa, H. David, S. Hava *et al.*, Support vector clustering, *Journal of Machine Learning Research*, **2**, 125–137, 2001.

[5] G.R. Liu and S.S. Quek, *The Finite Element Method: A Practical Course*, Butterworth-Heinemann, London, 2013.

[6] P. Fabian, V. Gae, G. Alexandre *et al.*, Scikit-learn: Machine learning in Python, *Journal of Machine Learning Research*, **12**(85), 2825–2830, 2011. http://jmlr.org/papers/v12/pedregosa11a.html.

[7] M.J.D. Powell, The theory of radial basis function approximation in 1990, *Advances in Numerical Analysis*, **II**, 105–210, 1992. https://ci.nii.ac.jp/naid/10008965650/en/.

[8] G.R. Liu, *Mesh Free Methods: Moving Beyond the Finite Element Method*, Taylor and Francis Group, New York, 2010.

[9] Y. Xiaowei, S. Lei, H. Zhifeng *et al.*, An extended Lagrangian support vector machine for classifications, *Progress in Natural Science*, **14**(6), 519–523, 2004.

Chapter 7

Activation Functions and Universal Approximation Theory

Activation functions are some of the most essential elements in machine learning models based on artificial neural networks. Activation functions are used for the purpose of bringing in must-have nonlinearity to the neural network to enable it for complex problems. We have discussed about this in Chapter 5. This chapter takes a close look at this topic. In this book, the activation function is generally denoted using $\phi(z)$ with an argument of z that is often an input to a neuron in a neural network and often an affine transformed output from the previous layer of neurons.

There are many types of activation functions that have been used, some are still in active use, and more are being developed. Our discussion will focus on the typical ones. After establishing a clear understanding of these activation functions in this chapter, it should be reasonably straightforward to understand other functions. A quite complete list of activation functions can be found at Wikipedia (https://en.wikipedia.org/wiki/Activation_function).

With a good understanding of the roles of the weights and bias of the neuron on the output of the activation function, we shall then be able to appreciate the basic capability of a neuron. Such capability offers a pictorial presentation of the universal approximation theorem [1, 2] of neural networks.

It is worth noting that in training a neural network, we would usually need the derivatives of the loss function with respect to all its training parameters, which is often part of the argument of the activation function. Therefore, the activation function should be differentiable or at least piecewise differentiable. All activation functions discussed in this chapter satisfy this requirement.

We first examine the famous sigmoid activation function.

7.1 Sigmoid Function ($\sigma(z)$)

The sigmoid function is the earliest activation function used in training neural networks. It is still widely used today, and we will use it in multiple chapters. It has a coined symbol σ and is defined as follows:

$$\phi(z) = \sigma(z) = \frac{1}{1 + e^{-z}} \tag{7.1}$$

It is clear that for any given argument of a real number z in $(-\infty, \infty)$, it returns a positive number within (0,1). In machine learning, the argument is often an array, and we use element-wise operations. Hence, $\sigma(z)$ is also an array, given an array input. The sigmoid activation function σ maps, or practically squashes, any argument value into (0,1). Hence, it is called squashing function. It is also called logistic function, because it is often used in logistic regression, giving a result in a kind of probability.

The derivative of the sigmoid function has a simple form of

$$\phi'(z) = \phi(z)(1 - \phi(z)) \tag{7.2}$$

We now write the following codes of the activation function and to demonstrate the behavior of the sigmoid function using `mxnet` and `matplotlib`.

```python
%matplotlib inline
import mxnet as mx
from mxnet import nd, autograd, gluon
import matplotlib.pyplot as plt
import numpy as np
from matplotlib import rc
def logistic0(z):     # also known as the sigmoid function
    return 1. / (1. + nd.exp(-z))

plt.figure(figsize=(4.0, 2.5),dpi=100)
z = nd.arange(-10, 10, .1)
y = logistic0(z)
plt.plot(z.asnumpy(),y.asnumpy())
plt.xlabel('z')
plt.ylabel(r'$\sigma(z) $')
plt.title('Sigmoid Function')
plt.grid(color='r',which='both',linestyle=':',linewidth=0.5)
plt.show()
```

```
10 = int(len (z)/2)      #take look at its value at the center
print('z=',z[10].asscalar(),'sigmoid(0)=',
      logistic0(z[10]). asscalar())
```

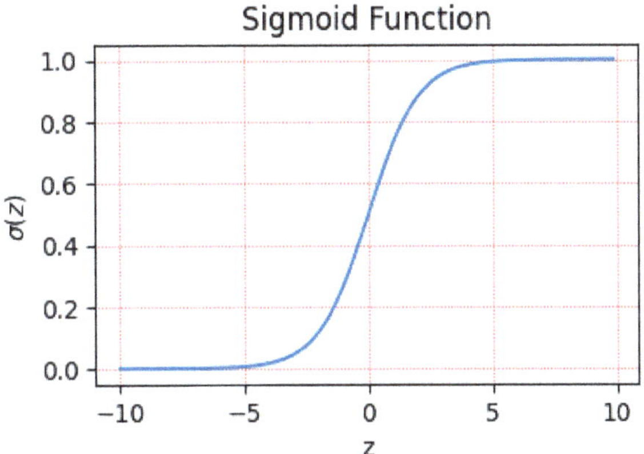

Figure 7.1: Variation of the sigmoid function: positive, monotonic, smooth, and differentiable.

```
z= 0.0 sigmoid(0)= 0.5
```

It is clear that the sigmoid outputs are between 0 and 1, and hence qualified for probability outputs. It has a value of 0.5 at $z = 0$. Therefore, if we set its output as positive when the probability is greater than 0.5, and negative whenever the output is less than 0.5, we have an adequate predictor for samples with ± 1 labels.

The derivative of the sigmoid function can be plotted using the following simple code:

```
yg = logistic0(z)*(1.-logistic0(z))
plt.figure(figsize=(4.0, 2.5),dpi=100)
plt.plot(z.asnumpy(),yg.asnumpy())
plt.xlabel('z')
plt.ylabel(r"$\sigma \ '(z) $")
plt.title('Derivative of the sigmoid Function')
plt.grid(color='r', linestyle=':', linewidth=0.5)
plt.show()
```

As shown in Figs. 7.1 and 7.2, the sigmoid activation function is monotonic, confined in $(0, 1)$, smooth, and differentiable. Its derivative is positive, smooth and further differentiable. These are all important and

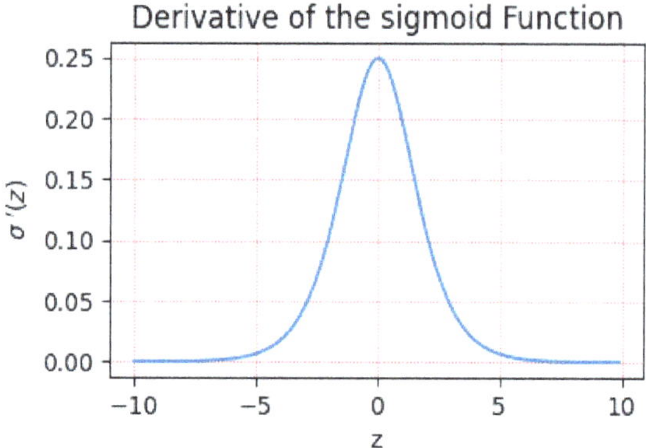

Figure 7.2: Variation of the derivative of the sigmoid function: positive, smooth, and further differentiable.

useful properties for ML models. The higher-order differentiability is useful for ML models using loss functions containing higher-order differentiations. It is also observed that for large arguments (positive or negative), the derivative of sigmoid function vanishes. This has implications when it is used in backward propagation processing when training a deepnet, where a gradient is needed.

7.2 Sigmoid Function of an Affine Transformation Function

In neural network-based machine learning, the inputs to the first layer take the direct inputs of samples or data-points. Therefore, no activation function is needed for the input layer. For all the subsequent layers, the inputs to a layer of neurons are an affine transformation of the output of the previous layer, as discussed in Chapter 5. Let us consider here one neuron at an output layer. We shall have

$$z = \mathbf{x} \cdot \mathbf{w} + b \tag{7.3}$$

where $\mathbf{x}$ is the input from the previous layer, $\mathbf{w}$ is the weight matrix that connects the previous layer to the current layer, and b is the bias for the neurons of the current layer. Both $\mathbf{w}$ and b are to be updated through training, and hence often referred to as training (or learning) parameters. In this chapter, we do not study how to update these parameter, but focus on the effects of them on the output of the neuron. When the sigmoid function is applied to produce the output of the current layer, we shall have the following general expression.

$$x^{out} = \frac{1}{1 + e^{-(\mathbf{x} \cdot \mathbf{w} + b)}} \tag{7.4}$$

7.3　Neural-Pulse-Unite (NPU)

Let us write a Python code to examine how the outputs of the activation function are influenced by the weights and biases. We also use the mxnet model to do the number crunching and plot out the results in graphics.

We first let w vary in a range, and b be fixed at 0.

```python
def logistic(w,x,b):
    return 1. / (1. + nd.exp(-(x*w + b)))

x = nd.arange(-10, 10, .1)
w = nd.arange(1.0, 50, 5.0)
b = nd.arange(0, 50, 10)
b0=b[0]
plt.figure(figsize=(4.0, 3.5),dpi=100.)
for wi in w:
    y = logistic(x,wi,b0)                        # b is fixed
    plt.plot(x.asnumpy(),y.asnumpy(),
            label="wi="+str(wi. asnumpy()))
plt.xlabel('x')
plt.ylabel(r"$\sigma(z=xw+b)$")
plt.title('Sigmoid Function with b='+str(b0.asscalar()))
plt.grid(color='r', linestyle=':', linewidth=0.5)
plt.legend()
plt.show()
```

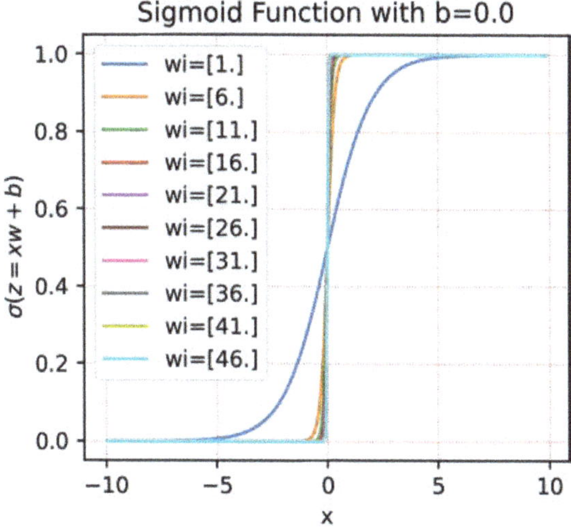

Figure 7.3:　Effects of weights on the sigmoid function.

Figure 7.3 shows clearly that a larger weight makes the sigmoid curve steeper near $x = 0$. We can practically make a function that is as closer as we want to the step function, by using a very large weight.

Let us now examine the influence of the bias on the shape of the activation function with a fixed weight.

```python
x = nd.arange(-10, 10, .1)
w = nd.arange(0.0, 50, 5.0)
b = nd.arange(-30, 30, 10)
w1=w[1].asscalar()
plt.figure(figsize=(4.0, 3.0),dpi=100.)
for bi in b:
    y = logistic(x,w1,bi)
    plt.plot(x.asnumpy(),y.asnumpy(),\
             label="b="+str(bi[0].asnumpy()))
plt.xlabel('x')
plt.ylabel(r"$\sigma(z=xw+b) $")
plt.title('Sigmoid Function with w='+str(w1))
plt.grid(color='r', linestyle=':', linewidth=0.5)
plt.legend(loc='center right', bbox_to_anchor=(1, 0.5))
plt.show()
```

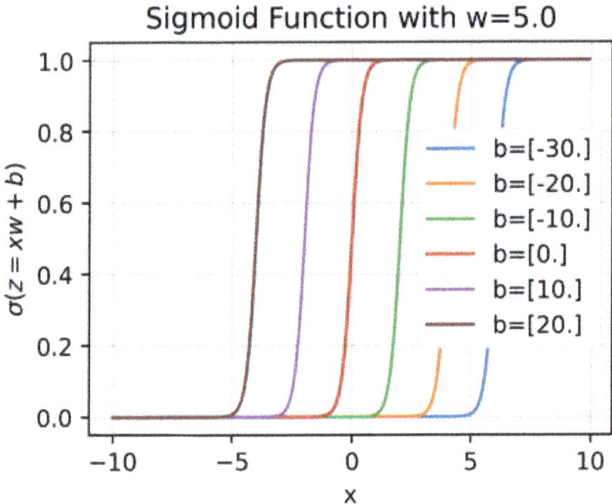

Figure 7.4:   Effects of the bias.

Figure 7.4 shows clearly that the bias makes the sigmoid curve shift: A positive bias value shifts the sigmoid curve leftwards and a negative value

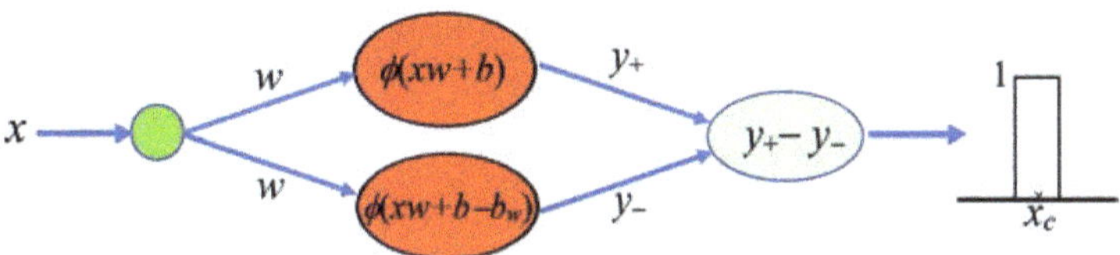

Figure 7.5: NPU: A pair of neurons is capable of producing a close-to-rectangular pulse when a large w value is used. The pulse location and its width are controlled by the base bias b_0, width of the bias b_w, and w.

shifts the curve rightwards. It practically controls where in space the output should appear. If we make use of these effects of both weight and bias, we can produce a close-to-rectangular pulse function using a pair of activation functions. We call it Neural-Pulse-Unit (NPU). It is schematically drawn in Fig. 7.5.

The width (in the x coordinate) at the middle point of the pulse, p_w, is controlled by the difference of the biases used in the two paired neurons and the weight. The formula can be derived in the following procedure.

First, the z value at the middle point of the sigmoid function should always be zero; we shall then have for the neuron (on the top)

$$z = x_+ \cdot w + b = 0 \tag{7.5}$$

where b is the base bias of the neuron pair, as shown in Fig. 7.5 above. For the neuron below,

$$z = x_- \cdot w + b - b_w = 0 \tag{7.6}$$

where b_w is the negative offset of the bias at the neuron below. The width at the middle point of the pulse, p_w, becomes

$$p_w = x_+ - x_- = b_w/w \tag{7.7}$$

It depends on b_w and w.

By altering the weight and bias values, one can also create such a pulse at any x. The center location of the pulse, x_c, can be calculated using

$$x_c = \frac{x_+ + x_-}{2} = -\frac{2b - b_w}{2w} \tag{7.8}$$

It depends on b, b_w, and w.

It is seen that the width and the location of the pulse depend only on the weight and bias, which are trainable parameters. This implies that once the neurons are trained with a set of fixed parameters, it will be capable of producing the function value for any given input x.

We now write the following code to generate a pulse:

```python
x = nd.arange(-8, 8, .1)
w = nd.arange(0.0, 30, 5.0)
w1=w[-1].asscalar()
b0=10.0                    # the base bias
bw=20.0                    # negative shift of b at the 2nd neuron
bc = 2*b0 - bw             # compute the center value of b
xc = -0.5* bc/w1           # compute x of the center of the pulse
pw = bw/w1                 # width of the pulse (at the middle)

y = logistic(x,w1,b0)-logistic(x,w1,b0-bw)
plt.figure(figsize=(4.5, 3.0),dpi=100.)
plt.plot(x.asnumpy(),y.asnumpy())
plt.xlabel('x')
plt.ylabel(r"$\sigma(x*w+b0)-\sigma(x*w+b0-bw) $")
plt.title('Neural Pulse, Sigmoid, w='
          +str(w1)+' b='+str(b0)+' bw='+str(bw))
plt.grid(color='r', linestyle=':', linewidth=0.5)
plt.show()
print('b0=',b0,'bc=',bc,'xc=',xc,'pw=',pw)
```

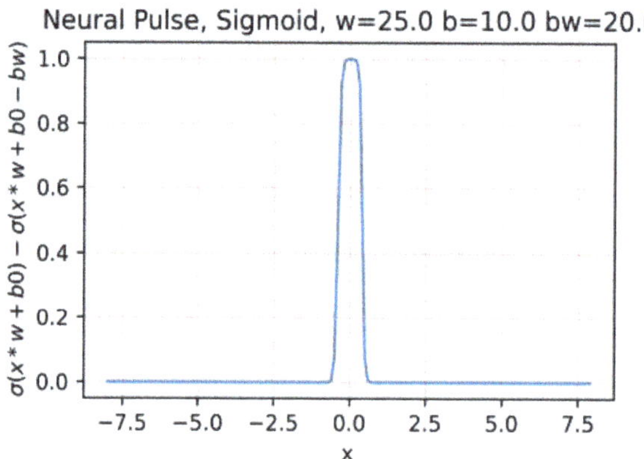

Figure 7.6:   A pulse generated using a pair of sigmoid functions.

```
b0= 10.0 bc= 0.0 xc= -0.0 pw= 0.8
```

We have successfully created a rectangular pulse function with unit height at $x = 0$, as shown in Fig. 7.6.

The above neural network has just one input neuron (the green filled circle), one hidden layer with two neurons (the two vertical orange filled ellipses in the middle), and one output layer with one neuron (orange filled ellipse on the right). To produce the pulse, we have set the weights for both hidden neurons as the same large value and let the bias shift. The outputs of these two neurons will all be close to step functions, but in opposite orientation and at different stepping-up locations. The final output neuron sums these two step functions and delivers a pulse. It functions as an NPU.

Using multiple such NPUs, one can generate as many NPUs located at different x_c as one desires. Below is a code for producing a lined-up rectangular unit pulse.

```python
plt.figure(figsize=(6.5, 3.0),dpi=200)
x = nd.arange(-8, 8, .1)
w = nd.arange(0.0, 51, 5.0)
b = nd.arange(-120, 190, 40)
w1=40. #w[-1].asscalar() #We use only one but large weights
                        #for all NPUs
db=20.0      #=bw            #define the width of the pulse
plt.figure(figsize=(6.5, 3.0),dpi=100.)
for bi in b:
    y = logistic(x,w1,bi)-logistic(x,w1,bi-db)
    plt.plot(x.asnumpy(),y.asnumpy(),
            label="b="+str(bi[0]. asnumpy()))

plt.xlabel('x')
plt.ylabel(r"$\sigma(x*w+b)-\sigma(x*w+b-bw) $")
plt.title('Subtraction of two Sigmoid Functions with w='+str(w1)
          +' bw='+str(db))
plt.grid(color='r', linestyle=':', linewidth=0.5)
plt.legend()
plt.show()
```

```
<Figure size 1300x600 with 0 Axes>
```

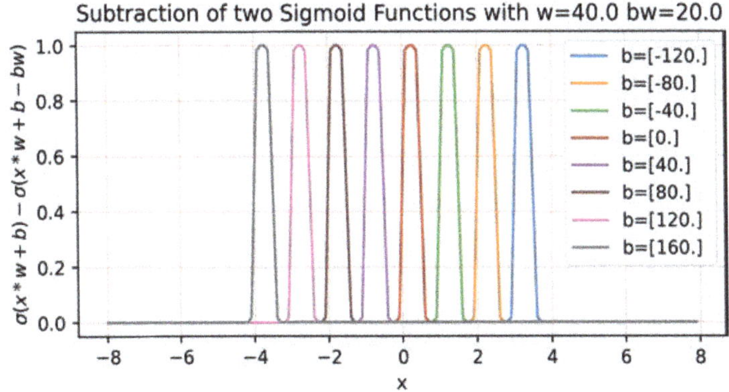

Figure 7.7: Eight pulses generated using sigmoid functions.

Figure 7.7 shows eight pulses lined up created using eight NPUs (eight pairs of neurons in the hidden layer). Each NPU is responsible for a pulse centered at its x_c value. As long as we have enough number of pair neurons in the hidden layer, one can create as many pulses as needed to cover the interest domain of x.

7.4 Universal Approximation Theorem

Universal approximation theorem [1] states that *a neural network with sufficiently large number of neurons in one hidden layer is capable of approximating any continuous function.*

7.4.1 *Function approximation using NPUs*

Now, when the outputs of these pairs of neurons are fed to the final output neuron, a linear combination using the following formula can be used to approximate an arbitrary given function:

$$\langle f(x) \rangle = \sum_{i=1}^{N_x} f(x_i) \cdot P(x_i) \tag{7.9}$$

where $f(x)$ is the given function, $\langle f(x) \rangle$ denotes the approximated function, $f(x_i)$ is the given function value at x_i, $P(x_i)$ is the unit rectangular pulse created by the ith neuron pair for x_i, and N_x is the number of x_i sampled in the domain of x.

Let us write another code for this single hidden layer neuron network to get this done.

```python
plt.figure(figsize=(6.5, 3.0),dpi=100)
x = nd.arange(-10, 10, .1)
w = nd.arange(0.0, 50, 5.0)
b = nd.arange(-400, 470, 40)
w1=w[-1].asscalar() # use one large weights for all NPUs
bw=40.0             # negative shift (width) of the bias
for bi in b:
    bc = 2*bi - bw              # center value of b
    xc = -0.5* bc/w1            # x at the center of pulse
    fcos = nd.cos(xc/2)         # value of cosine function
    pulse = (logistic(x,w1,bi)-logistic(x,w1,bi-bw))
```

```python
    y = fcos * pulse                    #linear combination of pulse
    plt.plot(x.asnumpy(),y.asnumpy(),
            label="b="+str(bi[0]. asnumpy()))


xi = -0.5*(2*b - bw)/w1
plt.plot(xi.asnumpy(),np.cos(xi.asnumpy()/2),c='b',
    linewidth=2.5)
plt.xlabel('x')
plt.ylabel("cos(x/2)")
plt.title('Approximating cos(x) using neuron pulses, w='
        +str(w1)+' bw='+str(bw))
plt.grid(color='r', linestyle=':', linewidth=0.5)
#plt.legend()
plt.show()
```

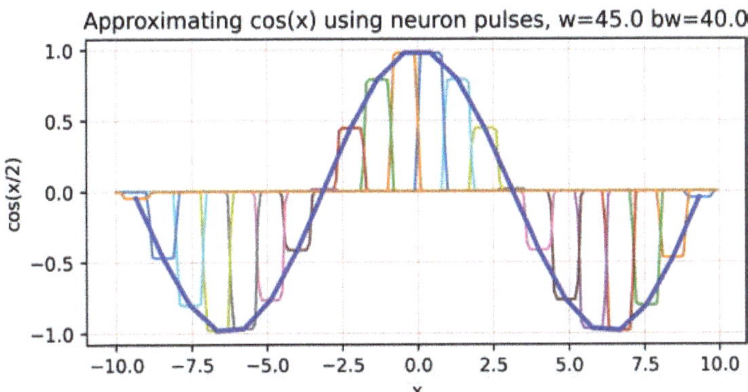

Figure 7.8:   A cosine function is approximated using a series of neuron pulses.

The above demonstrations, as plotted in Figs. 7.6–7.8, show that at most two neurons in the hidden layer can approximate one point in a curve. The number of neurons required in approximating a curve depends on the complexity of the curve varying with x. If 200 points needed to approximate the curve with desired accuracy, one would need (at most) to use 400 neurons in the hidden layer.

7.4.2 *Function approximations using neuron basis functions*

We now change our way to do the approximation using the *node-based* approximation idea in the meshfree methods [3]. In this case, we treat all the center points of the pulses as *nodes*, and all the pulse functions as continuous nodal shape functions. Our approximation of the function will become as follows:

$$\langle f(x)\rangle = \sum_{i=1}^{N_x} f(x_i) \cdot P(x) \tag{7.10}$$

where $f(x_i)$ is the nodal value of the function at x_i, and $P(x)$ is now a continuous neuron basis function of pulse-like. In this case, the approximated function $\langle f(x)\rangle$ becomes a continuous function, and the neuron pair become a basis function.

Using a series of NPUs, this universal approximation theorem (UAT) can be schematically drawn in Fig. 7.9. A UAT-Net can be constructed with one input layer, one hidden layer, and one output layer. If the hidden layer has sufficient number of neuron pairs, each pair can form one NPU unit, which is responsible to produce one pulse function at a location. When all

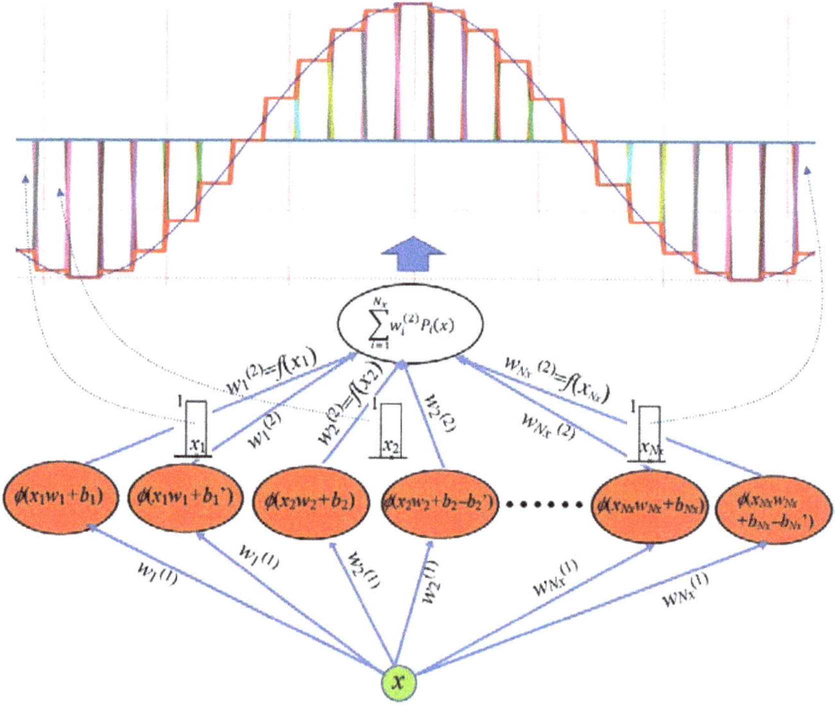

Figure 7.9: Schematic description of the Universal Approximation Theorem. This UAT-Net consists of one hidden layer with sufficient number of neuron pairs. Each pair forms one NPU unit responsible to produce one pulse at a location. When all these weights at the input and output layers and all these biases at the hidden layer neurons are set (trained) properly, any continuous function can be approximated for any input value of x.

these weights at input and output layers and all these biases at the hidden layer neurons are set (or trained) properly, the UAT-Net is capable of approximating any continuous function for any input value of x.

Let us plot this function to see what it looks like.

```python
plt.figure(figsize=(6.5, 3.0),dpi=200)
x = nd.arange(-10, 10, .05)      #we refined the points
w = nd.arange(0.0, 50., 5.0)
b = nd.arange(-400, 470, 40)


w1=w[-1].asscalar() # Use one large weights for all NPUs
bw= b[1]-b[0] #20.0                 # negative shift of bias
sx = int(x.size)
yfem = np.zeros(sx)
for bi in b:
    bc = 2*bi - bw          # center value of b
    xc = -0.5* bc/w1         # x at the center of the pulse
    fcos = nd.cos(xc/2)      # nodal function value of cosine
    pulse = (logistic(x,w1,bi)-logistic(x,w1,bi-bw))
    y = fcos * pulse         # linear combination of pulse
    plt.plot(x.asnumpy(),y.asnumpy(),
            label="b="+str(bi[0]. asnumpy()))
    yfem += y.asnumpy()

plt.plot(x.asnumpy(),yfem,c='r')
                            #plot the approximated function
xi = -0.5*(2*b - bw)/w1
plt.plot(xi.asnumpy(),np.cos(xi.asnumpy()/2),c='b',
        linewidth=0.5)
plt.xlabel('x')
plt.ylabel("cos(x/2)")
plt.title('Approximating cos(x) using neuron pulses, w='
        +str(w1)+' bw='+str(bw.asscalar()))
plt.grid(color='r', linestyle=':', linewidth=0.5)
#plt.legend()
plt.show()
```

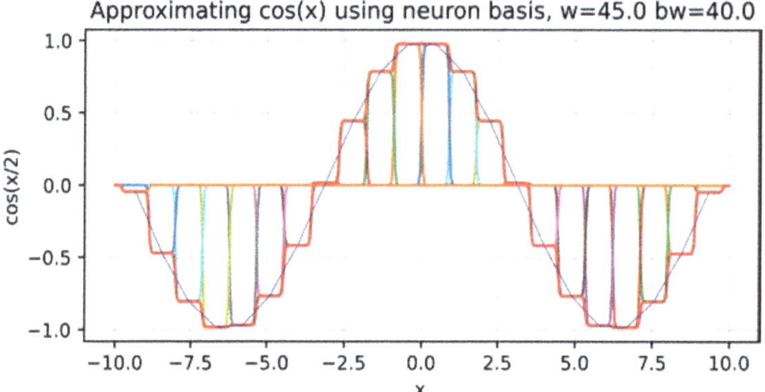

Figure 7.10:   A cosine function is approximated using a series of neuron basis functions that are pulse-like.

The approximated function using pulse-like neural basis functions becomes the thinker red line, as shown in Fig. 7.10. It is clearly continuous.

One may also use the FEM method do to a similar approximation [4]. In this case, we still treat all the center points of the pulses as *nodes*, and our elements can now be defined as the segments between the center point of a pulse and the center of its next pulse. Each of the pulse functions becomes a nodal shape function. The FEM approximation can then be done using only two pieces of pulse functions that cover the element. The outcome of the approximated results will be quite similar.

The above analysis clearly shows the capability of a neuron and a neural network. Let us end this section by mentioning the following points:

1. We found **one** possible way to approximate a function. It is not necessarily the best possible way.
2. In actual applications, if the weights and biases of a neural network are trained in a systematic **optimal** way, it should perform much better than the hand-designed neural network above.
3. It is not really necessary to create pulse functions to perform approximation in reality. Doing this here is for the purpose of showing the **concept** in an easy-to-understand manner.
4. The width of each pulse does not have to be the same. In a trained neural network, the training parameters in each of the neurons are **individually tuned** for an overall performance measured by a loss function.
5. All the neurons on the hidden layer in an actual trained neural network are **working together** in a system, not necessarily in pairs. Hence, it is expected to perform much better, because of this flexibility.

6. Our above analysis is for approximating a curve in one dimension. A similar idea is applicable to approximation of surfaces and even higher-dimensional hyper-surfaces.

7. When **more hidden layers** are used, one can significantly reduce the number of neurons in the hidden layers. Theoretical analysis has already shown that the total number of neurons used should be much less, provided such a deepnet can be properly trained. It is an issue of **trainability**. Deepnets have become popular and practical to may applications because we now have increasingly better ways to train them well with big datasets.

8. We **rarely** see people using the neural network to approximate a function. Our tasks in real-life problems are often a lot more complicated and practical.

9. The significance of the universal approximation theorem reveals the **capability** of a neural network in terms of function approximation.

The affine transformation applied in the neural network setting has created a connection between the data-prediction relationship $(\mathbf{x}, \hat{\mathbf{y}})$ and the model parameters $(\mathbf{w}, b)$. In other words, $(\mathbf{x}, \hat{\mathbf{y}})$ or the features in the data can be corded in $(\mathbf{w}, b)$. In addition, when activation functions are used for all the neurons in a layer, the outputs of all these neurons become linearly independent, and can be treated as new inputs to be fed further to the next layers, forming an MLP, leading to the Universal Prediction Theory for ML model creation. This forms the foundation of neural network-based machining learning models, as discussed in Chapter 5.

To support item (3), we can use a smaller weight to create the nodal shape functions and then approximate the cosine function as below.

```
plt.figure(figsize=(6.5, 3.0),dpi=100.)
x = nd.arange(-10, 10, .05)      # refined points
#w = nd.arange(0.0, 50., 5.0)
#b = nd.arange(-400, 470, 40)
w = nd.arange(0.0, 10., 5.0)
b = nd.arange(-400, 470, 5)
w1=w[-1].asscalar() # Use one but large weights for all NPUs
bw= b[1]-b[0] #20.0              # define the width of the bias
sx = int(x.size)
yfem = np.zeros(sx)
pu = np.zeros(sx)
```

```python
for bi in b:
bc = 2*bi - bw                # center value of b
    xc = -0.5* bc/w1          # x at the center of the pulse
    fcos = nd.cos(xc/2)       # nodal function value of cosine
    pulse = (logistic(x,w1,bi)-logistic(x,w1,bi-bw))
    y = fcos * pulse          # linear combination of pulse
    plt.plot(x.asnumpy(),y.asnumpy(),
            label="b="+str(bi[0]. asnumpy()))
    yfem += y.asnumpy()
    pu += pulse.asnumpy()   # Check on whether the partitions
                            # of unity (PU) is satisfied.
plt.plot(x.asnumpy(),yfem,c='r')
plt.plot(x.asnumpy(),pu,c='b')
print(pu[:60:10])
xi = -0.5*(2*b - bw)/w1
plt.xlabel('x')
plt.ylabel("cos(x/2)")
plt.title('Approximating cos(x) using neuron pulses, w='
            +str(w1)+' bw='+str(bw.asscalar()))
plt.grid(color='r', linestyle=':', linewidth=0.5)
#plt.legend()
plt.show()
```

```
[0.99999999 1.        0.99999999 1.        0.99999999 1.        ]
```

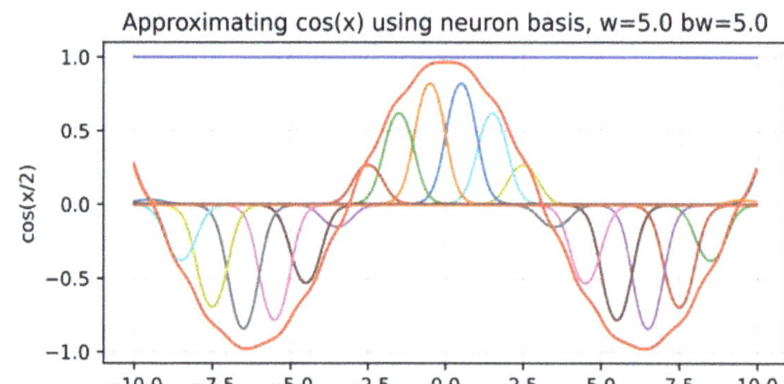

Figure 7.11:   A cosine function is approximated using a series of neuron basis functions as "nodal shape functions".

Figure 7.11 shows that the approximated function (the red line) is smoother and hence has better quality in approximating the cosine function.

This is because the neural pulse is used as a nodal shape function that is smooth and not necessarily being a sharp pulse.

Note that the partition of unity (PU) property/condition is one of the most important properties of nodal shape functions used in a numerical method for a mechanics problem [3]. The PU condition states that

$$\sum_{i=1}^{N_x} P(x) = 1 \tag{7.11}$$

This needs to be satisfied at any x. In the code above, we added one more computation to check whether this property is satisfied if we would use the neuron pair as a nodal shape function. As shown in Fig. 7.11, the PU condition is indeed naturally satisfied by these neuron basis.

If we further reduce the pulse width, we shall obtain a very accurate approximation of the function, as shown in Fig. 7.12.

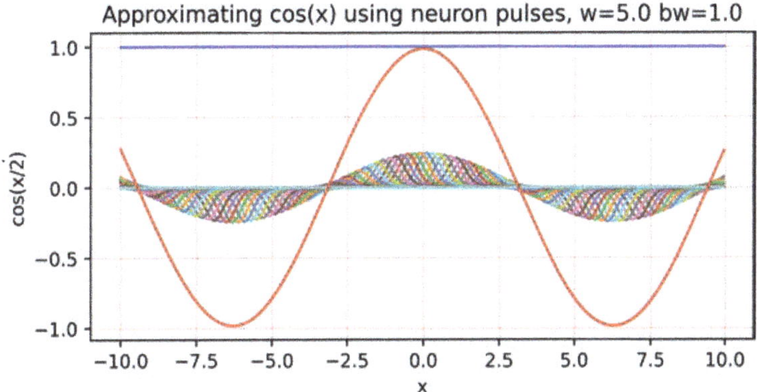

Figure 7.12: **Neuron Basis**: A pair of neurons can be used as nodal basis functions for function approximation. In this case, one does not have to use very large weight. The resolution can be controlled by the width of the bias used in the neuron pairs.

In the study above, we used the sigmoid activation function. Many other activation functions to be discussed in the following sections may also be used. In Ref. [2], triangular pulses are constructed and used in addition to the sigmoid pulses to approximate functions, and they worked better in some ways.

7.4.3 *Remarks*

Note that Eq. (7.9) uses NPUs to support the Universal Approximation Theory, which provide a nice intuition for understanding. However, Eq. (7.10) is more general. This is because the neuron basis function $P(x)$ used in

Eq. (7.10) do not have to be a pulse for function approximation, as shown in the previous two figures. Therefore, any activation function can be used for constructing $P(x)$, as long as it is monotonic for uniqueness (see Section 5.5.3) and nonlinear for linearly independence (see Section 5.8.2).

7.5 Hyperbolic Tangent Function (tanh)

The tanh function is another activation function widely used in neural networks to bring in nonlinearities. It is defined as follows:

$$\phi(z) = \tanh(z) = \frac{e^z - e^{-z}}{e^z + e^{-z}} \tag{7.12}$$

It is clear that for any given argument of a real number z in $(-\infty, \infty)$, it returns a real number within $(-1, 1)$. Again, in machine learning models, the argument is often an array. Hence, we use element-wise operations, and tanh(z) will also be an array. The tanh activation function maps any argument value into $(-1, 1)$, in comparison with the sigmoid function that maps to $(0, 1)$. It comes handy for many machine learning models that need outputs in real numbers within $(-1, 1)$.

The derivative of the tanh function has a simple form of

$$\phi'(z) = 1 - \phi(z)^2 \tag{7.13}$$

```python
def tanhf(z):
    return nd.tanh(z)


x = nd.arange(-10, 10, .1)
y = tanhf(x)
#plt.figure(figsize=(4.5, 3.0),dpi=100.)
plt.plot(x.asnumpy(),y.asnumpy())
plt.xlabel('z')
plt.ylabel('$tanh(z)$')
plt.title('Hyperbolic Tangent Function')
plt.grid(color='r', linestyle=':', linewidth=0.5)
plt.show()
yg = 1.-tanhf(x)**2
plt.plot(x.asnumpy(),yg.asnumpy())
plt.xlabel('x')
plt.ylabel("$tanh(z)\ '(z) $")
plt.title('Derivative of Hyperbolic Tangent Function')
plt.grid(color='r', linestyle=':', linewidth=0.5)
plt.show()
```

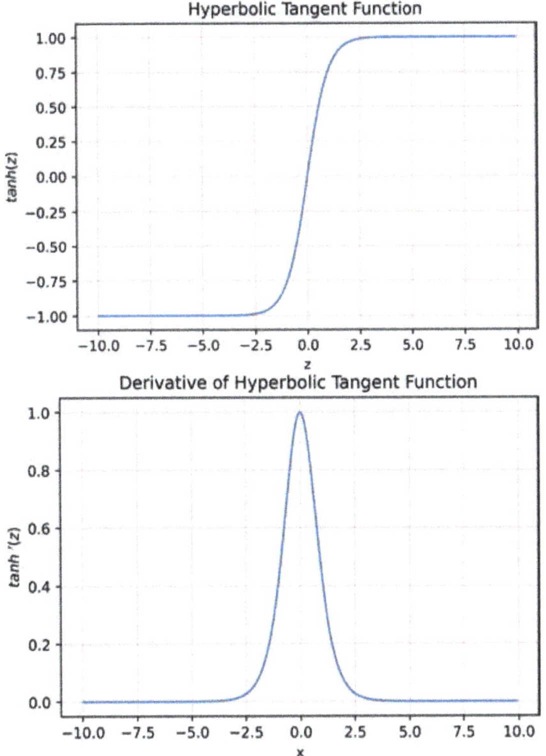

Figure 7.13: Hyperbolic tangent (tanh) activation function (monotonic, smooth, and differentiable) and its derivative (positive, smooth, and further differentiable).

```
10 = int(len (x)/2)
print('x=',x[10].asscalar(),'tanh(0)=',tanhf(x[10]). asscalar())
```

```
x= 0.0 tanh(0)= 0.0
```

As shown in Fig. 7.13, the hyperbolic tangent (tanh) activation function is monotonic, confined in $(-1, 1)$, smooth, and differentiable. Its derivative is positive, smooth and further differentiable.

7.6 Relu Functions

Relu stands for "rectified linear unit" [5]. It is widely used in deep neural nets in applications in computer vision, speech recognitions, etc. It is the most popular activation function for training deep neural networks, due to its effectiveness in mitigating the so-called gradient vanishing issues. It has the simple form of

$$\phi(z) = z^+ = \max(0, z) = \begin{cases} 0 & z < 0 \\ z & z \geq 0 \end{cases} \tag{7.14}$$

Relu function is also known as a ramp function. It is an analogy for half-wave rectification in electrical engineering. It simply wipes out the effects from the inputs that are negative, but keeps the non-negative inputs as it is, resulting in nonlinearity. Such a drastic discount to the inputs might be one of the reasons why it worked well for densely connected deepnets.

Relu function is piecewise differentiable. The derivative of the Relu function also has a very simple form of

$$\phi'(z) = \begin{cases} 0 & z < 0 \\ 1 & z \geq 0 \end{cases} \tag{7.15}$$

The unit gradient is helpful in mitigating the gradient vanishing in a deepnet, because it remains unchanged with the depth of the net.

Relu has a number of variations, including leaky Relu and parametric Relu. A general formulation can be given as follows:

$$\phi(z) = \begin{cases} k_n z & z < 0 \\ k_p z & z \geq 0 \end{cases} \tag{7.16}$$

where k_n and k_p are all positive constants, in which k_n represents the derivative of the negative portion and k_p represents the derivative of the positive portion. For the leaky Relus, one often uses $k_n = 0.01$ and $k_p = 1.0$. In parametric Relus, we make these parameters trainable.

The derivative of the generalized Relu function has the form of

$$\phi'(z) = \begin{cases} k_n & z < 0 \\ k_p & z \geq 0 \end{cases} \tag{7.17}$$

It is seen that for a deep net, the negative part effect can vanish quickly with depth because of the small value of k_n. In such cases, the leaky Relu may behave like the Relu.

We now write a simple code to demonstrate the generalized Relu function and its derivatives, with tunable parameters k_n and k_p.

```python
def reluf(z,kn,kp):
    f = [kn*zi if zi < 0.0 else kp*zi for zi in z]
    return f


def relug(z,kn,kp):
    g = [kn if zi < 0.0 else kp for zi in z]
    return g
```

```python
x = np.arange(-10, 10, .1)
y = reluf(x,0.1,1.0)
plt.plot(x,y)
plt.xlabel('x')
plt.ylabel("$relu(z)$")
plt.title('Relu Function')
plt.grid(color='r', linestyle=':', linewidth=0.5)
plt.show()
yg = relug(x,0.1,1.0)
plt.plot(x,yg)
plt.xlabel('x')
plt.ylabel("$relu(z)\ '(z) $")
plt.title('Derivative of the Relu Function')
plt.grid(color='r', linestyle=':', linewidth=0.5)
plt.show()
```

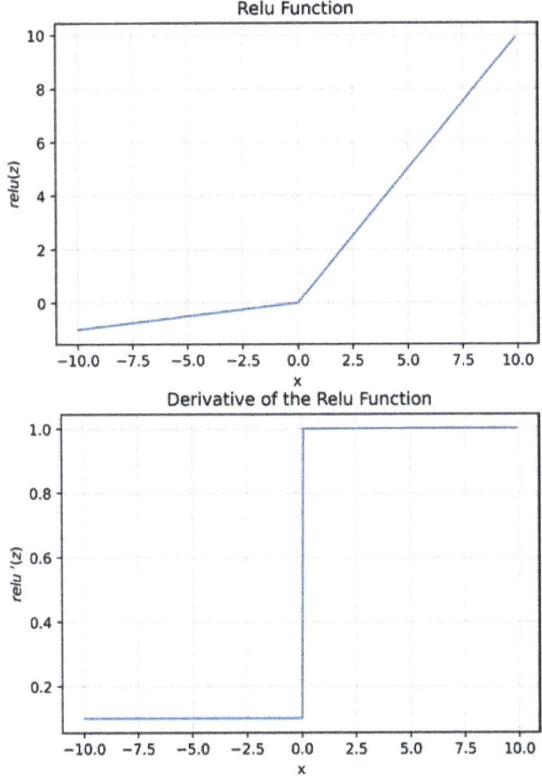

Figure 7.14: Relu activation function (monotonic, continuous, piecewise smooth, and differentiable), and its derivative (positive, discontinuous at the origin).

Note that Relu or leaky Relu function is not smooth, only piecewise differentiable, and not differentiable at the origin. Its gradient jumps at the origin as shown in Fig. 7.14. One would need to use the so-called *sub-gradient* in the optimization process (to be discussed in Chapter 9). The sub-gradient can be simply the average of the gradients on the both sides of the origin.

The non-smooth continuity of Relu function at the origin is similar to domain discretization via elements in the FEM [4] where the approximated function is continuous but not smooth on the elemental interfaces. The treatment of the non-smoothness in FEM is using the so-called weak form formulation.

7.7 Softplus Function

The softplus function has a similar shape as the rule, but is differentiable in the entire 1D space. It is defined as follows:

$$\phi(z) = \ln(1 + e^z) \tag{7.18}$$

It is clear that for any given argument of a real number z in $(-\infty, \infty)$, it returns a positive number within $(0, \infty)$.

The derivative of the softplus function is

$$\phi(z) = \sigma(z) = \frac{1}{1 + e^{-z}} \tag{7.19}$$

It is the sigmoid function (and hence it is also smooth and differentiable). We now plot the function and its derivative using `matplotlib`.

```python
import mxnet as mx
from mxnet import nd, autograd, gluon
import matplotlib.pyplot as plt
import numpy as np
from matplotlib import rc
%matplotlib inline

def softplus(z):
    return np.log(1. + np.exp(z))

def softplusg(z):
    return 1./(1. + np.exp(-z))

x = np.arange(-10, 10, .1)
y = softplus(x)
plt.plot(x,y)
plt.xlabel('x')
```

```python
plt.ylabel('Softplus')
plt.title('Softplus Function')
plt.grid(color='r', linestyle=':', linewidth=0.5)
plt.show()
plt.plot(x,softplusg(x))
plt.xlabel('x')
plt.ylabel('Derivative of Softplus function')
plt.grid(color='r', linestyle=':', linewidth=0.5)
plt.title('Derivative')
plt.show()
```

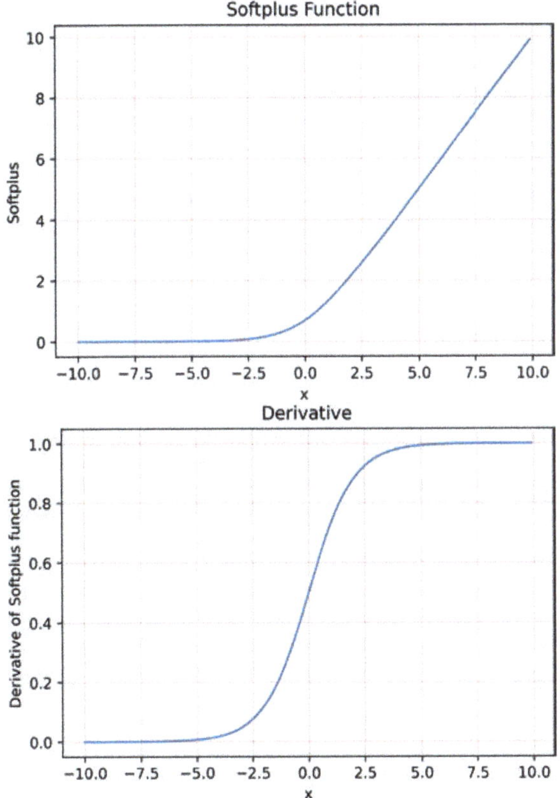

Figure 7.15: The softplus activation function (monotonic, continuous, smooth, and differentiable), and its derivative (positive, smooth, and further differentiable).

As shown Fig. 7.15, the softplus activation function is monotonic, continuous, smooth, and differentiable. Its derivative is positive, smooth, and further differentiable.

7.8 Conditions for activation functions

We now ready to list some conditions for an activation function.

(1) It should be monotonic for uniqueness requirement (see Section 5.5.3).
(2) It should be nonlinear for linearly independence requirement (see Section 5.8.2).
(3) Analytical formula is available for gradient computation, as in all the examples given in this chapter. Computation of gradients for ML models will be discussed in the next chapter.
(4) It does not contribute much in gradient vanishing. Relu is an excellent example. Its gradient stays at 1. Therefore, it does not contribute to gradient vanishing in a deepnet architecture.

7.9 Novel activation functions

Based on the conditions given in the previous section, we can now device some new activation functions. We present these functions below. Note that these functions have not yet be tested in machine learning models. Interested readers may give it a try.

7.9.1 *Rational activation function*

The ration function is a new type of activation function presented in this book for the first time (to the best knowledge of the author). It is equipped with parameter α that can be used to control the peak values of the derivation of the function. The α may also be treated as a trainable parameter, so that the derivative value also be trained. It has also a tunable function $Q(z)$. Therefore, it is a family of activation functions. The general form is defined as follows.

$$\phi(z) = \frac{Q(z)}{\alpha + |Q(z)|}; \quad z \in (-\infty, \infty) \tag{7.20}$$

where α is a constant in $\mathbb{R}$, and $Q(z)$ is an arbitrary function as long as it is (strictly) monotonically increasing with $z \in [0, \infty)$ and monotonically increasing with $z \in (-\infty, 0)$. Note that $\phi(z) \in (-1, 1)$. Its derivative can be easily found as

$$\phi'(z) = \frac{\alpha Q'(z)}{(\alpha + |Q(z)|)^2} \tag{7.21}$$

where $Q'(z)$ is the derivative of $Q(z)$.

Let, for example, $Q(z) = z$, we have the simplest rational activation function:

$$\phi(z) = \frac{z}{\alpha + |z|} \tag{7.22}$$

Its derivative can be easily found as

$$\phi'(z) = \frac{\alpha}{(\alpha + |z|)^2} \tag{7.23}$$

If we would like the rational activation function to be positive: $\phi(z) \in (0, 1)$, we need simply to do a positive shifting by 1.0 and then a scaling by 0.5, which gives,

$$\phi(z) = 0.5 \left(1 + \frac{z}{\alpha + |z|} \right) \tag{7.24}$$

In this case, its derivative becomes,

$$\phi'(z) = \frac{0.5\alpha}{(\alpha + |z|)^2} \tag{7.25}$$

The Python codes for this activation function and its derivative are given below.

```python
# Rational activation function by GR Liu; in (-1, 1)
def raf(z, alfa):
    f = [zi/(alfa-zi) if zi < 0.0 else zi/(alfa+zi) for zi in z]
    return f                  # or return z/(alfa+ np.abs(z))
    #return np.sign(z)*np.sqrt(np.abs(z))/(alfa+np.sqrt(np.abs(z)))
    #return np.sign(z)*z**2/(alfa+np.abs(z**2))


def d_raf(z,alfa):           # analytical derivative
    return alfa/(alfa+np.abs(z))**2


alfa = 2.0
x = np.arange(-10., 10., .1)     #x -> z
y = raf(x,alfa)
plt.plot(x,y)
plt.xlabel('z')
plt.ylabel('Function value')
plt.title('Rational activation function, in (-1, 1)')
plt.grid(color='r', linestyle=':', linewidth=0.5)
plt.savefig('raf.png',dpi=500,bbox_inches='tight')
plt.show()
plt.plot(x,d_raf(x,alfa))
plt.xlabel('z')
plt.ylabel('Derivative of the function')
```

```python
plt.grid(color='r', linestyle=':', linewidth=0.5)
plt.title('Derivative of the Rational activation function')
plt.savefig('d_raf.png',dpi=500,bbox_inches='tight')
plt.show()
```

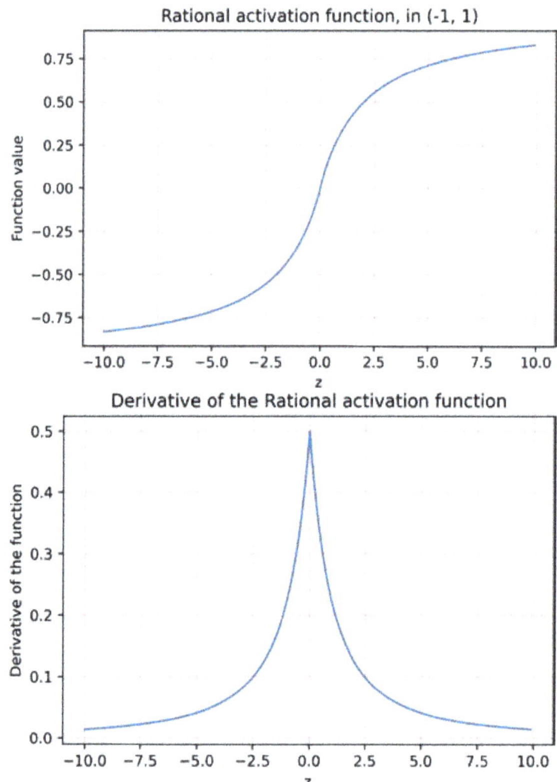

Figure 7.16: The rational activation function (monotonic, continuous, confined in $(-1, 1)$, smooth, and differentiable), and its derivative (positive, piecewise smooth, and further differentiable).

```python
# Rational activation function by GR Liu; in (0, 1)
def rafp(z, alfa):
#f=[.5*alfa/(alfa-zi) if zi<0. else (.5*alfa+zi)/(alfa+zi) for zi in z]
    f = [zi/(alfa-zi) if zi<0. else zi/(alfa+zi) for zi in z]
    return 0.5*(1.+np.array(f))


def d_rafp(z,alfa):             # analytical derivative
    return .5*alfa/(alfa+np.abs(z))**2


alfa = 2.0
```

```python
x = np.arange(-10., 10., .1)     #x -> z
y = rafp(x,alfa)
plt.plot(x,y)
plt.xlabel('z')
plt.ylabel('Function value')
plt.title('Rational activation function, in (0, 1)')
plt.grid(color='r', linestyle=':', linewidth=0.5)
plt.savefig('rafp.png',dpi=500,bbox_inches='tight')
plt.show()
plt.plot(x,d_rafp(x,alfa))
plt.xlabel('z')
plt.ylabel('Derivative of the function')
plt.grid(color='r', linestyle=':', linewidth=0.5)
plt.title('Derivative of the Rational activation function')
plt.savefig('d_rafp.png',dpi=500,bbox_inches='tight')
plt.show()
```

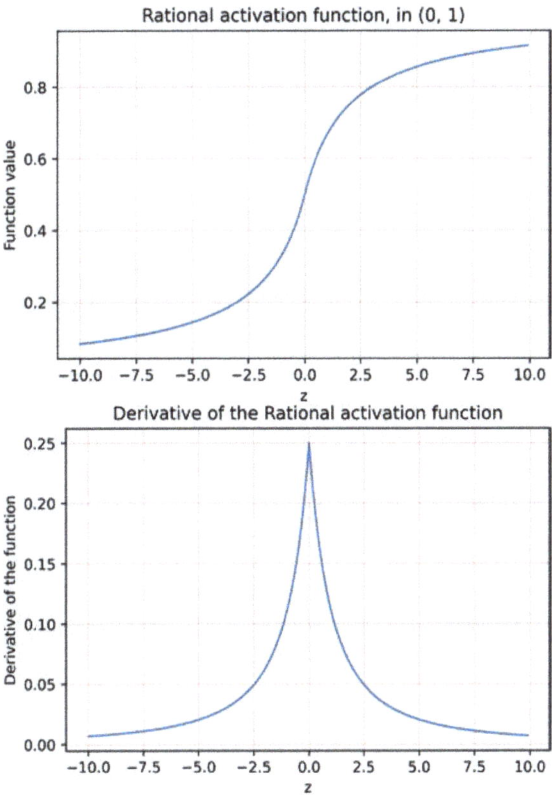

Figure 7.17: The rational activation function (monotonic, continuous, confined in $(0, 1)$, smooth, and differentiable), and its derivative (positive, piecewise smooth, and further differentiable).

7.9.2 *Power function*

The power function is another new type of activation function presented in this book (to be best knowledge of the author) for the first time. It is equipped with parameter α that can be used to control the degree of non-linearity for different nets and/or for different layers in a deepnet. This is also a family of activation functions. The general form is given as,

$$\phi(z) = \begin{cases} -(-z)^\alpha & z < 0 \\ z^\alpha & z \geq 0 \end{cases} \tag{7.26}$$

where α is a given positive constant limited by 1. Because $\alpha < 1$, the negative sign is needed when z is less than zero, or the output become a complex number. When $\alpha = 1$, it is linear. The smaller the α, the stronger the nonlinearity. The α may also be treated as a trainable parameter, so that the nonlinearity at different layers can also be trained.

Note that $\phi(z)$ defined in Eq.(7.26) is in $(-1, 1)$. If we would like it to be positive: $\phi(z) \in (0, 1)$, we need to do a shifting and then a scaling, as we have done earlier for the rational activation function.

Let us also write a code to examine the behavior of the power function.

```python
#Power function as an activation function

def powerf(z,alpha): # power function using list comprehension
    f = [-(-zi)**alpha if zi < 0.0 else zi**alpha for zi in z]
    return f

x0 = np.array([0.0,2.0])
x = np.arange(-2, 2, 0.11)
#alfa = np.arange(0.2, 1.2, .2)
alfa = 1.0/np.arange(1, 9, 1.0)
nx = 1
for ai in alfa:
    y = powerf(x,ai)
    plt.plot(x,y,label = r"$\alpha$="+"{:.2f}".format(ai))

plt.xlabel('z')
plt.ylabel("$\phi(z) $")
plt.title('Power Activation Function')
plt.grid(color='r', linestyle=':', linewidth=0.5)
plt.legend()
plt.savefig('paf.png',dpi=500,bbox_inches='tight')
plt.show()
```

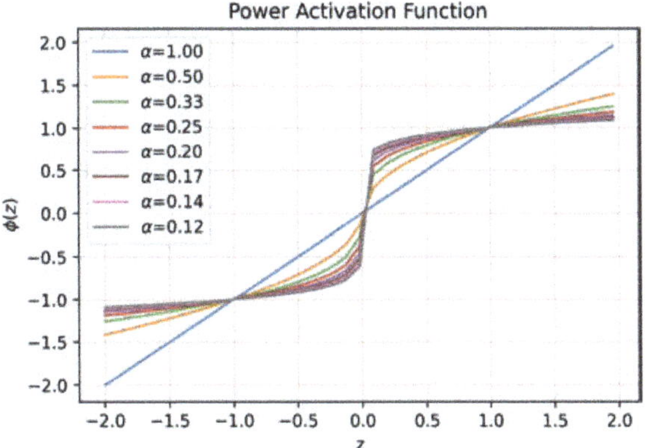

Figure 7.18: The power activation function. It is monotonic, continuous, piecewise smooth, and differentiable.

The above curves clearly show that when $\alpha \to 0$, it gives similar behavior as the tanh function. Therefore, we may choose a small α for the first hidden layer, and then let it grow when the net approaches the last layer. At the last layer we use $\alpha = 1$, a linear function that is exactly what we want.

The derivative of the power function is as follows.

$$\phi'(z) = \begin{cases} \alpha(-z)^{\alpha-1} & z < 0 \\ \alpha(z)^{\alpha-1} & z \geq 0 \end{cases} \tag{7.27}$$

We write the following code to examine the derivative of the power function.

```python
def powerg(z,alpha):
    a1 = alpha-1.
    g = [alpha*(-zi)**a1 if zi < 0.0 else alpha*zi**a1 for zi in z]
    return g


x0 = np.array([0.0,2.0])
x = np.arange(-2, 2, 0.11)
#alfa = np.arange(0.2, 1.2, .2)
alfa = 1.0/np.arange(1, 9, 1.0)


for ai in alfa:
    yg = powerg(x,ai)
    plt.plot(x,yg,label = r"$\alpha$="+"{:.2f}".format(ai))


plt.xlabel('z')
plt.ylabel("$\phi \ '(z) $")
plt.title('Derivative of the Power Activation Function')
```

```
plt.grid(color='r', linestyle=':', linewidth=0.5)
plt.legend()
plt.savefig('d_paf.png',dpi=500,bbox_inches='tight')
plt.show()
```

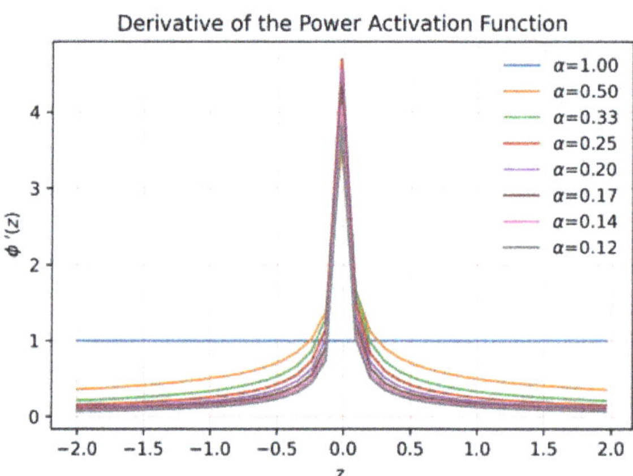

Figure 7.19: The derivative of the power activation function. It is positive, continuous, piecewise smooth, and further differentiable.

At a glance, the derivative of the power function is quite similar to that of the tanh function we have seen in the previous section, but it is not the same. The derivative of the power function goes to infinity at $z = 0$! Therefore, this can possibly lead a numerical problem.

We may now modify it, by introducing a linear piece near $z = 0$.

7.9.3 *Power-linear function*

The power-linear function is a modification to the power function, by using a linear function in the vicinity of $z = 0$, so that the derivative is bounded. It has the following form.

$$\phi(z) = \begin{cases} -(-z)^\alpha & z < -z_m \\ k_m z & -z_m \leq z < z_m \\ z^\alpha & z \geq z_m \end{cases} \tag{7.28}$$

where z_m is a positive value defining the half-width of the linear portion, and k_m is the derivative of the linear portion of the function near the vicinity of $z = 0$ computed using

$$k_m = z_m^{(\alpha-1)} \tag{7.29}$$

We examine the power-linear function, using the following code.

```python
#Power-linear(1) function as an activation function

def powerf1(z,alpha,xm):
    fm = xm**alpha
    km = fm / xm      # xm^(alpha-1)
    f = [-(-zi)**alpha if (zi<-xm) else km*zi if (-xm<=zi<=xm)\
        else zi**alpha for zi in z]
    return f

x0 = np.array([0.0,2.0])
x = np.arange(-1, 1, 0.01)
#alfa = np.arange(0.2, 1.2, .2)
alfa = 1.0/np.arange(1, 9, 1.0)
xm = 0.1
for ai in alfa:
    y = powerf1(x,ai,xm)
    plt.plot(x,y,label = r"$\alpha$="+"{:.2f}".format(ai))

plt.xlabel('z')
plt.ylabel("$\phi(z) $")
plt.title('Power-Linear Function')
plt.grid(color='r', linestyle=':', linewidth=0.5)
plt.legend()
plt.savefig('plaf.png',dpi=500,bbox_inches='tight')
plt.show()
```

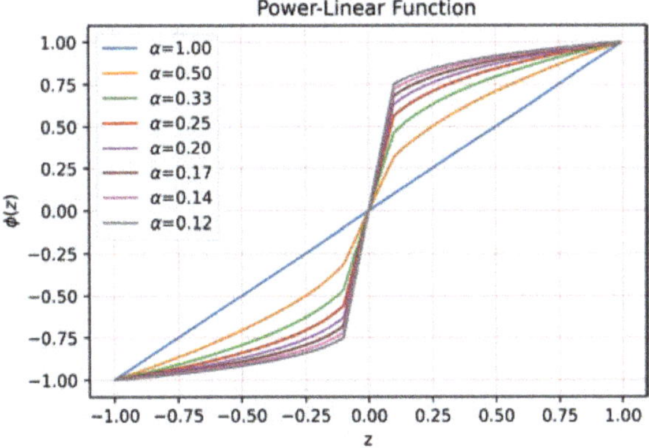

Figure 7.20:   The power-linear activation function. It is monotonic, continuous, piecewise smooth, and differentiable.

We do get a linear portion near $z = 0$, which connects the two pieces of power functions one each side. Let us look at the derivative of this power-linear function now. The formula is,

$$\phi'(z) = \begin{cases} \alpha(-z)^{\alpha-1} & z < -z_m \\ k_m & -z_m \leq z < z_m \\ \alpha(z)^{\alpha-1} & z \geq z_m \end{cases} \tag{7.30}$$

```python
#Power-linear(1) function, derivative of the function

def powerg1(z,alpha,xm):
    fm = xm**alpha
    km = fm / xm
    a1 = alpha-1.
    g = [alpha*(-zi)**a1 if zi<-xm else km if (-xm<=zi<=xm)\
        else alpha*zi**a1 for zi in z]
    return g

x0 = np.array([0.0,2.0])
x = np.arange(-1, 1, 0.01)
#alfa = np.arange(0.2, 1.2, .2)
alfa = 1.0/np.arange(1, 9, 1.0)

xm = 0.1
for ai in alfa:
    yg = powerg1(x,ai,xm)
    plt.plot(x,yg,label = r"$\alpha$="+"{:.2f}".format(ai))

plt.xlabel('z')
plt.ylabel("$\phi \' (z) $")
plt.title('Derivative of the Power-Linear Function')
plt.grid(color='r', linestyle=':', linewidth=0.5)
plt.legend()
plt.savefig('d_plaf.png',dpi=500,bbox_inches='tight')
plt.show()
```

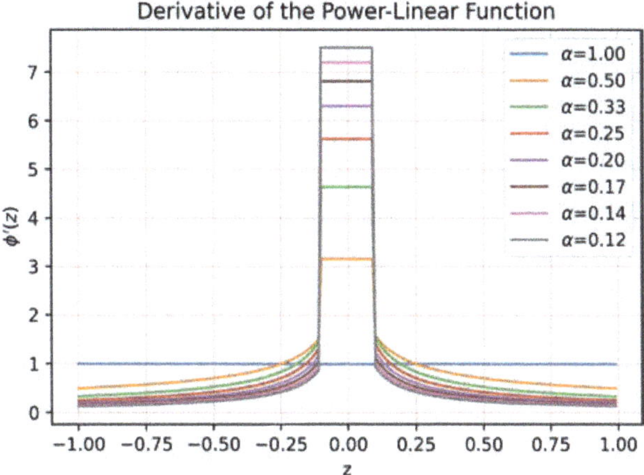

Figure 7.21:   The derivative of the power-linear activation function. It is positive, continuous, piecewise smooth, and differentiable.

Yes! The derivative is caped. We observe also that the smaller the α, the large the derivative value. This may be useful in mitigating the vanishing derivative problem in training deep nets. The vanishing derivative occurs when back-propagation is used to update the weights and biases using a gradient descent technique (to be discussed in great detail in Chapter 9), the derivatives get smaller and smaller due to the multiplication of the derivatives from the chain rule of differentiation (as shown in Chapter 8). With the power-linear function, one may get some help in reducing the vanishing rate, if it is placed properly in these layers.

We see also that the derivative has a plateau in the linear range. This can be improved further by the power-quadratic function.

7.9.4 *Power-quadratic function*

Finally, we examine the power-quadratic function. It is further modified from the power-linear function, by replacing the linear function portion with two pieces of quadratic function, so that the derivative can change linearly. This is done in the following process.

First, we compute the derivative at $z = 0$, which is the same as that for the power-linear function at $z = 0$:

$$k_m = z_m^{(\alpha-1)} \qquad (7.31)$$

Next, we compute the derivative at $z = z_m$, which gives,

$$k_p = \alpha z_m^{(\alpha-1)} \tag{7.32}$$

We now assume that the derivative varies linearly in $[-z_m, z_m]$, which give us

$$\phi'(z) = \begin{cases} -\dfrac{kp - km}{z_m}z + k_m & -z_m \leq z < 0 \\ \dfrac{kp - km}{z_m}z + k_m & 0 \leq z < z_m \end{cases} \tag{7.33}$$

We finally integrate the above function, and using the condition that it has to be zero at $z = 0$, we obtain,

$$\phi(z) = \begin{cases} -\dfrac{kp - km}{2z_m}z^2 + k_m z & -z_m \leq z < 0 \\ \dfrac{kp - km}{2z_m}z^2 + k_m z & 0 \leq z < z_m \end{cases} \tag{7.34}$$

Adding up the other two pieces on both side of the equation, we now have the full definition for the power-quadratic function:

$$\phi(z) = \begin{cases} -(-z)^\alpha & z < -z_m \\ -\dfrac{kp - km}{2z_m}z^2 + k_m z & -z_m \leq z < 0 \\ \dfrac{kp - km}{2z_m}z^2 + k_m z & 0 \leq z < z_m \\ z^\alpha & z \geq z_m \end{cases} \tag{7.35}$$

The derivative of the power-quadratic function becomes,

$$\phi'(z) = \begin{cases} \alpha(-z)^{\alpha-1} & z < -z_m \\ -\dfrac{kp - km}{z_m}z + k_m & -z_m \leq z < 0 \\ \dfrac{kp - km}{z_m}z + k_m & 0 \leq z < z_m \\ \alpha(z)^{\alpha-1} & z \geq z_m \end{cases} \tag{7.36}$$

Let us examine the power-quadratic function, using the following code.

```python
#Power-quadratic(2) function
def apowerf2(z,alpha,xm):
    a1 = alpha-1.
    fm = xm**alpha
    km = fm/xm
    kp= alpha*xm**a1
    kg = (kp-km)/xm
    f = [-(-zi)**alpha if (zi<-xm) else km*zi-0.5*kg*zi**2\
        if (-xm<=zi<0.) else km*zi+0.5*kg*zi**2 if (0.<=zi<=xm)\
        else zi**alpha for zi in z]
    return f

x0 = np.array([0.0,2.0])
x = np.arange(-2, 2, 0.02)
#alfa = np.arange(0.2, 1.2, .2)
alfa = 1.0/np.arange(1, 9, 1.0)

xm = 0.1
for ai in alfa:
    y = apowerf2(x,ai,xm)
    plt.plot(x,y,label = r"$\alpha$="+"{:.2f}".format(ai))

plt.xlabel('z')
plt.ylabel("$\phi(z) $")
plt.title('Power-Quadratic Activation Function')
plt.grid(color='r', linestyle=':', linewidth=0.5)
plt.legend()
plt.savefig('pqaf.png',dpi=500,bbox_inches='tight')
plt.show()
```

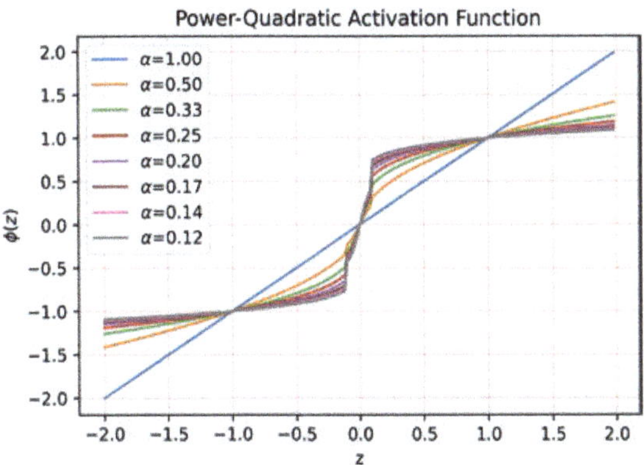

Figure 7.22: The power-quadratic activation function. It is monotonic, continuous, piecewise smooth, and differentiable.

```python
#Power-quadratic(2) function, derivative

def apowerg2(z,alpha,xm):
    a1 = alpha-1.
    fm = xm**alpha
    km = fm/xm
    kp= alpha*xm**a1
    kg = (kp-km)/xm
    g = [alpha*(-zi)**a1 if zi<-xm else -kg*zi+km\
         if (-xm<=zi < 0.) else kg*zi+km if (0.<=zi <xm)\
         else alpha*zi**a1 for zi in z]
    return g

#x0 = np.array([0.0,2.0])
x = np.arange(-1, 1, 0.002)
#alfa = np.arange(0.2, 1.2, .2)
alfa = 1.0/np.arange(1, 9, 1.0)

xm = 0.1
for ai in alfa:
    yg = apowerg2(x,ai,xm)
    plt.plot(x,yg,label = r"$\alpha$="+"{:.2f}".format(ai))

plt.xlabel('z')
plt.ylabel("$\phi \ '(z) $")
plt.title('Derivative Power-Quadratic Activation Function')
plt.grid(color='r', linestyle=':', linewidth=0.5)
plt.legend()
plt.savefig('d_pqaf.png',dpi=500,bbox_inches='tight')
plt.show()
```

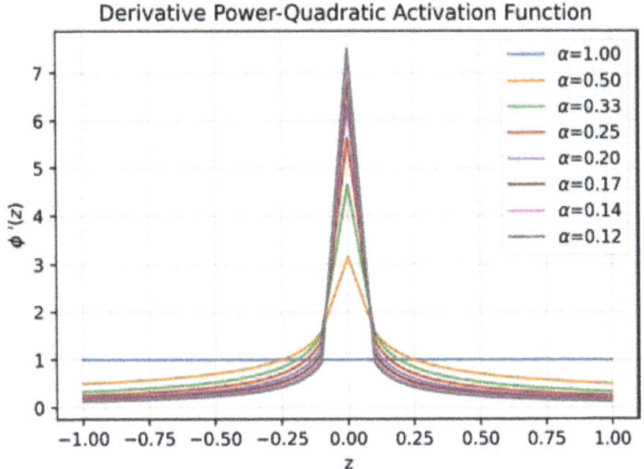

Figure 7.23: The derivative of the power-quadratic activation function. It is positive, continuous, piecewise smooth, and differentiable.

The plateau in the linear range is now removed with a nice linearly varying derivative. We still observe that the smaller the α, the large the derivative value. This may be useful in mitigating the vanishing derivative problem in training deepnets. Thorough tests are required for this proposed set of power functions, in its application to practical problems.

References

[1] G. Cybenko, Approximation by superpositions of a sigmoidal function, *Mathematics of Control, Signals and Systems*, **2**, 303–314, 1989.

[2] G.R. Liu, A neural element method, *International Journal of Computational Methods*, **17**(07), 2050021, 2020.

[3] G.R. Liu, *Mesh Free Methods: Moving Beyond the Finite Element Method*, Taylor and Francis Group, New York, 2010.

[4] G.R. Liu and S.S. Quek, *The finite element method: A practical course*, Butterworth-Heinemann, London, 2013.

[5] V. Nair and G.E. Hinton, Rectified Linear Units Improve Restricted Boltzmann Machines, *Proceedings of the 27th International Conference on Machine Learning*, 2010.

Chapter 8

Automatic Differentiation and Autograd

8.1 General Issues on Optimization and Minimization

In machine learning, we would like the models such as neural networks to learn by mistakes, through feeding it with teaching (or training) samples, so that it knows where the errors are made. The measurement of error uses the so-called **loss function** that evaluates, in some predefined formulas, the difference between the predicted results (the output of current model) and the ground truth (labels) given by training samples.

Loss function is sometimes also called cost function or objective function. They all are *essentially* the same, but can have different names to make better sense for problems of different purposes. The name of "objective function" is more neutral and can be used for both optimization and minimization settings. Loss or cost function implies a minimization problem, because the purpose is clearly for minimizing the cost or loss. From now on, we do not distinguish these names in our discussion, but use more often the name of loss function for machine learning models. The smaller the value of the loss function, we generally say the better the model (in training accuracy). Therefore, the training process is essentially a process of minimizing the loss function.

Optimization is equivalent to minimization in mathematics, because one can simply flip the sign of the objective function and then the optimization problem becomes a minimization problem or vice versa. Therefore, we do not distinguish the optimization and minimization techniques in theory. Care is needed when calling a routine function from an existing module to make sure whether it is for optimization or minimization. One may need to flip the sign of the objection function accordingly, before feeding it to the function.

The next question would be how to design optimization (or minimization) techniques, to effectively find the maximum (or minimum). In the past, quite a number of optimization techniques (https://en.wikipedia.org/wiki/Mathematical_optimization) had been developed. There are techniques that use gradient information of the objective function, and those that do not. In general, the techniques that used the gradient information work more efficiently, and hence it is used whenever the gradient information can be made available in a cost-effective manner. For machine learning models such as NNs, gradient-based techniques have been found effective. This is because the prediction functions (Chapter 5) and the activation function (Chapter 7) used in NNs are continuous functions of the learning parameters, and hence the gradient is computable. The applicability of a gradient-based minimizer depends largely on whether we can compute the gradient of the loss function efficiently.

In this chapter, we consider functions in general areas of study in science and engineering, including machine learning. Therefore, without losing generality, the function to be differentiated is denoted in general as $f(\mathbf{x})$ with $\mathbf{x}$ being the independent variables. Also, $\mathbf{x}$ is defined as a column vector as in a more conventional way. In machine learning, however, our function would be the loss function $\mathcal{L}(\hat{\mathbf{w}})$ and the independent variable would be the learning parameters $\hat{\mathbf{w}}$. Care is needed to avoid confusion.

There are three major types of methods to compute the gradient of a function: analytical method, numerical method, and automatic differentiation method or Autograd. We first briefly discuss the analytical method.

8.2 Analytic Differentiation

The analytical method explicitly gives the formulas for the derivatives of functions. Table 8.1 lists some scalar functions often used in ML, $f(x)$, with variable x also being a scalar, together with their derivatives $\frac{f(x)}{dx}$. These formulas can be coded directly for computing the derivatives, and symbolic computational tools such as SymPy can be used to obtain the expression of the derivatives. However, such formulas may not be available for all functions. Also, not all functions can be explicitly written in such a simple closed form,

Table 8.1: Analytical formulas for derivatives of simple functions (c, n are constants).

$f(x) = c$	cx^n	e^{cx}	$log(cx)$	$\dfrac{1}{1+e^{-cx}}$	$\dfrac{e^{cx} - e^{-cx}}{e^{cx} + e^{-cx}}$
$\dfrac{df}{dx} = 0$	ncx^{n-1}	ce^{cx}	$\dfrac{1}{x}$	$\dfrac{ce^{-cx}}{(e^{cx} + e^{-cx})^2}$	$c\left(1 - \left(\dfrac{e^{cx} - e^{-cx}}{e^{cx} + e^{-cx}}\right)^2\right)$

let alone their derivatives. Most importantly, expressions of the derivatives of many functions can be very complicated and hence difficult to implement in a code.

8.3 Numerical Differentiation

Numerical methods compute gradient or derivative of a function using essentially the finite difference method (FDM), curve fitting, and interpolation techniques. The smoothing domain based methods used in the smoothed finite element methods [1] and the meshfree methods [2] have been found effective for computing the gradient of functions in lower dimensions. Numerical methods usually give approximated gradient results for all differentiable functions, as long as their numerical values are available at the nodes of a mesh or at a set of points given in the vicinity of the location of interest. However, it can be a challenge for high dimensional space, and also for a chain of functions that we often encounter in machine learning. Although the approximation in the results may not be an issue, the complexity in the implementation could be. The numerical method is not used in this book for creating ML models.

8.4 Automatic Differentiation

8.4.1 *The concept of automatic or algorithmic differentiation*

Automatic differentiation (AD) is sometimes also called algorithmic differentiation (http://www.autodiff.org/?module=Publications&submenu=list%20publications&id=neidinger2010ita). It is a technique to evaluate the value of differentiation via a computer algorithm. The **essential idea** is to simultaneously compute the involved functions and their derivatives into numerical numbers, so that the arithmetic operations among them can be done simply in numerical numbers, avoiding such operations at expression level. This drastically simplifies coding. The results are numerical but is exact (in theory with machine accuracy), because all the rules of differentiation are still followed exactly, which is fundamentally different from the numerical differentiation mentioned earlier. It has the following features:

- It uses the chain rule of differentiation, so that the differentiation of the final loss function becomes a product of the *local derivatives* (derivatives of local function at the "node" in a computational graph).

- It constructs a process to split the complicated functions into elementary arithmetic operations (addition, subtraction, multiplication, division, analytic differentiation of simple functions, etc.), so that derivatives for those functions can be computed using exact analytical formulas.
- It records the results of differentiation with respect to a variable, together with the variable itself (as one of its attributes), for convenient recording, automation and computation. This is because the gradient and the variable have the same shape.

In neural network-based machine learning models, the AD is one of the key techniques for its success. Types of algorithms based on AD are readily available, and often known as autograd. It can be conveniently used to compute the gradients for a number of parameter variables in automatic fashion. Many libraries allow users to visualize a computational graph of the net constructed. Such a graph is essentially a logical path for computing the local derivatives in the chained nodes.

8.4.2 *Differentiation of a function with respect to a vector and matrix*

The loss function for machine learning is usually in a form of scalar function. Even if it is not, one can always make it a scalar function by, for example, measuring its norm in some way. However, their variables can often be vectors or matrices. Consider a scalar function $f(\mathbf{x}) \in \mathbb{R}^1$ defined in a P-dimensional space, the variable vector $\mathbf{x}$ will be in $\mathbb{R}^P$. The gradient of the function $\nabla f(\mathbf{x})$ is a vector and will also be in $\mathbb{R}^P$,

$$\nabla f(\mathbf{x}) = \frac{\partial f(\mathbf{x})}{\partial \mathbf{x}} = \frac{\partial f(\mathbf{x})}{\partial \begin{bmatrix} x_1 \\ x_2 \\ \vdots \\ x_m \end{bmatrix}} = \begin{bmatrix} \dfrac{\partial f(\mathbf{x})}{\partial x_1} \\ \dfrac{\partial f(\mathbf{x})}{\partial x_2} \\ \vdots \\ \dfrac{\partial f(\mathbf{x})}{\partial x_m} \end{bmatrix} \tag{8.1}$$

When the variables are in a matrix form, we shall have

$$\nabla f(\mathbf{x}) = \frac{\partial f(\mathbf{x})}{\partial \mathbf{x}} = \frac{\partial f(\mathbf{x})}{\partial \begin{bmatrix} x_{11} & x_{12} & \cdots & x_{1p} \\ x_{21} & x_{22} & \cdots & x_{2p} \\ \vdots & \vdots & \vdots & \vdots \\ x_{m1} & x_{m2} & \cdots & x_{mp} \end{bmatrix}} = \begin{bmatrix} \frac{\partial f(\mathbf{x})}{\partial x_{11}} & \frac{\partial f(\mathbf{x})}{\partial x_{12}} & \cdots & \frac{\partial f(\mathbf{x})}{\partial x_{1p}} \\ \frac{\partial f(\mathbf{x})}{\partial x_{21}} & \frac{\partial f(\mathbf{x})}{\partial x_{22}} & \cdots & \frac{\partial f(\mathbf{x})}{\partial x_{2p}} \\ \vdots & \vdots & \vdots & \vdots \\ \frac{\partial f(\mathbf{x})}{\partial x_{m1}} & \frac{\partial f(\mathbf{x})}{\partial x_{m2}} & \cdots & \frac{\partial f(\mathbf{x})}{\partial x_{mp}} \end{bmatrix}$$

$$(8.2)$$

When we seek the derivatives for a scalar function with respect to a vector or matrix of variables, what this really means is that we want the (partial) derivatives of the function with respect to each one of the variables in the vector (both row or column) or matrix. Therefore, all we need to do is to perform the differentiation of the function with respect to these variables one by one, as we do for the scalar variable case shown in Table 8.1. This can be easily done using the element-wise operations in Python. As a result, we simply replace x in Table 8.1 by the vector or matrix $\mathbf{x}$. In this case, the derivative of the function shall become a vector or matrix that contains the derivatives of the function with respect to each variable. Such a derivative vector or matrix can have the same shape as that of the variable vector of matrix, can be computed simultaneously, and stored together as an additional attribute. It is essentially what is done in Autograd.

Table 8.2 gives some often used functions and their gradient. In machine learning algorithms, we need to frequently compute the norm of vectors, and the summation of the elements in vectors, which results in special functions: $f(\mathbf{x}) = \|\mathbf{x}\|^2$, $f(\mathbf{x}) = sum(\mathbf{x})$. These special functions are all scalars, and the above arguments still hold. Because their variables are a vector, the gradient of these special functions will become a vector. For sum function of a vector $\mathbf{x}$, the gradient becomes a vector of ones. For the squared-norm function of a vector $\mathbf{x}$, the gradient becomes two times the $\mathbf{x}$, which is also a vector. In addition, when f is a constant vector $\mathbf{c}$, its gradient becomes the vector of zeros, as shown in Table 8.2.

In Table 8.2, b is a contact, c is a contact, $\mathbf{c}$ is a vector of constants, and $\mathbf{C}$ is a matrix of constants. All these constants do not change with $\mathbf{x}$. We assume all the matrices have compatible shape (dimensions). The C-scalar can also be a norm (C-norm, positive), if $\mathbf{C}$ is positive definite. The same is true for X-scalar. The $\nabla f(\mathbf{x})$ has the same shape of $\mathbf{x}$.

Table 8.2:   Analytical formulas for the gradients of some useful scalar functions.

Function Name	$f(\mathbf{x})$	$\nabla f(\mathbf{x})$
Constant	c	$\mathbf{0}$
Linear	$\mathbf{x}^\top\mathbf{c} = \mathbf{c}^\top\mathbf{x}$	$\mathbf{c}$
General exponential	$e^{\mathbf{x}^\top\mathbf{c}+b}$	$\mathbf{c}e^{\mathbf{x}^\top\mathbf{c}+b}$
General logarithm	$log(\mathbf{x}^\top\mathbf{c}+b)$	$\dfrac{-\mathbf{c}}{\mathbf{x}^\top\mathbf{c}+b}$
Sigmoid	$\dfrac{1}{1+e^{-\mathbf{x}^\top\mathbf{c}+b}}$	$\dfrac{\mathbf{c}e^{-\mathbf{x}^\top\mathbf{c}+b}}{(e^{\mathbf{x}^\top\mathbf{c}}+e^{-\mathbf{x}^\top\mathbf{c}+b})^2}$
tanh	$\dfrac{e^{\mathbf{x}^\top\mathbf{c}+b}-e^{-\mathbf{x}^\top\mathbf{c}+b}}{e^{\mathbf{x}^\top\mathbf{c}+b}+e^{-\mathbf{x}^\top\mathbf{c}+b}}$	$\mathbf{c}\left(1-\left(\dfrac{e^{\mathbf{x}^\top\mathbf{c}+b}-e^{-\mathbf{x}^\top\mathbf{c}+b}}{e^{\mathbf{x}^\top\mathbf{c}+b}+e^{-\mathbf{x}^\top\mathbf{c}+b}}\right)^2\right)$
summation	$sum(\mathbf{x})$	$\mathbf{1}$
norm (quadratic in $\mathbf{x}$)	$\|\mathbf{x}\|^2 = \mathbf{x}^\top\mathbf{x}$	$2\mathbf{x}$
C-scalar (quadratic in $\mathbf{x}$)	$\mathbf{x}^\top\mathbf{C}\mathbf{x}$	$2\mathbf{C}\mathbf{x}$
X-scalar (linear in $\mathbf{X}$)	$\mathbf{c}^\top\mathbf{X}\mathbf{c}$	$\mathbf{c}\mathbf{c}^\top$

Table 8.1 is obvious and writing it down needs only college calculus. However, writing Table 8.2 requires careful derivation. The best way may be using the tensor calculus, by first converting the matrix notation to (Ricci) index notation, performing the differentiations, and then converting back to matrix form. Using the tensor calculus, one can further derive formulas for vector or even matrix functions with tensor variables. Here, we will not discuss this in detail.

8.5 Autograd Implemented in Numpy

Autograd brings the automatic differentiation into Numpy (Oliphant, 2007) and Scipy (Jones *et al.*, 2001). Let us practice this. We first use the autograd.numpy to compute the derivatives of given analytical functions. For this, we need to install autograd (using pip install autograd or conda install-c conda-forge autograd). We then import the autograd.numpy model and grad() function.

```python
#import numpy as np
import autograd.numpy as np    # This is a thinly-wrapped numpy
from autograd import grad      # for computing grad(f)
import matplotlib.pyplot as plt
%matplotlib inline
```

```python
def f_sigma(z):              # The sigmoid function
    return 1./(1.+np.exp(-z))
def dfsa(z):
    return f_sigma(z)*(1.-f_sigma(z)) # analytical derivative

df1 = grad(f_sigma)          # function for the 1st derivative of f
df2 = grad(df1)              # for the 2nd derivative of f
df3 = grad(df2)              # ......
df4 = grad(df3)
df5 = grad(df4)
z = np.linspace(-5,5,200) # create values of arguments, z
fi = f_sigma(z)              # compute the discrete values of f()
df1i = []
for i in range(len(z)):   # compute df1 by passing z one-by-one
    df1i.append(df1(z[i]))

df1ia = grad(f_sigma)(z[0])
df2i = list(map(df2,z))     # compute df2
plt.figure(figsize=(4.5, 3.0),dpi=100)
plt.scatter(z, df1i,c='green',label='Autograd',alpha=0.2)
plt.plot(z, dfsa(z),c='red',label='Analytical')
plt.xlabel('z')
plt.ylabel(r"$\sigma'(z)$")
plt.title('Derivative of Sigmoid: analytic vs. autograd')
plt.grid(color='r', linestyle=':', linewidth=0.5)
plt.legend()
plt.show ()

plt.figure(figsize=(4.5, 3.0),dpi=100)
plt.plot(z, fi,label='Function')
plt.plot(z, df1i,label='1st derivative')
plt.plot(z, df2i,label='2nd derivative')
plt.plot(z, list(map(df3,z)),label='3rd derivative')
plt.plot(z, list(map(df4,z)),label='4th derivative')
plt.xlabel('z')
plt.ylabel(r'$\sigma(z) $'+' and its derivatives')
plt.title('Derivatives of sigmoid function via autograd')
plt.grid(color='r', linestyle=':', linewidth=0.5)
plt.legend()
plt.show ()
```

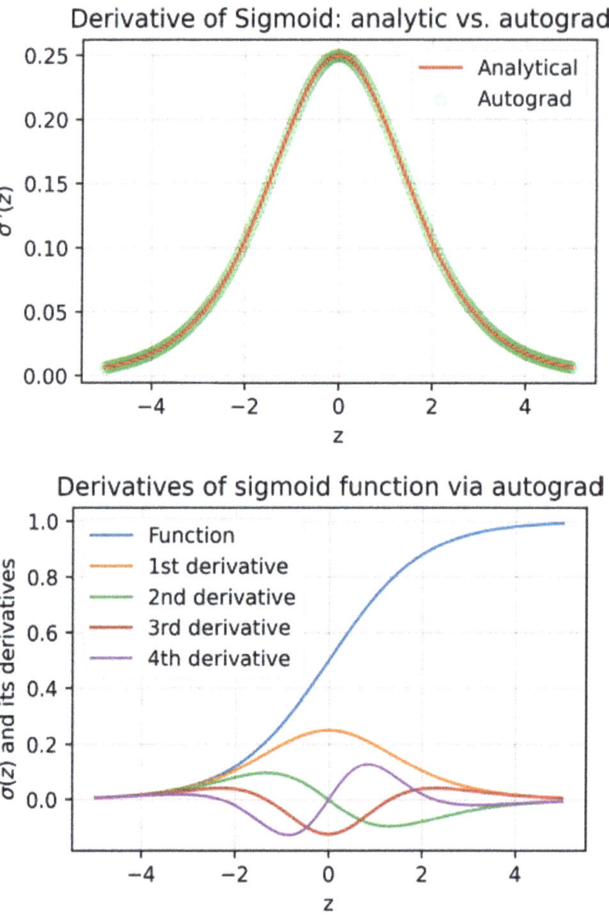

Figure 8.1:   Computed derivatives of functions using autograd.

As seen from Fig. 8.1, autograd is a powerful means to compute derivatives of functions. It is produces exact derivatives (to machine accuracy), and is capable of computing higher order of derivatives so long as the function is differentiable to the order.

8.6 Autograd Implemented in the MXNet

Autograd has been implemented in many well-established modules. Next, we use the mxnet.autograd module to demonstrate how to automatically calculate derivatives of a loss function with respect to its variables. Once a parameter variable is specified for gradients, and the chain of the sub-functions for the loss function is defined, the autograd builds a graph on the fly (https://d2l.ai/chapter_preliminaries/autograd.html). It then computes backwards the gradients of the loss function with respect to the variables. The following discussion and the codes are written in reference to these at mxnet-the-straight-dope (https://github.com/zackchase/mxnet-the-straight-dope), under the Apache-2.0 License:

```python
import numpy as np
import mxnet as mx
from mxnet import nd, autograd
mx.random.seed(1)
```

8.6.1 *Gradients of scalar functions with simple variable*

As a toy example, we take the gradient of a simple function defined as

$$f = 8(x^2) \quad \text{for } x \in \mathbb{R}^1 \tag{8.3}$$

with respect to parameter variable x in one dimension. The gradient is just the derivative in this one-dimensional case with only x, because there is only one parameter variable. For this simple function, we know the gradient (derivative) can be calculated analytically using the following equation,

$$\frac{df(x)}{dx} = 16x \quad \text{for } x \in \mathbb{R}^1 \tag{8.4}$$

for any given x value in $\mathbb{R}^1$.

In this demonstration, we start by assigning the values of x, at which the derivatives of $f(x)$ can be computed. If x is given in a vector or matrix or in general in a tensor, the corresponding derivatives are computed and will be in the same shape. This is quite similar to the general element-wise operations in Python: the same differentiation is done at all the x values in the tensor. We now define a matrix of x values as follows:

```python
x=nd.array([[1,5,10],[20,18,28]]) # initialization of x
                                  # in a matrix (tensor)
```

At all these values of x in the above matrix, we can easily compute the gradient using analytical formula given in Eq. (8.4).

```python
print('x=',x)
grad_at_x = 16.0*x                      # analytical gradient
print('Analytical grad_at_x=', grad_at_x)
```

```
x=
[[ 1.   5.  10.]
 [20. 18.  28.]]
<NDArray 2x3 @cpu(0)>
Analytical grad_at_x=
[[ 16.   80.  160.]
 [320. 288.  448.]]
<NDArray 2x3 @cpu(0)>
```

We note that the shape of x and grad_at_x is the same.

In MXNet, the gradient computation requires three steps.

First, we request a gradient for a variable, say x. We need it to be stored in x.grad(). This is done by first invoking

```
x.attach_grad()            # request for gradient w.r.t
                           # all entries in matrix x
```

Second, we need to define the function f, which is often given in a chain of functions $(x-> g-> f$, as shown in the example below).

```
with autograd.record():    # record down the path
    g = x * 8              # x -> g
    f = g * x              # g -> f
```

This defines a path for carrying out the differentiation and the related evaluations. This path of differentiation is also called *graph*. The definition of the chain or path builds a computation graph. The differentiation is then done using the well-known chain rule of differentiation. MXNet builds such a graph on the fly, using a kind of recording "device", which record the path.

Third, with the path defined, we can finally invoke

```
f.backward()    # compute the gradient in a back-propagation
```

which calls for differentiations to be carried out backwards in the defined path, known as backprop in machine learning. To this end, the gradient values are computed and stored at x.grad, as an attribute of object x.

We finally print out the gradient values stored at x.grad.

```
print('At x=',x)
print('The gradient values of f at x=', x.grad) # autograd
print('Analytical grad_at_x=', grad_at_x)        # analytical
```

```
At x=
[[ 1.   5. 10.]
 [20. 18. 28.]]
<NDArray 2x3 @cpu(0)>
The gradient values of f at x=
[[ 16.  80. 160.]
 [320. 288. 448.]]
<NDArray 2x3 @cpu(0)>
Analytical grad_at_x=
[[ 16.  80. 160.]
 [320. 288. 448.]]
<NDArray 2x3 @cpu(0)>
```

We note again that the shape of x and x.grad is the same. x stores all these x values, and x.grad stores the corresponding gradients at these x values. We can see that the gradient value obtained at x using autograd is exactly the same as those we got using the analytic formula.

8.6.2 *Gradients of scalar functions in high dimensions*

Let us now consider the gradients of a scalar function with multiple variables (multiple dimensional problems). We compute the gradients of some scalar functions listed in Table 8.2. The first is the linear function defined in p-dimensional space.

$$f(\mathbf{x}) = \mathbf{x}^\top \mathbf{c} \quad \text{for } \mathbf{x} \in \mathbb{R}^p \tag{8.5}$$

where $\mathbf{c}$ is vector of constants. It is also in $\mathbb{R}^p$, so that $f(\mathbf{x})$ become a scalar.

```python
c = nd.array([.1, .8, .18])      # 3 constants
x = nd.array([1., 2., 3.])       # 3 independent variables
x.attach_grad()                  # request gradient w.r.t x

with autograd.record():          # record the path
    f = x.T * c                  # or f = nd.dot(x, c)

f.backward()                     # compute gradient
print('At x=',x, '  Constants c = ',c)
print('The gradient values of f at x=', x.grad)
print('The analytical gradient values of f at x=', c)
```

```
At x=
[1. 2. 3.]
<NDArray 3 @cpu(0)>   Constants c =
[0.1  0.8  0.18]
<NDArray 3 @cpu(0)>
The gradient values of f at x=
[0.1  0.8  0.18]
<NDArray 3 @cpu(0)>
The analytical gradient values of f at x=
[0.1  0.8  0.18]
<NDArray 3 @cpu(0)>
```

We observe the agreement of the results obtained using autograd and the analytical method. We now examine the general exponential function in p-dimensional space.

$$f(\mathbf{x}) = exp(\mathbf{x}^\top \mathbf{c}) \quad \text{for} \ \ \mathbf{x} \in \mathbb{R}^p \tag{8.6}$$

where $\mathbf{c}$ is vector of constants. It is also in $\mathbb{R}^p$.

```python
x.attach_grad()               # Request gradient w.r.t x
                              # that is a vector
with autograd.record():       # Record down the path
    f = nd.exp(nd.dot(x,c))

f.backward()                  # compute gradient
print('At x=',x, '  Constants c = ',c)
print('The gradient values of f at x=', x.grad)
print('The analytical gradient values of f at x=', \
      c*nd.exp(nd.dot(x,c)))
```

```
At x=
[1. 2. 3.]
<NDArray 3 @cpu(0)>   Constants c =
[0.1  0.8  0.18]
<NDArray 3 @cpu(0)>
The gradient values of f at x=
[0.93933314 7.514665   1.6907997 ]
<NDArray 3 @cpu(0)>
The analytical gradient values of f at x=
[0.93933314 7.514665   1.6907997 ]
<NDArray 3 @cpu(0)>
```

We observe again the agreement of the results obtained using autograd and the analytical method (in machine accuracy). We now examine the general logarithmic function in p-dimensional space.

$$f(\mathbf{x}) = log(\mathbf{x}^\top \mathbf{c}) \quad \text{for} \ \ \mathbf{x} \in \mathbb{R}^p \tag{8.7}$$

where $\mathbf{c}$ is vector of constants. It is also in $\mathbb{R}^p$.

```python
c = nd.array([.1, .8, .18])      # 3 constants
x = nd.array([1, 2, 3])          # 3 independent variables
x.attach_grad()                  # request gradient w.r.t. x

with autograd.record():          # record down the path
    f = nd.log(nd.dot(x,c))

f.backward() # compute gradient via back-prop.
print('At x=',x, '  Constants c = ',c)
print('The gradient values of f at x=', x.grad)
print('The analytical gradient values of f at x=',\
      c/(nd.dot(x,c)))
```

```
At x=
[1. 2. 3.]
<NDArray 3 @cpu(0)>    Constants c =
[0.1  0.8  0.18]
<NDArray 3 @cpu(0)>
The gradient values of f at x=
[0.04464286 0.35714287 0.08035714]
<NDArray 3 @cpu(0)>
The analytical gradient values of f at x=
[0.04464286 0.35714287 0.08035715]
<NDArray 3 @cpu(0)>
```

Now, the general form of the sigmoid function is in Table 8.2.

```python
x.attach_grad()                  # request gradient w.r.t. x

def sigma_nd(z):                 # Define the sigmoid function
    return 1./(1.+nd.exp(-z))

def ds_nd(z):                    # analytical derivative
    return sigma_nd(z)*(1.-sigma_nd(z))
```

```python
with autograd.record():            # record down the path
    f = sigma_nd(nd.dot(x,c))

f.backward()                       # compute gradient via back-prop.
print('At x=',x, '  Constants c = ',c)
print('The gradient values of f at x=', x.grad)
print('The analytical gradient values of f at x=',\
      c*ds_nd(nd.dot(x,c)))
```

```
At x=
[1. 2. 3.]
<NDArray 3 @cpu(0)>   Constants c =
[0.1  0.8  0.18]
<NDArray 3 @cpu(0)>
The gradient values of f at x=
[0.00869581 0.06956648 0.01565246]
<NDArray 3 @cpu(0)>
The analytical gradient values of f at x=
[0.00869581 0.0695665  0.01565246]
<NDArray 3 @cpu(0)>
```

Finally, the general form of the tanh function is in Table 8.2.

```python
c = nd.array([.1, .8, .18])        # 3 constants
x = nd.array([1., 2., 3.])         # 3 variables
x.attach_grad()                    # request gradient

def tanh_nd(z):                    # Define the function
    return (nd.exp(z)-nd.exp(-z))/(nd.exp(z)+nd.exp(-z))

def dtanh_nd(z):
    return (1.-tanh_nd(z)**2)      # analytical derivative

with autograd.record():            # record down the path
    f = tanh_nd(nd.dot(x,c))

f.backward()                       # compute gradient
print('At x=',x, '  Constants c = ',c)
print('The gradient values of f at x=', x.grad)
print('The analytical gradient values of f at x=',\
      c*dtanh_nd(nd.dot(x,c)))
```

```
At x=
[1. 2. 3.]
<NDArray 3 @cpu(0)>   Constants c =
[0.1  0.8  0.18]
<NDArray 3 @cpu(0)>
The gradient values of f at x=
[0.00443234 0.03545868 0.0079782 ]
<NDArray 3 @cpu(0)>
The analytical gradient values of f at x=
[0.00443233 0.03545866 0.0079782 ]
<NDArray 3 @cpu(0)>
```

Next, we compute the gradient of a summation function with a vector of variables.

```python
from mxnet import autograd, nd
x1d = nd.arange(4)          # create a 1D vector
x1d.attach_grad()           # request gradients
print(x1d)


with autograd.record():
    f = x1d.sum()           # summation function.


f.backward()                # compute gradient via back-prop.
x1d.grad
```

```
[0. 1. 2. 3.]
<NDArray 4 @cpu(0)>

[1. 1. 1. 1.]
<NDArray 4 @cpu(0)>
```

It gives a vector of all ones, as expected (see Table 8.2).

Dot-product (the inner product) is one of the most often used operations, which also results in a scalar function. It is the same as the squared-norm function in Table 8.2. We compute the squared-norm function and its derivatives with respect to its vector variable.

```python
from mxnet import autograd, nd
x1d = nd.arange(4)          # create a 1D vector
x1d.attach_grad()           # request gradients
x1d
```

```
[0. 1. 2. 3.]
<NDArray 4 @cpu(0)>
```

```
x1d.grad                        # current gradient value
```

```
[0. 0. 0. 0.]
<NDArray 4 @cpu(0)>
```

```
with autograd.record():         # define computation path
    f = 8 * nd.dot(x1d, x1d)
    #f = (x1d.norm())**2         # alternative formula
```

```
f.backward()                    # compute gradient
x1d.grad                        # query the results.
```

```
[ 0. 16. 32. 48.]
<NDArray 4 @cpu(0)>
```

```
2 * x1d                         # analytical formula
```

```
[0. 2. 4. 6.]
<NDArray 4 @cpu(0)>
```

```
x1d.grad == 2* x1d              # correct?
```

```
[1. 0. 0. 0.]
<NDArray 4 @cpu(0)>
```

All correct.

8.6.3 *Gradients of scalar functions with quadratic variables in high dimensions*

Consider the gradients of the scalar functions that vary quadratically with variables in high dimensions. A typical quadratic function defined in a p-dimensional space can have the following form:

$$f(\mathbf{x}) = \mathbf{x}^\top \mathbf{C} \mathbf{x} \quad \text{for} \ \ \mathbf{x} \in \mathbb{R}^p \tag{8.8}$$

where $\mathbf{C}$ is matrix of a constant with a dimension of $p \times p$. It is clear that $f(\mathbf{x})$ is a scalar depending on $\mathbf{x}$ quadratically. We now use autograd to compute the gradient of this function, and compare it with the analytical solution given in Table 8.2.

```python
c = nd.array([[1.1, .8, .18],[.8, 2.8, .18],[.18, .18, 3.8]])
                              # 3 by 3 matrix of constants
x = nd.array([1., 2., 3.])    # 3 independent variables
x.attach_grad()               # request for gradient
with autograd.record():       # record down the path
    g = nd.dot(x,c)
    f = nd.dot(g,x)
f.backward()                             # compute gradient
print('At x=',x, '  Constants c = ',c)
print('The gradient values of f at x=', x.grad)
print('The analytical gradient values of f at x=',\
      2*nd.dot(c,x))
```

```
At x=
[1. 2. 3.]
<NDArray 3 @cpu(0)>    Constants c =
[[1.1  0.8  0.18]
 [0.8  2.8  0.18]
 [0.18 0.18 3.8 ]]
<NDArray 3x3 @cpu(0)>
The gradient values of f at x=
[ 6.48 13.88 23.88]
<NDArray 3 @cpu(0)>
The analytical gradient values of f at x=
[ 6.48 13.88 23.88]
<NDArray 3 @cpu(0)>
```

The autograd gradient is in agreement with the analytical gradient.

8.6.4 *Gradient of scalar function with a matrix of variables in high dimensions*

Finally, we construct a scalar function with a matrix of variables. One of such can be defined as follows:

$$f(\mathbf{X}) = \mathbf{c}^\top \mathbf{X} \mathbf{c} \quad \text{for} \ \ \mathbf{X} \in \mathbb{R}^{p \times p} \tag{8.9}$$

where $\mathbf{X}$ is a matrix of $p \times p$ variables, and $\mathbf{c}$ is a vector of p constants that do not change with any of the variables in $\mathbf{X}$. We use autograd to compute the gradient of this function, and compare it with the analytical solution given in Table 8.2.

```python
c = nd.array([1., 2., 3.])          # vector of 3 constants
c1 = nd.array([[1., 2., 3.]])
X = nd.array([[1.1, .8, .18],[.8, 2.8, .18],[.18, .18, 3.8]])
                    # 3 by 3 matrix of independent variables
X.attach_grad()                      # request for gradient
with autograd.record():              # record down the path
    g = nd.dot(X,c)
    f = nd.dot(g,c)
f.backward()                         # compute gradient
print('At x=',X, '  Constants c = ',c)
print('Gradient values of f at x=', X.grad)
print('Analytical gradient values of f at x=',\
     nd.linalg.gemm2(c1.T,c1))
```

```
At x=
[[1.1  0.8  0.18]
 [0.8  2.8  0.18]
 [0.18 0.18 3.8 ]]
<NDArray 3x3 @cpu(0)>   Constants c =
[1. 2. 3.]
<NDArray 3 @cpu(0)>
Gradient values of f at x=
[[1. 2. 3.]
 [2. 4. 6.]
 [3. 6. 9.]]
<NDArray 3x3 @cpu(0)>


Analytical gradient values of f at x=
[[1. 2. 3.]
 [2. 4. 6.]
 [3. 6. 9.]]
<NDArray 3x3 @cpu(0)>
```

8.6.5 *Head gradient*

In the above example, the chain rule can be written as

$$\frac{d}{dx}f(g(x)) = \frac{df(g)}{dg}\frac{dg(x)}{dx} \tag{8.10}$$

The function can be defined in more than one layer, which forms a chain functions, as follows:

$$g = x * 2 \tag{8.11}$$

$$f = g * x \tag{8.12}$$

$$h = f \tag{8.13}$$

In this case, we have

$$\frac{d}{dx}f(g(x)) = \frac{d}{dx}h(f(g(x))) = \frac{dh(f)}{df}\frac{df(g)}{dg}\frac{dg(x)}{dx} \tag{8.14}$$

The first part $\frac{dh}{df}$ is called *head gradient*, which is often used in machine learning. For the above simple example, we have

$$\frac{dh}{df} = 1 \tag{8.15}$$

If we know the head gradient of the function, the gradient of the function can be computed using f.backward(), by feeding the head gradient as an input argument:

```python
with autograd.record():
    g = x * 2
    f = g * x
    h = f

head_gradient=nd.ones_like(g)
        # default. hence is not necessary.
h.backward(head_gradient)
        # this allows adding in a constant matrix to the head.
print('At x=',x, '\n The gradient values of f at x=', x.grad)
```

```
At x=
[1. 2. 3.]
<NDArray 3 @cpu(0)>
 The gradient values of f at x=
[ 4.  8. 12.]
<NDArray 3 @cpu(0)>
```

```
with autograd.record():
    g = 2* x ** 2
    h = g
head_gradient=nd.ones_like(g)
h.backward(head_gradient)
print('At x=',x, '\n The gradient values of f at x=', x.grad)
```

```
At x=
[1. 2. 3.]
<NDArray 3 @cpu(0)>
 The gradient values of f at x=
[ 4.  8. 12.]
<NDArray 3 @cpu(0)>
```

The above example is simple, but demonstrates a very powerful tool for computing the exact gradients of complicated loss/objective functions one may encounter in real-life applications to train a neural network. As long as we can structure the loss function that is a chain of sub-functions, autograd can be used. All one needs is to tell the code which are the parameters (variables) that need their gradients to be "attached" to, and then "record" the chain relationship of the sub-functions. The code will compute the gradients, in a back-propagation process upon request, regardless of how many layers there may be.

8.7 Gradients for Functions with Conditions

In Python, we can build complicated functions, where sub-functions are controlled by conditions, allowing nonlinearity to be built into the formulations. Autograd can also be used to compute the gradients for such functions. Below is an example.

```
a = nd.random_normal(shape=6)
a
```

```
[ 0.03629 -0.49024 -0.9501   0.03751 -0.7298  -2.0401056 ]
<NDArray 6 @cpu(0)>
```

```
a.attach_grad()
with autograd.record():
    b = a * 88 + 5.0
```

```python
    while (nd.norm(b) < 8888).asscalar():
        b = b * 88
    if (mx.nd.sum(b) > 0).asscalar():
        c = b + 88
    else:
        c = 800 * b
```

```python
head_gradient = nd.array([0.5, 1.2, .18, 0.3, 0.6, 0.9])
c.backward(head_gradient)
```

```python
print(a.grad)
```

```
[3097600.  7434240.5 1115136.   1858560.1 3717120.2 5575680. ]
<NDArray 6 @cpu(0)>
```

Note there are operations and functions that may not be supported by autograd, such as in-place operations, depending on the module used. Readers are referred the online [document] (https://github.com/HIPS/ autograd/blob/master/docs/tutorial.md) and the links therein for more detail, when encountering strange behavior.

8.8 Example: Gradients of an L2 Loss Function for a Single Neuron

Let us consider the simplest network with only a single neuron, as shown in Fig. 8.2.

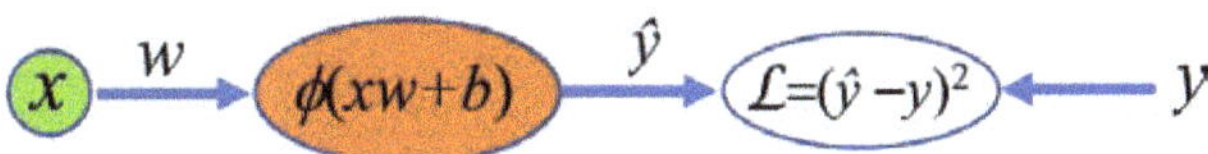

Figure 8.2: A 1-1-1 neuron network: One input layer, one hidden layer, and one output layer, each with a single neuron.

We first use hand calculation to get all the values at these local nodes and stages in the feed-forward process, together with all the gradients at the corresponding locations in the back-propagation process. The results are shown in Fig. 8.3.

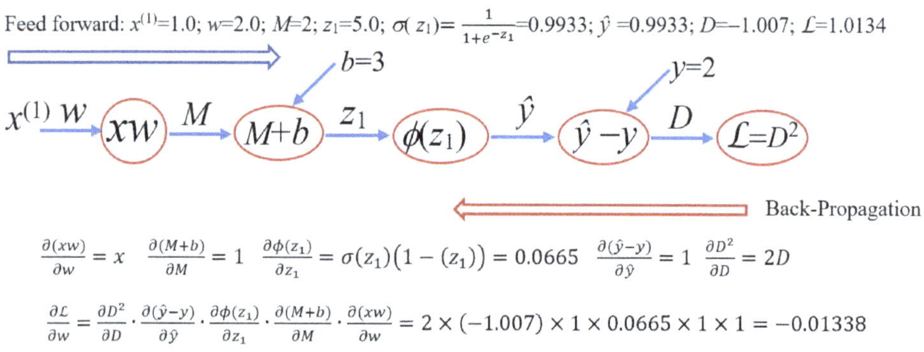

Figure 8.3: Feed-forward and Back-propagation for the simplest net with only a single neuron. The net is split into five local nodes (red elliptic circles), as shown in the middle of the figure. Feed-forward process: The input value of x, current values of the learning parameters w and b, as well as the label y value are all arbitrarily set for the calculation. All these intermediate values calculated using these values in the feed-forward process are given above the arrows leading to these nodes. Back-propagation: All the derivatives at the local nodes are computed backwards and the values are given in the bottom of the figure. The final gradient of the L2 function with respect to w is calculated. The same can be done with respect to b, and the result should be the same for this simple case.

In this case, we use the least squared error as the loss function (known as the L2 loss function) with $\phi(z)$ being the activation function.

$$\mathcal{L} = (\phi(\mathbf{x} \cdot \mathbf{w} + b) - y)^2 \tag{8.16}$$

where y is a given label at the out. In this case, we shall have

$$\frac{\partial\mathcal{L}}{\partial\mathbf{w}} = 2(\mathbf{x} \cdot \mathbf{w} + b - y)\mathbf{x}^{\top} \cdot \phi'(z) \tag{8.17}$$

and

$$\frac{\partial\mathcal{L}}{\partial b} = 2(\mathbf{x} \cdot \mathbf{w} + b - y) \cdot \phi'(z) \tag{8.18}$$

Let us write a code to compute all these, using the above analytic formulae and the autograd.

```python
import mxnet as mx
from mxnet import nd, autograd, gluon

def logistic(z):        #Define the sigmoid function
    return 1. / (1. + nd.exp(-z))
```

```python
def logisticg(z):          #Analytic gradient of the sigmoid
    return logistic(z)*(1-logistic(z))

def loss2(x,w,b,y):        #Define L2 loss function
    y_hat = logistic(nd.dot(x,w)+b)
    return (y_hat-y)**2

def lossdw(x,w,b,y):       #analytic derivative of L2 w.r.t w
    y_hat = logistic(nd.dot(x,w)+b)
    return 2*(y_hat-y)*x*logisticg(nd.dot(x,w)+b)

def lossdb(x,w,b,y):       #analytic derivative of L2 w.r.t b
    y_hat = logistic(nd.dot(x,w)+b)
    return 2*(y_hat-y)*logisticg(nd.dot(x,w)+b)

b = nd.arange(3, 4, 5)  # Set the current value for b
w1 = nd.arange(2, 3, 2) # Set the current value for w
w1.attach_grad()        # request for autograd w.r.t w
b.attach_grad()         # request for autograd w.r.t b
y = 2.                  # set the label value
x = nd.arange(1, 2, 2)  # set the input value
print(' w1=',w1,'\n b=',b,'\n x=',x)
```

```
 w1=
[2.]
<NDArray 1 @cpu(0)>
 b=
[3.]
<NDArray 1 @cpu(0)>
 x=
[1.]
<NDArray 1 @cpu(0)>
```

```python
with autograd.record():
    M = nd.dot(x, w1)
    x2 = M + b
    y_hat = logistic(x2)
    s = y_hat - y
    l2 = s*s
```

```python
head_gradient=nd.ones_like(l2)
l2.backward(head_gradient)
# print feed-forward results of the net at all local nodes
print('x=',x[0].asscalar,'w=',w1[0].asscalar,'M=',M[0].asscalar,
      'x2=',x2.asscalar, 'y_hat=',y_hat,'s=',s,'l2=',l2.asscalar)
# print the gradients from the back-propagation
print('Autograd, w1.grad',w1.grad,'  shape',np.shape(w1.grad))
print('Autograd, b.grad',b.grad)
#print the analytic results.
print('Analytic loss2=',loss2(x,w1,b,y))
print('Analytic lossdw=',lossdw(x,w1,b,y))
print('Analytic lossdb=',lossdb(x,w1,b,y))
```

```
x= <bound method NDArray.asscalar of
[1.]
<NDArray 1 @cpu(0)>> w= <bound method NDArray.asscalar of
[2.]
<NDArray 1 @cpu(0)>> M= <bound method NDArray.asscalar of
[2.]
<NDArray 1 @cpu(0)>> x2= <bound method NDArray.asscalar of
[5.]
<NDArray 1 @cpu(0)>> y_hat=
[0.9933072]
<NDArray 1 @cpu(0)> s=
[-1.0066929]
<NDArray 1 @cpu(0)> l2= <bound method NDArray.asscalar of
[1.0134306]
<NDArray 1 @cpu(0)>>
Autograd, w1.grad
[-0.0133851]
<NDArray 1 @cpu(0)>   shape (1,)
Autograd, b.grad
[-0.0133851]
<NDArray 1 @cpu(0)>
Analytic loss2=
[1.0134306]
<NDArray 1 @cpu(0)>
Analytic lossdw=
[-0.01338505]
<NDArray 1 @cpu(0)>
```

```
Analytic lossdb=
[-0.01338505]
<NDArray 1 @cpu(0)>
```

We see again that the autograd produces the exact solutions.

8.9 Examples: Differences Between Analytical, Autograd, and Numerical Differentiation

We now check out the differences between analytical, autograd, and numerical differentiation. We use the sigmoid function to do so, because it is one of the most often used functions in machine learning.

```python
import numpy as np


def logistic(z):              # Define the sigmoid function
    return 1. / (1. + nd.exp(-z))


x1 = nd.arange(-10, 10, 1)  # Define x1
x1.attach_grad()              # Request for gradient
with autograd.record():       # Define the path
    g = logistic(x1)
    h = g
head_gradient=nd.ones_like(g)
h.backward(head_gradient)
print('The gradient values of f at x=', x1.grad)
```

```
The gradient values of f at x=
[4.53958128e-05 1.23379359e-04 3.35237652e-04 9.10221133e-04
 2.46650912e-03 6.64805667e-03 1.76627077e-02 4.51766588e-02
 1.04993582e-01 1.96611941e-01 2.50000000e-01 1.96611971e-01
 1.04993574e-01 4.51766588e-02 1.76627059e-02 6.64805621e-03
 2.46650935e-03 9.10221308e-04 3.35237681e-04 1.23379359e-04]
<NDArray 20 @cpu(0)>
```

```python
import mxnet as mx
from mxnet import nd, autograd, gluon
import matplotlib.pyplot as plt
from matplotlib import rc
%matplotlib inline
```

```python
yg = logistic(x1)*(1.-logistic(x1))        # Analytic derivatives
nyg = nd.array(np.gradient(logistic(x1).asnumpy(),x1.asnumpy()))
                          # numerical gradient using np.gradient()
dgag=yg-x1.grad           # difference between the analytical and autograd
dgng=yg-nyg               # difference between the analytical and numerical
m = int(len(dgag)/10)
print('dgag=',dgag[0:len(dgag):m])
print('dgng=',dgng[0:len(dgng):m])
plt.plot(x1.asnumpy(),yg.asnumpy(),dashes=[30, 5, 5, 5],color='red')
plt.plot(x1.asnumpy(),x1.grad.asnumpy(),alpha=0.5,linewidth=7.0)
plt.plot(x1.asnumpy(),nyg.asnumpy(),alpha=0.9,linewidth=1.0,color='black')
plt.plot(x1.asnumpy(),dgag.asnumpy(), color='green')
plt.plot(x1.asnumpy(),dgng.asnumpy(), color='orange')
plt.xlabel('z')
plt.ylabel(r"$\sigma \ '(z) $")
plt.title('Gradient of the sigmoid Function')
plt.show()
l0 = int(len (x1)/2)   #take look at its value at the center
print('x=',x1[l0], 'sigmoid(0)=', logistic(x1[l0]))
```

dgag=
[-3.6379788e-12 2.9103830e-11 0.0000000e+00 -1.8626451e-09
  0.0000000e+00 0.0000000e+00 5.2154064e-08 2.7939677e-08
 -4.3539330e-08 -1.4406396e-08]
<NDArray 10 @cpu(0)>

dgng=
[-3.2600899e-05 -5.8590609e-05 -4.2439066e-04 -2.7038064e-03
 -5.7642013e-03 1.8941417e-02 -5.7641417e-03 -2.7037859e-03
 -4.2444887e-04 -5.8584614e-05]
<NDArray 10 @cpu(0)>

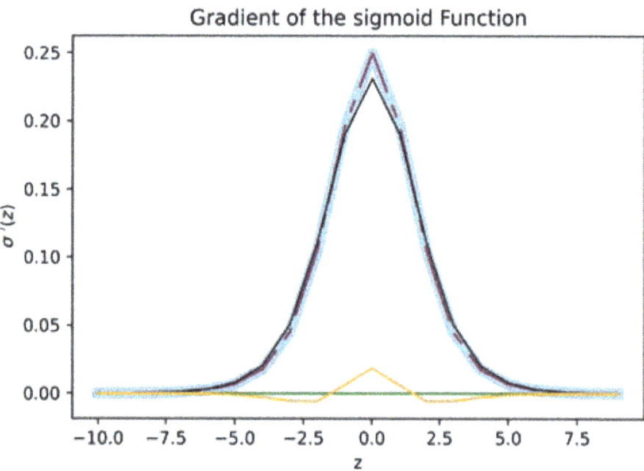

Figure 8.4:   Derivative of the sigmoid function computed using different methods, and the error in the results.

```
x=
[0.]
<NDArray 1 @cpu(0)> sigmoid(0)=
[0.5]
<NDArray 1 @cpu(0)>
```

The results plotted in Fig. 8.4 show clearly that the autograd gives the exact solution (the green line above is zero). The numerical gradient gives only an approximated solution (the orange line is not zero).

8.10 Discussion

The numerical autograd is a powerful tool for computing the gradient of a function and the result is exact (to machine accuracy). It can be used not only in machine learning but also for many other computations in engineering and sciences.

Our discussion focused on scalar functions with variables that can be a scalar, or a vector. When the variable is a scalar, we have a derivative, and when the variable is a vector, we have a gradient vector at a local node. In an MLP layer, the function itself at the layer can be a vector. In these cases, the gradient of the vector function can be formulated as a matrix, known as the Jacobian matrix. The formulation, procedure, and the chain rule still holds, but gradient vectors become Jacobian matrices.

References

[1] G.R. Liu and T.T. Nguyen, *Smoothed Finite Element Methods*. Taylor and Francis Group, New York, 2010.
[2] G.R. Liu, *Mesh Free Methods: Moving Beyond the Finite Element Method*. Taylor and Francis Group, New York, 2010.

Chapter 9

Solution Existence Theory
and Optimization Techniques

9.1 Introduction

Developing and training neural network models is to find a set of parameters (weights and biases) that minimize the loss function (or cost function or objective function). The first question that needs to be answered is on the existence of such a set of parameters for the model to be created given a dataset. Our theoretical study in Chapter 5 has concluded that such a set of parameters do exist, if affine transformation is used and the hypothesis space is sufficiently large in relation to the dataset. The uniqueness of the solution of the set of parameters needs further examination. This requires a good understanding on the hypothesis used in the model as well as the dataset. This chapter will first examine the solution existence and uniqueness using an analytical manageable ML problem, known as linear regression problem. Our analysis reveals important **solution existence theory, predictability of the solution**, and **effects of parallel data-points** in a dataset, which are applicable to general complex machine learning models.

Next, a proper tool known as optimization technique is required to find these parameters for general ML problems that do not have a closed form. Optimization techniques are not unique to machining learning algorithms and are widely used in many design and analysis problems in engineering and science. Developing more powerful new or using the existing techniques properly to their fullest potential is believed to be one of the most challenging works for a deep learning project. Techniques for optimization are essential to machine learning for a number of reasons. For one, the optimization efficiency largely controls the efficiency of training. Second, convergence of training is often rooted in the convergence property of the optimization techniques used.

In addition, optimization methods often with some tunable parameters and proper tuning of the optimization parameters can also be critical in training a model.

Our discussion will focus on gradient-based techniques for finding an optimal solution. For this part, we referenced excellent materials available at https://github.com/zackchase/mxnet-the-straight-dope/tree/master/chapter06_optimization (under the Apache License 2).

9.2 Analytic Optimization Methods: Ideal Cases

For optimization problems with very simple objective functions, one may be able to find analytical solutions. For example, for an objective function $f(w) = (w - a)^2$ with a given fixed real number a, one can immediately find the global and unique minimum at $w^* = a$. This function is positive and quadratic in w, and hence has one and only one solution in $\mathbb{R}^1$. This simple problem implies that finding the minimum is straightforward, if the function is quadratic.

9.2.1 *Least square formulation*

However, very few machine learning problems have such a simple objective function. There are problems that can be formulated with the least square type of objective functions, such as the linear regression problems (https://en.wikipedia.org/wiki/Linear_regression). This type of problem is quite common in sciences and engineering, yet simple enough to be formulated analytically to obtain kind of close-form solution. It is an excellent type of problem for us to reveal important theoretical properties on solution existence and predictability. These properties can be generalized for complex machine learning models that are too complex to analyze.

Given a dataset with m (measurement) data pair in the form of

$$[y_i, x_{i1}, x_{i2}, \ldots, x_{ip}], \quad i = 1, 2, \ldots, m \tag{9.1}$$

where $y_i \in \mathbb{Y}^1$ is the label obtained at the ith label (observed or measured), when p variables (features) are set at $x_{i1}, x_{i2}, \ldots, x_{ip}$. To predict y based on the given linearly independent variables $x_1, x_2, \ldots, x_p \in \mathbb{X}^p$, we can construct a simple linear regression model in p-dimensional space, by assuming that the predictor $\hat{y}_i$ is the affine transformation as discussed in Chapter 5:

$$\hat{y}_i \equiv z_i = w_0 + w_2 x_{i1} + w_2 x_{i2}, \ldots, + w_p x_{ip}, \quad i = 1, 2, \ldots, m \tag{9.2}$$

where $w_i, i = 0, 1, 2, \ldots, p$ are the learning parameters in $\mathbb{W}^{p+1}$. Equation (9.2) can be formulated in the following matrix form:

$$\hat{\mathbf{y}} = \overline{\mathbf{X}}\hat{\mathbf{w}} \tag{9.3}$$

where $\hat{\mathbf{y}}$ is a vector of predictions:

$$\hat{\mathbf{y}} = \{\hat{y}_1, \hat{y}_2, \ldots, \hat{y}_m\}^\top \tag{9.4}$$

and $\overline{\mathbf{X}}$ is an $m \times (p+1)$ matrix, and its ith row is given as

$$[1, x_{i1}, x_{i2}, \ldots, x_{ip}] \in \overline{\mathbb{X}}^p \tag{9.5}$$

and

$$\hat{\mathbf{w}} = [w_0, w_1, w_2, \ldots, w_p]^\top \in \mathbb{W}^{p+1} \tag{9.6}$$

Note that Eq. (9.3) requires $\hat{\mathbf{w}}$ being a column vector. This allows us to obtain a conventional form of the normal equation later. Our task is to find a vector $\hat{\mathbf{w}}$ that gives a best $\hat{\mathbf{y}}$ closest to the labels in the given m data pairs, $\mathbf{y}$:

$$[y_1, y_2, \ldots, y_m]^\top \tag{9.7}$$

For existence of a unique solution (see later), we require

$$m \geq (p+1) \tag{9.8}$$

Meaning that the number of rows in $\overline{\mathbf{X}}$ is at least no less than its number of columns. In other words, we require more (usually a lot more) observation/measurement data, and hence it results in a "tall" matrix $\overline{\mathbf{X}}$. Equation (9.8) also gives the basic relationship between the number of samples m and the number of training parameters $(p+1)$. More detailed discussion will be given in Section 13.2 for deepnets.

9.2.2 *L2 loss function*

We define now a loss function using the L2 norm that is the sum of the squared differences between the predictor $\hat{\mathbf{y}}$ and the label data $\mathbf{y}$ for all the observations. It is often called L2 loss function.

$$\mathcal{L}(\mathbf{y}, \hat{\mathbf{y}}(\hat{\mathbf{w}})) = ||\mathbf{y} - \overline{\mathbf{X}}\hat{\mathbf{w}}||_2^2 = (\mathbf{y} - \overline{\mathbf{X}}\hat{\mathbf{w}})^\top (\mathbf{y} - \overline{\mathbf{X}}\hat{\mathbf{w}}) \tag{9.9}$$

Notice Eq. (9.9) mimics the idea function discussed at the beginning of this section, and is essentially quadratic. Clearly, the loss function $\mathcal{L}$ is zero, if the prediction produces the dataset exactly. Otherwise it is a positive number.

The regression problem is casted as the following minimization problem using the **least-square formulation**:

$$\min_{\hat{\mathbf{w}} \in \mathbb{W}^{p+1}} \mathcal{L}(\mathbf{y}, \hat{\mathbf{y}}(\hat{\mathbf{w}})) = \min_{\hat{\mathbf{w}} \in \mathbb{W}^{p+1}} (\mathbf{y} - \overline{\mathbf{X}}\hat{\mathbf{w}})^T (\mathbf{y} - \overline{\mathbf{X}}\hat{\mathbf{w}}) \tag{9.10}$$

Because $\mathcal{L}$ is a function of $\hat{\mathbf{w}}$, and is also quadratic in $\hat{\mathbf{w}}$. It is thus hopeful that we can expect a unique set of optimal $\hat{\mathbf{w}}^* \in \mathbb{W}^{p+1}$ that minimize $\mathcal{L}$, which can be found analytically by evaluating its gradient (see Chapter 8), and then setting to 0:

$$\nabla_{\hat{\mathbf{w}}} \mathcal{L}(\mathbf{y}, \hat{\mathbf{y}}(\hat{\mathbf{w}})) = \frac{\partial \mathcal{L}(\mathbf{y}, \hat{\mathbf{y}}(\hat{\mathbf{w}}))}{\partial \hat{\mathbf{w}}} = -2\overline{\mathbf{X}}^T (\mathbf{y} - \overline{\mathbf{X}}\hat{\mathbf{w}}^*) = 0 \tag{9.11}$$

9.2.3 *Normal equation*

Equation (9.11) gives

$$\overline{\mathbf{X}}^\top \overline{\mathbf{X}} \hat{\mathbf{w}}^* = \overline{\mathbf{X}}^\top \mathbf{y} \tag{9.12}$$

This equation is known as **Normal Equation**. Assuming matrix $\overline{\mathbf{X}}^\top \overline{\mathbf{X}}$ is invertible ($\overline{\mathbf{X}}$ has full rank, as discussed in detail in Chapter 3), the solution can be found as

$$\hat{\mathbf{w}}^* = (\overline{\mathbf{X}}^\top \overline{\mathbf{X}})^{-1} \overline{\mathbf{X}}^\top \mathbf{y} \tag{9.13}$$

which is a kind of close-form solution.

Note that for large systems, we do not usually form the normal matrix and solve the normal equation. Instead, the QR transformation type of algorithms are used to compute numerically the least-square solution. This is because of the numerical instability reasons mentioned in Section 3.4.2. For our theoretical analysis here, this approach works well, because no numerical operations involved. It can reveal important inside on solution existence.

9.2.4 *Solution existence analysis*

In obtaining the above solution $\hat{\mathbf{w}}^*$, $\overline{\mathbf{X}}$ needs to have full rank so that $\overline{\mathbf{X}}^\top \overline{\mathbf{X}}$ is invertible. Let us examine what this really means, by considering a simple case of 2D feature space: $p = 2$, $m = p + 1$. If $\overline{\mathbf{X}}$ has full rank, the normal equation (9.12) can be reduced to

$$\overline{\mathbf{X}}\hat{\mathbf{w}}^* = \mathbf{y} \tag{9.14}$$

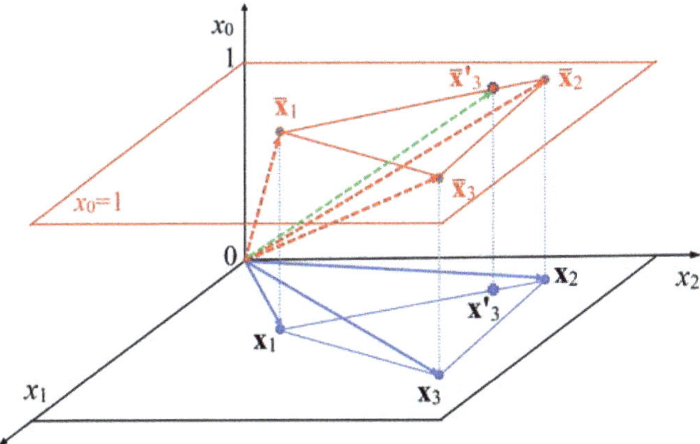

Figure 9.1: Vectors of data-points in the feature space $\mathbb{X}^2$ (blue) and in the augmented feature space $\overline{\mathbb{X}}^2$ (red). Vectors $\mathbf{x}_1$, $\mathbf{x}_2$, and $\mathbf{x}_3$ in space $\mathbb{X}^2$ are linearly dependent, but $\overline{\mathbf{x}}_1$, $\overline{\mathbf{x}}_2$, and $\overline{\mathbf{x}}_3$ on space $\overline{\mathbb{X}}^2$ in $\mathbb{R}^3$ are not, because of the elevation.

It can be written explicitly as

$$
\begin{bmatrix}
1 & x_{11} & x_{12} \\
1 & x_{21} & x_{22} \\
1 & x_{31} & x_{32}
\end{bmatrix}
\begin{bmatrix}
b^* \\
w_1^* \\
w_2^*
\end{bmatrix}
=
\begin{bmatrix}
y_1 \\
y_2 \\
y_3
\end{bmatrix}
\tag{9.15}
$$

It is clear now that $\overline{\mathbf{X}}$ is exactly the same as the "moment matrix" in the formulation of the triangular elements given in Eq. (7.10) in FEM [1]. The condition for $\overline{\mathbf{X}}$ having full rank is that the area formed by these 3 data-points in the feature space $\mathbb{X}^2$ (2-dimensional) is nonzero. Such an area is half of the determinate of the moment matrix. Figure 9.1 plots 3 data-points $\mathbf{x}_1$, $\mathbf{x}_2$, and $\mathbf{x}_3$ in space $\mathbb{X}^2$, the area for which the triangle is clearly nonzero. If we replace $\mathbf{x}_3$ by $\mathbf{x}_3'$, $\mathbf{x}_1$, $\mathbf{x}_2$, and $\mathbf{x}_3'$ become in line, the triangle becomes **degenerated**, the area becomes zero, $\overline{\mathbf{X}}$ will be singular, and its rank reduces to 2.

Notice that while $\mathbf{x}_1$, $\mathbf{x}_2$, and $\mathbf{x}_3$ are linearly dependent in space $\mathbb{X}^2$, vector $\mathbf{x}_3$ can be presented by a linear combination of $\mathbf{x}_1$ and $\mathbf{x}_2$, because these 3 vectors (in blue) are in plane. However, when these 3 data-points are projected onto the affine plane $\overline{\mathbb{X}}^2$ (see Section 1.4.2), these 3 vectors (in red) in $\mathbb{R}^3$ are no longer in plane and become linearly independent. Therefore, alternatively the condition for $\overline{\mathbf{X}}$ having a full rank is that the vectors of these 3 data-points on plane of $x_0 = 1$ on the space $\overline{\mathbb{X}}^2$ in $\mathbb{R}^3$ are linearly independent. If we replace $\overline{\mathbf{x}}_3$ by $\overline{\mathbf{x}}_3'$, $\overline{\mathbf{x}}_1$, $\overline{\mathbf{x}}_2$, and $\overline{\mathbf{x}}_3'$ are now in a plane, and they become linearly dependent. In this case, $\overline{\mathbf{X}}$ will become singular and its rank will become 2. Therefore, the rank of $\overline{\mathbf{X}}$ depends on the maximum number of the linearly independent vectors of the data-points in the $\overline{\mathbb{X}}^2$ space.

Consider now cases of $m > p + 1$ with $p = 2$. This means that we still have 2 features, but more than 3 data-points. In these cases, the rank of $\overline{\mathbf{X}}$ depends on the maximum number of the linearly independent vectors in $\mathbb{R}^3$ of all the data-points in the $\overline{\mathbb{X}}^2$ space. Hence, the chance should be higher.

For general high-dimensional feature spaces $\mathbb{X}^p$, the same argument shall hold for $\overline{\mathbf{X}}$ being full rank. If we examine the data-points in $\mathbb{X}^p$ space, we need the "volume" of the largest polyhedron with any set of $p + 1$ data-points as its vertexes to be non-zero. If we examine the data-points in $\overline{\mathbb{X}}^p$ space, we need the minimum number of the linearly independent vectors in $\mathbb{R}^{p+1}$ of all the data-points in the $\overline{\mathbb{X}}^p$ to be $p + 1$. Once $\overline{\mathbf{X}}$ has full rank, we shall have a least-square solution given by Eq. (9.13). A general analysis for arbitrary dimension can be found in [2].

We now summarize our discussion in the following solution existence theory.

9.2.5 *Solution existence theory*

Solution Existence Theory: *Consider a dataset with $m \geq p + 1$ data-points. If the maximum number of the linearly independent vectors among all the data-points in the dataset in the affine space $\overline{\mathbb{X}}^p$ is no-less than $p + 1$, then matrix $\overline{\mathbf{X}}$ will have full rank, and there exists a unique least-square solution given in by Eq. (9.13).*

Alternatively, the condition may also be set for non-degeneration of the largest polyhedron formed by any set of $p + 1$ data-points in the dataset as its vertexes in the feature pace $\mathbb{X}^p$. In high dimensions, the geometry of such a polyhedron becomes very complicated.

In practice, when we have many data-points, $\overline{\mathbf{X}}$ is usually a very tall matrix, and hence matrix $\overline{\mathbf{X}}^\top \overline{\mathbf{X}}$ is often invertible and SPD.

Remark: *The above analysis reveals also an important fact that the existence of unique solution depends solely on the number of data-points and the distribution of the data-points in $\mathbb{X}^p$.*

When $\overline{\mathbf{X}}$ has full rank, we can obtain the exact optimal value $\hat{\mathbf{w}}^*$ via single-step computation using Eq. (9.13), with one matrix multiplication, one matrix inversion, and two matrix-vector products.

If the dataset contains **higher-order latent features**, one can add in higher-order bases, such as $x_1, x_2, x_1^2, \ldots$. The solution existence theory still holds, and the solution existence depends on whether the resulting moment matrix $\overline{\mathbf{X}}$ has full rank. Alternatively, one can use a more powerful hypothesis, such as MLP a large number of learning parameters discussed in Section 13.2. Precise analysis of solution existence for MLP becomes more complicated, but we can assert that *it depends on whether or not the number and the distribution of the data-points support the MLP hypothesis with the learning parameters*. This assertion is important in ML model creation, because if one fails to train a model, checking and enriching the dataset, or reduce the complexity of MLP could be effective solutions.

9.2.6 *Effects of parallel data-points*

Let us dig in further into another important issue: the effects of duplicated or parallel data-points in datasets, which may bother many in building machine learning models. Assume in Eq. (9.15), that any two data-points are identical or parallel. The moment matrix will be singular, based on the Solution Existence Theory. If there are many data-points in the dataset, in which there still be at least three data-points linearly independent in its corresponding affine space $\overline{\mathbb{X}}^2$, we shall still have a least-square solution. In this case, the duplication (or parallelism) of the data-points has no effect on the solution existence. However, it may affect the value of the solution, because the same data-points are used twice in L2 loss function. If this is not the intention of the analyst, clearing up the dataset, using PCA for example, is needed. This finding applies to higher dimensions and to other complicated models.

In terms of obtaining a solution in a single step (without iteration) in the form of Eq. (9.13), this least square linear regression probably is as far as we can go. At most, we may add in some constraints for this type of optimization problem leading to quadratic programming problems, as we have done in studying the SVM.

9.2.7 *Predictability of the solution against the label*

Note that $y_i \in \mathbb{Y}$ does not affect the solution existence. It affects the values of the solution $\hat{\mathbf{w}}^*$. In constructing the loss function in Eq. (9.9), we compare $\hat{y}_i$ with y_i. This implies that the prediction $\hat{y}_i$ must be in the label space $\mathbb{Y}$. This relates to our discussion in Chapter 5 on predictability of the hypothesis using affine transformation. We have proved there that the prediction function given in Eq. (9.2) can predict any arbitrary linear function of feature variables $\mathbf{x}$ that may be hidden in the dataset. In this particular case, such a linear function gives the least error defined in Eq. (9.9) in fitting the dataset.

To predict higher-order and nonlinear latent features relating to the labels in a dataset, one has to either add in higher-order bases, or other types of nonlinear bases, or more powerful nonlinear models like MLP, as mentioned earlier. The predictions at the output layer of neurons will still be, in $\mathbb{Y}^k$. This is because of the continuous coverage over the affine spaces by each neuron in the hidden layers ensured by both affine transformations wrapped with activation functions. The prediction functions at the output layer are continuous and differentiable with respect to the learning parameters, as discussed in detail in Chapter 5 for affine transformations and in Chapter 7 for activation functions. In addition, the gradients can be found via autograd as demonstrated in Chapter 8. Thus, a smooth and continuous coverage of the prediction function can be realized by the learning parameters in hypothesis space $\mathbb{W}^P$. As results, the predictability of the solution against the label is ensured in theory. Regardless of the actual values of the labels in the label space, the prediction shall be able to match those values to the desired accuracy, by tuning the learning parameters in the hypothesis space. The Universal Prediction Theory (see, Chapter 5) has ensured the capability of an MLP, as long as proper configuration of the MLP is used with a sufficiently large number of learning parameters. Effective numerical techniques are, however, needed to find the optimal learning parameters that minimize the loss function.

For most of the machine training models, the loss function is complicated. It is often not possible to convert the minimization problem similar to Eq. (9.10) to a single normal equation system. Therefore, we have to find a way to solve the minimization problems directly by numerical means. Iterative methods are often used, and finding a set of the minimizers requires many steps.

9.3 Considerations in Optimization for Complex Problems

Careful considerations are needed to solve the minimization problems numerically. For example, the loss functions may not be convex globally, the optimum point is not unique, multiple local optima, and presence of saddle points.

In the rest of the discussion in this chapter, we consider general optimization techniques that can be used in many areas of study in science and engineering, including machine learning. Therefore, without losing generality, the function to be optimized is denoted in general as $f(\mathbf{x})$ with $\mathbf{x}$ being the independent variables. If there is only one variable, $\mathbf{x}$ simply becomes x. In machine learning, however, our function would be the loss function $\mathcal{L}(\hat{\mathbf{w}})$ and the independent variables would be the learning parameters $\hat{\mathbf{w}}$. Care is needed to avoid confusion.

9.3.1 *Local minima*

For most real-life machine learning, the objective function $f(x)$ with x being the variable may have a number of local minimum values, at each of which $f(x)$ is smaller than at its nearby points. Only the x^*, at which $f(x^*)$ has the smallest value over the entire domain, is regarded as the global minimizer, and is usually the one we would like to find.

Consider the following function:

$$f(x) = \frac{x}{2} \cdot \cos(\pi x), \quad -1.0 \le x \le 4.0. \tag{9.16}$$

Let us plot the curve of this function for an explicit view.

```python
%config InlineBackend.figure_format ='retina' # high quality plot
%matplotlib inline
import numpy as np
import matplotlib.pyplot as plt

def f(x):
    return 0.5*x * np.cos(np.pi * x)

x = np.arange(-1.0, 4.0, 0.1)
fig = plt.figure()
subplt = fig.add_subplot(111)
subplt.annotate('local minimum',xy=(-.3,-.1),xytext=(-.8,-.5),
            arrowprops=dict(facecolor='black', shrink=0.01))
subplt.annotate('local minimum',xy=(1.1,-.5),xytext=(.5, .05),
            arrowprops=dict(facecolor='black', shrink=0.05))
subplt.annotate('global minimum',xy=(3.,-1.5),xytext=(3.,.05),
            arrowprops=dict(facecolor='red', shrink=0.05))
plt.title('A cost function with multiple minima')
plt.plot(x, f(x))
plt.show()
```

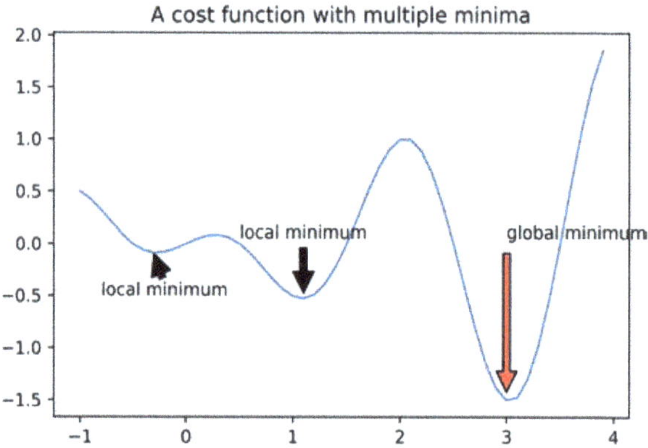

Figure 9.2: An example of cost functions with multiple minimums.

It is clear Fig. 9.2 that this function has two local minimums, and one global minimum in the domain we plotted. Existence of local minima presents a challenge, and unfortunately we do not have effective means to ensure the finding of the global minimum for general ML models. In practice, what we can do is to perform the optimization multiple times, each starting from a different initial point, and then take the minimum of these multiple minima.

9.3.2 *Saddle points*

Saddle points present another challenge for optimization techniques. The gradient of the loss function at the saddle points is zero, but the loss function itself may be minimum there along some directions and maximum along other directions. For high-dimensional problems (like machine learning), saddle points can be in numbers. The problem with saddle points can be evidenced using the following example.

Consider an objective function in one dimension defined as

$$f(x) = \frac{1}{2}x^3 + 2, \quad -2.0 \le x \le 2.0 \tag{9.17}$$

The derivative of this function is

$$f'(x) = \frac{3}{2}x^2, \quad -2.0 \le x \le 2.0 \tag{9.18}$$

which is zero at $x = 0$, but all positive elsewhere in $-2.0 \le x \le 2.0$. The 2nd derivative of this function is

$$f''(x) = 3x \quad -2.0 \le x \le 2.0 \tag{9.19}$$

which is zero at $x = 0$. However, it is negative in $[-2.0, 0.0)$, and positive in $(0.02.0]$. This means that $x = 0$ seems to be a maximizer when viewed from left towards 0 and seems to be a minimizer when viewed away from 0 to its right, as shown in Fig. 9.3. The gradients at both opposite sides of the saddle point are the same.

```python
x = np.arange(-2.0, 2.0, 0.1)
fig = plt.figure()
subplt = fig.add_subplot(111)
subplt.annotate('saddle point',xy=(0,1.8),xytext=(-.4,-1.),
            arrowprops=dict(facecolor='red', shrink=0.001))
plt.plot(x, 0.5 * x**3 + 2.0)
plt.show()
plt.annotate('saddle point', xy=(0., 0.1), xytext=(0., 2.),
            arrowprops=dict(facecolor='red', shrink=0.001))
plt.plot(x, 1.5 * x**2 )
plt.show()
```

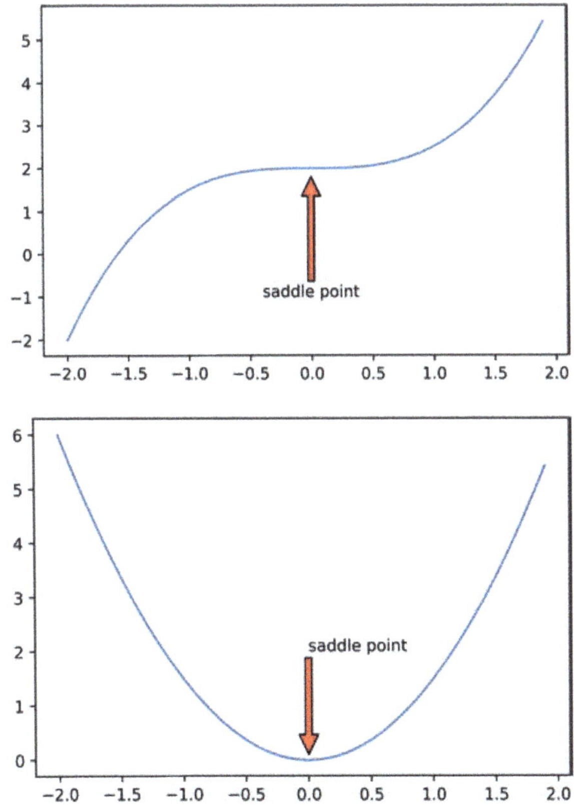

Figure 9.3: An example of cost functions with saddle points.

Figure 9.3 shows an example of cost functions with saddle points. We have seen saddle functions in 2D space earlier when studying the SVM. It was handled nicely via analytical means, which leads to a quadratic programming problem. In machine learning, many complicated functions can have multiple similar but more complicated saddle points. It is not likely we can find an analytical means for a set of minimizers. Let us write a code to generate such a function to get a feel for it.

```python
import matplotlib as mpl
#mpl.rcParams['figure.dpi']= 80
import matplotlib.pyplot as plt
from mpl_toolkits import mplot3d
from mpl_toolkits.mplot3d import axes3d
from IPython.core.interactiveshell import InteractiveShell
#InteractiveShell.ast_node_interactivity = "all"
#%matplotlib notebook #%matplotlib tk
x1 = np.linspace(.0 ,3.5,100) # np.arange(0.5, 5.0, 5.0)
x2 = np.linspace(-1.,4.0,100) # np.arange(2.0, 6.0, 5.0)
lx1, lx2 = len(x1), len(x2)
print('length of x1=',lx1,'length of x2=',lx2)
X1, X2 = np.meshgrid(x1, x2)
a, b = 1.0, 0.5
Z = a*X1 * np.cos(np.pi * X1) + b*X2 * np.cos(np.pi * X2)
fig_s = plt.figure(figsize=(8,5))
ax = fig_s.add_subplot(1,1,1,projection='3d')
ax.set_xlabel('$x_1$', fontsize=9, rotation=80)
ax.set_ylabel('$x_2$', fontsize=9)
ax.set_zlabel('Function Value', fontsize=9, rotation=0)
ax.yaxis._axinfo['label']['space_factor'] = 2.0
#ax.plot_wireframe(X1,X2,Z,color='b',rstride=5,cstride=5)
ax.plot_surface(X1,X2,Z,color='b',rstride=1,cstride=1,
                shade=False,cmap="jet", linewidth=1)
plt.title('Parabolic Cylinder function of $x_1$ and $x_2$'\
          'with, a='+str(a)+', b=' +str(b))
#plt.legend()
fig_s.tight_layout()   # otherwise right y-label is clipped
plt.show()
```

length of x1= 100 length of x2= 100

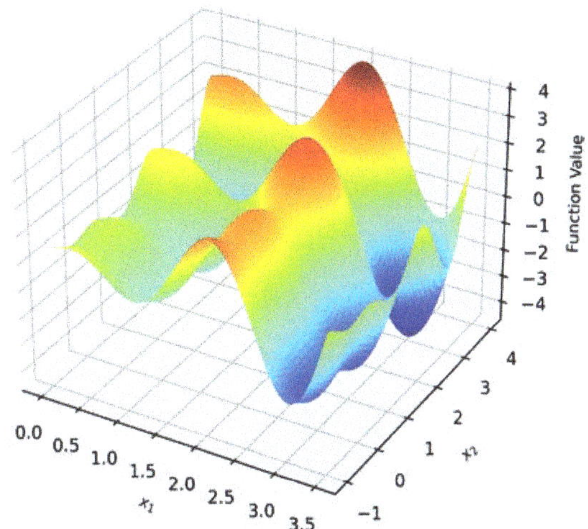

Figure 9.4:   An example of cost functions in 2D space with multiple saddle points.

For this 2D case plotted in Fig. 9.4, there are multiple saddle points, at which the gradient of the function is zero, but the values of the function are maxima along the x_1 direction and minima along the x_2 direction.

9.3.3 *Convex functions*

Elliptic paraboloidal functions are easy to deal with, because such a function is convex and has only one minimum. Let us write a code and plot one.

```python
a, b = 1.0, 2.0      # minor & major radii for an ellipse
x1 = np.linspace(-2.0,2.0,100)
x2 = np.linspace(-4.,4.0,100)
X1, X2 = np.meshgrid(x1, x2)        # Grides for 3D plot
Z = X1*X1/a**2 + X2*X2/b**2         # an ellipse
#%matplotlib notebook
%matplotlib inline
fig_s = plt.figure(figsize=(8,6))
ax = fig_s.add_subplot(1,1,1,projection='3d')
ax.set_xlabel('$x_1$', fontsize=12, rotation=80)
ax.set_ylabel('$x_2$', fontsize=12)
ax.set_zlabel('Function Value',fontsize=12,rotation=0)
ax.yaxis._axinfo['label']['space_factor'] = 3.0
ax.plot_wireframe(X1,X2,Z,color='b',rstride=5,cstride=5)
```

```
plt.title('Elliptic Paraboloidal function of $x_1$ and '\
          '$x_2$ with, a='+str(a)+', b=' +str(b))
#plt.legend()
fig_s.tight_layout()       # otherwise  y-label is clipped
plt.show();
```

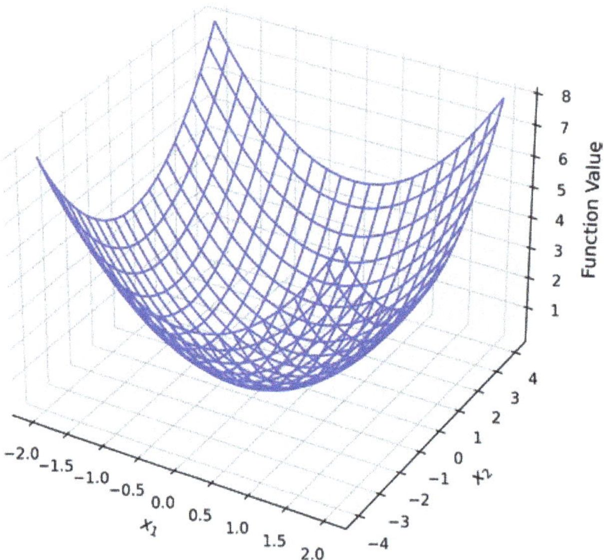

Figure 9.5: An ideal example of quadratic cost functions in 2D space with only one minimum.

As shown in Fig. 9.5, the ellipse function behaves very well and has only one minimum. Understanding this type of property is useful in dealing with complicated loss functions because near a local minimum, many complicated functions are locally elliptic, and hence can be taken advantage of. The only difficulty that may arise is when the ratio of the minor and major radii is too large (or too small). We shall discuss this again later.

9.4 Gradient Descent (GD) Method for Optimization

The *gradient descent* method is the basic technique for minimization of a function when its gradient is computable. It is widely used in science and engineering, including machine learning. It is in general an iterative method, meaning the solution (approximate) is obtained through a number of guided iterations. This type of iterative method is most practical especially for training machine learning models, because the parameter space is usually of extremely high dimension.

Consider a 2D space, where a cost function surface is defined. The surface of the cost function can be viewed as a terrain surface with many valleys and hills. Imagine that one is currently standing at a point on a hill and would like to get to the lowest point in the valley. The fastest path is going downhill in the direction where the slope is steepest. This is essentially the gradient descent method (sometimes called the steepest descent method). The gradient is just a formal and more rigorous term in mathematics for the slope.

A typical cost function defined in machine learning problems can be in much higher dimensions, possibly in the order of as much as millions. It is a space far beyond human imagination. However, the surface can still be viewed as a hyper-dimensional surface, and the direction should still be the steepest downhill direction (or negative gradient direction). To develop such a computer algorithm, we shall

- Compute the gradient that gives the learning direction.
- Determine the step to take in that direction, which gives the learning rate.

Let us examine how this would work for the simplest one-dimensional problem.

9.4.1 *Gradient descent in one dimension*

Assume a cost function $f(x)$ defined in a one-dimensional (1D) space with variable x. Assume also that it has at least the first derivative (that is the gradient in the 1D case) at any x in the domain of interest. We can then use the Taylor series expansion in the vicinity of x, which gives

$$f(x + \delta x) \approx f(x) + f'(x)\delta x \tag{9.20}$$

where (δx) is a small real number. Because the function has the first derivative, it must be a finite number (otherwise, it is not differentiable). Therefore, we can choose a very small positive real number $-\eta$ as a scalar, so that $-\eta f'(x)$ is as small as δx. This implies that η should carry a unit of $[(\delta x)f'^{-1}(x)]$. Equation (9.20) can now be rewritten as

$$f(x - \eta f'(x)) \approx f(x) - \eta(f'(x))^2. \tag{9.21}$$

Because η is chosen positive, we have

$$f(x - \eta f'(x)) \leq f(x). \tag{9.22}$$

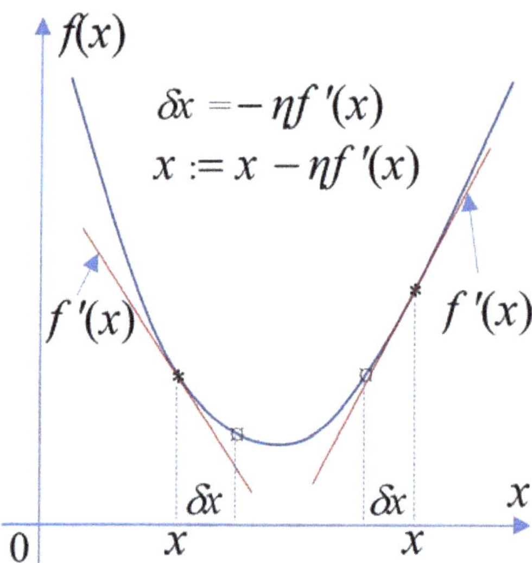

Figure 9.6: Gradient descent in a one-dimensional case.

This means that an update to x with

$$x := x - \eta f'(x) \tag{9.23}$$

would lead to a reduction of the value of $f(x)$. Note the negative sign, which implies that updating in x is in the negative (or downhill) direction of the gradient.

Figure 9.6 shows that regardless of which side the x is located on, the gradient descent takes a step closer to the minimum of the function that is convex.

9.4.2 *Remarks*

Based on the above analysis, we note the following important points:

1. Updating in x is in the negative direction of the gradient, and hence the name of *gradient descent*.
2. The amount of reduction is proportional to the gradient of the function. The larger the gradient, the larger the reduction, provided that $\eta f'(x)$ is sufficiently small so that the Taylor expansion (and our analysis) can still hold without overshooting.
3. Scalar η is called the *learning rate* or learning step size in machine learning, and choices of it can be tricky. It often requires some trial and error.

4. On the one hand, we must take the direction at which the derivative is the largest. On the other hand, we must not be too greedy to take too big an η that could undermine the basis of our analysis. A larger learning rate may lead to overshooting and hence oscillating behavior in the convergence process, which is often observed in practicing machine learning.
5. When the derivative value $f'(x)$ at x is zero, we make no progress. This means also that we are already at the minimum (including the saddle point discussed in the previous section).
6. If the derivative value $f'(x)$ at x is small, we make *very* (one more order smaller) little progress (note the $(f'(x))^2$ term). This implies that to speed up the process, one would need to access the higher-order derivatives of the cost function (such as the higher-order methods like Newton's method).

9.4.3 *Gradient descent in hyper-dimensions*

Consider a cost function $f(\mathbf{x})$, where argument $\mathbf{x} = [x_1, x_2, \ldots, x_p]^\top$ has p variables (or parameters in ML models). This means that $f(\mathbf{x})$, a *scalar*, is defined in a space with a dimension of p.

The gradient of $f(\mathbf{x})$ is thus with respect to all these variables/parameters $\mathbf{x}$, which is a *vector* (see Chapter 8) written in the form of

$$\nabla_{\mathbf{x}} f(\mathbf{x}) = \left[\frac{\partial f(\mathbf{x})}{\partial x_1}, \frac{\partial f(\mathbf{x})}{\partial x_2}, \ldots, \frac{\partial f(\mathbf{x})}{\partial x_p} \right]^\top. \tag{9.24}$$

where $\partial f(\mathbf{x})/\partial x_i$ is the partial derivative of the function with respect to the ith parameter. It is the change in f at $\mathbf{x}$ with respect only to a small change in x_i.

To measure the change in f at $\mathbf{x}$ with respect to a small of change in length (δl) in an arbitrary direction defined by a unit arbitrary vector $\mathbf{u}$, we may write

$$D_{\mathbf{u}} f(\mathbf{x}) = \lim_{(\delta l) \to 0} \frac{f(\mathbf{x} + (\delta l)\mathbf{u}) - f(\mathbf{x})}{(\delta l)} \tag{9.25}$$

which is in fact the derivative of $f(\mathbf{x})$ in an arbitrary direction $\mathbf{u}$. Notice that $D_{\mathbf{u}} f(\mathbf{x})$ is a *scalar* (for a scalar $f(\mathbf{x})$).

On the other hand, using the Taylor series expansion in the vicinity of $\mathbf{x}$ gives

$$f(\mathbf{x} + (\delta l)\mathbf{u}) \approx f(\mathbf{x}) + \nabla_{\mathbf{x}} f(\mathbf{x}) \cdot (\delta l)\mathbf{u} \tag{9.26}$$

which can be rewritten as

$$\nabla_{\mathbf{x}} f(\mathbf{x}) \cdot \mathbf{u} = \lim_{(\delta l) \to 0} \frac{f(\mathbf{x} + (\delta l)\mathbf{u}) - f(\mathbf{x})}{(\delta l)} \tag{9.27}$$

Using Eqs. (9.25) and (9.27), we obtain

$$D_{\mathbf{u}} f(\mathbf{x}) = \nabla_{\mathbf{x}} f(\mathbf{x}) \cdot \mathbf{u}. \tag{9.28}$$

This is expected, because the derivative of the function (scalar) in an arbitrary direction $\mathbf{u}$ is the projection (inner product) of the gradient of the function (vector) on the direction of $\mathbf{u}$.

For our minimization purposes, we want the change in cost function $D_{\mathbf{u}} f(\mathbf{x})$ as negative as possible. We thus minimize $D_{\mathbf{u}} f(\mathbf{x})$ with respect to all possible directions of the unit vector $\mathbf{u}$. Equation (9.28) is then written as

$$D_{\mathbf{u}} f(\mathbf{x}) = \|\nabla_{\mathbf{x}} f(\mathbf{x})\| \cdot \|\mathbf{u}\| \cdot \cos(\theta) = \|\nabla_{\mathbf{x}} f(\mathbf{x})\| \cdot \cos(\theta) \tag{9.29}$$

where θ is the angle between $\nabla_{\mathbf{x}} f(\mathbf{x})$ and $\mathbf{u}$, with $0 \leq \theta \leq 2\pi$. The minimum value of $\cos(\theta)$ is -1 at $\theta = \pi$. Therefore, $D_{\mathbf{u}} f(\mathbf{x})$ is minimized when $\mathbf{u}$ is at the opposite direction of the gradient $\nabla_{\mathbf{x}} f(\mathbf{x})$.

We can now reduce the value of f by updating $\mathbf{x}$ in the following manner:

$$\mathbf{x}_i := \mathbf{x}_{i-1} - \eta \nabla_{\mathbf{x}} f(\mathbf{x}) \tag{9.30}$$

where η is a positive scalar that shall carry a unit of $[(\delta x)\|\nabla_{\mathbf{x}} f(\mathbf{x}_i)\|^{-1}]$, the learning rate.

The analysis for hyper-dimensional problems is similar to what we have done for the one-dimensional problems, but needs an additional analysis on the direction. We also note that the gradient of a scalar function with respect to a vector variable is a vector of the same shape of the variable vector. In other words, taking the gradient to a scalar function is essentially the same as taking the derivative. All one needs to do is to change the scalar variable to a vector variable. By the same argument, all the remarks made in the previous subsection also hold for hyper-dimensional problems.

9.4.4 *Property of a convex function*

Convexity is an important feature of a function in terms of optimization, and many optimization algorithms work well for convex functions. If a function $f(\mathbf{x})$ is said to be **convex**, it means that (a) there is an $\mathbf{x}^*$ at which $f(\mathbf{x}^*)$ is a minimum and (b) for any $\mathbf{x}_a$ and $\mathbf{x}_b$ in the domain where $f(\mathbf{x})$ is defined, we always have

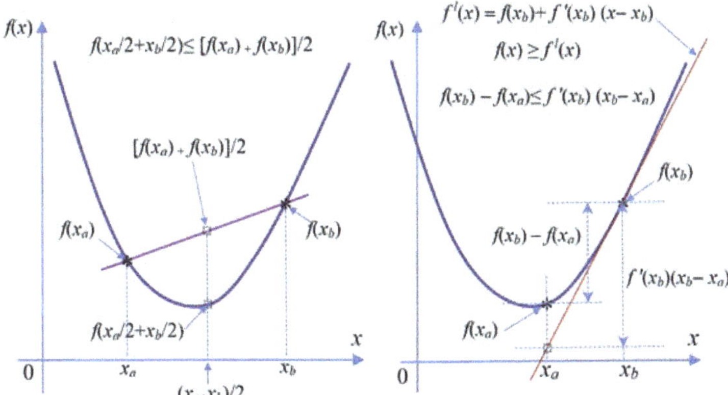

Figure 9.7: Pictorial demonstration of the properties and important inequalities of a convex function in one dimension.

$$f\left(\frac{\mathbf{x}_a + \mathbf{x}_b}{2}\right) \leq \frac{f(\mathbf{x}_a) + f(\mathbf{x}_b)}{2} \tag{9.31}$$

This condition can be given in a more general statement as follows:

$$f(\mathbf{x}_b) - f(\mathbf{x}_a) \leq \nabla_{\mathbf{x}_b} f(\mathbf{x}_b) \cdot (\mathbf{x}_b - \mathbf{x}_a) \tag{9.32}$$

These properties are useful to prove convergence theory for gradient descent methods. They are shown pictorially in Fig. 9.7.

9.4.5 *The convergence theorem for the Gradient Decent algorithm*

Theorem: Consider a Gradient Descent (GD) algorithm for minimizing function $f(\mathbf{x})$. At time $t+1$, it updates $\mathbf{x}$ using the following GD algorithm:

$$\mathbf{x}_{t+1} = \mathbf{x}_t - \eta \underbrace{\left[\nabla_{\mathbf{x}_t} f(\mathbf{x}_t)\right]}_{\nabla_t} = \mathbf{x}_t - \eta \nabla_t \tag{9.33}$$

where we denote for short

$$\nabla_t = \nabla_{\mathbf{x}_t} f(\mathbf{x}_t) \tag{9.34}$$

If (1) function $f(\mathbf{x})$ is convex;
(2) the norm of the gradient has an upper bound for all t:

$$\|\nabla_t\| = \|\nabla_{\mathbf{x}_t} f(\mathbf{x}_t)\| \leq G \tag{9.35}$$

where G is a constant independent of t;

(3) there is no overshooting in the updating process, meaning that the (Euclidean) distance between any point $\mathbf{x}_a$ in the domain and the minimum point $\mathbf{x}^*$ is bounded; We shall have

$$\|\mathbf{x}_a - \mathbf{x}^*\| \leq R \tag{9.36}$$

where R is a constant independent of t.

After T iterations, we obtain

$$f\left(\frac{1}{T}\sum_t^T \mathbf{x}_t\right) \leq f(\mathbf{x}^*) + \frac{RG}{\sqrt{T}} \tag{9.37}$$

by setting $\eta = \frac{R}{G\sqrt{T}}$ that has a unit of $[f^{-1}R]$.

Proof. We first examine the length (amplitude) of vector $\|\mathbf{x}_{t+1} - \mathbf{x}^*\|^2$.

$$\begin{aligned}
\|\mathbf{x}_{t+1} - \mathbf{x}^*\|^2 &= (\mathbf{x}^* - \mathbf{x}_{t+1}) \cdot (\mathbf{x}^* - \mathbf{x}_{t+1}) \\
&= (\mathbf{x}^* - \mathbf{x}_t + \eta\nabla_t) \cdot (\mathbf{x}^* - \mathbf{x}_t + \eta\nabla_t) \\
&= \|\mathbf{x}^* - \mathbf{x}_t\|^2 - 2\eta\nabla_t \cdot (\mathbf{x}_t - \mathbf{x}^*) + \eta^2\|\nabla_t\|^2 \\
&\leq \|\mathbf{x}^* - \mathbf{x}_t\|^2 - 2\eta\nabla_t \cdot (\mathbf{x}_t - \mathbf{x}^*) + \eta^2 G^2
\end{aligned} \tag{9.38}$$

The above equation gives

$$\nabla_t \cdot (\mathbf{x}_t - \mathbf{x}^*) \leq \frac{1}{2\eta}(\|\mathbf{x}^* - \mathbf{x}_t\|^2 - \|\mathbf{x}_{t+1} - \mathbf{x}^*\|^2) + \frac{\eta}{2}G^2 \tag{9.39}$$

We now examine

$$\begin{aligned}
f\left(\frac{1}{T}\sum_t^T \mathbf{x}_t\right) - f(\mathbf{x}^*) &\leq \frac{1}{T}\sum_t^T (f(\mathbf{x}_t) - f(\mathbf{x}^*)) \\
&\leq \frac{1}{T}\sum_t^T (\nabla_t \cdot (\mathbf{x}_t - \mathbf{x}^*)) \\
&\leq \frac{1}{2\eta T}\sum_t^T [\|\mathbf{x}^* - \mathbf{x}_t\|^2 - \|\mathbf{x}_{t+1} - \mathbf{x}^*\|^2] + \frac{\eta}{2}G^2 \\
&= \frac{1}{2\eta T}[\|\mathbf{x}^* - \mathbf{x}_0\|^2 - \|\mathbf{x}^* - \mathbf{x}_T\|^2] + \frac{\eta}{2}G^2 \\
&\leq \frac{R^2}{2\eta T} + \frac{\eta}{2}G^2 = \frac{RG}{\sqrt{T}}
\end{aligned} \tag{9.40}$$

In the last step, we have set $\eta = \frac{R}{G\sqrt{T}}$. This completes the proof. $\qquad\square$

9.4.6 *Setting or the learning rates*

In the proof given above, we simply assumed that the gradient is bounded by a constant $G < \infty$. The setting of η implies that the learning rate shall depend on step t. More detailed analysis can be performed by linking G with the so-called Lipschitz continuity constant for convex functions. Such an analysis would lead to the following conditions for general convex functions.

$$\sum_{n}^{\infty} \eta_t^2 < \infty \quad \text{and} \quad \sum_{n}^{\infty} \eta_t \to \infty \tag{9.41}$$

The first equation ensures a convergence, meaning that $f(\mathbf{x}_t)$ will eventually approaches to $f(\mathbf{x}^*)$, and the 2nd equation ensures the convergence can be achieved in finite steps. Note that in practice, the tuning rate can often be a challenging task. Equation (9.41) a theoretical guideline to design a schedule for learning rates. The schedule give below satisfies both foregoing equations.

$$\eta_t = \frac{\eta_0}{t^\beta} \tag{9.42}$$

in which η_0 is a pre-specified initial learning rate, and $1/2 < \beta < 1$, in order to satisfy conditions in Eq. (9.41). The following is a simple code for this (inverse) power scheduling.

```python
%matplotlib inline
import matplotlib.pyplot as plt
import numpy as np


def lr_schedulerP(epoch, lr0, beta):
    '''epoch: epoch number in the learning process
       lr0: starting linearing rate
       beta: (inverse) power '''
    return lr0/(epoch+1)**beta


ep_list = np.array(range(2000))
lr0, beta, lr_list= 0.01, 0.51, []
for epoch in ep_list:
    lr_list.append(lr_schedulerP(epoch, lr0, beta))


fig = plt.figure()
ax =  plt.axes()
ax.plot(ep_list, lr_list);
```

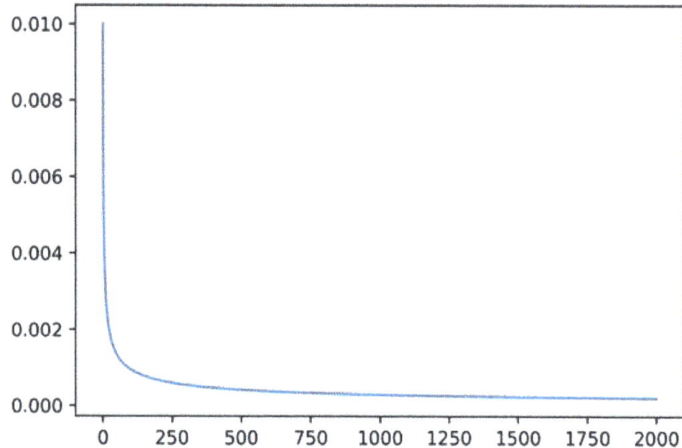

Figure 9.8:   An exponentially decaying learning rate.

Figure 9.8 plots an example of an exponentially decaying learning rate. The author often found a simple linear schedule can work well for many problems. Readers may try the following codes with modification for his/her problems.

```python
def lr_scheduler1(epoch, lr, lr1, lrT, ep_linear):
    '''Linear schedule of learning rates
       epoch: epoch number in the learning process
       lr: current learning rate
       lr1: starting point of the linear schedule
       lrT: learning rate at the final learning stage
       ep_linear: number of epochs for the linear schedule\
          portion
       lr1_T: learning rages in the linear portion from lr1\
          to lrT'''

    lr1_T = (lrT-lr1)/ep_linear * epoch + lr1
    lr = [lrT if epoch>ep_linear else lr if lr1_T>lr\
          else lr1_T][0]
    return lr


ep_list = np.array(range(1500))
lr, lr_list= 0.01, []
for epoch in ep_list:
    lr_list.append(lr_scheduler1(epoch,lr,0.02,1e-5,1000))
```

```
fig = plt.figure()
ax = plt.axes()
ax.plot(ep_list, lr_list)
```

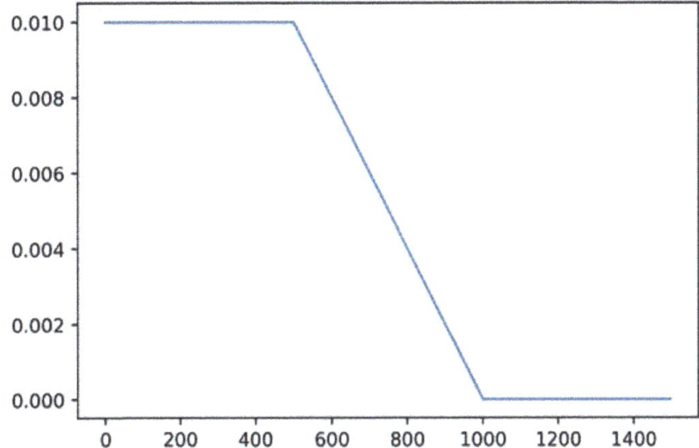

Figure 9.9: An example of piecewise linearly decaying learning rate.

This schedule shown in Fig. 9.9 has constant portion at the beginning, which can be useful to have a fast convergence at the initial stage. The learning rate used at the final stage is set at a minimum rate that is acceptable to the analyst. The learning rate in between varies linearly.

9.5 Stochastic Gradient Descent

Computation of the gradient in a gradient descent algorithm is the major consumption of the computer power. Especially for hyper-dimensional problems with extremely large number of variables with a huge dataset, the gradient descent methods can be too costly. The stochastic gradient descent (SGD) method offers an effective way to reduce computations. It makes use of the statistics property when the training datasets are sufficiently large. The key idea in SGD is as follows.

When training a model, we use a dataset with many data-points. The cost function is in fact a sum of a number of cost functions for each data-point. The gradient of the whole cost function is then estimated using the gradient of the cost function for the ith data-point, with i being randomly sampled at uniform from the dataset. Such a sampling gives, of course, less accurate gradient, but it is an unbiased estimation of the true gradient of the whole cost function. For a dataset with one million data-points, for example, the computation of the gradient at each iteration is reduced by one million times! Thus, this can be very cost-effective.

When the SGD is used in this kind of extreme manner, the convergence of the cost function may become less stable and behaves in an oscillatory manner. This is when the **mini-batch** concept comes in handy; instead of randomly sampling only one data-point, we can sample randomly at uniform a small batch of data-points at each iteration (epoch). This can significantly improve the convergence behavior with a little increase of cost, and hence the mini-batch technique can be very effective. It is one of the most efficient algorithms in machine learning when dealing with a big dataset.

The SGD is even more appealing when the training data-points have high redundancy. The stochastically sampled gradients can be a very good estimation of the true gradient of the whole cost function using a small batch. When the training data-points are large enough with high redundancy, a smaller batch size can be used, and the saving in cost can be very significant. In addition, using the stochastically sampled gradients can be considered as a type of regularization, providing some effect in alleviating overfitting.

9.5.1 *Numerical experiment*

We now demonstrate gradient-based algorithms, by creating a simple neural network model for linear regression, using the code made available at mxnet-the-straight-dope (https://github.com/zackchase/mxnet-the-straight-dope/blob/master/chapter01_crashcourse/autograd.ipynb), under the Apache-2.0 License.

We first define a function for minimization based on the SGD method with a mini-batch algorithm. The key steps in a basic mini-batch algorithm are as follows:

1. Randomly shuffle all the data-points or samples in the entire dataset.
2. Select batches each with a small number of samples (known as mini-batch) from the shuffled dataset.
3. Loop over the mini-batches, and compute the gradient of the loss function with respect to all its training parameters and perform minimization (update the training parameters) until the process is roughly converged. This completes one training *epoch*.
4. Select another set of mini-batches randomly from the entire training dataset, and repeat the above for another epoch of training. This is done

for multiple epochs, until all the samples in the entire dataset are more or less exhausted and the loss function is converged to an acceptable low level.

Because of the random sample selection for the mini-batches, one can hope that any mini-batch is statistically a good representation of the entire dataset. The following function is defined for the mini-batch SGD:

```python
def sgd(params, lr, batch_size): # Mini-batch SGD.
    for param in params:         # lr: learning rate
        param[:] = param-lr*param.grad/batch_size
```

```python
import mxnet as mx
import numpy as np
from mxnet import autograd,gluon
from mxnet import ndarray as nd
import random
%matplotlib inline
import matplotlib.pyplot as plt


mx.random.seed(1)    # seed value for random number generation
random.seed(1)
# Generate data for training and testing.
n_v = 1        # n_v = 2  # number of variables/features
               # or dimension of the space for regression.
n_s = 1000   # number of samples (data pints in the dataset)
true_w = [0.8]      # one may try this: true_w = [2, -3.4]
true_b = 4.2
start_w,start_b = 1.0,3.5 # initialize w and b
X = nd.random_normal(scale=1, shape=(n_s, n_v))
                 #generate coordinates in variable space
y = true_w[0] * X[:, 0] + true_b
                 # generate the function values
                 # using the coordinates
#y = true_w[0] * X[:,0]+true_w[1]*X[: 1]+true_b
y += .2 * nd.random_normal(scale=1, shape=y.shape)# add noise
dataset = gluon.data.ArrayDataset(X, y) #generate the dataset
```

```python
plt.scatter(X[:, 0].asnumpy(),y.asnumpy(),color='r')
plt.xlabel('$x$')
plt.ylabel("$\hat{y}$")
plt.title('data-points for Linear Regression')
plt.show()
```

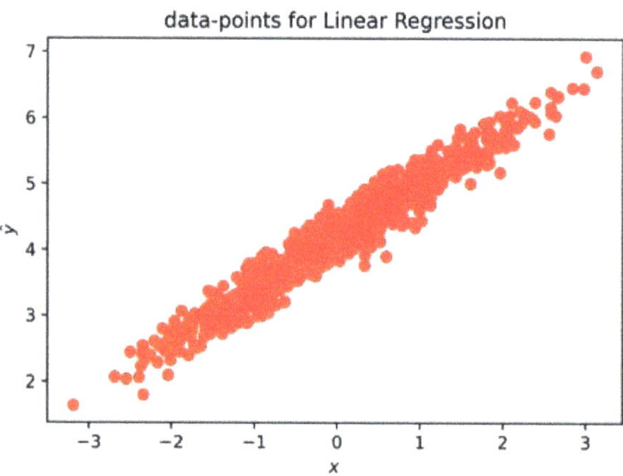

Figure 9.10:   Computer-generated data-points with noises for regression study.

```python
# Data iterator for randomly generating mini-batches of data-points
def data_iter(batch_size):
    idx = list(range(n_s))        # n_s: number of samples
    random.shuffle(idx)
    for batch_i,i in enumerate(range(0,n_s,batch_size)):
        j = nd.array(idx[i: min(i + batch_size, n_s)])
        yield batch_i, X.take(j), y.take(j) # take a mini-batch

# Initialize model training parameters.
def init_params():
    w = nd.random_normal(scale=1, shape=(n_v, 1))
    b = nd.zeros(shape=(1,))
    w[0,0] = start_w             # for examination, fix starting point.
    b[0] = start_b               # print('in init;',w[0,0],b[0])
    params = [w, b]
    for param in params:
        param.attach_grad()
    return params

# Linear regression net: an affine mapping.
def net(X, w, b):
    return nd.dot(X, w) + b
```

```python
# Least squared loss function.
def square_loss(yhat, y):
    return (yhat - y.reshape(yhat.shape)) ** 2 / 2


def cost_function(X,W11,B1,y): # for plotting cost function
    W12 = np.expand_dims(W11, axis=2)
                # W11:(100,100)->(100,100,1) for X:(1000,1)
    print('shape of W12:',W12.shape,'shape of X:',X.shape)
    yh = np.inner(X.asnumpy(), W12)+ B1
    yy = np.expand_dims(y.asnumpy(), axis=-1)
    yz = np.expand_dims(yy, axis=-1)
    print('shape of yh:',yh.shape,'shape of yz is:',yz.shape)
    yhy = np.mean((yh - yz) ** 2/2,axis=0)
    return yhy
```

With all the necessary functions defined for use, we now write the algorithm to train the model.

```python
%matplotlib notebook
import matplotlib as mpl
mpl.rcParams['figure.dpi']= 120
import matplotlib.pyplot as plt
from mpl_toolkits import mplot3d
from mpl_toolkits.mplot3d import axes3d
import numpy as np


def train(batch_size, lr, epochs, period):
    assert period >= batch_size and period % batch_size == 0
    w, b = init_params()
    total_loss=[np.mean(square_loss(net(X, w, b), y).asnumpy())]
    wi, bi = [], []
    wi.append(w.asnumpy()[0,0])
    bi.append(b.asnumpy()[0])

    # Epoch starts from 1.
    for epoch in range(1, epochs + 1):
        if epoch > 2:
            lr *= 0.9                    # Decay learning rate.
        for batch_i, data, label in data_iter(batch_size):
            #for samples in a mini-batch
            with autograd.record(): # define computational graph.
                output = net(data, w, b)
                loss = square_loss(output, label)
```

```
            loss.backward()                 # compute the gradient
            sgd([w, b], lr, batch_size)     # update the parameters

            if batch_i * batch_size % period == 0:
                total_loss.append(np.mean(square_loss
                        (net(X,w,b),y).asnumpy()))
                bi.append(b.asnumpy()[0])
                wi.append(w.asnumpy()[0,0])

        print("Batch size %d,Learning rate %f,Epoch %d,loss %.4e"
                        %(batch_size,lr,epoch, total_loss[-1]))

    return wi,bi,total_loss,epochs
```

```
Wi,Bi,T_cost,Epochs=train(batch_size=10,lr=.2,epochs=5,
        period=10)
```

```
print(Wi[-1],Bi[-1])  #the final converged weight and bias
```

```
Batch size 10,Learning rate 0.200000,Epoch 1,loss 2.0546e-02
Batch size 10,Learning rate 0.200000,Epoch 2,loss 2.0513e-02
Batch size 10,Learning rate 0.180000,Epoch 3,loss 2.0435e-02
Batch size 10,Learning rate 0.162000,Epoch 4,loss 2.1135e-02
Batch size 10,Learning rate 0.145800,Epoch 5,loss 2.1392e-02
0.78678846 4.246581
```

Finally, let us examine the training process.

```
nonlic =['linear','sigmoid','tanh','relu'] #nonlinearities
nsf = ['(a) ','(b) ','(c) ', '(d) ']

w11 = np.linspace(-2.0,4.0,100) # np.arange(0.5, 5.0, 5.0)
b1 = np.linspace(0.,8.0,100)    # np.arange(2.0, 6.0, 5.0)
lw, lb = len(w11), len(b1)
print('length of w11=',lw,'length of b1=',lb)
W11, B1 = np.meshgrid(w11, b1)
Z = cost_function(X,W11,B1,y)
```

```python
tw,tb = [true_w],[true_b]
true_z = cost_function(X,tw,tb,y)

print('length of Wi = ',len(Wi))
#%matplotlib notebook
%matplotlib inline

fig_s = plt.figure(figsize=(8,6))     # Convergence 3D plot
ax = fig_s.add_subplot(1,1,1,projection='3d')
ax.set_xlabel('$w11$', fontsize=12, rotation=80)
ax.set_ylabel('$b1$', fontsize=12)
ax.set_zlabel(r'$error$', fontsize=12, rotation=0)
ax.yaxis._axinfo['label']['space_factor'] = 3.0
ax.plot_wireframe(W11,B1,Z,color='b', rstride=5, cstride=5)
plt.title('Error function of $w11$ and
          $b1$ (' + nonlic[0] +')')
marker_style = dict(markersize=20)
ax.scatter3D(Wi,Bi,T_cost, color='red',marker='.',
    cmap='hsv',s=20)
ax.scatter3D(Wi[-1],Bi[-1],T_cost[-1],color='red',
    marker='X', s=80)
ax.scatter3D(Wi[0], Bi[0],T_cost[0],color='green',
    marker='o', s=50)
ax.scatter3D(true_w[0],true_b,true_z,color='green',
    marker='o', s=50)
#plt.legend()
fig_s.tight_layout()        # otherwise y-label is clipped
plt.show()
```

```
length of w11= 100 length of b1= 100
shape of W12: (100, 100, 1) shape of X: (1000, 1)
shape of yh is: (1000, 100, 100) shape of yz is: (1000, 1, 1)
shape of W12: (1, 1, 1) shape of X: (1000, 1)
shape of yh is: (1000, 1, 1) shape of yz is: (1000, 1, 1)
length of Wi =  501
```

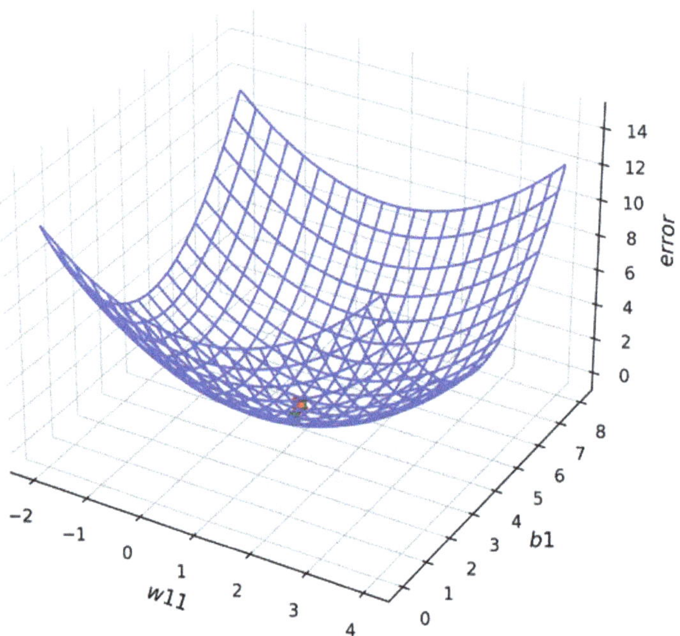

Figure 9.11: The loss function in 2D space varying quadratically with weight and bias for the linear regression problem.

```python
fig, ax = plt.subplots(figsize=(8,6))
plt.rcParams["font.size"] = "15"
CS = ax.contour(W11, B1, Z,20)
ax.clabel(CS, inline=1, fontsize=9)
ax.set_title('A cost function of least square error')
plt.scatter(Wi, Bi, s=20, c='r',marker='^', alpha=0.5)
plt.scatter(Wi[-1], Bi[-1], s=80, c='r',marker='X',alpha=0.9)
plt.scatter(Wi[0], Bi[0], s=80, c='r', marker='o', alpha=0.9)
plt.scatter(true_w[0],true_b,s=80,c='g',marker='o',alpha=0.5)
ax.set_xlabel('$w11$', fontsize=12, rotation=0)
ax.set_ylabel('$b1$', fontsize=12)
fig.tight_layout()
plt.show()
```

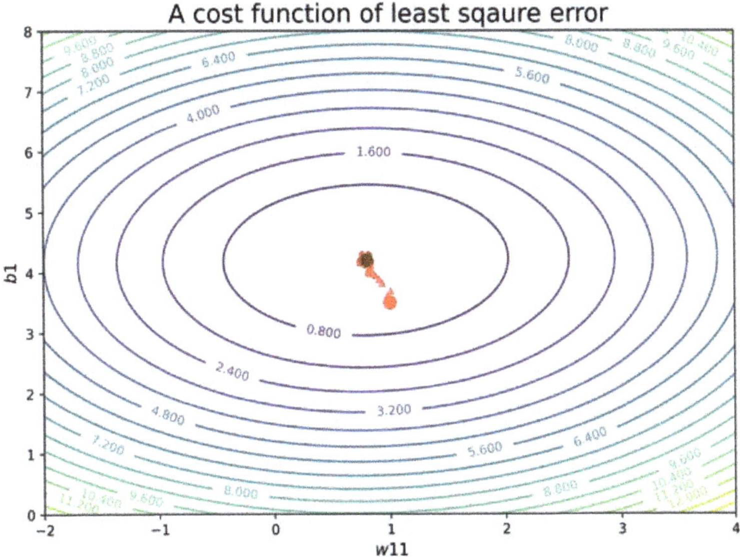

Figure 9.12:   Contours of the loss function in 2D space varying quadratically with weight and bias for the linear regression problem. A minimization algorithm (SGD) finds the minimum (green dot) starting from the initial values of weight and bias (red dot).

```python
#line plots: https://jakevdp.github.io/PythonDataScience
#Handbook/04.06-customizing-legends.html


fig, ax1 = plt.subplots(figsize=(8,6))
plt.rcParams["font.size"] = "15"
x_axis = np.linspace(0, Epochs, len(T_cost), endpoint=True)
plt.semilogy(x_axis, T_cost,color='black',linestyle='solid',\
            label='Loss function')
plt.xlabel('Epoch')
plt.ylabel('Loss')
leg = ax1.legend(loc='center', frameon=False)
ax2 = ax1.twinx()   # second axes that shares the same x-axis
color = 'tab:blue'
ax2.set_ylabel('w11 and b1 ', color=color)
ax2.plot(x_axis,Wi,color='red',linestyle='dotted',
        label='w11')
ax2.plot(x_axis,Bi,color='blue',linestyle='dashed',
        label='b1')
ax2.tick_params(axis='y', labelcolor=color)
```

```
ax1.grid() # linestyle='-', linewidth='0.5', color='red')
fig.tight_layout()  # otherwise y-label is slightly clipped
leg = ax2.legend()
plt.show()
```

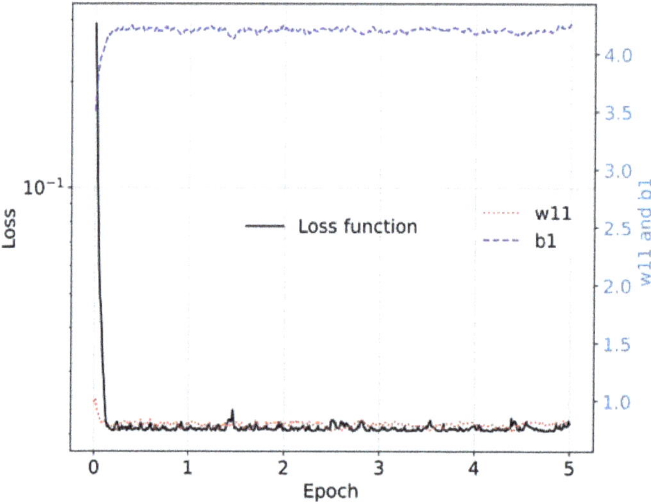

Figure 9.13:   Convergence of the loss function, the weight, and bias for the linear regression problem, during the SGD searching for the minimizer.

```
%matplotlib inline
import matplotlib.pyplot as plt
print('true_w:',true_w,' true_b:',true_b)
x = np.arange(-4, 4, .1)
yh = Wi[-1] * x + Bi[-1]
print('Predicted_w:', Wi[-1],'Predicted_b:',Bi[-1])
fig = plt.figure(figsize=(8,6))
plt.rcParams["font.size"] = "12"
plt.scatter(X[:, 0].asnumpy(),y.asnumpy(),color='r')
plt.plot(x,yh,label = "$\hat{y} = x w + b$")
plt.xlabel('$x$')
plt.ylabel("$\hat{y}$")
plt.title('Linear Regression by Minimizing the Distances')
plt.legend()
plt.show()
```

```
true_w: [0.8]  true_b: 4.2
Predicted_w: 0.78678846 Predicted_b: 4.246581
```

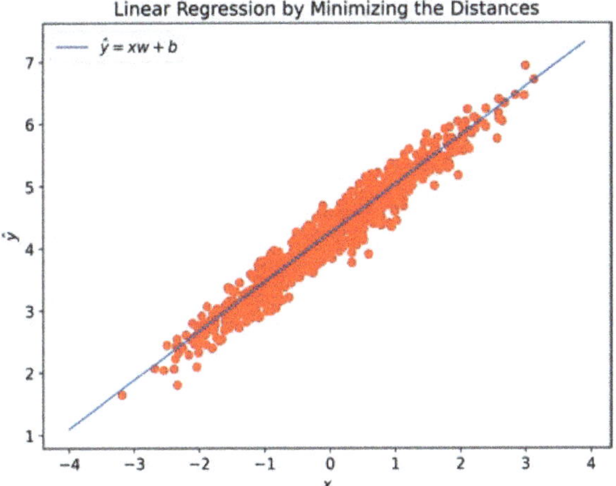

Figure 9.14: The results of the linear regression. It is found that a linear function fits best to the data-points in the sense of the least squares of errors.

9.6 Gradient Descent with Momentum

The gradient descent (GD) and its variation of the stochastic gradient descent (SGD) move in each iteration based solely on the current status of the gradient information of the cost function. It does not use any information from the past search history. Therefore, techniques that making use of the history may perform better. The method of gradient descent momentum (GDM) is one of these techniques.

9.6.1 *The most critical problem with GD methods*

Let us first examine the most critical problem with gradient descent type of methods, including the GD and SGD. We use a simple example in two-dimensional parameter space for easy intuitive analysis and understanding. Consider a cost function $f(\mathbf{x})$ with two parameters $\mathbf{x} = [x_1, x_2]$. In Fig. 9.15, we plotted the contours of the functions value in 2D space. On each contour line, the function has the same value. The green dot near the center is the true minimum point of the function. Let the GD algorithm start to search for the green dot from the initial point marked with a red star. Based on the concept of steepest descent, the negative gradient direction should be perpendicular to the contour line at the current point, because that direction is the steepest. Because of the highly elliptical shape of these contours, a GD step could overshoot and arrive at a contour line at the next lower level, and get to the other side of the hill. At this new position, GD makes the next

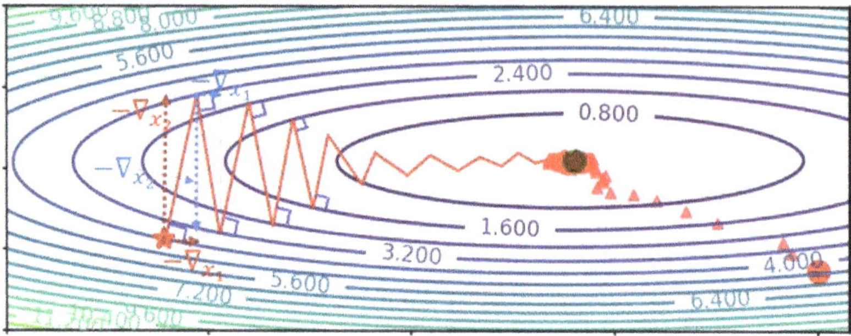

Figure 9.15:   Pictorial description of the zigzag behavior of the gradient descent algorithm for searching the minimizer of an elliptic loss function in an extreme case. The long axis is in the horizontal direction, and the short axis is in the vertical direction. "Productive" gradient components are in the horizontal direction, and they are all aligned in the positive direction towards the minimizer, but they are small, and hence progressing slowly. The "unproductive" gradient components are in the vertical direction, because they reverse directions each iteration resulting in a waste. The search traces on the right-lower part (starting from the red dot) are the actual case that we have seen in the previous example. We managed to reach the minimizer with rather a smoother path (at least at the earlier iterations). This was at a cost using a very small learning rate.

marching step. This time, the negative gradient point is yet again on the opposite side. This cycle continues, forming a zigzag path moving slowly toward the minimum point. It is clear that the GD method wasted quite a lot of effort in the process.

The root of the problem is the drastic change in direction of the consecutive (negative) gradient vectors, from one step to the next. For this type of cost functions with heavy elliptical contours, the two components of the gradient vector are very much different (it corresponds to the bad conditioning of Hessian matrix that contains the 2nd derivatives of the cost function). All these marching arrows have two components pointing to the x_1 (along the long axis of the ellipse) and x_2 (along the short axis of the ellipse) directions. They are basically two components of the (negative) gradient vector. It is easy to see that the x_1 components for all the marching arrows are largely aligned and pointing more or less to the target. However, the x_2 component of a marching arrow is largely opposite that of the next arrow.

With this insightful observation, we can now design an algorithm that uses some kind of weighted average of the gradient vectors in consecutive steps. If this can be done, all the x_1 components are still encouraged to point to the target, and all the x_2 components will cancel each other, leading to a significant reduction of the zigzag. This is essentially the idea of the method of gradient descent with momentum.

9.6.2 *Formulation*

The gradient descent with momentum can be found in Ref. [3]. It is given as follows:

$$\mathbf{v}_i := \gamma \mathbf{v}_{i-1} + \eta \nabla f(\mathbf{x}_i) \tag{9.43}$$

$$\mathbf{x}_i := \mathbf{x}_{i-1} - \mathbf{v}_i \tag{9.44}$$

where $\mathbf{v}$ is the velocity at the current step, and γ is the momentum parameter that is between 0 and 1, and is usually set to 0.9. The learning rate η and the gradient $\nabla f(\mathbf{x})$ are defined in the previous section.

To analyze the working behavior of the GDM, let us consider two simplified cases. The first case assumes that all the $\nabla f(\mathbf{x})$ at consecutive steps are pointing to the same direction and have the same values as a constant vector $\mathbf{g}$. This situation is quite similar to the component of the gradient in the x_1-direction for the case shown in Fig. 9.15. We now start the iteration as follows:

$$\mathbf{v}_0 := \mathbf{0}, \tag{9.45}$$

$$\mathbf{v}_1 := \eta \mathbf{g}, \tag{9.46}$$

$$\mathbf{v}_2 := \gamma \mathbf{v}_1 + \eta \mathbf{g} = \eta \mathbf{g}(\gamma + 1), \tag{9.47}$$

$$\mathbf{v}_3 := \gamma \mathbf{v}_2 + \eta \mathbf{g} = \eta \mathbf{g}(\gamma^2 + \gamma + 1), \tag{9.48}$$

$$\cdots \tag{9.49}$$

$$\mathbf{v}_t := \gamma \mathbf{v}_{t-1} + \eta \mathbf{g} = \eta \mathbf{g}(\gamma^{t-1} + \gamma^{t-2} + \cdots + \gamma^2 + \gamma + 1), \tag{9.50}$$

$$\cdots \tag{9.51}$$

$$\mathbf{v}_{\text{inf}} := \frac{\eta \mathbf{g}}{1 - \gamma}. \tag{9.52}$$

Let us now examine the following cases:

1. For a large γ that close to 1, such as $\gamma = 0.9$, the final velocity would be 10 times faster than the original gradient descent using the constant $\mathbf{g}$. Therefore, iterations with momentum can speed up the advancement in the direction at which all the gradients are aligning on the same direction, such as the component of the gradient in the x_1-direction shown in Fig. 9.15.
2. For a small γ that close to 0, such as $\gamma = 0.1$, the effect on the acceleration of the iteration is very small, and hence the GDM will not have much difference from the original GD algorithm.

3. For a middle ranged γ, such as $\gamma = 0.5$, the speed up is about 50% in the alignment direction.

This simple example shows that a momentum is built up to speed up the marching faster and faster, if the gradients are all well aligned and a larger γ is used.

In the second example, let us assume that all the $\nabla f(\mathbf{x})$ at consecutive steps are pointing to the opposite direction, but still have the same values as a constant vector $\mathbf{g}$. This is similar to the x_2 component under this assumption; the standard GD method will not make any advancement in that direction. Let us examine what would happen when the GDM is used.

We now start the iteration as follows:

$$\mathbf{v}_0 := \mathbf{0}, \tag{9.53}$$

$$\mathbf{v}_1 := \eta\mathbf{g}, \tag{9.54}$$

$$\mathbf{v}_2 := \gamma\mathbf{v}_1 - \eta\mathbf{g} = -\eta\mathbf{g}(1 - \gamma), \tag{9.55}$$

$$\mathbf{v}_3 := \gamma\mathbf{v}_2 + \eta\mathbf{g} = \eta\mathbf{g}(1 - \gamma + \gamma^2), \tag{9.56}$$

$$\mathbf{v}_4 := \gamma\mathbf{v}_3 - \eta\mathbf{g} = -\eta\mathbf{g}(1 - \gamma + \gamma^2 - \gamma^3), \tag{9.57}$$

$$\cdots \tag{9.58}$$

$$\mathbf{v}_{2i-1} := \eta\mathbf{g}(1 - \gamma + \gamma^2, \ldots, -\gamma^{2i-3} + \gamma^{2i-2}), \tag{9.59}$$

$$\mathbf{v}_{2i} := -\eta\mathbf{g}(1 - \gamma + \gamma^2, \ldots, +\gamma^{2i-2} - \gamma^{2i-1}), \tag{9.60}$$

For any $\gamma < 1$, we note the following:

1. The learning is always reduced, as long as $\gamma < 1$.
2. The series behind $\eta\mathbf{g}$ in Eqs. (9.59) and (9.60) will all bounded by 1, and hence we shall have

$$\mathbf{v}_{2i-1} \leq \eta\mathbf{g} \tag{9.61}$$

$$\mathbf{v}_{2i} \geq -\eta\mathbf{g} \tag{9.62}$$

Let us now examine the following cases:

1. For a large γ close to 1, such as $\gamma = 0.9$, the value of the (negative) velocity at the 2nd iteration $\mathbf{v}_2$ is reduced by 90%, because of the cancellation. Although $\mathbf{v}_3$ at the 3rd become larger again, it will always be smaller than the original velocity. The same trend is kept in the following iterations. Therefore, iterations with momentum will reduce the speed in the direction at which all the gradients are opposite to each other, such

as the component of the gradient in the x_2-direction as shown Fig. 9.15. Note that because the velocity in the x_1-direction is significantly speeding up, the zigzag behavior will be significantly reduced.

2. For a small γ that close to 0, such as $\gamma = 0.1$, the cancellation effect is very small, and hence the GDM will not have much difference from the original GD algorithm.

3. For a middle ranged γ, such as $\gamma = 0.5$, the cancellation at early iterations is about 50%. The cancellation effect is reduced in the later iterations, but will always be smaller than the original velocity. Because the velocity in the x_1-direction is speeding up about 50%, the zigzag behavior will be significantly reduced. The convergence is expected to be more than 50% faster.

Based on the above analysis, we can conclude that a large γ that close to 1, say $\gamma = 0.9$, is preferred. In summary, the gradient descent with momentum converges much faster, compared to the original GD, because updates in the long axis are much faster, and in the short axis there are some levels of cancellation. The zigzag behavior can be significantly suppressed.

From the algorithm, it is seen that the gradients obtained in all the previous iterations are involved in the current iteration. The next question one may ask is what the extent of such involvements. Let us analyze this further.

We start the iteration again as follows considering the gradient is changing in each iteration:

$$\mathbf{v}_0 := \mathbf{0}, \tag{9.63}$$

$$\mathbf{v}_1 := \eta \nabla f(\mathbf{x}_1), \tag{9.64}$$

$$\mathbf{v}_2 := \gamma \mathbf{v}_1 + \eta \nabla f(\mathbf{x}_2) = \gamma \eta \nabla f(\mathbf{x}_1) + \eta \nabla f(\mathbf{x}_2), \tag{9.65}$$

$$\mathbf{v}_3 := \gamma \mathbf{v}_2 + \eta \nabla f(\mathbf{x}_3) = \gamma^2 \eta \nabla f(\mathbf{x}_1) + \gamma \eta \nabla f(\mathbf{x}_2) + \eta \nabla f(\mathbf{x}_3), \tag{9.66}$$

$$\cdots \tag{9.67}$$

$$\mathbf{v}_t := \gamma \mathbf{v}_{t-1} + \eta \nabla f(\mathbf{x}_t) = \gamma^{t-1} \eta \nabla f(\mathbf{x}_1) + \gamma^{t-1} \eta \nabla f(\mathbf{x}_2)$$
$$+ \cdots + \gamma \eta \nabla f(\mathbf{x}_{t-1}) + \eta \nabla f(\mathbf{x}_t) \tag{9.68}$$

Because $\gamma < 1$, it is clear that the influence of the gradient of the earlier iterations slowly reduced at the rate of γ.

Finally, one may be inspired from this analysis that a properly varying γ could be even better! We also note that to solve this kind zigzag behavior entirely, the *conjugate gradient method* should be used, but it requires the valuation of the 2nd gradient (the Hessian matrix), which can be a lot more expensive and the scalability can also be a problem.

9.6.3 *Numerical experiment*

We now demonstrate an algorithm of GDM, by creating a linear regression model.

```python
def sgd_momentum(params, vs, lr, mom, batch_size):
    for param, v in zip(params, vs):
        v[:] = mom * v + lr * param.grad / batch_size
        param[:] = param - v
```

```python
import mxnet as mx
from mxnet import autograd, gluon
from mxnet import ndarray as nd
import random
import numpy as np

mx.random.seed(1); random.seed(1)
# Generate data.
n_v = 2                  # number of variables (features)
n_s = 1000               # number of samples

true_w, true_b = [2, -3.4], 4.2
X=nd.random_normal(scale=1,shape=(n_s,n_v))
y=true_w[0] * X[:, 0] + true_w[1] * X[:, 1] + true_b
y+=.01 * nd.random_normal(scale=1, shape=y.shape)
dataset = gluon.data.ArrayDataset(X, y)
# Construct data iterator.
def data_iter(batch_size):
    idx = list(range(n_s))
    random.shuffle(idx)
    for batch_i,i in enumerate(range(0,n_s,batch_size)):
        j = nd.array(idx[i: min(i + batch_size, n_s)])
        yield batch_i, X.take(j), y.take(j)

# Initialize model parameters.
def init_params():
    w = nd.random_normal(scale=1, shape=(n_v, 1))
    b = nd.zeros(shape=(1,))
```

```python
    params = [w, b]
    vs = []
    for param in params:
        param.attach_grad()
        #
        vs.append(param.zeros_like())
    return params, vs

# Linear regression.
def net(X, w, b):
    return nd.dot(X, w) + b

# Loss function.
def square_loss(yhat, y):
    return (yhat - y.reshape(yhat.shape)) ** 2 / 2
```

```python
%matplotlib inline
import matplotlib as mpl
mpl.rcParams['figure.dpi']= 120
import matplotlib.pyplot as plt
import numpy as np

def train(batch_size, lr, mom, epochs, period):
    assert period >= batch_size and period % batch_size == 0
    [w, b], vs = init_params()
    total_loss=[np.mean(square_loss(net(X,w,b),y).asnumpy())]
    # Epoch starts from 1.
    for epoch in range(1, epochs + 1):
        # Decay learning rate.
        if epoch > 2:
            lr *= 0.1
        for batch_i, data, label in data_iter(batch_size):
            with autograd.record():
                output = net(data, w, b)
                loss = square_loss(output, label)
            loss.backward()
            sgd_momentum([w, b], vs, lr, mom, batch_size)
            if batch_i * batch_size % period == 0:
                total_loss.append(np.mean(square_loss\
                (net(X,w,b),y).asnumpy()))
```

```python
    print("Batch size %d, Learning rate %f, Epoch %d,loss\
        %.4e" % (batch_size, lr, epoch, total_loss[-1]))
print('true_w:',true_w,' true_b:',true_b)
print('Predicted_w:', np.reshape(w.asnumpy(), (1, -1)),
    'Predicted_b:', b.asnumpy()[0], '\n')
x_axis=np.linspace(0,epochs,len(total_loss),endpoint=True)
plt.semilogy(x_axis, total_loss)
plt.xlabel('epoch')
plt.ylabel('loss')
plt.show()
```

```python
train(batch_size=10, lr=.2, mom=.9, epochs=3, period=10)
```

```
Batch size 10, Learning rate 0.20, Epoch 1,loss    1.4316e-02
Batch size 10, Learning rate 0.20, Epoch 2,loss    6.2213e-05
Batch size 10, Learning rate 0.02, Epoch 3,loss    5.2174e-05
true_w: [2, -3.4]  true_b: 4.2
Predicted_w: [[ 1.9999688 -3.4014332]] Predicted_b: 4.1995444
```

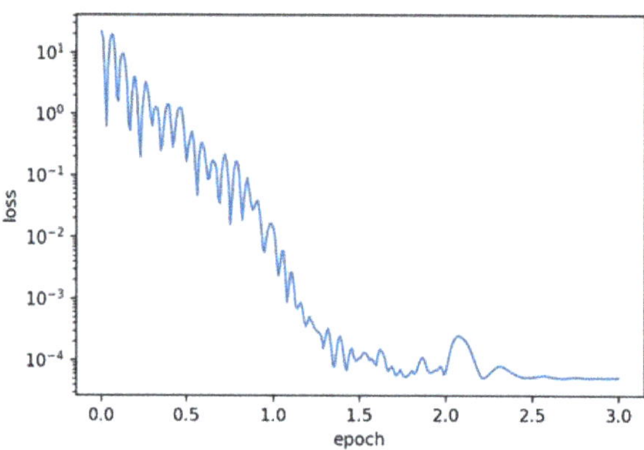

Figure 9.16:   Convergence of the loss function for the same linear regression problem, during the SGD with momentum searching for the minimizer.

9.7 Nesterov Accelerated Gradient

9.7.1 *Formulation*

The Nesterov accelerated gradient (NAG) [4] method may be viewed as a modified GDM. In computing the gradient in Eq. (9.43), instead of using $\mathbf{x}_i$, it uses $(\mathbf{x}_i - \gamma\mathbf{v}_{i-1})$. The equations become

$$\mathbf{v}_i := \gamma\mathbf{v}_{i-1} + \eta\nabla f(\mathbf{x}_i - \gamma\mathbf{v}_{i-1}) \tag{9.69}$$

$$\mathbf{x}_i := \mathbf{x}_{i-1} - \mathbf{v}_i \tag{9.70}$$

It is clear that it looks ahead in computing the gradient at a near future instead of at the current, aiming for faster convergence. We will observe its behavior in the case study section at the end of this chapter.

9.8 AdaGrad Gradient Algorithm

Adaptive gradient algorithm (AdaGrad) is another modified stochastic gradient descent (SGD) algorithm. It was first published in 2011 [5], allowing the use of per-iteration and even per-parameter learning rates. It is designed to increase the learning speed for sparser parameters and decrease it for dense ones. It is claimed that this strategy often improves convergence performance over standard SGD, and has been successfully applied to both convex and non-convex problems. More detailed discussions may be found at the wikepedia page (https://en.wikipedia.org/wiki/Stochastic_gradient_descent).

9.8.1 *Formulation*

The Adagrad scales the base learning rate η and updates the parameters using

$$\mathbf{x}_i := \mathbf{x}_{i-1} - \frac{\eta}{\sqrt{\mathbf{G}_i + \epsilon}}\nabla f(\mathbf{x}_i) \tag{9.71}$$

where ϵ is a small positive just for preventing a zero denominator during the computation. Note that the above operations for these vectors are all element-wise including the square-root operation, and $\mathbf{G}_i$ is also a vector given by

$$\mathbf{G}_i = \sum_{q=1}^{i}(\nabla f(\mathbf{x}_q))^2 \tag{9.72}$$

which is the sum of the element-wise product of the gradients of all the previous iterations (which are accumulated during the iteration).

Note that this is done for each parameter. For parameters that received excessive updates in the previous iterations, the current update is suppressed, while parameters that get small updates receive larger learning rates.

For the strong elliptical objective functions discussed earlier, the Adagrad tends promote advancement along the long axis (x_1-direction) and discourages moves along the short axis (x_2-direction). This practically suppresses the zigzag behavior shown in Fig. 9.15.

Let us examine the Adagrad algorithm using the same linear regression problem.

9.8.2 *Numerical experiment*

```python
# Adagrad.
def adagrad(params, sqrs, lr, batch_size):
    eps_stable = 1e-7
    for param, sqr in zip(params, sqrs):
        g = param.grad / batch_size
        sqr[:]+=nd.square(g) # Accumulate squared gradient
        div=lr*g/nd.sqrt(sqr+eps_stable)    #element-wise
        param[:] -= div


import mxnet as mx
from mxnet import autograd, gluon
from mxnet import ndarray as nd
import random


mx.random.seed(1); random.seed(1)
# Generate data.
n_v = 2              # number of variables (features)
n_s = 1000           # number of samples
true_w, true_b = [2, -3.4], 4.2
X=nd.random_normal(scale=1,shape=(n_s,n_v))
y=true_w[0] * X[:, 0] + true_w[1] * X[:, 1] + true_b
y+=.01 * nd.random_normal(scale=1, shape=y.shape)
dataset = gluon.data.ArrayDataset(X, y)


# Construct data iterator.
def data_iter(batch_size):
    idx = list(range(n_s))
    random.shuffle(idx)
    for batch_i,i in enumerate(range(0,n_s,batch_size)):
        j = nd.array(idx[i: min(i + batch_size, n_s)])
        yield batch_i, X.take(j), y.take(j)
```

```python
# Initialize model parameters.
def init_params():
    w = nd.random_normal(scale=1, shape=(n_v, 1))
    b = nd.zeros(shape=(1,))
    params = [w, b]
    sqrs = []
    for param in params:
        param.attach_grad()
        #
        sqrs.append(param.zeros_like())
    return params, sqrs

# Linear regression.
def net(X, w, b):
    return nd.dot(X, w) + b

# Loss function.
def square_loss(yhat, y):
    return (yhat - y.reshape(yhat.shape)) ** 2 / 2
```

```python
%matplotlib inline
import matplotlib as mpl
mpl.rcParams['figure.dpi']= 120
import matplotlib.pyplot as plt
import numpy as np

def train(batch_size, lr, epochs, period):
    assert period >= batch_size and period % batch_size == 0
    [w, b], sqrs = init_params()
    total_loss=[np.mean(square_loss(net(X, w, b),y).asnumpy())]

    # Epoch starts from 1.
    for epoch in range(1, epochs + 1):
        for batch_i, data, label in data_iter(batch_size):
            with autograd.record():
                output = net(data, w, b)
                loss = square_loss(output, label)
            loss.backward()
            adagrad([w, b], sqrs, lr, batch_size)
            if batch_i * batch_size % period == 0:
                total_loss.append(np.mean(square_loss\
                (net(X,w,b),y).asnumpy()))
```

```python
        print("Batch size %d, Learning rate %f, Epoch %d",
            "loss %.4e" %(batch_size,lr,epoch,total_loss[-1]))
    print('true_w:',true_w,' true_b:',true_b)
    print('Predicted_w:', np.reshape(w.asnumpy(), (1, -1)),
        'Predicted_b:', b.asnumpy()[0], '\n')
    x_axis=np.linspace(0,epochs,len(total_loss),endpoint=True)
    plt.semilogy(x_axis, total_loss)
    plt.xlabel('epoch')
    plt.ylabel('loss')
    plt.show()
```

```python
train(batch_size=10, lr=0.9, epochs=3, period=10)
```

```
Batch size 10, Learning rate 0.90, Epoch 1, loss 5.1843e-05
Batch size 10, Learning rate 0.90, Epoch 2, loss 5.2248e-05
Batch size 10, Learning rate 0.90, Epoch 3, loss 5.1507e-05
true_w: [2, -3.4]   true_b: 4.2
Predicted_w: [[ 2.0000997 -3.4004908]] Predicted_b: 4.199482
```

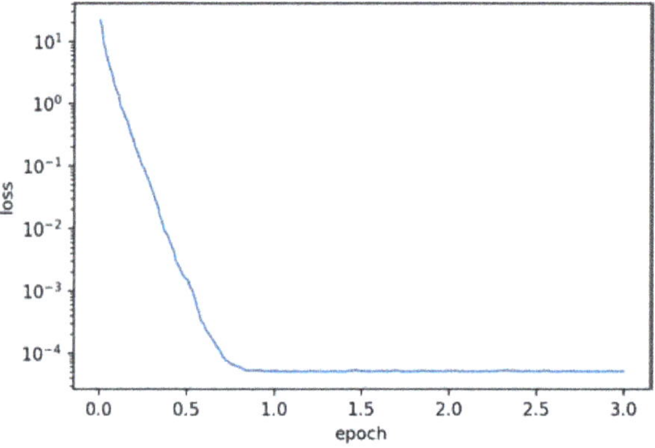

Figure 9.17: Convergence of the loss function for the same linear regression problem, during the AdaGrad searching for the minimizer.

9.9 RMSProp Gradient Algorithm

RMSProp is short for Root Mean Square Propagation [6]. It scales the learning rate for each of the parameters. It has been shown that RMSProp has good adaptation of learning rate for different applications. More details can be found at the Wikipedia page (https://en.wikipedia.org/wiki/Stochastic_gradient_descent).

9.9.1 *Formulation*

RMSProp scales the base learning rate η and updates the parameters using

$$\mathbf{x}_i := \mathbf{x}_{i-1} - \frac{\eta}{\sqrt{\mathbf{v}_i + \epsilon}} \nabla f(\mathbf{x}_i) \tag{9.73}$$

where ϵ is a small positive number for preventing a zero denominator during the computation. Notice again that the operations are element-wise. And, $\mathbf{v}_i$ at the ith iteration is given as follows:

$$\mathbf{v}_i := \gamma \mathbf{v}_{i-1} + (1 - \gamma)(\nabla f(\mathbf{x}_i))^2 \tag{9.74}$$

where γ is the tunable positive number called forgetting factor.

Let us observe the behavior.

9.9.2 *Numerical experiment*

```python
# RMSProp.
def rmsprop(params, sqrs, lr, gamma, batch_size):
    eps_stable = 1e-8
    for param, sqr in zip(params, sqrs):
        g = param.grad / batch_size
        sqr[:]=gamma*sqr+(1.-gamma)*nd.square(g)
                    #note the in-place computation here
        div = lr * g / nd.sqrt(sqr + eps_stable)
        param[:]  -= div


import mxnet as mx
from mxnet import autograd, gluon
from mxnet import ndarray as nd
import random


mx.random.seed(1); random.seed(1)
# Generate data.
n_v = 2                  # number of variables (features)
n_s = 1000               # number of samples
```

```python
true_w, true_b = [2, -3.4], 4.2
X = nd.random_normal(scale=1, shape=(n_s, n_v))
y = true_w[0] * X[:, 0] + true_w[1] * X[:, 1] + true_b
y += .01 * nd.random_normal(scale=1, shape=y.shape)
dataset = gluon.data.ArrayDataset(X, y)
# Construct data iterator.
def data_iter(batch_size):
    idx = list(range(n_s))
    random.shuffle(idx)
    for batch_i,i in enumerate(range(0,n_s,batch_size)):
        j = nd.array(idx[i: min(i + batch_size, n_s)])
        yield batch_i, X.take(j), y.take(j)


# Initialize model parameters.
def init_params():
    w = nd.random_normal(scale=1, shape=(n_v, 1))
    b = nd.zeros(shape=(1,))
    params = [w, b]
    sqrs = []
    for param in params:
        param.attach_grad()
        sqrs.append(param.zeros_like())
    return params, sqrs


# Linear regression.
def net(X, w, b):
    return nd.dot(X, w) + b


# Loss function.
def square_loss(yhat, y):
    return (yhat - y.reshape(yhat.shape)) ** 2 / 2
```

```python
%matplotlib inline
import matplotlib as mpl
mpl.rcParams['figure.dpi']= 120
import matplotlib.pyplot as plt
import numpy as np
```

```python
def train(batch_size, lr, gamma, epochs, period):
    assert period >= batch_size and period % batch_size == 0
    [w, b], sqrs = init_params()
    total_loss=[np.mean(square_loss(net(X,w,b),y).asnumpy())]

    # Epoch starts from 1.
    for epoch in range(1, epochs + 1):
        for batch_i, data, label in data_iter(batch_size):
            with autograd.record():
                output = net(data, w, b)
                loss = square_loss(output, label)
            loss.backward()
            rmsprop([w, b], sqrs, lr, gamma, batch_size)
            if batch_i * batch_size % period == 0:
                total_loss.append(np.mean(square_loss\
                (net(X, w, b), y).asnumpy()))
        print("Batch size %d,Learning rate %f, Epoch %d,loss\
            %.4e" %(batch_size, lr, epoch, total_loss[-1]))

    print('true_w:',true_w,' true_b:',true_b)
    print('Predicted_w:', np.reshape(w.asnumpy(), (1, -1)),
        'Predicted_b:', b.asnumpy()[0], '\n')
    x_axis=np.linspace(0,epochs,len(total_loss),
        endpoint=True)
    plt.semilogy(x_axis, total_loss)
    plt.xlabel('epoch')
    plt.ylabel('loss')
    plt.show()
```

```python
train(batch_size=10, lr=.02, gamma=.9, epochs=3, period=10)
```

```
Batch size 10,Learning rate 0.020, Epoch 1,loss      6.2608e+00
Batch size 10,Learning rate 0.020, Epoch 2,loss      5.9297e-01
Batch size 10,Learning rate 0.020, Epoch 3,loss      5.6944e-05
true_w: [2, -3.4]  true_b: 4.2
Predicted_w: [[ 2.0020406 -3.397886 ]] Predicted_b: 4.2007647
```

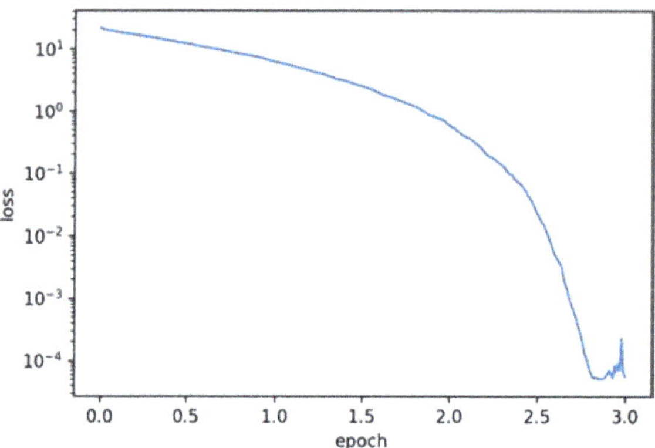

Figure 9.18:   Convergence of the loss function for the same linear regression problem, during the RMSProp searching for the minimizer.

9.10 AdaDelta Gradient Algorithm

9.10.1 *The idea*

Adadelta gradient algorithm is a more robust extension of Adagrad [7]. It adapts learning rates using a moving window of gradients, instead of accumulating all past gradients as in the Adagrad. In using AdaDelta, one does not have to set an initial learning rate. A short and clearly written note on AdaDelta can also be found at http://akyrillidis.github.io/notes/AdaDelta.

9.10.2 *Numerical experiment*

```python
# Adadelta.
def adadelta(params, sqrs, deltas, rho, batch_size):
    eps = 1e-5           # epsilon for stabilization
    for param, sqr, delta in zip(params, sqrs, deltas):
        g = param.grad / batch_size
        sqr[:] = rho * sqr + (1. - rho) * nd.square(g)
        cur_delta=nd.sqrt(delta+eps)/nd.sqrt(sqr+eps)*g
        delta[:]=rho*delta+(1.-rho)*cur_delta*cur_delta
                        # update weight
        param[:] -= cur_delta


import mxnet as mx
from mxnet import ndarray as nd
from mxnet import autograd, gluon
import random
```

```python
mx.random.seed(1)
# Generate data.
n_v = 2                    # number of variables (features)
n_s = 1000                 # number of samples
true_w, true_b = [2, -3.4], 4.2
X = nd.random_normal(scale=1,shape=(n_s,n_v))
y = true_w[0] * X[:, 0] + true_w[1] * X[:, 1] + true_b
y += .01 * nd.random_normal(scale=1, shape=y.shape)
dataset = gluon.data.ArrayDataset(X, y)
# Construct data iterator.
def data_iter(batch_size):
    idx = list(range(n_s))
    random.shuffle(idx)
    for batch_i,i in enumerate(range(0,n_s,batch_size)):
        j = nd.array(idx[i: min(i + batch_size, n_s)])
        yield batch_i, X.take(j), y.take(j)


# Initialize model parameters.
def init_params():
    w = nd.random_normal(scale=1, shape=(n_v, 1))
    b = nd.zeros(shape=(1,))
    params = [w, b]
    sqrs = []
    deltas = []
    for param in params:
        param.attach_grad()
        #
        sqrs.append(param.zeros_like())
        deltas.append(param.zeros_like())
    return params, sqrs, deltas


# Linear regression.
def net(X, w, b):
    return nd.dot(X, w) + b


# Loss function.
def square_loss(yhat, y):
    return (yhat - y.reshape(yhat.shape)) ** 2 / 2
```

```python
%matplotlib inline
import matplotlib as mpl
mpl.rcParams['figure.dpi']= 120
import matplotlib.pyplot as plt
import numpy as np

def train(batch_size, rho, epochs, period):
    assert period >= batch_size and period % batch_size == 0
    [w, b], sqrs, deltas = init_params()
    total_loss=[np.mean(square_loss(net(X,w,b),y).asnumpy())]

    # Epoch starts from 1.
    for epoch in range(1, epochs + 1):
        for batch_i, data, label in data_iter(batch_size):
            with autograd.record():
                output = net(data, w, b)
                loss = square_loss(output, label)
            loss.backward()
            adadelta([w, b], sqrs, deltas, rho, batch_size)
            if batch_i * batch_size % period == 0:
                total_loss.append(np.mean(square_loss\
                (net(X, w, b), y).asnumpy()))
        print("Batch size %d, Epoch %d, loss %.4e" %
            (batch_size, epoch, total_loss[-1]))

    print('true_w:',true_w,' true_b:',true_b)
    print('Predicted_w:', np.reshape(w.asnumpy(), (1, -1)),
        'Predicted_b:', b.asnumpy()[0], '\n')
    x_axis=np.linspace(0,epochs,len(total_loss), endpoint=True)
    plt.semilogy(x_axis, total_loss)
    plt.xlabel('epoch')
    plt.ylabel('loss')
    plt.show()
```

```python
train(batch_size=10, rho=.9999, epochs=3, period=10)
```

```
Batch size 10, Epoch 1, loss 5.3295e-05
Batch size 10, Epoch 2, loss 5.2909e-05
Batch size 10, Epoch 3, loss 5.2828e-05
true_w: [2, -3.4]  true_b: 4.2
Predicted_w: [[ 1.999908  -3.4017406]] Predicted_b: 4.19924
```

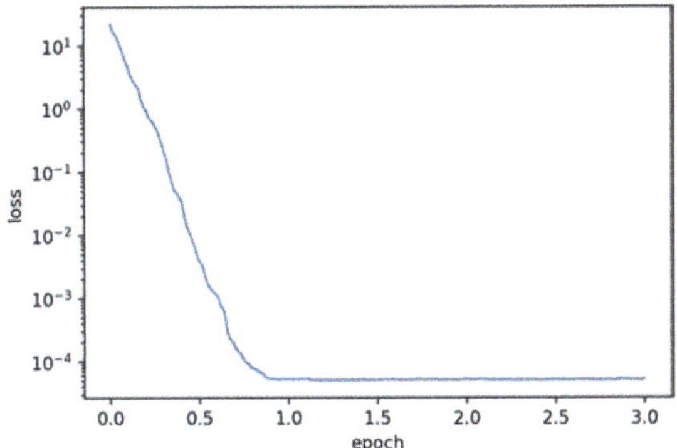

Figure 9.19: Convergence of the loss function for the same linear regression problem, during the AdaDelta searching for the minimizer.

9.11 Adam Gradient Algorithm

Adaptive Moment Estimation (Adam) gradient algorithm [8] is a modified version of the RMSProp algorithm. It uses running averages of both the RMSProp gradients and the second moments of the gradients.

9.11.1 *Formulation*

At the ith training iteration, for given parameters $\mathbf{x}_i$ and a loss function $f(\mathbf{x}_i)$, Adam algorithm scales the base learning rate η and updates the parameters using

$$\mathbf{x}_i := \mathbf{x}_{i-1} - \frac{\eta \mathbf{m}_i}{\sqrt{\hat{\mathbf{v}}_i} + \epsilon} \tag{9.75}$$

where ϵ is a small positive number for preventing a zero denominator during the computation, and $\mathbf{m}_i$ and $\hat{\mathbf{v}}_i$ are given as follows:

$$\mathbf{m}_i := \frac{\mathbf{m}_i}{1 - \beta_1} \tag{9.76}$$

$$\hat{\mathbf{v}}_i := \frac{\mathbf{v}_i}{1 - \beta_2} \tag{9.77}$$

in which $\mathbf{m}_i$ and $\mathbf{v}_i$, are, respectively, updated using

$$\mathbf{m}_i := \beta_1 \mathbf{m}_{i-1} + (1 - \beta_1)(\nabla f(\mathbf{x}_i)) \tag{9.78}$$

$$\mathbf{v}_i := \beta_2 \mathbf{v}_{i-1} + (1 - \beta_2)[\nabla f(\mathbf{x}_i)]^2 \tag{9.79}$$

In Eqs. (9.78) and (9.79), β_1 and β_2 are all positive constants of forgetting factors, respectively, for the gradients and the second moments of the gradients.

The Adam algorithm is essentially a combination of the GDM and the RMSProp. It has features from these two. It is carefully formulated with statistical bias corrected by dividing $(1 - \beta)$ for both the first and second momentums. To see this, let us examine the case of the first momentum, as an example.

$$t = 0 : \mathbf{m}_0 = 0 \tag{9.80}$$

$$t = 1 : \mathbf{m}_1 = (1 - \beta_1)\nabla f(\mathbf{x}_1) \tag{9.81}$$

$$t = 2 : \mathbf{m}_2 = \beta_1(1 - \beta_1)\nabla f(\mathbf{x}_1) + (1 - \beta_1)\nabla f(\mathbf{x}_2) \tag{9.82}$$

$$t = 3 : \mathbf{m}_3 = \beta_1^2(1 - \beta_1)\nabla f(\mathbf{x}_1) + \beta_1(1 - \beta_1)\nabla f(\mathbf{x}_2)$$

$$+ (1 - \beta_1)\nabla f(\mathbf{x}_3) \tag{9.83}$$

$$\ldots \tag{9.84}$$

$$t = t : \mathbf{m}_t = (1 - \beta_1) \sum_{i=1}^{t} \beta_1^{t-i}\nabla f(\mathbf{x}_i) \tag{9.85}$$

The expectation for Equation (9.85) becomes

$$E[\mathbf{m}_t] = E\left[(1 - \beta_1) \sum_{i+1}^{t} \beta_1^{t-i}\nabla f(\mathbf{x}_i)\right] = (1 - \beta_1)\frac{1 - \beta_1^t}{1 - \beta_1}E[\nabla f(\mathbf{x}_t)]$$

$$= (1 - \beta_1^t)E[\nabla f(\mathbf{x}_t)] \tag{9.86}$$

To ensure the statistical equivalence in expectation between $\mathbf{m}_t$ and $\nabla f(\mathbf{x}_t)$, $\mathbf{m}_t$ needs to be divided by $(1 - \beta_1^t)$.

Let us observe the behavior.

9.11.2 *Numerical experiment*

```
# Adam.
def adam(params, vs, sqrs, lr, batch_size, t):
    beta1, beta2 = 0.9, 0.999
    eps = 1e-8                   # epsilon for stabilization
    for param, v, sqr in zip(params, vs, sqrs):
        g = param.grad / batch_size
        v[:] = beta1 * v + (1.-beta1)*g       # momentum
        sqr[:] = beta2 * sqr + (1.-beta2)* nd.square(g)
        v_bias_corr = v / (1. - beta1 ** t)
        sqr_bias_corr = sqr / (1. - beta2 ** t)
```

```python
        div=lr*v_bias_corr/(nd.sqrt(sqr_bias_corr)+eps)
        param[:] = param - div    #RMSprop

import mxnet as mx
from mxnet import autograd, gluon
from mxnet import ndarray as nd
import random

mx.random.seed(1); random.seed(1)
# Generate data.
n_v = 2                         # number of variables (features)
n_s = 1000                      # number of samples
true_w, true_b = [2, -3.4], 4.2
X = nd.random_normal(scale=1, shape=(n_s, n_v))
y = true_w[0] * X[:, 0] + true_w[1] * X[:, 1] + true_b
y += .01 * nd.random_normal(scale=1, shape=y.shape)
dataset = gluon.data.ArrayDataset(X, y)


# Construct data iterator.
def data_iter(batch_size):
    idx = list(range(n_s))
    random.shuffle(idx)
    for batch_i, i in enumerate(range(0, n_s, batch_size)):
        j = nd.array(idx[i: min(i + batch_size, n_s)])
        yield batch_i, X.take(j), y.take(j)


# Initialize model parameters.
def init_params():
    w = nd.random_normal(scale=1, shape=(n_v, 1))
    b = nd.zeros(shape=(1,))
    params = [w, b]
    vs = []
    sqrs = []
    for param in params:
        param.attach_grad()
        vs.append(param.zeros_like())
        sqrs.append(param.zeros_like())
    return params, vs, sqrs
```

```python
# Linear regression.
def net(X, w, b):
    return nd.dot(X, w) + b


# Loss function.
def square_loss(yhat, y):
    return (yhat - y.reshape(yhat.shape)) ** 2 / 2
```

```python
%matplotlib inline
import matplotlib as mpl
mpl.rcParams['figure.dpi']= 120
import matplotlib.pyplot as plt
import numpy as np

def train(batch_size, lr, epochs, period):
    assert period >= batch_size and period % batch_size == 0
    [w, b], vs, sqrs = init_params()
    total_loss=[np.mean(square_loss(net(X,w,b),y).asnumpy())]

    t = 0
    # Epoch starts from 1.
    for epoch in range(1, epochs + 1):
        for batch_i, data, label in data_iter(batch_size):
            with autograd.record():
                output = net(data, w, b)
                loss = square_loss(output, label)
            loss.backward()
            # Increment t before invoking adam.
            t += 1
            adam([w, b], vs, sqrs, lr, batch_size, t)
            if batch_i * batch_size % period == 0:
                total_loss.append(np.mean(square_loss\
                (net(X, w, b), y).asnumpy()))
        print("Batch size %d, Learning rate %f, Epoch %d",\
            "loss %.4e"%(batch_size,lr,epoch,total_loss[-1]))

    print('true_w:',true_w,' true_b:',true_b)
    print('Predicted_w:', np.reshape(w.asnumpy(), (1, -1)),
        'Predicted_b:', b.asnumpy()[0], '\n')
```

```python
x_axis = np.linspace(0,epochs,len(total_loss),
    endpoint=True)
plt.semilogy(x_axis, total_loss)
plt.xlabel('epoch')
plt.ylabel('loss')
plt.show()
```

```python
train(batch_size=10, lr=0.1, epochs=3, period=10)
```

```
Batch size 10, Learning rate 0.100, Epoch 1, loss   5.7667e-04
Batch size 10, Learning rate 0.100, Epoch 2, loss   5.2377e-05
Batch size 10, Learning rate 0.100, Epoch 3, loss   5.1530e-05
true_w: [2, -3.4]   true_b: 4.2
Predicted_w: [[ 2.0000498 -3.4008262]] Predicted_b: 4.1996875
```

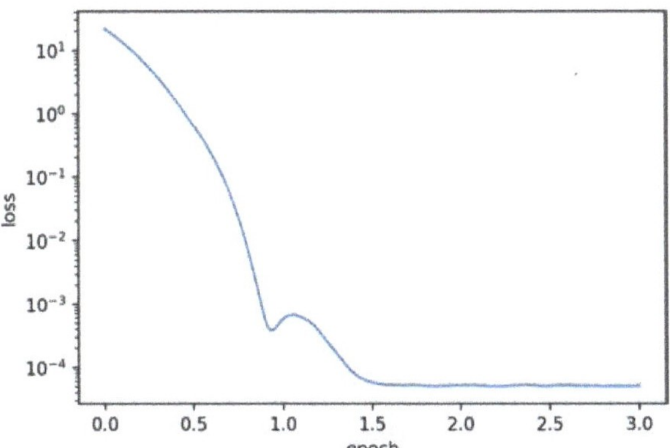

Figure 9.20:　Convergence of the loss function for the same linear regression problem, during the Adam searching for the minimizer.

9.12　A Case Study: Compare Minimization Techniques Used in MLPClassifier

We now present a case study done by the scikit-learn team [9]. This study examines the performance and plots the loss function evolution, using different stochastic minimization techniques, including SGD and Adam. The code is available at Sklearn example site (https://scikit-learn.org/stable/auto_examples/neural_networks/plot_mlp_training_curves.html#). Figure 9.21 is the result obtained using the code.

It is observed that SDM (momentum), Nesterov's SDM, and Adam are among the best performers, and Adam seems to be the overall best, based

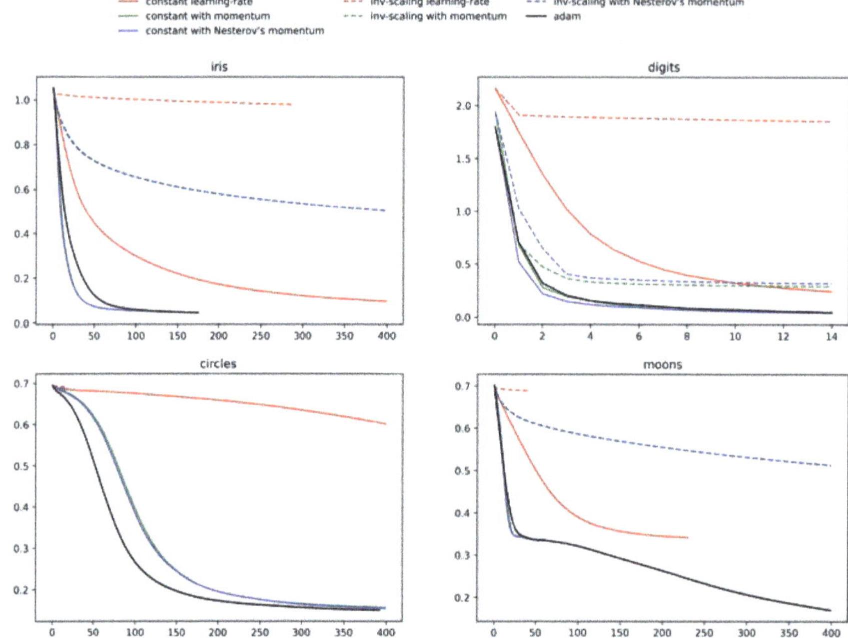

Figure 9.21: Results of a comparison study on minimization techniques based on gradient descent algorithms using Sklearn MLPClassifiers.

on this study on four datasets (iris, digits, circles, and moons). Note that there may be some bias to some techniques, and the outcome of the tests can change for different datasets. This study shall still give a good general indication on these different techniques. Note also that those results can be highly dependent on some parameters. A more detailed examination of this study can be found at the Sklearn example site.

9.13 Other Algorithms

- There are many other versions of gradient descent algorithms available in the open literature.
- Another direction of development is on higher-order methods and algorithms, including Newton Methods, Quasi-Newton methods, and Conjugate Gradient methods.
- These methods often use line search algorithms to ensure a reasonable quality solution at each iteration so that the matching can be significantly faster and also provide necessary conditions for convergence.

- In general, high-order methods can drastically reduce the number of iteration (by as much as hundreds of times).
- In each iteration, however, high-order methods take a lot more time for line search and new directions.
- In general, high-order methods converge very fast near the minimum, because of the improved local convexity there and also the quadratic convergence property.
- The robustness (sensitive to line search and noise data) and efficiency for higher-order methods for complex and large machine learning problems may need further improvements.
- It may be a good idea to use a first-order robust algorithm to drive the solution to near a minimum, and use a higher-order algorithm to finish it up.

References

[1] G.R. Liu and S.S. Quek, *The Finite Element Method: A Practical Course*, Butterworth-Heinemann, London, 2013.

[2] G.R. Liu, Solution existence theory for artificial neural networks, *International Journal of Computational Methods*, **19**(8), in-printing, 2022.

[3] D.E. Rumelhart, G.E. Hinton, and R.J. Williams, Learning representations by back-propagating errors, *Nature*, **323**(6088), 533–536, 1986. http://www.nature.com/articles/323533a0.

[4] Y. Nesterov, A method for unconstrained convex minimization problem with the rate of convergence o(1/k^2), *Doklady ANSSSR* (translated as Soviet.Math.Docl.), **269**, 543–547, 1983.

[5] J.C. Duchi, H. Elad and S. Yoram, Adaptive subgradient methods for online learning and stochastic optimization, *J. Mach. Learn. Res.*, **12**, 2121–2159, 2011. http://dblp.uni-trier.de/db/journals/jmlr/jmlr12.html#DuchiHS11.

[6] T. Tieleman and G. Hinton, Lecture 6.5-rmsprop: Divide the gradient by a running average of its recent magnitude, *COURSERA, Neural Networks for Machine Learning*, **4**(1), 26–31, 2012.

[7] M. Zeiler, ADADELTA: An adaptive learning rate method, arXiv, 1212.5701, 2012.

[8] D.P. Kingma and J. Ba, Adam: A method for stochastic optimization, 2014. http://arxiv.org/abs/1412.6980.

[9] P. Fabian, V. Gae, G. Alexandre *et al.*, Scikit-learn: Machine Learning in Python, *Journal of Machine Learning Research*, **12**(85), 2825–2830, 2011. http://jmlr.org/papers/v12/pedregosa11a.html.

Chapter 10

Loss Functions for Regression

Regression is one of the most widely used tools in analyses of engineering systems. It is also an important technique in the construction of numerical models for both physics-law-based methods (such as the point interpolation methods PIM [1], and the moving least square or MLS used in the meshfree methods [2]) and machine learning models. In a machine learning setting, it takes inputs of a dataset and produces a prediction of a real number, once a regression model is established/trained.

In Chapter 9, we discussed a linear regression problem that has an analytic close-form solution using an L2 loss function, revealing conditions for solution existence. This chapter introduces first various types of loss functions for regression problems. The common feature of all loss functions is that they all produce a positive real number for given learning parameters and a dataset. Our discussion will focus on their differences. Python codes are presented for solutions to the normal equation derived in Chapter 9. Linear regressions are performed on both linear and nonlinear datasets, using corresponding order of bases as features.

A simple neural network will then be built with one layer of input neurons and one neuron in the output layer. It is trained to perform a task of linear regression, using stochastic gradient descent (SGD) as minimizer to numerically obtain the solution. Detailed procedures will be presented using the materials and code from mxnet-the-straight-dope (https:// github.com/zackchase/mxnet-the-straight-dope/tree/master/chapter06_ optimization) under the Apache License 2. Codes developed by the scikit-learn team have also been used [3].

10.1 Formulations for Linear Regression

10.1.1 *Mathematical model*

The mathematical model for regression is to predict a real valued y for a given dataset with p linearly independent **features** defined in p-dimensional spaces $\mathbb{X}^p$. An arbitrary point in the feature space can be expressed as

$$\mathbf{x} = [x_1, x_2, \ldots, x_p] \tag{10.1}$$

In engineering design problems, these features may be the design parameters of an engineering structure, for example.

In linear regression, we **assume** that the prediction function $\hat{y}$ is the affine transformation $z(\mathbf{w}, b; \mathbf{x})$:

$$\hat{y} \equiv z(\mathbf{w}, b; \mathbf{x}) = w_1 x_1 + \cdots + w_p x_p + b = \sum_{i=1}^{p} w_i x_i + b = \mathbf{x} \cdot \mathbf{w} + b \tag{10.2}$$

where $\mathbf{w} = [w_1, w_2, \ldots, w_p]^\top \in \mathbb{W}^p$ is called weights and $b \in \mathbb{W}^1$ is called bias. The learning (or training) parameters are in $\mathbb{W}^{p+1}$.

10.1.2 *Neural network configuration*

If we build a neural network to perform linear regressions, the typical architecture of this type of nets can be shown as follows.

As shown in Fig. 10.1, the loss function $\mathcal{L}(\hat{\mathbf{y}}, \mathbf{y})$ needs to be minimized for a given set of data-points, so as to force the prediction as close as possible to

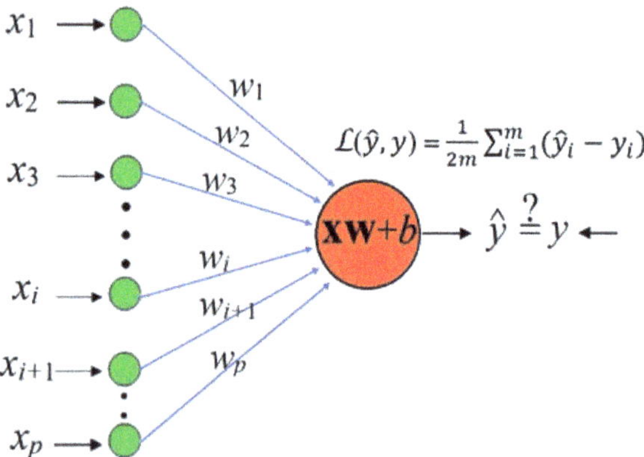

Figure 10.1: A simple $p \to 1$ neural network with one input layer of multiple neurons each takes one feature input, and one output layer of a single neuron that produces a prediction $\hat{y}$, using the xw+b formulation.

the label **y**. This is done through training of the network, using a dataset as inputs together with their corresponding label value of **y**. The data structure can be exactly the same as those discussed in Chapter 5, by simply replacing z by $\hat{y}$. This replacement is usually done for the last layer of output neurons where a comparison of the prediction is performed against the label y.

10.1.3 *The xw formulation*

By the xw formulation, Eq. (10.2) can be written as

$$\hat{y} = \sum_{i=1}^{p} w_i x_i + b = \sum_{i=0}^{p} w_i x_i = \overline{\mathbf{x}}\hat{\mathbf{w}} \tag{10.3}$$

in which $x_0 = 1$, and $w_0 = b$. It is more obvious to state that the information taken by a neuron is simply a weighted aggregation for the inputs. In this case, the neural network has the following architecture is shown in Fig. 10.2.

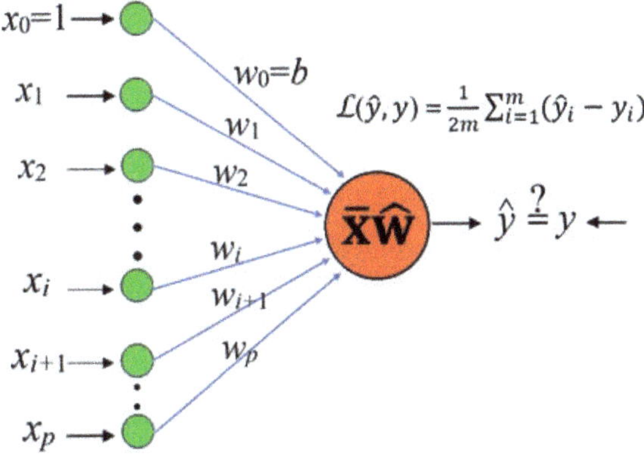

Figure 10.2: A simple $p \to 1$ neural network with one input layer of multiple neurons and one output layer of a single neuron, using the xw formulation.

10.2 Loss Functions for Linear Regression

An ideal loss function should be largely quadratic in learning parameters for a given type of dataset and hypothesis of the ML model used, so that a minimization technique can work effectively to find the minimizers. The L2 loss function is such a function for linear regression problems.

10.2.1 *Mean squared error loss or L2 loss function*

Loss (cost, objective) function is needed to measure how far the model predictions are from the true label data. It is used by the optimizer to tune the training parameters. Here, we introduce a widely used loss function in engineering and sciences, known as mean-squared-error (MSE) or L2 loss function, which is used in Chapter 9. Assume we have m labels or measured/observed actual data. The loss function can be defined as follows:

$$\mathcal{L}(\hat{\mathbf{y}}, \mathbf{y}) = \frac{1}{2m}\sum_{i=1}^{m}\underbrace{(\hat{y}_i - y_i)}_{r_i}{}^2 = \frac{1}{2m}\sum_{i=1}^{m}(r_i)^2 = \frac{1}{2m}(\mathbf{r}^\top \mathbf{r}) = \frac{1}{2m}\|\mathbf{r}\|_2^2 \quad (10.4)$$

where i is the dummy index for the ith training sample and m is the total number of samples in the training dataset. r_i is the ith entry in residual vector $\mathbf{r}$ and is the residual caused by the ith prediction against the label. Equation (10.4) gives a loss functional that maps m sets of data to a positive real number. The MSE loss function is called L2 loss function because it uses the L2 norm, as seen in Eq. (10.4).

The MSE or L2 loss function has the following properties:

1. It is quadratic in predictions, and hence will be quadratic in weights and biases when affine transformation is used in linear regression. We can have a close-form solution for the minimizers, as shown in the previous chapter.
2. It is smooth and convex with respect to the residual and hence convenient to use with optimization algorithms that use gradients.
3. The L2 loss is (Euclidean) distance based because it depends only on the residual, and hence it is also called residual loss. When the residual is zero, it is zero.
4. In addition, it is translation invariant, because the L2 loss is distance based. This means that

$$\mathcal{L}(\hat{\mathbf{y}} + \mathbf{c}, \mathbf{y} + \mathbf{c}) = \mathcal{L}(\hat{\mathbf{y}}, \mathbf{y}) \quad (10.5)$$

where $\mathbf{c}$ is an arbitrary constant vector. Therefore, it may not be used for measures using relative error, such as $\frac{\hat{y}_i - y_i}{y_i}$.

5. Because of the square operation, it overestimates the error when the residual is larger than 1, and hence it is sensitive to the outliers (few data samples that stand out of the reset). It underestimates the error when the residual is less than 1. When the error level is low, the loss function becomes insensitive to the change of the residual and in turn to

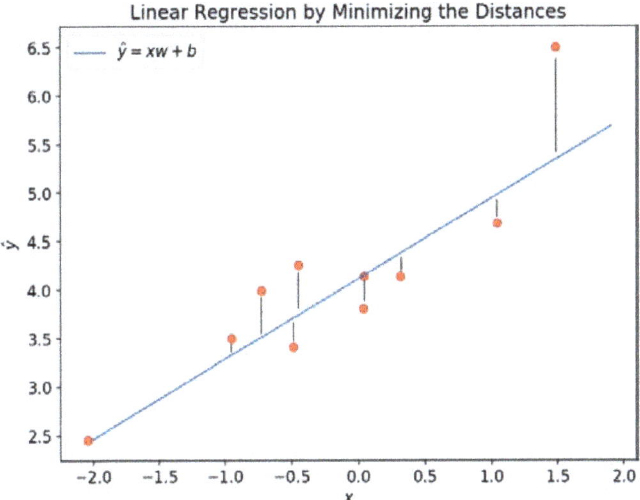

Figure 10.3: Schematic drawing for linear regression problems using loss function measuring the average squared distances from the data-points to the linear prediction function.

the training parameters. Therefore, one can expect a fast convergence at the beginning and slow convergence when coming near the minimum.

For our linear regression problems, the loss function measures the average squared distances from the data-points to the straight line of prediction, as shown in Fig. 10.3 for one-dimensional problems, where we have only one design parameter or feature, one weight, and one bias.

The error is linear in $\hat{\mathbf{y}}$, which is in turn linear in weights and biases. Therefore, the squared error loss function is quadratic in weights and biases. The minimization would lead to a set of linear system equations, and we can have a close-form solution for the minimizers, as shown in Chapter 9. In this chapter, we compute the solution numerically and demonstrate how a neural network can be trained to do this task.

10.2.2 *Absolute error loss or L1 loss function*

Another loss function is the mean absolute error (MAE) loss function or L1 loss for short. It also measures the distance between the model predictions and the true label data. Assume we have m labels or measured/observed actual data. The L1 loss function is given by

$$\mathcal{L}(\hat{\mathbf{y}}, \mathbf{y}) = \frac{1}{m}\sum_{i=1}^{m}(|\underbrace{\hat{y}_i - y_i}_{r_i}|) = \frac{1}{m}\sum_{i=1}^{m}|r_i| = \frac{1}{m}\|\mathbf{r}\|_1 \qquad (10.6)$$

The MAE or L1 loss function is also called Laplace loss. It has the following properties:

1. It is still convex with respect to the residual by definition or by the fact that all norms are convex.
2. The L1 loss is, however, not differentiable at the sample point where the residual is zero. Special techniques (sub-gradient) are needed to use gradient-based optimization algorithms.
3. It is distance based depending only on the residual. When the residual is zero, it is zero. It is also translation invariant (distance-based).
4. Because L1 measures the absolute residuals, it is linearly related to the residuals. It is thus more robust to outliers compared to its L2 counterpart.

10.2.3 *Huber loss function*

Huber loss is a combination of the L1 and L2 losses. It is less sensitive to outliers in the dataset and behaves more like the L1 in this regard. It is made differentiable at 0 by letting it be quadratic when the residual is small. The transition from linear to quadratic depends on a hyperparameter δ that can be tuned. Huber loss approaches the L1 loss when δ is near zero, and L2 loss when δ become a very large number. The formula is as follows:

$$\mathcal{L}(\hat{\mathbf{y}}, \mathbf{y}, \delta) = \begin{cases} \dfrac{1}{2m}\|\hat{\mathbf{y}} - \mathbf{y}\|_2^2 & \text{when} \quad \|\hat{\mathbf{y}} - \mathbf{y}\|_1 \leq \delta; \\ \dfrac{1}{m}\delta\|\hat{\mathbf{y}} - \mathbf{y}\|_1 - \frac{1}{2m}\delta^2 & \text{Otherwise.} \end{cases} \tag{10.7}$$

The Huber loss has the following properties:

1. It is convex, and is quadratic when the residual is near zero.
2. It is differentiable everywhere.
3. It has a tunable hyperparameter.
4. The error measure is linear in residuals when it is large. It is thus less sensitive to outliers compared to the L2 counterpart.

10.2.4 *Log-cosh loss function*

Log-cosh loss is a logarithm of the hyperbolic cosine of the residual. The formula is as follows:

$$\mathcal{L}(\hat{\mathbf{y}}, \mathbf{y}) = \frac{1}{m}\sum_{i=1}^{m}\log(\cosh(\underbrace{\hat{y}_i - y_i}_{r_i})) = \frac{1}{m}\sum_{i=1}^{m}\log(\cosh(r_i)) \tag{10.8}$$

1. It is approximately equal to $\frac{r^2}{2}$ for a small residual, and hence it behaves more like the L2 loss near zero.
2. It approaches $abs(\mathbf{r}) - \log(2)$ when the residual is large, and hence is more like the L1 loss.
3. It is convex, smooth, and differentiable everywhere.
4. It is less sensitive to outliers compared to the L2 loss.

Let us now write a Python code to examine these loss functions in more detail in numbers and in graphs, using only one sample. We first check all of them in numbers.

10.2.5 *Comparison between these loss functions*

```python
import numpy as np
huber=lambda r,dlt: np.where(np.abs(r)<dlt,0.5*((r)**2),\
                    dlt*np.abs(r)-0.5*(dlt**2))
for r in np.linspace(0.1,1.0,10): #range(0.1,1, 11):
    print(f'r={r:.3f}      |r|= {r:.3f}   r^2= {r*r:.3f}\
    Huber={huber(r,1.0):.3f} logcosh={np.log(np.cosh(r)):.3f}')
```

```
r=0.100    |r|= 0.100    r^2= 0.010    Huber=0.005 logcosh=0.005
r=0.200    |r|= 0.200    r^2= 0.040    Huber=0.020 logcosh=0.020
r=0.300    |r|= 0.300    r^2= 0.090    Huber=0.045 logcosh=0.044
r=0.400    |r|= 0.400    r^2= 0.160    Huber=0.080 logcosh=0.078
r=0.500    |r|= 0.500    r^2= 0.250    Huber=0.125 logcosh=0.120
r=0.600    |r|= 0.600    r^2= 0.360    Huber=0.180 logcosh=0.170
r=0.700    |r|= 0.700    r^2= 0.490    Huber=0.245 logcosh=0.227
r=0.800    |r|= 0.800    r^2= 0.640    Huber=0.320 logcosh=0.291
r=0.900    |r|= 0.900    r^2= 0.810    Huber=0.405 logcosh=0.360
r=1.000    |r|= 1.000    r^2= 1.000    Huber=0.500 logcosh=0.434
```

We notice that the L2, Huber, and log-cosh losses are very insensitive to small residuals.

```python
for r in np.linspace(10,100,10): #range(0.1,1, 11):
    print(f'r={r:.1f}      |r|= {r:.1f}      r^2= {r*r:.1f}\
    Huber={huber(r,1.0):.1f} logcosh={np.log(np.cosh(r)):.1f}')
```

```
r=10.0    |r|= 10.0    r^2= 100.0    Huber=9.5 logcosh=9.3
r=20.0    |r|= 20.0    r^2= 400.0    Huber=19.5 logcosh=19.3
r=30.0    |r|= 30.0    r^2= 900.0    Huber=29.5 logcosh=29.3
```

```
r=40.0     |r|= 40.0     r^2= 1600.0     Huber=39.5 logcosh=39.3
r=50.0     |r|= 50.0     r^2= 2500.0     Huber=49.5 logcosh=49.3
r=60.0     |r|= 60.0     r^2= 3600.0     Huber=59.5 logcosh=59.3
r=70.0     |r|= 70.0     r^2= 4900.0     Huber=69.5 logcosh=69.3
r=80.0     |r|= 80.0     r^2= 6400.0     Huber=79.5 logcosh=79.3
r=90.0     |r|= 90.0     r^2= 8100.0     Huber=89.5 logcosh=89.3
r=100.0    |r|= 100.0    r^2= 10000.0    Huber=99.5 logcosh=99.3
```

We notice this time that the L2 is very sensitive to large residuals.

10.2.6 *Python codes for these loss functions*

Next, we take a look at the graphs for all these loss functions by running
our codes.

```python
# The mean squared error loss (function)
def mse(ylabel, yhat):
    r = ylabel-yhat
    return 0.5*r**2


# The mean absolute error loss
def mae(ylabel, yhat):
    r = ylabel-yhat
    return np.abs(r)


# The huber loss
def huber(ylabel, yhat, dlt=1.0):
    r = ylabel-yhat
    abr = np.abs(r)
    loss=np.where(abr<dlt,0.5*((r)**2), dlt*abr-0.5*(dlt**2))
    return loss


# The log-cosh loss
def logcosh(ylabel, yhat):
    r = ylabel-yhat
    return np.log(np.cosh(r))
```

```python
%matplotlib inline
import matplotlib.pyplot as plt
import numpy as np
from matplotlib import rc
```

```python
plt.figure(figsize=(4.5, 2.8),dpi=100)

xleft,xright,xdelta =-1.5,1.6, 0.1
rs = np.arange(xleft,xright,xdelta) # Residuals
lxd = len(rs)
y = np.arange(xleft,xright,xdelta) # y_label


y_hat = y + rs    # simulated prediction

plt.plot(rs,mse(y,y_hat),label = "MSE loss")
plt.plot(rs,mae(y,y_hat),label = "MAE loss")
dlt = 1.0
plt.plot(rs,huber(y,y_hat,dlt),label="Huber loss, $\delta=$"\
        +str(f"{dlt:.1f}"))
plt.plot(rs,logcosh(y,y_hat),label = "logcosh loss")

plt.xlabel('Residual')
plt.ylabel('Loss (Residual)')
plt.title('Comparison of loss functions')
plt.grid(color='r', linestyle=':', linewidth=0.5)
plt.legend()
plt.show()
```

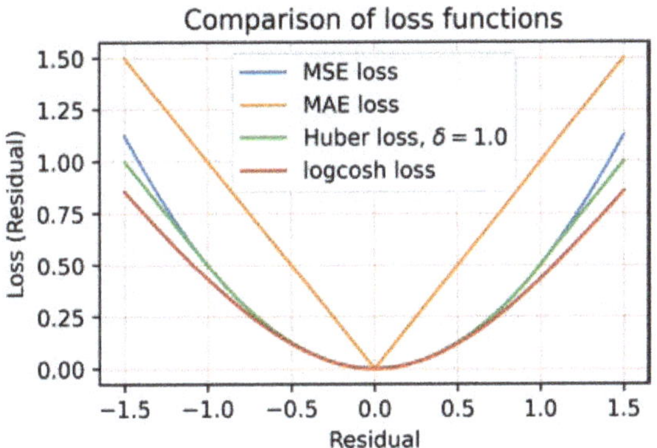

Figure 10.4.   Four typical loss functions based on residuals.

The key features mentioned earlier are evident in Fig. 10.4. Readers may play with the code, make changes to the hyperparameter, and have a different view of these loss functions. For more detailed discussions, readers are referred to the article entitled 5 Regression Loss Functions All Machine Learners Should Know (heartbeat.fritz.ai/5-regression-loss-functions-all-machine-learners-should-know-4fb140e9d4b0.

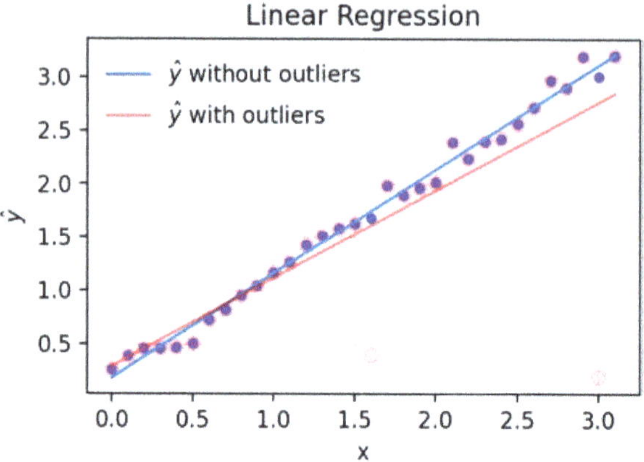

Figure 10.5:   Regression result using linear polynomial and noisy data-points.

10.3 Python Codes for Regression

Let us now write a code to perform linear regressions, based on the formulations given above. We first perform linear regression with a linear polynomial function using the following code by setting reg_type =1. At the same time, we can examine how sensitive the L2 loss is to the outlier data-points. The results are plotted in Fig. 10.5.

It is clearly shown that these two outliers have pushed the regression line significantly downward. Figure 10.5 is generated using the following code. Readers may play with the code using different feature functions by slightly modifying the code.

```python
import numpy as np
%matplotlib inline
import matplotlib.pyplot as plt

def datagen1(x,noise=0.3):
                    # Generate data with features of 1, x (linear)
    lx = len(x)

    One = np.ones(lx)
    np.random.seed(8)
    X = np.stack((One, x), axis=-1)     # for linear polynomial
    y = x + np.random.rand(lx)*noise    # y vector,
    return X,y
```

```python
def datagen2(x,noise=0.3):       # data with features of 1, x, x^2
    lx = len(x)
    One = np.ones(lx)
    np.random.seed(8)
    X = np.stack((One, x,x2), axis=-1)       # 2nd order polynomial
    y = x**2.+ x + np.random.rand(lx)*noise # form y vector
    return X, y

def datagen3(x,noise=0.3):       # data with features 1,x,sin(x)
    lx = len(x)
    One = np.ones(lx)
    np.random.seed(8)
    X = np.stack((One, x,np.sin(x)), axis=-1)
    y = 1.+ 0.1*x + np.sin(x) + np.random.rand(lx)*noise
    return X, y

xleft,xright,xdelta = 0.0, np.pi, 0.1
x = np.arange(xleft,xright,xdelta)
lx = len(x)
print('Length of x=',lx, x)
noise = 0.3
reg_type = 3     # 1:linear, 2:2nd order polynomial, 3:sin(x)

if reg_type ==1:
    X, y = datagen1(x,noise)  # Data, linear polynomial
elif reg_type ==2:
    X, y = datagen2(x,noise)  # Data, 2nd order polynomial
else:
    X, y = datagen3(x,noise=0.1)               # Data with sin(x)

yout = y.copy()
yout[int(lx/2)],yout[int(lx-2)] = 1.0, 0.8  # 2 outliers
print('y=',y,y.shape)

XTy = np.dot(X.T,y)              #compute X.T * y
XTyout = np.dot(X.T,yout)
print('XTy=',XTy,XTy.shape)

XTX = np.matmul(X.T,X)          #Compute X.T * X
print('XTX=',XTX,XTX.shape)

def y_hat(X,cr): # function for the predicted regression
                 # line for given solution cr*
    return np.dot(X,cr) # X = [1  x1] ;  cr* = [b*  w*]^T
```

```python
plt.figure(figsize=(4.5, 2.9),dpi=100)
c = np.linalg.solve(XTX,XTy)
cout = np.linalg.solve(XTX,XTyout)
print(' c*=',c,c.shape)
plt.plot(x,y_hat(X,c),label = "$\hat{y}$ without outliers")
plt.plot(x,y_hat(X,cout), c='r',alpha=0.5,
         label = "$\hat{y}$ with outliers")
# compute the predicted lines and plot out.

plt.scatter(x, y, s=15., c='b', alpha=0.8)
plt.scatter(x, yout, s=45., c='r', alpha=0.2)
plt.xlabel('x')
plt.ylabel('$\hat{y}$')
plt.title('Linear Regression')
plt.grid(color='r', linestyle=':', linewidth=0.3)
plt.legend()
plt.show()
```

```
Length of x= 32 [0.  0.1 0.2 0.3 0.4 0.5 0.6 0.7 0.8 0.9 1.
   1.1 1.2 1.3 1.4 1.5 1.6 1.7
 1.8 1.9 2.  2.1 2.2 2.3 2.4 2.5 2.6 2.7 2.8 2.9 3.  3.1]
y= [1.08734294 1.20668748 1.30558878 1.37860578 1.45269118
 1.53056542
 1.66768936 1.75445282 1.84962356 1.92116609 1.99700663
 2.05554596
 2.12812864 2.16479564 2.18741794 2.19010416 2.18848111
 2.25905033
 2.18722504 2.15818019 2.11587827 2.17149642 2.04128198
 2.00791829
 1.92255747 1.87094914 1.81486486 1.78699438 1.64953431
 1.62772427
 1.44399321 1.38674914] (32,)
XTy= [58.51029079 93.63832045 39.77958804] (3,)
XTX= [[ 32.            49.6           19.9954796 ]
 [ 49.6          104.16          31.42797769]
 [ 19.9954796    31.42797769   15.70789511]] (3, 3)
 c*= [1.06733004 0.09226871 0.98918366] (3,)
```

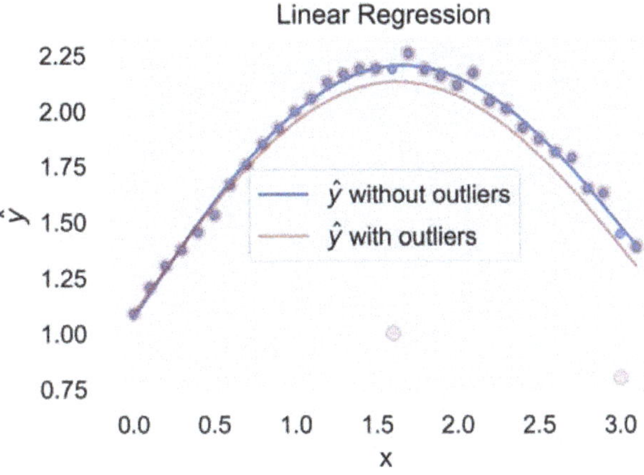

Figure 10.6:   Linear regression of data-points with a quadratic polynomial.

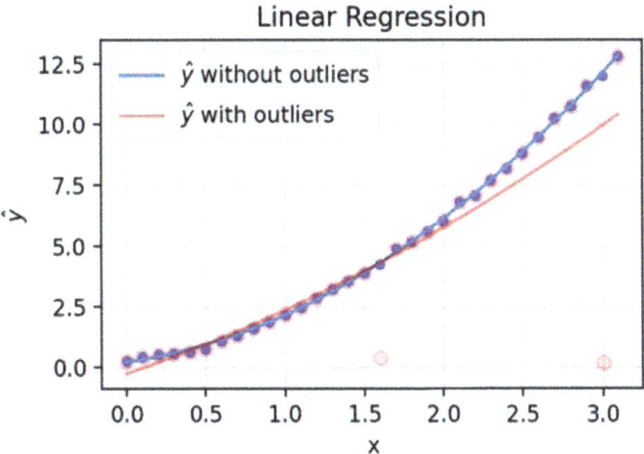

Figure 10.7:   Regression result using 2nd-order polynomial and noisy data-points.

10.3.1 *Linear regression using high-order polynomial and other feature functions*

We now use the code given above to do a regression using 2nd-order polynomials, simply by adding a quadratic term x^2 as the 2nd feature (basis) in the above code. In the code, we just set reg_type $= 2$. The results are plotted in Fig. 10.7.

Figure 10.8 shows regression results using sine feature (basis) function.

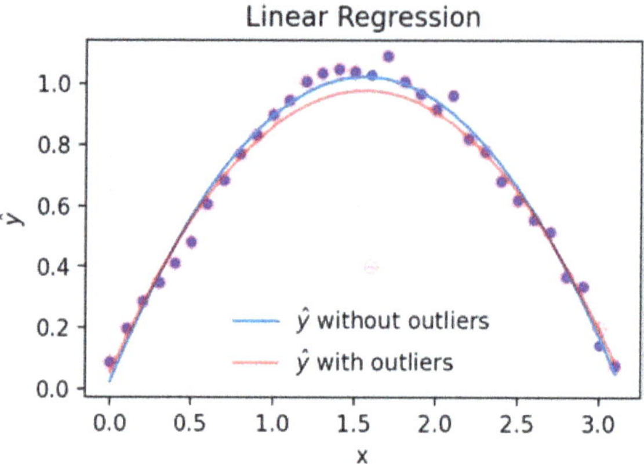

Figure 10.8: Regression result using sine feature function and noisy data-points.

It is convenient to use the classes built in Scikit-Learn to perform the regression (curve fitting).

```python
from sklearn.preprocessing import PolynomialFeatures
from sklearn.pipeline import make_pipeline
from sklearn.linear_model import LinearRegression
%matplotlib inline
import matplotlib.pyplot as plt
import seaborn as sns; sns.set()
import numpy as np
```

```python
# Create a 6th-degree polynomial model
poly7_model = make_pipeline(PolynomialFeatures(6),
    LinearRegression())
```

```python
rng = np.random.RandomState(1)
x = 10 * rng.rand(50)
y = np.sin(x) + 0.05 * rng.randn(50)
xfit = np.linspace(0, 10, 1000)
poly7_model.fit(x[:, np.newaxis], y)
yfit = poly7_model.predict(xfit[:, np.newaxis])
plt.figure(figsize=(3.5, 3.0),dpi=100)
plt.scatter(x, y, s=15., c='b', alpha=0.8)
plt.plot(xfit, yfit,c='b',label = "Fitted with 6th order\
        polynomial", alpha=0.9)
plt.plot(xfit, np.sin(xfit),c='r',label = "Original true sine\
        function,"alpha=0.9)
plt.grid(color='r', linestyle=':', linewidth=0.3)
```

```
plt.legend(bbox_to_anchor=(2.02, 0.5),loc='center right')
plt.show;
```

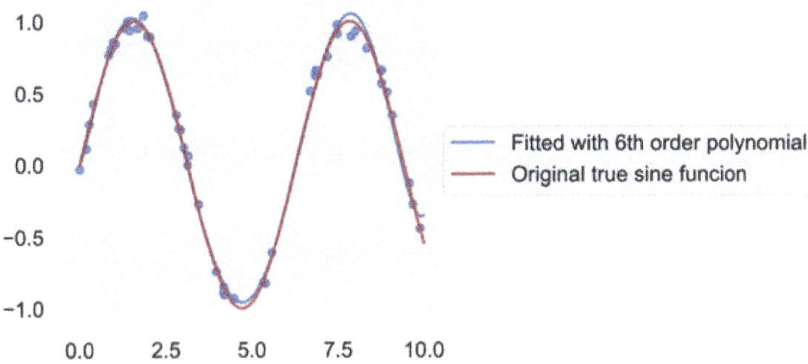

Figure 10.9: Linear regression of data-points with a higher-order polynomial using Sklearn.

It is seen from Fig. 10.9 that using a 6th-order polynomial basis functions, we can fit a set of nonlinear data created using a sine function and 5% white noise. Note that such a high-order polynomial fitting can be very dangerous when it is used for making predictions outside of the dataset. We can print out the features of a 6th-order polynomial (variable powered with all the orders):

```
x1 = np.arange(2,4,4)     # one-dimensional, 6 data-points
poly7_data = PolynomialFeatures(7, include_bias=False)
poly7_data.fit_transform(x1[:, None])
```

```
array([[  2.,    4.,    8.,   16.,   32.,   64.,  128.]])
```

We can see that it grows very fast with the increase of the order of the polynomial. Let us print out the prediction a little out of the fitted domain.

```
xfit = np.linspace(0, 11, 1000)
yfit = poly7_model.predict(xfit[:, np.newaxis])
plt.figure(figsize=(4.5, 2.9),dpi=100)
plt.scatter(x, y, s=15., c='b', alpha=0.8)
plt.plot(xfit, yfit,c='b',label = "Fitted with 6th order\
        polynomial")
plt.plot(xfit, np.sin(xfit),c='r',label = "Original true\
        sine function")
plt.legend();
```

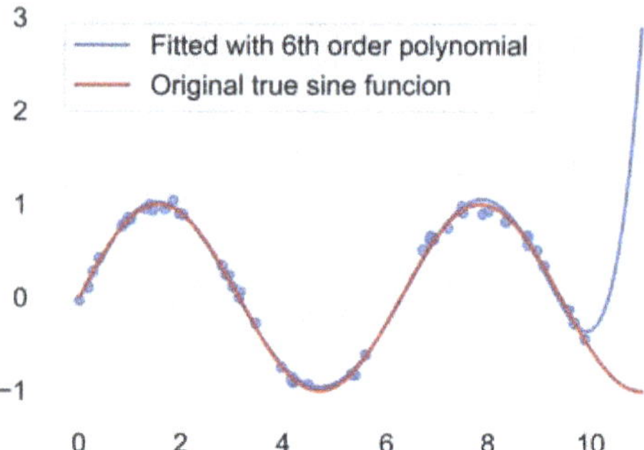

Figure 10.10: Linear regression of data-points with a higher-order polynomial. Note the danger of extrapolation.

It is clear from Fig. 10.10 that high-order polynomial fitting should be used with care especially when extrapolation is used.

10.3.2 *Linear regression using Gaussian basis functions*

We will now use the Scikit-Learn and the code for linear regression linear regression (https://jakevdp.github.io/PythonDataScienceHandbook/05.06-linear-regression.html), using Gaussian basis functions as the feature function.

```python
from sklearn.base import BaseEstimator, TransformerMixin
class GaussianFeatures(BaseEstimator, TransformerMixin):
    """Uniformly spaced Gaussian features for\
        one-dimensional input"""

    def __init__(self, N, width_factor=2.0):
        self.N = N
        self.width_factor = width_factor

    @staticmethod
    def _gauss_basis(x, y, width, axis=None):
        arg = (x - y) / width
        return np.exp(-0.5 * np.sum(arg ** 2, axis))

    def fit(self, X, y=None):
        # create N centers spread along the data range
        self.centers_ = np.linspace(X.min(), X.max(), self.N)
        self.width_=self.width_factor*(self.centers_[1]-self.
            centers_[0])
```

```python
    return self
    def transform(self, X):
        return self._gauss_basis(X[:, :, np.newaxis], self.
            centers_,self.width_, axis=1)
xfit = np.linspace(0, 10, 1000)
gauss_model = make_pipeline(GaussianFeatures(20),
                            LinearRegression())
gauss_model.fit(x[:, np.newaxis], y)
yfit = gauss_model.predict(xfit[:, np.newaxis])
plt.figure(figsize=(4.5, 2.9),dpi=100)
plt.scatter(x, y, s=15., c='b', alpha=0.8)
plt.plot(xfit,yfit,c='b',label="Fitted with Gaussian\
        basis")
plt.plot(xfit,np.sin(xfit),c='r',label="Original true\
        sine function")
plt.legend(bbox_to_anchor=(1.72, 0.5),loc='center right');
#plt.xlim(0, 10)
```

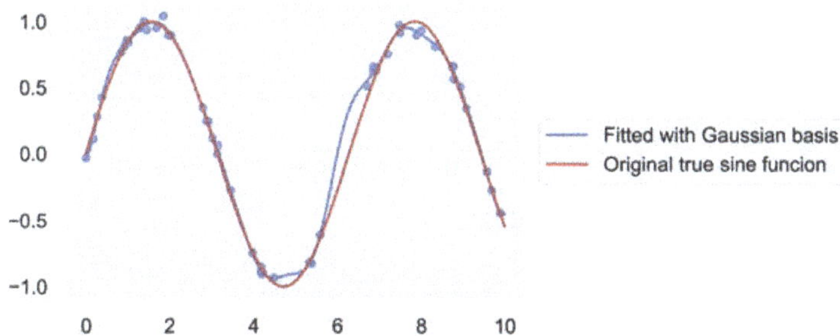

Figure 10.11:   Linear regression of data-points with RBFs.

This is indeed an excellent fit, as shown in Fig. 10.11. Let us print out the prediction a little out of the fitted domain.

```python
xfit = np.linspace(0, 11, 1000)
yfit = gauss_model.predict(xfit[:, np.newaxis])
plt.figure(figsize=(4.5, 2.9),dpi=100)
plt.scatter(x, y, s=15., c='b', alpha=0.8)
plt.plot(xfit,yfit,c='b',label="Fitted with Gaussian basis")
plt.plot(xfit,np.sin(xfit),c='r',label="Original true sine\
        function")
plt.legend()
plt.ylim(-1.5,3)
```

(-1.5, 3.0)

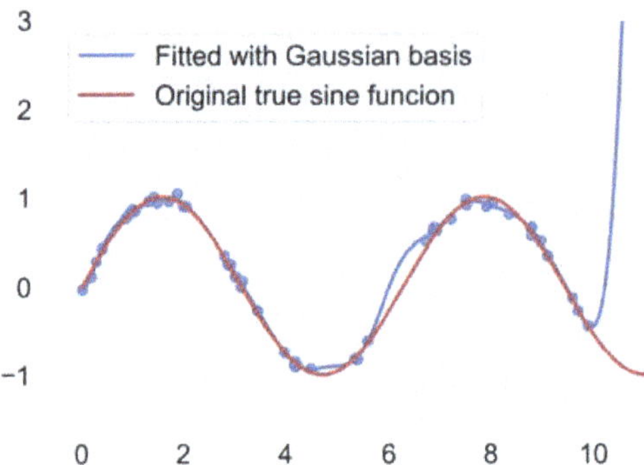

Figure 10.12: Linear regression of data-points with RBFs. Note the danger of extrapolation.

We observe a similar phenomenon when the Gaussian basis functions are used. Care is needed for curve fitting using nonlinear feature functions, especially when extrapolation is used.

10.4 Neural Network Model for Linear Regressions with Big Datasets

10.4.1 *Setting up neural network models*

A neural network model can be built to form a systematic procedure to effectively minimize the loss function that can have a number of forms as discussed earlier. The loss function is a function of the weights and biases of the neurons, which are the learning (or training) parameters. The training is to find the minimizers, that is, a set of the weights and biases at which the loss function is a minimum. Because our loss functions are differentiable (or sub-differentiable), we can use a gradient-based minimization technique to achieve the goal.

We now use the code provided by mxnet-the-straight-dope (https:// github.com/zackchase/mxnet-the-straight-dope/tree/master/chapter02_ supervised-learning), under the Apache-2.0 License, to complete the process of training a linear regression model using the neural network. We shall do the following:

- Generate a set of synthetic data and the corresponding labels, similar as what we did in Section 9.5.1.
- The dataset shall be generated using nd.random_normal with mean close to 0 and variance close to 1. Therefore, the covariance of the dataset will be close to diagonal, and the corresponding features in the dataset will thus be almost independent.

- The labels are generated using the "true" feature and with artificially added noise, synthesizing the measurement error. The noise generation uses a random Gaussian distribution with zero mean and a small percentage (say, 10%; readers may change it) of variance.

We first import necessary libraries for this task.

```python
# The following codes are modified from these at https://
# github.com/zackchase/ mxnet-the-straight-dope/tree/master/
# chapter02_supervised- learning
# Under Apache-2.0 License.

from __future__ import print_function
import mxnet as mx
from mxnet import nd, autograd, gluon
import random
import numpy as np
mx.random.seed(1)           # fix seed for repeatable random numbers


# Specify GPU or CPU computation
data_ctx = mx.cpu()
model_ctx = mx.cpu()
num_inputs = 2              # 2D space with two features: x1 and x2
num_outputs = 1            # one prediction y
num_samples = 1000        # Sample number, use 10 for demonstration,
                          # but 100 or more for actual running.
def real_fn(X):           # linear func.,
                          # w1,w2,b1: 3 learning parameters
    return 2*X[:,0]-3.4*X[:,1]+4.2   #2*x1-3.4*x2+4.2

X = nd.random_normal(shape=(num_samples, num_inputs), ctx=data_ctx)
                    # randomly generate samples for x1 and x2
noise = .1 * nd.random_normal(shape=(num_samples,), ctx=data_ctx)
                    # 10% noise, zero mean, 1 variance
y = real_fn(X) + noise   # Generate labels with noise.
```

To relate the data with the equations presented earlier, we have p=num_inputs, m=num_samples. Matrix **X** has a dimension of num_samples x num_inputs, and y is a one-dimensional array with num_samples entries.

As a good practice, we shall always try to understand the dataset as much as possible. First, to check the data structure, use the following:

```python
print('y=',y[0:10])
print(y.shape)
print(X[:5])
print(X.shape)
```

```
y=
[ 6.0136046  2.2423      9.592255   3.569859   2.2450843
  4.9734535  5.285636    6.4735103 10.942213   8.004087 ]
<NDArray 10 @cpu(0)>
(1000,)

[[ 0.03629482 -0.49024424]
 [-0.9501793   0.03751943]
 [-0.7298465  -2.0401056 ]
 [ 1.4821309   1.040828   ]
 [-0.45256865  0.3116043 ]]
<NDArray 5x2 @cpu(0)>
(1000, 2)
```

Next, let us compute the covariance matrix of X just to see the level of independence of these two variables.

```python
print('Covariance Matrix of X:\n', np.cov(X.asnumpy().T))
```

```
Covariance Matrix of X:
 [[ 1.05065641 -0.01452139]
 [-0.01452139  1.08663854]]
```

These two variables are quite independent, which is good news, and a quality model can likely be built. Further, let us check how far the prediction is from the label for the 1st sample:

```python
print('y_hat=',2 * X[0, 0] - 3.4 * X[0, 1] + 4.2,
      'Label y_1=', y[0])
```

```
y_hat=
[5.9394197]
<NDArray 1 @cpu(0)> Label y_1=
[6.0136046]
<NDArray 1 @cpu(0)>
```

These values are quite close. We can hope for quite a fast training.

Finally, let us use matplotlib to plot all the data-points for easy viewing. In order to use **matplotlib**, we need to convert data arrays in NDArray to NumPy arrays using the **.asnumpy()** function.

```python
%matplotlib inline
import matplotlib.pyplot as plt
plt.scatter(X[:, 0].asnumpy(),y.asnumpy(),color='r')
plt.scatter(X[:, 1].asnumpy(),y.asnumpy(),color='b')
plt.show()
```

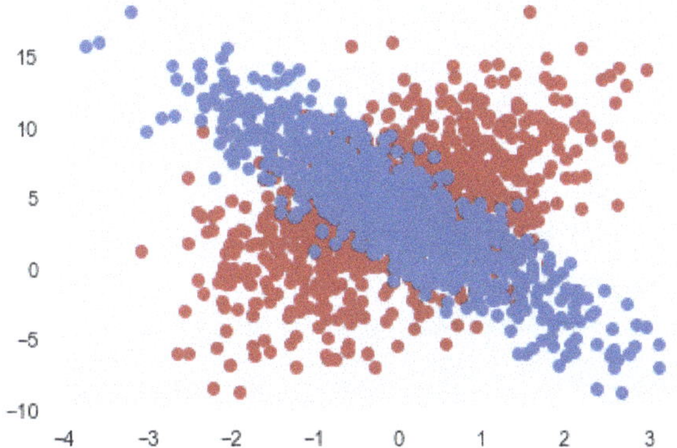

Figure 10.13:   Computer-generated data-points for linear regression study using NNs.

These data-points for two different features are quite distinct. Our model shall be able to learn these features.

10.4.2 *Create data iterators*

For fast computation, the data are packaged in ways for easy operation in bulk. In MXNet, data iterators provide utilities for fetching and manipulating data. In our case, we load training data pair X and y into an ArrayDataset, by calling `gluon.data.ArrayDataset(X, y)`. X can be a multi-dimensional input array (say, of images) and y can be just a one-dimensional array. They shall have equal lengths along the first axis, i.e., `len(X) == len(y)`.

Given an `ArrayDataset`, we create a DataLoader which grabs random batches of data from the `ArrayDataset`. We need decide the `batch_size` for group training samples, which specify how many examples we want to use at a time (epoch). We shall specify whether or not to shuffle over the dataset between the iterations.

```python
batch_size = 4
train_data = gluon.data.DataLoader(gluon.data.
    ArrayDataset(X, y), batch_size=batch_size, shuffle=True)
```

We have now `train_data` initialized using DataLoader. It becomes an iterable object, and can be easily fetched in batches, as if it were a Python list. To unpack the data, we simply use the following loop to iterate:

```python
for i, (data, label) in enumerate(train_data):
                # Get samples after shuffling the data pool.
    print(data, label)
    break
```

```
[[-0.7022906    0.6857335 ]
 [-0.02577175  0.43850085]
 [-0.38564655  0.6393674 ]
 [-0.6317411  -1.3817437 ]]
<NDArray 4x2 @cpu(0)>
[0.22829296 2.823702   1.2765092  7.6593714 ]
<NDArray 4 @cpu(0)>
```

When we run the same code again, we shall get a different set of 4 samples, because we have set **shuffle=True**.

```python
for i, (data, label) in enumerate(train_data):
    print(data, label)
    break
```

```
[[-2.206704     2.3855615 ]
 [ 0.7445208   -0.2434989 ]
 [-1.0826081   -1.027927  ]
 [ 0.09882921 -0.86426044]]
<NDArray 4x2 @cpu(0)>
[-8.413907    6.1686425  5.5676003  7.5225515]
<NDArray 4 @cpu(0)>
```

Let us see how many batches we have, and then ensure that makes sense.

```python
for i, (data, label) in enumerate(train_data):
    pass
print(i+1)
```

10.4.3 *Training parameters*

First, initialize the training parameters for both the weights and bias. Usually, this is done by assigning some random numbers.

```python
w = nd.random_normal(shape=(num_inputs, num_outputs),
    ctx=model_ctx)
b = nd.random_normal(shape=num_outputs, ctx=model_ctx)
params = [w, b]
print(params)
print('w=',w, '\n b=',b)
```

```
[
[[-2.3237102]
 [-1.109485 ]]
<NDArray 2x1 @cpu(0)>,
[-0.48563406]
<NDArray 1 @cpu(0)>]
w=
[[-2.3237102]
 [-1.109485 ]]
<NDArray 2x1 @cpu(0)>
 b=
[-0.48563406]
<NDArray 1 @cpu(0)>
```

Allocate some memory for the gradient of loss functions with respect to all learning parameters.

```python
for param in params:
    param.attach_grad()
print(param.grad)
```

```
[0.]
<NDArray 1 @cpu(0)>
```

It is seen that only the location is assigned.

10.4.4 *Define the neural network*

Following the formulas given in the formulation section, the net can be defined simply as follows:

```python
def net(X):
    return mx.nd.dot(X, w) + b
```

10.4.5 *Define the loss function*

We use the L2 loss function that is the squared distance between the prediction and the label value.

```python
def square_loss(yhat, y):
    return nd.mean((yhat - y) ** 2)
```

10.4.6 *Use of optimizer*

Let us use the stochastic gradient descent (SGD) to train the net. This is done in mini batches. At each iteration, a batch of training samples is randomly drawn from the dataset. We shall then compute the gradient of the loss function with respect to all the training parameters: the weights and biases. The gradient provides the direction for updating the training parameters, and a learning rate lr, usually a small number, will be specified to determine how fast the parameter should be updated at each step along that direction.

```python
def SGD(params, lr):      # lr: the learning rate determine
                          # how fast the parameters are updated
    for param in params:
        param[:] = param - lr * param.grad
```

10.4.7 *Execute the training*

The training is done in stages. Each stage is called an epoch, that is, the number of drawings of the data batches over the entire dataset. Then, for each pass, we iterate through the **train_data**, grabbing batches of examples and their corresponding labels.

```python
epochs = 10
learning_rate = .01
num_batches = num_samples/batch_size

for e in range(epochs):
    cumulative_loss = 0
    for i, (data, label) in enumerate(train_data):
        data = data.as_in_context(model_ctx)
        label = label.as_in_context(model_ctx).reshape((-1, 1))
        with autograd.record(): # record the path for gradient
            output = net(data)
            loss = square_loss(output, label)
        loss.backward()            # compute gradient via backward prop.
        SGD(params, learning_rate)         # perform optimization
        cumulative_loss += loss.asscalar() # update the loss.
    print(cumulative_loss / num_batches)
```

```
4.694164189037867
0.010493556420027745
0.010353110232390463
0.01032697731954977
0.010341777712805197
0.010346036787843332
0.010346328813116997
0.010331496173050254
0.01031649975432083
0.010330414514523
```

10.4.8 *Examining training progress*

```python
# Re-initialize parameters because they were already
# trained earlier
w[:] = nd.random_normal(shape=(num_inputs, num_outputs),
        ctx=model_ctx)
b[:] = nd.random_normal(shape=num_outputs, ctx=model_ctx)
# Function to plot the losses over epoch
def plot(losses, X, sample_size=100):
    xs = list(range(len(losses)))
    f, (fg1, fg2) = plt.subplots(1, 2)
    fg1.set_title('Loss during training')
    fg1.plot(xs, losses, '-r')
    fg2.set_title('Estimated vs real function')
```

```python
    fg2.plot(X[:sample_size, 1].asnumpy(),
        net(X[:sample_size,:]).asnumpy(),'or', label='Estimated')
    fg2.plot(X[:sample_size, 1].asnumpy(),
        real_fn(X[:sample_size,:]).asnumpy(),'*g', label='Real')
    fg2.legend()
    plt.show()

learning_rate = .01
losses = []
plot(losses, X)

for e in range(epochs):
    cumulative_loss = 0
    for i, (data, label) in enumerate(train_data):
        data = data.as_in_context(model_ctx)
        label=label.as_in_context(model_ctx).reshape((-1, 1))
        with autograd.record():
            output = net(data)
            loss = square_loss(output, label)
        loss.backward()
        SGD(params, learning_rate)
        cumulative_loss += loss.asscalar()

    print("Epoch %s, batch %s. Mean loss: %s" % (e, i,
        cumulative_loss/num_batches))
    losses.append(cumulative_loss/num_batches)

plot(losses, X)
```

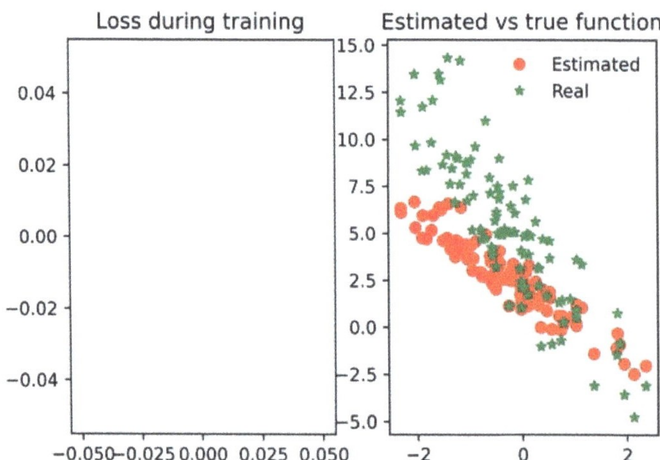

Figure 10.14:   Results from the NN before training.

```
Epoch 0, batch 249. Mean loss: 4.427614943831228
Epoch 1, batch 249. Mean loss: 0.010421961726155131
Epoch 2, batch 249. Mean loss: 0.010315687943017111
Epoch 3, batch 249. Mean loss: 0.01035601595134358
Epoch 4, batch 249. Mean loss: 0.01037310311215697
Epoch 5, batch 249. Mean loss: 0.010365772993071004
Epoch 6, batch 249. Mean loss: 0.01032915258151479
Epoch 7, batch 249. Mean loss: 0.0103718894142665752
Epoch 8, batch 249. Mean loss: 0.010340319244773128
Epoch 9, batch 249. Mean loss: 0.010389118599705397
```

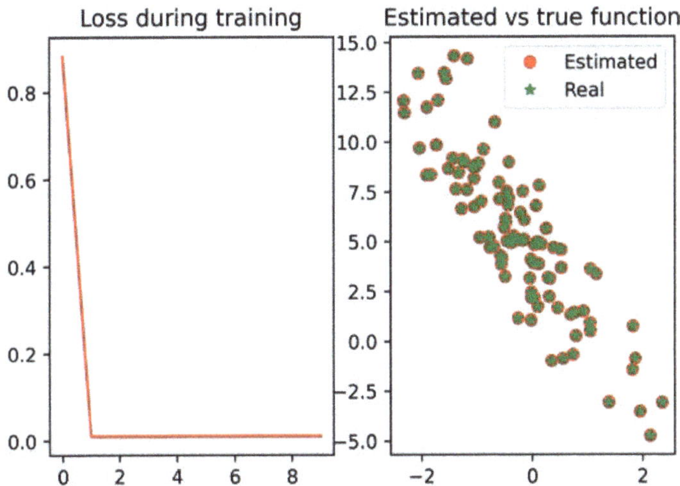

Figure 10.15:   Results from the NN after training.

10.5 Neural Network Model for Nonlinear Regression

We now present a case study done by the scikit-learn team [3]. This study
uses a multi-layer perceptron network (MLPRegressor class) to perform nonlinear regression using the Boston housing price dataset, together with the
decision tree regression [4, 5]. A code is provided to perform the regressions
and then plot the partial dependence curves. The `plot_partial_dependence`
function returns a `PartialDependenceDisplay` class object that contains
the necessary attributes, which can be used for plotting without recalculating
the partial dependence.

```python
%matplotlib inline
import pandas as pd
import matplotlib.pyplot as plt
from sklearn.datasets import load_boston
from sklearn.neural_network import MLPRegressor
from sklearn.preprocessing import StandardScaler
from sklearn.pipeline import make_pipeline
from sklearn.tree import DecisionTreeRegressor
from sklearn.inspection import plot_partial_dependence
```

10.5.1 *Train models on the Boston housing price dataset*

We train a decision tree (will not be discussed in this book) and a multi-layer perceptron on the Boston housing price dataset. One may use help to figure out these classes build in Sklearn. For example, use "help(MLPRegressor)" to find out the setting of the neural network, when using the MLPRegressor class.

```python
boston = load_boston()
X = pd.DataFrame(boston.data, columns=boston.feature_names)
y = boston.target
tree = DecisionTreeRegressor()
mlp = make_pipeline(StandardScaler(),
    MLPRegressor(hidden_layer_sizes=(100, 100), tol=1e-2,
    max_iter=500, random_state=0))     # 2 hidden layers, Relu.
tree.fit(X, y)
mlp.fit(X, y); # you may remove # to view outputs.
```

10.5.2 *Plotting partial dependence for two features*

We plot partial dependence curves for two features "LSTAT" and "RM" for the decision tree, using plot_partial_dependence(). The spacing of the grids of these two plots is defined by ax.

```python
fig, ax = plt.subplots(figsize=(12, 6))
ax.set_title("Decision Tree")
tree_disp=plot_partial_dependence(tree,X,["LSTAT", "RM"],ax=ax)
```

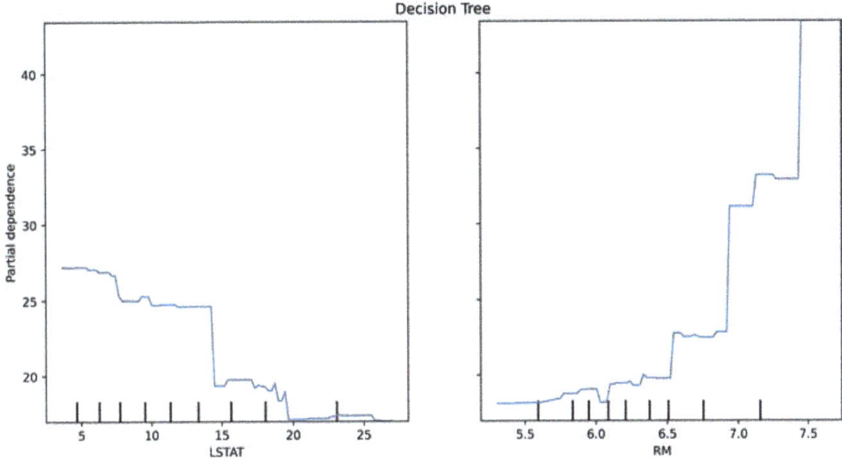

Figure 10.16: Results using the decision tree in Sklearn for the Boston housing price dataset.

Next, the partial dependence curves are plotted for the MLP.

```python
fig, ax = plt.subplots(figsize=(12, 6))
ax.set_title("Multi-layer Perceptron")
mlp_disp = plot_partial_dependence(mlp, X, ["LSTAT", "RM"], ax=ax,
                                   line_kw={"c": "red"})
```

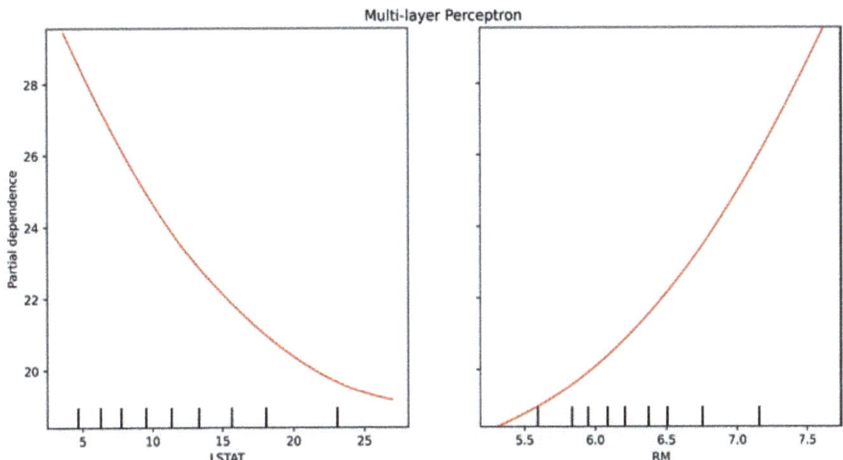

Figure 10.17: Results using the MLP in Sklearn for the Boston housing price dataset.

10.5.3 *Plot curves on top of each other*

Finally, we plot these partial dependence curves on top of each other using the following code:

```python
# Sets this image as the thumbnail for sphinx gallery
# sphinx_gallery_thumbnail_number = 4
fig, (ax1, ax2) = plt.subplots(1, 2, figsize=(10, 6))

tree_disp.plot(ax=[ax1,ax2],line_kw={"label":"Decision Tree"})
mlp_disp.plot(ax=[ax1, ax2], line_kw={"label":"Multi-layer
                                      Perceptron","c": "red"})

ax1.legend()
ax2.legend();
```

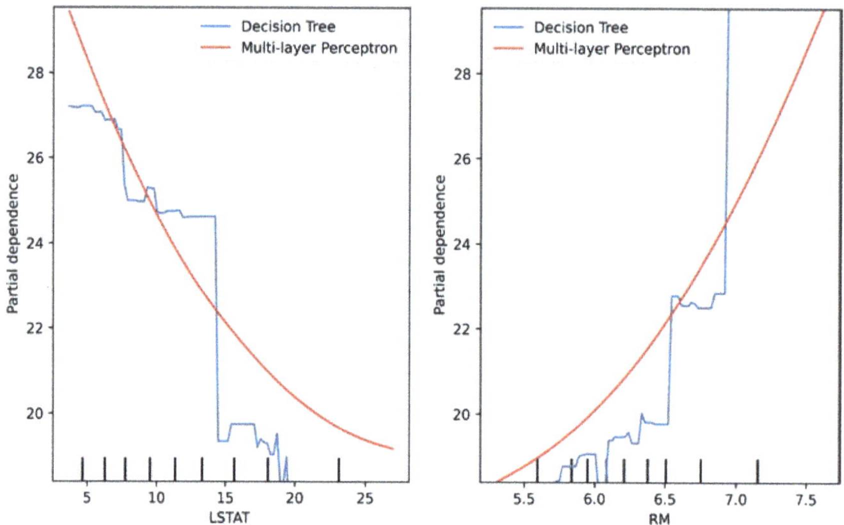

Figure 10.18:   Comparison of results obtained using the decision tree and MLP in Sklearn for the Boston housing price dataset.

10.6 On Nonlinear Regressions

Note that the above-discussed regression models are in fact linear models, even if we use nonlinear feature functions, such as higher-order polynomial, many other special feature functions, and kernels in SVMs. The term feature function used in regression is essentially the same as the basis function in FEM. It is just a different name.

We may also note here that when a regression model uses a nonlinear feature function, it is sometimes called nonlinear regression. This is different from the FEM types of models, where an FEM model is still called linear, even if nonlinear basis functions are used. When we say nonlinear FEM model, it is truly nonlinear because the system matrix will depend on the unknown field variables, and hence a solution to a nonlinear FEM model is usually iterative.

In fact, one should not be confused that the regression model itself is a linear one, even if a nonlinear feature function is used, because the system matrix $\mathbf{X}^\top\mathbf{X}$ does not depend on the regression parameter $[\hat{\mathbf{w}}]$, and $[\hat{\mathbf{w}}]$ can be obtained by a single step with a linear equation solver. The prediction is assumed to be a linear combination of the features and the regression parameters, shown in the formulation above and will also be seen explicitly in the code to be written later. This seems just to be a minor terminology problem, but it may have conceptual significance. Moreover, there are also true nonlinear regression models, in which the regression parameters and some (or all) features cannot be written in linear combination. For such true nonlinear regression models, the solution should be obtained via iterative or successive fitting processes.

10.7 Conclusion

We end this chapter with the following remarks:

1. Regression is a process of deriving a function of features from a dataset. The form of the function is set once the model is defined. The model parameters (e.g., weights and biases for MLP) are determined when the model is trained. These parameters now record the features of the dataset.
2. Linear regression models can use nonlinear feature functions to better fit complicated datasets. The use of nonlinear feature functions is similar to the use of nonlinear kernels in the SVM.
3. Regression can be performed using various machine learning models.
4. A properly built and trained neural network is capable of producing prediction functions from big datasets containing complicated label-feature relations. It is capable of extracting features that are both linear and nonlinear from datasets.

References

[1] G.R. Liu and G.Y. Zhang, *Smoothed Point Interpolation Methods: G Space Theory and Weakened Weak Forms*, World Scientific, Singapore, 2013.

[2] G.R. Liu, *Mesh Free Methods: Moving Beyond the Finite Element Method*, Taylor and Francis Group, New York, 2010.

[3] P. Fabian, V. Gae, G. Alexandre *et al.*, Scikit-learn: Machine Learning in Python, *Journal of Machine Learning Research*, **12**(85), 2825–2830, 2011. http://jmlr.org/papers/v12/pedregosa11a.html.

[4] X. Wu, R.J. Kumar Vipin *et al.*, Top 10 algorithms in data mining, *Knowledge and Information Systems*, **14**, 1–37, 2007.

[5] W. Pushkar and G.R. Liu, Real-time prediction of projectile penetration to laminates by training machine learning models with finite element solver as the trainer, *Defence Technology*, **17**(1), 147–160, 2021. https://www.sciencedirect.com/science/article/pii/S2214914720303275.

Chapter 11

Loss Functions and Models for Classification

In many practical applications, we often only need to make a "yes" or "no" type of decision. Probability prediction is often the best choice for making such a decision. For example, what is the likelihood that a machinery may fail in operation in the coming month? What is the probability that a virus will become a pandemic in a region in the coming season? This type of problem requires an assessment on probability of the occurrence of an event, and is a typical *classification* problem. The simplest classification problem is the *binary classification*: there are only two classes, "yes" or "no", for decision making. This chapter shall focus on this type of problem, focusing on necessary methods, formulation, and techniques that can be used for best prediction for binary labels, using neural networks. The reference materials for this chapter include the following:

- Lecture series by David S. Rosenberg, Office of the CTO at Bloomberg.
- Hastie, Tibshirani, and Friedman's book: The Elements of Statistical Learning.
- James, Witten, Hastie, and Tibshirani's book: An Introduction to Statistical Learning.
- Shalev-Shwartz and Ben-David's book, Understanding Machine Learning: From Theory to Algorithms.
- The mxnet-the-straight-dope (https://github.com/zackchase/mxnet-the-straight-dope) (under the Apache License 2).

11.1 Prediction Functions

To formulate proper loss functions, we must define a prediction function for the last layer of a neural network model. Thus, our discussion starts from formulation of different types of prediction functions that may be used for binary classification. The prediction function is also called score function and the value of the prediction function is called score achieved by the model.

11.1.1 *Linear function*

The first and simplest prediction function for a given input $\mathbf{x}$ is the affine transformation function discussed in Chapter 5:

$$z = \sum_{i=1}^{p} w_i x_i + b = \mathbf{x} \cdot \mathbf{w} + b = \mathbf{x}\,\mathbf{w} + b \tag{11.1}$$

Or by the xw formulation

$$z = \sum_{i=0}^{p} w_i x_i = \overline{\mathbf{x}}\hat{\mathbf{w}} \tag{11.2}$$

in which $x_0 = 1$, $w_0 = b$, and $\hat{\mathbf{w}}$ includes all the training parameters (both the weights and bias). Output values z are in general real numbers.

The linear prediction function uses the z value as it is at the output (last) layer of the neural network (linear):

$$\hat{y} = z \tag{11.3}$$

The values of the linear prediction function are in $\mathbb{Y}^1$, and are real numbers in $(-\infty, \infty)$.

11.1.2 *Logistic prediction function*

A two-classification problem has two labels 1 or 0 for a given input $\mathbf{x}_i$: positive class labeled with $y_i = 1$ and negative class labeled with $y_i = 0$. Our problem can be formulated to predict values of probability alike for an event against these labels. Therefore, it makes good sense to use the following logistic (or sigmoid) activation function σ that maps an arbitrary real output z to be within $(0, 1)$:

$$\hat{y} = \sigma(z) = \frac{1}{1 + e^{-z}} \tag{11.4}$$

It squashes any argument value z in $(-\infty, \infty)$ to be in $(0, 1)$. Using the affine transformation our prediction formula becomes

$$\hat{y} = \frac{1}{1 + e^{-(\mathbf{x}\mathbf{w}+b)}} = \frac{1}{1 + e^{-(\overline{\mathbf{x}}\hat{\mathbf{w}})}} \tag{11.5}$$

Because the value of a logistic prediction function falls in the region of $(0, 1)$, it is now comparable with the given labels.

11.1.3 *The tanh prediction function*

The positive and negative classes in a two-classification problem may also be labeled, respectively, with 1 and -1. This type of problem can be re-labeled to 1 and 0. Alternatively, the hyperbolic tangent (tanh) prediction function becomes handy. It is defined as follows:

$$\hat{y} = \tanh(z) = \frac{e^z - e^{-z}}{e^z + e^{-z}} \tag{11.6}$$

where z is given in Eq. (11.1) or (11.2). It is clear that for any given argument of a real number z in $(-\infty, \infty)$, the tanh prediction function returns a real number within $(-1, 1)$.

11.2 Loss Functions for Classification Problems

Loss function is a measure of the correctness of the prediction against the true label that is discrete for binary classification problems. Constructing a loss function requires careful considerations. We first define some terminology.

11.2.1 *The margin concept*

The margin $m(x)$ is also called margin function. It is often used to define loss functions for binary classification problems. Let $\hat{y}$ be the prediction function. There are two major cases of setting for binary classification problems.

Case I: the label is given as $y \in \{-1, +1\}$. In this case, the margin $m(x)$ is defined as

$$m_g(x) = y\hat{y}(x) = \begin{cases} -\hat{y}, & \text{when } y = -1 \\ \hat{y}, & \text{when } y = 1 \end{cases} \tag{11.7}$$

The above definition tells us the following:

- Assuming the label y and a prediction $\hat{y}$ have the same sign, the prediction is correct, and the margin m_g is positive.
- Assuming the label y and a prediction $\hat{y}$ have a different sign, the prediction is incorrect, and the margin m_g is negative.
- Therefore, margin m_g is a measure of the level of the correctness of a prediction. We thus want to maximize the margin $m_g(x)$, to achieve correct prediction with a largest possible margin.

Case II: the label is given as $y \in \{0, 1\}$. In this case, the margin $m(x)$ is defined as

$$m_g(x) = y\hat{y}(x) + (1-y)(1-\hat{y}(x)) = \begin{cases} (1-\hat{y}), & \text{when } y = 0 \\ \hat{y}, & \text{when } y = 1 \end{cases} \quad (11.8)$$

This definition ensures the following:

- When the label $y = 0$, $\hat{y}$ should be close to 0 for the prediction to be correct, and the margin m_g can be positive and maximized for the best possible prediction.
- When the label $y = 1$, $\hat{y}$ should be close to 1 for the prediction to be correct, and the margin m_g can be positive and maximized for the best possible prediction.
- In either situation, the margin m_g becomes a measure of how correct the prediction is. Maximizing margin $m_g(x)$ achieves correct prediction with the largest possible margin.

Once the margin is properly defined as above according to these two different label cases, the definition on the loss functions for binary classification problems can be unified for these two cases. All one needs is to have a maximized margin by minimizing the loss function. These types of loss functions are called margin-based loss, in contrast to the distance-based loss discussed in Chapter 10.

We have seen a similar concept in Chapter 6 when discussing SVM, where we call the margin the width of the decision street. We went through a procedure to maximize it, using a nice prime-dual (Lagrangian multipliers) formulation leading to a standard quadratic programming problem, which was solved using routinely available packages.

11.2.2 *0–1 loss*

For a given margin function, the 0–1 loss function can be defined as follows:

$$\mathcal{L}(m_g) = \mathbb{1}(m_g \leq 0) \quad (11.9)$$

where $\mathbb{1}()$ is the indicator function. Figure 11.1 shows schematically the 0–1 loss.

The 0–1 loss function has the following properties:

1. This function has 1 as its value when the margin is smaller or equal to zero. It is zero otherwise, where it gives the correct prediction. Minimization of the loss is to maximize the margin.

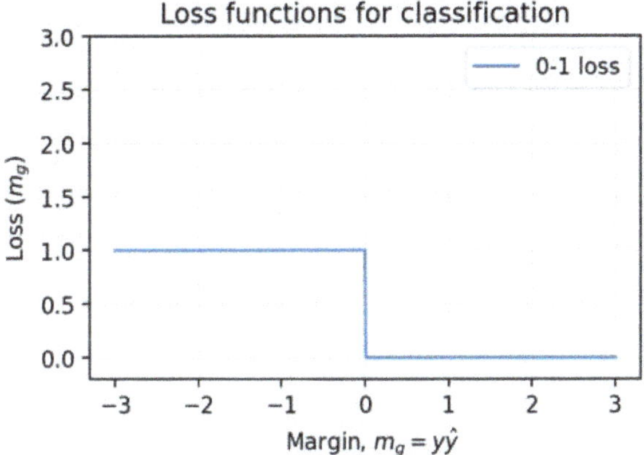

Figure 11.1:   0–1 loss function for classification.

2. It is clearly discontinuous and not differentiable. Therefore, it is difficult to be used with a gradient-based minimization algorithm.
3. It is also not convex, and hence there is no guarantee that a minimum can be found, even if a gradient-based minimization algorithm is workable for it.

11.2.3 *Hinge loss*

For a given margin function, the hinge loss function has the following form:

$$\mathcal{L}(m_g) = \max(1 - m_g, 0) \tag{11.10}$$

Figure 11.2 shows schematically the hinge loss together with the 0–1 loss.

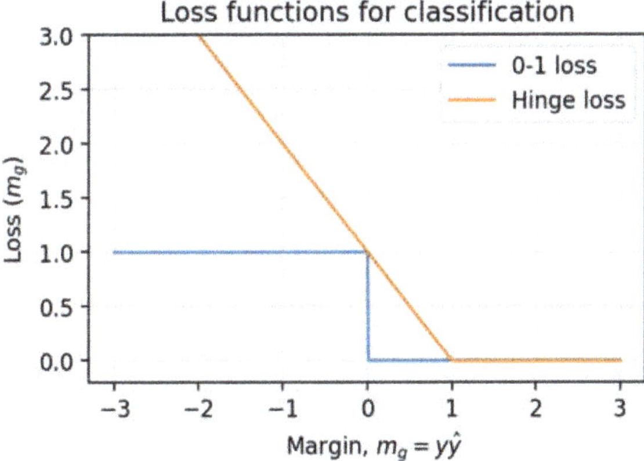

Figure 11.2:   Hinge loss and 0–1 loss functions for classification.

The hinge loss function has the following properties:

1. When the margin is smaller then 1, it is a linear function with a slope of -1 and passing through $[0, 1]$. When the margin is larger than 1, it is zero. We see again that minimizing the loss maximizes the margin.
2. It is convex, but not strictly and has multiple minima.
3. It is an upper bound of the 0–1 loss.
4. Not differentiable at $m_g = 1$.
5. It has a margin error when $0 < m_g < 1$: it has a loss even if it gives a correct prediction there.

The hinge loss can be used to train an SVM model using a gradient-based minimization algorithm.

11.2.4 *Logistic loss*

For a given margin function, the logistic loss function has the following form:

$$\mathcal{L}(m_g) = \log(1 + e^{-m_g}) \tag{11.11}$$

Figure 11.3 shows schematically the logistic loss together with the hinge loss and the 0–1 loss.

The logistic loss function has the following properties:

1. It is smooth, differentiable, and convex.
2. It never goes to zero (minimizer always wants more margin).
3. When the margin is negatively small, its slope is close to the hinge loss.

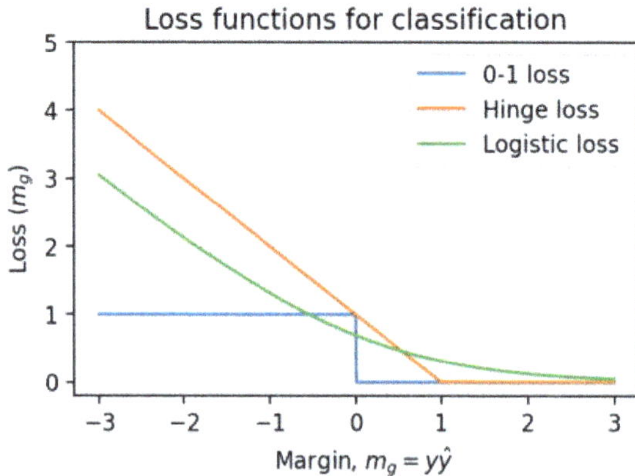

Figure 11.3:   Logistic, Hinge, and 0–1 loss functions for classification.

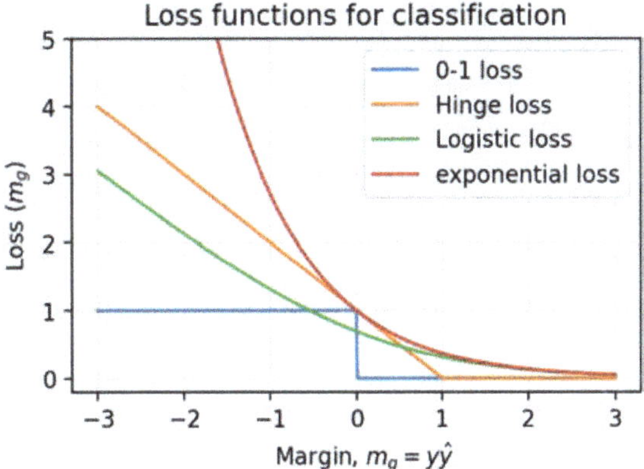

Figure 11.4:   Exponential, Logistic, Hinge, and 0–1 loss functions for classification.

11.2.5 *Exponential loss*

For a given margin function, the exponential loss function has the following form:

$$\mathcal{L}(m_g) = \exp(-m_g) \tag{11.12}$$

Figure 11.4 shows schematically the exponential loss together with the hinge loss and the 0–1 loss.

The exponential loss function has the following properties:

1. It is smooth, differentiable, and convex.
2. It never goes to zero (minimizer always wants more margin).
3. It is an upper bound of the 0–1 loss.
4. It penalizes the negative margins very heavily.

11.2.6 *Square loss*

Square loss function uses the L2 loss and it can be also written as a function of margin:

$$\mathcal{L}(\hat{y}, y) = (\hat{y} - y)^2 = (1 - \hat{y}y)^2 = (1 - m_g)^2 = \mathcal{L}(m_g) \tag{11.13}$$

This is because $y^2 = 1$ for the label $y \in \{-1, +1\}$.

The properties of the square loss function have been discussed in detail in Chapter 10:

1. It is smooth, differentiable, convex, and $m_g = 1$ is the minimizer of the loss function.

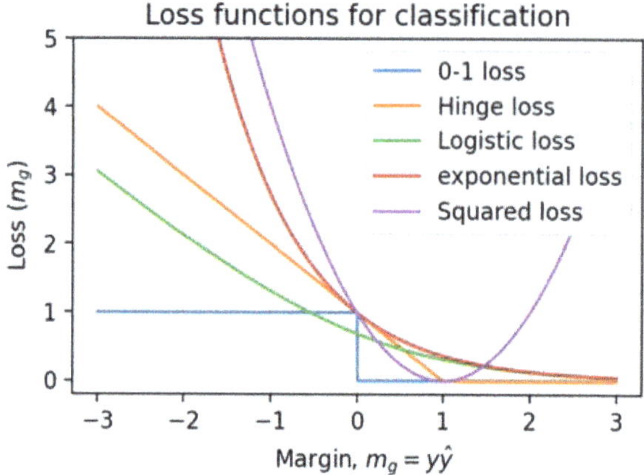

Figure 11.5:   A neural network for binary classification.

2. It is sensitive to outliers.
3. It may have higher complexity and hence need for samples compared to the hinge and logistic lasses [1].

Figure 11.5 plots all these four together for examination.

We write a code to compute these loss functions and plot figures in the above.

```python
# Loss functions for classification
# the 0-1 loss
def zerone(mg):
    return np.where(mg <= 0 , 1.0,0.)

# the hinge loss
def hinge(mg):
    return np.where(mg <= 1. , 1.-mg,0.) #np.max(1-mg,0)

# the logloss
def logloss(mg):
    return np.log(1.+np.exp(-mg))

# the exploss, exponential loss
def exploss(mg):
    return np.exp(-mg)
```

```python
# the squared error loss
def squared(mg):
    return (1-mg)**2
```

```python
%matplotlib inline
import matplotlib.pyplot as plt
import numpy as np
from matplotlib import rc

xleft,xright,xdelta =-3.0,3.01, .01
mg = np.arange(xleft,xright,xdelta) # Residuals
lxd = len(mg)
#print('Length of mg=',lxd, mg)

plt.figure(figsize=(4.5, 2.8),dpi=100)
plt.plot(mg,zerone(mg),label = "0-1 loss") #+str(f"{L:.2f}"))
plt.plot(mg,hinge(mg),label = "Hinge loss")
plt.plot(mg,logloss(mg),label = "Logistic loss")
plt.plot(mg,exploss(mg),label = "exponential loss")
plt.plot(mg,squared(mg),label = "Squared loss")
dlt = 1.0
plt.xlabel('Margin, $m_g=y\hat{y}$')
plt.ylabel('Loss ($m_g$)')
plt.title('Loss functions for classification')
plt.grid(color='r', linestyle=':', linewidth=0.2)
plt.legend()
plt.ylim(-0.2, 5)
plt.show()
```

The code above produces the previous figure.

11.2.7 *Binary cross-entropy loss*

Consider a given dataset of m samples, $\mathbf{x}_s, (s = 1, 2, \ldots, m)$. We now want to evaluate the overall probability of labels being true, given these m samples, using a neural network with training parameter $\hat{\mathbf{w}}$. This requires computing the following probability:

$$P_{\hat{\mathbf{w}}}((y_1, \ldots, y_m)|\mathbf{x}_1, \ldots, \mathbf{x}_m) \tag{11.14}$$

If each sample is independent of the rest, and each label is only for its own corresponding sample, these m events are independent. Thus, the overall probability is the product of all the probabilities for each sample. Equation (11.14) becomes

$$P_{\hat{\mathbf{w}}}(y_1|\mathbf{x}_1)P_{\hat{\mathbf{w}}}(y_2|\mathbf{x}_2)\dots P_{\hat{\mathbf{w}}}(y_m|\mathbf{x}_m) \tag{11.15}$$

This is a product of multiple probabilities, which is not very convenient to use directly as a loss function. In addition, the probabilities are all smaller or equal to 1.0, whose products can be a very small number, if m is a very large number. Taking a log for the product of the probabilities gives

$$\log P_{\hat{\mathbf{w}}}(y_1|\mathbf{x}_1) + \cdots + \log P_{\hat{\mathbf{w}}}(y_m|\mathbf{x}_m) \tag{11.16}$$

This is preferred, and we shall use it instead. Because log function is a monotonically increasing function with an increasing positive argument, it does not change the trend of the original function, and hence will not alter the locations of the extremes of the original function that fed to the log function. This can be observed using the following codes that produces Fig. 11.6:

```python
x = np.arange(0.001, 10, .1)
y = np.log(x)
plt.plot(x,y)
plt.xlabel('x')
plt.ylabel('$log(x) $')
plt.title('Log Function: Monotonic!')
plt.show()
print('log(0.5)=',np.log(0.5),'log(1.0)=',np.log(1.0))
```

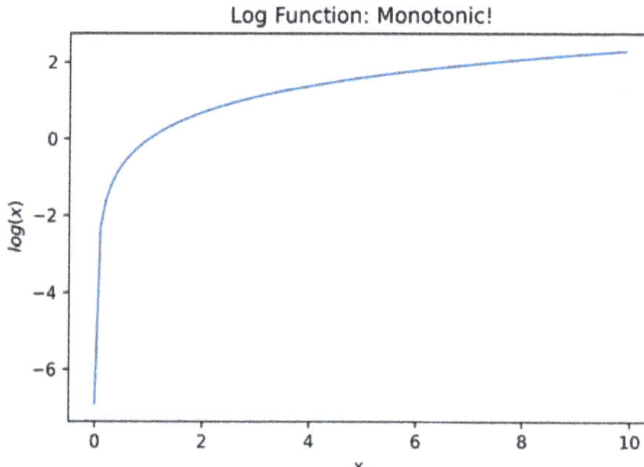

Figure 11.6: The curve of a logarithmic function. It varies monotonically.

```
log(0.5)= -0.6931471805599453 log(1.0)= 0.0
```

Now, our goal is to find the prediction $\hat{y}_i$ as close as possible to the labels y_i, but needs to be in terms of probability. Also, we already know that $\hat{y}_i$ will be a value between 0 and 1, when using the sigmoid logistic function to squash any input given. Moreover, because a label y_i is given as either 1 or 0 for a binary classification problem, the prediction $\hat{y}_i$ shall have the following correspondence to label y_i:

- When y_i belongs to the positive class (i.e., $y_i = 1$), the probability for y_i being observed for the given ith sample should be set as $\hat{y}_i$. This is because when $\hat{y}_i$ is maximized, over the training parameters $\hat{\mathbf{w}}$, we obtain the correct correspondence.
- On the other hand, when y_i belongs to the negative class (i.e., $y_i = 0$), the probability for y_i being observed for the given ith sample should be set as $1 - \hat{y}_i$. This is because when $\hat{y}_i$ is maximized, over the training parameters $\hat{\mathbf{w}}$, $1 - \hat{y}_i$ is minimized to approach 0. We, again, obtained the correct correspondence.

The above setting nicely covers both possible situations for our binary classification problem. Hence, for the ith sample, this setting can be expressed in the following formula:

$$P_{\hat{\mathbf{w}}}(y_i|\mathbf{x}_i) = \begin{cases} \hat{y}_i, & \text{if } y_i = 1 \\ 1 - \hat{y}_i, & \text{if } y_i = 0 \end{cases} \tag{11.17}$$

Using a mathematical trick, Eq. (11.17) can be rewritten in a single piece of

$$P_{\hat{\mathbf{w}}}(y_i|\mathbf{x}_i) = \hat{y}_i^{y_i}(1 - \hat{y}_i)^{1-y_i} \tag{11.18}$$

Finally, take a log for the probability above for all samples; our loss function can be expressed as

$$\mathcal{L}(\mathbf{y}, \hat{\mathbf{y}}) = -\sum_{i=1}^{m} (y_i \log \hat{y}_i + (1 - y_i) \log(1 - \hat{y}_i)), \tag{11.19}$$

where the minus sign is added, because the loss function will be minimized rather than optimized in the training process. Note also that log function is again used to make the power function easier to deal with in gradient computations. It is clear now that the above loss function is exactly the measure of the binary cross-entropy of the distribution of the label with respect to that of prediction, which are given in the last section of Chapter 4. This loss function is called "log loss" or "binary cross-entropy", or "negative log likelihood". It is a special case of cross-entropy, which can used for multi-classification problems.

11.2.8 *Remarks*

Note that the loss functions discussed above are basic ones. There are also problem-specified loss functions. For example, when we deal with k-classification problems, cross-entropy loss may be a better choice (see the next chapter). Also, when designing a facial recognition neural network, we may use a special loss function called triplet loss.

11.3 A Simple Neural Network for Classification

With all the concepts set properly, let us build a feed forward net to perform binary classifications. The neural network is schematically shown in Fig. 11.7.

This simple neural network has just one input and one output layer. It uses a combination of affine mapping, logistic prediction function, and binary cross-entropy loss. One may choose other types of combinations, depending on the application problem. The training of the net requires a backward process to update the learning parameters of weights and bias.

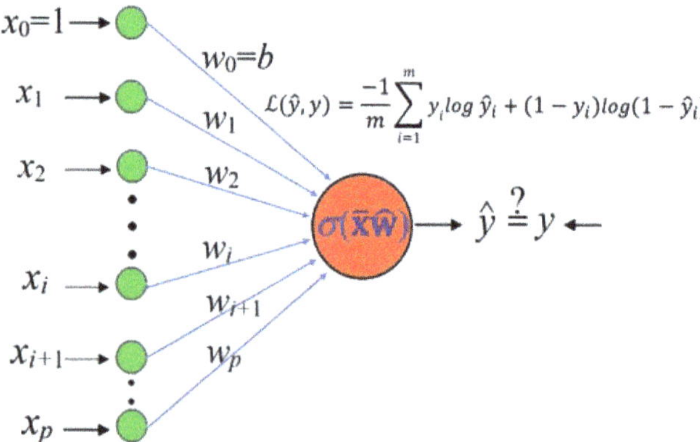

Figure 11.7: A simple neural network with just one input and one output layer for binary classification: affine mapping, logistic prediction function, and binary cross-entropy loss.

11.4 Example of Binary Classification Using Neural Network with mxnet

11.4.1 *Dataset for binary classification*

We demonstrate here an example of binary classification provided by mxnet-the-straight-dope (https://github.com/zackchase/mxnet-the-straight-dope) (under the Apache License 2). This time, we use a real dataset taken from the UCI repository (http://archive.ics.uci.edu/ml/datasets/). It was constructed by Barry Becker in 1994, containing 14 features, including age, education, occupation, sex, and native country. In the version hosted by National Taiwan University (https://www.csie.ntu.edu.tw/%7Ecjlin/libsvmtools/datasets/binary.html), the data have been re-processed to have 123 features. The label is a binary indicator on whether the person corresponding to each row made more ($y_i = 1$) or less ($y_i = 0$) than \$50,000 income in the year of 1994. The dataset contains 30,956 training and 1,605 testing samples.

We first read the following in the dataset:

```python
import numpy as np
import mxnet as mx
from mxnet import nd, autograd, gluon
import matplotlib.pyplot as plt

data_ctx = mx.cpu()
# Change this to mx.gpu(0) to train on an NVIDIA GPU
model_ctx = mx.cpu()

with open("datasets/a1a.train") as f:
    train_raw = f.read()

with open("datasets/a1a.test") as f:
    test_raw = f.read()

print(len(test_raw))
print(test_raw[0:216])
```

```
114816
-1 3:1 11:1 14:1 19:1 39:1 42:1 55:1 64:1 67:1 73:1 75:1 76:1 80:1 83:1
-1 3:1 6:1 17:1 27:1 35:1 40:1 57:1 63:1 69:1 73:1 74:1 76:1 81:1 103:1
-1 4:1 6:1 15:1 21:1 35:1 40:1 57:1 63:1 67:1 73:1 74:1 77:1 80:1 83:1
```

The first three lines of data are printed above. The first entry in each row is the label value. The following tokens are the indexes of the non-zero features. The number "1" is redundant. Let use the following code to process the dataset.

```python
def process_data(raw_data):
    train_lines = raw_data.splitlines()
    num_examples = len(train_lines)
    num_features = 123
    X = nd.zeros((num_examples, num_features), ctx=data_ctx)
    Y = nd.zeros((num_examples, 1), ctx=data_ctx)
    for i, line in enumerate(train_lines):
        tokens = line.split()
        label(int(tokens[0])+1)/2   #Change label:{-1,1} to {0,1}
        Y[i] = label
        for token in tokens[1:]:
            index = int(token[:-2]) - 1
            X[i, index] = 1
    return X, Y
```

Verify the data by checking the shape of the arrays.

```python
Xtrain, Ytrain = process_data(train_raw)
Xtest, Ytest = process_data(test_raw)
```

```python
print('Xtrain:',Xtrain.shape)
print('Ytrain:',Ytrain.shape)
num_sample = len(Xtrain[0:])
print('num_sample=',num_sample)
print('Xtest:',Xtest.shape)
print('Ytest:',Ytest.shape)
```

```
Xtrain: (30956, 123)
Ytrain: (30956, 1)
num_sample= 30956
Xtest: (1605, 123)
Ytest: (1605, 1)
```

It is confirmed that the dataset $\mathbf{X}$ has a total of $m = 30{,}956$ train samples, each of which has $p = 123$ figures. Corresponding to each training sample is a label y, with a total of 30,956 labels. The dataset for testing has a total of 1605 samples, each of which also has $p = 123$ figures. Corresponding to each test sample is a label y with a total of 1,605 labels.

The data value of each sample is given in either 1.0 or 0.0, corresponding to "yes" or "no". The same is true also for these labels.

Check the ratio of positive samples in the training and test datasets. This shall give us an indication of the overall distribution of the training and test data.

```
print(nd.sum(Ytrain)/len(Ytrain))
print(nd.sum(Ytest)/len(Ytest))
```

```
[0.24053495]
<NDArray 1 @cpu(0)>

[0.24610592]
<NDArray 1 @cpu(0)>
```

Let us instantiate a dataloader

```
batch_size = 64
train_data = gluon.data.DataLoader(gluon.data.ArrayDataset
    (Xtrain, Ytrain), batch_size=batch_size, shuffle=True)
test_data = gluon.data.DataLoader(gluon.data.ArrayDataset
    (Xtest, Ytest), batch_size=batch_size, shuffle=True)
```

11.4.2 *Define loss functions*

We write codes for loss functions discussed earlier for use and examinations. Readers may try out these function by simply changing the function name in the training. The trial outcomes by the author done earlier are given in the comment lines.

```
def logistic(z):                    # Sigmoid function
    return 1. / (1. + nd.exp(-z))

def cross_entropy(output,y):        # This will not work well, try
    yhat = logistic(output)         # for k-classification
    return - nd.nansum(y * nd.log(yhat+1e-6))

def log_loss(output, y):            # readers may try different loss
    yhat = logistic(output)
    #return nd.mean((1-y*yhat)**2)  # fast, not accurate: 0.241
    #return nd.sum(nd.maximum(1.-(y*yhat+(1-y)*(1-yhat)),
    # nd.zeros_like(y))) works: 0.837
```

```python
    return nd.nansum((1-y*yhat-(1-y)*(1-yhat))**2)
                                      #work best: 0.849.


    #return   - nd.nansum(  y * nd.log(yhat) + (1-y)
    #* nd.log(1-yhat)) standard: 0.848
```

```python
import numpy as np

# Define and initialize the neural network model
# When re-train the model from fresh, start from here,
# so that the learning parameters can be reset in a random.
net = gluon.nn.Dense(1)
net.collect_params().initialize(mx.init.Normal(sigma=1.),
    ctx=model_ctx)

# Instantiate an optimizer
# Choices on optimizer and the learning rate are made here.

trainer = gluon.Trainer(net.collect_params(),'sgd',
    {'learning_rate':0.01})

# Estimate the maximum epochs
max_epochs = int(num_sample/batch_size + 1)
# Decide the number of epochs, or use the max_epochs
epochs = 100     # max_epochs
print('num_sample=',num_sample,'epochs=',epochs,'max_epochs='
    ,max_epochs,' batch_size=',batch_size)
print('The initial loss in the order of',
    int(-np.log(0.5)*num_sample))
loss_sequence = []
num_examples = len(Xtrain)

for e in range(epochs):
    cumulative_loss = 0
    for i, (data, label) in enumerate(train_data):
        data = data.as_in_context(model_ctx)
        label = label.as_in_context(model_ctx)
        with autograd.record():
            output = net(data)          # output=z, net=x.w+b
            loss = log_loss(output, label)

        loss.backward()
        trainer.step(batch_size)
        cumulative_loss += nd.sum(loss).asscalar()
```

```
    if e%20 == 0 or e == epochs-1:
        print("Epoch %s, loss: %s" % (e, cumulative_loss ))
    loss_sequence.append(cumulative_loss)
```

```
num_sample= 30956 epochs= 100 max_epochs= 484  batch_size= 64
The initial loss in the order of 21457
Epoch 0, loss: 7092.165759086609
```

11.4.3 *Plot the convergence curve of the loss function*

```python
# plot the convergence of the estimated loss function
%matplotlib inline
import matplotlib
import matplotlib.pyplot as plt
plt.figure(num=None,figsize=(8, 6))
plt.plot(loss_sequence)
plt.grid(True, which="both")
plt.xlabel('epoch',fontsize=14)
plt.ylabel('average loss',fontsize=14)
```

11.4.4 *Computing the accuracy of the trained model*

The convergence curve shows the process of the learning parameters getting improvements during the training. It is not exactly the measure of the accuracy of the model trained. To assess how good the trained model is, we must use an independent set of the test data. This can be done using the following code. It is also a good practice to also check how good the model performs using the training data.

```python
num_correct = 0.0
num_total = len(Xtrain)
for i, (data, label) in enumerate(train_data):
    data = data.as_in_context(model_ctx)
    label = label.as_in_context(model_ctx)
    output = net(data)
    prediction = (nd.sign(output) + 1) / 2
    num_correct += nd.sum(prediction == label)

print("Accuracy: %0.3f (%s/%s)" % (num_correct.asscalar()/
        num_total,num_correct.asscalar(),num_total))
```

The accuracy looks good. It should be good, because we have used the data to train the net. Therefore, this is only an indication that the training itself is well done. Let us finally conduct a more objective assessment, using the test data, which gives the indication of the accuracy and usefulness of the trained model.

```python
num_correct = 0.0
num_total = len(Xtest)
for i, (data, label) in enumerate(test_data):
    data = data.as_in_context(model_ctx)
    label = label.as_in_context(model_ctx)
    output = net(data)
    prediction = (nd.sign(output) + 1) / 2
    num_correct += nd.sum(prediction == label)

print("Accuracy: %0.3f (%s/%s)" % (num_correct.asscalar()/
        num_total, num_correct.asscalar(), num_total))
```

We now see the accuracy of the trained model after the training is done for the specified epochs, using both the training and the test datasets. We have also run the same code using 483 epochs (the max_epochs), which allows the model to see almost all the training samples, and the accuracy can reach about 84% for the test dataset.

This model is simple, but it shall give one good experience in training neural networks for similar types of problems.

11.5 Example of Binary Classification Using Sklearn

We now introduce a case study done by the scikit-learn team [2]. It uses a total of 10 classifiers in scikit-learn on three synthetic datasets, and plots decision boundaries together for easy comparison.

```python
%matplotlib inline
print(__doc__)
# Code source: Gaël Varoquaux
#              Andreas Müller
# Modified for documentation by Jaques Grobler
# License: BSD 3 clause
```

```python
import numpy as np
import matplotlib.pyplot as plt
from matplotlib.colors import ListedColormap
from sklearn.model_selection import train_test_split
from sklearn.preprocessing import StandardScaler
from sklearn.datasets import make_moons,
    make_circles, make_classification
from sklearn.neural_network import MLPClassifier
from sklearn.neighbors import KNeighborsClassifier
from sklearn.svm import SVC
from sklearn.gaussian_process import
    GaussianProcessClassifier
from sklearn.gaussian_process.kernels import RBF
from sklearn.tree import DecisionTreeClassifier
from sklearn.ensemble import
    RandomForestClassifier, AdaBoostClassifier
from sklearn.naive_bayes import GaussianNB
from sklearn.discriminant_analysis import
    QuadraticDiscriminantAnalysis

h = .02  # step size in the mesh
names = ["Nearest Neighbors", "Linear SVM", "RBF SVM",
        "Gaussian Process", "Decision Tree", "Random Forest",
        "Neural Net", "AdaBoost", "Naive Bayes", "QDA"]
classifiers = [
    KNeighborsClassifier(3),
    SVC(kernel="linear", C=0.025),
    SVC(gamma=2, C=1),
    GaussianProcessClassifier(1.0 * RBF(1.0)),
    DecisionTreeClassifier(max_depth=5),
    RandomForestClassifier(max_depth=5, n_estimators=10,
        max_features=1),
    MLPClassifier(alpha=1, max_iter=1000),
    AdaBoostClassifier(),
    GaussianNB(),
    QuadraticDiscriminantAnalysis()]

X, y = make_classification(n_features=2, n_redundant=0,
    n_informative=2,random_state=1,n_clusters_per_class=1)
rng = np.random.RandomState(2)
X += 2 * rng.uniform(size=X.shape)
linearly_separable = (X, y)
```

```python
datasets = [make_moons(noise=0.3, random_state=0),
            make_circles(noise=.2, factor=.5, random_state=1),
            linearly_separable
            ]

figure = plt.figure(figsize=(27, 9))
i = 1
# iterate over datasets
for ds_cnt, ds in enumerate(datasets):
    # preprocess dataset, split into training and test part
    X, y = ds
    X = StandardScaler().fit_transform(X)
    X_train, X_test, y_train, y_test = \
        train_test_split(X, y, test_size=.4, random_state=42)

    x_min, x_max = X[:, 0].min() - .5, X[:, 0].max() + .5
    y_min, y_max = X[:, 1].min() - .5, X[:, 1].max() + .5
    xx, yy = np.meshgrid(np.arange(x_min, x_max, h),
                         np.arange(y_min, y_max, h))

    # just plot the dataset first
    cm = plt.cm.RdBu
    cm_bright = ListedColormap(['#FF0000', '#0000FF'])
    ax = plt.subplot(len(datasets), len(classifiers) + 1, i)
    if ds_cnt == 0:
        ax.set_title("Input data")
    # Plot the training points
    ax.scatter(X_train[:, 0], X_train[:, 1], c=y_train,
        cmap=cm_bright,edgecolors='k')
    # Plot the testing points
    ax.scatter(X_test[:,0],X_test[:,1],c=y_test, cmap=cm_bright,
        alpha=0.6,edgecolors='k')
    ax.set_xlim(xx.min(), xx.max())
    ax.set_ylim(yy.min(),yy.max())
    ax.set_xticks(())
    ax.set_yticks(())
    i += 1

    # iterate over classifiers
    for name, clf in zip(names, classifiers):
        ax=plt.subplot(len(datasets),len(classifiers)+1,i)
        clf.fit(X_train, y_train)
        score = clf.score(X_test, y_test)
```

```python
    # Plot the decision boundary. We assign a color to each
    # point in the mesh [x_min, x_max]x[y_min, y_max].
    if hasattr(clf, "decision_function"):
        Z = clf.decision_function(np.c_[xx.ravel(),
            yy.ravel()])
    else:
        Z = clf.predict_proba(np.c_[xx.ravel(),1]

    # Put the result into a color plot
    Z = Z.reshape(xx.shape)
    ax.contour f(xx, yy, Z, cmap=cm, alpha=.8)

    # Plot the training points
    ax.scatter(X_train[:,0],X_train[:,1],c=y_train,
        cmap=cm_bright,edgecolors='k')

    # Plot the testing points
    ax.scatter(X_test[:,0],X_test[:,1],c=y_test,cmap=cm_bright,
        edgecolors='k',alpha=0.6)

    ax.set_xlim(xx.min(), xx.max())
    ax.set_ylim(yy.min(), yy.max())
    ax.set_xticks(())
    ax.set_yticks(())
    if ds_cnt == 0:
        ax.set_title(name)
    ax.text(xx.max()-.3,yy.min()+.3,('%.2f'
    %score).lstrip('0'),
        size=15,horizontalalignment='right')
    i += 1

plt.tight_layout()
plt.show()
```

Automatically created module for IPython interactive environment

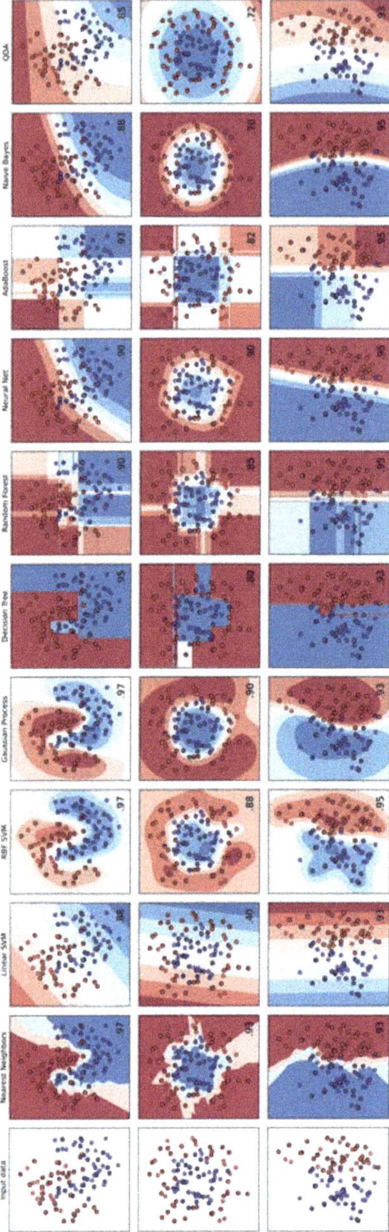

Figure 11.8: Comparison of the classification results using various classifiers. A study by Sklearn team.

Three randomly generated datasets are used in this study, and the results are plotted in three row in Fig. 11.8. The methods used are Nearest neighbors, Linear SVM, RBF SVM, Gaussian Process, Decision Tree, Random Forest, MLP Neural Network, Ada Boost, Gaussian Naive Bayes, and Quadratic Discriminant Analysis (QDA). The training data-points are in solid colors, and the testing data-points are semi-transparent. The number in the lower-right corner is the accuracy of the classification on the test datasets. Although we did not discuss some of these classification methods, the decision boundaries obtained by these different methods give some intuitive indication of how these methods work. Readers may read the documentation of Sklearn for more details.

11.6 Regression with Decision Tree, AdaBoost, and Gradient Boosting

Decision tree, AdaBoost, and Gradient boosting can also be applied to regression problems. Scikit Learn has provided a number of examples that are quite easy to follow. Readers may take a look at these examples:

- Decision Tree Regression.
- Decision Tree Regression with AdaBoost [3].
- Gradient boosting regression.
- A study on real-time prediction of projectile penetration to laminates, using both neural network and decision tree [4].

References

[1] R. Lorenzo, De Vito Ernesto, C. Andrea *et al.*, Are loss functions all the same?, *Neural Computation*, **16**(5), 1063–1076, May 2004. https://doi.org/10.1162/0899766 04773135104.

[2] P. Fabian, V. Gae, G. Alexandre *et al.*, Scikit-learn: Machine learning in Python, *Journal of Machine Learning Research*, **12**(85), 2825–2830, 2011. http://jmlr.org/papers/v12/pedregosa11a.html.

[3] H. Drucker, *Improving regressors using boosting techniques*, Proc. 14th International Conference on Machine Learning, 1997.

[4] W. Pushkar and G.R. Liu, Real-time prediction of projectile penetration to laminates by training machine learning models with finite element solver as the trainer, *Defence Technology*, **17**(1), 147–160, 2021. https://www.sciencedirect.com/science/article/pii/S2214914720303275.

Chapter 12

Multiclass Classification

In the previous chapter, we discussed neural networks for binary classification, useful for "yes" or "no" types of problems. It is also a basis for handling many types of multi-classification problems, because one can often change a multi-classification problem into a set of binary classification problems. The techniques include one-to-rest, all-pairs, and their variation, as we have discussed in the Chapter 6 on SVM. There are many well-established modules for this type of purpose, such as Scikit learn. In this chapter, we discuss a systematic means to handle multi-classification problems, also known as **k-classification** problems, where we have in general a dataset that has k classes.

12.1 Softmax Activation Neural Networks for k-Classifications

For binary logistic regression problems, we often use the following activation function for the neuron at the final layer to predict the output:

$$\hat{y} = \sigma(z) = \frac{1}{1 + e^{-z}} = \frac{1}{1 + e^{-(\mathbf{x}\cdot\mathbf{w}+b)}} = \frac{1}{1 + e^{-(\overline{\mathbf{x}}\cdot\hat{\mathbf{w}})}} \qquad (12.1)$$

where σ stands for the sigmoid function. It squashes an arbitrarily real number into a number between 0 and 1, which becomes a type of probability output.

For k-classification problems, we create a neural network with k neurons at the output layer. If there are p inputs $x_i (i = 1, 2, \ldots, p)$, the input layer shall have p neurons. The structure of the simplest neural network can be shown in Fig. 12.1.

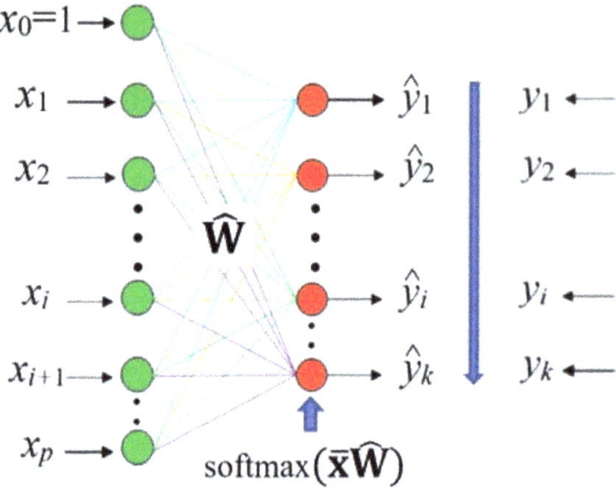

Figure 12.1:   A simple one-layer network for k-classifications.

In order to have a probability type of output, we would need to use a special activation function (instead of the sigmoid) to force the output layer to produce a set (not just one) of probabilities for all these k classes. This is the well-known softmax function defined as

$$\text{softmax}(\mathbf{z}) = \frac{e^{\mathbf{z}}}{\sum_{j=1}^{k} e^{z_j}} \tag{12.2}$$

where $\mathbf{z}$ can be a vector with k components $z_j (i = 1, 2, \ldots, k)$, and the computation of the exponentiates is all element-wise. In matrix form, $\mathbf{z}$ can be given, for example, in the following form:

$$\underset{1\times k}{\mathbf{z}} = \underset{1\times p}{\mathbf{x}}\,\underset{p\times k}{\mathbf{W}} + \underset{1\times k}{\mathbf{b}} = \underset{1\times(p+1)}{\bar{\mathbf{x}}}\,\underset{(p+1)\times k}{\hat{\mathbf{W}}} \tag{12.3}$$

The jth component z_j can be expressed as

$$z_j = \bar{\mathbf{x}}\,\hat{\mathbf{W}}[j] \tag{12.4}$$

Readers my refer to Chapter 5 for these notations. For image classification problems, p is the total number of pixels in the image.

It is clear that the softmax function uses $e^{\mathbf{z}}$ to convert all values to be strictly positive followed by a normalization, so that all values can sum to 1.

The outputs at these k neurons on the final layer become a vector of

$$\hat{\mathbf{y}} = \text{softmax}(\overline{\mathbf{x}}\,\hat{\mathbf{W}}) = \frac{e^{(\overline{\mathbf{x}}\,\hat{\mathbf{W}})}}{\sum_{j=1}^{k} e^{(\overline{\mathbf{x}}\,\hat{\mathbf{W}}[j])}} \tag{12.5}$$

The softmax activation function is widely used in k-classification, also known as softmax regression or multinomial regression.

12.2 Cross-Entropy Loss Function for k-Classifications

In a k-classification problem, one of the k labels is 1 (the correct one or the hot one) and the rest are all 0. Therefore, we can use the following cross-entropy function (see Chapter 4) as the loss function:

$$\mathcal{L}(\mathbf{y},\hat{\mathbf{y}}) = \frac{1}{m}\sum_{s=1}^{m}\left(\underbrace{-\sum_{j=1}^{k} y_j \log \hat{y}_j}_{\mathbf{y}_s \cdot \log \hat{\mathbf{y}}_s}\right) = -\frac{1}{m}\sum_{s=1}^{m}(\mathbf{y}_s \cdot \log \hat{\mathbf{y}}_s) \tag{12.6}$$

where s stands for the sth sample in the dataset. The above loss function essentially cares only about the loss related to the correct label. Note that this cross-entropy loss function is still a scalar function.

Compared to the loss function used in the binary classification problems, we can expect that the binary-cross-entropy loss function is a special case of the k-classification loss function. To proof this, we simply let $k = 2$ in Eq. (12.6), which gives

$$\mathcal{L}(\mathbf{y},\hat{\mathbf{y}}) = -\frac{1}{m}\sum_{s=1}^{m}\left(\sum_{j=1}^{2} y_j \log \hat{y}_j\right)_s \tag{12.7}$$

$$= -\frac{1}{m}\sum_{s=1}^{m}\left(y_{j=1}\log \hat{y}_{j=1} + y_{j=2}\log \hat{y}_{j=2}\right)_s$$

Notice that index j is for the class, and s stands for the sth sample. Now, in the case of binary classifications, we must have

$$y_{j=2} = 1 - y_{j=1}, \quad \text{and} \quad \hat{y}_{j=2} = 1 - \hat{y}_{j=1} \tag{12.8}$$

This is true for any sample. Substituting Eq. (12.8) into (12.7), dropping $j = 1$ because it is the only one left, and then moving the index s inside, we have

$$\mathcal{L}(\mathbf{y}, \hat{\mathbf{y}}) = -\frac{1}{m} \sum_{s=1}^{m} (y_s \log \hat{y}_s + (1 - y_s) \log(1 - \hat{y}_s)), \qquad (12.9)$$

which is exactly the same equation for binary classification, as we seen in Chapter 11 (except the normalization by m). This proof implies that if one just uses two labels ($k = 1, 2$) and arranges the dataset in accordance with a multi-classifier, one should be able to perform a binary classification.

12.3 Case Study 1: Handwritten Digit Classification with 1-Layer NN

We are now ready to perform a demonstration of k-classification: to classify handwritten digits. We have done this earlier using the Naive Bayes Classifier. Now, we do the same, but using a simply neural network with a single (input and output, no hidden) layer. We will discuss the detailed procedure using the codes available at mxnet-the-straight-dope (under the Apache License 2), with some minor changes. As usual, we import the necessary libraries to begin with.

```python
# Import necessary libraries
from __future__ import print_function
import numpy as np
import mxnet as mx
from mxnet import nd, autograd, gluon
mx.random.seed(1)
```

12.3.1 *Set contexts according to computer hardware*

We can set the compute context, using either `model_ctx` or `mx.gpu(0)` of your choice. In this demonstration, we use cpu.

```python
data_ctx = mx.cpu()
model_ctx = mx.cpu()   # model_ctx = mx.gpu() # alternative
```

12.3.2 *Loading the MNIST dataset*

We again use the real MNIST data for this demonstration. The MNIST dataset contains a total of 70,000 images of handwritten digits (0–9), each image is a 28 by 28 centrally cropped black&white photograph. We are to train the k-classification model to classify handwritten digits in $\{0-9\}$.

We first use MXNet's utility to get a copy of the MNIST dataset and then preprocess each item in it. The data and label are casted to floats and normalized to the range of $[0, 1]$. The 70,000 images are divided, in a random fashion, into a training dataset with 60,000 and a test dataset with 10,000 images. Both x_train and x_test parts contain grayscale RGB codes (from 0 to 255), while y_train and y_test parts contain labels (from 0 to 9), representing the actual number of the handwriting. To visualize these numbers, we can use matplotlib.

```python
def transform(data, label):
    return data.astype(np.float32)/255, label.astype(np.float32)
                        # data type conversion & normalization
mnist_train=gluon.data.vision.MNIST(train=True,transform=transform)
                        #get the data for training
mnist_test=gluon.data.vision.MNIST(train=False,transform=transform)
                        #get the data for testing
```

Each item in the train (and test) dataset is a tuple of an image paired with a label:

```python
print(len(mnist_train))
image,labelmnist_train[100]    # unpack the 100th data pair
print(image.shape, label)      # check the shape and label
#print(image)                  # print the image in floats
```

```
60000
(28, 28, 1) 5.0
```

This shows that each image is formatted as a three-tuple (height, width, channel). The channel here is one dimension, because the image is black&white. For color images, the channel would have three dimensions (red, green, and blue).

We next define variables for the numbers of inputs and outputs.

```python
num_inputs = 784      # 28×28=784
num_outputs = 10      # 10 digits
num_examples = 60000  # number of training samples
```

Because matplotlib expects either (height, width) or (height, width, channel) with RGB channels, we reshape the data by broadcasting the single channel to 3.

```python
im = mx.nd.tile(image, (1,1,3))    #This should be a 5
print(im.shape)
```

```
(28, 28, 3)
```

We shall now visualize the image to see whether the image tallies with the label.

```python
import matplotlib.pyplot as plt
plt.imshow(im.asnumpy())
plt.show()
print('label=',label)
```

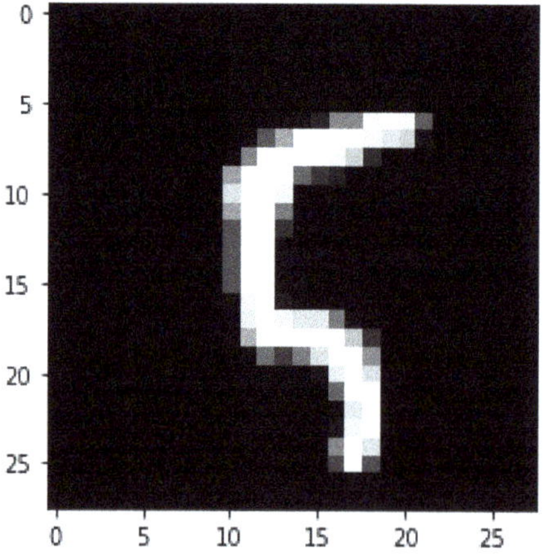

Figure 12.2:   A sample image of handwritten digit from the MNIST dataset.

```
label= 5.0
```

Let us load the training dataset of images in batches (for stochastic gradient descent optimization) with a batch size specified. This is done in a random fashion (by setting shuffle to True). We also load the test dataset but without shuffling.

```
batch_size = 64
train_data=mx.gluon.data.DataLoader(mnist_train,batch_size,\
        shuffle=True)
test_data=mx.gluon.data.DataLoader(mnist_test,batch_size,\
        shuffle=False)
```

12.3.3 *Set model parameters*

Our model parameters should be as follows:

1. We need to do a 10-classification, thus $k = 10$.
2. We decided to use 64 training samples in a batch.
3. Because the image data are in a matrix of 28×28, we should flatten it into a 1D row vector with $28 \times 28 = 784$ components. Therefore, p for this case is 784.
4. The dimension of any of these samples is a row vector $\mathbf{x}$ with 784 dimensions.
5. Because we have 10 classes, the weight matrix $\mathbf{W}$ should be 784×10.
6. The prediction outputs of our model should be 10 probability values for each of these 10 digits $\mathbf{c}$ to be the label digit for a given image $\mathbf{x}$: $P(\mathbf{y} = \mathbf{c} \mid \mathbf{x})$.
7. Finally, the row vector for the bias $\mathbf{b}$ is 10 in dimension.

12.3.4 *Multiclass logistic regression*

Define softmax function for our 10-classification problem.

```
def softmax(y_linear):
    exp=nd.exp(y_linear-nd.max(y_linear,axis=1).reshape((-1,1)))
    norms = nd.sum(exp, axis=1).reshape((-1,1))
    return exp / norms
```

```
sample_y_linear = nd.random_normal(shape=(2,10))
sample_yhat = softmax(sample_y_linear)
print(sample_yhat)
print(nd.sum(sample_yhat, axis=1))
```

```
[[0.08024886 0.04739863 0.02992393 0.08034719 0.03729992
  0.01006166 0.3406885  0.2191301  0.04921847 0.10568278]
 [0.02349378 0.02465977 0.06156655 0.04537923 0.11654365
  0.04362861 0.5023322  0.02725256 0.1258423  0.02930132]]
<NDArray 2x10 @cpu(0)>

[1. 1.]
<NDArray 2 @cpu(0)>
```

This confirms that each of the rows sums to 1, as expected.

12.3.5 *Defining a neural network model*

We define now our 10-classification model.

```
def net(X):
    y_linear = nd.dot(X, W) + b
    yhat = softmax(y_linear)
    return yhat
```

12.3.6 *Defining the cross-entropy loss function*

Because our k-classification problem is to predict probabilities, the relevant loss function would be the cross-entropy function. In digit classification case, label vector $\mathbf{y}$ always has a 1 (hot) in its entries. Hence, it is sometimes called one-hot vector. The value corresponding to the correct label digit is set to 1 and the rest are set to 0. For example, if the label is 2, we set

$$\mathbf{y} = [0, 1, 0, 0, 0, 0, 0, 0, 0, 0] \tag{12.10}$$

Because we only care about the component in $\hat{\mathbf{y}}$ corresponding to 2, and the cross-entropy counts only the hot 1. The minimization algorithm can then drive $\hat{\mathbf{y}}$ to approach $\mathbf{y}$, by updating the weights in $\mathbf{W}$ and biases in $\mathbf{b}$ in the net.

The code definition of the cross-entropy is as follows:

```
def cross_entropy(yhat, y):               # cross- entropy loss
    return - nd.sum(y * nd.log(yhat+1e-6))
    # return nd.sum((y - yhat)**2)         # one may try this too
```

12.3.7 *Optimization method*

We use the stochastic gradient descent (SGD) for optimization.

```python
def SGD(params, lr):
    for param in params:
        param[:] = param - lr * param.grad
```

12.3.8 *Accuracy evaluation*

We can compute the accuracy of a model with its current learning parameters, by finding out the ratio of the number of correct answers with the total number of tests. We use the following evaluation loop to do this:

```python
def evaluate_accuracy(data_iterator, net):
    numerator = 0.
    denominator = 0.
    for i, (data, label) in enumerate(data_iterator):
        data = data.as_in_context(model_ctx).reshape((-1,784))
        label = label.as_in_context(model_ctx)
        label_one_hot = nd.one_hot(label, 10)
        output = net(data)
        predictions = nd.argmax(output, axis=1)
        numerator += nd.sum(predictions == label)
        denominator += data.shape[0]
    return (numerator / denominator).asscalar()
```

For our randomly initialized model, roughly one tenth of all examples may belong to each of the 10 classes. We thus expect an accuracy of 0.1. Now, we are ready to train the model.

12.3.9 *Initiation of the model and training execution*

```python
# Initialize the learning parameters randomly
W=nd.random_normal(shape=(num_inputs, num_outputs),ctx=model_ctx)
b=nd.random_normal(shape=num_outputs,ctx=model_ctx)

params = [W, b]
print(W.shape,b.shape)
```

```python
# Let MXNet know that the gradients with respect to each of
# these parameters will be needed during training.

for param in params:
    param.attach_grad()

# Estimate the accuracy of the un-trained model
print("Accuracy of untrained model:",
    evaluate_accuracy(test_data,net))

import time        # To time the performance
epochs = 10        #20
learning_rate = .005

print('Parameter setting: epochs =',epochs, ' learning_rate =',\
      learning_rate,'  batch_size=',batch_size)

start_t = time.process_time()
for e in range(epochs):
    cumulative_loss = 0
    for i, (data, label) in enumerate(train_data):
        data = data.as_in_context(model_ctx).reshape((-1,784))
        label = label.as_in_context(model_ctx)
        label_one_hot = nd.one_hot(label, 10)
        with autograd.record():
            output = net(data)
            loss = cross_entropy(output, label_one_hot)
        loss.backward()
        SGD(params, learning_rate)
        cumulative_loss += nd.sum(loss).asscalar()

    test_accuracy = evaluate_accuracy(test_data, net)
    train_accuracy = evaluate_accuracy(train_data, net)
    if e%3 == 0 or e == epochs-1:
        print("Epoch %s. Loss: %s, Train_acc %s,
                Test_acc %s" %
        (e,cumulative_loss/num_examples,train_accuracy,
                test_accuracy))

t_elapsed = (time.process_time() - start_t)
print('One-layer neural network, training time =',
      f'{t_elapsed}','s')
```

```
(784, 10) (10,)
Accuracy of untrained model: 0.1152
Parameter setting: epochs = 10 learning_rate = 0.005 batch_size= 64
Epoch 0. Loss: 1.3851381640116374, Train_acc 0.8584833,
      Test_acc 0.8635
Epoch 3. Loss: 0.4689176872412364, Train_acc 0.898, Test_acc 0.8941
Epoch 6. Loss: 0.39240473754405975, Train_acc 0.9094, Test_acc 0.9035
Epoch 9. Loss: 0.3527593985239665, Train_acc 0.9142333,
      Test_acc 0.9077
One-layer neural network, training time = 1696.734375 s
```

12.3.10 *Prediction with the trained model*

We pick 10 samples randomly from the test dataset, and then use our trained
model to make a prediction.

```python
# Define the function to do prediction
def model_predict(net,data):
    output = net(data)
    return nd.argmax(output, axis=1)


# let us sample 10 random data-points from the test set

plt.figure(figsize=(15, 60))

sample_data = mx.gluon.data.DataLoader(mnist_test,10,shuffle=True)
start_t = time.process_time()
for i, (data, label) in enumerate(sample_data):
    data = data.as_in_context(model_ctx)
    print(data.shape)
    im = nd.transpose(data,(1,0,2,3))
    im = nd.reshape(im,(28,10*28,1))
    imtiles = nd.tile(im, (1,1,3))

    plt.imshow(imtiles.asnumpy())
    plt.show()
    pred=model_predict(net,data.reshape((-1,784)))
    print('model predictions are:', pred)
    break

t_elapsed = (time.process_time() - start_t)
print('One-layer neural network, prediction time=',
      f'{t_elapsed}','s')
```

```
(10, 28, 28, 1)
```

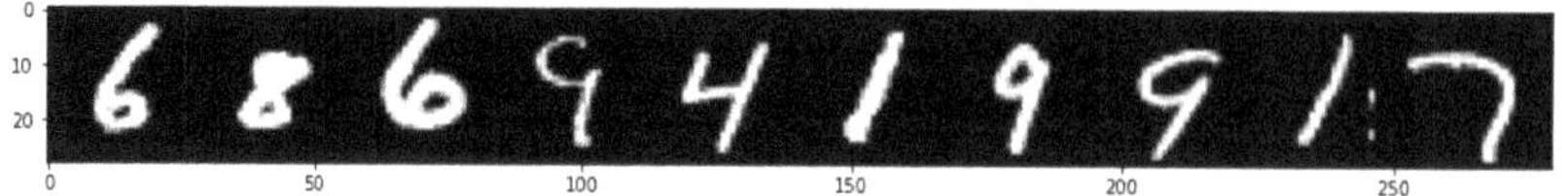

Figure 12.3:   Predicated digits from the trained one-layer NN, using the testing dataset of MNIST.

```
model predictions are:
[6. 8. 6. 4. 4. 1. 9. 9. 1. 7.]
<NDArray 10 @cpu(0)>
One-layer neural network, prediction time= 0.5 s
```

Summary of this study: The accuracy is about 90% after five epochs of training, and the time taken on the author's laptop for the training is about 500 s. The time taken for the prediction of 10 digits is only about 0.55 s. When using 10 epochs, the test accuracy increases to 91%, and the time taken for the training is 1,100 s (about double). When using 50 epochs, the test accuracy increases to 92%. When using 100 epochs, the test accuracy increases to 92.3%. Further training using this model may not make much difference. To improve further, one may need to increase the learning ability of the net to capture more nonlinear features for the images of handwritten digits. Based on the Universal Prediction Theory, this can be done using more hidden layers known as the multilayer perceptron (MLP, see the next chapter).

12.4 Case Study 2: Handwritten Digit Classification with Sklearn Random Forest Multi-Classifier

For comparison, let us do the same digit prediction using the gradient boosting classifier. It is one of the powerful techniques for classification problems. Readers may read an online article by Harshdeep Singh at towards datascience. We will not discuss this technique in detail, but will simply use the model and codes provided by scikit learn (or Sklearn) [1] for this comparison study. We slightly modified the code to allow readers to view more detailed differences in the results for different parameter settings.

```python
import numpy as np
import pandas as pd
from matplotlib import pyplot as plt
from sklearn.ensemble import RandomForestClassifier
from sklearn.model_selection import train_test_split
%matplotlib inline
```

```python
# Read-in and take a look at the data
data=pd.read_csv('mnist.csv') # the mnist data already in a
                              # csv file under the local direction
data.head()                   # take a look at the first few lines
```

```
   label  1x1  1x2  1x3  1x4  1x5  1x6  1x7  1x8  1x9  ...  28x19  28x20  \
0      5    0    0    0    0    0    0    0    0    0  ...      0      0
1      0    0    0    0    0    0    0    0    0    0  ...      0      0
2      4    0    0    0    0    0    0    0    0    0  ...      0      0
3      1    0    0    0    0    0    0    0    0    0  ...      0      0
4      9    0    0    0    0    0    0    0    0    0  ...      0      0

   28x21  28x22  28x23  28x24  28x25  28x26  28x27  28x28
0      0      0      0      0      0      0      0      0
1      0      0      0      0      0      0      0      0
2      0      0      0      0      0      0      0      0
3      0      0      0      0      0      0      0      0
4      0      0      0      0      0      0      0      0

5 rows x 785 columns
```

```python
# Take look at the image of a digit.
digit_array = data.iloc[4,1:].values
digit_image = digit_array.reshape(28,28).astype('uint8')
plt.imshow(digit_image)
```

```
<matplotlib.image.AxesImage at 0x1eea6883dd8>
```

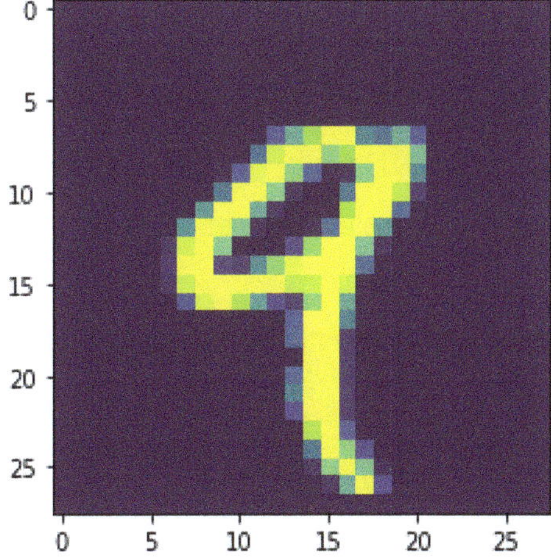

Figure 12.4: A sample image of handwritten digit in the MNIST dataset.

```python
# Split the data into train and test datasets.
df_x=data.iloc[:,1:]
df_y=data.iloc[:,0]
x_train, x_test, y_train, y_test = train_test_split(df_x, df_y,\
                                  test_size=0.25, random_state=4)
y_train.head()   # Take a look at it
```

```
50965    8
1315     3
57499    4
11420    2
1328     5
Name: label, dtype: int64
```

```python
# Use sklearn RandomForestClassifier() to train the model.
rf=RandomForestClassifier()
                    #(n_estimators=200,min_samples_split=4)
rf.fit(x_train,y_train)
# Predict the digits in the test dataset.
predicted_digits =rf.predict(x_test)
```

```python
# Print out the results and image
print('First 10 true digits in the test set:',y_test.values[0:10])
fig, figs = plt.subplots(1, 10, figsize=(15, 15))
for i in range(10):
    digit_array=x_test.iloc[i,:].values
    figs[i].imshow(digit_array.reshape(28,28).astype('uint8'))
    figs[i].axes.get_xaxis().set_visible(False)
    figs[i].axes.get_yaxis().set_visible(False)

plt.show()
print('Predicated digits for the first 10 in the test set:',
      predicted_digits[0:10])
```

```
First 10 true digits in the test set: [0 6 5 6 2 8 9 5 0 9]
```

Figure 12.5:   Predicated handwritten digits using the Sklearn Random forest and the testing dataset of MNIST.

```
Predicated digits for the first 10 in the test set:
    [0 6 5 6 2 7 9 5 0 9]
```

```python
# compute the accuracy for the whole test set
print('Total number of digits in the test set:',
    len(predicted_digits))
correct = 0
for i in range(len(predicted_digits)):
    if predicted_digits[i] == y_test.values[i]:
        correct += 1

print('Total number of correctly predicted_digitsicted digits:',
    correct)
print('The accuracy is:',100*correct/len(predicted_digits),'%')
```

```
Total number of digits in the test set: 17500
Total number of correctly predicted_digitsicted digits: 16964
The accuracy is: 96.93714285714286 %
```

Summary of this study: The result is better than the one-layer neural network. Without discussing the details, further tests have given the following findings:

- When n_estimators = 50, and min_samples_split=2 are used, the accuracy is: 96.11%.
- When n_estimators = 50, and min_samples_split=2 are used, the accuracy is: 96.81%.
- When n_estimators = 100, and min_samples_split=2 are used (this is the default setting), the accuracy is: 96.96%.
- When n_estimators = 100, and min_samples_split=4 are used, the accuracy is: 96.91%.
- When n_estimators = 200, and min_samples_split=2 are used, the accuracy is: 97.15%.
- When n_estimators = 400, and min_samples_split=2 are used, the accuracy is: 97.14%.
- When n_estimators = 200, and min_samples_split=4 are used, the accuracy is: 97.01%.
- When n_estimators = 400, and min_samples_split=4 are used, the accuracy is: 97.14%.

12.5 Case Study 3: Comparison of Random Forest, Extra-Forest, and Gradient Boosting for Multi-Classifier

We now introduce a study on comparison between the random-forest, extra-forest, and gradient boosting methods for multi-classification problems, using the same MNIST digit prediction and the modules provided by the scikit learn team [1].

```python
#from sklearn.datasets import load_digits
from sklearn.ensemble import RandomForestClassifier
from sklearn.ensemble import ExtraTreesClassifier
from sklearn import ensemble
from sklearn import metrics
from sklearn.model_selection import train_test_split
from matplotlib import pyplot as plt
import numpy as np
import pandas as pd
import time
%matplotlib inline
```

```python
# Read-in and take a look at the data
data=pd.read_csv('mnist.csv')
#data.head()
```

```python
# Split the data into train and test datasets.
df_x=data.iloc[:,1:]
df_y=data.iloc[:,0]
x_train,x_test,y_train,y_test=train_test_split(df_x, df_y,\
                        test_size=0.25,  random_state=4)
y_train.head()  # Take a look at it
```

```
50965    8
1315     3
57499    4
11420    2
1328     5
Name: label, dtype: int64
```

```python
# Using the classifiers in sklearn to train the model, and timeit
# %%timeit is not working, use time
n_e=10 #n_e = 100: very slow for the GradientBoosting Classifier
m_s=2
print('Parameters:n_estimators=',n_e,' min_samples_split=',m_s)

rf=RandomForestClassifier(n_estimators=n_e,min_samples_ split=m_s)
start_t = time.process_time()
rf.fit(x_train,y_train)
t_elapsed = (time.process_time() - start_t)
print('RandomForestClassifier, training time =',f'{t_elapsed}','s')

ef = ExtraTreesClassifier(n_estimators=n_e, min_samples_split=m_s)
start_t = time.process_time()
ef.fit(x_train,y_train)
t_elapsed = (time.process_time() - start_t)
print('ExtraTreesClassifier, training time =',f'{t_elapsed}','s')

gf = ensemble.GradientBoostingClassifier(n_estimators=n_e,\
                                min_samples_split=m_s)
start_t = time.process_time()
gf.fit(x_train,y_train)
t_elapsed = (time.process_time() - start_t)
print('GradientBoostingClassifier,training time=',\
        f'{t_elapsed}','s')
```

```
Parameters:n_estimators= 10   min_samples_split= 2
RandomForestClassifier, training time = 4.5625 s
ExtraTreesClassifier, training time = 3.65625 s
GradientBoostingClassifier,training time= 187.71875 s
```

The above test conditions are as follows:

- $n\_estimators = n\_e = 100$, $min\_samples\_split = m\_s = 2$ for all classifiers.
- All other parameters are defaults set by the corresponding classifiers.

The test results are as follows:

- RandomForestClassifier, training time $= 40.625$ s, which is about 10 times faster than the one-layer neural network.
- ExtraTreesClassifier, training time $= 39.141$ s.
- GradientBoostingClassifier, training time $= 1958.8$ s, which is about four times slower than the one-layer neural network.

When the test conditions are set to the following:

- $n\_estimators = n\_e = 10$, min_samples_split $= m\_s= 2$ for all classifiers.
- All other parameters are defaults set by the corresponding classifiers.

The test results are as follows:

- RandomForestClassifier, training time $= 5.2969$ s.
- ExtraTreesClassifier, training time $= 4.8594$ s.
- GradientBoostingClassifier, training time $= 211.97$ s.

Time scalability is roughly linear with $n\_estimators$.

```python
# Predict the digits in the test dataset, and time it.
print('Parameter setting:n_estimators=',n_e,
      'min_samples_split=',m_s)

start_t = time.process_time()
rf_predicted_digits =rf.predict(x_test)
t_elapsed = (time.process_time() - start_t)
print('RandomForestClassifier, prediction time=',
      f'{t_elapsed:.5f}','s')

start_t = time.process_time()
ef_predicted_digits =ef.predict(x_test)
t_elapsed = (time.process_time() - start_t)
print('ExtraTreesClassifier, prediction time =',
      f'{t_elapsed:.5f}','s')

start_t = time.process_time()
gf_predicted_digits =gf.predict(x_test)
t_elapsed = (time.process_time() - start_t)
print('GradientBoostingClassifier,prediction time=',
      f'{t_elapsed:.5f}','s')
```

```
Parameter setting:n_estimators= 10  min_samples_split= 2
RandomForestClassifier, prediction time= 0.14062 s
ExtraTreesClassifier, prediction time = 0.09375 s
GradientBoostingClassifier,prediction time= 0.17188 s
```

The test conditions for the training are as follows:

- $n_$estimators $= n\_e = 100$, min$_$samples$_$split $= m\_s= 2$ for all classifiers.
- All other parameters are defaults set by the corresponding classifiers.

The test results on prediction time of the classifiers are as follows:

- RandomForestClassifier, prediction time $= 1.40625$ s.
- ExtraTreesClassifier, prediction time $= 1.12500$ s.
- GradientBoostingClassifier, prediction time $= 1.50000$ s.

When the test conditions for the training are as follows:

- $n_e$stimators $= n\_e = 10$, min$_$samples$_$split $= m\_s= 2$ for all classifiers.
- All other parameters are defaults set by the corresponding classifiers.

The test results on prediction time of the classifiers are as follows:

- RandomForestClassifier, prediction time $= 0.20312$ s.
- ExtraTreesClassifier, prediction time $= 0.20312$ s.
- GradientBoostingClassifier, prediction time $= 0.21875$ s.

It is clear that the time for prediction is much less than linear with $n_$estimators, and they all are very fast in general.

```python
print('Total number of digits in the test set:',
      len(rf_predicted_digits))
rf_accuracy = metrics.accuracy_score(y_test, rf_predicted_digits)
ef_accuracy = metrics.accuracy_score(y_test, ef_predicted_digits)
gf_accuracy = metrics.accuracy_score(y_test, gf_predicted_digits)
print('The rf_accuracy is:',f'{rf_accuracy:.5f}','%')
print('The ef_accuracy is:',f'{ef_accuracy:.5f}','%')
print('The gf_accuracy is:',f'{gf_accuracy:.5f}','%')
```

```
Total number of digits in the test set: 17,500
The rf_accuracy is: 0.94657 %
The ef_accuracy is: 0.94829 %
The gf_accuracy is: 0.83806 %
```

The conditions for the training are as follows:

- $n_$estimators $= n\_e = 100$, min$_$samples$_$split $= m\_s= 2$ for all classifiers.
- All other parameters are defaults set by the corresponding classifiers.

The test accuracy results on prediction of the classifiers are as follows:

- Total number of digits in the test set: 17,500.
- The rf_accuracy is: 0.97023%.
- The ef_accuracy is: 0.97160%.
- The gf_accuracy is: 0.94651%.

When the following conditions are used for the training:

- n_estimators = n_e = 10, min_samples_split = m_s= 2 for all classifiers.
- all other parameters are defaults set by the corresponding classifiers.

The test accuracy results on prediction of the classifiers become as follows:

- Total number of digits in the test set: 17,500.
- The rf_accuracy is: 0.94577%, which is about 4% higher than the neural network with a single layer.
- The ef_accuracy is: 0.95011%.
- The gf_accuracy is: 0.83806%, which is about 6% lower than the neural network with a single layer.

```python
# Print out the results and image
print('True digits for the 10 first in the test set:',
      y_test.values[0:10])
print('rf_predicated digits for first 10 in testset:',
      rf_predicted_digits[0:10])
print('ef_predicated digits for first 10 in testset:',
      ef_predicted_digits[0:10])
print('gf_predicated digits for first 10 in testset:',
      gf_predicted_digits[0:10])
```

```
True digits for the 10 first in the test set: [0 6 5 6 2 8 9 5 0 9]
rf_predicated digits for first 10 in testset: [0 6 5 6 2 9 9 3 0 9]
ef_predicated digits for first 10 in testset: [0 6 5 6 2 3 9 5 0 9]
gf_predicated digits for first 10 in testset: [0 6 5 6 2 7 9 8 0 9]
```

12.6 Multi-Classification via TensorFlow

Due to rapid development over the past decades, many Python packages have already been developed for k-classification problems. TensorFlow is one such excellent package. Readers may take a look at the TensorFlow tutorial problems of classification images of clothing, at https://www.tensorflow.org/tutorials/keras/classification. After going through this chapter, readers shall not have much problem in understanding this TensorFlow tutorial.

12.7 Remarks

Note that the performance of a module can depend on a list of factors, including settings in computer hardware, datasets, condition of the computer system, and even on when it is run. The setting parameters used in the comparison tests presented above may not be entirely fair for some classifiers. The test outcome is therefore highly subjective. When developing large-scale machine learning models, for which computational resources are a concern, one may use a smaller-scale model (such as setting $n_$estimators at a smaller number) and quickly test the models for their datasets and then choose a proper one for the large-scale project.

Reference

[1] P. Fabian, V. Gae, G. Alexandre *et al.*, Scikit-learn: Machine learning in Python, *Journal of Machine Learning Research*, **12**(85), 2825–2830, 2011. http://jmlr.org/papers/v12/pedregosa11a.html.

Chapter 13

Multilayer Perceptron (MLP) for Regression and Classification

In the previous chapter, we have seen examples of using a simple (input and output layers, only one layer has learning parameters) neural network for k-classification of handwritten digits. We found that there is room for improvements, and we have shown that other classifiers like the random forest and the extra-forest performed better than the one-layer neural network. This chapter will show that a neural network with more layers (by adding in some hidden layers) is one of the ways to make an improvement. This type of neural networks is often known as multilayer perceptron (MLP) [1–5].

The fundamental theoretical basis for MLPs is the Universal Prediction Theory discussed in Chapter 5. It uses a chain of stacked affine transformations wrapped with nonlinear activation functions grows the dimension of hypothesis space, increases the learning parameters, giving as much as needed learning ability. It is regarded as a universal model with unlimited learning abilities, at least in theory, that can be trained and applied for all types of problems [1–3], including classification, regression, and inverse analysis of mechanical problems [6–9].

13.1 The General Architecture and Formulations of MLP

13.1.1 *The general architecture*

The difference in the configuration of an MLP from the one-layer neural networks is that an MLP has a number of **hidden layers** in addition to the two (input and output) layers. It is the base network for many other types

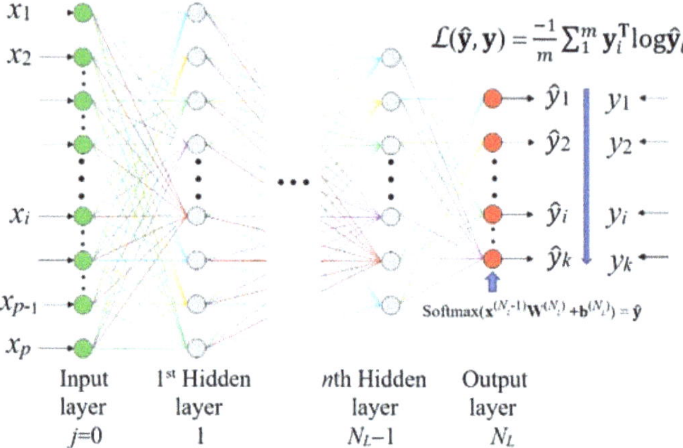

Figure 13.1: An MLP with multiple hidden layers with a chain of stacked affine transformations. All the neurons are connected with weights (dense, or fully connected), and a bias is also added (not shown) to each of the neurons in all the layers (except the input layer). Here cross entropy loss is used for classification, but loss function discussed in Chapter 12 may also be used. When the MLP is used for regression, L2 loss or any other loss function discussed in Chapter 10 may be used.

of modern configurations of neural networks. The typical configurations of an MLP is shown in Fig. 13.1.

The MLP shown in Fig. 13.1 has n_h **hidden layers** with neurons in gray color. Together with the input layer of p green neurons and output layer of k red neurons, the net has a total of $N_L = n+2$ layers. Only $N_L = n+1$ layers has learning parameters $\hat{\mathbf{W}}$. It is thus called N_L-layer network. Beginning from the input layer, each layer feeds leftward (forward) into the next layer sequentially, until the output layer. This a typical architecture for the MLP networks for $p \to k$ mapping.

We may have an arbitrary number of hidden layers, each of which can have an arbitrary number of neurons. Each neuron in a layer is fully connected to neurons in the next layer, known as fully connected (unless we use special techniques, such as dropouts, to make the connection sparse, mainly for regularization purposes). A fully connected layer is also called dense layer.

The use of more hidden layers leads to an increase in the complexity of the neural network and hence the learning capacity. In principle, a dense MLP can have a large number of training parameters to model complicated problems.

13.1.2 *The xw+b formulation*

At the input layer, we have a input vector of training samples with p features:

$$\mathbf{x}^{(0)} = \mathbf{x} = [x_1, x_2, \ldots, x_p] \tag{13.1}$$

At the output layer, we can have a single neuron or multiple neurons, depending on the need of the problem to be modeled. In general, let us have k neurons.

The optimization algorithms needed to find the minimizers (of all the learning parameters) for the loss function are in principle the same as these neural networks studied earlier. One shall expect increasing difficulties during the training of such deepnets, mostly because of the vanishing gradient problems. The Relu activation function becomes a frequent choice for the neurons in the hidden layers to overcome such problems, which will be discussed in detail in the next section.

Recall that in the k-classification problem, we used the softmax as the prediction function at the **output layer** of a neural network. It is defined as

$$\hat{\mathbf{y}} = \text{softmax}(\mathbf{z}^{(N_L)}) = \frac{e^{\mathbf{z}^{(N_L)}}}{\sum_{i=1}^{k} e^{z_i^{(N_L)}}} = \frac{e^{(\overline{\mathbf{x}}^{(N_L-1)}\hat{\mathbf{W}}^{(N_L)})}}{\sum_{i=1}^{k} e^{(\overline{\mathbf{x}}^{(N_L-1)}\hat{\mathbf{W}}^{(N_L)}[i])}} \tag{13.2}$$

where $\mathbf{z}^{(N_L)}$ is an affine transformed vector with k components $z_i^{(N_L)}$ ($i = 1, 2, \ldots, k$), and the computation of the exponentiates is element-wise. The dimensions of all these matrices can be seen in the following form:

$$\underset{1\times k}{\mathbf{z}^{(N_L)}} = \underset{1\times p}{\mathbf{x}^{(N_L-1)}} \underset{p\times k}{\mathbf{W}^{(N_L)}} + \underset{1\times k}{\mathbf{b}^{(N_L)}} = \underset{1\times(p+1)}{\overline{\mathbf{x}}^{(N_L-1)}} \underset{(p+1)\times k}{\hat{\mathbf{W}}^{(N_L)}} \tag{13.3}$$

For an MLP network, $\mathbf{x}^{(N_L-1)}$ is the output from the last hidden layer and can be written as a vector of

$$\mathbf{x}^{(N_L-1)} = [x_1^{(N_L-1)}, x_2^{(N_L-1)}, \ldots, x_{n_h}^{(N_L-1)}] \tag{13.4}$$

where the substrate n_h is the number of neurons in the last hidden layer of the MLP.

For an MLP, in the feed-forward process, the values that the neurons receive and produce are

$$
\begin{aligned}
\mathbf{x}^{(0)} &= \mathbf{x} = [x_1, x_2, \ldots, x_p] && \text{feature at the input layer} \\
\mathbf{x}^{(1)} &= \phi^{(1)}(\underbrace{\mathbf{x}^{(0)}\mathbf{W}^{(1)} + \mathbf{b}^{(1)}}_{\mathbf{z}^{(1)}}) && \text{feature at the 1st hidden layer} \\
\mathbf{x}^{(2)} &= \phi^{(2)}(\underbrace{\mathbf{x}^{(1)}\mathbf{W}^{(2)} + \mathbf{b}^{(2)}}_{\mathbf{z}^{(2)}}) && \text{feature at the 2nd hidden layer} \\
&\cdots \\
\mathbf{x}^{(i)} &= \phi^{(i)}(\underbrace{\mathbf{x}^{(i-1)}\mathbf{W}^{((i))} + \mathbf{b}^{((i))}}_{\mathbf{z}^{(i)}}) && \text{feature at the } i\text{th hidden layer} \\
&\cdots \\
\hat{\mathbf{y}} &= \mathbf{x}^{(N_{Li})} \\
&= \phi^{(N_{Li})}(\underbrace{\mathbf{x}^{(N_L-1)}\mathbf{W}^{(N_{Li})} + \mathbf{b}^{(N_{Li})}}_{\mathbf{z}^{(N_{Li})}}) \quad \text{prediction at the output layer}
\end{aligned}
\tag{13.5}
$$

Here, the number in the parentheses in the superscript stands for the layer number. The terms above the curly brackets are the affine transformation functions $\mathbf{z}^{(i)}$ $(i = 1, 2, \ldots, N_L)$, which can change from layer to layer and bring in information for the past layers. After fitted to the activation function, it becomes new independent "features" for the next layer. The dimension of the new feature space changes accordingly.

The above chain equations for the network flow can also be expressed as

$$
\hat{\mathbf{y}} = \phi^{(N_L)}(\cdots \phi^{(2)}(\phi^{(1)}(\mathbf{x}\mathbf{W}^{(1)} + \mathbf{b}^{(1)})\mathbf{W}^{(2)} + \mathbf{b}^{(2)}) \cdots \mathbf{W}^{(N_L)} + \mathbf{b}^{(N_L)})
\tag{13.6}
$$

We now see explicitly that our MLP model is indeed a giant function with k components in the feature space $\mathbb{X}^p$ and controlled (parameterized) by the training parameters in $\mathbb{W}^P$, as mentioned in Section 1.5.5. When these parameters $\mathbf{W}^{(i)}$ $(i = 1, 2, \ldots, N_L - 1)$ are tuned, one gets k giant functions over the feature space $\mathbb{X}^p$. On the other hand, this set of k giant functions can also be viewed as differentiable functions of these parameters for any given data-point in the dataset, which can be used to form a differentiable loss function using the corresponding k labels given in the dataset. The training is to minimize such a loss function for all the data-points in the dataset, by updating the training parameters to become minimizers.

This feed-forward network creates a chain "reaction", and such a nice flowing structure is made use of in computing the gradients in the so-called backward propagation or backprop or BP [10], using the chain rule of differentiation. The backprop process can be achieved via the autograd discussed in detail in Chapter 8. Each layer in an MLP has its own set of learning parameters (in the weight matrix and bias vector). As the layer number grows, the total number of learning parameters can grow fast. Notice also that the activation function used in each layer can be in theory different, although in many current practices, the hidden layer often uses the same type of activation function, typically Relu and tanh.

For the last output layer, the activation function is often chosen differently based on the application problem the network is built for. For many engineering problems of the regression type, we may simply use a linear activation function, meaning that we do nothing for the last layer, and output whatever is received.

$$\hat{\mathbf{y}} = \mathbf{x}^{(N_L)} = \mathbf{z}^{(N_L)} = \mathbf{x}^{(N_L-1)}\mathbf{W}^{(N_L)} + \mathbf{b}^{(N_L)} = \overline{\mathbf{x}}^{(N_L-1)}\hat{\mathbf{W}}^{(N_L)} \tag{13.7}$$

In this case, the mean square error (or L2) loss function is often used and minimized.

For classification problems, we may use the sigmoid or tanh function for binary classification. In general, one can use the softmax as the prediction function, as given in Eq. (13.2). Note that we have proved in the previous chapter that a binary classification problem can be treated as a special case of k-classification problem.

13.1.3 *The xw formulation, use of affine transformation weight matrix*

Using the *affine transformation weight matrix* $\overline{\mathbf{W}}$ defined in Chapter 5, we have for the ith layer,

$$\overline{\mathbf{W}}^{(j)} = \begin{bmatrix} 1 & \mathbf{b}^{(j)} \\ \mathbf{0} & \mathbf{W}^{(j)} \end{bmatrix}, \quad j = 1, 2, \ldots, N_L \tag{13.8}$$

We can then perform a chain of ATA transformations. The feed-forward process an MLP can have the following neat formulation.

$$\overline{\mathbf{x}}^{(0)} = [1, x_1, x_2, \ldots, x_p] \qquad \in \overline{\mathbb{X}}^{n_0} \text{ at the input layer}$$

$$\overline{\mathbf{x}}^{(1)} = \phi^{(1)}\left(\overline{\mathbf{x}}^{(0)}\overline{\mathbf{W}}^{(1)}\right) \qquad \in \overline{\mathbb{X}}^{n_1} \text{ at the 1st hidden layer}$$

$$\overline{\mathbf{x}}^{(2)} = \phi^{(2)}\left(\overline{\mathbf{x}}^{(1)}\overline{\mathbf{W}}^{(2)}\right) \qquad \in \overline{\mathbb{X}}^{n_2} \text{ at the 2nd hidden layer}$$

$$\cdots \tag{13.9}$$

$$\overline{\mathbf{x}}^{(j)} = \phi^{(j)}\left(\overline{\mathbf{x}}^{(j-1)}\overline{\mathbf{W}}^{(j)}\right) \qquad \in \overline{\mathbb{X}}^{n_j} \text{ at the } i\text{th hidden layer}$$

$$\cdots$$

$$\hat{\mathbf{y}} = \phi^{(N_L)}\left(\overline{\mathbf{x}}^{(N_L-1)}\hat{\mathbf{W}}^{(N_L)}\right) \in \mathbb{Y}^{n_{N_L}} \text{ prediction at the output layer}$$

where n_j is the *pseudo-dimension of the affine space* in the j layer, or the number of neurons for the interlayer features plus 1. For the input layer, $n_0 = p + 1$, and for the output layer, $n_{N_L} = k$, where the connection terminates and an affine transformation is no longer needed for these k output neurons.

Notice that in the xw formulation, we assume the linear (i.e., no) activation function is applied to constant 1. Under this condition, we can easily prove that

$$\phi^{(j)}\left(\overline{\mathbf{x}}^{(j-1)}\overline{\mathbf{W}}^{(j)}\right) = \phi^{(j)}\left(\overline{\mathbf{x}}^{(j-1)}\begin{bmatrix} 1 & \mathbf{b}^{(j)} \\ \mathbf{0} & \mathbf{W}^{(j)} \end{bmatrix}\right)$$
$$= \phi^{(j)}\left(\begin{bmatrix} 1 & \mathbf{x}^{(j-1)} \end{bmatrix}\begin{bmatrix} 1 & \mathbf{b}^{(j)} \\ \mathbf{0} & \mathbf{W}^{(j)} \end{bmatrix}\right)$$
$$= \phi^{(j)}\left(\begin{bmatrix} 1 & \mathbf{x}^{(j-1)}\mathbf{W}^{(j)} + \mathbf{b}^{(j)} \end{bmatrix}\right) \quad (13.10)$$
$$= \begin{bmatrix} 1 & \phi^{(j)}\left(\mathbf{x}^{(j-1)}\mathbf{W}^{(j)} + \mathbf{b}^{(j)}\right) \end{bmatrix}$$
$$= \begin{bmatrix} 1 & \mathbf{x}^{(j)} \end{bmatrix} = \overline{\mathbf{x}}^{(j)}$$

In the 3rd line in Eq. (13.10), we moved $\phi^{(j)}$ inside the array, because we assumed the constant 1 does not subject to activation and the fact that $\phi^{(j)}$ operation is element-wise. It is clear that Eq. (13.10) achieves the same results as in Eq. (13.5), but with an extra constant 1 component in the array. The constant 1 is automatically generated when moving to the next layer. This is because an affine transformation stays in the affine space, as demonstrated in Chapter 5. The affine transformation weight matrix $\hat{\mathbf{W}}^{(j)}$ performs the transformation from one affine space to another. Therefore, when our xw formulation is used, there is no need to inject the bias b to each neuron, which is one major difference from the xw+b formulation.

Note also that at the output layer, affine transformation ends and we use only $\hat{\mathbf{W}}^{(N_L)}$ as discussed in Chapter 5, producing predictions naturally back to a vector label space $\mathbf{Y}^{(k)}$, where a loss function can now be constructed for "terminal" control, using given labels.

Using the affine transformation matrix, Eq. (13.6) becomes neatly to,

$$\hat{\mathbf{y}} = \phi^{(N_L)}\left(\cdots\phi^{(2)}\left(\phi^{(1)}\left(\overline{\mathbf{x}}\,\overline{\mathbf{W}}^{(1)}\right)\overline{\mathbf{W}}^{(2)}\right)\cdots\hat{\mathbf{W}}^{(N_L)}\right) \quad (13.11)$$

Assuming the number of (total) neurons in the jth layer is n_j, the dimension of the affine transformation weight matrix $\overline{\mathbf{W}}^{(j)}$ is $n_{j-1} \times n_j$, offers a natural match in matrix computations for chained ATAs.

13.1.4 *MLP configuration with affine transformation weight matrix*

Using the affine transformation weight matrix, our MLP can have a configuration shown in Fig. 13.2.

The general formula for calculating the total number of learning parameters of an MLP becomes,

$$P = \underbrace{[n_0(n_1 - 1)]}_{\text{layer 1}} + \underbrace{[n_1(n_2 - 1)]}_{\text{layer 2}} + \cdots + \underbrace{[n_{i-1}(n_i - 1)]}_{\text{layer } i}$$
$$+ \cdots + \underbrace{[n_{N_L-1}(n_{N_L} - 1)]}_{\text{layer } N_L} \tag{13.12}$$

The reason for subtracting 1 in the parenthesis is because the first column in the affine transformation weight matrix $\overline{\mathbf{W}}^{(j)}$ contains all constants (1 or zeros) that are not trainable, as shown in Eq. (13.8). Equation (13.12) is an alternative equation to Eq. (5.32) that is based on the xw+b formulation. This number is usually reported in the summary report when an MLP model is created in a module. The vector of trainable parameters $\hat{\mathbf{w}}$ is in space $\mathbb{W}^P$, as discussed in Section 1.5.5.

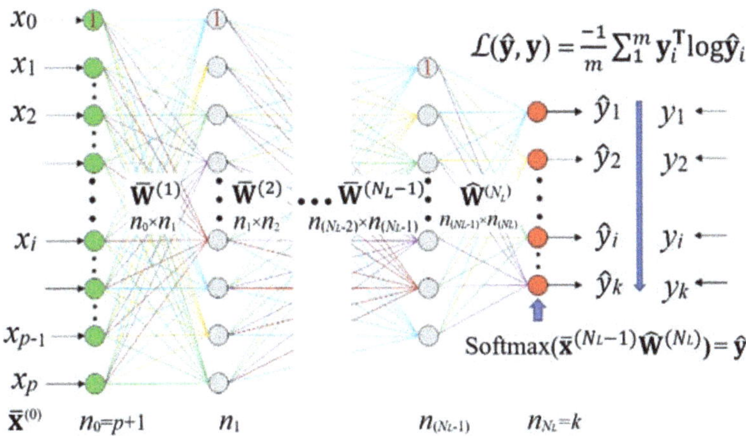

Figure 13.2: An MLP with multiple hidden layers with a chain of stacked affine transformations for a $n_0 \to k$ mapping. When affine transformation weight matrix is used, the constant feature 1 in the top neuron of each layer is automatically generated. The network flows naturally without injection of biases, and the dimensions of all these weight matrices between layers match naturally. Here cross entropy loss is used for classification, but loss function discussed in Chapter 12 may also be used. When the MLP is used for regression, L2 loss or any other loss function discussed in Chapter 10 may be used.

13.1.5 *Space evolution process in MLP*

We discussed at the beginning in Chapter 1 about spaces in machine learning models. We are now ready put the detailed connections in the following equation.

$$
\begin{aligned}
&\overset{\overline{\mathbf{W}}^{(1)}}{\underset{n_0 \times n_1}{\Longrightarrow}} \; \overset{\overline{\mathbf{W}}^{(2)}}{\underset{n_1 \times n_2}{\Longrightarrow}} \quad \overset{\overline{\mathbf{W}}^{(N_L-1)}}{\underset{n_{(N_L-2)} \times n_{(N_L-1)}}{\Longrightarrow}} \\[-2pt]
&\overline{\mathbf{x}}^{(0)} \qquad \overline{\mathbf{x}}^{(1)} \qquad \overline{\mathbf{x}}^{(2)}, \ldots, \qquad\qquad \overline{\mathbf{x}}^{(N_L-1)} \\
&\in \overline{\mathbb{X}}^{p+1} \quad\; \in \overline{\mathbb{X}}^{n_1} \quad\; \in \overline{\mathbb{X}}^{n_2} \qquad\qquad\qquad \in \overline{\mathbb{X}}^{n_{N_L-1}} \\[8pt]
&\overset{\hat{\mathbf{W}}^{(N_L)}}{\underset{n_{(N_L-1)} \times n_{(N_L)}}{\Longrightarrow}} \; \mathbf{x}^{(N_L)} \xrightarrow{\phi()} \hat{\mathbf{y}} \overset{\mathcal{L}(\hat{\mathbf{y}}(\hat{\mathbf{w}}),\mathbf{y})}{\Longleftrightarrow} \mathbf{y} \\
&\qquad\qquad\qquad \in \mathbb{X}^{n_{(N_L)}} \quad\;\; \in \mathbb{Y}^k \qquad\quad \in \mathbb{Y}^k
\end{aligned}
\tag{13.13}
$$

Equation (13.13) shows clearly the chained structure for a $p \to k$ mapping. The mapping is controlled by the learning parameters $\hat{\mathbf{w}} \in \mathbb{W}^P$, through a gigantic loss function $\mathcal{L}(\hat{\mathbf{y}}(\hat{\mathbf{w}}), \mathbf{y})$ chosen based on type of the problems to be modeled. The discussion on how $\hat{\mathbf{w}}$ relates the weight matrices in Eq. (13.13) are discussed in Section 1.5.5.

We emphasize again that the loss function is continuous and differentiable with respect to all the learning parameters, because all the prediction and activation functions used in all the layers are continuous and differentiable with respect to the local arguments. In addition, the chained structure of MLP allows the Autograd to work effectively through the layers to compute the gradient, by the well-known chain rule of differentiation. Therefore, the minimization techniques discussed in Chapter 9 can be used for finding the minimizers in terms of these learning parameters. The only subtlety is when the Relu function is used. It is continuous, piecewise differentiable, but not differentiable at the origin. The gradient jumps at the origin, as shown graphically in Section 7.6. We thus would need to compute its sub-gradient, that is, the average of the gradients on the both sides of the origin, and use it in the minimization process, as discussed at the end of Section 7.6.

13.2 Neurons-Samples Theory

The most often asked question in the machine learning community is on the relationship between the number neurons/layers in an NN and the number of samples (or data-points) in the dataset needed to train the NN. However, no concrete answers were available, until now. The author has searched for such a convincing answer but failed. In the past years, the author studied various NNs, which has led the Neurons-Samples Theory [13] presented in this section.

13.2.1 *Affine spaces and the training parameters used in an MLP*

Using Eq. (13.12), we can calculate the total number of trainable parameters P for a given MLP. The P number does relate to the sample number m of the dataset, but only loosely. The direct relationship is given by our *Neurons-Samples Theory*, which uses a P^*-number that is the total *pseudo-dimension of the affine spaces* involved in a machine learning model. The formula for an MLP is given as follows.

$$P^* = \underbrace{n_0}_{\text{layer 1}} + \underbrace{n_1}_{\text{layer 2}} + \cdots + \underbrace{n_{j-1}}_{\text{layer } j} + \cdots + \underbrace{n_{N_L-1}}_{\text{layer } N_L} \tag{13.14}$$

The P^*-number increases with the number of layers and the number of neurons in the previous layers. In other words, the P^*-number is also the *total number of neurons* in the MLP, including neurons in the input layer but excluding the neurons in the output layer where affine transformation is no longer needed.

Deriving Eq. (13.14) requires a careful analysis and deep understanding on the relationship between the pseudo-dimension of the affine space n_{j-1}, dataset $\overline{\mathbf{X}}_{(j-1)}$ in the affine space, and its corresponding affine transformation weight matrix $\overline{\mathbf{W}}^{(j)}$ in the jth layer.

Optimal learning parameters in a layer: Consider a given MLP, from which we isolate a $n_{j-1} \to 1$ neural network (an ATU discussed in Section 5.2) with an interlayer input of n_{j-1} neurons and a single output neuron at the jth layer, as shown in Fig. 5.2. The single output neuron is the ith neuron in the layer. Using Eq. (9.12), the optimal solution for the learning parameters $\hat{\mathbf{w}}_i^*$ for that neuron can be written as follows.

$$\left[\overline{\mathbf{X}}_{(j-1)}^\top \overline{\mathbf{X}}_{(j-1)}\right] \hat{\mathbf{w}}_i^* = \overline{\mathbf{X}}_{(j-1)}^\top \mathbf{y}_i \tag{13.15}$$

where $\overline{\mathbf{X}}_{(j-1)}$ denotes the interlayer dataset with m data-points in the affine space, with the original dataset at the input layer as $\overline{\mathbf{X}}_{(0)}$. And $\mathbf{y}_i$ is an assumed label vector corresponding to the ith neuron in the layer. It is a vector for these m data-points in the dataset. We do not usually know the content of $\mathbf{y}_i$ for these hidden layers. Fortunately, we do not need to know, because its content is not relevant in this analysis.

Now, for the $(i+1)$th neuron in the same jth layer, we shall have

$$\left[\overline{\mathbf{X}}_{(j-1)}^\top \overline{\mathbf{X}}_{(j-1)}\right] \hat{\mathbf{w}}_{i+1}^* = \overline{\mathbf{X}}_{(j-1)}^\top \mathbf{y}_{i+1} \tag{13.16}$$

where $\mathbf{y}_{i+1}$ an assumed label vector corresponding to the $(i+1)$th neuron in the same layer.

Comparison of Eqs.(13.15) and (13.16) finds that the existence of (unique) solutions $\hat{\mathbf{w}}_i^*$ and $\hat{\mathbf{w}}_{i+1}^*$ all depend on the same interlayer dataset $\overline{\mathbf{X}}_{(j-1)}$: whether or not $[\overline{\mathbf{X}}_{(j-1)}^\top \overline{\mathbf{X}}_{(j-1)}]$ is invertible. The terms in the right hand-side of these two equations are irrelevant. This reveals a very important fact that $\hat{\mathbf{w}}_i^*$ for all the neurons in a given layer, depend only on the same dataset with m data-points. An $n_{(j-1)} \to n_j$ net is the same as an $n_{(j-1)} \to 1$ net in this regard. In other words, all these $\hat{\mathbf{w}}_i^*$ live in the same hypotheses space $\mathbb{W}^{n_{(j-1)}}$, where $n_{(j-1)}$ is the pseudo-dimension of the affine space for the jth layer (with $n_{(0)} = p + 1$ for the input layer).

From another view point, we know that the affine space for the jth layer is $\overline{\mathbb{X}}^{n_{(j-1)}}$, the corresponding hypotheses space can only be $\mathbb{W}^{n_{(j-1)}}$.

Note that $\hat{\mathbf{w}}_i^*$ may be a different vector for different i, but they are all just vectors living in the column-space of matrix $[\overline{\mathbf{X}}_{(j-1)}^\top \overline{\mathbf{X}}_{(j-1)}]$. When the column-space of matrix $[\overline{\mathbf{X}}_{(j-1)}^\top \overline{\mathbf{X}}_{(j-1)}]$ is of full rank (when m is sufficiently large), it has zero null-space, and $\hat{\mathbf{w}}_i^*$ will be unique. Therefore, the pseudo-dimension of the affine space for the jth layer should be the number directly related to m for a layer. The optimal learning parameters for the jth layer should be: $P_{(j-1)}^* = n_{(j-1)}$.

Optimal learning parameters in MLPs: The above discussion is applicable to each individual layer in an MLP. However, when multiple layers are connected together to form the MLP (using nonlinear activation functions in all the hidden layers), these interlayer inputs are linearly independent from layer to layer, meaning the ranges of variations of $\hat{\mathbf{w}}_i$ in a layer is determined only by the pseudo-dimension of the affine space in that layer, which is n_{j-1}. In addition, the values in $\hat{\mathbf{w}}_i$ of a layer will be influenced by those in other layers. Therefore, the total optimal training parameters is effectively increased, which shall sum up the dimensions of the affine spaces of all layers, leading to Eq. (13.14). This again shows the importance of using nonlinear activation functions in the hidden layers for increasing optimal training parameters in an MLP, and hence its learning ability.

13.2.2 *Neurons-Samples Theory for MLPs*

We are now ready to state the Neurons-Samples Theory.

Neurons-Samples Theory: The number of samples m in the dataset for training an MLP capable of producing a unique solution must be no-less than the P^*-number, which is the sum of the dimensions of all the affine spaces used in $1 \sim N_L$ layers.

$$m \geq P^* \tag{13.17}$$

In other words, the P^*-number is the lower bound of m.

Alternatively, this theorem can be stated as: The number of samples m in the dataset for training an MLP capable of producing a unique solution must be no-less than the total number of neurons in the MLP. In this statement, the total number of neurons include the neuron for constant 1 on the top of each layer. It includes the neurons in the input layer, but excludes those in the output layer. It is defined as the P^*-number in Eq. (13.14).

Based on our analysis, we note the following remarks:

1. The P^*-number is essentially the total number of neurons in the net. In other words, the number of neurons is the number of data-points for an ideal model.
2. The P^*-number is the sum of the dimensions of all the affine spaces used in the net.
3. The P^*-number is independent of the number of the output neurons.
4. Equation (13.14) can also be used to estimate the needed number of layers N_L for an MLP:

$$N_L = \frac{P^*}{\overline{n}} \leq \frac{m}{\overline{n}} \tag{13.18}$$

where $\overline{n}$ is the average number of neurons used in $0 \sim (N_L - 1)$ layers.

We mention that Eq. (13.14) is the most important and essential equation for estimating the minimum number of data-points for training an ML model based on affine transformations, including the standard MLP, RNN and CNN.

Note that in the openly available ML modules, the learning parameters used in an MLP are the total number P given in Eq. (13.12). In all these MLP or deepnet algorithms, P parameters are indeed allowed to vary independently. However, because of the special construction of the MLP, $\hat{\mathbf{w}}_i$ for all the neurons in the jth layer lives only in the same hypothesis-space $\mathbb{W}^{n_{(j-1)}}$, which is only a small sub-space of $\mathbb{W}^{n_{(j-1)} \times (n_{(j)}-1)}$, as discussed in this section. Therefore, P^* given by Eq. (13.14), and not Eq. (13.12), relates directly the number of samples in the dataset. The P^*-number is the lower bound of m.

Note that the above analysis is based on regression formulations. For classification problems, there are some subtleties, because the loss function may use probability. In such cases, a correct prediction may not necessarily need a perfect match in values for the predicted probability and that of the given label. However, the principle of our above analysis shall apply.

13.3 Nonlinear Activation Functions for the Hidden Layers

For hidden layers in MLP, one has to use some nonlinear activation functions to take the advantage of multilayer effects. If the whole network uses only linear function, it would be equivalent to using the simple one-layer network, because an output in a hidden layer will be linearly dependent on that of the previous layer. This can be seen more clearly in the derivation below, using the xw formulation:

$$\hat{\mathbf{y}} = (\cdots((\overline{\mathbf{x}}\,\overline{\mathbf{W}}^{(1)})\overline{\mathbf{W}}^{(2)})\cdots\cdot\hat{\mathbf{W}}^{(N_L)})$$
$$= \overline{\mathbf{x}}\,\overline{\mathbf{W}}^{(1)} \cdot \overline{\mathbf{W}}^{(2)} \cdots\cdot \hat{\mathbf{W}}^{(N_L)} = \overline{\mathbf{x}}\mathbf{W}^{combined} \tag{13.19}$$

where $\mathbf{W}^{combined}$ is a product of weight matrices:

$$\mathbf{W}^{combined} = \overline{\mathbf{W}}^{(1)} \cdot \overline{\mathbf{W}}^{(2)} \cdots\cdot \hat{\mathbf{W}}^{(N_L)} \tag{13.20}$$

which is nothing but a single weight matrix for a one-layer network. The use of such hidden layers does not increase the hypothesis space dimension and the independent learning parameters. Therefore, there is no point at all in using the linear activation function in any layer in an MLP. Using the linear activation function in a layer of an MLP is effectively the same as removing the layer from the MLP.

13.4 General Rule for Estimating Learning Parameters in an MLP

Based on the Neurons-Samples Theory, we can now determine the number of layers and the number of neurons in each layer. In practice, we shall consider also the type of the problem to be modeled. Below is a general rule.

For a given dataset with m data-points, the upper bound of the P^*-number used in an MLP should be m.

$$P^* \leq m \tag{13.21}$$

where P^* is computed using Eq. (13.14). For the simplest linear regression model with a single output neuron, $P^* = p + 1$, and Eq. (13.21) is the equality part of Eq. (9.8) in Chapter 9. To estimate the number of layers needed, Eq. (13.7) may be used.

The dataset quality is defined as its representativeness to the underlaying problem to be modeled, including correctness, size, data-point distribution over the features space, and noise level. This guideline is very simple, because it depends only on the size of the dataset. This assumes that (1) the m data-points in the dataset are all linearly independent and (2) the training parameters in the model are linearly independent following the Universal Prediction Theory (see Chapter 5). For an MLP, if $P^* < m$, a trained MLP may not pass the data-points, and generalizes better. If $P^* = m$, the data-points may be reproduced by the MLP when it is fully trained. If $P^* > m$, a fully trained MLP is capable of producing the data-points that may have noise, leading possibly to overfitting (see Chapter 14) and may not be used in general. Note in the practice that we may use MLP with $P^* > m$ and may not observe overfitting, because the MLP has not fully trained.

It is worth mentioning again that m is only the upper bound for P^*. In practice, P^* can be much smaller than m.

13.5 Key Techniques for MLP and Its Capability

We have discussed the Universal Approximation Theorem earlier. It states that a network with a single hidden layer is capable of approximating any function to a desired accuracy, as along as the hidden layer is sufficiently "wide" with enough number of neurons. Based on our discussion on the Universal Prediction Theory, increasing the layers can further increase the learning ability of MLP. There is thus a question on whether a wide (more neurons in a layer) net or a deeper (more layers) net should be used. The general understanding is that: (1) when the number of layers increases, one can significantly reduce the width of the net; (2) it has been found that one may be able to approximate more complicated functions more "compactly" if we use deeper neural networks compared to wider ones, meaning that deepnets can use a smaller number of neurons in total. This is because of the nonlinearity introduced in the MLP. Therefore, it is more capable of modeling nonlinear behavior, and also it can produce decision boundaries that may be highly nonlinear.

However, compared with wide nets, MLP is found more difficult to train because of the well-known vanishing (or explosion) gradients of the loss function. Therefore, in the past, wide nets were used more, until recent breakthrough on techniques or algorithms for training deepnets. The major techniques may include (but are not limited to) the following:

1. **Relu activation function**. Because the Relu function is linear with a gradient of 1 (in the positive region), it allows the affine transformed information in neurons in a layer to reach farther unaffected in the depth of the net. There will be no squashing like in the sigmoid-type activation functions near $z = 1$ where the gradients would become nearly zero. In addition, the Relu function vanishes in the negative region and hence still offers the needed nonlinearity for deepnets. Such a cut-off may also offer some regularization effects. Moreover, the vanishing in the negative region is for both the z function value and its local gradients together, which eliminates other possible complications. It is the author's understanding that simply omitting the negative half of the information in an MLP should not give rise to many problems, based on the Neurons-Samples Theory. The number of the training parameter P in an MLP is usually many times more than the P^*-number. The MLP has plenty of room to adjust the learning parameters to find the minimizers, even if the negative half of the information is discarded.

2. **Sparse connection**. This technique reduces the "density" of the training parameters, such as the convolution neural networks that use filters leading to sparse connections and hence a drastic reduction of the learning parameters (weights and biases) in a layer. When the learning parameters are not so crowded, the numerical conditioning improves. The legitimacy of discarding some of the connections is also rooted in the Neurons-Samples Theory, and the successive P number in an MLP.

3. **Skip connection (or short cut)**. This is another technique that enables the network to go further in depth. It is used in the development of the so-called ResNet, which will be discussed more in Chapter 15. Essentially, it allows the activated values of neurons in one layer to feed to the next-next layer (skip one layer) before the activation function is applied. This well mitigates the vanishing of gradients in deepnets.

4. **Long short-term memory or LSTM** [11]. This technique is useful for overcoming the gradient vanishing problem. It is widely used in the recurrent neural network (RNN, Chapter 16) that often has very deep connections for handling time sequential inputs, such as in language translation models.

Because of the nicely chained stacked structure of the MLP, simple affine transformation, activation functions with analytical formula for their differentials, and the Autograd algorithms, there is no additional difficulty for us to perform feed forward computation and backward propagation for computing the gradients. This is done practically in the same way as we have done for wide nets in the earlier chapters. Because the vanishing (or explosion) gradients problem are mitigated effectively, one can now build up and successfully train very deep neural networks that can have the needed complexity for modeling complicated problems. This is why deepnets were developed very fast in the past few years.

13.6 A Case Study on Handwritten Digits Using MXNet

Let us now build an MLP with two hidden layers and one output layer for the same task of identification of handwritten digits. We use the code (with slight modifications) provided at mxnet-the-straight-dope under the Apache-2.0 License, which allows us to go through the process step by step. We will use the same MNIST dataset that is familiar to us.

13.6.1 *Import necessary libraries and load data*

```python
from __future__ import print_function
import mxnet as mx
import numpy as np

from mxnet import nd, autograd, gluon
# Set contexts according to computer hardware
ctx = mx.gpu() if mx.test_utils.list_gpus() else mx.cpu()
data_ctx = ctx
model_ctx = ctx
# Load the MNIST dataset
num_inputs = 784
num_outputs = 10
batch_size = 64
num_examples = 60000


def transform(data, label):
    return data.astype(np.float32)/255, label.astype(np.float32)


train_data = gluon.data.DataLoader(mx.gluon.data.vision.
        MNIST(train=True, transform=transform),
        batch_size, shuffle=True)
test_data = gluon.data.DataLoader(mx.gluon.data.vision.
        MNIST(train=False, transform=transform),
        batch_size, shuffle=False)
```

13.6.2 *Set neural network model parameters*

```python
# Here we set the model with two-hidden layers
# One can easily modify the network and try
num_hidden = 256
weight_scale = .01
#  Allocate parameters for the first hidden layer
W1 = nd.random_normal(shape=(num_inputs, num_hidden),
      scale=weight_scale, ctx=model_ctx)
b1 = nd.random_normal(shape=num_hidden,
      scale=weight_scale, ctx=model_ctx)
#  Allocate parameters for the second hidden layer
W2 = nd.random_normal(shape=(num_hidden,
      num_hidden), scale=weight_scale,ctx=model_ctx)
b2 = nd.random_normal(shape=num_hidden,
      scale=weight_scale, ctx=model_ctx)
#  Allocate parameters for the output layer
W3 = nd.random_normal(shape=(num_hidden, num_outputs),
      scale=weight_scale, ctx=model_ctx)

b3 = nd.random_normal(shape=num_outputs,
      scale=weight_scale, ctx=model_ctx)
params = [W1, b1, W2, b2, W3, b3]
# Allocate now the space for the gradients of each parameter.
for param in params:
    param.attach_grad()
```

13.6.3 *Softmax cross entropy loss function*

When computing the jth components of the output for a k-classification problem, we use the following softmax function:

$$\hat{y}_j = \frac{e^{z_j}}{\sum_{i=1}^{k} e^{z_i}} \tag{13.22}$$

where z_j is the jth element of the input $\mathbf{z}$ in Eq. (13.2), and $j = 1, 2, \ldots, k$.

We may have a numerical problem in computing these exponentials, because the argument z_i can be both very large and small. Hence, its exponential e^{z_i} can be extremely large or small, leading to possible over- or underflow in the computer that has limited precision. The solution to this is to use the so-called LogSumExp trick (https://en.wikipedia.org/wiki/LogSumExp).

As we have shown in the previous chapter, we know that log function is monotonic and will not affect the location of extremes of an argument function that is positive (and $\hat{y}_j$). We thus take logarithm to both sides of Eq. (13.22), which gives

$$\log(\hat{y}_j) = \log\left(\frac{e^{z_j}}{\sum_{i=1}^{k} e^{z_i}}\right) = \log(e^{z_j}) - \log\left(\sum_{i=1}^{k} e^{z_i}\right) = z_j - \log\left(\sum_{i=1}^{k} e^{z_i}\right) \tag{13.23}$$

Note that e^{z_i} is still there in the last term. We next compute the last term using

$$\log\left(\sum_{i=1}^{k} e^{z_i}\right) = z^* + \log\left(\sum_{i=1,i\neq i^*}^{k} e^{z_i-z^*}\right) \tag{13.24}$$

where we simply factor out e^{z^*} from the first sum with $z^* = max(z_1, z_2, \ldots, z_k)$ with i^* being the index for z^*.

It is clear now that all the numbers involved in the computation are now bounded. In these computations, we need only $\mathbf{z}$ as inputs. This formula is known as softmax cross-entropy, because both ideas of softmax and log cross-entropy are used. Using mxnet, it is defined as follows:

```python
def softmax_cross_entropy(yhat, y):
    return -nd.nansum(y*nd.log_softmax(yhat), axis=0, exclude=True)
```

13.6.4 *Define a neural network model*

```python
def relu(z):
    return nd.maximum(z, nd.zeros_like(z))
```

```python
def net(X):
    h1_linear = nd.dot(X, W1) + b1      # 1st hidden layer
    h1 = relu(h1_linear)                # Relu activation
    h2_linear = nd.dot(h1, W2) + b2     # 2nd hidden layer
    h2 = relu(h2_linear)
    yhat_linear = nd.dot(h2, W3) + b3   # output layer
    return yhat_linear
```

13.6.5 *Optimization method*

Here, we choose to use the stochastic gradient descent (SGD) method. Readers may try other methods.

```python
def SGD(params, lr):
    for param in params:
        param[:] = param - lr * param.grad
```

13.6.6 *Model accuracy evaluation*

The following function is defined for model accuracy evaluation.

```python
def evaluate_accuracy(data_iterator, net):
    numerator = 0.
    denominator = 0.
    for i, (data, label) in enumerate(data_iterator):
        data=data.as_in_context(model_ctx).reshape((-1, 784))
        label = label.as_in_context(model_ctx)
        output = net(data)
        predictions = nd.argmax(output, axis=1)
        numerator += nd.sum(predictions == label)
        denominator += data.shape[0]
    return (numerator / denominator).asscalar()
```

13.6.7 *Training the neural network and timing the training*

```python
import time                     # timing the performance
num_inputs = 784
num_outputs = 10
epochs = 10                     # readers may change this and try
learning_rate = .001            # readers may change this and try
smoothing_constant = .01        # readers may change this and try
print('Parameter setting: epochs=',epochs,' num of neurons in
      hidden layers =', num_hidden,'\n learning_rate =',
      learning_rate, 'batch_size=',batch_size,
      'smoothing_constant=',smoothing_constant)
start_t = time.process_time()


for e in range(epochs):
    cumulative_loss = 0
    for i, (data, label) in enumerate(train_data):
        data = data.as_in_context(model_ctx).reshape((-1,
                num_inputs))
```

```python
        label = label.as_in_context(model_ctx)
        label_one_hot = nd.one_hot(label, num_outputs)
        with autograd.record():
            output = net(data)
            loss = softmax_cross_entropy(output, label_one_hot)

        loss.backward()
        SGD(params, learning_rate)
        cumulative_loss += nd.sum(loss).asscalar()

    test_accuracy = evaluate_accuracy(test_data, net)
    train_accuracy = evaluate_accuracy(train_data, net)
    if e%3 == 0 or e == epochs-1:
        print("Epoch %s. Loss: %s, Train_acc %s, Test_acc %s" %
        (e,cumulative_loss/num_examples,train_accuracy,
            test_accuracy))

t_elapsed = (time.process_time() - start_t)
print('3-layer neural network, training time =',f'{t_elapsed}','s')
```

```
Parameter setting: epochs= 10   num of neurons in hidden layers = 256
 learning_rate = 0.001   batch_size= 64   smoothing_constant= 0.01
Epoch 0. Loss: 1.2388756741285325, Train_acc 0.8823, Test_acc 0.8849
Epoch 3. Loss: 0.1648619899849097, Train_acc 0.95958334,
    Test_acc 0.9578
Epoch 6. Loss: 0.08768035567005475, Train_acc 0.9797, Test_acc 0.973
Epoch 9. Loss: 0.056695277426143484, Train_acc 0.98615,
    Test_acc 0.9746
3-layer neural network, training time = 2798.078125 s
```

When parameters are set as epochs $= 10$, learning_rate $= 0.001$, batch_size $= 64$, and smoothing_constant $= 0.01$, we found the following:

- at the 5th epoch, Loss: 0.12915, Train_acc 0.96988, Test_acc 0.9654
- at the 10th epoch, Loss: 0.056414, Train_acc 0.98768, Test_acc 0.9757.

The 3-layer neural network (with two hidden layers each with 256 neurons) needs a training time of 1,653 s, and produces test accuracy of about 97.6%. Compared to the 1-layer net without a hidden layer (in the previous chapter) that took 1100 s to train and with 91% accuracy, the accuracy is as much as 5.6% higher, which is quite a significant improvement. This is achieved by capturing the nonlinear features of the handwritten digits. Note that these numbers can change depending on computer system and business of the computer.

13.6.8 *Prediction with the model trained*

We use some randomly selected data-points from the test set to perform predictions.

```python
%matplotlib inline
import matplotlib.pyplot as plt
# Define the function to do prediction
def model_predict(net,data):
    output = net(data)
    return nd.argmax(output, axis=1)

samples = 10
mnist_test=mx.gluon.data.vision.MNIST(train=False,
            transform=transform)

# Sample randomly "samples"  data-points from the test set
sample_data=mx.gluon.data.DataLoader(mnist_test,samples,
            shuffle=True)
plt.figure(figsize=(10, 60))
for i, (data, label) in enumerate(sample_data):
    data = data.as_in_context(model_ctx)
    im = nd.transpose(data,(1,0,2,3))
    im = nd.reshape(im,(28,samples*28,1))
    imtiles = nd.tile(im, (1,1,3))
    plt.imshow(imtiles.asnumpy())
    plt.show()
    pred=model_predict(net,data.reshape((-1,784)))
    print('model predictions are:', pred)
    print('true labels :', label)
    break
```

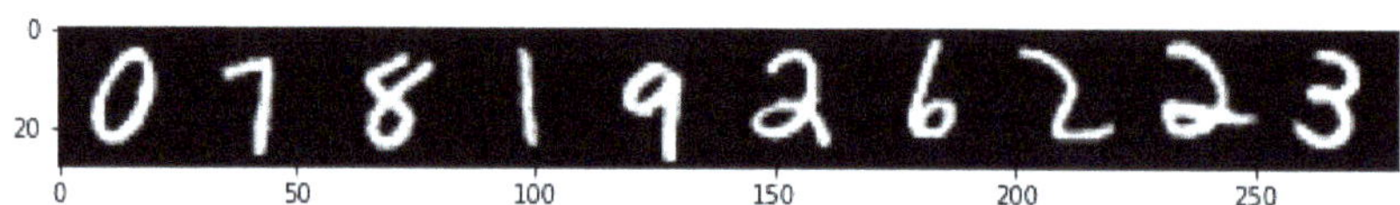

Figure 13.3:   Predicted digits using the 3-layer MLP on the testing dataset of MNIST.

```
model predictions are:
[0. 7. 8. 1. 9. 2. 6. 2. 2. 3.]
<NDArray 10 @cpu(0)>
true labels :
[0. 7. 8. 1. 9. 2. 6. 2. 2. 3.]
<NDArray 10 @cpu(0)>
```

One can also try predictions using the training dataset. It should reflect how well the model is trained.

```python
mnist_test=mx.gluon.data.vision.MNIST(train=True,
        transform=transform)
# Sample randomly "samples"  data-points from the test set
sample_data=mx.gluon.data.DataLoader(mnist_test,samples,
            shuffle=True)
plt.figure(figsize=(10, 60))
for i, (data, label) in enumerate(sample_data):
    data = data.as_in_context(model_ctx)
    im = nd.transpose(data,(1,0,2,3))

    im = nd.reshape(im,(28,samples*28,1))
    imtiles = nd.tile(im, (1,1,3))
    plt.imshow(imtiles.asnumpy())
    plt.show()
    pred=model_predict(net,data.reshape((-1,784)))
    print('model predictions are:', pred)
    print('true labels :', label)
    break
```

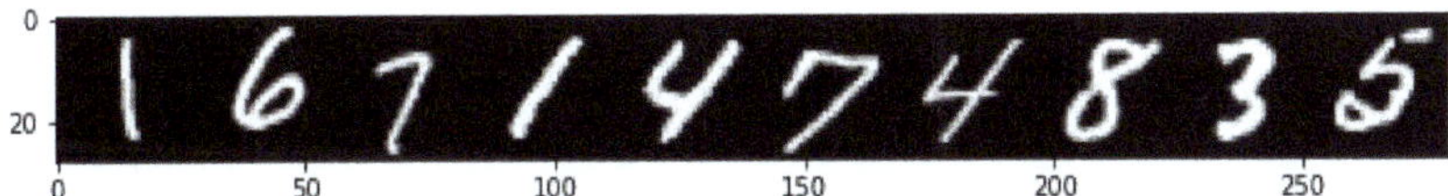

Figure 13.4:   Predicted digits using the 3-layer MLP on the training dataset of MNIST, just to see how good the training is.

```
model predictions are:
[1. 6. 7. 1. 4. 7. 4. 8. 3. 5.]
<NDArray 10 @cpu(0)>
true labels :
[1. 6. 7. 1. 4. 7. 4. 8. 3. 5.]
<NDArray 10 @cpu(0)>
```

13.6.9 *Remarks*

With two hidden layers (three layers with Ws), each containing 256 neurons, the MLP model has achieved over 97% accuracy, compared to the 1-layer net used in the previous chapter, and we had about 6% improvement.

When parameters are set as epochs = 10, learning_rate = 0.001, batch_size = 64, and smoothing_constant = 0.01, this 3-layer neural network needs training time = 1,653 s, which is about 3 times slower than the random forest model used in the previous chapter. The accuracy is about 0.5% higher than the random forest model.

The same handwritten Digits MNIST and the Fashion MNIST recognition can also be easily done using the Tensorflow and Keras modules. Readers may refer to the following reference materials for more details:

- For Digits MNIST: https://www.youtube.com/watch?v=wQ8BIBpya2k.
- For Fashion MNIST: https://www.tensorflow.org/tutorials/keras/classifi cation.

13.7 Visualization of MLP Weights Using Sklearn

We now present a case study done by the scikit-learn team [12] on visualization of MLP weights on the MNIST dataset. To have the model run faster, we use only one hidden layer, and train it only for a small number of iterations.

13.7.1 *Import necessary Sklearn module*

```python
import matplotlib.pyplot as plt
from sklearn.datasets import fetch_openml
from sklearn.neural_network import MLPClassifier
import time
```

13.7.2 *Load MNIST dataset*

```python
%matplotlib inline
# Load data from https://www.openml.org/d/554
X, y = fetch_openml('mnist_784', version=1, return_X_y=True)
X = X / 255.
# rescale the data, use the traditional train/test split
X_train, X_test = X[:60000], X[60000:]
y_train, y_test = y[:60000], y[60000:]
```

13.7.3 *Set an MLP model*

```python
hls= 50          # hidden_layer_sizes
mx_iter=8        # Maximum number of iterations for optimization
alpha=1e-2       # L2 penalty parameter for L2 regularization
lri=.1           # initial learning rate
mlp = MLPClassifier(hidden_layer_sizes=(hls,), max_iter=mx_iter,
                    alpha=alpha, solver='sgd', verbose=10,
                    random_state=1, learning_rate_init=lri)
print('Parameter setting: epochs=',epochs,'max_iter=',mx_iter,
      ' learning_rate_init =',lri)
```

```
Parameter setting: epochs= 10 max_iter= 8  learning_rate_init = 0.1
```

13.7.4 *Training the MLP model and time the training*

```python
start_t = time.process_time()
mlp.fit(X_train, y_train)
print("Training set score: %f" % mlp.score(X_train, y_train))
print("Test set score: %f" % mlp.score(X_test, y_test))
t_elapsed = (time.process_time() - start_t)
print('One-layer neural network, training time=',
      f'{t_elapsed}','s')
```

```
Iteration 1, loss = 0.32484982
Iteration 2, loss = 0.15960803
Iteration 3, loss = 0.12264513
Iteration 4, loss = 0.10188910
Iteration 5, loss = 0.08910487
Iteration 6, loss = 0.08259557
Iteration 7, loss = 0.07394721
Iteration 8, loss = 0.06810929

Training set score: 0.987083
Test set score: 0.970700
One-layer neural network, training time= 27.78125 s
```

13.7.5 *Performance analysis*

When parameters are set as epochs $= 10$, max_iter $= 10$, learning_rate_init $=$ 0.1, at the 10th epoch, we obtain in the following:

Training set score: 0.9868, and Testset score: 0.9700.

This one-layer neural network needs only 30 s to train, which is about 30% faster than the random forest model. The accuracy is about the same as the random forest model we used in the previous chapter.

13.7.6 *Viewing the weight matrix as images*

Sometimes, looking at the parameters learned in a trained neural network can provide some insight into the learning behavior. For example, if the weights look unstructured, these weights may not be very useful. If very large weights are observed, the regularization may be too low, or the learning rate may be too high. In the following, we plot weights of some of the first layers in the MLPClassifier trained on the MNIST dataset. Let us look at weights in the form of image. The input data in the MNIST dataset consist of handwritten digits in an image with 28×28 pixels. Therefore, it has 784 (pixel) features in the dataset. The weight matrix in the first layer net shall have a shape of (784, hidden_layer_sizes[0]). We reshape the single column of 784 weights back to a 28×28 pixel image, so that we can show it.

```python
#plt.figure(figsize=(50, 100))
fig, axes = plt.subplots(5, 10, figsize=(20, 10))
# use global min/max to ensure all weights are shown on
# the same scale
print(mlp.coefs_[0].shape,mlp.coefs_[1].shape)
vmin, vmax = mlp.coefs_[0].min(), mlp.coefs_[0].max()
for coef, ax in zip(mlp.coefs_[0].T, axes.ravel()):
    ax.matshow(coef.reshape(28, 28), cmap=plt.cm.gray,
        vmin=.5 * vmin, vmax=.5 * vmax)
    ax.set_xticks(())
    ax.set_yticks(())

plt.show()
```

(784, 50) (50, 10)

13.8 MLP for Nonlinear Regression

MLP is also a powerful tool regression. As we have discussed, MLP always uses nonlinear activation functions in all these hidden layers. Therefore, MPL regression is nonlinear and can handle complicated problems. Here, we introduce a case study done by the scikit-learn team [12]. It studies

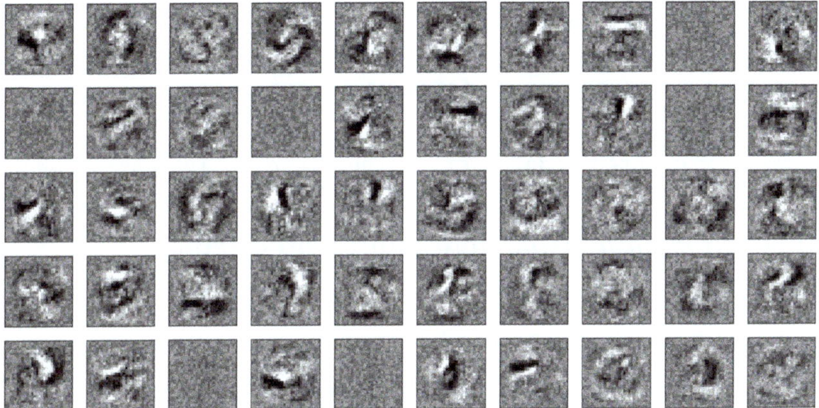

Figure 13.5: Images of the weight matrix in the layer of the one-layer MLP trained on the MNIST dataset.

the dependence between the target function and a set of "target" features, marginalizing over the values of all other features (the complement features). For possible visualization of the results, the target features should be one or two. We thus choose the important target features to plot.

The study uses the California housing dataset [3]. The dataset has a total of 8 features, and 4 of them are found relatively more influential to the house price. We will build MLP models to reveal these influences. For comparison purposes, we will also build a model of gradient boosting regressor to do the same study.

```python
# import necessary modules
%matplotlib inline
print(__doc__)
from time import time
import numpy as np
import pandas as pd
import matplotlib.pyplot as plt
from mpl_toolkits.mplot3d import Axes3D

from sklearn.model_selection import train_test_split
from sklearn.preprocessing import QuantileTransformer
from sklearn.pipeline import make_pipeline
from sklearn.inspection import partial_dependence
from sklearn.inspection import plot_partial_dependence
from sklearn.experimental import enable_hist_gradient_boosting
from sklearn.ensemble import HistGradientBoostingRegressor
```

```python
from sklearn.neural_network import MLPRegressor
from sklearn.tree import DecisionTreeRegressor
from sklearn.datasets import fetch_california_housing
```

```
Automatically created module for IPython interactive environment
```

13.8.1 *California housing data and preprocessing*

```python
# get the dataset
cal_housing = fetch_california_housing()

X = pd.DataFrame(cal_housing.data, columns=cal_housing.
    feature_names)
y = cal_housing.target
print(' data-points:',y.shape,'\n Some sample sof labels:', y)
                            # check the raw label data
```

```
data-points: (20640,)
Some sample sof labels: [4.526 3.585 3.521 ... 0.923 0.847 0.894]
```

```python
y -= y.mean()                           # gradient boosting
      # with 'recursion' method does not account for initial
      # estimator (here the average target, by default)
X_train, X_test, y_train, y_test = train_test_split(X, y,
      test_size=0.1, random_state=0)  #split the data
X.head()
```

	MedInc	HouseAge	AveRooms	AveBedrms	Population	AveOccup	Latitude	Longitude
0	8.3252	41.0	6.984127	1.023810	322.0	2.555556	37.88	-122.23
1	8.3014	21.0	6.238137	0.971880	2401.0	2.109842	37.86	-122.22
2	7.2574	52.0	8.288136	1.073446	496.0	2.802260	37.85	-122.24
3	5.6431	52.0	5.817352	1.073059	558.0	2.547945	37.85	-122.25
4	3.8462	52.0	6.281853	1.081081	565.0	2.181467	37.85	-122.25

There are a total of eight features, which means that the regression is over an eight-dimensional space, and hence is it not possible to view all of them in such a high-dimensional space. We thus plot in price-dependence curve one by one, or plot contour plots two by two. The target features for the plots are 4 relatively important features: median income (`MedInc`), average occupants per household (`AvgOccup`), median house age (`HouseAge`), and average rooms per household (`AveRooms`). We have added in also two less important features "AveBedrms" and "Population" to the plots, for comparison purposes.

Note that this tabular dataset has very different value ranges for these features. Because neural networks can be sensitive to features with varying scales, preprocessing these numeric features is critical.

```
print(' data-points:',y.shape,'\n Some samples of labels:', y)
                                    # check if zero centered
```

```
data-points: (20640,)
Some samples of labels: [ 2.45744183  1.51644183  1.45244183
    ... -1.14555817 -1.22155817  -1.17455817]
```

```
print(X_train.shape, X_test.shape, y_train.shape, y_test.shape)
```

```
(18576, 8) (2064, 8) (18576,) (2064,)
```

13.8.2 *Configure, train, and test the MLP*

Let us fit an MLPRegressor and compute single-variable partial dependence plots.

```
print("Training MLPRegressor...")
tic = time ()
# a pipeline to scale the numerical input
# features and tuned the neural network size and learning rate.
mlp = make_pipeline(QuantileTransformer(),
      MLPRegressor(hidden_layer_sizes=(50, 50),
      learning_rate_init=0.01, early_stopping=True))
                                    #configure the MLP
mlp.fit(X_train, y_train)          #Train the MLP
print("Done in {:.3f}s".format(time() - tic))
print("Test R2 score: {:.2f}".format(mlp.score(X_test,
      y_test)))                    # Check the performance
```

```
Training MLPRegressor...
Done in 20.779s
Test R2 score: 0.80
```

One can increase the complexity of an MLP for stronger learning ability. However, to avoid overfitting, the complexity of the MLP should be in accordance with the number of the data-points in the training set.

13.8.3 *Compute and plot the partial dependence*

Let us now compute and plot the partial dependence using the MLP.

```
print('Compute and plot the  partial dependence...')
tic= time()
# If compute the 2-way PDP (5, 1), it would be much slower
# with the brute method.
features=['MedInc','AveOccup', 'HouseAge', 'AveRooms',
         ('AveOccup', 'HouseAge'),('AveBedrms', 'MedInc')]
          #Select features to plot

plot_partial_dependence(mlp,X_train,features,n_jobs=3,
                        grid_resolution=20)
print("done in {:.3f}s".format(time() - tic))
fig = plt.gcf()
fig.suptitle('Partial dependence of house value on\n
             non-location features''for the California\n
             housing dataset, with MLPRegressor')
fig.subplots_adjust(wspace=0.4,hspace=0.4)
```

```
Compute and plot the partial dependence...
done in 60.972s
```

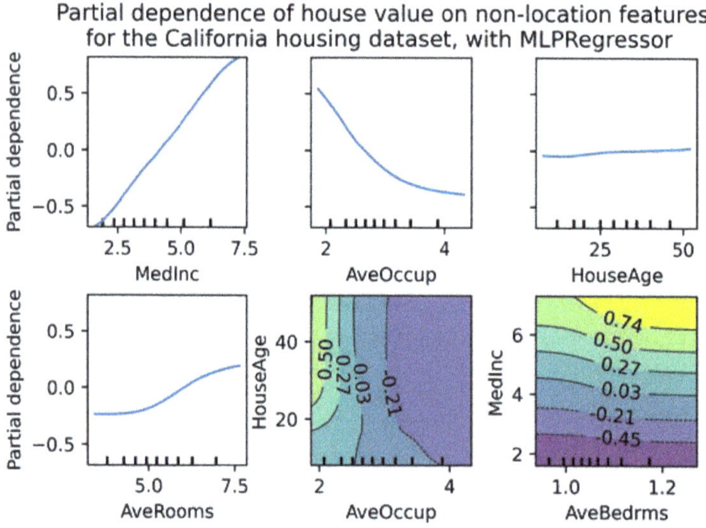

Figure 13.6: Results on price-feature dependence obtained using the MLP regressor in Sklearn for the California housing dataset.

The tick marks on the x-axis in the above plots represent the deciles of the feature values in the dataset. We can observe the following findings:

- The median house price is approximately linearly dependent on the median income (top left plot).
- The house price drops with the increase of the average occupants per household (top middle plot).
- The house age does not have a strong influence on the house price, nor do the average rooms per household.

The contour plots show the interactions of two target features on the house price. For example, for average occupancy greater than two, the house price is nearly independent of the house age. For average occupancy less than two, there is some dependence.

13.8.4 *Comparison studies on different regressors*

For comparison purposes, we also perform regressions on the same dataset using the GradientBoostingRegressor and the DecisionTreeRegressor at the Scikit Learn package, and plot these results.

13.8.5 *Gradient boosting regressor*

Now, we train a model of gradient boosting regressor.

```python
print("Training GradientBoostingRegressor...")
tic = time()
gbr = HistGradientBoostingRegressor()
gbr.fit(X_train, y_train)
print("done in {:.3f}s".format(time() - tic))
print("Test R2 score: {:.2f}".format(gbr.score(X_test, y_test)))
```

```
Training GradientBoostingRegressor...
done in 1.600s
Test R2 score: 0.85
```

For this tabular dataset, the Gradient Boosting Regressor is found both significantly faster to train and more accurate on the test dataset, compared to the MLP. It is also relatively easier to tune the hyperparameters, and the defaults usually work well.

```python
print('Computing partial dependence plots...')
tic = time()
features = ['MedInc', 'AveOccup', 'HouseAge', 'AveRooms',
            ('AveOccup', 'HouseAge'),('AveBedrms', 'MedInc')]
plot_partial_dependence(gbr, X_train, features,
                        n_jobs=3, grid_resolution=20)
print("done in {:.3f}s".format(time() - tic))
#fig = plt.figure(figsize=(45, 29))
fig = plt.gcf()
fig.suptitle('Partial dependence of house value on\n
             non-location features' 'for the California\n
             housing dataset, with Gradient Boosting')
fig.subplots_adjust(wspace=0.4, hspace=0.4)
```

```
Computing partial dependence plots...
done in 0.530s
```

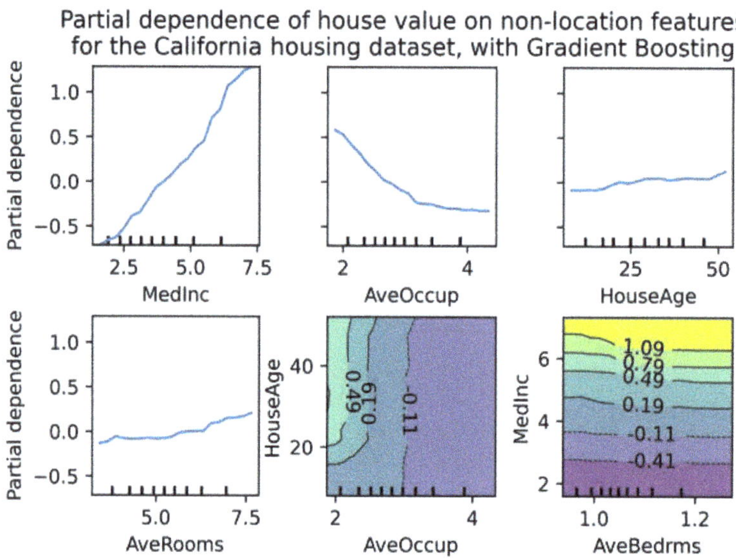

Figure 13.7:   Results on price-feature dependence obtained using the gradient boosting regressor in Sklearn for the California housing dataset.

```python
fig, ax = plt.subplots(figsize=(8, 4))
ax.set_title("Gradient Boosting Regressor")
gbr_disp=plot_partial_dependence(gbr,X_train,
    ["MedInc", "AveOccup"],ax=ax)
```

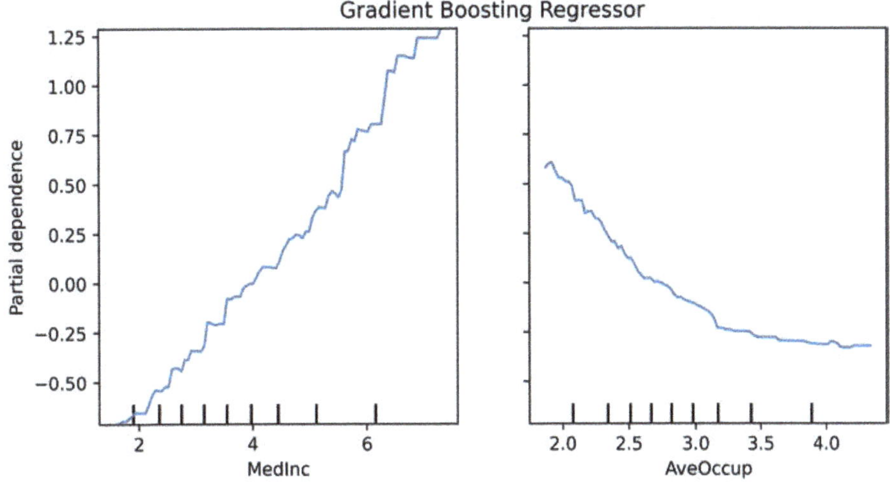

Figure 13.8:   Results using the gradient boosting regressor in Sklearn for the California housing dataset.

```
fig, ax = plt.subplots(figsize=(8, 4))
ax.set_title("Multi-layer Perceptron")
mlp_disp = plot_partial_dependence(mlp, X, ["MedInc", "AveOccup"],
    ax=ax, line_kw={"c": "red"})
```

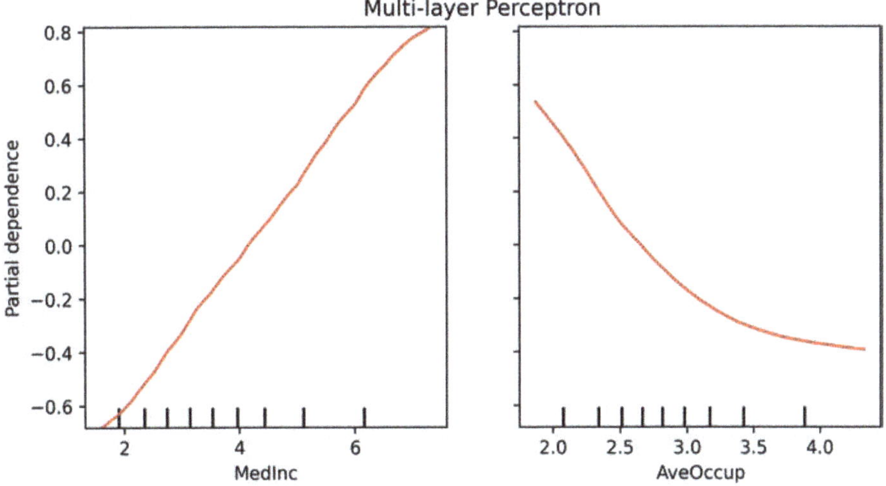

Figure 13.9:   Results using the MLP in Sklearn for the California housing dataset.

We observe that the MLP results are smooth.

13.8.6 *Decision tree regressor*

We next train a decision tree regressor.

```python
print("Training DecisionTreeRegressor...")
tic = time()
tree = DecisionTreeRegressor()
tree.fit(X_train, y_train)
print("done in {:.3f}s".format(time()- tic))
print("Test R2 score: {:.2f}".format(tree.score(X_test, y_test)))
```

```
Training DecisionTreeRegressor...
done in 0.243s
Test R2 score: 0.61
```

```python
fig, ax = plt.subplots(figsize=(8, 4))
ax.set_title("Decision Tree Regressor")
tree_disp=plot_partial_dependence(tree,X,["MedInc",
        "AveOccup"],ax=ax, line_kw={"c": "m"})
```

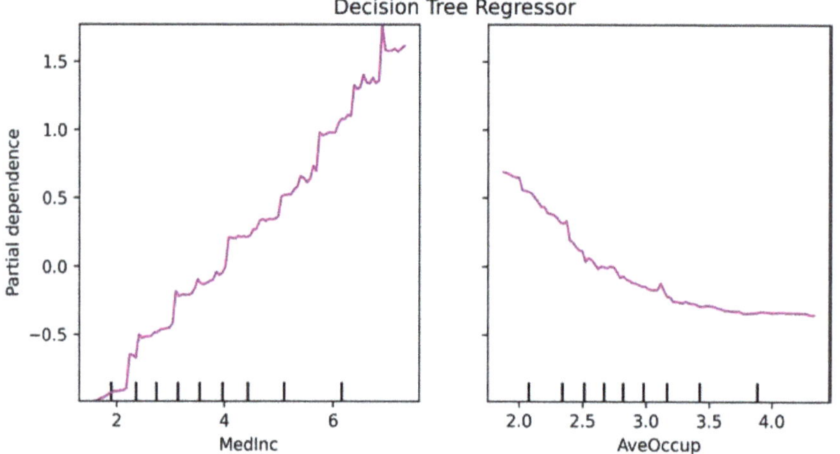

Figure 13.10: Results using the decision tree regressor in Sklearn for the California housing dataset.

```python
fig, (ax1, ax2) = plt.subplots(1, 2, figsize=(10, 5))
gbr_disp.plot(ax=[ax1, ax2], line_kw={"label":\
                        "Gradient Boosting Regressor"})
```

```
mlp_disp.plot(ax=[ax1, ax2], line_kw={"label":\
                    "Multi-layer Perceptron", "c": "red"})
tree_disp.plot(ax=[ax1, ax2], line_kw={"label":
                    "Decision Tree Regressor", "c": "m"})
ax1.legend()
ax2.legend()
```

```
<matplotlib.legend.Legend at 0x18e35abb128>
```

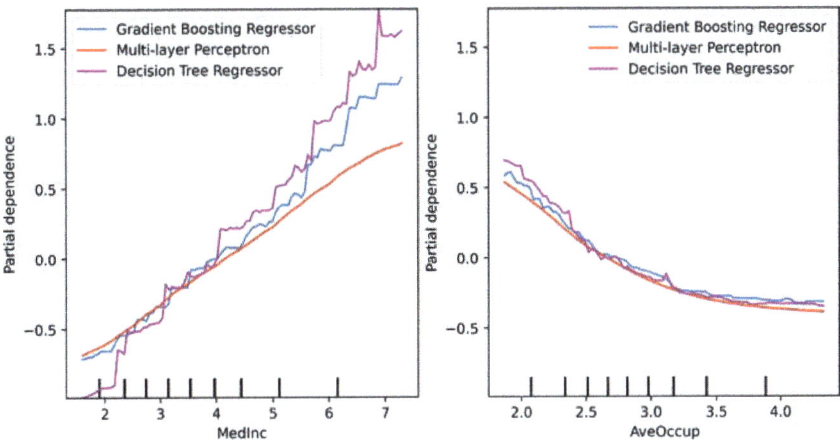

Figure 13.11: Comparison of results using three regressors in Sklearn for the California housing dataset.

Figure 13.11 shows that MLP prediction curves are much smoother than the gradient boosting and the decision tree regressors.

Note that all the test results depend heavily on settings of the hyperparameters used to set up the model, datasets, computer system, and even on when it is run. The setting parameters used in the above tests may not be fair for some models. Thus, the test results are subjective.

References

[1] D.E. Rumelhart and J.L. McClelland, Learning internal representations by error propagation, in *Parallel Distributed Processing: Explorations in the Microstructure of Cognition: Foundations*, pp. 318–362, MIT Press, Cambridge, MA, 1987.

[2] J. Orbach, Principles of neurodynamics: Perceptrons and the theory of brain mechanisms, *Archives of General Psychiatry*, **7**(3), 218–219, 09 1962. https://doi.org/10.1001/archpsyc.1962.01720030064010.

[3] T. Hastie, R. Tibshirani and J. Friedman, *Elements of Statistical Learning Ed.* p. 2, Springer, New York, 2009.

[4] G.R. Liu, FEA-AI and AI-AI: Two-way deepnets for real-time computations for both forward and inverse mechanics problems, *International Journal of Computational Methods*, **16**(08), 1950045, 2019.

[5] G.R. Liu, S.Y. Duan, Z.M. Zhang *et al.*, Tubenet: A special trumpetnet for explicit solutions to inverse problems, *International Journal of Computational Methods*, **18**(01), 2050030, 2021. https://doi.org/10.1142/S0219876220500309.

[6] G.R. Liu and X Han, *Computational Inverse Techniques in Nondestructive Evaluation.*, Taylor and Francis Group, New York, 2003.

[7] D. Shuyong, W. Li, G.R. Liu *et al.*, A technique for inversely identifying joint-stiffnesses of robot arms via two-way TubeNets, *Inverse Problems in Science & Engineering*, **29**, 3041–3061, 2021.

[8] D. Shuyong, H. Zhiping, G.R. Liu *et al.*, A novel inverse procedure via creating tubenet with constraint autoencoder for feature-space dimension-reduction, *International Journal of Applied Mechanics*, Revised, 2021.

[9] L. Shi, F. Wang, G. Liu *et al.*, Two-way tubeNets uncertain inverse methods for improving positioning accuracy of robots based on interval, *The 11th International Conference on Computational Methods (ICCM2020)*, 2020.

[10] R. David, H. Geoffrey and W. Ronald, Learning representations by back-propagating errors, *Nature*, **323**(6088), 533–536, October 1986.

[11] H. Sepp and S. Jürgen, Long short-term memory, *Neural Computation*, **9**(8), 1735–1780, 1997. https://doi.org/10.1162/neco.1997.9.8.1735.

[12] P. Fabian, V. Gae, G. Alexandre *et al.*, Scikit-learn: Machine Learning in Python, *Journal of Machine Learning Research*, **12**(85) 2825–2830, 2011. http://jmlr.org/papers/v12/pedregosa11a.html.

[13] G.R. Liu, Neurons-Samples Theorem, *International Journal of Computational Methods*, **19**(9), in-printing, 2022.

Chapter 14

Overfitting and Regularization

14.1 Why Regularization

Regularization in machine learning is closely related to the so-called "overfitting" that happens often in practice in supervised training. Overfitting depends on mainly two aspects: number of the training data-points m and the dimension of the hypothesis space $\mathbb{W}^P$ (the complexity of the neural network or other machine learning model). A quality model should have just enough complexity to capture the important features from the dataset and not be sensitive to the noise in the data. If a model merely reproduces all or most of the data-points in the training dataset, it may become overfitting. Such a model is of little practical use because it cannot be generalized for deployment. A rough **general guideline** may be given as follows:

$$m \geq P^* \tag{14.1}$$

where P^* is calculated using Eq. (13.14) in Chapter 13. When $m < P^*$, the prediction by a fully trained model may, in theory, pass through all the data-points, the labels are exactly produced, and the loss is zero. There may be chances of overfitting and some type of regularization is needed.

For Eq. (14.1) to be an effective guide, we assume that the dataset is of reasonably good quality (defined at the end of Section 5.9). For example, if the dataset has too many parallel data-points, the number of the data-points does not mean much. In such cases, m should count only these linearly independent samples. In other words, there may still be overfitting, even if Eq. (14.1) is satisfied, due to the insufficient quality of the dataset.

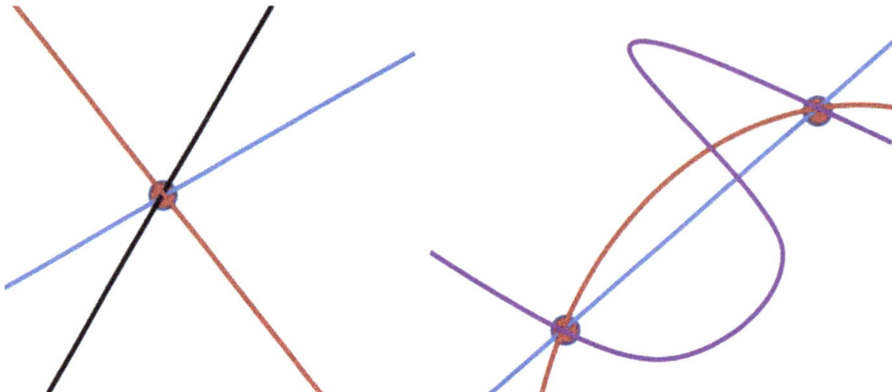

Figure 14.1: Fitting to data-points. Left: one data-point, infinite number of lines can be used to fit this data; Right: two data-points, one straight line fits perfectly to these data-points, but there are infinite numbers of higher-order curves can fit these two data-points.

Figure 14.1 illustrates schematically simple cases of overfitting. Consider the simplest case with only one data-point. If one would use a linear line (or any other types of curves) to fit perfectly the data-point, we shall have an infinite number of lines. Any of these lines is unlikely predictive to any other test data-point. To produce a robust predictive line, one would need more data-points to generate a predictive line. A regularization technique might be of help to obtain a unique line, but one would need to have some information on the feature of the data, if the data are so scare.

Similarly, when there are two data-points, one straight line perfectly fits these data-points, but there are infinite numbers of higher-order curves that can fit these two data-points. All these high-order curves can be an overly fitted prediction because it can predict test data-points incorrectly.

Overfitting can also occur in ML models for classifications. Figure 14.2 shows possible cases for given data-points in the 2D space. The orange line gives an overly simplified boundary, the green line gives an overly fitted boundary, and the black line gives a better fitted boundary for the given data-points and possibly for the test data-points not used in training the model.

Therefore, care is needed when using such an overly fitted machine learning model for practical problems, because when applying it to other data-points outside of the training dataset, or when the data-points have noises, the performance is not going to be reliable. For a given dataset, we may be able to train a model with extremely high accuracy, even with zero loss. Such a model, however, cannot be used in general for prediction for

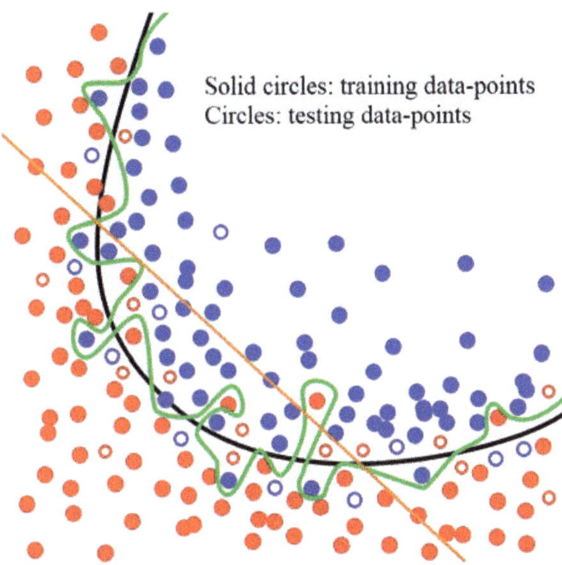

Figure 14.2: Fitting to find decision boundaries for classification problems. Orange line: overly simplified boundary; Green line: overly fitted boundary; Black line: better fitted boundary. Modified based on image from Wikimedia Commons by Chabacano (https:// en.wikipedia.org/wiki/Overfitting) under the CC BY-SA 4.0 license.

real-life problems. It is thus of importance to conduct **objective tests**: test the trained model using a sufficient number of randomly selected data (from the entire dataset), that was not used in training the model.

To overcome overfitting, various types of regularization techniques are used. However, introducing regularization into a model gives some of your biases to the features of your model. It thus unavoidably introduces additional errors to the model. Hence, one should use it with care. To have a regularization work well, one should also pay attention to the following matters:

- Always be aware of the number of trainable parameters in the model. It is the number of degrees of freedom of your model. When this number is large, the model has a chance to be overly fitted.
- In contrast, the number of (independent) training examples plays a critical role. When this number is too small compared to the P^*-number in the model, the model has a chance to be overly fitted.
- Consider the number and quality of the training datasets you have and then build a model accordingly, making sure that the number of the quality samples is sufficiently large. The P^*-number is only a lower bound. In

practice, m can be much larger than the P^*-number. This lets the data do the job. Use the regularization as a preventive tool or as a last resort.

Commonly used regularization techniques include the following:

1. Early stop during training: This is done by using a randomly chosen independent validation dataset to monitor the training. When the validation error comes across the training errors, consider stopping the training.
2. Dropout: Simply randomly drop neurons along with their connections from the net during training to limit the overfitting ability.
3. Tikhonov regularization that has a well-established mathematical foundation.

The early-stop technique is straightforward and easy to implement. The dropout technique needs to determine the ratio of neurons to be dropped out. This will depend on the Neurons-Samples Theory and how many successive training parameters there are in the model. A trial-and-error type of approach may be required for the model to be trained. We will discuss in great detail the Tikhonov regularization that has a clear mathematical foundation.

14.2 Tikhonov Regularization

Tikhonov regularization is a widely used regularization technique. It is named after the Russian scientist, Andrey Tikhonov. It is typically used for regularizing the solutions for ill-posed problems, such as the inverse problems in engineering [1]. It is also known as ridge regression in statistics. It is widely used in machine learning for regularizing the training parameters.

Let us revisit the general formulation for linear regressions that we presented at the beginning of Chapter 9, where we try to find solution for $\hat{\mathbf{w}}$ by solving the following equation:

$$\hat{\mathbf{y}} = \overline{\mathbf{X}}\hat{\mathbf{w}} \tag{14.2}$$

For given dataset $\overline{\mathbf{X}}$ and label $\mathbf{y}$, we built a loss function: $\mathcal{L}(\mathbf{y}, \hat{\mathbf{y}}(\hat{\mathbf{w}})) = [\mathbf{y} - \overline{\mathbf{X}}\hat{\mathbf{w}}]^\top [\mathbf{y} - \overline{\mathbf{X}}\hat{\mathbf{w}}]$. We then went through an analytical minimization process, and the solution is found in the following matrix form:

$$\hat{\mathbf{w}}^* = (\overline{\mathbf{X}}^T \overline{\mathbf{X}})^{-1} \overline{\mathbf{X}}^T \mathbf{y} \tag{14.3}$$

If one is careful, there will naturally be three important questions to ask:

1. Is $\overline{\mathbf{X}}^T\overline{\mathbf{X}}$ invertible? What if not?
2. Assuming $\overline{\mathbf{X}}^T\overline{\mathbf{X}}$ is invertible, and we do get the solution, is the solution usable for a test dataset?
3. Assuming $\overline{\mathbf{X}}^T\overline{\mathbf{X}}$ is invertible, and we do get the solution, how does the solution behave when the test dataset is noisy?

We are interested in providing answers to these questions, and will see where the Tikhonov regularization method can be of help.

When the Tikhonov regularization method (the simplest form) is used, our formulation starts from re-writing the loss function:

$$\mathcal{L}(\mathbf{y}, \hat{\mathbf{y}}(\hat{\mathbf{w}}), \lambda) = [\mathbf{y} - \mathbf{X}\hat{\mathbf{w}}]^\top [\mathbf{y} - \mathbf{X}\hat{\mathbf{w}}] + \lambda [\hat{\mathbf{w}} - \hat{\mathbf{w}}_0]^\top [\hat{\mathbf{w}} - \hat{\mathbf{w}}_0] \qquad (14.4)$$

The first term on the right-hand side is the data loss. The 2nd term is added as a regularization loss. λ is the regularization parameter that is a pre-specified positive real number. Vector $\hat{\mathbf{w}}_0$ is also pre-specified for the preferred the parameter $\hat{\mathbf{w}}$. $\hat{\mathbf{w}}_0$ is often set to zero, because we usually do not know what is preferred. If we have some knowledge on $\hat{\mathbf{w}}_0$ we can put it in, and we shall have the shifted regularization. Hence, $\hat{\mathbf{w}}_0$ is also a regularization parameter (more on this in the example studies).

Adding of the regularization term means that if the parameter $\hat{\mathbf{w}}$ departs from the preferred vector, there will be penalty to the loss function. The farther it departs, the more the penalty is scaled by the regularization parameter. Therefore, a compromise needs to be arrived at to fit the data and also with least regularization penalty.

We now go through the same analytical minimization process to find a regularized solution that is the minimizer to the above loss function:

$$\min_{\hat{\mathbf{w}}} \mathcal{L}(\mathbf{y}, \hat{\mathbf{y}}(\hat{\mathbf{w}}), \lambda) = \min_{\hat{\mathbf{w}}}([\mathbf{y} - \overline{\mathbf{X}}\hat{\mathbf{w}}]^T [\mathbf{y} - \overline{\mathbf{X}}\hat{\mathbf{w}}] + \lambda [\hat{\mathbf{w}} - \hat{\mathbf{w}}_0]^\top [\hat{\mathbf{w}} - \hat{\mathbf{w}}_0]) \quad (14.5)$$

It is obvious that this function is also quadratic in $\hat{\mathbf{w}}$. This time, we can be quite sure that there is a unique $\hat{\mathbf{w}}^*$ that minimizes the modified loss function, regardless of the data $\overline{\mathbf{X}}$. This is because at least the regularization term is strictly positive, as long as the λ is not zero. Such a regularized solution can be found by setting the derivative of objective function to 0:

$$\frac{\partial \mathcal{L}(\mathbf{y}, \hat{\mathbf{y}}(\hat{\mathbf{w}}), \lambda)}{\partial \hat{\mathbf{w}}} = -2\overline{\mathbf{X}}^T(\mathbf{y} - \overline{\mathbf{X}}\hat{\mathbf{w}}^*) + 2\lambda [\hat{\mathbf{w}}^* - \hat{\mathbf{w}}_0] = 0 \qquad (14.6)$$

which gives a regularized solution:

$$\hat{\mathbf{w}}_R^* = [\overline{\mathbf{X}}^T\overline{\mathbf{X}} + \lambda\mathbf{I}]^{-1}\{\overline{\mathbf{X}}^T\mathbf{y} - \lambda\hat{\mathbf{w}}_0\} \tag{14.7}$$

which is a find of close-form solution.

Now, even if, for some reason (too small dataset, data-points are closely correlated, etc.), matrix $\overline{\mathbf{X}}^T\overline{\mathbf{X}}$ is singular or close to singular, $\lambda\mathbf{I}$ is strictly positive-definite regardless. In addition, by adjusting λ, one can make its "positivity" sufficiently strong so that the matrix in the square blankets is always invertible, to ensure the existence of a regularized solution. This answers the first question.

Use of norms to add terms into the loss function is convenient because the loss function needs to be a positive functional and norms by definition satisfy the positivity requirement. Possible norms are

$$\text{norm} = \left(\sum_{i=0}^{P}|w_i|^q\right)^{\frac{1}{q}} \tag{14.8}$$

where P is the total number of learning parameters. The term in the parentheses in Eq. (14.8) multiplied by a regularization parameter is added into the loss function. Figure 14.3 gives contours of the functions using these norms defined in the foregoing equation for different q values.

In our modified loss function Eq. (14.4), we used the L2 norm for the regularization term, which is quadratic and popular in current practices. It has a good convex property, and is easy in formulation and implementation. One may choose to use other norms, such as the L1 norm (called Lasso), to regularize the absolute values of the training parameters. The L1 norm function is still convex, but its derivatives are not continuous.

When the loss function is modified with the regularization term, we would need to find the minimizer for the combined loss function. This situation is

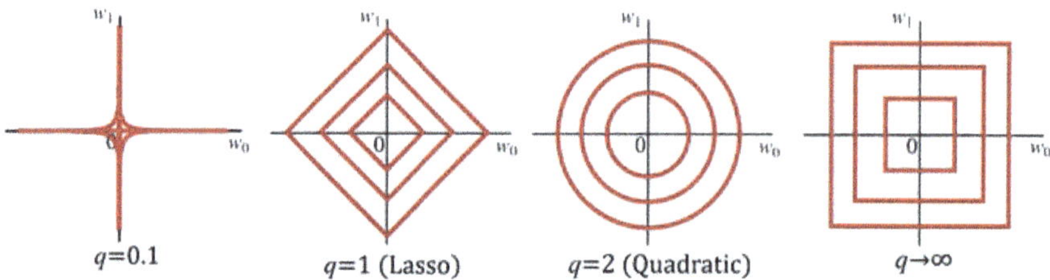

Figure 14.3: Contourfs of the norms in simple two dimension.

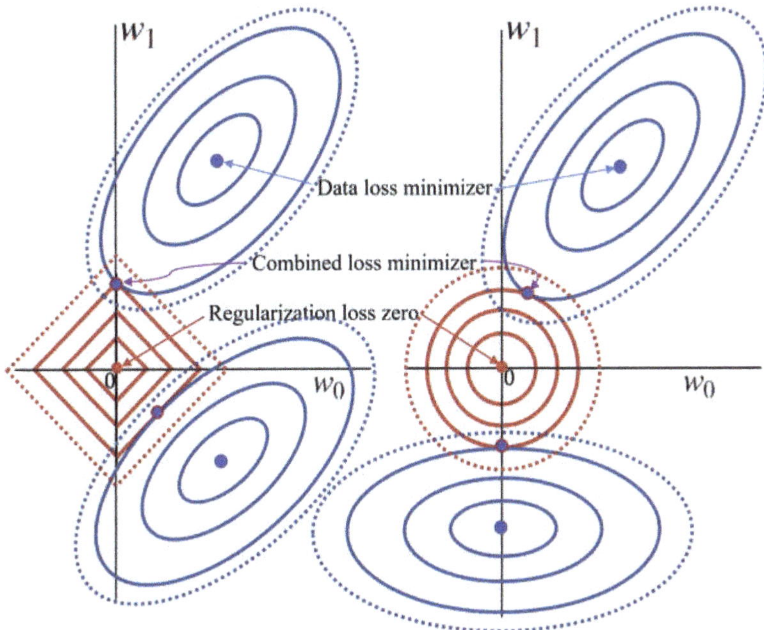

Figure 14.4:   Contours of both the data loss function and the regularization loss function.

schematically drawn in Fig. 14.4. The combined minimizer should be at the *kissing* point of the contour of the *data loss function* and that of the *regularization loss function*. When the quadratic regularization function is used, the kissing point is usually with multiple nonzero feature parameters, unless the data loss minimizer is located exactly on one of the feature axes, which is not likely to happen. When the L1 norm is used, its contours have sharp vortexes. Therefore, the oval contour of the data loss function can kiss at a vortex, even if the data loss minimizer is not located exactly on any of the feature axes. Because of this, the combined minimizer tends to select some of the features and make the other features zero, creating a sparse model (with many zero parameters) in the minimization process. Therefore, L1 regularization can also be used for making the machine learning model sparse.

In Eq. (14.4), we have applied the same λ equally to all the parameters in the above formulation. This does not have to be this way. If you know the features of your model well, you may choose different λ values for individual parameters. In this case, λ should be a diagonal matrix. In Python, one can just define a vector to store these λs and use its element-wise products (as will be shown in the example codes below) to apply different λ to different features.

In some practices, regularizations are only applied to the weights not the biases. This is equivalent to using a diagonal λ matrix, but set zero for these diagonal terms corresponding to the biases. We will demonstrate this in the following example too.

We are now ready to test out this method using a very simple example, so that we can see through the process and feel how the regularization is at work.

14.2.1 *Demonstration examples: One data-point*

Case 1: Consider the simplest possible one-dimensional problem with only one data-point (x_1, y_1). We would like to find a linear regression $y = xw + b$ based on this data-point. In this case, we shall have $\hat{\mathbf{w}} = [w_0, w_1]^\top = [b, w]^\top$. Clearly, the linear line has two model parameters: w and b. Thus, we can have an infinite number of lines that satisfy the requirement if you use Eq. (14.3). This can be clearly seen using **Part I** of the code attached below, by setting xdata $=$ np.arange(2, 5, 6), which gives only one data-point $x_1 = 2.$; with $x_0 = 1$, we then have $\overline{\mathbf{X}} = [1 \quad x_1] = [1., \quad 2.]$. Let also $y = [2.]$.

Note that our code is written for multiple data-points. One can use just one data-point to see what we get, and then try out using multiple data-points.

```python
import numpy as np
import random


# Part I code: No regularization, one data-point,
             # two regression parameters, b and w

xdata = np.arange(2, 5, 6)   # for 1 data-point
#xdata = np.arange(1, 5, 2) # for 2 data-points
#xdata = np.arange(1, 7, 2) # for 3 data-points


lxd = len(xdata)
One = np.ones(lxd)
print('Length of xdata=',lxd, '   Value of xdata=', xdata)
X = np.stack((One, xdata), axis=-1)    # form X matrix
print('X=',X,X.shape)
```

```python
np.random.seed(8)
y=xdata.T+np.random.randn(lxd)*0. # Label y, 1 data-point
#y=xdata.T+np.random.rand(lxd)*2. # Label y, >=3 data-points,
    # using random number so that [x_i, y_i] will not be inline.
#y=2.*xdata.T+np.random.randn(lxd)*2.
    # form y, for >= 3 data-points,
    # using random number so that [x_i, y_i] will not be inline.
print('y=',y,y.shape)


XTy = np.dot(X.T,y)                     # Compute X.T * y
print('XTy=',XTy,XTy.shape)


XTX = np.matmul(X.T,X)                  # Compute X.T * X
print('XTX=',XTX,XTX.shape)


cd = np.linalg.cond(XTX) # c=np.linalg.solve(XTX,XTy) will not
                    # work for 1 data-point. Check condition number


print('Condition number=',cd,' Rank=',np.linalg.matrix_rank(XTX))
                            # check the rank also
if lxd >= 2:
    w = np.linalg.solve(XTX,XTy)        # only for data-points >=2.
    print('w*=', w, w.shape)
```

```
Length of xdata= 1    Value of xdata= [2]
X= [[1. 2.]] (1, 2)
y= [2.] (1,)
XTy= [2. 4.] (2,)
XTX= [[1. 2.]
 [2. 4.]] (2, 2)
Condition number= 4.804857307547117e+16  Rank= 1
```

It is clear that when only one data-point is used, the condition number of the $\overline{\mathbf{X}}^\top \overline{\mathbf{X}}$ matrix is very large, and the rank of the $\overline{\mathbf{X}}^\top \overline{\mathbf{X}}$ matrix is only 1. It is not solvable for $\hat{\mathbf{w}}^* = [w_0^*, w_1^*]^\top = [b^*, w^*]^\top$. This means that there are infinite number of $[w_0, w_1]^\top = [b, w]^\top$ that can be the solution, which honor the data.

We now use Eq. (14.7) to compute regularized solutions for this linear regression, using different settings for the regularization parameter λ. We used Part II of our code given below to perform the computation and Part III to plot the results. Here, we shall have three cases to be studied, by setting different values for lb0 and lw0 in vector L0=np.array([lb0, lw0]) in the codes below. For all these cases, we will get a unique solution because of the effects of the regularization. However, the solution behavior will also be different, affected by the setting of the regularization parameters for b and/or for w. Let us first examine Case 2.

```python
# Part II code: Regularized linear regression, 2 parameters, b, w
    # The code works for multiple data-points. Try one point first.
    # For multiple data-points, use proper settings in Part I code.

w0 = np.array([.0,.0]) # Case 2,3,4; pre-specified parameters: b,w

#w0 = np.array([.4,.8]) # Case 5; with setting
                       # L0=np.array([1.,1.])
#w0 = np.array([.6,1.0]) # Case 5-1: 2 data, L0=np.array([1.,1.])
#w0 = np.array([.45341,1.]) # Case 5: 2 data, L0=np.array([1.,1.])
#w0 = np.array([.0,1.]) # Case 5: 2 data, L0 = np.array([1.,1.])
#w0 = np.array([1.8138,.99788]) # Case 5: 3 data,
                              # L0=np.array([1.,1.])
#w0 = np.array([0.65, 2.0]) # Case 5: 3 data, L0=np.array([1.,1.])

print('w0=',w0,w0.shape)

L0 = np.array([1.,0.]) # Case 2; # define base lambdas for b and w
#              [lb0, lw0])   # One may try 3 cases: regularize b
                            #   only set [1.,0]; [0.,1]; [1.,1.]

#L0 = np.array([0.,1.])    # Case 3; # regularize w only

#L0 = np.array([1.,1.])    # Case 4; # regularize both b and w

                          # Case 5;   with w0 = np.array([.4,.8])
print('Lambda for b w =',L0, L0.shape)
L = 0.5 * L0                    # set lambda value
I = np.identity(2)
print('I=',I,' L*I=',L*I)   # regularization matrix lambda

K = XTX+L*I                      # regularized system matrix

XTy0 = XTy+L*w0                  # regularized y vector
print('XTy=',XTy,XTy.shape,'w0=',w0,'XTy0=',XTy0)

crd = np.linalg.cond(K)          # condition number of regularized
                                 # system matrix. Should be small.
```

```python
print('crd=',np.linalg.cond(K),' Rank=', np.linalg.matrix_rank(K))
                              # Check rank
wr = np.linalg.solve(K,XTy0)      # regularized solution
print('wr=',wr)
```

```
w0= [0. 0.] (2,)
Lambda for b w = [1. 0.] (2,)
I= [[1. 0.]
 [0. 1.]]  L*I= [[0.5 0. ]
 [0.  0. ]]
XTy= [2. 4.] (2,) w0= [0. 0.] XTy0= [2. 4.]
crd= 13.048362028288917  Rank= 2
wr= [0. 1.]
```

Note in the code above, that the input XTy is a 1D numpy array, and the result is also a 1D array, which is not the convention of linear algebra, as discussed in Section 2.9.13. One can also purposely define a column vector (a 2D array with only on column) following the convention of linear algebra, and get the solution. The solution will be the same, but is in a column vector. Use of 1D numpy array will be more efficient. We have also seen an example in Section 3.1.11.

Case 2: Using the same data as case 1 (one data-point $x_0 = 1, x_1 = 2., \overline{\mathbf{X}} = [1 \quad 2.], y = [2.]$) but set the regularization parameters as L0 = np.array([1.0, 0.]), which regularizes only the bias b.

We write the following code to compute and plot the results.

```python
# Part III: plot the regression linears.


%matplotlib inline
import matplotlib.pyplot as plt
import numpy as np
from matplotlib import rc


def y_hat(X, w):    # function for the predicated regression
                    # line for given solution wr*
    return np.dot(X, w)  # X = [1   x1] ;   wr* = [b*   w*]^T


x = np.arange(0, 9, 1.)  # points on x-axis
lx = len(x)
One = np.ones(lx)
```

```python
print('Length of x=',lx, x)
Xm = np.stack((One, x), axis=-1) #build up X using points x.

#Lmda = np.arange(0.1, 1.5, 0.4) #control the range of lambda
#Lmda = np.arange(0.01, 15., 4)
Lmda = np.arange(0.1, 20., 6)

I = np.identity(2)
print('w0=', w0, w0.shape)
print('Lambda base for b, and w =',L0, L0.shape)
print('X=',X,X.shape)
print('y=',y,y.shape)

plt.figure(figsize=(4.5, 2.9),dpi=100)
for L in Lmda:
    lmd = L*L0
    K = XTX+lmd*I                       #regularized system matrix.
    XTy0 = XTy +lmd*w0                   #regularized y vector.
    wr = np.linalg.solve(K,XTy0)
    print('Lambda='+str(f"{L:.2f}"), ' wr=', wr,XTy.shape,\
          w0.shape,XTy0.shape,L.shape)
    plt.plot(x,y_hat(Xm, wr),label="Lambda="+str(f"{L:.2f}"))
    # compute the predicted lines and plot out.

plt.scatter(xdata, y, s=35., c='r', alpha=0.5)
plt.xlabel('x')
plt.ylabel('$\hat{y}$')
plt.title('$\^{w}_0=$['+str(f"{w0[0]:.3f}")+','+\
      str(f"{w0[1]:.3f}")+'], lb0='+str(L0[0])+',lw0 ='+str(L0[1]))
plt.grid(color='r', linestyle=':', linewidth=0.5)
plt.legend()
plt.show()
```

```
Length of x= 9 [0. 1. 2. 3. 4. 5. 6. 7. 8.]
w0= [0. 0.] (2,)
Lambda base for b, and w = [1. 0.] (2,)
X= [[1. 2.]] (1, 2)
y= [2.] (1,)
Lambda=0.10  wr= [0. 1.] (2,) (2,) (2,) ()
Lambda=6.10  wr= [0. 1.] (2,) (2,) (2,) ()
Lambda=12.10  wr= [0. 1.] (2,) (2,) (2,) ()
Lambda=18.10  wr= [0. 1.] (2,) (2,) (2,) ()
```

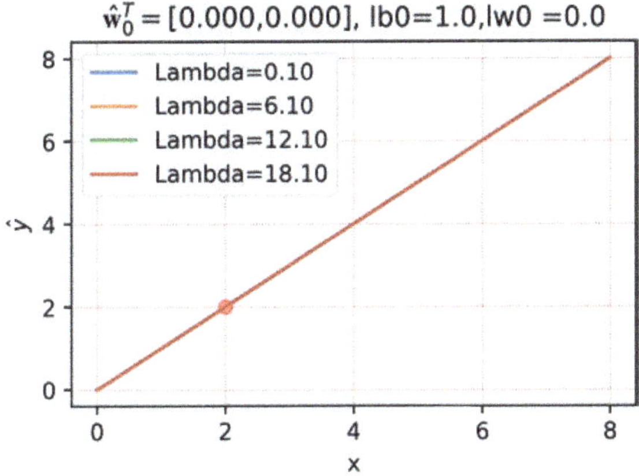

Figure 14.5: Simple linear regression for one data-point, with bias regularized at various levels.

In this case, we regularize b only and leave w free (from regularization). The results are plotted in Fig. 14.5. We shall observe the following points:

- This solution would produce a zero solution for b, because it is regularized, and some value for w, because it is allowed to change freely.
- As we can see, it is a line passing through the origin with a slope. This is because the solution for b is zero, and w (responsible for the slope) is not.
- The regression line passes through the one data-point. This is because we regularize one parameter and the other parameter is free. Therefore, we have a total of two conditions: one is passing the data-point, and one is zero bias b. Both conditions determine uniquely two regression parameters, b and w.
- The magnitude of the λ has no effect on the solution, because of the setting of this case with two conditions and two parameters. The amount of the regularization is immaterial.
- It is clear that the Tikhonov regularization helped us obtain a unique solution for the problem (Case 1) that has an infinite number of solutions. This is why the Tikhonov regularization technique is also used to obtain *pseudo-inversion* of an un-invertible matrix.

Using Part II and III of our code again, we now study Case 3:

Case 3: Use the same dataset as Case 2, but set L0 = np.array([0.0, 1.0]), which regularizes w_0 only.

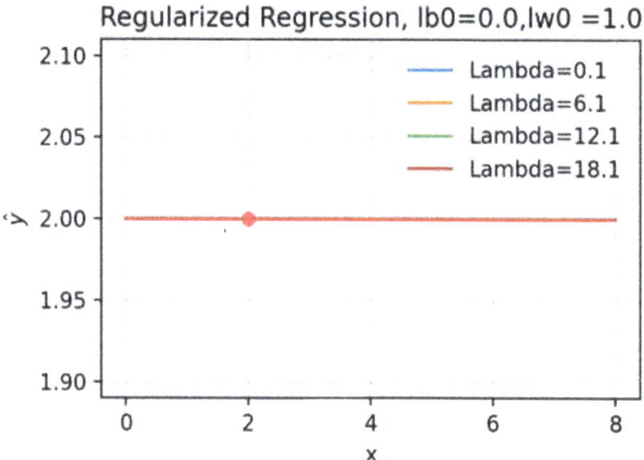

Figure 14.6: The regression line for Case 3: only w is regularized, but the results are not affected by the regularization parameter λ (these 4 lines are overlapping). b is set free from regularization.

In this case, b is left free (from regularization). The results are shown in Fig. 14.6. We shall observe the following points:

- This solution would produce a zero solution for w (hence the slope will be zero), because it is regularized, and some value for b, because it is allowed to change freely.
- As we can see, it is a horizontal line, as expected. This is because the solution for w is zero and it is responsible for the slope.
- The line is no longer passing the origin, because b is no longer zero.
- The regression line still passes through the one data-point. This is because we regularize one parameter and the other parameter is free. Therefore, we have a total of two conditions: one is passing the data-point, and one is zero slope w. Both conditions determine uniquely two regression parameters, b and w.
- The magnitude of the λ has, again, no effect on the solution, because of the setting with two conditions and two parameters. The amount of the regularization is immaterial.
- It is clear that the Tikhonov regularization helped us again obtain a unique solution for the problem (Case 1) that has an infinite number of solutions. But, the solution is different because of the different way in which the regularization is applied.

Using Part II and III of our code again, we now study Case 4 where we regularize both b and w.

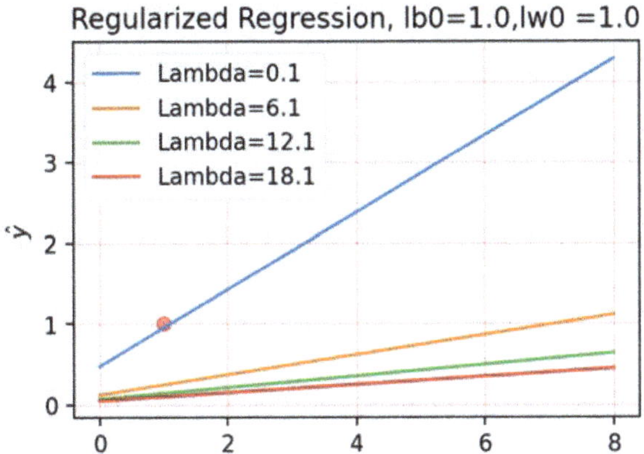

Figure 14.7:   The regression line for Case 4: both b and w are all regularized.

Case 4: Use the same dataset as Case 2, but set L0 = np.array([1.0, 1.0]) in code Part II.

In this case, both b and w are all regularized, as shown in Fig. 14.7. We shall observe the following points:

- This solution would produce a nonzero solution for both b and w, and hence the intersection and the slope will all be nonzero. This is because both cannot change freely.
- The regression line is no longer passing through the one data-point. This is because we regularize both parameters. Therefore, we have a total of three conditions: one is passing the data-point, one is a nonzero bias b, and one is nonzero slope w. Because we have only two regression parameters b and w, none of these conditions will be satisfied. The solution is a compromise.
- This time, the magnitude of the λ matters. When it is very small (0.1 for example), the line is nearly passing through the data-point. Otherwise, the line will not pass the data-point, for the same reason mentioned in the above point.
- It is clear that the Tikhonov regularization helped us again obtain a unique solution for the problem (Case 1) that has an infinite number of solutions. But, the solution is different, depending on the level of the regularization parameters used.

Figure 14.8 plots regression lines using small regularization parameters. This re-emphasizes that the level of regularization is controlled by the regularization parameter. Thus, setting proper a regularization parameter is important.

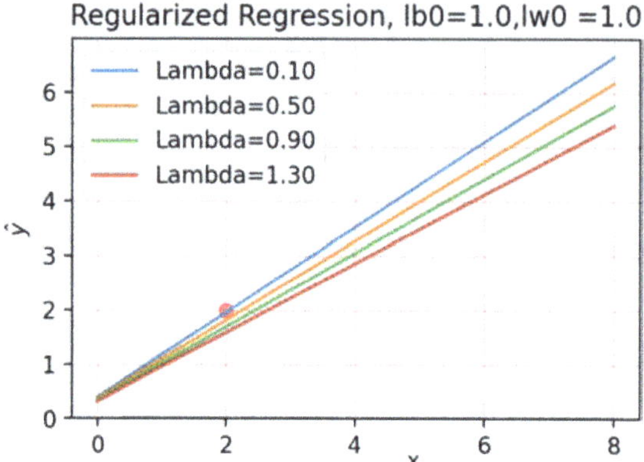

Figure 14.8:   The regression line for Case 4: both b and w are all regularized with a small regularization parameter.

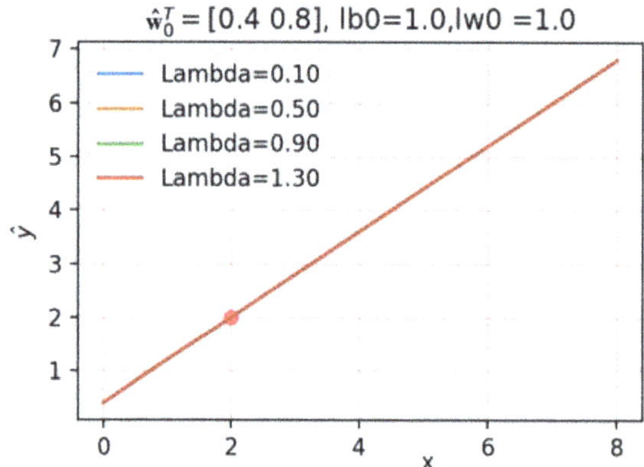

Figure 14.9:   The regression line for Case 5: both b and w are all regularized, with respect to the preferred solution set at the true solution of $(0.4, 0.8)$.

Using our codes, we found that when we use a very small Lambda=0.01 for Case 4 where both b and w are all regularized, the resulting regularized solution becomes $[0.3992016\ 0.79840319]$. We can then guess that the true solution should be $[0.4, 0.8]$. Let us now study the following case.

Case 5: Set L0 = np.array($[1.0, 1.0]$) and $\hat{w}_0 = [0.4, 0.8]^\top$ in the Part II code.

In this case, both b and w are all regularized with respect to a preferred solution that is the true solution. The results are plotted in Fig. 14.9.

We shall observe the following points:

• This solution becomes the true solution for both b and w, meaning that if we know the true solution, we can put it in the regularization term, and

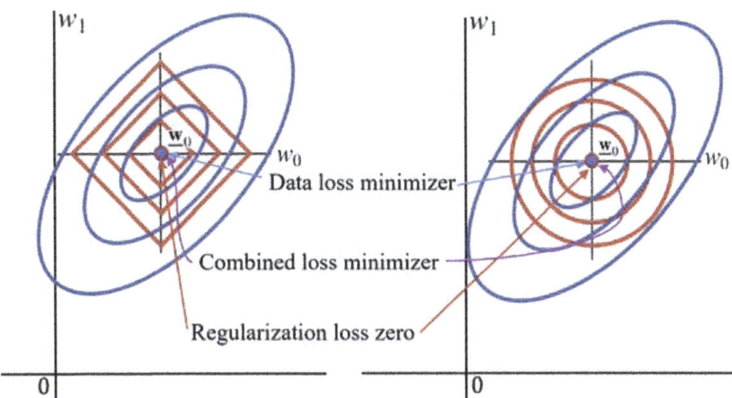

Figure 14.10: The regression line for Case 5: both b and w are all regularized, but with respect to the preferred solution set at the true solution of (0.4, 0.8).

our code will reproduce it. The regression line passes through the data-point. Figure 14.10 illustrates schematically what has happened in this case.

- As shown in Fig. 14.10, these minimizers are for both the data loss and the regularization loss, and thus the combined loss is located at the same place (the true solution).

- In reality, it is not possible to know where the true solution for complex problems is (if we do, we will not need any model). However, if we have some but not exact knowledge about the true solution, using this shifted regularization may be effective, because the trained model can be more representative to the data, and yet biased to the knowledge. Because of this, $\hat{\mathbf{w}}_0$ can also be a regularization parameter.

- Notice that $\hat{\mathbf{w}}_0$ is a vector, and hence the specification on it can be done per parameter/feature.

- The magnitude of the λ does not matter in this case. This is because our data loss and regularization loss are essentially the same for this simple problem. When the data loss differs from the regularization loss (which is true for practical complex problems), the magnitude of the λ shall have effects.

14.2.2 *Demonstration examples: Two data-points*

With the understanding established for the simple examples using one data-point, we can now extend the study to cases with two data-points, which shall enforce our understanding of the regularization effects and the relationship

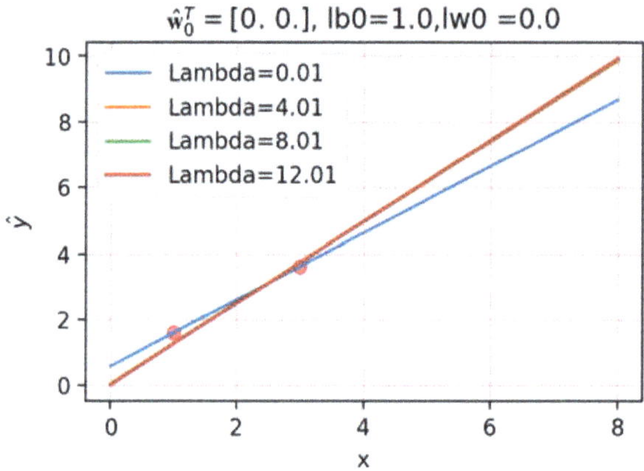

Figure 14.11: The regression line for Case 2 with 2 data-points: only b is regularized, and w set free from regularization.

with the data. We shall do this in reference to all these 5 cases we have studied for one data-point.

For **Case 1**, when we have two data-points, and still using the linear regression model in one-dimensional space, we shall have a unique solution as long as these two data-points are not coinciding. This is because the rank of the system matrix $\overline{\mathbf{X}}^\top \overline{\mathbf{X}}$ is 2. The solution will be passing exactly these two data-points. When these two data-points are X = [[1. 1.], [1. 3.]] and y = [1.4534 3.4534] (note randomly generated), the true (un-regularized) is $\hat{\mathbf{w}}^* = [0.45341172, 1.]^\top$.

For **Case 2** using two data-points, we also set L0 = np.array([1.0, 0.]). In this case, we regularize b only and leave w free (from regularization). The solution is plotted in Fig. 14.11.

We shall observe the following points:

- The regression line does not pass through these two data-points unless the regularization parameter is set to zero. This is because we regularize one parameter (and the other parameter is free). Therefore, we have a total of three conditions: two for passing these two data-points, and one is for zero bias b. The regularized solution is a compromise.
- When the regularization parameter is very small (0.01 for this case, blue line in Fig. 14.11), the solution line closely passes these two points and the result is close to Case 1 using two data-points.
- When the regularization parameter is large, the line is turned to give a nearly zero bias b while minimizing the data loss (the sum of the distances between these two data-points and the regression line).

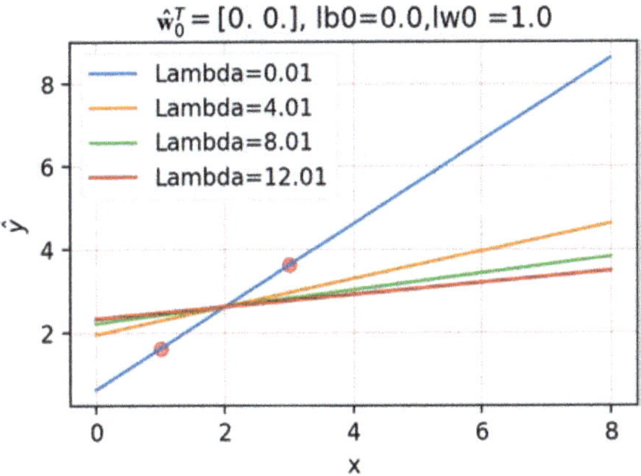

Figure 14.12: The regression line for Case 3: only w is regularized, and b set free from regularization.

- The magnitude of the λ has effects on the solution. The larger the λ, the closer the b to zero.
- The Tikhonov regularization helped us obtain a compromise solution. It uniquely depends on the data and the regularization parameter.

Case 3 for two data-points: Set L0 = np.array([0.0, 1.0]).

In this case, we regularize w only and leave b free (from regularization), while the data loss is for both data-points. The results are plotted in Fig. 14.12.

We shall observe the following points:

- The regression lines do not pass through these two data-points unless the regularization parameter is set to zero. This is because we regularize one parameter (and the other parameter is free). Therefore, we have a total of three conditions: two for passing these two data-points, and one is for small weight w. The regularized solutions are compromises.
- When the regularization parameter is very small (0.01 for this case, blue line in Fig. 14.12), the solution line closely passes these two data-points and the result is close to Case 1 using two data-points.
- When the regularization parameter is large, the line is turned to give a small slope controlled by w while minimizing the data loss (the sum of the distances between these two data-points and the regression line).
- The magnitude of the λ has effects on the solution. The larger the λ, the closer the slope w to zero.

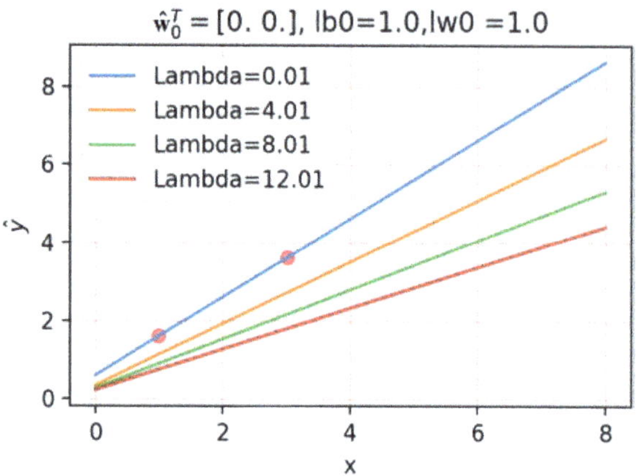

Figure 14.13:   The regression line for Case 4: both b and w are all regularized.

Case 4 with two data-points: Set L0 = np.array([1.0, 1.0]) in code Part II, and using two data-points.

In this case, both b and w are all regularized. The result from our code is plotted as follows.

We shall mention the following points:

- The regression line does not pass through these two data-points, unless the regularization parameter is set to zero. This is because we regularize two parameters. Therefore, we have a total of four conditions: two for passing these two data-points, and two for small weight w. The regularized solution is a compromise.
- When the regularization parameter is very small (0.01 for this case, blue line in Fig. 14.13), the solution line closely passes these two data-points and the result is close to Case 1 using two data-points.
- When the regularization parameter is large, the line is turned to give a small slope controlled by w, and also shifted downward to give a smaller intersection controlled by b, while minimizing the data loss (the sum of the distances between these two data-points and the regression line).
- The magnitude of λ has effects on the solution. The larger the λ, the smaller the intersection and the closer the slope w to zero.

From the study of Case 1 with two data-points, we obtained the true (un-regularized) solution $\hat{\mathbf{w}}^* = [0.4534, 1.]^\top$. We can then use the true solution for a shifted regularization.

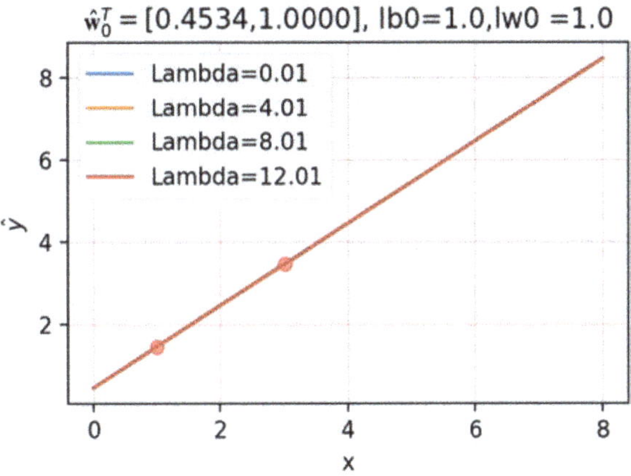

Figure 14.14: The regression line for Case 5 with two data-points: both b and w are all regularized, with respect to the preferred solution set at the true solution of $[0.4534, 1.0]$.

Case 5 with two data-points: Set L0 = np.array($[1.0, 1.0]$) and $\hat{\mathbf{w}}_0 = [0.4534, 1.0]^\top$ in Part II code.

In this case, both b and w are all regularized, with respect to a preferred solution that is the true solution. The results are plotted in Fig. 14.14.

We shall observe the following point:

- This solution becomes the true solution for both b and w, meaning that if we know the true solution, we can put it in the regularization term, and our code will reproduce it. The regression line passes through these two data-points, regardless of the level of regularization.

14.2.3 *Demonstration examples: Three data-points*

We can now extend the study to cases with three data-points.

For **Case 1**, when we have three data-points, and are still using the linear regression model in one-dimensional space, we shall have a unique solution, as long as these three data-points are not coinciding. This is because the rank of the system matrix $\overline{\mathbf{X}}^\top \overline{\mathbf{X}}$ become 2. However, the solution will not be passing these three data-points exactly, because it is a least-square solution, ensuring only the distances between these points to the linear line being minimum. When these three data-points are $\overline{\mathbf{X}} = [[1.\ 1.], [1.\ 3.], [1.\ 5.]]$ and $y = [2.7469\ 4.9379\ 6.7389]$ (randomly generated), the true least-square solution (un-regularized) is $\hat{\mathbf{w}}^* = [1.8138, 0.9979]^\top$.

                Machine Learning with Python: Theory and Applications

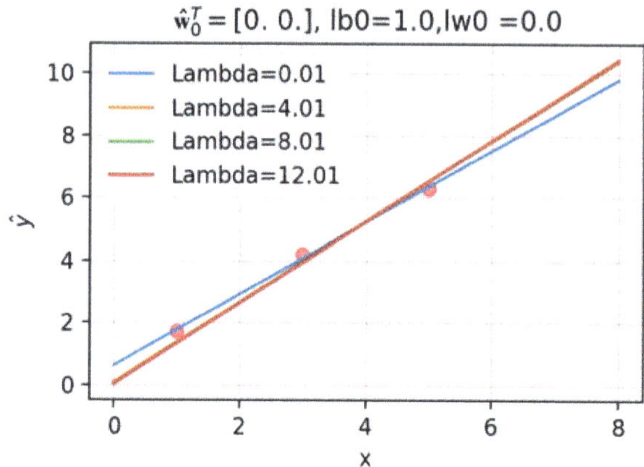

Figure 14.15:   The regression line for Case 2 with 3 data-points: only b is regularized, and w set free from regularization.

For **Case 2** using three data-points, we also set L0 = np.array([1.0,0.]).
In this case, we regularize b only and leave w free (from regularization). The
solution is plotted in Fig. 14.15.

We shall observe the following points:

- The regression lines do not pass through these three data-points, even if
  the regularization parameter is set to zero. This is because we have a total
  of four conditions/equations: these three data-points and one for zero bias
  b. Therefore, the regularized solution is a compromise.
- When the regularization parameter is very small (0.01 for this case, blue
  line in Fig. 14.15), the solution line is close to the un-regularized true
  least-square solution.
- When the regularization parameter is large, the line is turned to give a
  nearly zero bias b while minimizing the data loss (the sum of the distances
  between these three data-points and the regression line).
- The magnitude of the λ has effects on the solution. The larger the λ, the
  closer the b to zero.
- The Tikhonov regularization helped us obtain a compromise solution. It
  uniquely depends on the data and the regularization parameter.

Case 3 for three data-points: Set L0 = np.array([0.0,1.0])

In this case, we regularize w only and leave b free (from regularization),
while the data loss is for all the data-points. The results are plotted in
Fig. 14.16.

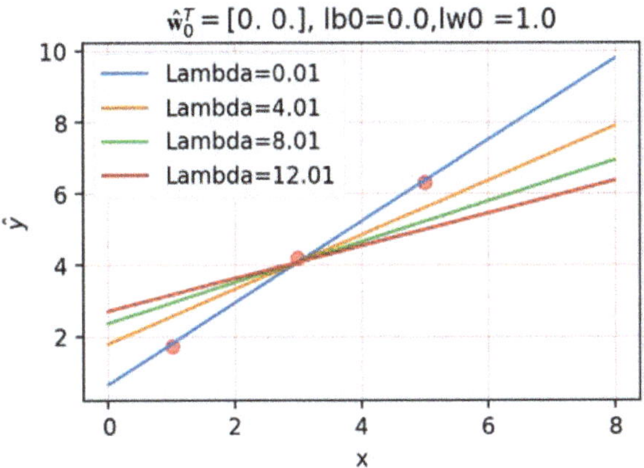

Figure 14.16: The regression line for Case 3 with three data-points: only w is regularized, and b set free from regularization.

We shall observe the following points:

- The regression lines do not pass through these three data-points, even if the regularization parameter is set to zero. This is because we have a total of four conditions/equations: these three data-points and one on slope w. Therefore, the regularized solution is a compromise.
- When the regularization parameter is very small (0.01 for this case, blue line in Fig. 14.16), the solution line is close to the un-regularized true least-square solution.
- When the regularization parameter is large, the line is turned to give a small slope controlled by w while minimizing the data loss (the sum of the distances between these three data-points and the regression line).
- The magnitude of λ has effects on the solution. The larger the λ, the closer the slope w to zero.

Case 4 with three data-points: Set L0 = np.array($[1.0,\ 1.0]$) in Part II code.

In this case, both b and w are all regularized. The result from our code is plotted as follows.

We shall mention the following points:

- The regression lines do not pass through these three data-points, even if the regularization parameter is set to zero. This is because we have a total of five conditions/equations: these three data-points, and one for small b and the other for small slope w. Therefore, the regularized solution is a compromise.

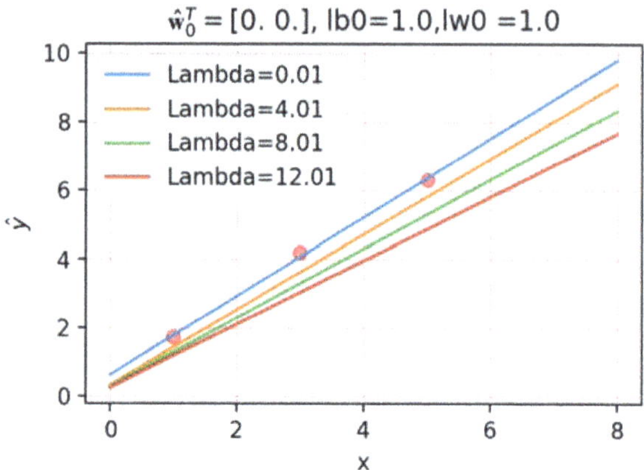

Figure 14.17:　　The regression line for Case 4 with three data-points: both b and w are all regularized.

- When the regularization parameter is very small (0.01 for this case, blue line in Fig. 14.17), the solution line is close to the un-regularized true least-square solution.
- When the regularization parameter is large, the line is turned to give a small slope controlled by w, and also shifted downward to give a smaller intersection controlled by b, while minimizing the data loss.
- The magnitude of λ has effects on the solution. The larger the λ, the smaller the intersection and the closer the slope w to zero.

From the study of Case 1 with three data-points, we obtained the true (un-regularized) solution $\hat{\mathbf{w}}^* = [1.8138, 0.9979]^\top$. We can then use the true solution for a shifted regularization.

Case 5 with three data-points: Set L0 = np.array([1.0, 1.0]) and $\hat{\mathbf{w}}_0 = [1.8138, 0.9979]^\top$ in Part II code.

In this case, both b and w are all regularized, with respect to a preferred solution that is the true solution. The results are plotted in Fig. 14.18.

We shall observe the following point:

- This solution becomes the true least-square solution for both b and w, meaning that if we know the true solution, we can the put it in the regularization term, and our code will reproduce it. The regression line passes through these three data-points, regardless of the level of regularization.

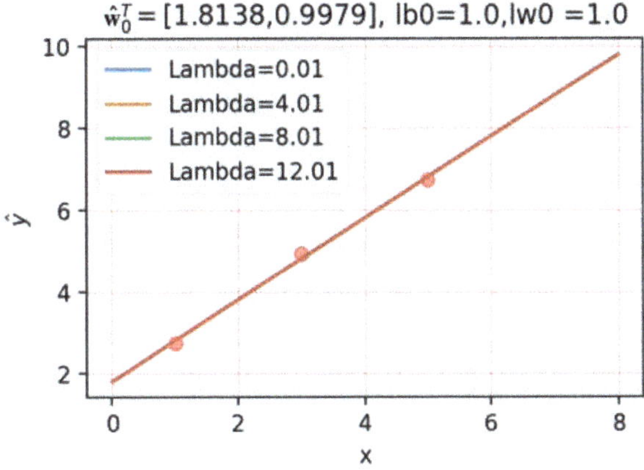

Figure 14.18: The regression line for Case 5 with three data-points: both b and w are all regularized, with respect to the preferred solution set at the true solution of $[1.8138, 0.9979]^\top$.

14.2.4 *Summary of the case studies*

These studies show that the Tikhonov regularization has the following major effects:

- For small datasets, it allows one to make use of knowledge of the data to make up the shortfall in information to obtain a unique solution.
- For excessive datasets, it offers means to control the magnitudes of the training parameters to prevent overfitting.
- For noisy datasets, the regularization offers means for mitigating the error. Based on our study on the universal approximation theory, we found that the weights and biases are responsible for producing the pulses for approximating a function (see Section 7.3). We have also demonstrated that the larger the weights, the steeper the pulse, hence offering more capability in approximating more complex functions. If the weight values are sufficiently large, it may even pick up the noises, which generally have higher variation in frequencies. When the Tikhonov regularization is applied, the values of the weights are generally reduced as shown explicitly in these case studies. Therefore, the model will be less sensitive to noise.
- All these are done via the use of regularization parameters including the following:

  (1) Parameter λ or λ matrix of parameters to control the norms of all or partial or individual features.

(2) Shifting parameter $\hat{\mathbf{w}}_0$ that can also be specified for individual features, to allow the regularization loss to be more in alignment with the data loss.

- Regularization parameters can be set differently based on the types of the features.
- Other norms may be used for accounting the regularization loss.

14.3 A Case Study on Regularization Effects using MXNet

Based on the above detailed study using the simple examples, we shall have a good understanding of how a regularization may work for a machine learning model. We are ready for a study on its effects on a real machine learning model. We now revisit the handwritten digit classification problem on the MNIST dataset, which was studied earlier.

Note that our earlier models do not overfit because we used all 60,000 training examples, which is far more than the P^*-number and sometimes even the P-number in those models. For example, we used a one-layer net that has $P = 7,850$ parameters: $784 \times 10 = 7,840$ weights plus 10 biases, and $P^* = 785$ (which is the pseudo-dimension of the affine space for the single layer). Thus, $m \gg P^*$ and $m \gg P$.

Let us do a case study to examine what might happen if we use fewer training samples, say 2,000. For the one-layer net, we have $m > P^*$ but $m \ll P$. This study will show in detail the effects of the regularization technique on mitigating the over-fitting. It is done following the study and using the code at mxnet-the-straight-dope (https://github.com/zackchase/mxnet-the-straight-dope/blob/master/chapter02_supervisedlearning/regularization-scratch.ipynb), under the Apache-2.0 License.

```python
from __future__ import print_function
import mxnet as mx
import mxnet.ndarray as nd
from mxnet import autograd
import numpy as np
ctx = mx.cpu()
mx.random.seed(1)
# for plotting purposes
```

```
%matplotlib inline
import matplotlib
import matplotlib.pyplot as plt
```

14.3.1 *Load the MNIST dataset*

```
mnist = mx.test_utils.get_mnist()
num_examples = 2000
batch_size = 64
train_data = mx.gluon.data.DataLoader(mx.gluon.data.ArrayDataset(
    mnist["train_data"][:num_examples], mnist["train_label"]
    [:num_examples].astype(np.float32)), batch_size, shuffle=True)

test_data = mx.gluon.data.DataLoader(mx.gluon.data.ArrayDataset(\
    mnist["test_data"][:num_examples], mnist["test_label"]
    [:num_examples].astype(np.float32)), batch_size, shuffle=False)
```

14.3.2 *Define a neural network model*

We use a simple linear model with the softmax as activation as the prediction function. We set up the following neural network model:

```
W = nd.random_normal(shape=(784,10))       #Allocate model parameters
b = nd.random_normal(shape=10)
params = [W, b]

for param in params:
    param.attach_grad()                      # request for gradient

def net(X):
    y_linear = nd.dot(X,    W) + b           # Define the affine mapping
    yhat = nd.softmax(y_linear, axis=1)
    return yhat                              # return the prediction function
```

14.3.3 *Define loss function and optimizer*

We use the cross entropy, which we have discussed in detail earlier, as the loss function.

```python
def cross_entropy(yhat, y):
    return - nd.sum(y * nd.log(yhat), axis=0, exclude=True)


def SGD(params, lr):
    for param in params:
        param[:] = param - lr * param.grad
```

14.3.4 *Define a function to evaluate the accuracy*

We use the following function to calculate the average loss function as a measure of the accuracy of the model during training:

```python
def evaluate_accuracy(data_iterator, net):
    numerator = 0.
    denominator = 0.
    loss_avg = 0.
    for i, (data, label) in enumerate(data_iterator):
        data = data.as_in_context(ctx).reshape((-1,784))
        label = label.as_in_context(ctx)
        label_one_hot = nd.one_hot(label, 10)
        output = net(data)
        loss = cross_entropy(output, label_one_hot)
        predictions = nd.argmax(output, axis=1)
        numerator += nd.sum(predictions == label)
        denominator += data.shape[0]
        loss_avg=loss_avg*i/(i+1)+nd.mean(loss).asscalar()/(i+1)
    return (numerator / denominator).asscalar(), loss_avg
```

14.3.5 *Define a utility function plotting convergence curve*

The following function is used to plot out the change of the loss functions against the iterations during the minimization process:

```python
def plot_learningcurves(loss_tr,loss_ts, acc_tr,acc_ts):
    xs = list(range(len(loss_tr)))
    f = plt.figure(figsize=(12,6))
    fg1 = f.add_subplot(121)
    fg2 = f.add_subplot(122)
```

```python
fg1.set_xlabel('epoch',fontsize=14)
fg1.set_title('Comparing loss functions')
fg1.semilogy(xs, loss_tr)
fg1.semilogy(xs, loss_ts)
fg1.grid(True,which="both")
fg1.legend(['training loss', 'testing loss'],fontsize=14)

fg2.set_title('Comparing accuracy')
fg1.set_xlabel('epoch',fontsize=14)
fg2.plot(xs, acc_tr)
fg2.plot(xs, acc_ts)
fg2.grid(True,which="both")
fg2.legend(['training accuracy', 'testing accuracy'],
           fontsize=14)
```

14.3.6 *Train the neural network model*

We now train the neural network model to its fullest learning ability.

```python
epochs = 1000
moving_loss = 0.
niter=0
loss_seq_train = []
loss_seq_test = []
acc_seq_train = []
acc_seq_test = []

for e in range(epochs):
    for i, (data, label) in enumerate(train_data):
        data = data.as_in_context(ctx).reshape((-1,784))
        label = label.as_in_context(ctx)
        label_one_hot = nd.one_hot(label, 10)
        with autograd.record():
            output = net(data)
            loss = cross_entropy(output, label_one_hot)
        loss.backward()
        SGD(params, .001)
        # Keep a moving average of the losses
        niter +=1
        moving_loss=.99*moving_loss+.01*nd.mean(loss).asscalar()
        est_loss = moving_loss/(1-0.99**niter)
```

```python
test_accuracy, test_loss = evaluate_accuracy(test_data, net)
train_accuracy, train_loss=evaluate_accuracy(train_data, net)
# save them for later
loss_seq_train.append(train_loss)
loss_seq_test.append(test_loss)
acc_seq_train.append(train_accuracy)
acc_seq_test.append(test_accuracy)

if e % 300 == 299:
    print("Epoch %s. Train Loss:%.2e, Test Loss:%.2e,
            Train_acc:%.2e, Test_acc:%.2e" %
        (e+1,train_loss, test_loss,train_accuracy,
            test_accuracy))

# Plotting the learning curves
plot_learningcurves(loss_seq_train,loss_seq_test, acc_seq_train,
                    acc_seq_test)
```

```
Epoch 300. Train Loss:1.61e-01, Test Loss:1.16e+00,
    Train_acc:9.64e-01, Test_acc:7.75e-01
Epoch 600. Train Loss:6.72e-02, Test Loss:1.15e+00,
    Train_acc:9.90e-01, Test_acc:7.83e-01
Epoch 900. Train Loss:3.73e-02, Test Loss:1.16e+00,
    Train_acc:9.98e-01, Test_acc:7.85e-01
```

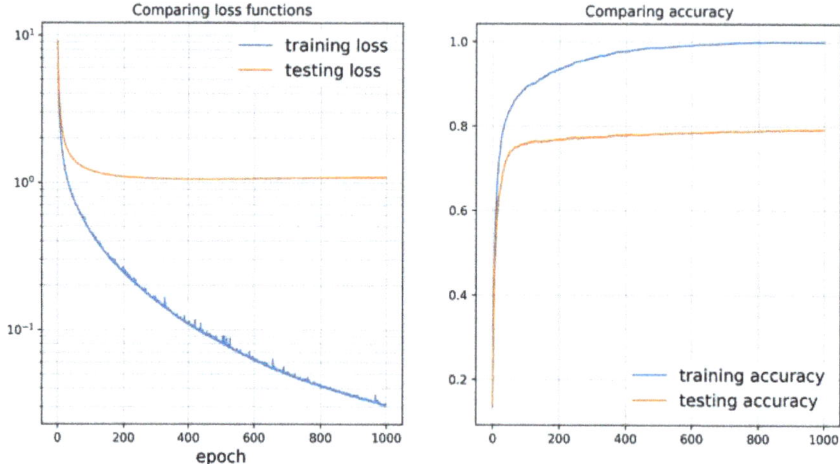

Figure 14.19:   A case of over-fitting when the one-layer net is used for a reduced dataset of MNIST that has only 2,000 samples.

14.3.7 *Evaluation of the trained model: A typical case of overfitting*

In the above example, it is seen that at the 1,000th epoch, the MLP model achieves 100% accuracy on the training data (the loss function is still quite far from zero, partially because $m > P^*$). However, it classifies only $\sim$79% of the test data accurately. This is a typical case of overfitting. Clearly, such a "well" trained model is not possible to perform well on the test dataset or dataset in the real world the model did not seen during the training.

If the sample is reduced to 1,000 with all other settings unchanged, this MLP model would achieves 100% accuracy on the training data at the 700th epoch, but it classifies only $\sim$75% of the test data accurately.

14.3.8 *Application of L2 regularization*

We now apply the L2 regularization by just adding in a penalized L2 norm of the parameters to the original loss function. We use the following function to do so:

```python
def l2_penalty(params):
    penalty = nd.zeros(shape=1)
    for param in params:
        penalty = penalty + nd.sum(param ** 2)
    return penalty
```

14.3.9 *Re-initializing the parameters*

We re-initialize the parameters randomly to erase these in the trained model.

```python
for param in params:
    param[:] = nd.random_normal(shape=param.shape)
```

14.3.10 *Training the L2-regularized neural network model*

```python
epochs = 1000
moving_loss = 0.
l2_lambda = 0.1 #0.3                      # regularization parameter
niter=0
```

```python
loss_seq_train = []
loss_seq_test = []
acc_seq_train = []
acc_seq_test = []

for e in range(epochs):
    for i, (data, label) in enumerate(train_data):
        data = data.as_in_context(ctx).reshape((-1,784))
        label = label.as_in_context(ctx)
        label_one_hot = nd.one_hot(label, 10)
        with autograd.record():
            output = net(data)
            loss = nd.sum(cross_entropy(output, label_one_hot))+\
            l2_lambda*l2_penalty(params) # regularization
                                         # loss added

        loss.backward()
        SGD(params, .001)

        #  Keep a moving average of the losses
        niter +=1
        moving_loss=.99*moving_loss+.01*nd.mean(loss).asscalar()
        est_loss = moving_loss/(1-0.99**niter)

    test_accuracy, test_loss = evaluate_accuracy(test_data, net)
    train_accuracy,train_loss= evaluate_accuracy(train_data, net)

    # save them for later
    loss_seq_train.append(train_loss)
    loss_seq_test.append(test_loss)
    acc_seq_train.append(train_accuracy)
    acc_seq_test.append(test_accuracy)
                if e % 300 == 299:
        print("Epoch %s. Train Loss:%.2e, Test Loss:%.2e,
                Train_acc:%.2e, Test_acc:%.2e" %
        (e+1,train_loss,test_loss,train_accuracy, test_accuracy))

# Plotting the learning curves
plot_learningcurves(loss_seq_train,loss_seq_test,acc_ seq_train,
                    acc_seq_test)
print('Regularization parameter=',l2_lambda)
```

```
Epoch 300. Train Loss:1.93e-01, Test Loss:5.19e-01,
    Train_acc:9.65e-01, Test_acc:8.38e-01
Epoch 600. Train Loss:1.91e-01, Test Loss:5.03e-01,
    Train_acc:9.67e-01, Test_acc:8.45e-01
```

```
Epoch 900. Train Loss:1.91e-01, Test Loss:5.03e-01,
    Train_acc:9.67e-01, Test_acc:8.46e-01
Regularization parameter= 0.1
```

14.3.11 *Effect of the L2 regularization*

When we use 2,000 training samples, addition of the L_2 regularization resulted in the following effects, compared to the unregulated overfitted case:

- When the regularization parameter is set at 0.1 with all other settings unchanged, at the 1,000th iteration, the accuracy of our MLP model on the test dataset increased from 78.6% to 84.5%, a 5.7% increase. The accuracy on the training dataset is reduced to 94.7% percent from 100%. The regularized model is more robust and shall generalize better for unseen data.
- When the regularization parameter is set at 0.3, the accuracy on the test dataset increased from 78.6% to 84.4%, a 5.8% increase. The accuracy on the training dataset is reduced to 93.6% percent from 100%. This regularized model is about unchanged. This suggests that a regularization parameter in between 0.1 and 0.3 may be a proper choice for this problem.

When only 1,000 training samples are used in the training (with all the other settings unchanged in the above code), the findings are as follows, compared to the corresponding unregulated overfitted case:

- For the regularization parameter set at 0.1, the accuracy of our MLP model on the test dataset increased from 75% to 83.3%, an 8.3% increase.

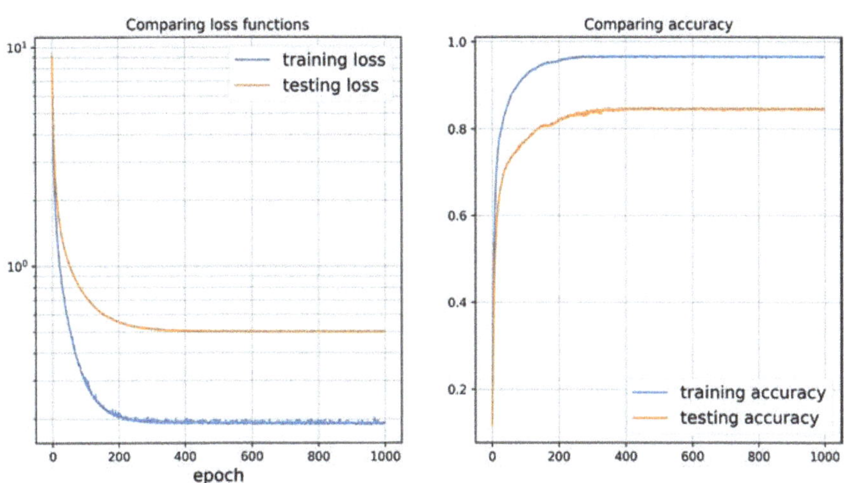

Figure 14.20: The L2 regularization has reduced the gap between the training and testing accuracy. One-layer net using the reduced dataset of MNIST that has only 2,000 samples.

The accuracy on the training dataset is reduced to 99.1% percent from 100%. The regularized model is more robust and shall generalize better for unseen data.

- When the regularization parameter is set at 0.3, the accuracy on the test dataset increased from 75% to 84.9%, a 9.9% increase. The accuracy on the training dataset is reduced to 96.7% percent from 100%. This regularized model is even more robust for unseen data compared to the case of using a regularization parameter of 0.1. This may suggest that when the number of samples becomes small, the regularization parameter should be increased accordingly.

Ideally, we would want a model having the same level of accuracy for both the training and test datasets. Tuning the regularization parameter can help to achieve this goal, but it can often be a challenging task. Readers may give it a try using the above code.

We finally note that the choice of the regularization parameter is an issue. Experiences may help, or trial and error may be needed to train a robust model. Below is another case study.

14.4 A Case Study on Regularization Parameters Using Sklearn

We now introduce another case study done by the scikit-learn team [2] for classification to investigate the influence of the regularization parameters on the predicted decision boundary. We have made minor changes to the original code to fix issues possibly caused by module version differences. We have also done some tuning on the parameters. This study is on the effects of the regularization parameter "alpha" (equivalent to the lambda in our formulation). This study uses synthetic datasets for classification, and the plots will show different decision boundaries produced when using different alpha values.

```python
%matplotlib inline
print(__doc__)
# Author: Issam H. Laradji, License: BSD 3 clause
import numpy as np
from matplotlib import pyplot as plt
from matplotlib.colors import ListedColormap
from sklearn.model_selection import train_test_split
from sklearn.preprocessing import StandardScaler
from sklearn.datasets import make_moons,make_circles,
    make_classification
from sklearn.neural_network import MLPClassifier
```

```python
h = .02  # step size in the mesh
alphas = np.logspace(-5, 3, 5)
names = ['alpha ' + str(i) for i in alphas]

classifiers = []
for i in alphas:
    classifiers.append(MLPClassifier(solver='lbfgs', alpha=i,
      max_iter=1500,random_state=1, hidden_layer_sizes=[100, 100]))

X, y = make_classification(n_features=2, n_redundant=0,
        n_informative=2, random_state=0, n_clusters_per_class=1)
rng = np.random.RandomState(2)
X  += 2 * rng.uniform(size=X.shape)
linearly_separable = (X, y)

datasets = [make_moons(noise=0.2, random_state=0),
            make_circles(noise=0.1, factor=0.5, random_state=1),
            linearly_separable]

figure = plt.figure(figsize=(17, 9))
i = 1
# iterate over datasets
for X, y in datasets:
    # preprocess dataset, split into training and test part
    X = StandardScaler().fit_transform(X)
    X_train,X_test,y_train,y_test=train_test_split(X,y,
            test_size=.4)

    x_min, x_max = X[:, 0].min() - .5, X[:, 0].max() + .5
    y_min, y_max = X[:, 1].min() - .5, X[:, 1].max() + .5
    xx, yy = np.meshgrid(np.arange(x_min, x_max, h),
                         np.arange(y_min, y_max, h))
    # just plot the dataset first
    cm = plt.cm.RdBu
    cm_bright = ListedColormap(['#FF0000', '#0000FF'])
    ax = plt.subplot(len(datasets), len(classifiers) + 1, i)
    # Plot the training points
    ax.scatter(X_train[:,0],X_train[:, 1], c=y_train )
    # and testing points
    ax.scatter(X_test[:,0],X_test[:,1], c=y_test, alpha=.4)
    ax.set_xlim(xx.min(), xx.max())
    ax.set_ylim(yy.min(), yy.max())
    ax.set_xticks(())
    ax.set_yticks(())
    i += 1
```

```python
    # iterate over classifiers
    for name, clf in zip(names, classifiers):
        ax=plt.subplot(len(datasets),len(classifiers)+1,i)
        clf.fit(X_train, y_train)
        score = clf.score(X_test, y_test)
        # Plot the decision boundary. Assign a color to each
        # point in the mesh [x_min, x_max]x[y_min, y_max].
        if hasattr(clf, "decision_function"):
            Z = clf.decision_function(np.c_[xx.ravel(),
                yy.ravel()])
        else:
            Z = clf.predict_proba(np.c_[xx.ravel(),
                yy.ravel()])[:,1]

        # Put the result into a color plot
        Z = Z.reshape(xx.shape)
        ax.contourf(xx, yy, Z, cmap=cm, alpha=.8)

        # Plot also the training points
        ax.scatter(X_train[:,0],X_train[:,1], c=y_train,
          cmap=cm_bright,edgecolors='black')
        # and testing points

        ax.scatter(X_test[:,0], X_test[:,1], c=y_test,
          cmap=cm_bright,alpha=0.4, edgecolors='black')

        ax.set_xlim(xx.min(), xx.max())
        ax.set_ylim(yy.min(), yy.max())
        ax.set_xticks(())
        ax.set_yticks(())
        ax.set_title(name)
        ax.text(xx.max()-.3,yy.min()+.3,
            ('%.2f' % score).lstrip('0'), size=15,
                horizontalalignment='right')
        i += 1

figure.subplots_adjust(left=.02, right=.98)
plt.show();
```

```
Automatically created module for IPython interactive environment
```

Figure 14.21 shows the effects of the regularization parameters used.

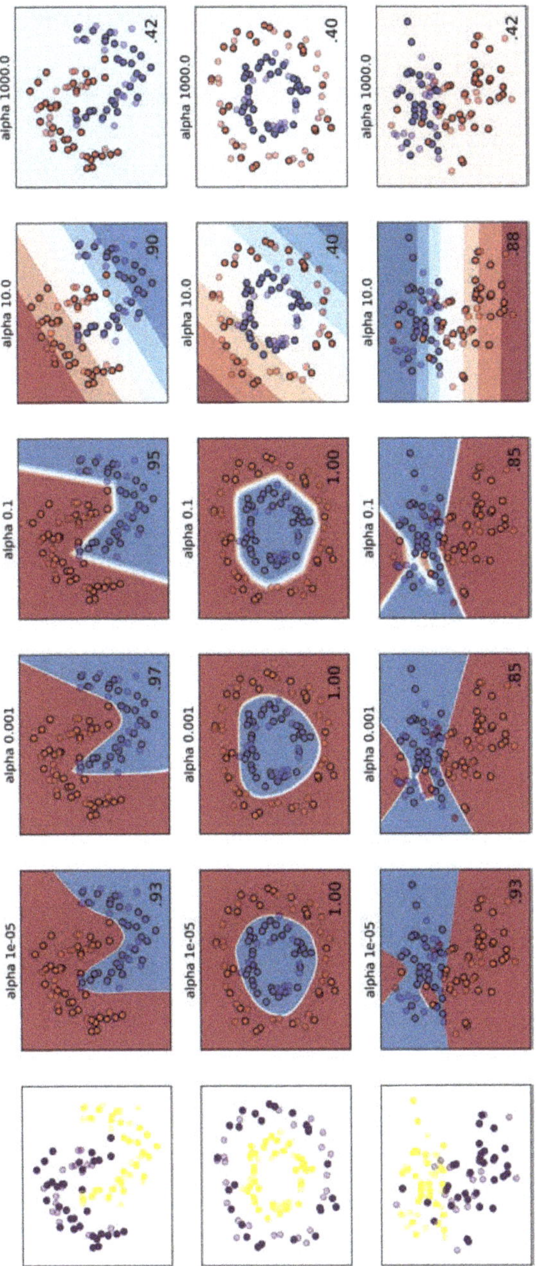

Figure 14.21: Effects of regularization parameters used in an MLPclassifier, based on a study done by Sklearn team.

It is found that a larger alpha (that suppresses large weights) results in less sharper decision boundaries, which helps to avoid overfitting. On the other hand, a smaller alpha leaves larger room for the weights, resulting in sharper decision boundaries, which helps to mitigate underfitting. This study shows again that it is important to choose a proper regularization parameter, which can often be a challenge.

References

[1] G.R. Liu and X. Han, *Computational Inverse Techniques in Nondestructive Evaluation*, Taylor and Francis Group, New York, 2003.

[2] P. Fabian, V. Gae, G. Alexandre *et al.*, Scikit-learn: Machine learning in Python, *Journal of Machine Learning Research*, **12**(85), 2825–2830, 2011. http://jmlr.org/papers/v12/pedregosa11a.html.

Chapter 15

Convolutional Neural Network (CNN) for Classification and Object Detection

Convolutional neural network (CNN) or ConvNet [1–6] is one of the most powerful tools in machine learning, especially for processing multi-dimensional images and image-based classifications. It is currently widely used, and effective modules are made available at many packages/libraries, such as Scikit learn, PyTouch, TensorFlow, and Keras. The CNN uses quite a number of special techniques, which have very much different net configurations, compared to the neural networks discussed in the previous chapters. CNNs still use affine transformations, but these are specially designed with spatial filters to capture the spatial features of images. These details are often hidden in the black boxes of the modules available at various libraries. This chapter offers a concise description of the key ideas and techniques used in CNN and then a demonstration of CNN. More detailed information can be found in the rich open literature and the original papers given for each CNN network. An excellent online course by Andrew Ng is also available.

Our discussion starts from a brief description of the general structure of CNN, some landmark CNN net, a demonstration of image classification, and finally some examples of object detection using CNN.

15.1 Filter and Convolution

As discussed in Chapter 5, the most fundamental hypothesis made in a machine learning model is the affine transformation. For different types of problems, one naturally needs to design proper affine transformation units. CNN works particularly well for image processing related problems, because the key techniques used are rooted in computer vision-related techniques. Filtering in a convolutional manner is one of those. Consider an idealized "image" with 6 × 6 pixels, as shown in Fig. 15.1.

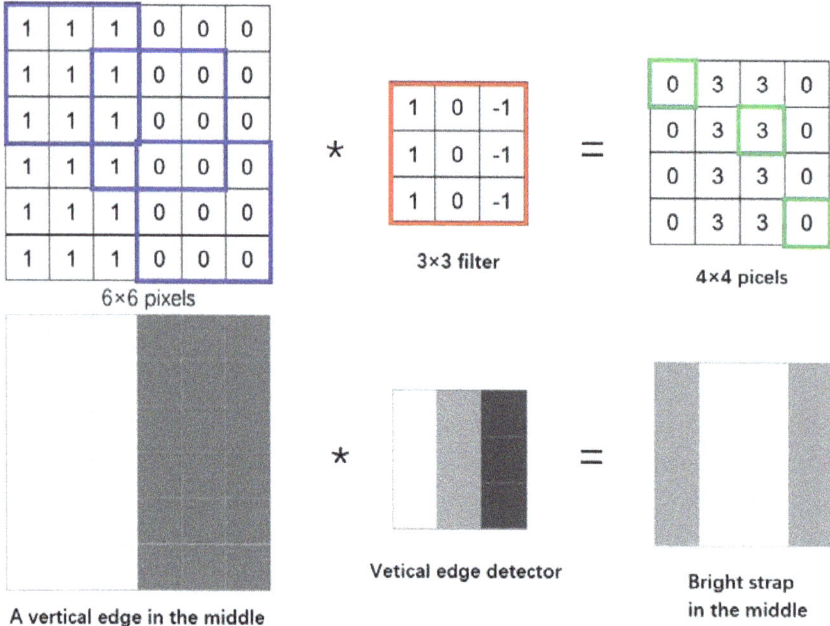

Figure 15.1: A 3 × 3 filter (in the middle of the figure) acting like an edge detector that captures the vertical edge line in the middle of the 6 × 6 pixel image as a 4 × 4 bright strap, when the filter slides over and within the 6 × 6 pixel image.

The **filter** (sometimes called kernel) in used in Fig. 15.1 is a 3 × 3 2D matrix in the red frame in the middle of the figure. It has a 1-vector on the left, a 0-vector in the middle, and a -1-vector on the right. The **convolution** operator is denoted by "*" that performs the following operation with the elements of the 2D sub-matrix in the blue frame in the 6 × 6 pixel image, with the red frame sliding pixel by pixel over and within the 6 × 6 image. In many machine learning modules, it is termed conv2D.

$$\sum_{i=1}^{3}\sum_{j=1}^{3} x_{ij} \times w_{ij} = value\ in\ a\ green\ box$$ corresponding to the filter center

$$(15.1)$$

The above computation is a "kind" of "dot-product" of the blue matrix and the red matrix (of the same shape): summation of all the element-wise products in these two matrices. Such a sliding (convolution) "2D-matrix-dot-product" produces a 4 × 4 pixel image. It captures the vertical edge line in the middle of the 6 × 6 pixel image as a 4 × 4 image with a bright strap in the middle. Therefore, it acts like a vertical edge detector. We can expect the following:

- If we rotate the red filter matrix, we shall have a horizontal edge detector.
- If we rotate the red filter matrix in an arbitrary angle, we shall have an inclined edge detector.
- One can have many other types of filters, such as the "Sobel" filter and "Scharr" filter.

Essentially, the filter is a matrix with desirable values in its entry. Changing these values changes the functionality of the filter. In a CNN, the **key** here is that we are not using this kind of manually designed filter. Instead, we will make the network learn these values in the filter by feeding it with a large number of images, as will be discussed in the next section. Here, let us also note the following:

- In the above case, the filter slides per-pixel, or the "stride" is 1. One may have multiple strides, such as two strides per sliding.
- The filter size can also change, and 5×5 (but usually an odd number, in order to always have a central pixel) is also an often used filter size.
- The above convolution results in a reduction in size in the filtered image. To avoid this, one may use a technique call "padding": extending the original 6×6 pixel image by filling in zeros to extend pixels on its boundaries, and make the original image bigger, so that the filtered image can have the same size.

Figure 15.2 is a picture made (https://github.com/vdumoulin/conv_arithmetic) by Dumoulin and Visin [7] under the MIT License.

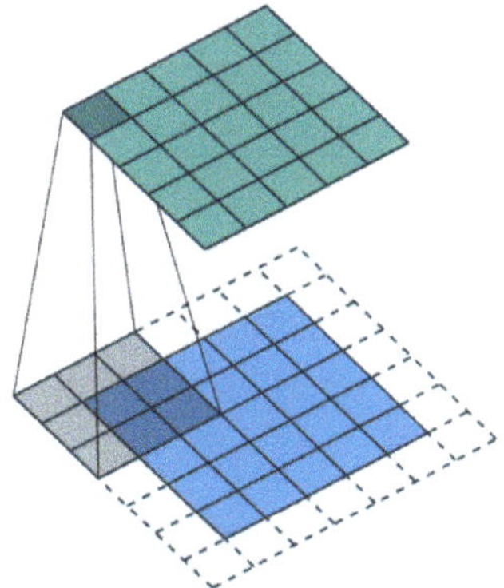

Figure 15.2: A 3×3 filter (gray) sliding over a 5×5 pixel image (blue) with stride=1 and padding=1 (padding part is not colored). It generates a cyan image of the same (5×5) size as the blue image.

The settings for different strides and paddings are shown in Fig. 15.3.

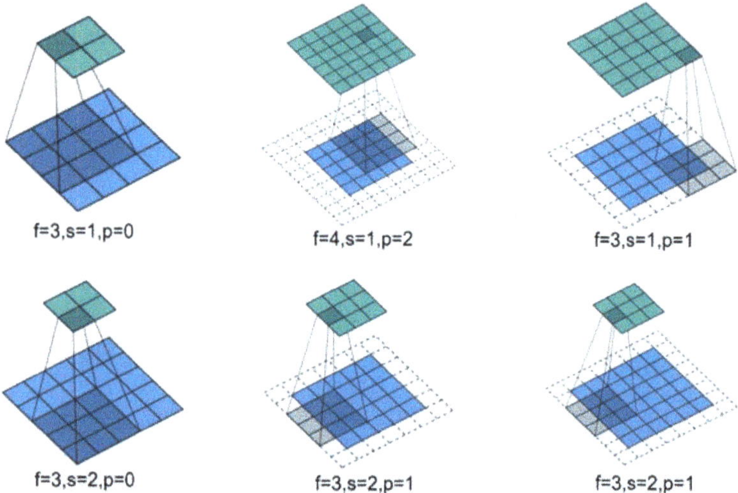

Figure 15.3: In the upper row, from left to right: f=3,s=1,p=0; f=4,s=1,p=2; f=3,s=1,p=1. In the bottom row, from left to right: f=3,s=2,p=0; f=3,s=2,p=1; f=3,s=2,p=1.

where f stands for filter, s for stride, and p for padding. Readers may take a look at cartoons and pictures for more cartoons to get a better understanding.

15.2 Affine Transformation Unit in CNNs

In a CNN, we do not use the handcrafted filters. Instead, we let elements in the filter matrix be trainable parameters (the **w** and **b**). This may be one of the most important tricks in CNN: we let the sample-based training eventually decide what kind of filters to use, in order to get the correct label from the training samples. This parametrization of the filter matrix creates a special ATU for CNNs. A CNN model for one channel of covn2d in a convolution layer is schematically illustrated in Fig. 15.4.

We mention the following key points for CNN models:

- The same set of weights and bias (total of 10 learning parameters in this case) is used for filtering the entire image, regardless of the size of the image. This is known as parameter sharing. Therefore, the training parameters in a CNN are usually much smaller compared to the densely

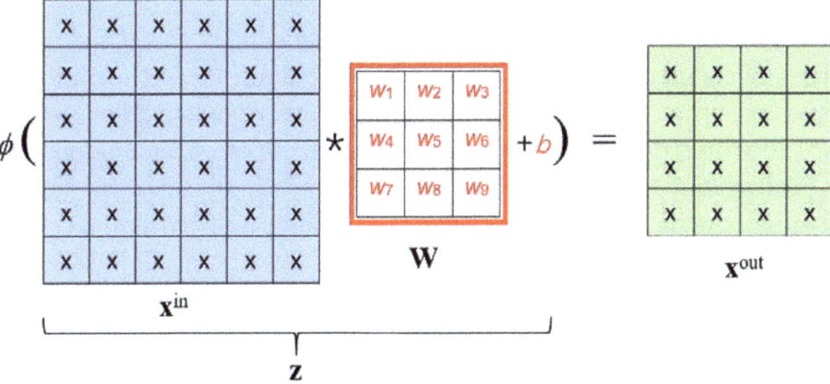

Figure 15.4:   Schematic of a typical affine transformation unit (ATU) wrapped with an activation function. Learning parameters, weights w_i, and bias b, in a single channel of a conv2D using a 3×3 filter in one layer of CNN. ϕ stands for an activation function (usually the Relu). For a 3×3 filter, we have a total of 9 weights, and one bias, resulting in a hypothesis space $\mathbb{W}^{10}$ for the ATU. For this 6×6 pixel image with 1 stride and no padding, the output is a 4×4 image. This output image may be subjected to a "pooling" and then to another layer of convolution.

connected neural networks (such as the standard MLP). This leads to a drastic reduction of learning parameters. Based on the Neurons-Samples Theory given in Section 13.2.2, we know the number of the learning parameters in an MLP can be huge, because P is usually much larger than P^*. Hence, there is plenty room for reduction.

- A CNN is less prone to overfitting because of the reduction in learning parameters.

- The parameter sharing works particularity well for image processing, because the same filter is capable of capturing the features (such as edges) in different parts of the same image.

- The parameter sharing leads to a sparse connection: each set of the learning parameters connects only to very small part of the input image at a time. This is also very much different from the densely connected neural networks.

- One often uses multiple channels (it is also termed depths in the literature) in one convolution layer. The number of learning parameters will then increase proportionally with the increasing channel number. This enables the training of different kinds of filters (one channel is a different filter with its own $\mathbf{w}$) in a CNN convolution layer, to capture different features in the image.

15.3 Pooling

Another often used technique in a CNN is pooling. It uses a similar sheet like the filter (but no parameters involved), called pooling filter, to cover a part of the filtered image. There are two major types of pooling operations: max pooling and average pooling. Max pooling simply takes the maximum pixel value among all the pixels that the pooling filter covers, as shown in Fig. 15.5.

Average pooling is very similar to max pooling, but it takes the average of the covered pixels, instead of the maximum, as shown in Fig. 15.6.

For pooling operations, we note the following:

- There is no training parameter introduced in the pooling operation. Hence, it may be treated as a part of one CNN layer.
- It seems that max pooling is capable of getting out the outstanding features from the image, and hence it is used more often than average pooling.

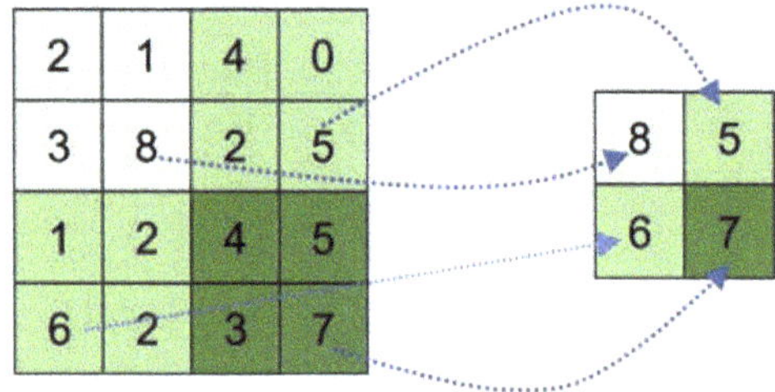

Figure 15.5:   Max pooling in a CNN: a 2 × 2 pooling filter covers 2 × 2 pixels in a filtered 4 × 4 image. It takes the maximum pixel value from the 2 × 2 pixels of each of these four covers, and forms a 2 × 2 new image.

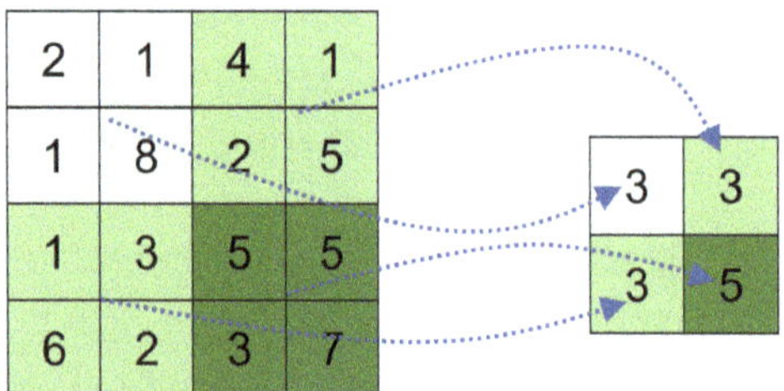

Figure 15.6:   Average pooling in a CNN: a 2 × 2 pooling filter covers 2 × 2 pixels in a filtered 4 × 4 image. It gets the average pixel value of these covered 2 × 2 pixels. This is done for each of these four covers, resulting in a 2 × 2 new image.

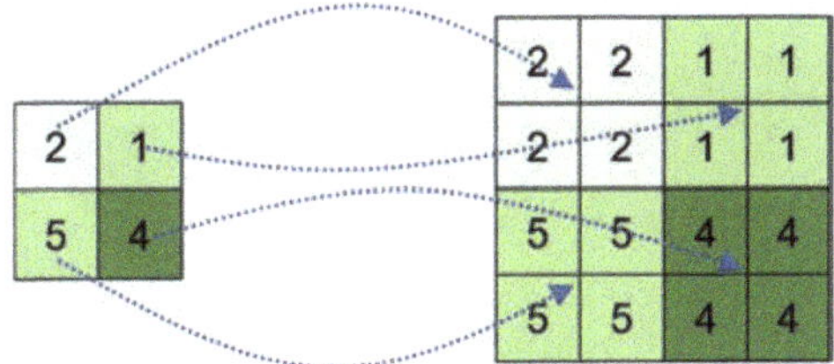

Figure 15.7: Up sampling in a CNN: an image with 2 × 2 pixels is expanded to a new one with 4 × 4 pixels. In this case, the value of a pixel in the original image is copied four times in the corresponding locations in the enlarged image.

- One may also take a different number of strides, when covering the image.
- One may also use a different size of covers.

15.4 Up Sampling

Another often used technique in a CNN is up sampling (or up pooling). It enlarges images by expanding one pixel to four with the same value, as shown in Fig. 15.7. This is used when there is a need to enlarge an image such as in the decoder part of an Autoencoders (that will be discussed in Chapter 17).

Note that there are quite a number of other similar operations in image processing. With the basic ones introduced above, we are now ready to configure a CNN network.

15.5 Configuration of a Typical CNN

The typical configuration of a CNN is shown in Fig. 15.8. An image in black-white or in RGB is first fed to a set of filters (F) consisting of a number (6–64) of filter channels, each having its own set of weights and a bias. The filter size may be 3 × 3, 5 × 5 or another odd number in one direction. The filtered image may be subjected to a possible pooling (P) operation that is usually of size 2 × 2. This reduces (in half) both the height and width, but the number of the channels is kept the same. The pooling performs fixed operations: either max pooling or average pooling. It does not introduce any additional training parameters. Another set of filters may be applied, which further increases the number of filter channels. If another

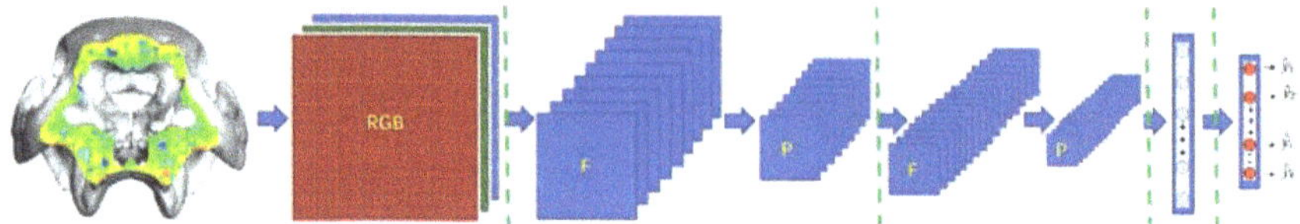

Figure 15.8: Configuration of a CNN: an RGB image is first fed to a set of filters (F) and is then subjected to a possible pooling (P) operation. Another set of filters may be applied, followed by another possible pooling. An F-P pair may consist of a CNN layer. The output of the final CNN layer may be fed to few normal dense layers producing a prediction.

pooling is applied, it reduces the height and width again, but keeps the number of channels unchanged. Usually, an F-P pair may consist of a CNN layer, and we can have quite a large number of CNN layers. The output of the final CNN layer may (or may not) be fed to few normal dense layers, and then produces a prediction. The following operation is essentially the same as those in an MLP.

The network in Fig. 15.8 has 1 input layer, 2 CONV layers, 1 hidden dense layer, and 1 output dense layer. In practice, many CNNs have a large number of CONV layers.

15.6 Some Landmark CNNs

With the building blocks we have discussed so far, one can build a really complex neural network for very complicated tasks of computer vision and image-based object detection. The development in this area is very fast and many useful special networks have already been proposed. This section discusses briefly some of the widely used landmark CNN networks. These networks were built upon the basic configurations of dense layers, CONV layers, and their variations and combinations. Many new special techniques and tricks have been invented to improve the learning capacity and efficiency. In fact, there is practically no limit to the types of neural networks that we can build, but some work well and some may not for some problems. Having an overall knowledge of these successful landmark networks can be very useful before one starts to build a new network. The source codes of many of these networks are made openly available at GitHub, which can be effectively made use of based on the specified license there.

We will not be able to cover all of the good landmark CNN networks, but readers can find more in the open sources with the leads given in the following discussions, often by simply googling with a keyword. The online courses by Andrew Ng also provide very clear discussions on this topic. The intention of this section is to just provide an abstract discussion. To begin with, we take a look at the LeNet-5.

15.6.1 *LeNet-5*

This famous CNN was proposed in 1998 by LeCun *et al.* [8]. The basic (not exactly the same) structure is given in Fig. 15.9. It uses a black-white image with a size of $(32 \times 32 \times 1)$ as the input, the sigmoid activation function for the hidden layers, and the softmax at the output.

The detailed numbers related to the configuration of the LeNet-5 network are listed in Fig. 15.10.

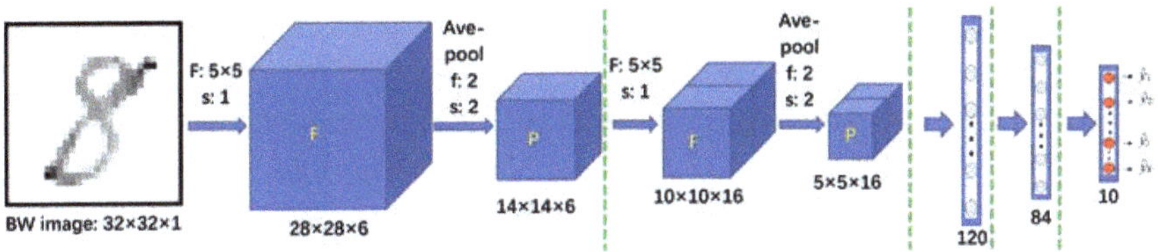

Figure 15.9:   LeNet-5 for handwritten digit recognition using black-white images. It has 1 input layer, 2 CONV layers, 2 hidden dense layers, and 1 output dense layer.

	Model settings	Image data shape	Data size	Learning parameters		Total learning parameters
	Input layer	(32,32,1)	3072	0	0	
Layer 1	CONV-1 (f=5, s=1)	(28,28,6)	4704	1×5×5×6+6=	156	
Layer 2	Ave-pool-1 (f=2, s=2)	(14,14,6)	1176	0	0	
Layer 3	CONV-2 (f=5, s=1)	(10,10,16)	1600	6×5×5×16+16=	2416	
Layer 4	Ave-pool-2 (f=2, s=2)	(5,5,16)	400	0	0	
Layer 5	Dense Layer 1	(120,1)	120	400×120+120=	48120	
Layer 6	Dense Layer 2	(84,1)	84	120×84+84=	10164	
	Output	(10,1)	10	84×10+10=	850	**61706**

Figure 15.10:   Data size and learning parameters for LeNet-5. It has a total of 61,706 training parameters. The CONV layers have very few training parameters, and most of the learning parameters are due to the dense layers.

Figure 15.10 shows clearly how the number of data flowing forward across the network and the number of learning parameters in each layer and in total are calculated. Similar calculations can be used to examine other networks.

15.6.2 *AlexNet*

Another famous landmark CNN network was proposed in 2012 by Alex Krizhevsky, Ilya Sutskever, and Geoffrey E. Hinton. This network won the 2012 ImageNet LSVRC-2012 competition. Its configuration is shown in Fig. 15.11. The details can be found in the original paper [9]. It is a widely used paper and can be easily found online. It has some similarities with LeNet-5, but with 3 more CONV layers, and one more dense layer. These 3 dense layers have much more neurons. It was built for 1000-classification on the ImageNet. The AlexNet is much large in scale. It also uses a number of new techniques, including the Relu activation function to deal with the vanishing gradient problem and dropout techniques for the first 2 fully connected dense layers to mitigate over-fitting.

Reader may read the original paper to find more details. Good analysis of the AlexNet is also given by Andrew Ng's online lectures and Hao Gao's article.

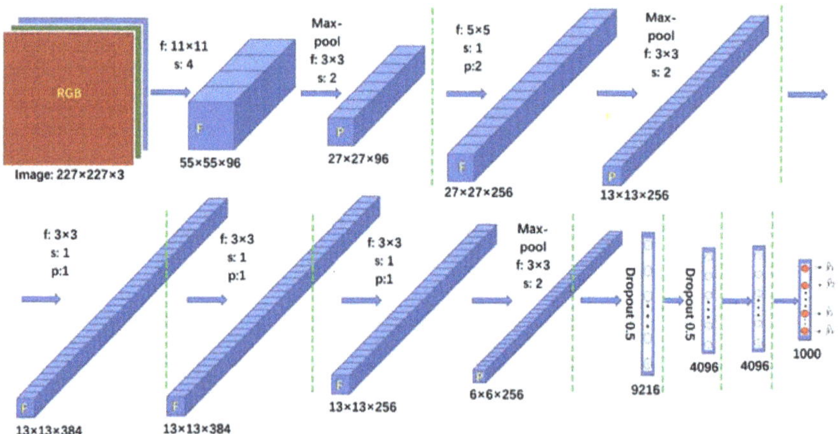

Figure 15.11: AlexNet: It has 1 input layer, 5 CONV layers, 3 hidden dense layers, and 1 output dense layer. The total learning parameters are about 62.3 million, about 6% of which are from the CONV layers, and 94% from the fully connected dense layers.

15.6.3 *VGG-16*

Another popular legend CNN network is VGG-16, which has a number of improvements upon the AlexNet. It increases the layers from 8 to 16, with nicely staged convolution and max pooling. Its configuration has the following appealing uniformity:

- All the CONV layers are unified with the same 3×3 filter size, stride 1, and 1 padding, followed by a max pooling.
- All the max pooling is with the same 2×2 size and stride 2.
- The height and width of the net block are roughly halved from one CONV layer to the next.
- The number of filter channels always doubles from one CONV layer to the next.

VGG-16 was proposed by K. Simonyan and A. Zisserman in their paper [10]. VGG-16 was one of best models submitted to ILSVRC-2014. It achieved 92.7% accuracy on ImageNet with over 14 million images of 1,000 classes. Interested readers may read the original paper and online articles, such as the one at Nerohive. An implementation of VGG-16 is available at the TensorFlow-vgg. It also has implementations at Keras and Pytorch.

15.6.4 *ResNet*

ResNet stands for residual neural network. It was proposed by He, Kaiming; Zhang, Xiangyu; Ren, Shaoqing; and Sun, Jian in 2015 [11]. The major difference for the ResNet from the nets discussed above, such as the VGG-16, is the use of **skip connection**: the activation of one layer (CONV or dense) can be connected to the next-next layer, by skipping one layer and then applying the activation (often the Relu). This well mitigates vanishing of gradients and enables the net going even deeper, and thus it made up to 152 layers. It has about 23 million learning parameters in total. The capability of going deep is of importance for many visual recognition tasks. The ResNet has obtained 28% relative improvement on the COCO object detection dataset. It is the foundation for the ILSVRC & COCO 2015 competitions, where the authors won the 1st place in the tasks of ImageNet detection, ImageNet localization, COCO detection, and COCO segmentation.

The skip connection is a useful technique and can be implemented with ease. For example, for a dense MLP, in the feed-forward process, the activated values at a ResNet become (see, Eq. (13.5) in Chapter 13 for comparison)

$$
\begin{aligned}
\mathbf{x}^{(0)} &= \mathbf{x} = [x_1, x_2, ..., x_p] && \text{feature at input} \\
\mathbf{x}^{(1)} &= \phi^{(1)}\big(\underbrace{\mathbf{x}^{(0)}\mathbf{W}^{(1)} + \mathbf{b}^{(1)}}_{\mathbf{z}^{(1)}}\big) && \text{1st hidden layer} \\
\mathbf{x}^{(2)} &= \phi^{(2)}\big(\underbrace{\mathbf{x}^{(1)}\mathbf{W}^{(2)} + \mathbf{b}^{(2)}}_{\mathbf{z}^{(2)}}\big) && \text{2nd hidden layer} \\
\mathbf{x}^{(3)} &= \phi^{(3)}\big(\underbrace{\mathbf{x}^{(2)}\mathbf{W}^{(3)} + \mathbf{b}^{(3)} + \mathbf{x}^{(0)}\mathbf{W}^{(1)}}_{\mathbf{z}^{(3)}}\big) && \text{3rd hidden layer} \\
\mathbf{x}^{(4)} &= \phi^{(4)}\big(\underbrace{\mathbf{x}^{(3)}\mathbf{W}^{(4)} + \mathbf{b}^{(4)} + \mathbf{x}^{(1)}\mathbf{W}^{(2)}}_{\mathbf{z}^{(4)}}\big) && \text{4th hidden layer} \\
&\ldots \\
\mathbf{x}^{(n)} &= \phi^{(n)}\big(\underbrace{\mathbf{x}^{(n-2)}\mathbf{W}^{(n-1)} + \mathbf{b}^{(n-1)} + \mathbf{x}^{(n-4)}\mathbf{W}^{(n-3)}}_{\mathbf{z}^{(n)}}\big) && n\text{th hidden layer} \\
\hat{\mathbf{y}} &= \mathbf{x}^{(N_L)} \\
&= \phi^{(N_L)}\big(\underbrace{\mathbf{x}^{(N_L-2)}\mathbf{W}^{(N_L-1)} + \mathbf{b}^{(N_L-1)} + \mathbf{x}^{(N_L-4)}\mathbf{W}^{(N_L-3)}}_{\mathbf{z}^{(N_L)}}\big) && \text{prediction at output}
\end{aligned}
$$

$$(15.1)$$

Here the number in the parentheses in the superscript stands for the layer number. The terms above the curly brackets are the affine transformation functions $\mathbf{z}^{(i)}$ ($i = 1, 2, \ldots, N_L - 1$), which can change from layer to layer and bring in information for the past layers, as new independent "features" for the next layer after fed to an activation function. The dimension of the new feature space changes accordingly. For layers that take inputs from the previous layers, the dimensionality adds up. This may be the reason for mitigating gradient vanishing issues.

Equation (15.1) assume that the skipping is applied to all the layers starting from the 3rd hidden layer. One may choose not to skip some layers. In that case, the term in blue in the corresponding layer should be removed. It is also assumed that the skips are only over one layer. When multiple-layer skipping is performed, Eq. (15.1) can be easily adjusted accordingly. Note that the activation function used in each layer can be in theory different, although we typically use Relu for all the layers in a ResNet. Also, the activation in any layer $\mathbf{z}_l$ can be replaced by that of a CONV layer. This similarly applies to a net with mixed dense and CONV layers.

A more detailed description of the ResNet can be found in the original paper and also an article at the website towards data science, where a detailed architecture of the ResNet is given, in comparison with the VGG-19 (a later version of VGG-16) and the so-called plain network (without skipping).

Readers may also take a look at a clean Keras implementation of residual network.

15.6.5 *Inception*

The Inception network is another milestone in CNN development. It was proposed in 2014 by Christian Szegedy and Wei Liu and seven other co-authors [12], where the detailed architecture is given. It has been improved over the years, and the current version is Inception v4 and the Inception-ResNet.

Inception set a new state of the art for classification and detection in the ImageNet Large-Scale Visual Recognition Challenge 2014 (ILSVRC14). It was also called GoogLeNet. The following key ideas are used in the Inception network compared to the networks discussed above:

- It uses the so-called 1×1 convolution across the channels. This allows a configuration of a densely connected 1D network across the channel within a CONV layer, termed as network-in-network. The 1×1 convolution was proposed by Min Lin, Qiang Chen, and Shuicheng Yan in 2014 [13].
- The use of network-in-network configuration enables the reduction in channel numbers within a CONV layer, which leads to drastic saving in computation.
- It constructs **Inception Module** that is packaged with multiple convolutional operations, including 1×1, 3×3, 5×5, and max pooling all in a CONV layer, which allows the net to learn which are the best operations and filter (or kernel) sizes to use in the CONV layer. This is made possible and efficient with the help of 1×1 convolutions.
- The Inception modules become new building blocks for constructing a deep Inception network.

Readers may find more details from the original papers and an introduction article at towards data science.

15.6.6 *YOLO: A CONV net for object detection*

The development of CNN is getting faster and faster, driven by the competitions in the related industry, such as self-driven cars. For many real applications, such as in self-driven cars, we must have a fast and reliable real-time object detection based on images. YOLO is one of the outstanding deepnets for such tasks. YOLO stands for "You Only Look Once" [14], and was proposed by Joseph Redmon, Santosh Divvala, Ross Girshick, and Ali

Farhadi. The current version is YOLO-v3. Here, we summarize a number of the key techniques that are used in the YOLO network:

- It applies a single CONV neural network to a full image given to perform the detection, which eliminates the need for scanning over the image and processes the sub-image frame by frame. This allows very fast predictions.
- Different types of predictions needed for the objects, including the types of the objects (classes), locations of the objects, and (box) sizes of the objects, are all labeled, so that the network can be trained for fast detections at one go (You Only Look Once).
- It divides the given image into regions and predicts the probabilities of the presence of classes and the bounding boxes for each region.

There are many other techniques and tricks developed and implemented in YOLO. Interested readers may read the original paper and online articles, such as the one at towards data science. One may also visit the YOLO project website, where one finds a benchmark study on the performance of object detection on the COCO dataset. One may also follow up with the latest development there.

This course has prepared readers with quite a large amount of fundamentals on machine learning. We have so many building blocks now, and we have seen some of the outstanding implementations. It is the time to try to put these building blocks together, to solve some problems at hand. When the network becomes deep, there are many different ways to add in different types of connections, and to put things together for complicated tasks. We shall also continue the study and invent new techniques and tricks. It may also be productive to follow up with current work of the front-runners in this very active area of development. There are many novel techniques and tricks developed every day, and some of them can be useful not only for projects that you may working on but also for developing new ideas if one is interested in research in the related areas. The author and collaborators have also conducted some study in the related area [6].

Finally, let us look at a CNN network proved by the TensorFlow.

15.7 An Example of Convolutional Neural Network

This tutorial demonstrates training a simple CNN to classify CIFAR images. Because this tutorial uses the Keras Sequential API (Application Programming Interface), creating and training a CNN model will take just a few lines of code. The material is Licensed under the Apache License, Version 2.0.

15.7.1 *Import TensorFlow*

```python
import tensorflow as tf
from tensorflow.keras import datasets, layers, models
import matplotlib.pyplot as plt
```

15.7.2 *Download and preparation of a CIFAR10 dataset*

The CIFAR10 dataset contains 60,000 color images in 10 classes, with 6,000 images in each class. The dataset is divided into 50,000 training images and 10,000 testing images. The classes are mutually exclusive and there is no overlap between them.

```python
(train_images, train_labels), (test_images, test_labels) =\
                              datasets.cifar10.load_data()
# Normalize pixel values to be between 0 and 1
train_images,test_images=train_images/255.,test_images/255.
```

15.7.3 *Verification of the data*

To verify the dataset, let us plot the first 25 images from the training set and display the class name below each image.

```python
class_names = ['airplane', 'automobile', 'bird', 'cat', 'deer',
               'dog', 'frog', 'horse', 'ship', 'truck']

plt.figure(figsize=(10,10))

for i in range(36):
    plt.subplot(6,6,i+1)
    plt.xticks([])
    plt.yticks([])
    plt.grid(False)
    plt.imshow(train_images[i], cmap=plt.cm.binary)
    # The CIFAR labels happen to be arrays,
```

```python
    # which is why you need the extra index
    plt.xlabel(class_names[train_labels[i][0]])

plt.show()
```

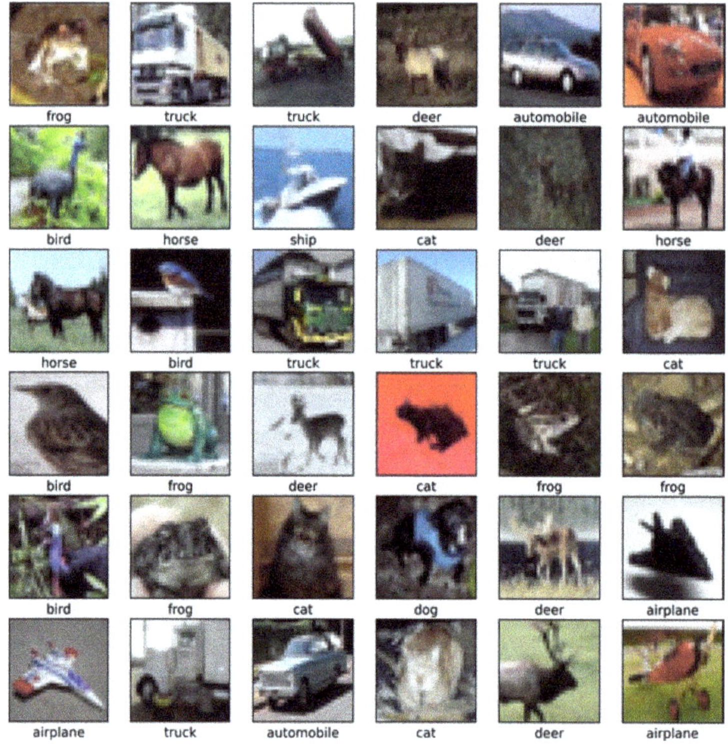

Figure 15.12:　Sample images from the CIFAR10 dataset.

15.7.4　*Creation of Conv2D layers*

The code below defines a CNN using a common pattern: a stack of Conv2D and MaxPooling2D layers. It takes in the image in the form of tensors of shape (image_height, image_width, color_channels). Color_channels refer to (R,G,B). This example configures a CNN to process inputs of shape (32, 32, 3), which is the format of CIFAR images. This is done by passing the argument **input_shape** to the first layer.

```python
model = models.Sequential()
model.add(layers.Conv2D(32, (3, 3), activation='relu', \
                        input_shape=(32, 32, 3)))
model.add(layers.MaxPooling2D((2, 2)))
model.add(layers.Conv2D(64, (3, 3), activation='relu'))
model.add(layers.MaxPooling2D((2, 2)))
model.add(layers.Conv2D(64, (3, 3), activation='relu'))
```

Let us display the architecture of our CNN model.

```python
model.summary()
```

```
Model: "sequential"
---------------------------------------------------------------
Layer (type)                 Output Shape              Param #
===============================================================
conv2d (Conv2D)              (None, 30, 30, 32)        896

max_pooling2d (MaxPooling2D) (None, 15, 15, 32)        0

conv2d_1 (Conv2D)            (None, 13, 13, 64)        18496

max_pooling2d_1 (MaxPooling2D (None, 6, 6, 64)         0

conv2d_2 (Conv2D)            (None, 4, 4, 64)          36928
===============================================================
Total params: 56,320
Trainable params: 56,320
Non-trainable params: 0
---------------------------------------------------------------
```

It is shown that the output of every Conv2D and MaxPooling2D layer is a 3D tensor with its own shape (height, width, channels). The dimensions of width and height are often set to shrink and those of the channels are set to grow as the net gets deeper in the network. Naturally, as the width and height of the Conv2D layer shrink, more output channels can be added. The number of output channels (e.g., 32 or 64 for this example) for each Conv2D layer is controlled by the first argument.

15.7.5 *Add Dense layers to the Conv2D layers*

The output tensor from the last Conv2D layer of shape (4, 4, 64) is fed into one or more dense layers to perform multi-classification. Because the dense layers take 1D vectors as input, the 3D Conv2D output shall be flattened to 1D. Since the CIFAR has 10 classes at the output, the final Dense layer shall have 10 output neurons with a softmax activation.

```python
model.add(layers.Flatten())
model.add(layers.Dense(64, activation='relu'))
model.add(layers.Dense(10))
```

The complete architecture of our CNN model is listed below:

```python
model.summary()
```

```
Model: "sequential"
_________________________________________________________________
Layer (type)                 Output Shape              Param #
=================================================================
conv2d (Conv2D)              (None, 30, 30, 32)        896
_________________________________________________________________
max_pooling2d (MaxPooling2D) (None, 15, 15, 32)        0
_________________________________________________________________
conv2d_1 (Conv2D)            (None, 13, 13, 64)        18496
_________________________________________________________________
max_pooling2d_1 (MaxPooling2D (None, 6, 6, 64)         0
_________________________________________________________________
conv2d_2 (Conv2D)            (None, 4, 4, 64)          36928
_________________________________________________________________
flatten (Flatten)            (None, 1024)              0
_________________________________________________________________
dense (Dense)                (None, 64)                65600
_________________________________________________________________
dense_1 (Dense)              (None, 10)                650
=================================================================
Total params: 122,570
Trainable params: 122,570
Non-trainable params: 0
_________________________________________________________________
```

As shown above, the 3D (4, 4, 64) outputs at conv2d_2 are flattened into a 1D vector of shape (1024) before feeding to the first dense layer.

15.7.6 *Compile and train the CNN model*

```python
model.compile(optimizer='adam',
        loss=tf.keras.losses.SparseCategoricalCrossentropy(
        from_logits=True), metrics=['accuracy'])

history = model.fit(train_images, train_labels, epochs=10,
        validation_data=(test_images, test_labels))
```

```
Epoch 1/10
1563/1563 [=================] - 45s 28ms/step - loss: 1.7221 -
accuracy: 0.3648 - val_loss: 1.2347 - val_accuracy: 0.5573
Epoch 2/10
1563/1563 [=================] - 42s 27ms/step - loss: 1.1582 -
accuracy: 0.5869 - val_loss: 1.0298 - val_accuracy: 0.6363

. . . . .
Epoch 9/10
1563/1563 [=================] - 39s 25ms/step - loss: 0.5681 -
accuracy: 0.7993 - val_loss: 0.8510 - val_accuracy: 0.7178
Epoch 10/10
1563/1563 [=================] - 39s 25ms/step - loss: 0.5337 -
accuracy: 0.8114 - val_loss: 0.9123 - val_accuracy: 0.6919
```

The training of our CNN model is done for 10 epochs with about 40 s running time for each.

15.7.7 *Evaluation of the trained CNN model*

```python
plt.plot(history.history['accuracy'], label='accuracy')
plt.plot(history.history['val_accuracy'],label='val_accuracy')
plt.xlabel('Epoch')
plt.ylabel('Accuracy')
plt.ylim([0.5, 1])
plt.legend(loc='lower right')
test_loss,test_acc=model.evaluate(test_images,test_labels, verbose=2)
```

```
313/313 - 3s - loss: 0.9123 - accuracy: 0.6919
```

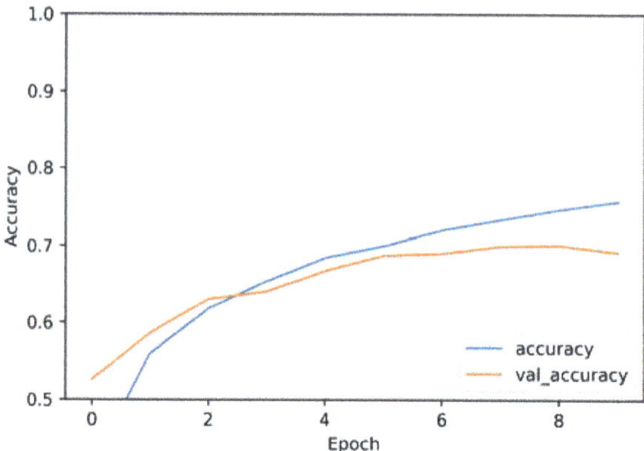

Figure 15.13:   Accuracy evolution of the CNN model during training.

This simple CNN has achieved a test accuracy of about 70%, as shown in Fig. 15.13. Not bad for a few lines of code! For another CNN model, readers may take a look at an example using the Keras subclassing API and a `tf.GradientTape` here.

15.8 Applications of YOLO for Object Detection

Object detection involves identifying the objects, including their presence, identities, dimensions, and locations from a given image. We would need efficient techniques, such as object recognition, classification, localization, and dimension determination. For practical applications such as self-driven cars, we would need to perform such an object detection in real time. YOLO is one of the best choices.

Sophisticated source codes for versions of YOLO and pre-trained models are available, many at the official DarkNet GitHub repository written in C, with tutorials on the usage. There are also third-party implementations of YOLO in Keras. A widely used project is the "keras-yolo3: Training and Detecting Objects with YOLO3" by Huynh Ngoc Anh. The project is called experiencor for short. The codes in the project are available under the MIT open source license, which is permissive. It provides scripts to load, uses pre-trained YOLO models, and transfers learning for developing new YOLOv3 models on new datasets.

In this section, we will introduce the basic procedure using a pre-trained YOLOv3 model for object detection in a given image. The materials and codes used in this section are based on a very clear and detailed online

Figure 15.14: YOLOv3 object detection: cars, persons, traffic light around a traffic light junction.

article by Jason Brownlee, on the experiencor YOLO3 Project. The code is a little lengthy and thus will not be listed here, but it should be quite easy to follow after the fundamental understanding is established. The sources are also listed in the additional reference section.

First, we take a photo with some interested objects to detect if it contains persons, cars, and traffic lights. We use the trained YOLOv3 model to make predictions on the objects in the photo. The results are shown in Fig. 15.14.

The YOLOv3 located 3 cars out of 4. The missed one has too much blockage, and even a human may not be able to see it. All the three persons are correctly located. It has located 4 traffic lights, 3 out of 4 are correct. The small box detected as a traffic light is box container for park users. It is not exactly a traffic light, but quite similar. Thus, this may be arguable. Overall, the YOLOv3 did an excellent job in locating all these interest objects from such a messy image. The time taken for the detection is about 20 s on author's laptop.

Using the same code, we detected a few more photos, and the results are summarized below.

For the above case, YOLOv3 found a person on the truck with 95.86% confidence. It also located the truck with 66.15% confidence (because it is in fact a trailer) and all the four cars with confidences of 61.95%, 84.14%, 99.63%, and 98.79%. All these objects are located and boxed as shown in Figs. 15.15 and 15.18.

Figure 15.15:   YOLOv3 has successfully detected a man standing on a truck (on the right side of the photo and quite difficult for humans to see), despite that part of the image being rather dark.

Figure 15.16:   Persons in winter clothes detected by the trained YOLOv3.

Additional references and further readings:

- Jason Brownlee, 2019, How to Perform Object Detection With YOLOv3 in Keras.
- experiencor/keras-yolo3, GitHub.
- You Only Look Once: Unified, Real-Time Object Detection, 2015.
- YOLO9000: Better, Faster, Stronger, 2016.
- YOLOv3: An Incremental Improvement, 2018.
- matplotlib.patches.Rectangle API.
- YOLO: Real-Time Object Detection, Homepage.
- Official DarkNet and YOLO Source Code, GitHub.

Figure 15.17:   Four cars and one fire hydrant detected by the trained YOLOv3.

Figure 15.18:   Two birds on marsh land detected by the trained YOLOv3.

- Official YOLO: Real Time Object Detection.
- Huynh Ngoc Anh, experiencor, Home Page.
- allanzelener/YAD2K, GitHub.
- qqwweee/keras-yolo3, GitHub.
- xiaochus/YOLOv3 GitHub.
- Blog of Rahmad Sadli.

Before ending this chapter, we may note that from MLP to conv2D, there is quite a significant change. Such a change has led to huge advancements in ML. This tells us that our mind needs to be wide open for advancements in sciences and technology. One may ask now: Can we have conv1D? The answer is yes. The interested reader may take a look at the online article by

Jason Brawnlee at https://machinelearningmastery.com/cnn-models-for-human-activity-recognition-time-series-classification/. Further, what about conv3D? Yes. You have guessed it.

References

[1] K. Fukushima, Neocognitron: A self-organizing neural network model for a mechanism of pattern recognition unaffected by shift in position, *Biological Cybernetics*, **36**, 193–202, 2004.

[2] D. Ciresan, M. Ueli and J. Schmidhuber, Multi-column deep neural networks for image classification, *2012 IEEE Conference on Computer Vision and Pattern Recognition*, 3642–3649, 2012.

[3] I. Goodfellow, B. Yoshua and C. Aaron, Deep learning, *Nature*, **521**, 436–444, 2015.

[4] M.V. Valueva, N.N. Nagornov, P.A. Lyakhov *et al.*, Application of the residue number system to reduce hardware costs of the convolutional neural network implementation, *Mathematics and Computers in Simulation*, **177**, 232–243, 2020. https://www.sciencedirect.com/science/article/pii/S0378475420301580.

[5] Duan Shuyong, Ma Honglei, G.R. Liu *et al.*, Development of an automatic lawnmower with real-time computer vision for obstacle avoidance, *International Journal of Computational Methods*, Accepted, 2021.

[6] Duan Shuyong, Lu Ningning, Lyu Zhongwei *et al.*, An anchor box setting technique based on differences between categories for object detection, *International Journal of Intelligent Robotics and Applications*, 1–14, 2021.

[7] V. Dumoulin and F. Visin, A guide to convolution arithmetic for deep learning, arXiv, 1603.07285, 2018.

[8] Y. Lecun, L. Bottou, Y. Bengio *et al.*, Gradient-based learning applied to document recognition, *Proceedings of the IEEE*, **86**(11), 2278–2324, 1998.

[9] A. Krizhevsky, I. Sutskever and G. E., Imagenet classification with deep convolutional neural networks, *Advances in Neural Information Processing Systems*, 2012.

[10] S. Karen and Z. Andrew, Very deep convolutional networks for large-scale image recognition, arXiv preprint arXiv:1409.1556, 2014. https://www.bibsonomy.org/bibtex/2bc3ee27a1dd159f48b10ac3555879865/buch_jon.

[11] He Kaiming, Zhang Xiangyu, Ren Shaoqing *et al.*, Deep residual learning for image recognition, *CoRR*, abs/1512.03385, 2015. http://arxiv.org/abs/1512.03385.

[12] Christian Szegedy, Wei Liu, Yangqing Jia *et al.*, *Going Deeper with Convolutions*, 2014.

[13] Min Lin, Qiang Chen and Shuicheng Yan, *Network In Network*, 2014. https://arxiv.org/abs/1312.4400.

[14] R. Joseph, D. Santosh, G. Ross *et al.*, You only look once: Unified, real-time object detection, *CoRR*, abs/1506.02640, (1), 2015. http://arxiv.org/abs/1506.02640.

Chapter 16

Recurrent Neural Network (RNN) and Sequence Feature Models

Recurrent neural networks (RNNs) are yet another quite special class of artificial neural networks (NNs) for datasets with features of sequence or temporal significance. An RNN typically has an internal state recorded in a memory cell, so that it can process sequential inputs, such as video and speech records. Affine transformations are used in an extended affine space that includes memorized states as additional features. RNNs have important applications in various areas including natural language processing, speech recognition, translation, music composition, robot control, and unconstrained handwriting recognition [1], to name just a few. A recent review on RNNs can be found in [2].

Different types of RNNs have been developed [2]. This chapter focuses on the so-called long short-term memory networks (LSTMs) presented originally by Sepp Hochreiter and Jürgen Schmidhuber [3]. This is because (1) LSTM is most widely used and studied; (2) when LSTM is well understood, it is relatively easy to understand other RNNs; and (3) most publicly available modules have LSTM classes built in for ready use.

A typical LSTM unit is composed of a **cell**, an **update gate**, a **forget gate**, and an **output gate**. The cell remembers values over time sequence corresponding to the sequential data inputs. These three gates regulate the information exchange between the memory cell and newly inputted data. The level of the regulation is controlled by nested neural network (NN) layers with learning parameters. These parameters are trained via a supervised process similar to the NN or MLP models discussed in previous chapters.

LSTMs were developed to deal with the vanishing gradient problem encountered in training traditional NNs, because they allow information to travel deep in the layers through interconnections built in the LSTM.

563

In writing this chapter, the following materials are referenced in addition to those listed in the reference section: Keras documentation on LSTM, Wikipedia page on LSTM, etc.

16.1 A Typical Structure of LSTMs

Figure 16.1 shows a schematic drawn of an unfolded LSTM in processing a sequential dataset. Consider a dataset with p dimensional vectors varying in time. Let

$$T: \text{the number of the time sequences}$$
$$p: \text{the dimension of the feature vectors} \qquad (16.1)$$
$$l: \text{the dimension of LSTM output spaces}$$

We denote,

Input data:
$$\mathbf{x} = [\mathbf{x}^{(1)}, \mathbf{x}^{(2)}, \ldots, \mathbf{x}^{(t)}, \ldots, \mathbf{x}^{(T)}]^\top \in \mathbb{X}^{T \times p}, \qquad \mathbf{x}^{(t)} \in \mathbb{X}^p$$

Activation states:
$$\mathbf{a} = [\mathbf{a}^{(0)}, \mathbf{a}^{(1)}, \mathbf{a}^{(2)}, \ldots, \mathbf{a}^{(t)}, \ldots, \mathbf{a}^{(T)}] \in \mathbb{X}^{(T+1) \times l}, \quad \mathbf{a}^{(t)} \in \mathbb{X}^l \qquad (16.2)$$

Memory cell states:
$$\mathbf{c} = [\mathbf{c}^{(0)}, \mathbf{c}^{(1)}, \mathbf{c}^{(2)}, \ldots, \mathbf{c}^{(t)}, \ldots, \mathbf{c}^{(T)}] \in \mathbb{X}^{(T+1) \times l}, \quad \mathbf{c}^{(t)} \in \mathbb{X}^l$$

In an LSTM, the initial vectors $\mathbf{a}^{(0)}$ and $\mathbf{c}^{(0)}$ are usually set to zero. These activations can be outputted at each time sequence or only at the final time T, depending on the type of labels used in the training for the problem at hand.

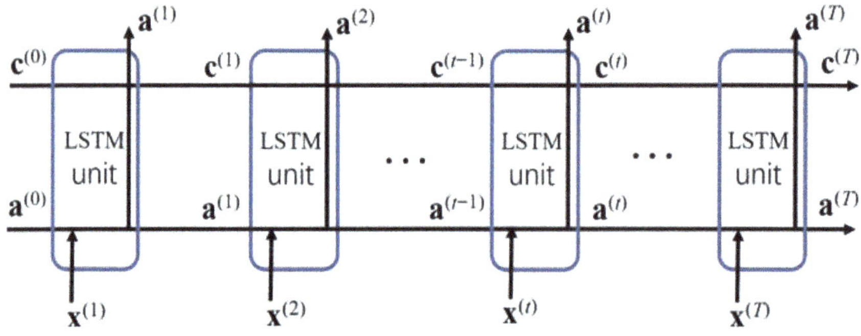

Figure 16.1: Unfolded identical LSTM units for processing a sequential dataset in an LSTM RNN. For a given sequential dataset $\mathbf{x}$, the LSTM uses a memory cell to memorize the state $\mathbf{c}$ at any time. The corresponding activation becomes $\mathbf{a}$, which is updated and can be outputted at each time sequence or only at the final time T.

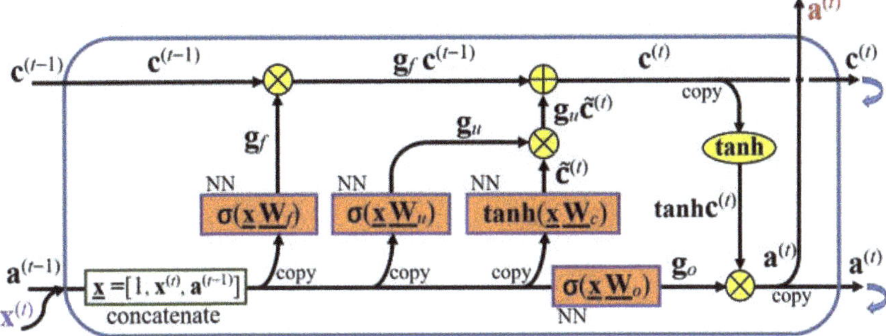

Figure 16.2: An LSTM unit. It has, recurrently, a memory cell $\mathbf{c}^{(t-1)}$ that memorizes the state and an activation state $\mathbf{a}^{(t-1)}$, both in $\mathbb{X}^l$. The unit corresponds to data input $\mathbf{x}^{(t)} \in \mathbb{X}^p$ at time t. The orange blocks are neural network layers, or an MLP, that perform affine transformations in an extended affine space $\overline{\mathbb{X}}^{1+p+l}$ producing a vector in $\mathbb{X}^l$. Yellow circles and ellipse denote element-wise operations.

These gates are equipped with independent learning parameters, and used to control the information exchange between $\mathbf{x}$, $\mathbf{a}$ and $\mathbf{c}$.

Note that Fig. 16.1 is used to show the sequential process inside an LSTM. In actual computation, only one LSTM unit is needed in a loop, by feeding back the $\mathbf{a}^{(t)}$ and $\mathbf{c}^{(t)}$ to the next time sequence. A typical unit is shown in Fig. 16.2, where all the detailed operations are shown.

16.2 Formulation of LSTMs

16.2.1 *General formulation*

Consider time t. At the start, the activation state is $\mathbf{a}^{(t-1)}$, and the memory cell is $\mathbf{c}^{(t-1)}$. Let l be the dimension of the output of our LSTM. Data $\mathbf{x}^{(t)}$ is a vector of p components, and is now inputted. Date $\mathbf{x}^{(t)}$ and previous activation $\mathbf{a}^{(t-1)}$ are concatenated to form an extended affine space together, 1, which shall have a dimension of $1 + p + l$. We perform the following operations using all the current learning parameters:

$$
\begin{aligned}
\overline{\mathbf{x}}_a &= [1, \mathbf{x}^{(t)}, \mathbf{a}^{(t-1)}] \in \overline{\mathbb{X}}^{1+l+p} && \text{extended affine space} \\
\tilde{\mathbf{c}} &= \tanh(\overline{\mathbf{x}}_a \hat{\mathbf{W}}_c) \in (-1,1)^l && \text{candidate memory} \\
\mathbf{g}_u &= \sigma(\overline{\mathbf{x}}_a \hat{\mathbf{W}}_u) \in (0,1)^l && \text{update gate} \\
\mathbf{g}_f &= \sigma(\overline{\mathbf{x}}_a \hat{\mathbf{W}}_f) \in (0,1)^l && \text{forget gate} \\
\mathbf{g}_o &= \sigma(\overline{\mathbf{x}}_a \hat{\mathbf{W}}_o) \in (0,1)^l && \text{output gate} \\
\mathbf{c}^{(t)} &= \mathbf{g}_u * \tilde{\mathbf{c}} + \mathbf{g}_f * \mathbf{c}^{(t-1)} \in (-1,1)^l && \text{new memory} \\
\mathbf{a}^{(t)} &= \mathbf{g}_o * \tanh(\mathbf{c}^{(t)}) \in (-1,1)^l && \text{new activation}
\end{aligned}
\tag{16.3}
$$

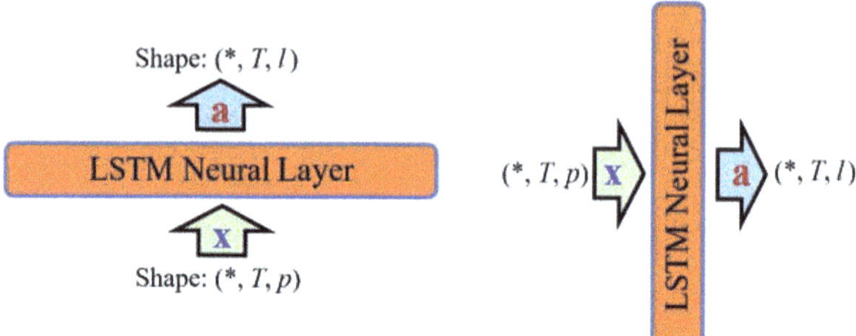

Figure 16.3: LSTM layer. An LSTM can be simply regarded as a normal NN layer that can be placed horizontally (left) or vertically (right). The input $\mathbf{x}$ has typically a shape of (m, T, p) and the output $\mathbf{a}$ has a shape of (m, T, l), where m stands for mini-batch size. If only the final activation output is needed, the shape of $\mathbf{a}^{(T)}$ has a shape of (m, l).

We highlight the input in blue, and output in red. These two are the connection points between LSTM units. The learning parameters are $\hat{\mathbf{W}}_c, \hat{\mathbf{W}}_u, \hat{\mathbf{W}}_f$, and $\hat{\mathbf{W}}_o$. If single NN layers are used in an LSTM, they all are in $\mathbb{W}^{(1+l+p)\times l}$, and thus the total number of training parameters is $P = 4 \times (1 + l + p) \times l$. Equation (16.3) is practically a computational graph of LSTM, which gives both forward and backward paths. Since all these operations are chained and all the derivatives of these activation functions are available, computing the gradients with respect to any of these training samples can be done in the standard way using autograd, as discussed in Chapter 8.

16.2.2 *LSTM layer and standard neural layer*

It is important to note that Eq. (16.3) and the figures may looks complicated, but it can be simply regarded as a single NN layer. The input to LSTM is only $\mathbf{x}^{(t)}$, and the output from it is just $\mathbf{a}^{(t)}$. All the others are the internal variables. An LSTM layer can be shown in the Fig. 16.3. Therefore, an LSTM layer is very easy to use, and can be used as a hidden layer in a neural network model that has a proper loss function defined at the terminal output layer of the entire model.

16.2.3 *Reduced LSTM*

Consider now a special case when the number of the time sequences $T = 1$. In this case, $\mathbf{a}^{(t-1)} = \mathbf{c}^{(t-1)} = 0$. Our formulation is reduced to

$$\overline{\mathbf{x}} = [1, \mathbf{x}^{(t)}] \in \overline{\mathbb{X}}^{1+p} \qquad \text{standard affine space}$$

$$\tilde{\mathbf{c}} = \tanh(\overline{\mathbf{x}}\,\hat{\mathbf{W}}_c) \in (-1,1)^l \qquad \text{candidate memory}$$

$$\mathbf{g}_u = \sigma(\overline{\mathbf{x}}\,\hat{\mathbf{W}}_u) \in (0,1)^l \qquad \text{update gate}$$

$$\mathbf{g}_f = \sigma(\overline{\mathbf{x}}\,\hat{\mathbf{W}}_f) \in (0,1)^l \qquad \text{forget gate} \qquad (16.4)$$

$$\mathbf{g}_o = \sigma(\overline{\mathbf{x}}\,\hat{\mathbf{W}}_o) \in (0,1)^l \qquad \text{output gate}$$

$$\mathbf{c}^{(t)} = \mathbf{g}_u * \tilde{\mathbf{c}} \in (-1,1)^l \qquad \text{new memory}$$

$$\mathbf{a}^{(t)} = \mathbf{g}_o * \tanh(\mathbf{c}^{(t)}) \in (-1,1)^l \qquad \text{new activation}$$

which can be simplified as

$$\mathbf{a}^{(t)} = \sigma(\overline{\mathbf{x}}\,\hat{\mathbf{W}}_o) * \tanh\left(\sigma(\overline{\mathbf{x}}\,\hat{\mathbf{W}}_u) * \tanh(\overline{\mathbf{x}}\,\hat{\mathbf{W}}_c)\right) \in (-1,1)^l \ \text{new activation}$$

$$(16.5)$$

Note that $*$ stands for element-wise multiplication. The learning parameters become $\hat{\mathbf{W}}_c$, $\hat{\mathbf{W}}_u$, and $\hat{\mathbf{W}}_o$. They are all now in $\mathbb{W}^{(1+p)\times l}$. It is essentially a mapping from $\overline{\mathbb{X}}^{1+p}$ to $(-1,1)^l \in \mathbb{X}^l$ on the standard affine space. The reduced LSTM is equipped with three times more learning parameters compared to a standard NN layer that maps from $\overline{\mathbb{X}}^{1+p}$ to $(-1,1)^l \in \mathbb{X}^l$. The total number of training parameters are $P = 3 \times (1+p) \times l$.

The 1st term on the right-hand side of Eq. (16.5) is essentially a standard NN layer with sigmoid activation, which is regulated by a tanh function that, in turn, is a function of another NN regulated by tanh activation of yet another NN. This configuration makes all these three groups of learning parameters independent. Therefore, the reduced LSTM is an NN regulated by the other two nested regulated NNs, resulting in three times more learning parameters.

16.3 Peephole LSTM

There are many other versions of LSTM, and peephole LSTM [4] is one of them. Peephole LSTM is said to allow the gates to access the constant error carousel, using the cell state $\mathbf{c}^{(t-1)}$ instead of activation $\mathbf{a}^{(t-1)}$. Note that $\mathbf{c}^{(t-1)}$ and $\mathbf{a}^{(t-1)}$ have the same shape, as discussed earlier. The formulation is thus quite similar and is given as follows:

$$\overline{\mathbf{x}} = [1, \mathbf{x}^{(t)}] \in \overline{\mathbb{X}}^{1+p} \qquad \text{standard affine space}$$

$$\overline{\mathbf{x}}_c = [\overline{\mathbf{x}}, \mathbf{c}^{(t-1)}] \in \overline{\mathbb{X}}^{1+l+p} \qquad \text{extended affine space}$$

$$\tilde{\mathbf{c}} = \tanh(\overline{\mathbf{x}}\,\hat{\mathbf{W}}_c) \in (-1, 1)^l \qquad \text{candidate memory}$$

$$\mathbf{g}_u = \sigma(\overline{\mathbf{x}}_c\,\hat{\mathbf{W}}_u) \in (0, 1)^l \qquad \text{update gate} \qquad (16.6)$$

$$\mathbf{g}_f = \sigma(\overline{\mathbf{x}}_c\,\hat{\mathbf{W}}_f) \in (0, 1)^l \qquad \text{forget gate}$$

$$\mathbf{g}_o = \sigma(\overline{\mathbf{x}}_c\,\hat{\mathbf{W}}_o) \in (0, 1)^l \qquad \text{output gate}$$

$$\mathbf{c}^{(t)} = \mathbf{g}_u * \tilde{\mathbf{c}} + \mathbf{g}_f * \mathbf{c}^{(t-1)} \in (-1, 1)^l \qquad \text{new memory}$$

$$\mathbf{a}^{(t)} = \mathbf{g}_o * \tanh(\mathbf{c}^{(t)}) \in (-1, 1)^l \qquad \text{new activation}$$

All the other operations of the peephole LSTM are similar to the LSTM.

16.4 Gated Recurrent Units (GRUs)

Gated recurrent units (GRUs) were introduced by Kyunghyun Cho *et al.* [5]. It may be viewed as a version of LSTM without a dedicated memory cell and hence with less learning parameters than LSTM. The formulation is as follows.

Consider time t. The activation state at its previous time is $\mathbf{a}^{(t-1)}$ with $\mathbf{a}^{(0)} = \mathbf{0}$. Let l be the dimension of the output of the GRU. Data $\mathbf{x}^{(t)}$ is a vector of p components, and is now inputted. Data $\mathbf{x}^{(t)}$ and previous activation $\mathbf{a}^{(t-1)}$ are concatenated to form an extended affine space together, 1, which shall have a dimension of $1 + p + l$. We perform the following operations:

$$\overline{\mathbf{x}}_a = [1, \mathbf{x}^{(t)}, \mathbf{a}^{(t-1)}] \in \overline{\mathbb{X}}^{1+l+p} \qquad \text{extended affine space}$$

$$\mathbf{g}_u = \sigma(\overline{\mathbf{x}}_a\,\hat{\mathbf{W}}_u) \in (0, 1)^l \qquad \text{update gate}$$

$$\mathbf{g}_r = \sigma(\overline{\mathbf{x}}_a\,\hat{\mathbf{W}}_r) \in (0, 1)^l \qquad \text{reset gate}$$

$$\overline{\mathbf{x}}_{ra} = [1, \mathbf{x}^{(t)}, \mathbf{g}_r\mathbf{a}^{(t-1)}] \in \overline{\mathbb{X}}^{1+l+p} \qquad \text{reset extended affine space} \qquad (16.7)$$

$$\tilde{\mathbf{a}} = \tanh(\overline{\mathbf{x}}_{ra}\,\hat{\mathbf{W}}_a) \in (-1, 1)^l \qquad \text{candidate activation}$$

$$\mathbf{a}^{(t)} = (1 - \mathbf{g}_u)\mathbf{a}^{(t-1)} + \mathbf{g}_u\tilde{\mathbf{a}} \in (-1, 1)^l \qquad \text{new output activation}$$

The learning parameters in a GRU are $\hat{\mathbf{W}}_u$, $\hat{\mathbf{W}}_r$, and $\hat{\mathbf{W}}_a$, 3/4 of those in an LSTM. Alternative versions of GRUs are also available. Interested readers my visit the Wiki page on GRUs and then the links therein.

16.5 Examples

16.5.1 *A simple reduced LSTM with a standard NN layer for regression*

Let us first look at an example for the reduced LSTM that can be easily handcrafted for comprehension. We will use the simple and familiar regression problem examined step by step in Chapter 10, using a synthesis dataset and the MxNet. The details on the problem setting will not be repeated here. We will follow our xw formulation in the following code:

```python
from __future__ import print_function
from mxnet import nd, autograd, gluon
import numpy as np
import mxnet as mx
import matplotlib.pyplot as plt
%matplotlib inline
np.set_printoptions(precision=4)


mx.random.seed(1)          # fix seed for repeatable random numbers.


# Specify GPU or CPU for the computation, mxnet's syntax.
data_ctx, model_ctx = mx.cpu(), mx.cpu()
num_inputs = 2             # p, 2D space with two features: x1, x2
num_outputs = 1           # k, one prediction y
num_samples = 1000        # Sample number, m, use 10 for debugging


p1 = num_inputs + 1                # dimension of the affine space


wr=nd.array([[4.2],[2.0],[-3.4]]) # true w_=[b,w0,w1].T,1 neuron
print(f" True w:{wr},{wr.shape}")


def true_fn(X, w): # linear func, 3 learning parameters:w1,w2,b
    return nd.dot(X,w)             # X is the X_; 2*x1-3.4*x2 + 4.2


X=nd.random_normal(shape=(num_samples,p1),ctx=data_ctx)
                     # randomly generate samples for x1 and x2
noise=.1*nd.random_normal(shape=(num_samples,num_outputs),
                    ctx=data_ctx)
                     # 10% noise, zero mean, 1 variance
X[:,0] = 1.0 # / num_samples
print(f" X in affine space:{X[0:4]},{X.shape}")


y = true_fn(X, wr) + noise         # Generate labels with noise.
print(f"y={y[0:4]}{y.shape}")      # A peek at the dataset
```

```
 True w:
[[ 4.2]
 [ 2. ]
 [-3.4]]
<NDArray 3x1 @cpu(0)>,(3, 1)
 X in affine space:
[[ 1.      -0.4902 -0.9502]
 [ 1.      -0.7298 -2.0401]
 [ 1.       1.0408 -0.4526]
 [ 1.      -0.8367 -0.7883]]
<NDArray 4x3 @cpu(0)>,(1000, 3)
y=
[[6.5203]
 [9.5923]
 [7.7648]
 [5.2164]]
<NDArray 4x1 @cpu(0)>(1000, 1)
```

```python
# Plot the data points.
plt.scatter(X[:, 1].asnumpy(),y.asnumpy(),color='r') # 1st feature
plt.scatter(X[:, 2].asnumpy(),y.asnumpy(),color='b') # 2nd feature
plt.show()
```

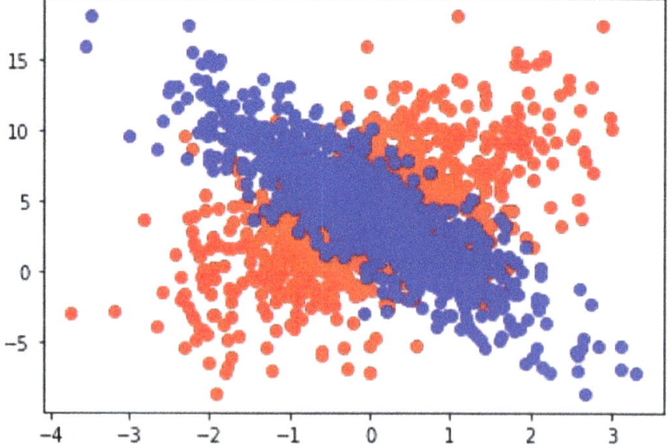

Figure 16.4:   Computer-generated data-points for study LSTM.

```python
# Create data iterators
batch_size=32
train_data=gluon.data.DataLoader(gluon.data.ArrayDataset(X,y),
        batch_size=batch_size, shuffle=True)

# Initialize the training parameters, only W_ is needed!
def init_wb(p1,l,k):          # p1: affine space dimension
    '''p:model num_inputs; l:lstm outputs; k:model num_outputs'''
    wo = nd.random_normal(shape=(p1,l),ctx=model_ctx)
    wu = nd.random_normal(shape=(p1,l),ctx=model_ctx)
    wc = nd.random_normal(shape=(p1,l),ctx=model_ctx)
    w  = nd.random_normal(shape=(l,k),ctx=model_ctx)
    return w, wo, wu, wc


l = 50
w, wo, wu, wc = init_wb(p1,l,num_outputs)  #p1 = p+1
params = [w, wo, wu, wc]

# Request for gradients
for param in params:
    param.attach_grad()
#print(param.grad)             # check initial gradients
```

```python
# Define a reduced LSTM layer

def rd_lstm(X):                           #only X_ is needed!
    '''Reduced LSTM, no T-loop'''
    tc = nd.tanh(nd.dot(X, wc))
    su = nd.sigmoid(nd.dot(X, wu))
    rd_lstm = nd.sigmoid(nd.dot(X, wo))*nd.tanh(su*tc)
    return rd_lstm

# Define a standard NN layer
def net(X):                               # X_ is needed
    return nd.dot(X, w)                    # only w_ is needed!

# Define a L2 loss function for regression
def square_loss(yhat, y):
    return nd.mean((yhat - y) ** 2)

# Optimizer using the stochastic gradient descent (SGD)
def SGD(params, lr):                       # lr: learning rate
```

```python
    for param in params:
        param[:] = param - lr * param.grad
```

```python
# Training and plot the training process and results.

epochs = 50  # times of getting batch-data from dataset
num_batches = num_samples/batch_size

# Re-initialize parameters. They may be trained earlier
w, wo, wu, wc = init_wb(p1,1,num_outputs)    # p1 = p+1
params = [w, wo, wu, wc]
for param in params:
    param.attach_grad()

# Function to plot the losses over time
def plot(losses, X, s_s = 100):                      #s_s: sample_size
    xs = list(range(len(losses)))
    f, (fg1, fg2) = plt.subplots(1, 2)
    fg1.set_title('Loss during training')
    fg1.plot(xs, losses, '-r')
    fg2.set_title('Estimated vs real function')
    fg2.plot(X[:s_s,2].asnumpy(),net(rd_lstm(X[:s_s,:])).asnumpy(),
            'or',label='Estimated')
    fg2.plot(X[:s_s, 2].asnumpy(), true_fn(X[:s_s,:],wr).asnumpy(),
            '*g',label='Real')
    fg2.legend()
    plt.show()

learning_rate = .1
losses = []
plot(losses, X)

for e in range(epochs):
    cumulative_loss = 0
    for i, (data, label) in enumerate(train_data):
        data = data.as_in_context(model_ctx)
        label = label.as_in_context(model_ctx).reshape((-1,1))

        with autograd.record():                      #Computational graph
            output = net(rd_lstm(data))
            loss = square_loss(output, label)

        loss.backward()
        SGD(params, learning_rate)
        cumulative_loss += loss.asscalar()
```

```
if e%10 ==0:
    print("Epoch %s, batch %s. Mean loss: %s" %
        (e, i, cumulative_loss/num_batches))

losses.append(cumulative_loss/num_batches)

plot(losses, X)
```

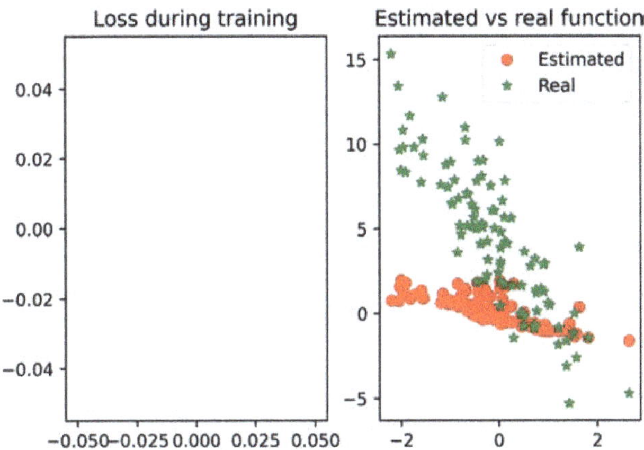

Figure 16.5:   Prediction using LSTM before training.

```
Epoch 0, batch 31. Mean loss: 3.1009296717643737
Epoch 10, batch 31. Mean loss: 0.03779914233088493
Epoch 20, batch 31. Mean loss: 0.020572829380631447
Epoch 30, batch 31. Mean loss: 0.01705670604109764
Epoch 40, batch 31. Mean loss: 0.01468234208971262
```

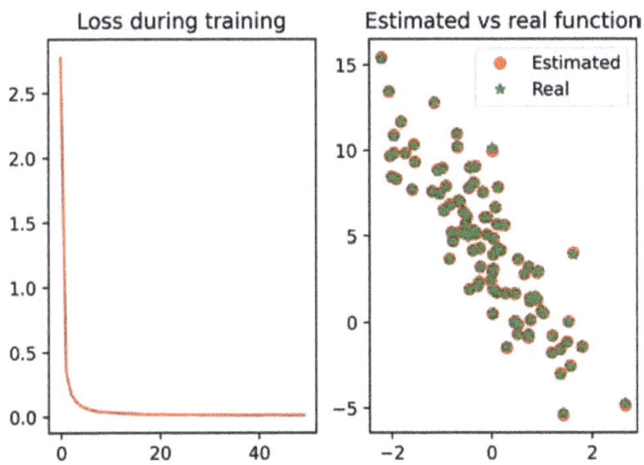

Figure 16.6:   Prediction using the trained LSTM.

This example demonstrates that a reduced LSTM together with a standard NN layer can perform a regression task. The use of LSTM for this simple example may not be helpful. In fact, it makes the model unnecessarily more complex, and it is overkill. However, this example does show clearly that an LSTM can have multiple learn parameters built into it in a nested fashion, which may have more capability for complicated problems.

We can easily create a loop in our simple code and turn our reduced LSTM to a full LSTM. However, is would be much easier to just make use of the well-developed LSTM classes available in a publicly available module.

16.5.2 *LSTM class in tensorflow.keras*

Let us this time use the LSTM class in tensorflow.keras. We first examine the dimensionality of the input and outputs to LSTM using a randomly generated synthetic dataset.

```python
import numpy as np
import tensorflow as tf
from tensorflow.keras.models import Sequential
from tensorflow.keras.layers import LSTM, Dense
```

```python
np.set_printoptions(precision=3)
tf.keras.backend.clear_session()

m, T, p = 32, 100, 28   # T: timesteps; p: features; m: mimi-batch
l = 4                   # l: dimension of the LSTM output

tf.random.set_seed(8)
inputs = tf.random.normal([m, T, p])
#inputs: A 3D tensor with shape [m, T, p].

lstm1 = tf.keras.layers.LSTM(l) # create a LSTM instance
output0 = lstm1(inputs)

print(inputs[-1, T-1,0:p:10],'\n',inputs.shape)
print(output0[-1,:],'\n',output0.shape)  #(32, 4)
```

```
tf.Tensor([ 0.521 -1.34    1.215], shape=(3,), dtype=float32)
 (32, 100, 28)
tf.Tensor([ 0.113  0.059 -0.321  0.248], shape=(4,), dtype=float32)
 (32, 4)
```

```
lstm2=tf.keras.layers.LSTM(1,return_sequences=True,return_state=True)

whole_seq_output, final_memory_state, final_carry_state=lstm2(inputs)

print(f"whole_seq_output.shape: {whole_seq_output.shape}")      #(32,10,4)
print(f"final_memory_state.shape:{final_memory_state.shape}")   #(32,4)
print(f"final_carry_state.shape:{final_carry_state.shape}")     #(32,4)
print(f"final_memory_states:{final_memory_state[-1,:]}")
print(f"final_carry_stfinal_memory_stateate",
      f"{final_carry_state[-1,:]}")
```

```
whole_seq_output.shape: (32, 100, 4)
final_memory_state.shape:(32, 4)
final_carry_state.shape:(32, 4)
final_memory_states:[ 0.079  0.01  -0.295  0.048]
final_carry_stfinal_memory_stateate [ 0.17   0.018 -0.863  0.099]
```

16.5.3 *Using LSTM for handwritten digit recognition*

We now use LSTM for handwritten digit recognition. We first train an LSTM
model using the training dataset of MNIST and perform the testing using
the test dataset to examine the accuracy of the recognition of the trained
LSTM model.

We used the MNIST dataset four times. It contains 28x28 images of digits
with labels. It is a static dataset. However, it can be treated as a dynamic
one. We first treat the image pixels in a row of the image as a vector of
features, and thus $p = 28$. Each row is then treated and a time sequence,
which gives $T = 28$. We simply use the default mini-batch size for our LSTM
model, which is $m = 32$.

```
mnist=tf.keras.datasets.mnist       # 28×28 images with labels
(x_train,y_train),(x_test,y_test)=mnist.load_data()

x_train, x_test = x_train/255., x_test/255.    #normalization

print(x_train.shape, x_train.shape[1:])
T = x_train.shape[1:][0]
p = x_train.shape[1:][1]
k = len(np.unique(y_train))          # k-classes of MNIST dataset
l = int(x_train[0].shape[0]*x_train[0].shape[1]/10)
# use 1/10th the total image features as the LSTM output, l
p1 = 1 + p + l      # dimension of the extended affine space
print(f"Number of classes k ={k}")
```

```python
print(f"Number of features p ={p}")
print(f"Dimension of the affine space ={p1}")
print(f"Number of outputs from the LSTM layer ={l}")
print(f"Training Parameters in LSTM ={4*p1*l}")

model = Sequential()
# LSTM layer to process sequential data [m, T, k]
# It produces an output [m, l]. Use default activation:tanh
# Outputs only the final activation a^T.
model.add(LSTM(l, input_shape=(x_train.shape[1:])))
# Add a dense layer for k-classification, using LSTM outputs.
model.add(Dense(k, activation='softmax')) # a^T is feed here
optimizer=tf.keras.optimizers.Adam(learning_rate=.01,decay=1e-6)

# Compile model: 1-LSTM, 1-Dense, use Adam
model.compile(loss='sparse_categorical_crossentropy',
    optimizer=optimizer, metrics=['accuracy'])

model.summary()
```

```
(60000, 28, 28) (28, 28)
Number of classes k =10
Number of features p =28
Dimension of the affine space =107
Number of outputs from the LSTM layer =78
Training Parameters in LSTM =33384
Model: "sequential"
_________________________________________________________________
Layer (type)                 Output Shape              Param #
=================================================================
lstm_2 (LSTM)                (None, 78)                33384
_________________________________________________________________
dense (Dense)                (None, 10)                790
=================================================================
Total params: 34,174
Trainable params: 34,174
Non-trainable params: 0
_________________________________________________________________
```

Our model has 33,384 training parameters for the LSTM layer, same as our calculation. The whole model consists of one LSTM layer and one dense NN layer. We shall now train the model.

```
model.fit(x_train,y_train,epochs=3,validation_data=(x_test,y_test));
# Using the default m_size 32
```

```
Epoch 1/3
1875/1875 [==============================] - 32s 16ms/step - loss:
   0.2583 - accuracy: 0.9175 - val_loss: 0.1020 - val_accuracy: 0.9703
Epoch 2/3
1875/1875 [==============================] - 29s 16ms/step - loss:
   0.1091 - accuracy: 0.9683 - val_loss: 0.0897 - val_accuracy: 0.9716
Epoch 3/3
1875/1875 [==============================] - 30s 16ms/step - loss:
   0.0882 - accuracy: 0.9731 - val_loss: 0.0792 - val_accuracy: 0.9772
```

This model achieved an accuracy of $\sim 98\%$, which is a quite good performance. One can easily add in additional LSTM layers and/or dense layers to form a deep net. The following code builds an LSTM-MLP, just for demonstration purposes:

```
Lmlp = Sequential()
l = int(l/2)    #reduce LSTM output, because using more layers
Lmlp.add(LSTM(l, input_shape=(x_train.shape[1:]),
    return_sequences=True)) # True: allows feed to next layer
Lmlp.add(LSTM(l, input_shape=(x_train.shape[1:])))
Lmlp.add(Dense(2*k, activation='relu'))    # a^T is feed here
Lmlp.add(Dense(k, activation='softmax'))   # for classification
optimizer=tf.keras.optimizers.Adam(learning_rate=.001,decay=1e-6)

# Compile our Lmlp: 2-LSTM layers, 2-Dense layers, use Adam
Lmlp.compile(loss='sparse_categorical_crossentropy',
    optimizer=optimizer, metrics=['accuracy'])

Lmlp.summary()
```

```
Model: "sequential_1"
```

Layer (type)	Output Shape	Param #
lstm_3 (LSTM)	(None, 28, 39)	10608
lstm_4 (LSTM)	(None, 39)	12324

```
-----------------------------------------------------------------------
dense_1 (Dense)               (None, 20)                    800
-----------------------------------------------------------------------
dense_2 (Dense)               (None, 10)                    210
=======================================================================
Total params: 23,942
Trainable params: 23,942
Non-trainable params: 0
-----------------------------------------------------------------------
```

```
Lmlp.fit(x_train,y_train,epochs=3,validation_data=(x_test,y_test));
```

```
Epoch 1/3
1875/1875 [====================] - 39s 19ms/step - loss:
  0.4861 - accuracy: 0.8447 - val_loss: 0.1857 - val_accuracy: 0.9420
Epoch 2/3
1875/1875 [====================] - 36s 19ms/step - loss:
  0.1394 - accuracy: 0.9597 - val_loss: 0.1105 - val_accuracy: 0.9674
Epoch 3/3
1875/1875 [====================] - 36s 19ms/step - loss:
  0.0965 - accuracy: 0.9711 - val_loss: 0.0818 - val_accuracy: 0.9755
```

The "deep" LSTM-MLP achieved a similar level of accuracy with about 2/3 training parameters.

16.5.4 *Using LSTM for predicting dynamics of moving vectors*

This example builds an LSTM for predicting the movements in time of vectors in 2D space.

```python
import numpy as np
import keras
import tensorflow as tf
from keras.models import Sequential
from keras.layers.core import Dense, Activation
from keras.layers.recurrent import LSTM
import matplotlib.pylab as plt
import sys
%matplotlib inline
```

```python
print(f"keras:{keras.__version__}, tensorflow: {tf.__version__}")
```

```
keras:2.6.0, tensorflow: 2.6.2
```

```python
np.set_printoptions(precision=5)
tf.keras.backend.clear_session()

# Generate a raw dataset of moving 2D vectors
x1=np.array(np.sin(  2*np.pi*np.arange(0,10,.001))) #component 1
x2=np.array(np.cos(2.3*np.pi*np.arange(0,10,.001))) #component 1

noise_level = 0.1                     # 10% Gaussian
noise = np.random.normal(0, 1, len(x1)) * noise_level
x1 = x1 + noise
noise = np.random.normal(0, 1, len(x1)) * noise_level
x2 = x2 + noise
print(x1[:5],x1.shape, x2.shape)

X = np.vstack((x1,x2)).T            # Form the dataset
print(X[:5],X.shape,len(X))
```

```
[ 0.00639 -0.04602  0.06577  0.07202  0.04981] (10000,) (10000,)
[[ 0.00639  0.8971 ]
 [-0.04602  0.9104 ]
 [ 0.06577  1.22828]
 [ 0.07202  0.982  ]
 [ 0.04981  1.01548]] (10000, 2) 10000
```

```python
# Set configurational parameters for the model
T, p, L = 100, 2, 20  # T: timesteps; p: features
                    #L: dimension of the LSTM output
out_d = 2        # output dimension for the whole model, or k
p1 = 1 + p + L  # dimension of the extended affine space
print(f"Final output dimension ={out_d}")
print(f"Number of time sequences T={T}")
print(f"Number of features p ={p}")
print(f"Dimension of the extended affine space ={p1}")
print(f"Number of outputs from the LSTM layer ={L}")
print(f"Training Parameters in LSTM ={4*p1*L}")
```

```
Final output dimension =2
Number of time sequences T=100
Number of features p =2
Dimension of the extended affine space =23
Number of outputs from the LSTM layer =20
Training Parameters in LSTM =1840
```

```python
# Take a look a the raw data
plt.rcParams["figure.figsize"] = (4, 2.5)
plt.figure(dpi=300)
plt.plot(X[:1000:10][:,0],"-")
plt.plot(X[:1000:10][:,1],"--")
plt.xlabel('Time t')
plt.ylabel('Coordinates of 2D vectors')
plt.legend(["x1", "x2"]);
```

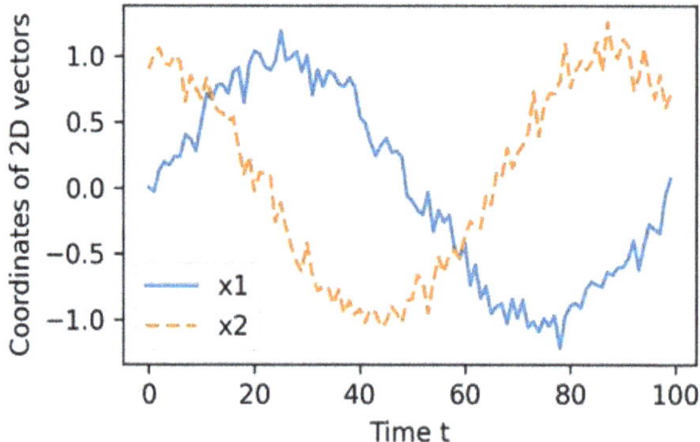

Figure 16.7:   Sample coordinates of the trajectory of a moving vector with noise.

```python
def createDataset(X, T = 100):
    '''Create dataset with proper shape for keras LSTM class
    input: X[*,p]; output: Xt[*,T,p]'''
    Xt, yt = [], []
    for i in range(len(X)-T):
        Xt.append(X[i:i+T])
        yt.append(X[i+T])
    Xt = np.array(Xt)
    yt = np.array(yt)
    return Xt, yt
```

```python
def sequentialSplit(X, y, train_rate=0.8):
    '''Sequentially split data, without random shuffling.
       1st part for training, the rest for test'''
    n_train = round(len(X) * train_rate)
    X_train, y_train = X[0:n_train], y[0:n_train]
    X_test, y_test = X[n_train:], y[n_train:]
    return X_train, y_train, X_test, y_test

def randomSplit(Xt, yt):                    # not used in this example
    ''' This code may be used for reshuffled data batches '''
    from sklearn.model_selection import train_test_split
    X_train, X_test, y_train, y_test = train_test_split(
            Xt, yt, train_size=.8, random_state=8)
    return X_train, y_train, X_test, y_test
```

```python
Xt, yt = createDataset(X, T = T )
print(Xt[1][0],Xt.shape,Xt.shape[1])
print(yt[1],yt.shape)
```

```
[-0.04602  0.9104 ] (9900, 100, 2) 100
[0.61192 0.61808] (9900, 2)
```

We split the dataset sequentially, so that we can train the model using the first part of the data, and then predict the future movements of the 2D vectors. One may shuffle the dataset and then split the dataset. In this case, we train the model for predicting the hidden features of the dataset.

```python
X_train, y_train, X_test, y_test = sequentialSplit(Xt, yt)
#X_train, y_train, X_test, y_test = randomSplit(Xt, yt)
```

```python
print(X_train[1][0],X_train.shape)
print(X_test[1][0],X_test.shape)
```

```
[-0.04602  0.9104 ] (7920, 100, 2)
[-0.62915  0.92939] (1980, 100, 2)
```

```python
# Build the LSTM-NN model
model = Sequential()
model.add(LSTM(L, input_shape=(T, p)))
model.add(Dense(out_d, input_dim=L))
model.add(Activation("linear"))
model.compile(loss="mean_squared_error", optimizer="rmsprop")

model.summary()
```

```
Model: "sequential"
_________________________________________________________________
Layer (type)                 Output Shape              Param #
=================================================================
lstm (LSTM)                  (None, 20)                1840
_________________________________________________________________
dense (Dense)                (None, 2)                 42
_________________________________________________________________
activation (Activation)      (None, 2)                 0
=================================================================
Total params: 1,882
Trainable params: 1,882
Non-trainable params: 0
_________________________________________________________________
```

```python
model.fit(X_train,y_train,batch_size=128,epochs=5,validation_split=.05);
```

```
Epoch 1/5
59/59 [==============================] - 8s 78ms/step - loss:
    0.1552 - val_loss: 0.0290
Epoch 2/5
59/59 [==============================] - 4s 73ms/step - loss:
    0.0151 - val_loss: 0.0154
Epoch 3/5
59/59 [==============================] - 4s 73ms/step - loss:
    0.0124 - val_loss: 0.0126
Epoch 4/5
59/59 [==============================] - 4s 73ms/step - loss:
    0.0121 - val_loss: 0.0128
```

```
Epoch 5/5
59/59 [==============================] - 4s 73ms/step - loss:
    0.0119 - val_loss: 0.0125
```

```python
# Accuracy assessment
from numpy.linalg import norm
predicted = model.predict(X_test)
rmse = np.sqrt((((predicted - y_test) ** 2).mean(axis=0))
print(f"Root Mean Square Error = {rmse}")
print(f"Relative Root Mean Square Error= {rmse/norm(y_test)}")
```

```
Root Mean Square Error = [0.10676 0.11551]
Relative Root Mean Square Error= [0.00238 0.00257]
```

```python
# Plot the prediction results
nt, ns = len(y_test), 50
plt.rcParams["figure.figsize"] = (4, 2.5)
plt.figure(dpi=300)
plt.plot(predicted[:nt:ns][:,0],"--")
plt.plot(y_test[:nt:ns][:,0],":")
plt.legend(["Predict",  "Test"])
plt.xlabel('Time t')
plt.ylabel('Coordinates of vectors, x1');
```

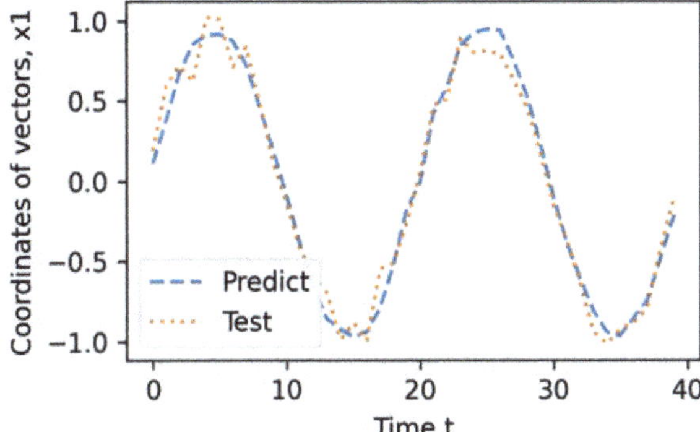

Figure 16.8: LSTM predicted coordinate x_1 of the trajectory of a moving vector, in comparison with the testing data.

```python
plt.rcParams["figure.figsize"] = (4, 2.5)
plt.figure(dpi=300)
plt.plot(predicted[:nt:ns][:,1],"--")
```

```
plt.plot(y_test[:nt:ns][:,1],":")
plt.legend(["Predict",  "Test"])
plt.xlabel('Time t')
plt.ylabel('Coordinates of vectors, x2');
```

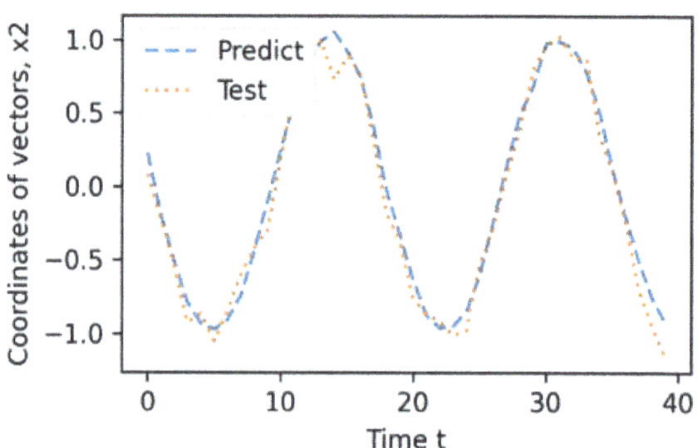

Figure 16.9: LSTM predicted coordinate x_2 of the trajectory of a moving vector, in comparison with the testing data.

It is seen in Fig. 16.9 that our LSTM model gives a reasonable prediction based on this dataset. It captures the major waving features of the moving vectors.

16.6 Examples of LSTM for Speech Recognition

LSTM is one of the most powerful tools for speech recognition. There are many open-source examples. Interested readers may take a look at the mxnet on Speech LSTM. The source code is also available at their GitHub site.

References

[1] G. Alex, L. Marcus, F. Santiago *et al.*, "A Novel Connectionist System for Unconstrained Handwriting Recognition", *IEEE Transactions on Pattern Analysis and Machine Intelligence*, **31**, pp. 855–868, 2009.
[2] Yu Yong, Si Xiaosheng, Hu Changhua *et al.*, "A Review of Recurrent Neural Networks: LSTM Cells and Network Architectures", *Neural Computation*, **31**(7), 1235–1270, 2019.
[3] H. Sepp and S. Jürgen, "Long Short-Term Memory", *Neural Computation*, **9**(8), 1735–1780, 1997. https://doi.org/10.1162/neco.1997.9.8.1735.
[4] F.A. Gers and E. Schmidhuber, "LSTM recurrent networks learn simple context-free and context-sensitive languages", *IEEE Transactions on Neural Networks*, **12**(6), 1333–1340, 2001.
[5] Cho KyungHyun, On the Properties of Neural Machine Translation: Encoder-Decoder Approaches, CoRR, abs/1409.1259, 2014. http://arxiv.org/abs/1409.1259.

Chapter 17

Unsupervised Learning Techniques

17.1 Background

The world now has a massive amount of data, and it is growing. How to make use of these data becomes very important. There are mainly two ways to make the data useful. One is to have the data examined by experts in the related areas, and have it labeled, and then the data can be used to train machine learning models. Labeling data, however, is a very expensive and time-consuming task. The other way is to develop machine learning algorithms that read the (unlabeled) raw data, and try to extract some latent features or characteristics from the data. This is the unsupervised learning that we are discussing in this chapter.

There are many applications for unsupervised learning, including data compression, de-noising, clustering, recommendation, abnormality detection, classification, just to name a few.

Unsupervised machine learning methods include principle components analysis (PCA) for principal value extraction from datasets, the family of K-means clustering methods, mean-shift methods, and the family of Autoencoders. We have already discussed PCA in Chapter 3 and hence will simply use it here for clustering algorithms. In this chapter, we shall discuss in detail K-means clustering, mean-shift clustering, and Autoencoders. We shall focus more on the fundamentals of these methods to help readers understand other related methods and techniques that are not covered in this book.

17.2 K-means for Clustering

K-means clustering is an unsupervised machine learning algorithm using unlabeled datasets. It is originally from signal processing for partitioning a cloud of data-points into k clusters. In each cluster, data-points have the nearest mean with respect to its cluster centers or centroid. K-means clustering minimizes within-cluster variances, that is, the squared (Euclidean) distances (hence, it becomes a least squares minimization problem, which is quadratic). Such an algorithm essentially partitions these data-points into Voronoi cells generated using the k centroids.

The clustering problem is in general NP-hard, meaning that it is computationally intractable in theory. However, efficient heuristic algorithms have been developed to effectively find local optimal solutions. The K-means is one such algorithm that clusters given unlabeled data-points into pre-specified k clusters. It is loosely related to the k-nearest neighbor classifier and it has a number of variations. The mean-shift clustering algorithm is one such variation, in which the number of clusters need not be pre-specified. More details on K-means and its relation to other algorithms can be found at the Wikipedia page (https://en.wikipedia.org/wiki/K-means_clustering) and the widely used Sklearn sites.

The typical K-means algorithm uses an iterative updating process. It is referred to as Lloyd's algorithm. Here, we discuss in detail this basic algorithm, hoping this can be of help in understanding and using other related and more advanced algorithms. The K-means algorithm starts with an initialization of k means.

17.2.1 *Initialization of means*

Consider a dataset with a cloud of n data-points in the feature space $\mathbb{X}^p$ with p features. Our objective is to group these data-points into k clusters (sub-clouds), by extracting k geometrical distributive characteristics of these data-points. A typical K-means algorithm starts with generating k initial means randomly. A discussion on random initiation methods is given in a paper by Hamerly and Elkan [1]. One of the methods is to randomly choose k points from the given dataset and use these as the initial means, which of course can be far away from the true ones. Another method randomly assigns clusters and then computes the initial means for these clusters. In this case, this initial clustering will also be far away from the true clustering. In either case, the initial start has some randomness involved. Hence, it is often necessary to run the K-means for a number of times each with a random set of initial means and then choose the best one based on some criterion.

There are a number of specially designed strategies for K-means initiation, including centroids of random subsamples, group representative points, random farthest points, or k-means++. Interested readers may refer to this online discussion page (https://stats.stackexchange.com/questions/317493/ methods-ofinitializing-k-means-clustering) for more details. We will use k-means++ in our example problems later in benchmark studies.

The PCA (discussed in Chapter 3) can be a good choice for generating the initial k means. One can conduct a PCA to obtain k principal components using the given dataset, and then use those principal components as the initial k means. In this case, the initiation becomes somewhat deterministic, and only one K-means run is conducted. It is believed to improve the accuracy of the clustering results because the K-means is known to be sensitive to scaling, and PCA can offer more stable scaling and also noise reduction features. PCA can also help in convergence behavior because of possible better initial guesses. Moreover, PCA is used for visualizing the results of K-means clustering. As discussed in Chapter 3, PCA can be expensive. Fortunately, in K-means applications, k is usually not a big number (compared to the number of samples in big datasets), and hence the PCA cost is usually not a big issue for many problems. We shall examine this using example problems later. Let us now look at the basic procedure, formulation, and algorithm for typical K-means clustering. It is iterative, and each iteration has mainly two steps.

17.2.2 *Assignment of data-points to clusters*

At $t = 0$, we have a set of initial k means $\mathbf{m}_1^{(0)}, \mathbf{m}_2^{(0)}, \ldots, \mathbf{m}_k^{(0)}$ corresponding to these initial k clusters for a given cloud of data-points in $\mathbb{X}^p$. These means are also referred to as centroids or centers of the clusters. Note that in K-means clustering, we pre-specify the number of clusters k. Also, $\mathbf{m}_i^{(t)}$ is in general a vector in $\mathbb{X}^p$.

At step t, we compute squared Euclidean distances between a data-point $\mathbf{x}_q$ to these means, and then assign this data-point to the cluster with the "nearest mean", meaning that the Euclidean distance between the data-point and the cluster mean is the shortest.

$$\mathbb{S}_i^{(t)} = \{\mathbf{x}_q : \|\mathbf{x}_q - \mathbf{m}_i^{(t)}\|^2 \leq \|\mathbf{x}_q - \mathbf{m}_j^{(t)}\|^2 \ \forall j, 1 \leq j \leq k\}, \quad i = 1, 2, \ldots, k \tag{17.1}$$

If there is more than one nearest means, we choose one of those, so that data-point $\mathbf{x}_q$ is assigned only to one set $\mathbb{S}_i^{(t)}$. This process is done for all the data-points in the dataset, which leads to a partitioning of all these data-points by the edges of the Voronoi diagram generated by these means (this will be shown more clearly in the case study examples later). Each Voronoi cell hosts a cluster with data-points in set $\mathbb{S}_i^{(t)}$.

17.2.3 *Update of means*

When partitioning is done, we re-compute the mean for each of the k clusters using these data-points assigned to the cluster. For the ith cluster, we have

$$\mathbf{m}_i^{(t+1)} = \frac{1}{n_i} \sum_{\mathbf{x}_j \in \mathbb{S}_i^{(t)}} \mathbf{x}_j, \qquad i = 1, 2, \ldots, k \qquad (17.2)$$

where n_i is the number of data-points in set $\mathbb{S}_i^{(t)}$.

This leads to an updated set of k means for the $t+1$ step, which is then used for a new round of iteration: re-assignment of data-points to a new set of k clusters using Eq. (17.1), and then re-update the k means for the $t+2$ step. This is done until the process converges, meaning that these k means do not change significantly based on some criteria.

Note that this algorithm does not guarantee finding the global optimum [2]. In practice, however, the K-means algorithm is fast, and it may be one of the fastest clustering algorithms available for local minima. Because the initiation of the k means is of random nature, one may need to perform the clustering several times and choose the best result.

Lloyd's algorithm discussed above has an average complexity of $O(kmT)$, where m is the number of data-points and T is the number of iterations. Even faster variations of Lloyd's algorithm have been developed, one of which is Elkan's algorithm, which uses the triangular inequality property to significantly improve the efficiency. Elkan's algorithm is quite frequently used, and we will demonstrate Elkan's algorithm in the case study examples.

Note also that one may use a different distance norm measure other than the squared Euclidean distance for these K-means type of algorithms. This may change the convergence behavior. More details on this can be found at the Wikipedia page (https://en.wikipedia.org/wiki/K-means_clustering) and the links therein.

Figure 17.1 is a picture taken from a nicely made animation by Chire with CC BY-SA 4.0 (https://creativecommons.org/licenses/by-sa/4.0) via the Wikimedia Commons (https://commons.wikimedia.org/wiki/File:K-means_convergence.gif). This animation shows clearly how the iteration is performed in a typical K-means algorithm.

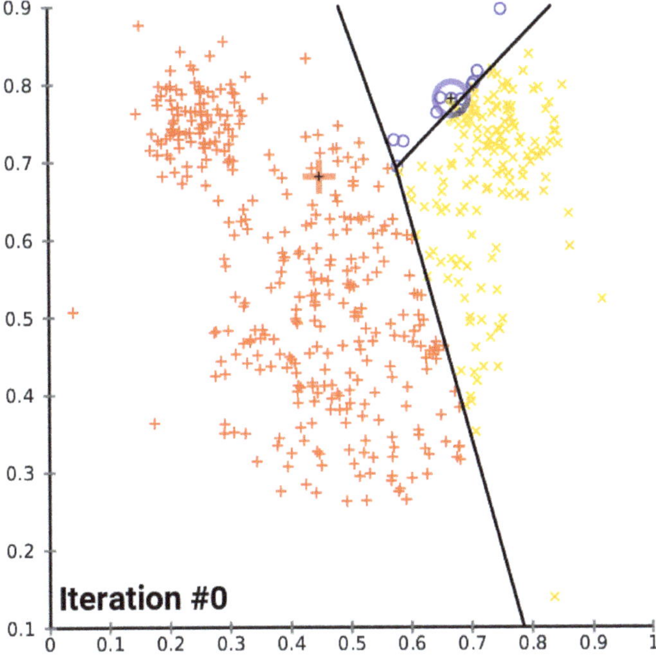

Figure 17.1: Convergence process of a typical K-means algorithm. The data-points are given and fixed in 2D feature space, which are to be grouped in $k = 3$ clusters: blue, yellow, and red ones.

To examine the process more closely, we plot snapshots at four iterations: 0th (initial), 2nd, 5th, and 14th, as shown in the Fig. 17.2.

As shown in Fig. 17.1, the data-points are given and fixed in 2D space, which are to be grouped in $k = 3$ clusters. At the beginning, a set of 3 means is generated (randomly or otherwise) based on these data-points. These three means (cluster centers) are marked with a blue circle, yellow x, and red cross. Based on these 3 means, a Voronoi diagram is formed, via the "nearest mean" criterion by computing the squared Euclidean distances of the data-points to these 3 means. The edges (these 3 black lines) of the Voronoi diagram divide the data-points into 3 clusters: the blue, yellow, and red ones. At the 0th iteration, these 3 means are quite randomly placed. The blue circle is very close to the yellow x, and both are far apart from the red cross. Next, 3 means of the coordinates of the data-points for these 3 clusters are computed, using Eq. (17.2). This results in 3 updated means. At the 2nd iteration, these 3 means are more reasonably separated and the data-points are also better clustered. With the updated 3 means, the data-points are re-clustered via the nearest mean criterion. This process iterates until the update becomes sufficiently small. The clustering process converges. At the

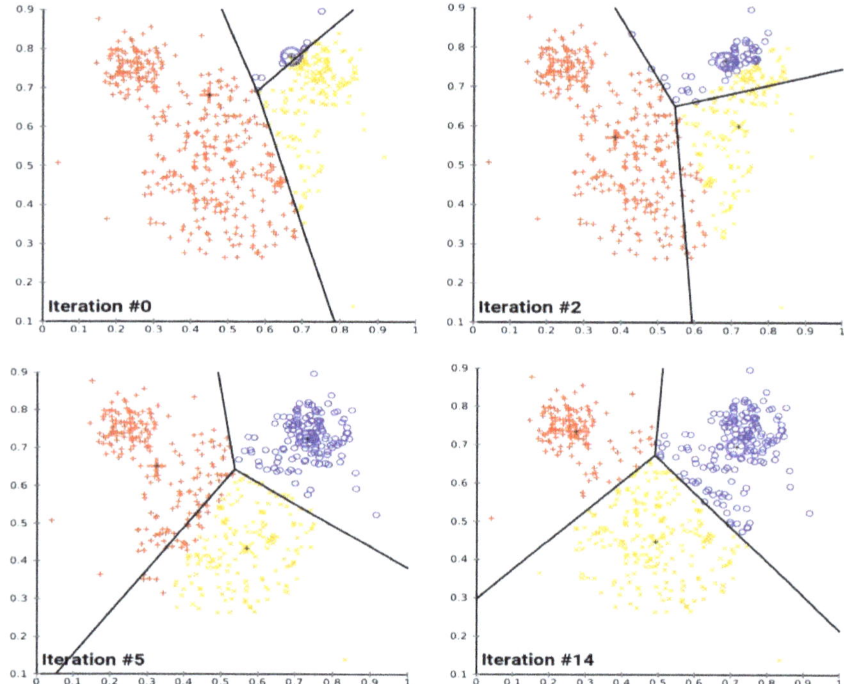

Figure 17.2: Examination of the converging process of a typical K-means algorithm. The data-points are given in 2D feature space, and are to be grouped into $k = 3$ clusters: blue, yellow, and red ones.

5th iteration, the clustering is already quite good and not too far from that achieved at the final 14th iteration.

Note that when the number of the clusters k increases, the Voronoi diagram will become more complicated, as will be shown in one of the examples later for a 10-digit clustering problem.

17.2.4 *Example 1: Case studies on comparison of initiation methods for K-means clustering*

In this first example, we compare the various initialization methods for K-means clustering in terms of computation time and quality of the clustering results, using various evaluation metrics. We will use randomly generated synthetic data for this study, so that we can design four different cases for this study. We will write a simple code for this study using routines available at Scikit-learn [3].

17.2.4.1 *Define a function for benchmarking study*

We will use the following function to evaluate the performance of the method. It uses the SKlearn class make_pipeline to compute the evaluation metrics. This function will be called when a K-means run is completed using an initiation means.

```python
# From Sklearn online examples
# import all necessary modules
import numpy as np
import matplotlib.pyplot as plt
from sklearn.cluster import MeanShift, estimate_bandwidth
from sklearn.datasets import make_blobs
from sklearn.datasets import load_digits
from sklearn import metrics
from sklearn.pipeline import make_pipeline
from sklearn.preprocessing import StandardScaler
from time import time
%matplotlib inline


def bench_k_means(kmeans, name, data, labels):
    """To evaluate the KMeans initialization methods.

    Parameters
    ----------
    kmeans : KMeans instance
             class:`~sklearn.cluster.KMeans` instance with the
             initialization already set.
      name : str
             Name given to the strategy. It will be used to show
             the results in a table.
      data : ndarray of shape (n_samples, n_features)
             The data for clustering.
    labels : ndarray of shape (n_samples,)
             The labels used to compute the clustering metrics
             which require some supervision.
    """
    t0 = time()
    (n_samples, n_features), n_k = data.shape,
        np.unique(labels).size
    estimator = make_pipeline(StandardScaler(), kmeans).fit(data)
    fit_time  = time() - t0
    results   = [name, fit_time, estimator[-1].inertia_]
```

```python
    # Define the metrics which require only the true labels
    # and estimated labels
    clustering_metrics = [metrics.homogeneity_score,
                          metrics.completeness_score,
                          metrics.v_measure_score,
                          metrics.adjusted_rand_score,
                          metrics.adjusted_mutual_info_score,]

    results+=[m(labels,estimator[-1].labels_) for m in
    clustering_metrics]

    # The silhouette score requires the full dataset
    results+=[metrics.silhouette_score(data, estimator[-1].labels_,
            metric="euclidean", sample_size=n_samples,)]

    # Show the results
    formatter_result = ("{:9s}\t{:.3f}s\t{:.0f}\t{:.3f}\t{:.3f}"
                        "\t{:.3f}\t{:.3f}\t{:.3f}\t{:.3f}")
    print(formatter_result.format(*results))
```

```python
# function to print out key information about the dataset

def print_data_info(data, labels,n_features,n_k,n_samples,n_comp):
    print('data=',data[0:1,0:10], '\n data.shape=', data.shape)

    print(f"No of clusters k:{n_k}; No of samples:{n_samples};
          "+ f"No of features p:{n_features};
          No of PCA  comps:{n_comp}")

    print('data.shape:',data.shape)
    print('labels:',labels,' Shape:',labels.shape)


#_____________________________________________________________________

# Function to print out evaluation metrics
def print_evaluation_metrics():
    print('inertia: sum of squared distances of samples to their
          centroid')
    print('homo: homogeneity [0,1] of the clusters with their own
          data-points')
    print('compl: completeness [0,1], how well the same
          class points fit the clusters')
    print('v_meas: v_measure score [0,1], consistence btw two
          clustering results')
```

```python
    print('ARI: adjusted rand index [-1,1], distances btw
          different sample splits')
    print('AMI: adjusted mutual info index [0,1], the mutual
          infor. for two splits')
    print('silht: silhouette [-1,1] mean-distance ratio of
          in- & btw-clusters points')


#____________________________________________________________
# Define a function to plot the clusters
# The data needs to be reduced to 2D, if it not already 2D
# kmeans needs already been fitted

def plot_clusters(reduced_data,kmeans,fig_title):

    # Mesh step size. Decrease to increase the quality of VQ.
    h = .02      # points in [x_min, x_max]x[y_min, y_max].

    plt.figure(figsize=(4.0, 4.0),dpi=100)
    # Plot the decision boundary. Assign a color to each
    x_min, x_max = reduced_data[:, 0].min() - 1,
                     reduced_data[:, 0].max() + 1
    y_min, y_max = reduced_data[:, 1].min() - 1,
                     reduced_data[:, 1].max() + 1
        xx, yy = np.meshgrid(np.arange(x_min, x_max, h),
                     np.arange(y_min, y_max, h))

    # Labels for each point in mesh. Use last trained model.
    Z = kmeans.predict(np.c_[xx.ravel(), yy.ravel()])

    # Put the result into a color plot
    Z = Z.reshape(xx.shape)
    plt.figure(1)
    plt.clf()
    plt.imshow(Z, interpolation="nearest",
               extent=(xx.min(), xx.max(), yy.min(), yy.max()),
               cmap=plt.cm.Paired, aspect="auto", origin="lower")

    plt.plot(reduced_data[:, 0], reduced_data[:, 1], 'k.',
             markersize=2)

    # Plot the centroids as a white X
    centroids = kmeans.cluster_centers_
    plt.scatter(centroids[:, 0], centroids[:, 1], marker="x",
                s=169, linewidths=3, color="w", zorder=10)

    plt.title(fig_title)
```

```
#xyd = 3.5
xyd = min(abs(x_min), x_max, abs(y_min), y_max)
x_min, x_max, y_min, y_max = -xyd, xyd, -xyd, xyd
plt.xlim(x_min, x_max)
plt.ylim(y_min, y_max)

plt.xticks(())
plt.yticks(())
plt.show()

#print('centroids=',centroids)
```

17.2.4.2 *Generation of synthetic data-points*

We now generate a set of synthetic data-points using the SKlearn make_blobs class in a random manner. In this example, we designed a total of four study cases, which are detailed in the cell below. Readers may simply assign a number (from 1 to 4) to a variable "Case", and the date points for this case will then be generated.

```
# Choose a case to generate a set of synthetic data-points.
# Number of features (n_features) and number of clusters (k)
# will be computed after the data-points are generated

Case=3 # 1 or 2 or 3 or 4 # 4 cases designed for this example

if Case == 1:
    #_____________________________________________________________
    # Case 1: synthetic sample with 2 groups of data-points
    # in 2D space, n_features=2, n_k=2
    centers = [[1, 1], [-1, -1]] # centers for 2D points
    #_____________________________________________________________
elif Case == 2:
    # Case 2: synthetic sample data that has 3 groups of
    # data-points in 3D space, n_features=3, n_k=3
    centers = [[1, 1, 1], [-1,-1,-1], [1,-1,0.5]] # for 3D points
    #_____________________________________________________________
elif Case == 3:
    # Case 3: synthetic sample data that has 3 groups of
    # data-points in 2D space, n_features=2, n_k=3
    centers = [[1, 1], [-1,-1], [1,-1]]   # set 3 centers 2D points
    #_____________________________________________________________
```

```python
elif Case == 4:
    # Case 4: synthetic sample data that has 2 groups of
    # data-points in 6D space, n_features=6, n_k=5
    centers = [[ 1, 0, 1, 1, 1, 0], [-1,-1,-1,-1, 0,-1],
               [1,-1,-1, 0,-1,-1],  [ 1, 1, 0,-1,-1,-1],
               [ 0, 1, 1, 0,-1, -1]]
            # set 5 centers for 5 group of data-points in 6D
    #_________________________________________________________
else:
    print('There are a total of 4 cases for this example!!!')

print('Cluster centers set for the data-points =', centers)

# Generation of data-points
n_s, c_std = 1888, 0.4888        # n_s: number of samples;
    #c_std: standard deviation for random data-points generation
data,labels=make_blobs(n_samples=n_s,centers=centers,
    cluster_std=c_std)           # number of samples

(n_samples, n_features), n_k = data.shape, np.unique(labels).size

n_comp = min(n_features, n_k)   # number of prin. cmpnts when
            # PCA is used to create initial means for K-means

# print out key data information
print('This example has a total of 4 cases. This is Case-'
      +str(Case)+'; Data:'+str(n_features)+'D')

print_data_info(data, labels,n_features,n_k,n_samples,n_comp)
```

```
Cluster centers set for the data-points =
    [[1, 1], [-1, -1], [1, -1]]
This example has a total of 4 cases. This is Case-3; Data:2D
data= [[ 0.60389228 -1.62706035]]
 data.shape= (1888, 2)
No of clusters k:3; No of samples:1888; No of features p:2;
    No of PCA comps:2
data.shape: (1888, 2)
labels: [2 0 2 ... 1 0 2]  Shape: (1888,)
```

17.2.4.3 *Examination of different initiation methods*

We conduct a comparison study on different initialization methods for K-means clustering. This includes three initiation methods:

- Initialization using the `kmeans++` method. This is a random-farthest-point for initial mean generation. We will run the initiation and clustering for n_i times, and choose the best results based on the inertia value.
- Initialization using "random" option. This is also a pure random method. We will run the initiation and clustering for n_i times, and choose the best results based on the inertia value.
- Initialization using PCA. The principal components of the PCA will be used as the initial means. This is a deterministic method, and a single run shall suffice.

```python
# Comparison study runs
from sklearn.cluster import KMeans
from sklearn.decomposition import PCA

print('This example has a total of 4 cases. This is Case-'+
        str(Case)+'; Data:'+str(n_features)+'D')
print_data_info(data, labels,n_features,n_k,n_samples,n_comp)
print(78 * '_')
print('init\t\ttime\tinertia\thomo\tcompl\tv-meas\tARI\
      tAMI \tsilht')
n_i = 5   # The times the k-means algorithm will run with
          # different centroid seeds. The final results will be the
          # best output of n_i consecutive runs in terms of inertia.

if Case != 3:   # (2D, n_features=2, n_k=3, PCA not applicable
    pca = PCA(n_components=n_comp).fit(data)
    kmeans = KMeans(init=pca.components_, n_clusters=n_k, n_init=1)
    bench_k_means(kmeans=kmeans,name="PCA-init",data=data,
                labels=labels)
kmeans = KMeans(init="random",n_clusters=n_k,n_init=n_i,
                random_state=0)
                # by default it uses the Elkan algorithm
bench_k_means(kmeans=kmeans, name="random", data=data,
                labels=labels)


kmeans = KMeans(init="k-means++", n_clusters=n_k, n_init=n_i,
                random_state=0)
```

```python
bench_k_means(kmeans=kmeans, name="k-means++",data=data,
            labels=labels)
r_data = PCA(n_components=n_comp).fit_transform(data)
bench_k_means(kmeans=kmeans,name="k-means++pca",data=r_data,
            labels=labels)

print(78 * '_')
print_evaluation_metrics()
```

```
This example has a total of 4 cases. This is Case-3; Data:2D
data= [[ 0.60389228 -1.62706035]]
 data.shape= (1888, 2)
No of clusters k:3; No of samples:1888; No of features p:2;
    No of PCA comps:2
data.shape: (1888, 2)
labels: [2 0 2 ... 1 0 2]  Shape: (1888,)
________________________________________________________________
init            time    inertia homo  compl v-meas ARI   AMI    silht
random          0.018s  763     0.890 0.890 0.890  0.929 0.890 0.561
k-means++       0.015s  763     0.890 0.890 0.890  0.929 0.890 0.561
k-means++pca    0.013s  892     0.830 0.830 0.830  0.878 0.830 0.555

________________________________________________________________
inertia: sum of squared distances of samples to their centroid
   homo: homogeneity [0,1] of the clusters with their own data-points
  compl: completeness [0,1], how well the same class points fit the clusters
v_meas: v_measure score [0,1], consistence btw two clustering results
   ARI: adjusted rand index [-1,1], distances btw different sample splits
   AMI: adjusted mutual info index [0,1], the mutual infor. for two splits
  silht: silhouette [-1,1] mean-distance ratio of in- & btw-clusters points
```

Set Case $= 1$ in the codes given above; the clustering has been completed on the author's laptop and the results are summarized in the same output table above. We may observe the following:

- First is the computation time for clustering. They are all very fast in the order of 20 ms. The K-means with PCA initiated means (the PCA-init method) takes about 7 ms, and it runs fastest (without counting the time for the PCA). This is because it runs only once. The time for the other three methods is roughly the same, and slower than the PCA-init, because they are set to run for 5 times. Because our toy problem with synthetic data is very small in scale, the measure of computation time is not accurate. We cannot make much point.

- Next is the quality of clustering. These first three methods listed in the output table give the same quality results in all the measuring metrics. Because this toy problem is too simple, there may just be one global optimal solution, and any of these methods give the same answer. However, the k-means++pca gives a result that is different from that of all the other three methods, especially on the inertia measure. This is because the K-means is done using the PCA processed data. For Case-1, the PCA did not reduce the data dimension, but projected the dataset to its two principle axes. The dataset in the principle component space become flatter (see Chapter 3). Thus, the measured inertia becomes much larger. The scores measured in other metrics have some change but not very much.

- Using the same code, we set the n_init to 1 (instead for 5) and run. We obtained the same results. This also supports the argument that there is likely just one optimal solution to this toy problem, because randomly selected initial means do not give a different solution for all the methods used. Readers can easily confirm this using the code given.

Readers may set Case to other numbers (2 or 3 or 4). Similar observations can be made for all these toy cases.

17.2.4.4 *Visualize the clustering results*

Our toy example problem has two cases (Case-2 and Case-4) with higher-dimensional data in the feature space ($p = 3$ and $p = 6$). K-means can have all these datasets clustered in these high dimensions. However, it is difficult to visualize these clusters in high dimension. Therefore, we will use PCA to project the datasets into a 2D principal component space, conduct K-means clustering, and then plot the data-points and their clusters on a 2D plane. This is done using the following codes and the plot_clusters() defined earlier:

```python
import matplotlib.pyplot as plt

if Case == 1 or Case == 3: # Case 1 or 3: data in 2D space,
    n_k =2 or 3
    #_________________________________________________________
    pca_compf = 0              # no PCA used for plotting the data
    reduced_data = data     # no dimension reduction
    #_________________________________________________________
elif Case == 2 or Case == 4:  # Case 2: 3 group data in 3D space,
                              #         n_features=3, n_k =3
                              # Case 4: 5 group data in 6D space,
                              #         n_features=6, n_k=5
    pca_compf = 2              # dimension reduction to show in 2D
    reduced_data = PCA(n_components=pca_compf).fit_transform(data)
    #_________________________________________________________
```

```python
else:
    print('There are a total of 4 cases for this example!!!')

print_data_info(data, labels,n_features,n_k,n_samples,n_comp)
kmeans = KMeans(init="k-means++", n_clusters=n_k, n_init=n_i)
kmeans.fit(reduced_data)
fig_title = "Case-"+str(Case)
plot_clusters(reduced_data,kmeans,fig_title)
print('Cluster centers set for the data-points =', centers)
```

```
data= [[ 0.60389228 -1.62706035]]
 data.shape= (1888, 2)
No of clusters k:3; No of samples:1888; No of features p:2;
    No of PCA comps:2
data.shape: (1888, 2)
labels: [2 0 2 ... 1 0 2]  Shape: (1888,)
```

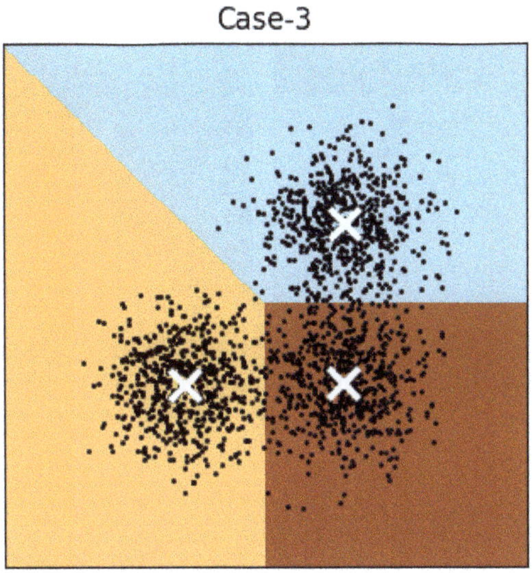

Case-3

Figure 17.3:   Clustered data-points for Case-3 using the K-means.

```
Cluster centers set for the data-points = [[1,1], [-1,-1], [1,-1]]
```

Figure 17.4 plots the clusters and the data-points for all these four cases. We note the following:

- All these cases are well clustered using K-means algorithm, with the converged centroids (marked with white X) each for a cluster.

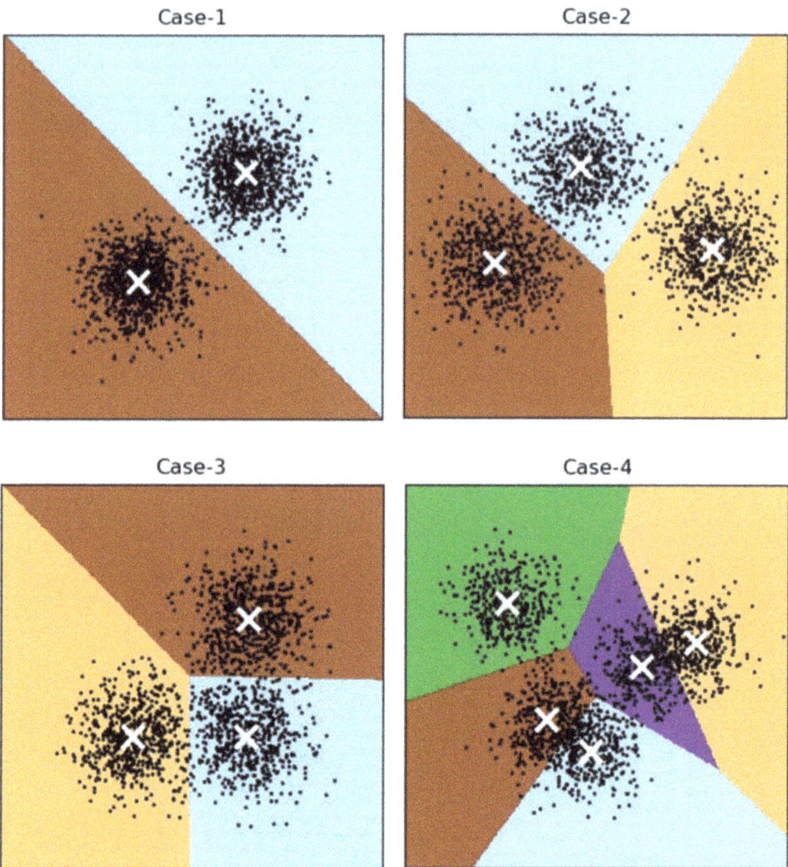

Figure 17.4: *K*-means clusters for synthetic data-points generated randomly for four different cases of datasets. The original datasets for Case-2 and Case-4 are in higher-dimensional feature spaces. For these datasets, its feature space is reduced to 2D and then the *K*-means clustering is performed.

- These clusters are hosted in the colored Voronoi cells (one cluster per color), and the boundaries between these Voronoi cells divide these clusters.
- The line that connects these centroids (for each of the cases) is perpendicular (orthogonal) to the Voronoi cell boundary (or its extended straight line). This orthogonality is proof that these cells are essentially the Voronoi cells by definition. It is produced by minimizing the squared Euclidean distances of a point in cluster to its centroid in the *K*-means clustering algorithm.

We are now ready to look at a more complicated real-life example.

17.2.5 *Example 2: K-means clustering on the handwritten digit dataset*

We now apply the K-means clustering algorithm to a set of images of hand-written digits. This dataset is the test set of the UCI ML hand-written digits (https://archive.ics.uci.edu/ml/datasets/Optical+Recognition+of+Handwritten+Digits). The functions defined earlier for our toy dataset example can be used as is for this study. We can also use the same metric for evaluation of the efficiency and quality of the clustering.

17.2.5.1 *Load handwritten digit dataset*

We first load the dataset using the SKlearn load_digits() and perform the clustering using the same SKlearn's K-means. This dataset contains images of 10 handwritten digits from 0 to 9. We would like each cluster to contain the images of the same digits. We thus have $k = 10$ clusters for the problem. Each of these images has 8×8 pixel, meaning that the number of features is 64.

```python
# Import necessary module for this task
import numpy as np
from sklearn.datasets import load_digits
import matplotlib.pyplot as plt
%matplotlib inline
# load the digits dataset
data, labels = load_digits(return_X_y=True)
(n_samples,n_features),n_digits=data.shape,np.unique(labels).size
n_k = n_digits
n_comp = 2
print_data_info(data, labels,n_features,n_k,n_samples,n_comp)
print('Take a look at the image for digit 9:')
plt.imshow(data[9].reshape(8,8))
```

```
data= [[ 0.  0.  5. 13.  9.  1.  0.  0.  0.  0.]]
 data.shape= (1797, 64)
No of clusters k:10; No of samples:1797; No of features p:64;
    No of PCA comps:2
data.shape: (1797, 64)
labels: [0 1 2 ... 8 9 8]  Shape: (1797,)
Take a look at the image for digit 9:

<matplotlib.image.AxesImage at 0x1fdcd0ca1d0>
```

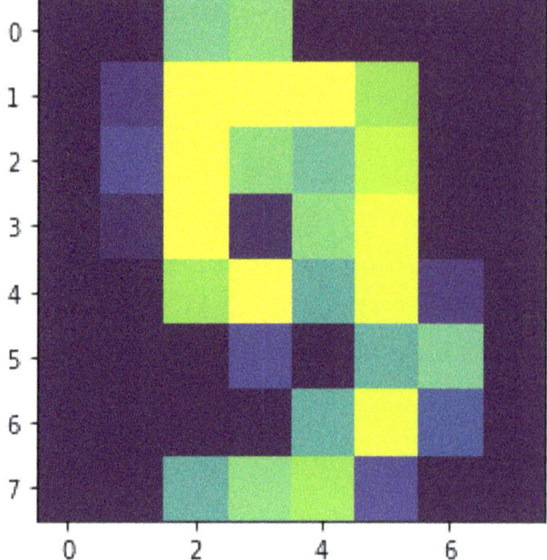

Figure 17.5: Sample image of a handwritten digit in the dataset of UCI ML hand-written digits.

As shown in Fig. 17.5, in this dataset, each of the images has 64 features that are the image values at the 8×8 pixels.

17.2.5.2 *Examination of different initiation methods*

We conduct a comparison study on different initialization methods for K-means clustering. We compare the same three initiation methods as in the previous example and in a similar manner.

```python
from sklearn.cluster import KMeans
from sklearn.decomposition import PCA

print('data.shape:',data.shape)
print(f"Number of digits (k):{n_digits}; Number of samples (n):\
{n_samples};Number of features (p) {n_features}")
print(78 * '_')
print('init\t\ttime\tinertia\thomo\tcompl\tv-meas\tARI\
    tAMI\tsilht')
n_i = 5
pca = PCA(n_components=n_digits).fit(data)
kmeans = KMeans(init=pca.components_, n_clusters=n_digits,
        n_init=1)
bench_k_means(kmeans=kmeans, name="PCA-init", data=data,
        labels=labels)  # by default it uses the Elkan algorithm
kmeans = KMeans(init="random",n_clusters=n_digits,n_init=n_i,
        random_state=0)
bench_k_means(kmeans=kmeans, name="random", data=data,
        labels=labels)
```

```
kmeans = KMeans(init="k-means++", n_clusters=n_digits, n_init=n_i,
        random_state=0)
bench_k_means(kmeans=kmeans, name="k-means++", data=data,
        labels=labels)


n_compr = 10 # n_digits
r_data = PCA(n_components=n_compr).fit_transform(data)
bench_k_means(kmeans=kmeans,name="k-means++pca",data=r_data,
            labels=labels)


print(78 * '_')
print_evaluation_metrics()
```

```
data.shape: (1797, 64)
Number of digits (k):10; Number of samples (n):1797;
    Number of features (p) 64
```

init	time	inertia	homo	compl	v-meas	ARI	AMI	silht
PCA-init	0.065s	72686	0.636	0.658	0.647	0.521	0.643	0.146
random	0.089s	69952	0.545	0.616	0.578	0.415	0.574	0.137
k-means++	0.143s	69485	0.613	0.660	0.636	0.482	0.632	0.162
k-means++pca	0.072s	9169	0.722	0.727	0.724	0.650	0.721	0.246

```
inertia: sum of squared distances of samples to their centroid
   homo: homogeneity [0,1] of the clusters with their own data-points
  compl: completeness [0,1], how well the same class points fit the clusters
v_meas: v_measure score [0,1], consistence btw two clustering results
    ARI: adjusted rand index [-1,1], distances btw different sample splits
    AMI: adjusted mutual info index [0,1], the mutual infor. for two splits
  silht: silhouette [-1,1] mean-distance ratio of in- & btw-clusters points
```

The results in the above output table tell us the following:

- First is the computation time taken for the clustering. They are all very fast for this handwritten digit dataset. The K-means with PCA initiated means (the PCA-init method) takes only $\sim$20 ms. It runs fastest (without counting the time for the PCA). This is because it runs only once. The time for the other three methods is roughly the same, and slower than the PCA-init, because they were set to run for 5 times. The k-means++ method took about 5 times more time. Note that the runtime can also change depending on whether or not the computer is on other tasks at the same time.

- The inertia value is the sum of squared distances of samples to their centroid. The random and k-means++ methods give quite close inertia values. The PCA-init gives a higher value and the k-means++pca gives a much smaller value. This is because the use of PCA has reduced the feature space dimension from 64 to 10, before the k-means++ clustering, leading to significant reduction in inertial value.

- The other five evaluation metrics, homo, compl, v-meas, ARI, and AMI, are objective measures on the quality of the clustered results, because these measures all use the true labels of the original data as the basis for comparison, although the measurement methods are different. Based on the output table above, PCA-init is of least quality, partially because it runs only once. The random method achieved better scores for all these measures compared to PCA-init, partially because it ran five times. Readers may change n_init number to 1 and rerun the code, and we shall still find that the random method performs better for this example. The k-means++ method is slightly better than the random method. The k-means++pca gives the best results, that is, quite significantly better than the k-means++ on all these measures. This is largely due to the dimension reduction to the original dataset before the k-means++ clustering.

- The silhouette score (shown in the last column in the output table) is computed without the use of the true labels. It measures the ratio of the mean distances of the data-points within the clusters and that between the clusters, based on the clustered results. This measure is less objective, because the true labels are not used as the basis for comparison. However, this measure is useful because we do not usually have true labels in unsupervised learning. In this silhouette measure, the PCA-init gives least score. Both random and k-means++ methods give a higher score. The best performer is still the k-means++pca method. Note that the silhouette measure is also useful in K-means methods that do not pre-specify the number of the clusters k. It can be used to determine the best k number for unlabeled datasets.

Readers can easily try out different setting and the run this example using the code given.

Let us now plot the clustered data-points in 2D plane with the help of (again) the PCA.

17.2.5.3 *Visualize the results for handwritten digit clustering using PCA*

The dataset for the handwritten digit is 64-dimensional in the feature space. It is not possible for us to visualize the clustered results is such a high dimension. We thus use the PCA to reduce the feature space to a two-dimensional PCA principal components space, and then plot the data together with the clusters.

```python
import matplotlib.pyplot as plt
pca_components = 2      # we can only view this well in 2D space
reduced_data = PCA(n_components=pca_components).
                fit_transform(r_data)
kmeans = KMeans(init="k-means++", n_clusters=n_digits, n_init=n_i)
kmeans.fit(reduced_data)
fig_title = str(n_digits)+" handwritten digits"
plot_clusters(reduced_data,kmeans,fig_title)
```

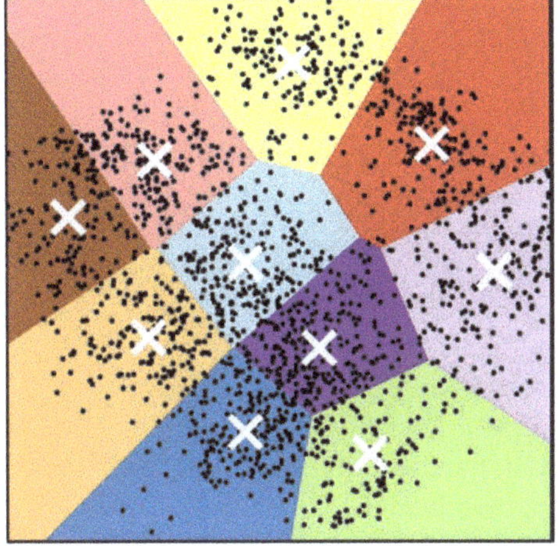

Figure 17.6:   Results of the 10-means clustering using the dataset of UCI ML hand-written digits.

Notice from Fig. 17.6 that we have a more complicated Voronoi diagram for the 10-means clustering problem.

17.3 Mean-Shift for Clustering Without Pre-Specifying k

In using a K-means type of algorithm, we usually need to pre-specify the number of clusters k. This implies that we do know some information about the dataset. In many unsupervised learning applications, we do not even know k, and we need to cluster the data-points in a dataset. This section discusses one such method, called mean-shift method, for such a task. Mean shift clustering aims to discover "blobs" in a "cloud" of data-points. It is a centroid-based algorithm, which works by updating candidates for centroids to be the mean of the data-points within a given region. These candidates are then filtered in a post-processing stage to eliminate near duplicates to form the final set of centroids. More details can be found in the Sklearn documentation and Ref. [4].

Let us look at a demonstration of the mean-shift clustering algorithm that uses a flat kernel. This demonstration is available at Scikit-learn [3].

```python
%matplotlib inline
print(__doc__)
import numpy as np
from sklearn.cluster import MeanShift, estimate_bandwidth
from sklearn.datasets import make_blobs

# Generate synthetic sample data that has 3 groups of data-points
n_s, c_std = 1888, 0.4888
centers = [[1, 1], [-1, -1], [1, -1]] # set 3 centers of these
                                      # data-points

X, _ = make_blobs(n_samples=n_s, centers=centers,
                  cluster_std=c_std)
print('X=',X[0:2:], ' X.shape=', X.shape)
# This dataset is the same as Case-3 in Example 1

# Compute clustering with MeanShift
# First, estimate the bandwidth, it is needed in the MeanShift
# algorithm
bandwidth = estimate_bandwidth(X, quantile=0.2, n_samples=500)
print('Bandwidth=', bandwidth)

# MeanShift clustering
ms = MeanShift(bandwidth=bandwidth, bin_seeding=True)
ms.fit(X)
labels = ms.labels_
cluster_centers = ms.cluster_centers_
# print('Predicted cluster centers=', cluster_centers)

labels_unique = np.unique(labels)
                          # Find the unique elements in an array
n_clusters_ = len(labels_unique)

print("Number of estimated clusters : %d" % n_clusters_)
# Plot the clustering result
import matplotlib.pyplot as plt
from itertools import cycle

fig_title ='MeanShift Clusters'
plot_clusters(X,ms,fig_title)
print('Cluster centers set for generating the dataset =', centers)
centroids_kmeans = [[ 0.98774496,  0.99979977],
    [-0.96779894 -0.9892344 ], [ 1.02407913, -0.98301746]]
```

```python
print('Cluster centers found by the kmeans++ was =',
        centroids_kmeans)
```

```
Automatically created module for IPython interactive environment
X= [[ 0.55586883 -0.56830437]
   [ 1.02971177 -1.1907716 ]]  X.shape= (1888, 2)
Bandwidth= 0.8892415258145057
Number of estimated clusters : 3
```

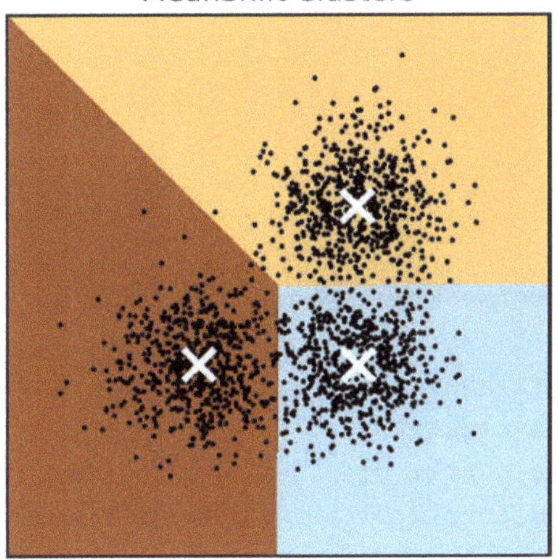

Figure 17.7:   An example of MeanShift clustering resulting in three clusters.

```
Cluster centers set for generating the dataset = [[1, 1],
    [-1, -1], [1, -1]]
Cluster centers found by the kmeans++ was = [[0.98774496,
    0.99979977], [-1.95703334], [1.02407913, -0.98301746]]
```

```python
# Compute clustering with MeanShift
# Estimate the bandwidth, needed in the MeanShift algorithm
# The complexity of estimate_bandwidth function is at
# least quadratic in n_samples. For large datasets, use a
# small value.
bandwidth = estimate_bandwidth(reduced_data, quantile=0.0519,
            n_samples=450)
# Note: estimate_bandwidth can be sensitive to the
# parameters: quantile and n_samples.
print('Bandwidth=', bandwidth)
```

```python
# MeanShift clustering
ms = MeanShift(bandwidth=bandwidth, bin_seeding=True)
ms.fit(reduced_data)
labels = ms.labels_
cluster_centers = ms.cluster_centers_
# print('Predicted cluster centers=', cluster_centers)

labels_unique = np.unique(labels)
                # Find the unique elements in an array
n_clusters_ = len(labels_unique)
print("Number of estimated clusters : %d" % n_clusters_)
fig_title ='MeanShift for Digits'
plot_clusters(reduced_data,ms,fig_title)
print('Centroids by MeanShift is:    Centroids by
        kmeans++ was:\n')
ms_cntr = np.sort(ms.cluster_centers_,axis=0)
                # sort for easy comparison
km_cntr = np.sort(kmeans.cluster_centers_,axis=0)
for i in range(n_clusters_):
    print (f'{ms_cntr[i,0]:12.4f}{ms_cntr[i,1]:9.4f}'
            f'{km_cntr[i,0]:19.4f}{km_cntr[i,1]:9.4f}')
```

```
Bandwidth= 5.722875000219844
Number of estimated clusters : 10
```

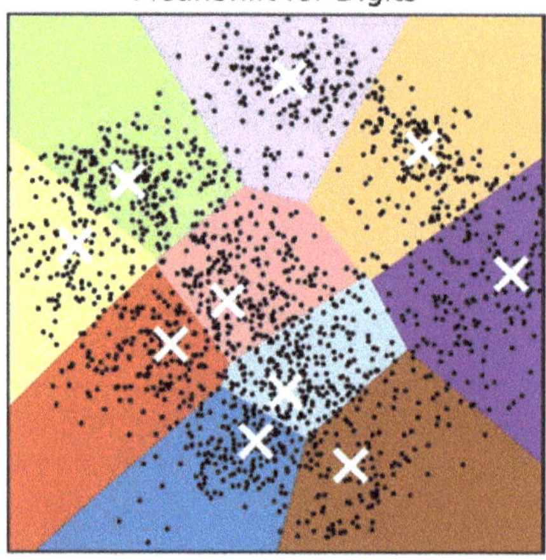

Figure 17.8:   Results of a MeanShift clustering using the dataset of UCI ML hand-written digits.

```
Centroids by MeanShift is:       Centroids by kmeans++ was:

  -21.2030 -19.2417               -22.0921 -19.5846
  -15.6402 -16.6971               -14.1853 -16.6444
  -11.0635 -11.4488               -12.8868  -8.2211
   -5.0131  -6.4602                -3.7937  -6.8557
   -1.9861  -1.9128                -3.6150  -0.3548
    1.1829   1.0722                 1.4639   0.3682
    1.5387   4.0261                 4.6894   5.7448
    8.0474  10.8061                 9.2011  11.3140
   15.6139  14.2532                15.9470  12.9644
   25.0669  21.7812                22.6392  21.6084
```

We note the following points from this study:

- This handwritten digit dataset has 64 features. To simply this problem, we used PCA to reduce the dimension number to 10. This also allows us to compare the MeanShift results with the K-means results that we obtained in the previous example.

- It is found that the clustered results obtained using the MeanShift are similar but quite different from these obtained using K-means, as shown in results for the centroids listed in the above table.

- Note also that the estimate_bandwidth can be quite sensitive to the parameters of quantile and n_samples. The setting with quantile=0.0519 and n_samples=450 produces 10 clusters for the handwritten digit dataset. Changing these to other numbers can produce totally different results first for the bandwidth and then for the final clustering results. For example, when quantile is changed to 0.04, we obtained 16 clusters. Therefore, care is needed when running this kind of prediction.

- This example has also demonstrated that constructing unsupervised machine learning models is in general a quite difficult task. Getting some kind of information on unlabeled datasets can be helpful. More concrete research is needed in this area, and hence it is one of the hottest topics of study.

17.4 Autoencoders

Compressing of data is widely used, because storing and transferring bigdata are expensive and can be very time consuming, despite advancements in computer telecommunication technology. Techniques for compressing data without much loss in features are of importance. A number of compression techniques for different forms of data have already been developed. The principle component analysis (PCA) technique is an excellent tool for compressing data with controllable loss of accuracy. We have seen some examples in Chapter 3. The PCA is a very general and universally useful tool for compressing data with features that are mostly linear. Neural network based Autoencoders [5–9] can also be useful for a variety of types of data, including huge datasets with linear or nonlinear features.

17.4.1 *Basic structure of autoencoders*

An autodecoder is a technique to encode data automatically using an artificial neural network that is trained without labeled data. It has essentially three major parts, an **encoder**, **bottleneck**, and **decoder**, as shown in Fig. 17.9.

The encoder can have one or more layers with training parameters of weights and biases. It takes the original input dataset, encodes it with these parameters, and then feeds it to the bottleneck neurons. The compressed

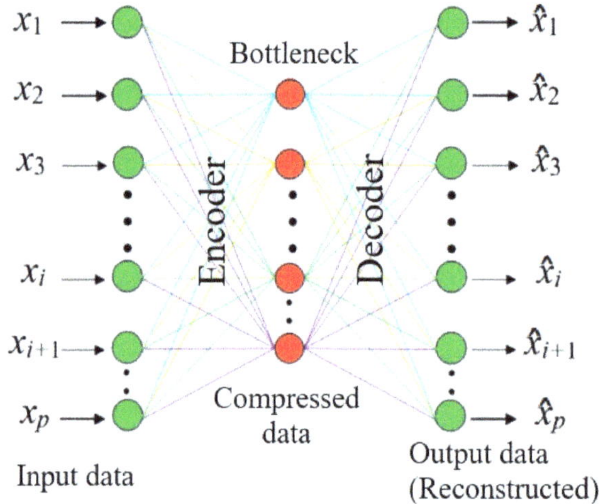

Figure 17.9:   A neural network for autodecoder. It consists of two sub-nets, one for the encoder and one for the decoder, which are bridged by the bottleneck layer $\mathbf{z}$. An input data $\mathbf{x}$ into the encoder, with the current training parameters, produces latent features $\mathbf{z}$. The same $\mathbf{z}$ is then feed into the decoder and produces an output $\tilde{\mathbf{x}}$. The input $\mathbf{x}$ itself is used as the label at the final output layer, and the residual $\mathbf{r} = \tilde{\mathbf{x}} - \mathbf{x}$ is minimized to force the output $\tilde{\mathbf{x}}$ close to the input $\mathbf{x}$. Once trained properly with a dataset, the autoencoder produces the latent features at the bottleneck, that are the extracted/hidden features in the dataset.

data is then feeds to the decoder that may have one or more layers and their own training parameters. The decoder decodes the compressed data to reconstruct the data.

The network is trained with a simple criterion that the decoded (reconstructed) data at the output layer must be as close as possible to the original input data. This is why the training does not require the input data to be labeled. Cost functions defined in the previous chapter can then be used to satisfy this criterion for different types of data. The training process is essentially the same as training any other neural network, via a back-propagation process. Once the training is completed, all the training parameters in these three parts are set, and the autodecoder is capable of reconstructing the data with the compressed data when it is needed. This is the basic strategy for an autoencoder.

Autoencoders can be built with various types of layers including dense layers, convolution layers, their combinations, and other forms of layers.

17.4.2 *Example 1: Image compression and denoising*

One can easily build an Autoencoder using an existing ML package such as Keras, by simply stacking up layers of neurons in a configuration similar to Fig 17.9. Reader may take a look at an example and the code provided by Ali Abdelaal in his online article "Autoencoders for Image Reconstruction in Python and Keras" (https://stackabuse.com/autoencoders-for-image-reconstruction-in-python-and-keras/). It uses the LFW (http://vis-www.cs.umass.edu/lfw/) dataset and shows a detailed procedure with code for image compression and denoising.

17.4.3 *Example 2: Image segmentation*

Image segmentation can be useful in autonomous vehicles, where one may need to segment objects such as persons, animals, bicycles, and cars. Techniques of CNNs and Autoencoders are useful to creating effective models for image segmentations. The following are some examples of image segmentation using pixel libraries (https://github.com/ayoolaolafenwa/PixelLib):

```python
import matplotlib.pyplot as plt
import numpy as np
from PIL import Image
%matplotlib inline
```

```python
import pixellib
from pixellib.semantic import semantic_segmentation
segment_image = semantic_segmentation()
segment_image.load_pascalvoc_model
    ('deeplabv3_xception_tf_dim_ordering_ tf_kernels.h5')
segment_image.segmentAsPascalvoc('../images/inkedcars15.jpg',
    output_image_name = '../images/cars15-s.jpg')
img = Image.open('../images/inkedcars15.jpg')
plt.figure(figsize=(10, 15))
plt.imshow(img);
```

Figure 17.10:   Original image for segmentation.

```python
img = Image.open('../images/cars15-s.jpg')
plt.figure(figsize=(10, 15))
plt.imshow(img);
```

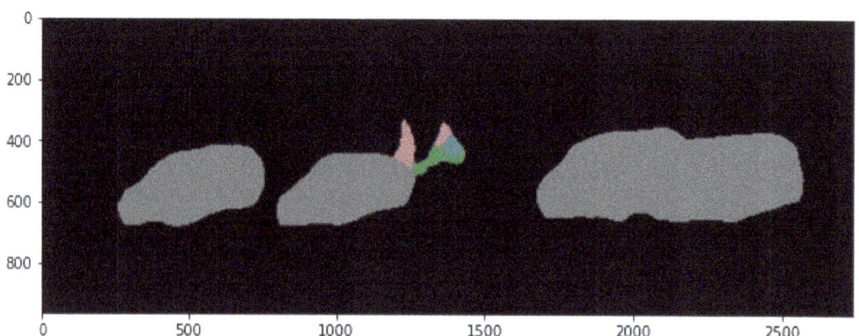

Figure 17.11:   Resulting image after segmentation. The object type of the image is color coded.

The color code is used to distinguish the type of objects. The details of the color codes can be found at pixel libraries site. One can also overlay the segmented objects with the original image

```python
segment_image.segmentAsPascalvoc('../images/inkedcars15.jpg',
    output_image_name = '../images/cars15-s.jpg', overlay = True)
img = Image.open('../images/cars15-s.jpg')
plt.figure(figsize=(10, 15))
plt.imshow(img);
```

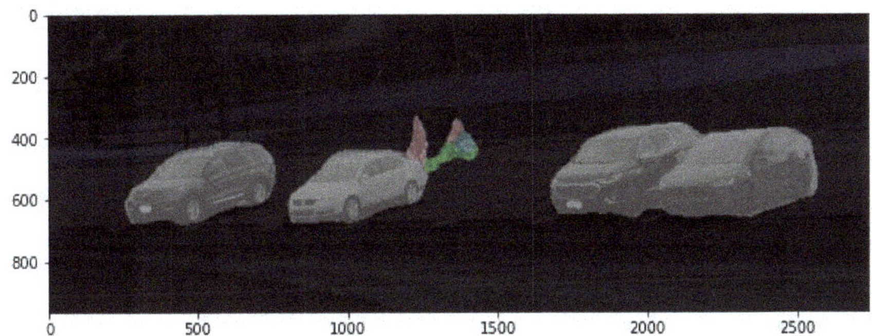

Figure 17.12:   Overlaid image of the original and the segmented images.

```python
import pixellib
from pixellib.semantic import semantic_segmentation
import time
from pixellib.instance import instance_segmentation
segment_image = instance_segmentation()
segment_image.load_model("mask_rcnn_coco.h5")
start = time.time()
segment_image.segmentImage("../images/inkedcars-blocked.jpg",
            output_image_name = "../images/cars-blocked-s.jpg")
end = time.time()
print(f"Inference Time: {end-start:.2f}seconds")
img = Image.open("../images/inkedcars-blocked.jpg")
plt.figure(figsize=(10, 15));
plt.imshow(img);
```

```
Processed image saved successfully in your current working
    directory.
Inference Time: 19.08seconds
```

Figure 17.13:   The original image for segmentation.

```python
img = Image.open("../images/cars-blocked-s.jpg")
plt.figure(figsize=(10, 15))
plt.imshow(img)
```

```
<matplotlib.image.AxesImage at 0x1fa39721108>
```

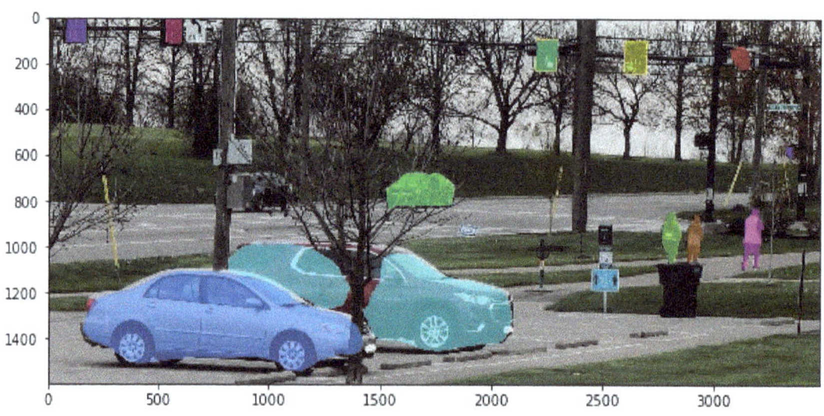

Figure 17.14:   Overlaid image of the original and segmented images. The object type is color coded.

```python
segment_image.segmentImage("../images/inkedcars-blocked.jpg",
        output_image_name = "../images/cars-blocked-sf.jpg",
        show_bboxes = True)
img = Image.open("../images/cars-blocked-sf.jpg")
plt.figure(figsize=(10, 15))
plt.imshow(img);
```

Figure 17.15: Overlaid image of the original and segmented images. The object type is color coded. Objects are boxed.

Examples of Autoencoders using the MNIST dataset and the codes by the Keras Team are available at The Keras Blog (https://blog.keras.io/building-autoencoders-in-keras.html). Variational Autoencoders (VAE) can also be used for segmentations. The theoretical discussion about VAE will be given in the last section of this chapter. Autoencoders have many other applications, including Text Embeddings (http://yaronvazana.com/2019/09/28/training-an-autoencoder-to-generate-text-embeddings/), Anomaly detection, and Popularity prediction, just to name a few.

17.5 Autoencoder vs. PCA

The above examples demonstrate how an Autodecoder is built, trained, and used. To build a high-quality and well-posed Autoencoder, one would need to have a good understanding of its mathematical foundation. Here, we try to establish a better mathematical understanding of an Autoencoder, and examine the similarity and difference between a single-layer Autoencoder and the PCA that we have studied in Chapter 3. This study follows an excellent article by Ranjan (https://towardsdatascience.com/build-the-right-Autoencodertune-and-optimize-using-pca-principles-part-i-1f01f821999b). Readers may refer to the original article for more details. Figure 17.16 is from this article and illustrates quite clearly the mathematical operations that are used in both an Autoencoder and a PCA. Note that the formulation is a little different from that in our book.

Figure 17.16 shows a single-layer linear Autoencoder together with the mathematical operations involved. The bottom of the figure shows

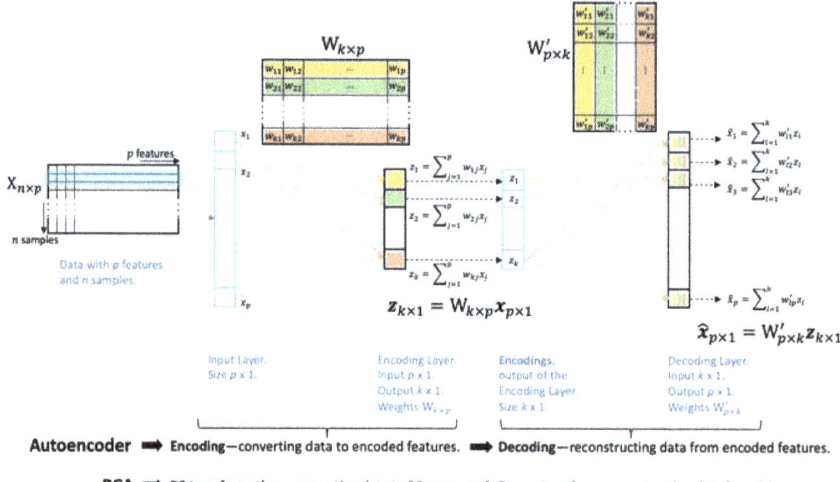

Figure 17.16:   Relationship between an Autoencoder and PCA [10] (with permission).

the similarity of the encoding process against the PC transformation. PC transformation projects the original input data on their principal components to yield orthogonal features, called principal scores or latents. The decoding process is also similar to the PCA reconstructing process using their principal scores. These weights in both Autoencoder and PCA models are determined by minimizing the errors between the p features. Both models use the same input data:

- The Autoencoder has p neurons in its input layer.
- The PCA uses the same p input samples.

For the encoder in an Autoencoder and the eigenvalue decomposition in PCA, the outcome of the mathematical operations is equivalent. In particular, the following points may be noted:

- The code-size of the encoder layer is k in the Autoencoder.
- In PCA, k is the number of the selected principal components (PCs, or latents). In both models, we shall have $k < p$, so as to achieve dimension reduction.
- When $k \geq p$, it can lead to over-representative models, and the reconstruction error can be made zero, if the training or reconstruction is successful. Because of the existence of multiple solutions, the solution obtained using one of these two models may be different from the other.
- The w_{ij} in the colored cells in the encoder in the foregoing figure is for the ith neuron in the bottleneck corresponding to the jth feature (parameter)

of the input data, where $i = 1, 2, \ldots, k$ and $j = 1, 2, \ldots, p$. The $\mathbf{W}_{k \times p}$ is equivalent to the matrix of the first k eigenvectors generated in a PCA algorithm.

- If the linear activation function is used in the bottleneck neurons, the output of the bottleneck of an Autoencoder becomes $\mathbf{z}_{k \times 1} = \mathbf{W}_{k \times p} \mathbf{x}_{p \times 1}$, which is equivalent to the k principal components (or scores) in a PCA.

For the decoder in an Autoencoder and for the reconstruction process in a PCA, the outcome of the mathematical operations is also equivalent. In particular, the following points may be noted:

- The number of neurons in the output layer of the decoder in the Autoencoder and the number of outputs in PCA reconstruction are the same, and all are equal to p, that is, the number of the features in the input data.
- The output (reconstructed) data from the decoder (after taking the outputs from the bottleneck neurons) become $\hat{\mathbf{x}}_{p \times 1} = \mathbf{W}'_{p \times k} \mathbf{z}_{k \times 1}$, equivalent to the p outputs in PCA, which are the principle scores projected back to the original space (from the principal component space), using the transpose of the matrix of the first k eigenvectors.

The multi-colors in the output neurons in the decoder indicate that the weights related to the bottleneck neurons may all contribute to a neuron of the output in the Decoder.

The above comparison uses words like "similar" and "equivalent". If one uses linear activation functions, it is possible to train an Autoencoder to be the same as the linear PCA, by properly enforcing a set of constraints during the training including tying the weights in the encoder and decoder, and orthogonal conditions on the weights. For more details, one may refer to the article by Ranjan. Constraint Autoencoder [9] is used for feature-space dimension-reduction for inverse analysis using Tubenets [11–13].

17.6 Variational Autoencoder (VAE)

Variational autoencoders are a recent interesting version of Autoencoder. Instead of training to encode usual *discrete* features from a dataset, a VAE learns the parameters of a probability *distribution*. When samples from the learned distribution, one can reconstruct, and also generate new data samples. Thus, VAE is thus said a "generative model". It has an architecture shown in Fig. (17.17), which is quite similar to a standard autoencoder.

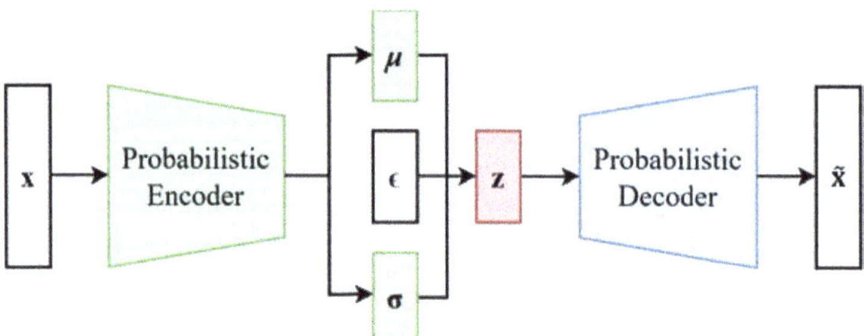

Figure 17.17: A variational autoencoders (VAE). It consists of two sub-nets, one for the encoder and one for the decoder, which are bridged by the bottleneck layer $\mathbf{z}$ that consists of three components: vector of means $\boldsymbol{\mu}$, covariance matrix $\boldsymbol{\Sigma}$, and vector $\boldsymbol{\epsilon}$ drawn from the standard normal distribution. An input data $\mathbf{x}$ into the encoder, with the current training parameters, produces $\boldsymbol{\mu}$ and $\boldsymbol{\Sigma}$ that is used together with $\boldsymbol{\epsilon}$ to form latent features $\mathbf{z}$ that is a normal distribution. The same $\mathbf{z}$ is then feed into the decoder and produces an output $\tilde{\mathbf{x}}$. The input $\mathbf{x}$ itself is used as the label at the final output layer, and the residual $\mathbf{r} = \mathbf{x} - \tilde{\mathbf{x}}$ is minimized to force the output $\tilde{\mathbf{x}}$ close to the input $\mathbf{x}$, while the KL-divergence of the standard normal distribution from the distribution of $\mathbf{z}$ is also minimized. Once trained properly with a dataset, the autoencoder produces the latent distributive features at the bottleneck, that can be used to reconstruct data-points in the input dataset, or to generate new data-points that may not in the dataset. [Image modified based on that of EugenioTL from Wikimedia Commons, under the CC BY-SA 4.0 license].

17.6.1.1 *Key ideas in VAE*

The key ideas used in the VAE is as follows.

- First, a VAE encoder converts the input samples $\mathbf{x}$ into in a latent space of distribution variables controlled by two sets of latent features: means of distribution $\boldsymbol{\mu}$ and covariance matrix $\boldsymbol{\Sigma}$, at the bottleneck.
- Next, we sample randomly points $\mathbf{z}$ from the normal distribution $\mathcal{N}(\boldsymbol{\mu}, \boldsymbol{\Sigma})$,

$$\mathbf{z} = \boldsymbol{\mu} + \boldsymbol{\Sigma}^{1/2}\boldsymbol{\epsilon}$$

where $\boldsymbol{\epsilon}$ is randomly generated vector from a standard normal distribution with zero means and identify standard variations $\mathcal{N}(\mathbf{0}, \mathbf{I})$. This is because for normal distributions, we have

$$\mathcal{N}(\boldsymbol{\mu}, \boldsymbol{\Sigma}) = \boldsymbol{\mu} + \boldsymbol{\Sigma}^{1/2}\mathcal{N}(\mathbf{0}, \mathbf{I}) \tag{17.3}$$

- Finally, a VAE decoder maps these sampled latent space points to reconstruct the input data or generate new data.
- The parameters of a VAE model are trained using the following loss function.

$$\mathcal{L}_{vae}\left(\mathbf{W}, \tilde{\mathbf{W}}; \mathbf{x}, \mathcal{N}(\mathbf{0}, \mathbf{I})\right) = \mathcal{L}(\tilde{\mathbf{x}}, \mathbf{x}) + D_{KL}\left(q_{\mathbf{W}}(\mathbf{z}|\mathbf{x}) \| p_{\tilde{\mathbf{W}}}(\tilde{\mathbf{x}}|\mathbf{z})\right) \tag{17.4}$$

where $\mathbf{W}$ is the training parameters used in the encoder, and $\tilde{\mathbf{W}}$ is that used in the decoder. This loss function consists of two parts: one is the reconstruction loss forcing the reconstructed samples to match the inputs. A loss function defined in Chapters 10, 11 and 12 may be used. The other is a KL-divergence defined in Chapter 4, which measures the differences between the latent distribution $q_{\mathbf{W}}(\mathbf{z}|\mathbf{x})$ and the prior distribution $p_{\tilde{\mathbf{W}}}(\tilde{\mathbf{x}}|\mathbf{z})$ acting as a regularization term. The KL-divergence needs to minimized so that the distributions is forced to match the prior distribution.

Note that the KL-divergence for any two normal distributions has a simple closed-form in terms of only their means and variances, which is critical for the practical implementation of VAEs. To show this, we use the KL-divergence of normal distributions in continuous form.

17.6.1.2 *KL-divergence for two single-variable normal distributions*

Consider two normal distributions $p(x)$ and $q(x)$ of a single-variable $x \in \mathbb{R}^1$. Their probability density functions are given by

$$
\begin{aligned}
p(x) &= \mathcal{N}(\mu_p, \sigma_p^2) = \frac{1}{\sqrt{2\pi}\sigma_p} e^{-\left(\frac{x-\mu_p}{\sqrt{2}\sigma_p}\right)^2} ; \\
q(x) &= \mathcal{N}(\mu_q, \sigma_q^2) = \frac{1}{\sqrt{2\pi}\sigma_q} e^{-\left(\frac{x-\mu_q}{\sqrt{2}\sigma_q}\right)^2}
\end{aligned}
\tag{17.5}
$$

where μ and σ are, respectively, the mean and the standard deviation of the distribution specified by the subscript. Note in this case, both $p(x)$ and $p(x)$ are scalar functions of x, and their distributions are full controlled by their means and standard deviations.

The KL-divergence from $q(x)$ to $p(x)$ can be written as

$$
\begin{aligned}
D_{KL}(q\|p) &= \int q(x)\left[\log(q(x)) - log(p(x))\right] dx \\
&= \int q(x)\left[-\log(\sigma_q) - \frac{1}{2}\left(\frac{x-\mu_q}{\sigma_q}\right)^2 + \log(\sigma_p) + \frac{1}{2}\left(\frac{x-\mu_p}{\sigma_p}\right)^2\right] dx \\
&= \int q(x)\left[\log\left(\frac{\sigma_p}{\sigma_q}\right) + \frac{1}{2}\left(\frac{x-\mu_p}{\sigma_p}\right)^2 - \frac{1}{2}\left(\frac{x-\mu_q}{\sigma_q}\right)^2\right] dx \\
&= E_q\left[\log\left(\frac{\sigma_p}{\sigma_q}\right) + \frac{1}{2}\left(\left(\frac{x-\mu_p}{\sigma_p}\right)^2 - \left(\frac{x-\mu_q}{\sigma_q}\right)^2\right)\right]
\end{aligned}
$$

$$= \log\left(\frac{\sigma_p}{\sigma_q}\right) + \frac{1}{2\sigma_p^2}E_q\left[(x-\mu_p)^2\right] - \frac{1}{2\sigma_q^2}E_q\left[(x-\mu_q)^2\right]$$

$$= \log\left(\frac{\sigma_p}{\sigma_q}\right) + \frac{1}{2\sigma_p^2}E_q\left[(x-\mu_p)^2\right] - \frac{1}{2}$$

$$= \log\left(\frac{\sigma_p}{\sigma_q}\right) + \frac{\sigma_q^2+(\mu_q-\mu_p)^2}{2\sigma_p^2} - \frac{1}{2}$$

$$= \frac{1}{2}\left[2\log\left(\frac{\sigma_p}{\sigma_q}\right) + \frac{\sigma_q^2}{\sigma_p^2} + \frac{(\mu_q-\mu_p)^2}{\sigma_p^2} - 1\right] \tag{17.6}$$

In the last step we used the following simple manipulation:

$$(x-\mu_p)^2 = (x-\mu_q+\mu_q-\mu_p)^2 = (x-\mu_q)^2 + 2(x-\mu_q)(\mu_q-\mu_p) + (\mu_q-\mu_p)^2, \tag{17.7}$$

Its expectation over $q(x)$ thus becomes

$$E_q[(x-\mu_p)^2] = E_q[(x-\mu_q)^2] + E_q[2(x-\mu_q)(\mu_q-\mu_p)] + E_q[(\mu_q-\mu_p)^2]$$

$$= \sigma_q^2 + 0 + (\mu_q-\mu_p)^2 \tag{17.8}$$

The 2nd term in the right-hand-side of Eq. (17.8) vanishes, because $(x-\mu_q)(\mu_q-\mu_p)$ is an odd function, and $q(x)$ is symmetric. It is easy to check if $q(x)$ and $p(x)$ are the same distribution, the KL-divergence becomes zero, as expected.

Now, if $p(x)$ is standard normal distribution: $\mu_p = 0$ and $\sigma_p = 1$, we shall have,

$$D_{KL}(q\|p) = \frac{\sigma_q^2+\mu_q^2}{2} - \log\sigma_q - \frac{1}{2}, \tag{17.9}$$

Further, when $q(x)$ is also standard normal distribution, the KL-divergence becomes zero.

17.6.1.3 *KL-divergence for two multi-variable normal distributions*

Consider now two normal distributions of $p(\mathbf{x})$ and $q(\mathbf{x})$ of a multi-variable $\mathbf{x} \in \mathbb{R}^k$. The dimension of the domain becomes k, and $\mathbf{x} = [x_1, x_2, \dots, x_k]^\top$ in $\mathbb{R}^k$. The probability density functions are given by

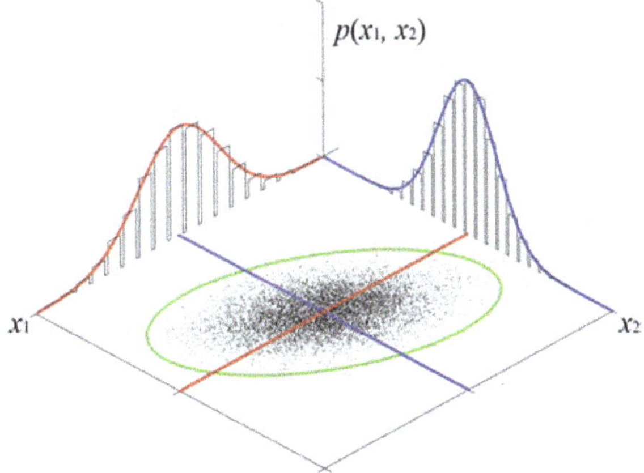

Figure 17.18: An example of multi-variable normal distribution with $k = 2$. The probability distribution of the samples along the red and blue straight lines are, respectively, given in red and blue Gaussian bell curves. [Image modified based on that of IkamusumeFan from Wikimedia Commons, under the CC BY-SA 3.0 license].

$$p(\mathbf{x}) = \mathcal{N}(\mathbf{x}; \boldsymbol{\mu}_p, \boldsymbol{\Sigma}_p) = \frac{1}{\sqrt{(2\pi)^k |\boldsymbol{\Sigma}_p|}} \exp\left(-\frac{1}{2}(\mathbf{x} - \boldsymbol{\mu}_p)^\top \boldsymbol{\Sigma}_p^{-1}(\mathbf{x} - \boldsymbol{\mu}_p)\right)$$

$$q(\mathbf{x}) = \mathcal{N}(\mathbf{x}; \boldsymbol{\mu}_q, \boldsymbol{\Sigma}_q) = \frac{1}{\sqrt{(2\pi)^k |\boldsymbol{\Sigma}_q|}} \exp\left(-\frac{1}{2}(\mathbf{x} - \boldsymbol{\mu}_q)^\top \boldsymbol{\Sigma}_q^{-1}(\mathbf{x} - \boldsymbol{\mu}_q)\right)$$

$$(17.10)$$

where $\boldsymbol{\mu} = [\mu_1, \mu_2, \ldots, \mu_k]^\top$ is a vector of means in $\mathbb{X}^k$, and $\boldsymbol{\Sigma}$ is the covariant matrix in $\mathbb{X}^{k \times k}$. Both $p(\mathbf{x})$ $p(\mathbf{x})$ are still scalar functions, and their distributions are controlled by their means and covariances. An example of multi-variable normal distribution with $k = 2$ is shown in Fig. 17.18. The KL-divergence from $q(\mathbf{x})$ to $p(\mathbf{x})$ can be written as the following starting with a multidimensional integral.

$$D_{KL}(q\|p) = \int q(\mathbf{x})\left[\log(q(\mathbf{x})) - log(p(\mathbf{x}))\right] d\mathbf{x}$$

$$= \int q(\mathbf{x})\frac{1}{2}\left[\log\frac{\det \boldsymbol{\Sigma}_p}{\det \boldsymbol{\Sigma}_q} + (\mathbf{x} - \boldsymbol{\mu}_p)^\top \boldsymbol{\Sigma}_p^{-1}(\mathbf{x} - \boldsymbol{\mu}_p)\right.$$

$$\left. - (\mathbf{x} - \boldsymbol{\mu}_q)^\top \boldsymbol{\Sigma}_q^{-1}(\mathbf{x} - \boldsymbol{\mu}_q)\right] d\mathbf{x}$$

$$
= \frac{1}{2} E_q \left[\log \frac{\det \mathbf{\Sigma}_p}{\det \mathbf{\Sigma}_q} + (\mathbf{x} - \boldsymbol{\mu}_p)^\top \mathbf{\Sigma}_p^{-1}(\mathbf{x} - \boldsymbol{\mu}_p) \right.
$$

$$
\left. - (\mathbf{x} - \boldsymbol{\mu}_q)^\top \mathbf{\Sigma}_q^{-1}(\mathbf{x} - \boldsymbol{\mu}_q) \right]
$$

$$
= \frac{1}{2} \left(\log \frac{\det \mathbf{\Sigma}_p}{\det \mathbf{\Sigma}_q} + E_q[(\mathbf{x} - \boldsymbol{\mu}_p)^\top \mathbf{\Sigma}_p^{-1}(\mathbf{x} - \boldsymbol{\mu}_p)] \right.
$$

$$
\left. - E_q[(\mathbf{x} - \boldsymbol{\mu}_q)^\top \mathbf{\Sigma}_q^{-1}(\mathbf{x} - \boldsymbol{\mu}_q)] \right)
$$

$$
= \frac{1}{2} \left(\log \frac{\det \mathbf{\Sigma}_p}{\det \mathbf{\Sigma}_q} + E_q[(\mathbf{x} - \boldsymbol{\mu}_p)^\top \mathbf{\Sigma}_p^{-1}(\mathbf{x} - \boldsymbol{\mu}_p)] - k \right)
$$

$$
= \frac{1}{2} \left(\log \frac{\det \mathbf{\Sigma}_p}{\det \mathbf{\Sigma}_q} + tr(\mathbf{\Sigma}_p^{-1}\mathbf{\Sigma}_q) + (\boldsymbol{\mu}_q - \boldsymbol{\mu}_p)^\top \mathbf{\Sigma}_p^{-1}(\boldsymbol{\mu}_q - \boldsymbol{\mu}_p) - k \right)
\tag{17.11}
$$

In the 4th step, we used properties of trace and expectation manipulations on products of matrices:

$$
\begin{aligned}
E_q \left[(\mathbf{x} - \boldsymbol{\mu}_q)^\top \mathbf{\Sigma}_q^{-1}(\mathbf{x} - \boldsymbol{\mu}_q) \right] &= E_q \left[tr \left((\mathbf{x} - \boldsymbol{\mu}_q)^\top \mathbf{\Sigma}_q^{-1}(\mathbf{x} - \boldsymbol{\mu}_q) \right) \right] \\
&= tr \left[E_q \left((\mathbf{x} - \boldsymbol{\mu}_q)^\top \mathbf{\Sigma}_q^{-1}(\mathbf{x} - \boldsymbol{\mu}_q) \right) \right] \\
&= tr \left[E_q \left((\mathbf{x} - \boldsymbol{\mu}_q)(\mathbf{x} - \boldsymbol{\mu}_q)^\top \mathbf{\Sigma}_q^{-1} \right) \right] \\
&= tr \left[\mathbf{\Sigma}_q \mathbf{\Sigma}_q^{-1} \right] = tr[\mathbf{I}] = k
\end{aligned}
\tag{17.12}
$$

In the last step, we used the matrix version of manipulations similar to Eq. (17.7).

It is easy to check if $q(\mathbf{x})$ and $p(\mathbf{x})$ are the same distribution, the KL-divergence becomes zero, as expected.

Now, if $p(\mathbf{x})$ is standard normal distribution, we shall have

$$
D_{KL}(q\|p) = \frac{1}{2} \left(-\log(\det \mathbf{\Sigma}_q) + tr(\mathbf{\Sigma}_q) + \boldsymbol{\mu}_q^\top \boldsymbol{\mu}_q - k \right)
\tag{17.13}
$$

Further, when $q(\mathbf{x})$ is also standard normal distribution, the KL-divergence becomes zero.

In VAE, we often assume the covariance matrix $\mathbf{\Sigma}_q$ is diagonal: $\mathbf{\Sigma}_q = diag(\Sigma_{q1}, \Sigma_{q2}, \ldots, \Sigma_{qk})$. Therefore, the trace of it will be sum of these variances. The determinant of it will be product of these variances. Therefore, Eq. (17.13) can be further simplified to

$$
\begin{aligned}
D_{KL}(q\|p) &= \frac{1}{2}\left(-\log(\prod_i^k \Sigma_{qi}) + \sum_i^k \Sigma_{qi} + \sum_i^k \mu_{qi}^2 - \sum_i^k 1\right) \\
&= \frac{1}{2}\left(-\sum_i^k \log(\Sigma_{qi}) + \sum_i^k \Sigma_{qi} + \sum_i^k \mu_{qi}^2 - \sum_i^k 1\right) \qquad (17.14) \\
&= \frac{1}{2}\sum_i^k \left(-\log(\Sigma_{qi}) + \Sigma_{qi} + \mu_{qi}^2 - 1\right)
\end{aligned}
$$

Finally, for numerical stability reason, we often replace Σ_{qi} with $\exp(\Sigma_{qi})$, and the final equation for KL-divergence often used in VAE in Eq. (17.4) is given as follows.

$$
D_{KL}(q\|p) = \frac{1}{2}\sum_i^k \left(\exp(\Sigma_{qi}) + \mu_{qi}^2 - \log(\Sigma_{qi}) - 1\right), \qquad (17.15)
$$

where the means and variances are computed using the current learning parameters $\mathbf{W}$ for q, and $\tilde{\mathbf{W}}$ for p for the deterministic part. The standard normal distribution is used for the stochastic part as shown in Eq. (17.3). This allows the back-propagation during training by-passing through the bottleneck layer without the stochastic part effecting the computation of gradients with respect to $\mathbf{W}$ in a VAE model. This is known as the so-called *re-parameterization trick*.

With the above formulation, a VAE can now be built with minimum change to the standard autoencoder. An example code is available at https://keras.io/examples/generative/vae/ where a step by step how to create, train and make use of a VAE model.

References

[1] G. Hamerly and C. Elkan, Alternatives to the k-means algorithm that find better clusterings, 2002. https://doi.org/10.1145/584792.584890.

[2] J.A. Hartigan and M.A. Wong, Algorithm AS 136: A K-Means Clustering Algorithm, *Journal of the Royal Statistical Society. Series C (Applied Statistics)*, **28**(1), 100–108, 1979. http://www.jstor.org/stable/2346830.

[3] P. Fabian, V. Gae, G. Alexandre *et al.*, Scikit-learn: Machine learning in Python, *Journal of Machine Learning Research*, **12**(85), 2825–2830, 2011. http://jmlr.org/papers/v12/pedregosa11a.html.

[4] D. Comaniciu and P. Meer, Mean shift: A robust approach toward feature space analysis, *IEEE Transactions on Pattern Analysis and Machine Intelligence*, **24**(5), 603–619, 2002.

[5] A. Kramer Mark, Nonlinear principal component analysis using autoassociative neural networks, *AIChE Journal*, **37**(2), 233–243, 1991. https://aiche.onlinelibrary.com/doi/abs/10.1002/aic.690370209.

[6] I. Goodfellow, Y. Bengio and A. Courville, Deep Learning, 2016.

[7] P. Diederik and W. Max, An introduction to variational autoencoders, *CoRR*, abs/1906.02691, 2019. http://arxiv.org/abs/1906.02691.

[8] G.E. Hinton, A. Krizhevsky and S.D. Wang, Transforming auto-encoders, *Artificial Neural Networks and Machine Learning — ICANN 2011*, 2011.

[9] D. Shuyong, H. Zhiping, G.R. Liu *et al.*, A novel inverse procedure via creating tubenet with constraint autoencoder for feature-space dimension-reduction, *International Journal of Applied Mechanics*, **13**(8), 2150091, 2021.

[10] C. Ranjan, *Understanding Deep Learning: Application in Rare Event Prediction*, Connaissance Publishing, 2020. www.understandingdeeplearning.com.

[11] G.R. Liu, S.Y. Duan, Z.M. Zhang *et al.*, Tubenet: A special trumpetnet for explicit solutions to inverse problems, *International Journal of Computational Methods*, **18**(01), 2050030, 2021. https://doi.org/10.1142/S0219876220500309.

[12] L. Shi, F. Wang, G. Liu *et al.*, Two-way TubeNets Uncertain Inverse methods for improving Positioning Accuracy of robots Based on Interval, *The 11th International Conference on Computational Methods (ICCM2020)*, 2020.

[13] D. Shuyong, S. Lutong, G.R. Liu *et al.*, An uncertainty inverse method for parameters identification of robot arms based on two-way neural network, *Inverse Problems in Science & Engineering*, Revised, 2021.

Chapter 18

Reinforcement Learning (RL)

18.1 Basic Underlying Concept

18.1.1 *Problem statement*

We shall have a pretty good idea about the supervised and unsupervised machine learning techniques. This chapter discusses another important technique called reinforcement learning (RL).

When a child is around the age of 1, he/she starts to learn walking. If one observes the learning process carefully, the child is trying to adjust his/her steps forward by moving different parts of muscles, without failing down or avoiding being punished by gravity that is an environment he/she dost not know. We may also notice that if a parent is squatted down in front of him/her, he/she will take bolder steps, and the learning often progresses faster. This is because he/she sees a higher safety and a reward, which reinforces the learning process. In a way, machine RL is a mimic of this process of learning to walk, and the machine-child is called **agent**. An agent learns to take actions in an environment with unknown distributed punishments or awards, and the learning is reinforced through the process of cumulating rewards and/or avoiding punishments.

The RL differs from the supervised learning mainly in the learning guiding principle. Supervised learning needs a dataset with predefined input-label pairs, and the learning objective it to minimize the differences between the given labels and the predictions using the corresponding inputs. In RL, however, the agent does not have such a dataset. It is given an environment that is unknown to the agent. It needs to learn the environment by taking trial **actions** that can lead to some **awards** when proper action is taken at **states** in the environment.

A number of techniques related to RL have been developed in various disciplines including the game theory, operational research, control theory, and optimal control. Techniques include the Monte Carlo method, Q-learning, Deep Q-Network, Deep Deterministic Policy Gradient, and Trust Region Policy Optimization. [1–4]. There are both model-based and model-free RLs. If a simulation model for predicting the dynamics of the environment is available, model-based RL may be a good choice, because the agent can predict the next state with a probability from the current state when an action is taken. If such a predictive model is not available, one has to use model-free RL. In this chapter, we will brief first on the fundamental principle and theory for reinforcement learning. Our focus will be on the so-called Q-learning method, which is a basic representative technique and is model-free. We will also introduce neural network implementation of Q-learning: Q-Network. In the last section, we will discuss about some currently most popular policy gradient methods, including the powerful Proximal Policy Optimization (PPO). Readers may refer to Reinforcement Learning: An Introduction [1] and the wikipedia page and the reference links therein for more details on various RL techniques.

18.1.2 *Applications in sciences, engineering, and business*

Reinforcement learning algorithms can be used to solve problems that arise in sciences, engineering, and business settings where operation automation is required.

Service and manufacturing robots: The agent (robot) senses and interacts with the environment and learns to complete a task in the most effective manner.

Automatic and optimal control: The agent learns to take the most stable or optimal positions and movements in an environment, by trial and error.

Delivery drones: The agent (drone) learns to find a safe and most economic path and navigates to the destination.

Operational research: The agent learns to find the best possible operations to accomplish tasks related to resource management.

Personalized recommendations: The agent learns to make the best recommendations of news or advertisements to users, by learning and predicting the behavior of the users.

Games: The agent learns to take the best actions to maximize the score. Each action will affect the states of the agent in the gaming environment. A typical example is the widely publicized AlphaGo.

18.1.3 *Reinforcement learning approach*

Figure 18.1 is a schematic drawing of a reinforcement learning process. An environment is given with some distributions of rewards and/or punishments. Such distributions are unknown to the agent. The agent sets to explore over it. It takes actions and then observes environment. Because the environment is initially unknown to the agent, it can only take actions at random at the beginning. By chance, it may make a wrong move and needs to restart. Or, by chance it makes a good move and gets awarded, and tries again. This trial-and-error learning circle iterates aiming to achieve optimal accumulated rewards. In each trial, it needs to interpret the environment and update its states. An algorithm is needed to ensure that such an updating leads to the best accumulation of rewards (or effective avoidance of the punishment). To this end, we need a number theory to govern the construction of such algorithms.

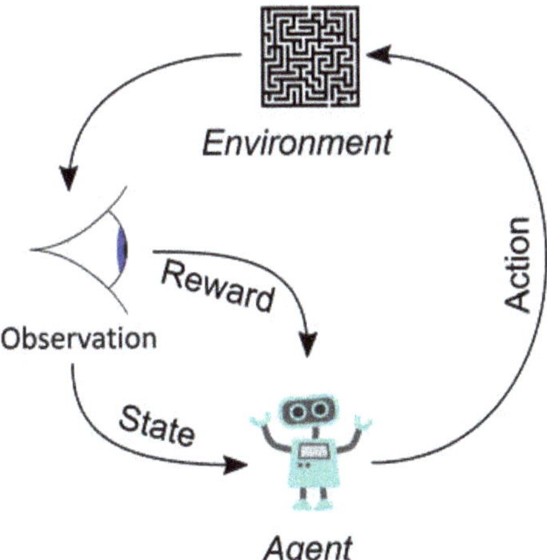

Figure 18.1: A schematic draw of a Reinforcement Learning (RL) process: an agent takes actions at a state in an environment with distributed reward (or punishment). The agent iterates a trial-and-error learning circle, aiming to achieve optimal accumulated rewards. Modified based on the original image by Megajuice under the [CC0] (https://commons.wikimedia.org/w/index.php?curid=57895741).

18.1.4 *Actions in discrete time: Solution strategy*

We know from the previous chapters that any optimization problem has an objective function, which is given in terms of the learning parameters. The learning process is essentially finding the minimum, making use of the gradient information of the objective function. In a reinforcement learning process, the objective is to accumulate rewards as much as possible, but the agent does not know where the award is in the given environment.

Clearly, the agent needs to take actions in steps at different points in time. It must keep track of how the *state* of the action-outcomes is evolving over time. At each time, the current state is the basis for making an action that updates the state, which shall result in a new state for the next time. Clearly, the outcomes at each time are partially random and partially depending on the actions taken. Therefore, the Markov decision process or **MDP** can be a proper description for our problem.

At any point in time, we need a rule that tells the agent how to act, given any possible values of the state. Such a rule, determining the actions as a function of the states, is called a **policy** or policy function [5], and the very fundamental equation known as the Bellman equation.

We naturally want the state to evolve in the best possible way, so that actions on the evolving states can maximize our objective, which is accumulating rewards. The best possible value of the accumulated rewards, written as a function of the state, is called the **state-value function**. When it is written as a function of the action (and hence also implicitly of the state), it is called the **action-value function**. Our reinforcement learning problem is now casted as an optimization problem with the action-value function as the objective function, in discrete time.

The final important strategy is how to find the optimizer (the optimal action and state) that optimizes the action-value function. For this, we use the **Bellman equation**, which gives the relationship between the action-value function at a time point and that at the next time point. Our optimization problem in discrete time is stated in a step-by-step recursive form (known as backward induction). This leads to the so-called value iterations, known as *value-based algorithms.*

Alternatively, RL can also be casted as a policy optimization problem and let the agent to learn an optimal policy. This is because when the policy is optimized and converged in an MDP process, the value function is also converged at the optimal. The policy and value function are directly interconnected in the MDP processes. This leads to *policy-based algorithms.*

For effective implementations, various types of neural networks (NN), which are familiar to our readers by now, are widely used in both value-based and policy-based RL algorithms/methods.

The following sections will formulate all these key pieces of strategy: MDP, policy, action-value function, and the Bellman equation. Examples and codes of both value-based and policy-based algorithms will be presented and examined.

18.2 Markov Decision Process

The Markov decision process (MDP) is a discrete-time stochastic decision process. It is a mathematical model for decision making for problems where outcomes depend on both random variables and decision variables. Detailed discussions on MDP can be found in multiple sources, including an article by Bellman, a book Dynamic Programming and Markov Processes by Ronald Howard, and wikipedia pages. It is an extension of the Markov chains.

The MDP considers a general dynamic process. At each time step, the process is in a state at which the agent takes an action. The process moves into the next state in responding to the action and some random variables, while the agent receives a reward. The probability of the process moving into the next state is determined by the current action taken and also the random variables at the current time step. The important assumption is that the dynamic process has the Markov property, meaning that the probability of moving into the next state from the current state does not conditionally depend on all the previous states and actions. This assumption offers one practical means to model our reinforcement learning process, and makes it possible algorithmically.

Mathematically, an MDP in a RL is defined as follows.

- *State space* $\mathbb{S}$ for the agent is interacting with and observing from.
- *Action space* $\mathbb{A}$ defines possible actions that agent may take.
- *Transition probability function* $P(s \to s'; a)$ defines the probability of transition from state s to state s' under action a.
- *Reward function* $R(s \to s'; a)$ defines the immediate reward after transition from s to s' under action a.
- *Discount factor* $\gamma \in (0, 1)$ that discounts awards from future steps in the process.

The process is essentially award driven, and convergence is ensured in theory by the discount factor that bounds the total awards obtainable in the entire process.

The *challenges* are:

1. the state of the environment is entirely unknown to the agent initially;
2. the choice of actions (the policy) is basically stochastic (although action space is deterministic); and
3. the transition from one state to the next is also stochastic. The agent has to learn the state and the policy in some way (value-optimized, policy-optimized, or a combination), so that its actions can get the maximized reward.

Therefore, the learning needs to be done via a series of explorations and exploitations.

18.3 Policy

Policy, π, defines how the agent makes an action selection $a \in \mathbb{A}$ in state $s \in \mathbb{S}$. It is defined as the following map.

$$\pi : \mathbb{S} \times \mathbb{A} \rightarrow [0, 1] \tag{18.1}$$

It is a conditional probability:

$$\pi(a, s) = \Pr(a_t = a \mid s_t = s) \tag{18.2}$$

Optimal policy: There can be a large number of possible policies (the combinations of variables in the state space and that in the action space). The agent needs to find an optimal policy that maximizes the expected return in terms of *cumulative reward*. In value-based algorithms, the simplest "optimal" policy for the agent is the greedy policy, which takes the action that gives the best values among possible choices at each step. However, this at-single-time best choice may not be the best in the entire MDP process. Thus, in policy-based algorithms, the goal is set for agent to learn a smoother optimal policy over multiple consecutive states in the MDP process, which can be done using MLPs (Chapter 13), while the agent explores the environment.

18.4 Value Functions

When the agent takes an action, it shall receive an immediate reward for the current action. In addition, the agent is going to take more actions in the coming time steps, for which the agent should also receive rewards. However, the future reward should be discounted when it is taken into consideration currently. Such a discount not only makes sense realistically but also has mathematical implications. If these is no discount for the future rewards, the sum of all these future rewards can be unbounded and hence mathematically not allowable. Therefore, we need a proper definition for measuring the return that the agent receives for the current and future rewards.

Return: We now formally define *return* R_t at state s_t, considering possible rewards from the future:

$$R_t = \sum_{k=0}^{\infty} \gamma^k r_{t+k+1} \tag{18.3}$$

where $\gamma \in (0, 1)$ is the *discount rate* considering the reward r_{t+k+1} from the future, which should be valued less currently. Note also that the return of the rewards from the far future terminal state (if any) should vanish.

When the policy π is followed by the agent at a state, the state-value function $V_\pi(s)$ can now be defined as the *expected return* from the future starting with state s_t. It estimates the total return from all these future rewards:

$$V_\pi(s) = \mathrm{E}\left[R \mid s_t = s, \pi\right] = \mathrm{E}\left[\sum_{k=0}^{\infty} \gamma^k r_{t+k+1} \mid s_t = s, \pi\right] \tag{18.4}$$

This is the **state-value function** under the policy π.

The **action-value function** under policy π, $Q_\pi(s, a)$, can be defined in the similar manner:

$$Q_\pi(s, a) = \mathrm{E}\left[R \mid s_t = s, a_t = a, \pi\right] = \mathrm{E}\left[\sum_{k=0}^{\infty} \gamma^k r_{t+k+1} \mid s_t = s, a_t = a, \pi\right] \tag{18.5}$$

18.5 Bellman Equation

In the MDPs, the action-value function Eq. (18.5) used in reinforcement learning has a recursive relationship. For the greedy policy, for example, we have the Bellman equation written as:

$$Q(s, a) = \max_{a \in \mathbb{A}} \left(r(s, a) + \gamma Q(s', a)\right) \tag{18.6}$$

The Bellman equation gives $Q(s, a)$ values at the current time step in terms of those at the next time step $Q' = Q(s', a)$, known as backward induction. Using Eq. (18.6), we can device the following simple but very basic algorithm, which is the base for a Q-learning algorithm.

- **Initialization**: At time $t = 0$, $Q(s, a), \forall s \in \mathbb{S}, a \in \mathbb{A}$ is initialized simply with zeros. The action variable of the agent a^* is computed following the optimal policy, which gives $a^* = \text{argmax}_{a \in \mathbb{A}} Q(s_0, a)$, added with a randomly generated small value. Because Q is null at this initial stage, a^* has only the random value. This means that this initial action is a random one, and the agent gets randomly into a new state s_1. Now, we can search for the *future reward* $\max_{a \in \mathbb{A}} Q(s_1, a)$, and then update Q values as $Q(s_0, a_0)$ using Eq. (18.6). This completes the initialization.
- **A typical iteration**: Consider at an arbitrary time step $t \geq 1$, the current $Q(s_t, a_t)$ is known. We compute $a^* = \text{argmax}_{a \in \mathbb{A}} Q(s_t, a)$, added with a smaller random value. The agent takes action with a^*, and gets into the next state s_{t+1}. We can now search for the *future reward* $\max_{a \in \mathbb{A}} Q(s_{t+1}, a)$, and update the Q values as $Q(s_t, a_t)$ using Eq. (18.6). This completes one typical iteration, and it moves to the next time step $t+1$. We see clearly here the important **backward induction** mechanism: the agent at the current state gets into the next state, and then has its current state updated using Eq. (18.6). If the current state has zero value, and the next state has a value (or reward), this iteration will give back to the current state some value! In other words, some of the next-state value is "induced" back to the current state. Because Q is initialized with all zeros, the agent has to make sufficient random moves to get into a state where there is some reward. That reward can then start to be back-induced gradually to previous states in future iterations. We make a remark that the essential mechanism of the Q-learning algorithm is that the Q values are updated backward in state space.
- The iteration continues until the Q values converge. Note that we shall control the randomly generated values in practice. The random value is gradually reduced with the increasing number of iteration and vanishes when the iteration gets to infinity.

Finally, we may have a simple intuitive analysis on the convergence of the algorithm. First, because $\gamma < 1$, the return given in Eq. (18.3) will be finite for all k, if the reward r is finite for all possible policy π, including the optimal policy. Therefore, Q value from Eq. (18.6) will always be bounded. Second, because the optimal policy is used at all time steps, the iteration using Eq. (18.6) can push the Q values to its upper bound further with the increase of iterations. Therefore, Q has to converge, because it is pushed to larger and larger by the algorithm to its upper bound.

The above algorithm based on the Bellman equation will be used in the code given in the example section.

18.6 Q-learning Algorithm

Q-learning algorithm is a basic and useful reinforcement learning process proposed by Watkins (1989) [2] in his PhD thesis "Learning from Delayed Rewards", Cambridge, UK. The convergence proof of this algorithm was refined in [3]. It is said to be "model-free" because the updating process does not require a predefined model for the environment. The algorithm is based on MDP, with an optimal policy, and uses the Bellman equation. The agent learns iteratively taking improved actions, while updating the environment value function.

"Q" is the name of the action-value function that is the maximum expected accumulative rewards used in the algorithm. It is a matrix of shape $(\dim \mathbb{S}, \dim \mathbb{A})$ and is updated during the iterative process. We shall use the following example to introduce the Q-algorithm.

18.6.1 *Example 1: A robot explores a room with unknown obstacles with Q-learning algorithm*

Consider a robot (as the agent) that wants to get to a goal in a room. There are, however, obstacles in the room. To make the problem simple, let us use a uniform regular grid to mesh the floor of the room into 4×4 regular cells. Therefore, the dimension of the state space is $16(= 4 \times 4)$. These obstacles occupy some of the cells, but the robot does not know which ones. The robot is capable of walking from any empty cell to the next cell in four directions: up, down, left, and right. Therefore, the dimension of the action space is 4. It is the robot's decision on which direction to go to. It starts at the up-leftmost corner cell (square-one) and walks to a goal cell where a reward is placed. The robot will be rewarded if it arrives at the goal cell. It will then go back to the starting cell and try the same again. The attempt (called episode) continues. If it hits on an obstacle, this attempt is considered failed, and it has to go back to the starting cell and try all over again. The robot is allowed to try as many times as required. The objective is to have the robot learn by itself that the environment can get the rewards at a higher and higher probability with an increased number of attempts.

We now design a Q-algorithm so that the robot equipped with it is capable of finding a valid path of reaching the goal cell. Clearly, the robot needs to fail and try for multiple times, and the only thing that allows it to have better trials is getting the rewards. We use a Q as a matrix of variables to record the accumulative reward received by the robot. This record must be a discrete function of space in the room for each possible action that the robot can take, and has a value for each cell. It also has to choose one of the four actions that the robot takes. Therefore, we can build a table of record, and let us call it Q-table with shape (16, 4). At the beginning, nothing has happened, and hence the Q-table is initialized with all zeros. At the goal cell, we give it a value of 1.0 as the reward. All the cells occupied by obstacles (the robot does not know where it is at the beginning) will send the robot back to square one.

With this setting, and the formulations that are presented in the previous sections, the formula for updating Q in the Q-algorithm can be easily written as

$$Q^{new}(s_t, a_t) \leftarrow Q^{old}(s_t, a_t) + l_r \cdot \left(\overbrace{r_t + \gamma \cdot \underbrace{\overbrace{\max_a Q(s_{t+1}, a)}^{\text{optimal value at t+1}} - Q^{old}(s_t, a_t)}_{\text{temporal-target (label-like)}}}^{\text{temporal-difference (gradient-like)}} \right)$$

$$(18.7)$$

where l_r is the learning rate ($0 < l_r \leq 1$) and it is a predetermined parameter. The reward r_t and the discount rate γ are also predetermined parameters. Note that Eq. (18.7) is essentially the same as Eq. (18.6). If l_r is set to 1.0, both are the same. Equation (18.7) shows explicitly the learning concept, which is very similar to the standard loss function used in a supervised training algorithm. The temporal target is something like the label in the standard loss function, and the temporal difference acts like the gradient. When the learning rate is set near 1, Q values change faster. The difference is that Q-learning algorithm is a dynamic process; when the episode (time step) advances, the optimal value at $t + 1$ (that is the discounted maximum reward from the future state s_{t+1}) is changing and hence the temporal target.

With this understanding of Eq. (18.7), we can also construct a neural network and different types of deepnets such as CNN to perform reinforcement learning. We will discuss this in detail in the next section on a Q-Network.

Based on the theory discussed earlier in this chapter, the discount rate must be set smaller than 1, so that the value for the action variable a is finite even if the episode gets infinite. In a Q-learning algorithm, we shall set a maximum number for the episodes, at which the iteration terminates.

Note that at each episode, an inner loop is used to control the exploration over the state space $\mathbb{S}$. The limit (299 for example) for this inner loop should be set to a number that is larger than the dimension of $\mathbb{S}$ (that is 16 for our example). This is because the robot may go back and forth (wondering) during the learning process, and hence when it arrives at the goal cell (if it does), the number of the steps it takes can be quite large (larger than 16). Even if it failed to arrive at the goal cell because of hitting on an obstacle and ends the episode, the number can also be quite large, because of the possibility of "wondering".

18.6.2 *OpenAI Gym*

We are now ready for coding our Q-learning algorithm. We would now need a module called Gym under the MIT License Copyright (c) 2016 [OpenAI] (https://openai.com). It is a tool kit for developing and comparing reinforcement learning algorithms. For our example, we will use OpenAI Gym to set up the environment, the room with obstacles. We will also use TensorFlow to build the algorithm and matplotlib to plot the results. First, we import necessary modules. The following code is from awjuliani/DeepRL-Agent under the MIT License:

```python
# https://github.com/awjuliani/DeepRL-Agents
# awjuliani/DeepRL-Agents is licensed under the MIT License
# import necessary modules
import numpy as np
import gym
import random
import tensorflow as tf
import matplotlib.pyplot as plt
%matplotlib inline
```

Next, we load the environment, FrozenLake-v0, available at Gym module. This environment was set for people walking on a frozen lake with a hole. The settings are fixed by Gym and cannot be changed, but it fits perfectly with our problem without the need for a change.

```python
env = gym.make('FrozenLake-v0')   # create an environment instance
```

The environment has a simple mesh with 4×4 cells:

- SFFF (S: starting cell, safe).
- FHFH (F: free cell, safe to walk).
- FFFH (H: hard obstacle, failed and back to starting point).
- HFFG (G: goal cell, mission accomplished, get a rewards and back to starting point).

Note that the robot does not know this setting before starting.

We shall now examine the Q-learning algorithm for the robot exploring a room with obstacles.

18.6.3 *Define utility functions*

```python
# Compute the moving average curve of a curve
env=gym.make('FrozenLake-v0') # create environment instance

def mv_avg(x, n):    # move average over past n points
    return [sum(x[i:i+n])/n for i in range(len(x)-n)]

def print_state(Q,ns,na):
    #Q = (env.observation_space.n, env.action_space.n)
    print('Initial Q-Table Values: (',ns,',',na,')')
    print('Norm of Q=',np.linalg.norm(Q,np.inf))
    for s in range(ns//na):
        for a in range(na):
            print (f'{Q[4*a,s]:7.4f}{Q[4*a+1,s]:7.4f}'
                   f'{Q[4*a+2,s]:7.4f}{Q[4*a+3,s]:7.4f}')

def tweak_reward(reward, done):
    if reward == 0:
        reward = -0.01
    if done:
        if reward < 1:
            reward = -1
    return reward

def schedule(p0,n_episodes,beta): # schedule parameter decay
    return p0/(np.arange(1,episodes+2))**beta
```

18.6.4 *A simple Q-learning algorithm*

```python
# Set learning parameters for Q-learning
np.set_printoptions(formatter={'float': '{:  0.3f}'.format})

episodes = 2000      # maximum episodes (trials)
jwSteps = 299        # maximum walk steps in an episode
```

```python
lr_0 = 0.90 #0.85      # initial learning rate (lr)
beta_lr = 0.01         # lr decay power

gamma_0 = .98          # initial discount rate (back reduction)
beta_g = 0.001         # gamma decay power

eps_0 = 0.01           # initial epsilon (random action)
beta_eps = 0.80        # epsilon decay power


lrv = schedule(lr_0,episodes,beta_lr)
gav = schedule(gamma_0,episodes,beta_g)
epsv = schedule(eps_0,episodes,beta_eps)


print(f'lrv_last={lrv[episodes]:.4e}', f'gav_last=
    {gav[episodes]:.4e}',f'epsv_last={epsv[episodes]:.4e}')
# initialize lists for recording the total rewards and steps
jList = []             # walked steps in episodes

rList = []             # total rewards received in episodes
norm_Q = []            # maximum (inf norm) value in Q-table
# Initialize the Q-table with all zeros
Q = np.zeros([env.observation_space.n,env.action_space.n])
    # Q: array of shape (env.observation_space.n,env.action_space.)
    # both env.observation_space.n and env.action_space are
    # attributes from Gym once the evn instance is created.
    # For FrozenLake-v0, the values are in (16,4),cells
    # For our example: observation space is state space


np.random.seed(1)


for e in range(episodes):          # episodes+1: maximum episodes
    # reset the environment, which gives an initial state
    s = env.reset()
    #print('e=',e,' s=',s)
    rAll = 0
        # to record the total rewards received in an episode
    done = False                   # is the attempt over?
    j = 0
    lrr = lrv[e]
    gam = gav[e]
    eps = epsv[e]
    #The Q-learning algorithm
    while j < jwSteps:
        # maximum walk steps over the state space in an episode
        #env.render('human')     # visualizing the training
```

```python
        j+=1
        # compute the action values using the greedy policy
        # using the current Q-table

        a=np.argmax(Q[s,:]+np.random.randn(1,env.
            action_space.n)*eps)
        # The action values are added with random values
        # The random value is a must at the initial episode
        # because the robot has no choice but walk randomly
        # It should be reduced with increase of episodes.
        # It shall vanish when the episode gets infinite.

        # Take a step with a, move to a new state s1 and get a
        # reward r from the environment, and check where the
        # attempt is over (either hits a obstacle or arrive
        # at the goal cell)
        s1,r,done,_ = env.step(a)
        # Tweaking the reward to help the agent learn faster
        # r = tweak_reward(r0, done)    # one may try this

        if done and e%500 == 0: #%100   # monitoring the progress
            if r == 1:
                print("episode:{}/{},score:{:.2f},goal!".
                    format(e,episodes,r))
                #print_state(Q,env.observation_space.n,
                    env.action_space.n)
            else:
                print("episode:{}/{},score:{:.2f}".
                    format(e, episodes, rAll))
        # Update Q-Table using the Bellman equation with a
        # learning rate lr
        Q[s,a] = Q[s,a] + lrr*(r + gam*np.max(Q[s1,:]) - Q[s,a])

        #if np.max(Q[s1,:]) != 0 and e%500 == 0:
        #    print('e=',e,'j=',j,' s1=',s1,' s=',s,' a=',a)
        #    print('Q:',Q,'\n Q[s1,:]:',Q[s1,:],' \n  qm:',
        #    np.max(Q[s1,:]))

        rAll += r
        s = s1                           # update the state
        if done: break

    norm_Q.append(np.linalg.norm(Q,np.inf))   # max value in
                                              # Q-table
```

```python
    jList.append(j)        # record walked steps in episodes
    rList.append(rAll)     # record total rewards received
                           # in episodes
print("Score over time: " +  str(sum(rList)/episodes))
#print_state(Q,env.observation_space.n,env.action_space.n)
N_avg = 100
plt.plot(rList,label="Current Reward")
plt.plot(mv_avg(rList, N_avg),label="Average reward over
        "+str(N_avg))
plt.title('Reward received')
plt.legend(loc='lower right')
plt.show()

plt.plot(norm_Q, label="Max Q value")
plt.plot(mv_avg(norm_Q, N_avg),label="Averaged max Q over"
        +str(N_avg))
plt.title('Maximum Q value')
plt.legend()
plt.show()
```

```
lrv_last=8.3412e-01  gav_last=9.7258e-01  epsv_last=2.2856e-05
episode:0/2000,score:0.00
episode:500/2000,score:0.00
episode:1000/2000,score:1.00, goal!
episode:1500/2000,score:0.00
Score over time: 0.4445
```

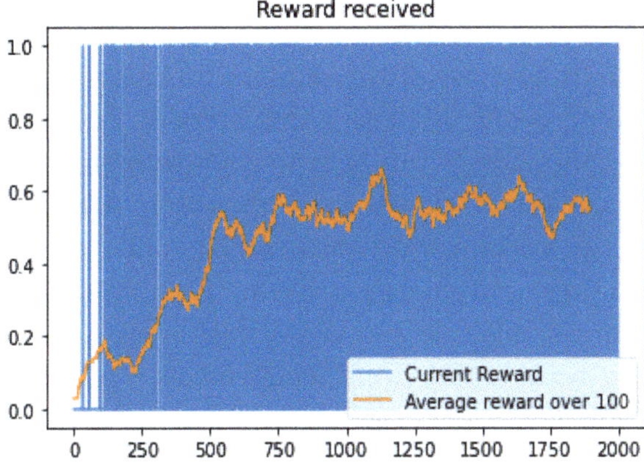

Figure 18.2:   Reward received by the agent in the FrozenLake-v0 environment through Q-learning.

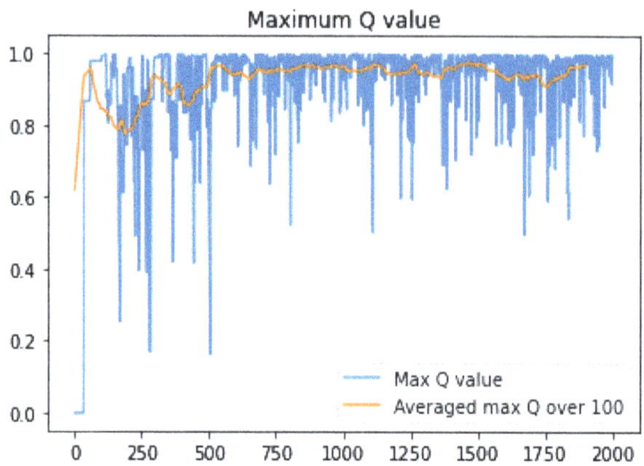

Figure 18.3: Q value evolution in the FrozenLake-v0 environment during Q-learning.

Figure 18.2 shows the record on rewards received over each episode of attempt by the robot starting with a random action (randomly generated Q-table). It is shown that the robot is wondering at the initial few hundred episodes. It seems to learn its way to reach the goal cell with a good success rate.

Figure 18.3 shows the evolution of the maximum value in the Q-table over each episode. Such values become quite close to 1.0 after a few hundred episodes.

18.6.5 *Hyper-parameters and convergence*

Note that the Q-learning algorithm above has some level of instability, meaning that its performance depends on the settings of the hyper-parameters (learning rate, discount rate, etc.) and the given environment. This may be partially because of the random process used in the algorithm. A more sophisticated choice of these parameters or designing a proper time schedule for these parameters can help to achieve more stable convergence. This is at the expense of slower convergence to tread for more stable convergence. For the learning rate, for example, one can let it decay slowly with episodes. The general rule is given in Eq. (9.41) in Chapter 9. For Q-learning algorithms, this rule may not always work well, because the "loss function" here can be quite far from being convex.

A similar tuning is also possible for the discount rate [3] and the hyper-parameter controlling the random actions. The basic underlying principle is that when the Q-algorithm is converged ideally, all these learning, backward induction, and random actions are no longer needed. All these tuning can be difficult.

18.7 Q-Network Learning

With a good understanding of the Q-learning algorithm, and the knowledge established in earlier chapters on neural networks, we are now ready to introduce a neural network for Q-learning, called Q-Network. The major difference between the Q-Network and the networks we studied earlier is the loss function, as shown in Eq. (18.7).

We show how a Q-Network can be established and trained for the same Example 1, but now use a Q-Network for the robot. We will also use OpenAI Gym to set up the room environment with obstacles. We will use the TensorFlow graph to build the Q-Network structure and execute the training with TensorFlow sessions. The following code is from awjuliani/DeepRL-Agent under the MIT License. It has been modified with more detailed explanations for easy comprehension for beginners. Most of the explanation is given together with the code lines as comments so that it can be followed with ease.

18.7.1 *Example 2: A robot explores a room with unknown obstacles with Q-Network*

```python
# Import necessary modules
from __future__ import division
import gym
import numpy as np
import random
#import tensorflow as tf
import tensorflow.compat.v1 as tf
                    # This code works only for tf version 1
tf.disable_v2_behavior()
from tensorflow.keras.models import Sequential
from tensorflow.keras.layers import Dense, InputLayer
import matplotlib.pyplot as plt
%matplotlib inline
```

```python
# Create the environment instant using Gym module
env = gym.make('FrozenLake-v0')
```

```python
# a utility function
def mv_avg(x, n):    # move average over past n points
    return [sum(x[i:i+n])/n for i in range(len(x)-n)]
```

18.7.2 *Building TensorFlow graph*

```
tf.reset_default_graph()     # define the graph for Q-Network
#tf.compat.v1.reset_default_graph()
```

The following procedure is for setting up the graph for our Q-Network. It should have an array of 16 neurons at the input layer, a 16×4 weight matrix, and an array of 4 neurons at the output layer. The structure has a simple configuration of $16 \times 4 \times 1$.

```
# Graph for our Q-Network
# First, a placeholder for a tensor to-be-fed. This is for the
# input layer (with 16 inputs) for our Q-Network
inputs1 = tf.placeholder(shape=[1,16],dtype=tf.float32)

# variables in the graph for the Q-Network. Initiated with random
# values and to-be updated during the learning process, when the
# session is run
W = tf.Variable(tf.random_uniform([16,4],0,0.01))

# A  matrix-multiply function to produce the output for the
# Q-Network
Qout = tf.matmul(inputs1,W)

# An instance for a prediction following the greedy optimal policy
predict = tf.argmax(Qout,1)

# A placeholder for a tensor to-be-fed. This is for the
# output layer (with 4 outputs) for our Q-Network
nextQ = tf.placeholder(shape=[1,4],dtype=tf.float32)

# A loss function using the tensorflow mean-squared-difference
# between the temporal-target Q and the predicted Q values from
# the Q-Network.
loss = tf.reduce_sum(tf.square(nextQ - Qout))

# A trainer instance using the gradient descent optimizer with lr
trainer = tf.train.GradientDescentOptimizer(learning_rate=0.1)

# A training instance for our Q-Network
updateModel = trainer.minimize(loss)
```

With the TensorFlow graph defined with necessary arrays (tensors), variables, instances, and functions for our Q-Network, we are now ready to create and run a session following the graph for training the Q-Network, based on the Q-learning algorithm.

```python
# Set learning parameters
gamma = .99              # discount rate
epsi = 0.1               # epsilon to control random actions
episodes = 2000          # maximum episodes (trials)
jwSteps = 99             # maximum walk steps in an episode

# initialize lists for recording the total rewards and steps
jList = []               # walked steps in episodes
rList = []               # total rewards received in episodes
jRate = []

init=tf.global_variables_initializer()
# instance for initializing variables one more piece for the graph

with tf.Session() as sess:               # Create a session
    sess.run(init) # variable initialization for the session

    for i in range(episodes):
        # Reset the room environment, which gives an initial
        # state for robot agent
        s = env.reset()

        rAll = 0    # initialization variable for the episode
        done = False
        j = 0

        # The algorithm for the Q-Network
        while j < jwSteps:
            j+=1
            # Run the "predict" and 'Qout' defined in the
            # graph for the Q-network
            a,allQ = sess.run([predict,Qout],
                feed_dict={inputs1:np.identity(16)[s:s+1]})
                # feed values to placeholder inputs1.
                # It is a zero vector but with 1 at entry s.

            if np.random.rand(1) < epsi: # sample a small
                                         # random action
                a[0] = env.action_space.sample()

            # Take the action with a, gets into a new state,
            # receive a reward from the room environment,
            # and check whether or not this attempt
```

```python
            # (episode) is over (done)
            s1,r,done,_ = env.step(a[0])

            # Compute the Q' values in the new state through
            # our network
            Q1 = sess.run(Qout,feed_dict={inputs1:np.
                identity(16)[s1:s1+1]})

            # Obtain the greedy maxQ' and set our target value
            # for chosen action.
            maxQ1 = np.max(Q1)      # Obtain the greedy maxQ'
            targetQ = allQ
            targetQ[0,a[0]] = r + gamma*maxQ1 # target value
            #Train the Q-Network using target and predicted
            #Q values
            _,W1 = sess.run([updateModel,W],
                    feed_dict={inputs1:np.identity(16)[s:s+1],
                    nextQ:targetQ})
            rAll += r
            s = s1
            if done:
                #Reduce chance of random action as we train
                #the model.
                epsi = 1./((i/50) + 10)
                break

        jList.append(j)
        rList.append(rAll)
        jRate.append(rAll/j)

print("Score over time: " +  str(sum(rList)/episodes))
```

```
Score over time: 0.433
```

18.7.3 *Results from the Q-Network*

We now plot the results in a similar manner as in Example 1.

```python
N_avg = 100
plt.plot(rList,label="Current Reward")
plt.plot(mv_avg(rList, N_avg),label="Average reward over"
    +str(N_avg))
plt.title('Reward received')
plt.legend(loc='lower right')
plt.show()
```

```python
plt.plot(norm_Q, label="Max Q value")
plt.plot(mv_avg(norm_Q, N_avg),label="Averaged max Q over"
    +str(N_avg))
plt.title('Maximum Q value')
plt.legend()
plt.show()
```

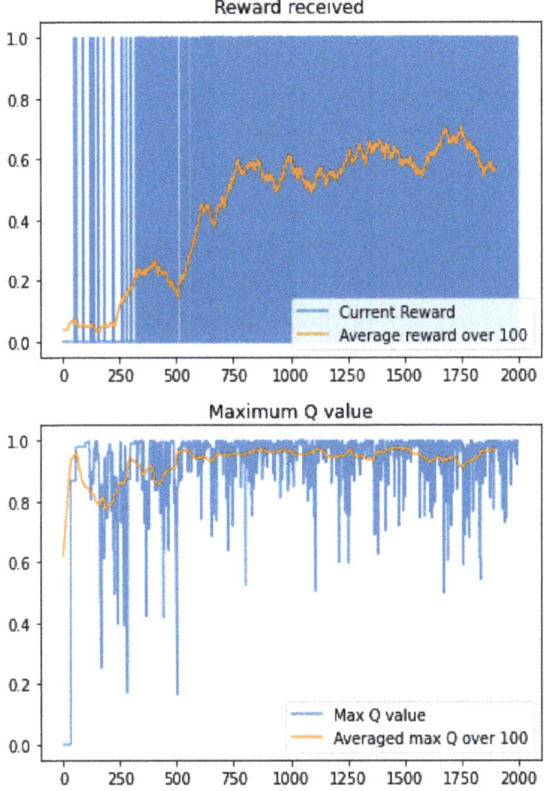

Figure 18.4: Award received (top) by the agent and Q value evolution (bottom) in the FrozenLake-v0 environment during Q-learning using an NN.

The results and learning process are shown in Fig. 18.4. Quite similar observations can be made as Example 1.

With the understanding of how to build a Q-Network, one should not have much difficulty in learning to construct deepnets for Q-learning. Our study has found that when a greedy policy is used at each step, such an at-single-time best choice may not be the best in the entire process. The agent may be trapped in local optimal and fail to arrive to the global optimal, as shown in the above examples. Policy-based algorithms can overcome this problem.

18.8 Policy gradient methods

The Q-learning and DQN studied in the previous sections is known as value-based aiming to maximize the Q values. Instabilities can often be observed in this type of algorithms. Alternatively, one can optimize the policy instead, known as policy-based methods, such as the policy gradient methods. These methods have been studied quite intensively in the past few years, and some significant improvements are made. These methods aim to optimize the policy, instead of the value. Because the transition probability $P(s \to s'; a)$ determines the return R, and is under action a that is in turn controlled (conditioned) by the policy π. Therefore, if we can find an optimal policy that maximize the return, our goal is achieved. There are many policy gradient methods and techniques developed in the past years, and study all these can be a challenge. In this section, we introduce first one of the best performers, Proximal Policy Optimization (PPO) [6], and then derive a formulation procedure that outlines the major path leading to PPO.

18.8.1 *PPO with NN policy*

The Advantage Actor Critic (A2C), Asynchronous Advantage Actor Critic (A3C) [7], Trust Region Policy Optimization (TRPO) [7] and the Proximal Policy Optimization (PPO) [6] are typical type of policy gradient methods. The PPO is an improvement on TRPO. Readers may take a look at the excellent on-line lecture series by Pieter Abbeel on this topic.

It is found that policy gradient methods are, in general, also quite sensitive to hyper-parameters, such as the step-size, which limits the performance and application, in addition to its sample efficiency issues. We know that supervised learning has quite good convergence and uses relatively less hyper-parameters. In addition, reinforcement learning is usually much less stable because of the absence of firm labels. Careful sampling strategies are thus required to smooth the searching process. These strategies can be complicated, expensive and with additional hyperparameters. PPO aims to find a balance among simple formulation, ease of implementation and sample efficiency. It computes an update at each step while ensuring the updated policy is not too far from the old policy to reduce variance and increase stability in training. This is done via "clipping". The loss function is designed as follows.

$$\mathcal{L}^{CLIP}(\hat{\mathbf{w}}) = \mathbb{E}_t \left[min \left(r_t(\hat{\mathbf{w}}) A_t, clip \left(r_t(\hat{\mathbf{w}}), 1 - \varepsilon, 1 + \varepsilon \right) A_t \right) \right] \qquad (18.8)$$

where

- $\hat{\mathbf{w}}$ is the vector of all parameters used for the policy model.
- $\mathbb{E}_t$ denotes an empirical expectation over time-steps.
- r_t is the ratio of the probabilities under the current and old policies.
- A_t is the estimated advantage (the expected return of a state with its baseline subtracted).
- ε is a hyperparameter, usually set as 0.1 or 0.2.

The clip function is defined as

$$clip(x, 1 - \varepsilon, 1 + \varepsilon) = \begin{cases} 1 - \varepsilon & \text{if } x < 1 - \varepsilon \\ 1 + \varepsilon & \text{if } x > 1 + \varepsilon \\ x & \text{else} \end{cases} \tag{18.9}$$

18.8.2 *Strategy used in policy gradient methods and PPO*

18.8.2.1 *Build an NN model for policy*

In a typical policy gradient method, such as PPO, we first build a neural network model (such as MLP, CNN, etc.) that maps $\dim \mathbb{S} \to \dim \mathbb{A}$. This is done by letting the agent to explore the environment first by itself for, say m time-steps. All the data (states, actions, values, rewards, and dones) generated during these m steps are stored. The stored dataset is now used to train one (or two) neural networks for the $\dim \mathbb{S} \to \dim \mathbb{A}$ mapping. The training of such NNs is essentially the same as we discussed in previous chapters for classifications and regressions. Care is needed in defining the loss functions for various policy gradient methods. The trained NNs are next used by the agent for further exploration for the next m time-steps, and a new dataset will be generated which is used to train a new policy of $\dim \mathbb{S} \to \dim \mathbb{A}$ mapping. This process continues, we shall have a new and old policies at every m time-steps. Readers may refer to the codes made public by philtabor for more details. We denote such an NN model as $\pi_{\hat{\mathbf{w}}}$ where $\hat{\mathbf{w}}$ stands for the training parameters. The following key formulations are useful in understanding the policy gradient methods. In particular, both TRPO and PPO use two (new and old) policies to for a so-called ratio policy for better controlling stability.

18.8.2.2 *P and R formulation*

Let τ denotes a state-action sequence, $s_0, a_0, s_1, a_1, \ldots, s_T, a_T$. Starting from Eq. (18.4), the problem can be casted as

$$\max_{\hat{\mathbf{w}}} \mathbb{E}\left[\underbrace{\sum_{t=0}^{T} R(s_t, a_t)}_{R(\tau)} \mid \pi_{\hat{\mathbf{w}}}\right] \Rightarrow \max_{\hat{\mathbf{w}}} \mathbb{E}\left[R(\tau) \mid \pi_{\hat{\mathbf{w}}}\right] \Rightarrow \max_{\hat{\mathbf{w}}} \underbrace{\sum_{\tau} P(\tau; \hat{\mathbf{w}}) R(\tau)}_{U(\hat{\mathbf{w}})}$$

$$(18.10)$$

To solve the above problem, we need to evaluate the gradient of $U(\hat{\mathbf{w}})$ with respect to $\hat{\mathbf{w}}$.

$$\nabla_{\hat{\mathbf{w}}} U(\hat{\mathbf{w}}) = \nabla_{\hat{\mathbf{w}}} \sum_{\tau} P(\tau; \hat{\mathbf{w}}) R(\tau) = \sum_{\tau} \nabla_{\hat{\mathbf{w}}} P(\tau; \hat{\mathbf{w}}) R(\tau)$$

$$= \sum_{\tau} P(\tau; \hat{\mathbf{w}}) \frac{\nabla_{\hat{\mathbf{w}}} P(\tau; \hat{\mathbf{w}})}{P(\tau; \hat{\mathbf{w}})} R(\tau) \qquad (18.11)$$

$$= \sum_{\tau} P(\tau; \hat{\mathbf{w}}) \left[\nabla_{\hat{\mathbf{w}}} \log P(\tau; \hat{\mathbf{w}})\right] R(\tau)$$

Using m sample paths and policy $\pi_{\hat{\mathbf{w}}}$, the above expectation can be approximated as a summation, and we obtain,

$$\nabla_{\hat{\mathbf{w}}} U(\hat{\mathbf{w}}) \approx \frac{1}{m} \sum_{i=1}^{m} \left(\left[\nabla_{\hat{\mathbf{w}}} \log P(\tau^{(i)}; \hat{\mathbf{w}})\right] R(\tau^{(i)})\right) \qquad (18.12)$$

Note here that the gradient is applied only to the P. Thus, R needs not be smooth and can be discrete.

$P \to \pi$

We now ready to make a connection between the transition probability function P to policy π, using the states and actions.

$$\nabla_{\hat{\mathbf{w}}} \log P(\tau^{(i)}; \hat{\mathbf{w}}) = \nabla_{\hat{\mathbf{w}}} \log \left[\prod_{t=0}^{T} \underbrace{P\left(s_{t+1}^{(i)} \mid s_t^{(i)}, a_t^{(i)}\right)}_{\text{transition probability}} \cdot \underbrace{\pi_{\hat{\mathbf{w}}}\left(a_t^{(i)} \mid s_t^{(i)}\right)}_{\text{policy}}\right]$$

$$= \nabla_{\hat{\mathbf{w}}} \left[\sum_{t=0}^{T} \log P\left(s_{t+1}^{(i)} \mid s_t^{(i)}, a_t^{(i)}\right) + \sum_{t=0}^{T} \log \pi_{\hat{\mathbf{w}}}\left(a_t^{(i)} \mid s_t^{(i)}\right)\right]$$

$$= \underbrace{\sum_{t=0}^{T} \nabla_{\hat{\mathbf{w}}} \log \pi_{\hat{\mathbf{w}}}\left(a_t^{(i)} \mid s_t^{(i)}\right)}_{\text{policy only}} \qquad (18.13)$$

$R \to A$

Equation (18.12) can now written as

$$\nabla_{\hat{\mathbf{w}}} U(\hat{\mathbf{w}}) \approx \frac{1}{m} \sum_{i=1}^{m} \left(\left[\sum_{t=0}^{T} \nabla_{\hat{\mathbf{w}}} \log \pi_{\hat{\mathbf{w}}} \left(a_t^{(i)} \mid s_t^{(i)} \right) \right] \left[\underbrace{R(\tau^{(i)}) - b_R}_{A_t} \right] \right) \tag{18.14}$$

where A is called **advantage**, which is R subtracted by b_R that is a *baseline* of the return. It can be calculated for example using

$$b_R \approx \frac{1}{m} \sum_{i=1}^{m} R(\tau^{(i)}) \tag{18.15}$$

Because b_R is an expectation, this subtraction does not introduce any bias. It enhances the effect of returns apart from the baseline, and hence widely used in policy gradient algorithms. The advantage term can be further improved:

$$
\begin{aligned}
A_t = R(\tau^{(i)}) - b_R &= \sum_{t=0}^{T-1} R\left(s_t^{(i)}, a_t^{(i)}\right) - b_R \\
&= \underbrace{\sum_{k=0}^{t-1} R\left(s_k^{(i)}, a_k^{(i)}\right)}_{\text{independent of } a_t^{(i)},\ \text{removed}} + \sum_{k=t}^{T-1} R\left(s_k^{(i)}, a_k^{(i)}\right) - b_R \\
&= \sum_{k=t}^{T-1} R\left(s_k^{(i)}, a_k^{(i)}\right) - b_R
\end{aligned}
\tag{18.16}
$$

The removal of the terms independent of the current action helps to lower the variance.

Using Eqs. (18.10) and (18.14), our problem can now re-casted as

$$\max_{\hat{\mathbf{w}}} \mathbb{E}_t \left[\pi_{\hat{\mathbf{w}}}(a_t \mid s_t) A_t \right] \tag{18.17}$$

A number of outstanding algorithms were developed based on Eq. (18.17), including the Advantage Actor Critic (A2C), Asynchronous Advantage Actor Critic or A3C [7], and other Actor-Critic Methods.

18.8.3 *Ratio policy*

Using now the importance sampling, Eq. (18.17) is modified by making use of the old model from the previous iteration.

$$\max_{\hat{\mathbf{w}}} \mathbb{E}_t \left[r_t(\hat{\mathbf{w}})(a_t \mid s_t) A_t \right]$$
$$\text{subject to } \mathbb{E}_t \left(KL[\pi_{\hat{\mathbf{w}}old}(\cdot \mid s_t), \pi_{\hat{\mathbf{w}}}(a_t \mid s_t)] \right) \leq \delta$$

where the KL-divergence (discussed in Chapter 4, used also in Chapter 17 for VAEs) are used to constrain the loss to prevent the current policy getting too far apart from the old one, and r_t is the ratio of policy π with respect to policy π_{old} that is the NN model with previous trained parameters.

$$r_t(\hat{\mathbf{w}}) = \frac{\pi_{\hat{\mathbf{w}}}(a_t \mid s_t)}{\pi_{\hat{\mathbf{w}}old}(a_t \mid s_t)} \tag{18.18}$$

Equation (18.18) is used in the TRPO method.

Now, the KL constraint can be implemented using a penalty method, which leads the early version of PPO. When the constraint is imposed using the clip function we obtain the PPO with loss defined in Eq. (18.8).

This objective function with clipping implements a Trust Region update with first order approximation, which is compatible with the widely used effective Stochastic Gradient Descent (SGD) algorithm. With such an objective function defined, an NN can be conveniently used in the implementation. The PPO with clip demonstrated good performances on continuous control tasks and many other types of tasks. We demonstrate it in two examples: CartPole and CarRacing.

18.8.4 *PPO: Controlling a pole staying upright*

Consider a pole attached to a cart via a hinge joint. The cart can move along a frictionless one-dimensional track. Our goal is to have the pole stay vertically up by controlling the cart moving $+1$ or -1. When an RL agent learns to achieve this goal, it is placed in an environment that gives a reward of $+1$ at every time-step when the pole stays upright. The episode ends when the pole inclines more than 15 degrees from the vertical position, or the cart moves more than 2.4 units away from the center. More detailed on this environment can be found at the OpenAI Gym.

This time we use the stable-baselines3 module to train the RL agent. Some codes have also made public by philtabor, and Nicholas Renotte at github to perform these tasks. Examples introduced below uses stable-baselines3 (which require an install of stable-baselines3).

```python
#!pip install stable-baselines3[extra]  #an useful model for RL
```

```python
import os
import gym
from stable_baselines3 import PPO
```

```python
from stable_baselines3.common.evaluation import evaluate_policy
from stable_baselines3.common.vec_env import DummyVecEnv
import matplotlib.pyplot as plt
%matplotlib inline
```

```python
#Load and then create an environment
Env_str = "CartPole-v0"
Environment2Solve = Env_str #One of the gym environments
                #https://gym.openai.com/envs/#classic_control
Env = gym.make(Environment2Solve)
```

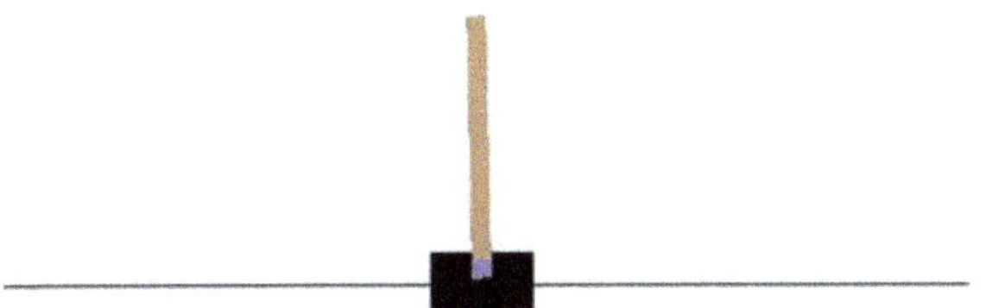

Figure 18.5:   A random agent on the CartPole-v0 environment.

Figure 18.5 shows an agent at a random state on the CartPole-v0 environment. The following code produces an animation of samples from the CartPole environment. It simply repeats falling and being rest.

```python
# Sample some episodes of the environment before training
episodes = 2                    # one may try more
    print(f"Take look {episodes} samples for {Env_str}")
    for episode in range(1, episodes+1):
        s = Env.reset()   # current state
        done = False
        rAll = 0

        while not done:
            Env.render()
            action = Env.action_space.sample()
            n_state, reward, done, info = Env.step(action)
            rAll+=reward

        print(f"Episode {episode}: Score={rAll}")

#Env.close()                     # close env gently when needed
```

```
Take look 2 samples for CartPole-v0
Episode 1: Score=41.0
Episode 2: Score=20.0
```

```python
"Understanding the Environment
"action-0: push cart to left, action-1: push to the right
print(f"Type of the action_space:{Env.action_space}")
print(f"A sample from the space:{Env.action_space.sample()}")
```

```
Type of the action_space:Discrete(2)
A sample from the space:1
```

```python
np.set_printoptions(precision=3)
#[cart position, cart velocity, pole angle, pole angular velocity]
print(f"Type of the observation_space:{Env.observation_space}")
print(f"A sample from the space:{Env.observation_space.sample()}")
```

```
Type of the observation_space:Box(4,)
A sample from the space:[-4.199e+00 -3.231e+38  2.745e-01
    -1.295e+38]
```

```python
Env = DummyVecEnv([lambda: Env])
    "model = PPO('MlpPolicy', Env, verbose = 2)"
```

```
Using cpu device
```

```python
model.learn(total_timesteps=50_000)  # let the agent to learn
```

```
---------------------------------
| time/             |      |
|    fps            | 995  |
|    iterations     | 1    |
|    time_elapsed   | 2    |
|    total_timesteps | 2048 |
---------------------------------


-----------------------------------------
| time/                |          |
|    fps               | 679      |
|    iterations        | 2        |
|    time_elapsed      | 6        |
|    total_timesteps   | 4096     |
```

```
| train/                   |               |
|    approx_kl             | 0.0033051167  |
|    clip_fraction         | 0.0277        |
|    clip_range            | 0.2           |
|    entropy_loss          | -0.305        |
|    explained_variance    | 0.123         |
|    learning_rate         | 0.0003        |
|    loss                  | 196           |
|    n_updates             | 1240          |
|    policy_gradient_loss  | -0.00145      |
|    value_loss            | 169           |
------------------------------------------------

......

------------------------------------------------
| time/                    |               |
|    fps                   | 625           |
|    iterations            | 25            |
|    time_elapsed          | 81            |
|    total_timesteps       | 51200         |
| train/                   |               |
|    approx_kl             | 0.0022214411  |
|    clip_fraction         | 0.0128        |
|    clip_range            | 0.2           |
|    entropy_loss          | -0.241        |
|    explained_variance    | 0.391         |
|    learning_rate         | 0.0003        |
|    loss                  | 83.3          |
|    n_updates             | 1470          |
|    policy_gradient_loss  | -0.000732     |
|    value_loss            | 154           |
------------------------------------------------
```

```
<stable_baselines3.ppo.ppo.PPO at 0x1aeda592518>
```

The training is quite fast. It took about three minutes on authors laptop to train 200k steps.

18.8.5 *Save and reload the learned model*

```python
model_path = os.path.join('Trained_Models','PPO_'+Env_str),
model.save(model_path)
```

```python
model = PPO.load(model_path, env=Env)    # re-load trained model
```

18.8.6 *Evaluate and view the trained model*

```python
from stable_baselines3.common.evaluation import evaluate_policy
evaluate_policy(model, Env, n_eval_episodes=2, render=True)
```

```
(200.0, 0.0)
```

```python
Env.close()
```

To perform a thorough quantitative test on the trained model, we write
the following code. It runs a number of tests of episodes, and in each episode
we put the trained (or untrained) model (agent) in the rest environment for
a maximum number of steps, and receives awards. The total awards received
in each test episode is recorded and plotted in a figure.

```python
test_episodes = 200      # number of tests of episodes
jwSteps = 100            # maximum steps over the state
rList = []               # total rewards received in episodes
for e in range(1, test_episodes+1):
    rAll = 0      # to record the total rewards received
    done = False
    s = Env.reset()
    j = 0
    while j < jwSteps:   # maximum steps over the state
        #a=[Env.action_space.sample()]    # by untrained samples
        a, _ = model.predict(s)             # action by trained model
        s1, r, done, info = Env.step(a)   # s1: the next state
        j += 1
        if done:
            # #print(f"Done! j={j}; info)
            break
        rAll += r          # accumulating rewards
        s = s1             # update the state & continue next step
```

```
    rList.append(rAll/jwSteps) # total rewards received
                               # in an episode

N_avg = 100
x,y=np.array([range(N_avg,len(rList))]).T, mv_avg(rList,N_avg)
plt.plot(rList,label="Current Reward")
plt.plot(x, y, label="Average reward over "+str(N_avg))
plt.title('Reward received, after 10k training')
plt.legend(loc='upper left')   #'lower right')
plt.savefig('images/'+Env_str+'_50k.png', dpi=300)
plt.show()
```

Figure 18.6 shows the performance of an untrained agent on the CartPole-v0 environment. It acts randomly. The average score is around 0.2.

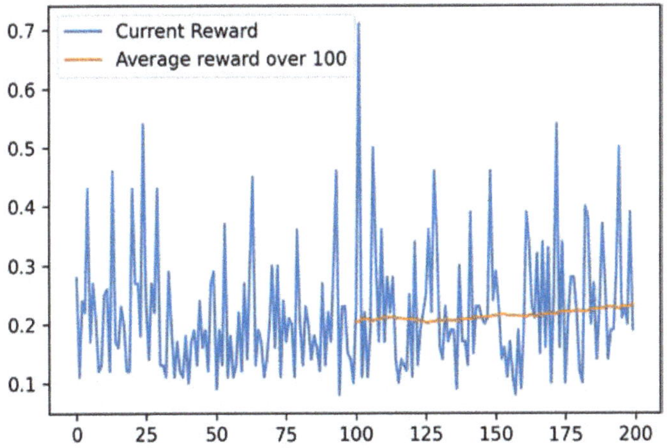

Figure 18.6:   Score of an untrained agent on the CartPole-v0 environment.

After 10k steps of training the performance of the agent is significantly improved, as shown in Fig. 18.7. The average score is around 0.97. After 50k steps of training, the agent achieved perfect scores by this test, as shown in Fig. 18.8.

The following code (or the code given below Section 17.8.5) can generate animations, which are difficult to put in a book. Readers may run the code, and should find that a CartPole balances itself quite well after 200k steps of training.

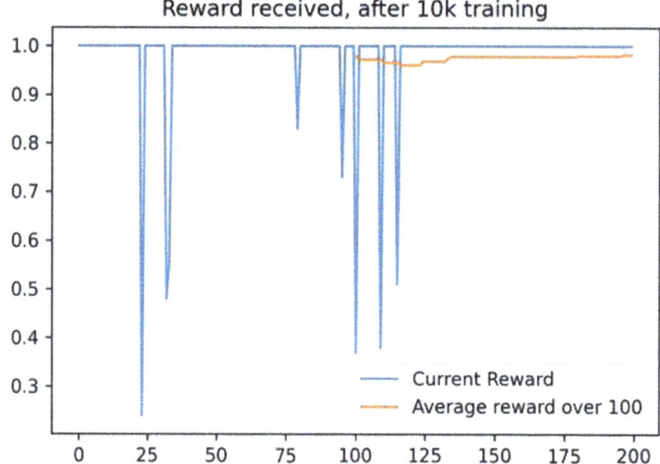

Figure 18.7: An agent trained with 10k steps on the CartPole-v0 environment.

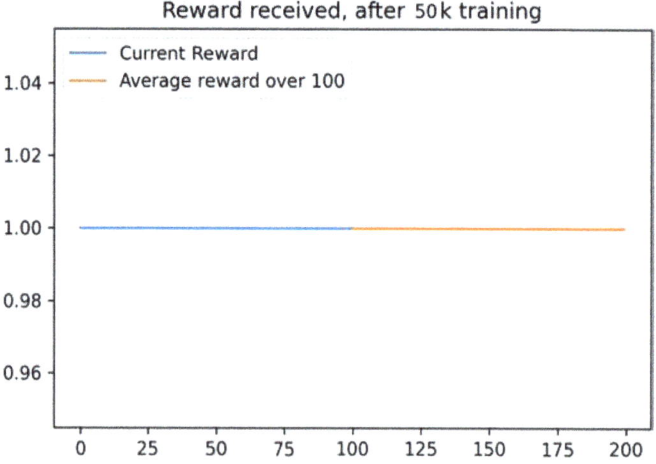

Figure 18.8: An agent trained with 50k steps on the CartPole-v0 environment.

```
observed = Env.reset()
frames = []
jwSteps = 100
while j < jwSteps:  # maximum steps over the state
    action, _states = model.predict(observed)
    observed, rewards, done, info = Env.step(action)
```

```
#frames.append(Env.render(mode="rgb_array") #for recording
Env.render()        #for viewing the states
if done:
    print(f"Done! {info}")
    break
j += 1
```

One may also use an alternate algorithm, such as the deep Q-Network (DQN) to train the model. The code is as simple as follows.

```
#from stable_baselines3 import DQN
#model = DQN('MlpPolicy',Env,verbose=2)
```

18.8.7 *PPO: Self-driving car*

We finally look at an example of a car that learns all by itself to drive on a track environment. For this example we would need to install SWIG. We need also to install gym[box2d] and pyglet==1.3.2, in addition to the stable-baselines3. The codes made public by Nicholas Renotte at github will also be used.

The environment to be used is CarRacing-v0. Figure 18.9 shows the track in the CarRacing environment. The state space is a square field of 96×96 pixels with an enclosed waving track in it. The car needs to learn to stay on track. The reward is -0.1 every frame and $+1000/N$ for every track tile visited by the car, where N is the total number of tiles in the track. For example, if the car finished in 732 frames, the reward is $1000 - 0.1*732 = 926.8$ points. An episode ends when all tiles are visited.

```
#!pip install gym[box2d] pyglet==1.3.2
import gym
from stable_baselines3 import PPO
from stable_baselines3.common.vec_env import VecFrameStack
from stable_baselines3.common.evaluation import import evaluate_policy
import os
import matplotlib.pyplot as plt
%matplotlib inline
```

Figure 18.9:   The track in the CarRacing environment.

18.8.8 *View samples of the racing car before training*

This following code shall produce an animation of samples from the
CarRacing environment with a car running. The car simply moves straight
before training.

```python
# Sample some episodes of the environment before training
episodes = 2            # one may try a few more
print(f"Take look {episodes} samples for {Env_str}")

for episode in range(1, episodes+1):
    state = Env.reset()
    done = False
    rAll = 0
    frames = []
    while not done:
        Env.render() # for in-window real-time render
        action = Env.action_space.sample()
        n_state, reward, done, info = Env.step(action)
        rAll+=reward
    print(f"Episode {episode}: Score={rAll}")
#Env.close()            #for gentle close the environment
```

```
Take look 2 samples for CarRacing-v0
Track generation: 1130..1417 -> 287-tiles track
Episode 1: Score=-30.069930069930493
```

```
Track generation: 1130..1416 -> 286-tiles track
Episode 2: Score=-33.333333333333826
```

```
Env.close()      #for gentle close the environment
```

We can check the environment using the following code.

```
print(f"action_space:{Env.action_space})
print(f"A sample in action_space:{Env.action_space.sample()}")
```

```
action_space:Box(3,)
A sample in action_space:[0.5832531  0.9261694  0.27739018]
```

The action space is a three-dimensional box, allowing the car turning left and right, and speed.

```
print(f"observation_space:{Env.observation_space}")
print(f"A part of a sample in observation:\
      {Env.observation_space.sample()[0,0:5,:]}")
```

```
observation_space:Box(96, 96, 3)
A part of a sample in observation:
[[139 246 145]
 [ 18 144 155]
 [ 95 226  46]
 [215  70  49]
 [105  88   1]]
```

18.8.9 *Train the racing car using the CNN policy*

```
log_path = os.path.join('Trained_Models','Logs_'+Env_str)
model_path = os.path.join('Trained_Models','PPO_500k'+Env_str)
```

```
model=PPO("CnnPolicy",Env,verbose=2,tensorboard_log=log_path)
```

```
Using cpu device
Wrapping the env with a 'Monitor' wrapper
Wrapping the env in a DummyVecEnv.
Wrapping the env in a VecTransposeImage.
```

```
model.learn(total_timesteps=500_000)
                # try smaller steps first model.save(model_path)
```

```
Using cpu device
Wrapping the env with a `Monitor` wrapper
Wrapping the env in a DummyVecEnv.
Wrapping the env in a VecTransposeImage.
Track generation: 1041..1324 -> 283-tiles track
retry to generate track (normal if there are not many of
    this messages)
Track generation: 1084..1359 -> 275-tiles track
Logging to Trained_Models\Logs_CarRacing-v0\PPO_1
Track generation: 1284..1609 -> 325-tiles track
Track generation: 1129..1418 -> 289-tiles track
retry to generate track (normal if there are not many of
    this messages)
Track generation: 1292..1619 -> 327-tiles track
-------------------------------------
| rollout/            |          |
|     ep_len_mean     | 1e+03    |
|     ep_rew_mean     | -54.4    |
| time/               |          |
|                     |          |
|     fps             | 39       |
|     iterations      | 1        |
|     time_elapsed    | 51       |
|     total_timesteps | 2048     |
-------------------------------------
```

18.8.10 *Evaluate and view the learned model*

The following code shall produce animations of the CarRacing car running on the track.

```python
evaluate_policy(model,Env,n_eval_episodes=2,render=True)
```

```
Track generation: 1214..1522 -> 308-tiles track
Track generation: 1219..1538 -> 319-tiles track
Track generation: 996..1258 -> 262-tiles track

(-93.59801837056875, 0.11267495155334473)
```

```python
Env.close()                 #for gentle close the environment
```

```python
model = PPO.load(model_path, env=Env)     # re-load trained model
```

```
Wrapping the env with a `Monitor` wrapper
Wrapping the env in a DummyVecEnv.
Wrapping the env in a VecTransposeImage.
```

```python
episodes = 2 #5
for episode in range(1, episodes+1):
    s = Env.reset()      # initial state
    done = False
    rAll = 0
    frames = []
    while not done:
        Env.render()     # for in-window real-time render
        action, _ = model.predict(s.copy())
        s1, reward, done, info = Env.step(action)
        rAll+=reward
        s = s1
print(f"Episode {episode}: Score={rAll}")
```

```
Track generation: 1151..1443 -> 292-tiles track
Episode 1: Score=-55.32646048110042
Track generation: 1140..1429 -> 289-tiles track
Episode 2: Score=-54.86111111111186
```

We have video recorded the trained car using a screen recorder. The video
plays when the following code are executed with the recorded files.

```python
from IPython.display import Video
#Video('./images/PPO_10k_Driving.mp4', width=600, height=600)
Video('./images/PPO_500k_Driving.mp4', width=600, height=600)
```

```
<IPython.core.display.Video object>
```

Our tests found that a not-well-trained car with small training steps ($<$20k)
runs wildly. When it is trained 500k steps, it runs reasonably well. The
training took a number of hours on the author's laptop. Interested readers
may run the above codes, or contact the author for these videos. Our tests
found that the PPO is much more stable compared to the Q-algorithm.

18.9 Remarks

Finally, we mention that tremendous progress has indeed been made so far in machine learning, but challenges have always accompanied with the advancements. Our quest will continue as always in the journey of developing machine learning techniques for increasing challenging problems, for the well-being of humanity. As mentioned numerous times in this text, significant advances require open-minded researchers in all the fields related to machine learning, including incorporating ideas and techniques from the well-established and still developing physics-law-based methods. Quests never end.

References

[1] R. Sutton and A. Barto, *Reinforcement Learning: An Introduction*, MIT Press, Cambridge, MA, 2018.

[2] C.J.C.H. Watkins, *Learning from Delayed Rewards, PhD thesis*, May 1989, Cambridge, UK. http://www.cs.rhul.ac.uk/~chrisw/new_thesis.pdf.

[3] C.J.C.H. Watkins and P. Dayan, Q-learning, *Machine Learning*, **8**(1), 279–292. https://doi.org/10.1007/BF00992698.

[4] Duan Shuyong, Zhang Linxin, G.R. Liu *et al.*, A smoothed-shortcut Q-learning algorithm for optimal robot agent path planning, *Journal of Mechanical Engineering*, Accepted, 2021.

[5] R.E. Bellman, *Dynamic Programming*, Dover, 1957.

[6] Schulman John, *"Proximal Policy Optimization Algorithms"*, CoRR, vol. abs/1707. 06347, arXiv, 2017. online.

[7] Mnih Volodymyr, *"Asynchronous Methods for Deep Reinforcement Learning"*, CoRR, vol. abs/1602.01783, 2016. online.

[8] Schulman John, *"Trust Region Policy Optimization"*, CoRR, vol. abs/1502.05477, arXiv, 2015. online.

Index

block structure, 84
boolean operators, 42
boolean values, 41
boston housing price dataset, 416
bottleneck, 610, 618
broadcasting, 67
built-in functions, 40

C

10-classification, 451
candidate memory, 565
CarRacing, 655
CartPole, 649
case, 197
chain multiplication, 185
chain of stacked affine transformations, 215, 473
chained structure, 474
chaining ATA, 215
CIFAR images, 552
CIFAR10 dataset, 553
class inheritance, 86, 90
classification, 5
clip function, 645
close-form solution, 334, 392
closed-form, 619
CNN policy, 657
COCO dataset, 552
code performance, 93
column-space of matrix, 476
comment line, 21
comparison operators, 77, 460
complete linear bases, 8
computation complexity, 258
computational graph, 305
concatenation, 42, 565
condition number, 116–117
conditional probability, 181
conditions for activation functions, 288
configuration of a CNN, 545–546
confusion matrix, 254
conjugate gradient method, 367, 386
controlled random sampling, 158–159
CONV layers, 546
Conv2D layer, 556
convergence process, 347, 589
convergence theorem, 349
convex functions, 343, 348
ConvNet, 539
convolution filter, 540

convolution operator, 540
convolutional neural network (CNN), 539
covariance matrix, 408, 622
cross-entropy, 173–175, 188
cross-entropy loss function, 447, 452
curve fitting, 120, 402
CVXOPT, 249

D

data compression, 133, 211, 585
data encoded parameter, 211
data iterator, 356, 368, 372, 376, 379, 383, 409
data loss function, 507
data scaling (normalization), 149
data type, 11
data-based model, 3
data-parameter converter, 10, 190, 210
data-point, 5–7, 228, 226
dataset, 5–7
de-noising, 585
decision boundaries for classification problems, 241, 443, 503, 538
decision rule, 226
decision tree, 443
decoder, 610
deeper (more layers) net, 479
denoising, 611
dense layers, 556
densely connected, 213
derivative of the function, 348
diagonal matrix, 129
different strides and paddings, 542
discount factor, 627
discount rate, 629
distance function, 239, 258
distance-based, 424
distances, 189
distributed reward, 625
doc-strings, 21
dot-product, 102, 106, 115, 167, 225, 317
double-star, 54

E

edge detector, 540–541
effect of the L2 regularization, 533
effects of parallel data-points, 331, 337
eigenvalue decomposition, 113, 136
element-wise computations, 61

policy gradient methods, 644–645
policy-based algorithms, 643
polynomial kernels, 257
pooling, 544
possible norms, 506
power activation function, 288
power scheduling, 351
power-linear function, 288
power-quadratic function, 288
predictability for constants, 192
predictability for linear functions, 192
predictability of high-order functions, 214
predictability of the solution, 331
predicting complex nonlinear functions, 219
prediction function gradient, 213
prediction functions, 189, 193, 421
prediction of linear functions, 193
principal component analysis (PCA), 135, 585
principal components, 135, 140
prior distribution, 619
probability and statistics, 157
proper regularization parameter, 538
property of a convex function, 348
proximal policy optimization (PPO), 644
pseudo-dimension of the affine space, 8, 472, 475–476
pulse location, 271
pulse width, 271
Python code for the perceptron, 226
Python environment, 15
Python language, 19

Q

Q-algorithm, 632
Q-learning, 624
Q-learning algorithm, 630–631, 633–634
Q-Network, 624, 639
Q-table, 632
QR decomposition, 130
QR transformation, 334
quadratic discriminant analysis (QDA), 443
quadratic programming (QP), 249
quadratic programming problem, 245
Quasi-Newton methods, 386

R

radial basis functions (RBFs), 126
random distributions, 164
random forest, 443, 456, 460
random sampling, 158
randomly initialized model, 453
rank deficiency, 118
rank of a matrix, 118
ratio policy, 647
rational activation function, 288
ratios of distances, 189
RBF SVM, 443
recommendation, 585
reconstructing the data, 611
reconstruction, 143
recurrent neural networks (RNNs), 563
reduced LSTM, 566
regression, 5
regularization effects, 501, 526
regularization loss function, 507
regularization parameter, 505, 533–534
regularization techniques, 504
regularized model, 533–534
regularized solution, 506
reinforcement learning (RL), 623
Relu functions, 283
ResNet, 480, 549–550
return, 629
reward function, 627
right-singular vectors, 129
RMSProp, 374
root finding, 143
rotation matrix, 119
rule for estimating learning parameters, 478

S

saddle point, 247–248, 340
sequence feature models, 563
sequential dataset, 564
sigmoid curve shift, 270
sigmoid function ($\sigma(z)$), 266, 268
sigmoid wrapped affine transformation, 208
similarity function, 258
singular value decomposition (SVD), 112, 129

www.ingramcontent.com/pod-product-compliance
Ingram Content Group UK Ltd.
Pitfield, Milton Keynes, MK11 3LW, UK
UKHW051852150726
7214IPUK00021B/388